THEORY AND EMPIRICAL PERFORMANCE

Economic Paradigm and performance in the long run (18th to 21st century)

Edited by
Dominique Barjot, Harm G. Schroeter
& Yago Kazuhiko
with the collaboration of Cécile Coursiéras-Jaff
and Boris Vinogradov

THEORY AND EMPIRICAL PERFORMANCE

Economic Paradigm and performance in the long run (18th to 21st century)

THÉORIE ET PERFORMANCE EMPIRIQUE
Paradigme économique et performance
à long terme (du XIXe au XXIe siècle)

Collection de la revue française d'histoire économique II

SPM

2022

ISBN : 978-2-37999-013-7

Conception graphique et mise en page huguesvollant.com
Ouvrage composé en Heldane text (Klim Type Foundry)

Éditions SPM
16, rue des Écoles 75005 Paris
Tél. : 06 86 95 37 06 - courriel : lettrage@free.fr
site : www.editions-spm.fr

DIFFUSION – DISTRIBUTION :
L'Harmattan 5-7 rue de l'École-Polytechnique 75005 Paris
Tél. : 01 40 46 79 20 – télécopie : 01 43 25 82 03
site : www.editions-harmattan.fr

Preface/Préface

Yago Kazuhiko
Waseda University

The great economists formulated their doctrines in relation to the historical background of the time in which they lived: Adam Smith described the division of labor at the dawn of the Industrial Revolution; Friedrich List legitimized protectionism in the awakening of modern Germany as an industrial power; Joseph Schumpeter founded the economics of general equilibrium and innovation witnessing the turmoil of capitalism in 20th century Europe and America. The central theme they tackled was, above all, industrialization and economic development. Although criticized and shadowed by quite recent social protests against inequality and global warming, it is still worth questioning, following the above intellectual giants, *how industrialization happened and how economic development started.* The answers to these questions might not solve everything, but they will give us an important key to approaching the challenges we face today. History, which is our *métier*, should be one of the strongest tools available for inquiring into the above questions.

This book approaches industrialization and economic development globally, taking into account the emerging economies represented by BRICS (Brazil, Russia, India, China, and South Africa) and MIST (Mexico, Indonesia, South Korea, and Turkey), together with emerging nations in Latin America and Africa. The experiences of the Western European forerunners, along with the paths taken by the United States, Canada, Japan, and Central and Eastern European countries, are revisited under a new light of historical studies. The Industrial Revolution in the late 18th century, which started in Great Britain, spread Europe-wide and then world-wide, but the wave of industrialization was complex and intertwined, not at all a linear process. Proto-industrialization in the European core preceded the Industrial Revolution; the British case itself was, according to recent historical studies, something unique and rather exceptional; in the wave of transmission of industrialization, the "Invisible

Hand" view of Adam Smith, used to describe the market mechanism, was replaced by the "Visible Hand" view of Alfred Chandler; and market-oriented industrialization ceded, in many cases, to state-led growth formulated by W.W. Rostow and Alexander Gerschenkron. The subject of "development" became powerful after WWII, paving the way for the rise of emerging economies.

In order to challenge the above-mentioned process, which is huge in terms of time and space, we paid attention to mobilizing plural points of view: theory (economics) and history (economic history), a quantitative approach and qualitative approaches, macroeconomic policy decisions of governments and microeconomic decision making of firms, European experiences and non-European processes, cyclical and structural moves, "outward" and "inward" industrialization, capital export and import, and "path dependency" representing continuity and "creative destruction" triggering discontinuity. This book, in fact, is a result of the above encounters of various sets of viewpoints, often opposing each other. Careful readers will find that the above antagonisms are often hypothetical and, in reality, interrelated: state-led growth often strengthened market-oriented industrialization; the "path-dependent" character of one nation invited "creative" innovation; and a European-style "take-off" took place in non-European countries in an almost similar and slightly different manner. In history, to sum up, both happened simultaneously.

The title of this book, *Theory and Empirical Performance,* demonstrates our special attention to theories and their historical background. Hand in hand, economics and economic history dealt with industrialization and economic development. Along with the "big names" forecited, the great thinkers, classical as well as contemporary, appear in the volume: Alfred Marshall, Karl Marx, Karl Polanyi together with Raymond Aron and François Perroux; and economists belonging to different schools and approaches gather in chapters: Dieter Senghaas, Samir Amin, Raoul Prebisch and Arthur Lewis along with Ronald Coase, Oliver Williamson and Douglas North. This variety of theorists represents a wide scope of issues in industrialization and economic growth in history. Historical theories are also tested: Harold Innis and William A. MacKintosh theories for Canada, Sánchez-Albornoz theories for Spainish "dualism" or the Akamatsu theory "in flight of the wild goose" over Asian economic development. The theories often surpass the borders of their home country: The Midelfarth-Knarvik model to explain proto-industrialization; the Cobb-Douglas function to view French productivity; Michael Porter's "the double diamond" theory for Hungary; or New Deal economist Lauchlin Currie's influence on Columbia. The above list of theories, which does not cover everyone in this volume, represents the immense product of thinking on industrialization and economic development, which is itself a mirror in which to reflect the contemporary situation of industry and the economy.

Many of the contributors to this volume are both economic and business historians. The authors are proud of presenting their "micro" view on business, to be coupled with a "macro" view on the economy and politics. How many of the firms listed below are familiar to the readers? Huawei, Xiaomi, Lenovo, Petrobras, Votorantim, Natura,

Mittal, Tata, Gazprom, Rusal, Severstal, Bidvest, Sappi, Sasol, Cemex, Bimbo, and El Seweby. The above list of firms, referred to in this volume, extends to cover well-known Western firms such as VW, GE and Westinghouse, or even to Alcan and Rio Tinto. Well-known South Korean conglomerates such as Samsung, LG, and Posco are contrasted to various state-owned companies or joint ventures in emerging countries. Historical firms in Japan, either in transport or textiles, are contrasted with the contemporary Chinese High Speed Railway enterprise. States, usually an actor of "macro" policies, are at the same time a "micro" actor in the global market, such as the case of Algeria, Senegal and Côte d'Ivoire. This book aims to explore a new field of historical research, through the above "micro" approaches, to amalgamate economic history with business history, and finally to integrate these two methods.

After all, what was the "motor" of industrialization, development and growth? This kind of "finding the origin" question is clear but sometimes misleading. Instead of taking out only one decisive force and neglecting others, the volume presents all possible factors in history, sometimes contradictory to each other in theory, but co-existing in reality. Natural resource, abundance of land and/or capital, technology, either innovated or imported, domestic and foreign markets, foreign aid and the geo-political context, ability of the government, "K", "L" or "residual" in Robert Solow's equation, and above all the entrepreneurship of firms fulfilled the list of the "motors". Some of the "motors" were effective while others were not, some of them avoided the other factors to rise. Some "motors" fit well in a framework of theories, some do not. It is our aim in this book to present the list of "motors" and put them all in their historical context.

This book is a product of encounters, as described above, of theories and empirical performance, of economics and economic history. Above all, however, it is the outcome of encounters among scholars world-wide. Historians of different continents, belonging to different intellectual traditions and sometimes to different political regimes, gathered in meetings held in global cities and conferences. The authors highly appreciate the academic organizations and funds which helped us to arrange the congresses all over the world. We all wish that the product of this friendship and collaboration between the contributors will serve as a key to making this world something better, to overcome divisions and crises.

Introduction

To what extent are European development-theories on industrialization valid from a World point of view?

Dominique Barjot
Sorbonne University, Renmin National University
and French Academy of Overseas Sciences

Introduction

Our world became global.[1] Today, the impressive growth of China and, more generally, of the BRICS (Brazil, Russia, India, China, South Africa) and MIST (Mexico, Indonesia, South Korea, Turkey) constitutes a good illustration of the profound change of this globalizing world. The spectacular development of the "Global Challengers" –i.e. the 100 companies "disrupting the world economic order" (Boston Consulting Group) – is demonstrating the pursuit of the rapid change of the world economy.[2] These "Global Challengers" are coming from late-industrialized countries such as China (Huawei, Xiaomi, Lenovo, China Communications Construction, etc.), Brazil (Petrobras, Votorantim, Natura), India (Mittal, Tata Group), Russia (Gazprom, Rusal, Severstal) or South Africa (Bidvest, Sappi, Sasol), but more and more also from other countries like Mexico (Cemex or Bimbo) or Egypt (El Seweby Electric). Because the emergence of new economic powers has been a fundamental motor of the human development, the importance of these phenomena is constituting today a very exciting question for economic historians.

1 Dominique Barjot, Harm G. Schroeter (eds), « La circulation de l'information et des connaissances », *Entreprises et Histoire*, juin 2014, n° 75.

2 The New Global Challengers – BCG, https://www.bcg.com/documents/file14801.pdf; Global Challengers Lead Digital Business Revolution - The Boston Consulting Group - BCG, https://www.bcg.com/.../17may2018-global-challenges-business-revolution.

This constitutes a major reason of our worldwide project.[3]

Scientific issues: Questioning traditional theories

The project combines the macroeconomic with the microeconomic dimension. The main question is: to what extent can these traditional theories be meaningfully applied to non-European countries? The approach used is that of economic actors: enterprises and their environment. Indeed, the micro-economic point of view was not yet systematically applied in a comparative perspective.

Classical theories of industrialization and development:

Traditional theories on the World's development, especially industrialization, have a Western Europe-biased design. Into these we count theories by Alexander Gerschenkron,[4] Walt Wittman Rostow,[5] Raymond Aron,[6] Paul Bairoch,[7] Karl Polanyi,[8] and even Karl Marx.[9] They took Europe and its offshoots for a general benchmark of success and development. Also, later theories, such as by Dieter Senghaas[10] or dependency theory (Eduardo Galeano[11] and others), structuralists (Raoul Prebisch[12]) and of the uneven development (Samir Amin,[13] Paul Bairoch and even François Perroux[14]) placed Europe and its institutions into their center of their analysis and explication. All these approaches claim general or even world-wide validity. The basic idea of our book is to evaluate to what extent these theories are useful in explaining by East and South Eastern Asian or South American and, today perhaps, African industrialization above all from the perspective of their actors. Consequently, we look at institutional actors, such as industrial firms, banks and financial institutions, households, public or private administrations within their economic, social and political environment.

3 Harm G. Schroeter, "Foreword: Theory and Empirical Performance Or: did development theories hold their promise?", in Dominique Barjot (ed.), "Theory and Empirical Performance. Economic Paradigm and Performance in the Long Run (18th to 21st century)", *Revue française d'histoire économique – The French Economic History Review*, n° 11-12 (n°1-2, 2019), p. 6-9.

4 Alexander Gerschenkron, *Economic backwardness in historical perspective, a book of essays*, Cambridge, Massachusetts: Belknap Press of Harvard University Press, 1962.

5 Walt Whitman Rostow, *The Stages of Economic Growth: A Non-Communist Manifesto*. Cambridge University Press, 1960.

6 Raymond Aron, *Dix-huit leçons sur la société industrielle*, Paris: Gallimard, 1963; *Eighteen Lectures on Industrial Society*, London: Weidenfeld & Nicolson, 1967.

7 Paul Bairoch, *Economics and World History: Myths and Paradoxe*, University of Chicago Press, 1993.

8 Karl Polanyi, *The Great Transformation: The Political and Economic Origins of Our Time*, 2nd ed. Foreword by Joseph E. Stiglitz; introduction by Fred Block. Boston: Beacon Press, 2001.

9 Karl Marx, *Le Capital (livre I)*, Paris, Garnier-Flammarion, 1969.

10 Dieter Senghaas (ed.), *Imperialismus und strukturelle Gewalt*, Frankfurt: Suhrkamp Verlag 1972 (7th edition. 1987); (ed.), *Peripherer Kapitalismus. Analysen über Abhängigkeit und Unterentwicklung*, Frankfurt: Suhrkamp Verlag 1974 (2nd edition. 1977); (ed.) *Kapitalistische Weltökonomie. Kontroen über ihren Ursprung und ihre Entwicklungsdynamik*, Frankfurt: Suhrkamp Verlag 1979 (2nd edition. 1982).

11 Eduardo Galeano, *Open Veins of Latin America: Five Centuries of the Pillage of a Continent*, (25th anniversary ed.). Monthly Review Press, 2010.

12 Raúl Prebisch, *The Economic Development of Latin America and Its Principal Problems* (New York: United Nations, 1950); Raúl Prebisch, *Change and Development : Latin America's Great Task*, Inter-American Development Bank, 1970.

13 Samir Amin, *L'accumulation à l'échelle mondiale*, Éditions Anthropos, Paris 1970. Translated and published as *Accumulation on a world scale*, Abe Books, 1970.

14 *François Perroux, œuvres complètes*, 6 tomes, Presses universitaires de Grenoble, 1993 ; François Perroux, *L'Économie du XXe siècle*, Presses universitaires de Grenoble, 1961.

Four good reasons to re-visit these theories

There exist four reasons for revisit traditional theories on the World's development.

1/ It seems valuable to mobilize the recent achievements in business history and of microeconomic research on companies, the state and consumers. The purpose is to evaluate the role of business, both large and small, in the growth dynamic of both industrialized and emerging nations; by exploring their performance, strategies and types of organization, together with the social, cultural and environmental implications of their behaviour as actors.

2/ Because it fundamentally concerns the behaviour of economic actors, the project amounts to a study of decision making. It comprehends consideration from a macroeconomic standpoint as well as that of institutional agents of national accounting and microeconomic action at the background of the theories mentioned above. Contributors are asked to primarily evaluate actions of individual agents' behaviour in the neoclassical sense: industrial firms, banks and financial institutions, households, public or private administrations.

3/ The issue of the emergence of globalization bears upon many fundamental questions: the growth of mass consumption and Americanization; public policy, both cyclical and structural; firms' investment policies and, more broadly, operational and strategic decisions (according to the famous Ansoff's distinction[15]), taking into account transaction costs (Ronald Coase,[16] Oliver Williamson[17]); the interaction of social networks and/or techniques, spatial dynamics (industrial districts, local productive systems and clusters); path dependency (as described by Arrows[18] or, above all, Nelson and Winter[19]).

4/ At the same time the specific contribution of the historians can also be made fruitful, such as the approaches of proto-industrialization (Mendels[20], Kriedtke, Medick & Schlumbohm[21]). The idea is to test traditional European theories to evaluate to what extent they can be applied fruitfully in Asia, Africa, or Latin America. Our approach is also a reflection on a recent fashion in history-writing. Many authors try to promote a non-European biased view (*History of the World* edited by Iriye and Osterhammel[22]). The change is based on the simple moral aspect that also the less powerful have an equal right to history. Is there also a *theoretical foundation* to this moral change? If European theory is not good enough for explaining the rest of the World the fashionable moral approach is necessary. If not, it is still nice, but much less important and urgent.

15 H. Igor Ansoff, *Corporate strategy: an analytic approach to business policy for growth and expansion*, New York, McGraw-Hill, 1965.

16 Ronald Coase, "The Nature of the Firm", *Economica*, 4 (16), 1937, p. 386-405.

17 Oliver Williamson, *Markets and Hierarchies: Analysis and Antitrust Implications*, 1975; *The Economic Institutions of Capitalism*, 1985; (co-edited with Sidney Winter), *The Nature of the Firm: Origins, Evolution, and Development* , 1991.

18 Kenneth J. Arrow, "The economic implications of learning by doing", *The Review of Economic Studies*. Oxford Journals, 29 (3), June 1962, p. 155-173.

19 Richard R. Nelson, Sydney G. Winter, *An Evolutionary Theory of Economic Change*, Cambridge (Mas.), Harvard University Press, 1982.

20 Franklin F. Mendels, *Industrialization and population pressure in eighteenth-century Flanders.*, Front Cover, University of Wisconsin--Madison, 1970.

21 Peter Kriedte, Hans Medick, Jurgen Schlumbohm, *In Industrialization before Industrialization*, Cambridge, Cambridge University Press, 1981.

22 Emily S. Rosenberg, Akira Iriye, Jürgen Osterhammel (eds), *A History of the* World by joint publication of Harvard University Press and C. H. Beck, 2014.

Scientific and organizational goals

These questions led to the definition of both scientific and organizational objectives.

Scientific goals

In this context two issues are important in our approach: our focus is on the side of success, it does not include excuse-stories like that by the Californian school (Kenneth Pomeranz et al.[23]); the approach is mainly one of business history: how single enterprises developed their specific path of growth under the special conditions and environment of their countries. The idea of the session is to test the traditional point of view: Is European biased theory sufficient to reflect industrial success in Asia, South America or other continents? Indeed, the basic question is whether economic paradigm corresponds with success or failure. There were three main types of cases:

- Case 1 – Adam Smith and open competition: Anglo-Saxon world, Denmark, Norway, Latin American states
- Case 2 – Friedrich List and the idea of temporary protection of "infant industry": Germany, Sweden, Finland, China, Italy, Hungary
- Case 3 – State-backed path: France, Japan, South Korea, Russia, Spain), South Africa, Turkey and Gulf States, Latin American states.

From an actor's point of view the contributions will combine a microeconomic and a macroeconomic approach: Change cannot be explained without actors, while actors' movements cannot be explained without their environment. The project does neither exclude space-approaches (regional economy, economic geography, otherwise geo-strategy), nor those from sociology (social structures and mobility, action sociology), nor other ones coming under the history of sciences and technology or historical demography. Such approaches need to consider microeconomic approaches. The purpose is to better understand the role of the firms and other actors, such as state authorities, in the emergence of the modern economy (opposed to traditional one, according to Arthur B. Lewis[24]). No approaches, which deal with business history, are to be excluded: microeconomics of the firm; economics and history of innovation; sociology of organizations ; social psychology ; history of labor ; anthropology of entrepreneurs, workers and consumers.

Organizational Issues

In order to carry out the project, it was decided to put in place an organizational scheme involving the holding of four preparatory conferences for a final session to be held in Boston, in the framework of WEG 2018. These four pre-conferences were the following:

1/ Rio de Janeiro, Brazil, August 17th and 18th, 2017 at Federal University of Rio de Janeiro. Local organizer: Luiz Carlo Delorme Prado, Professor, IE-UFRJ, Institute of Economics, Federal University of Rio de Janeiro

23 Kenneth Pomeranz, *The Great Divergence: China, Europe, and the Making of the Modern World Economy*. Princeton University Press, 2000.

24 William Arthur Lewis, *The Theory of Economic Growth*, London Taylor and Francis, 2003.

2/ Beijing, China, October 21st & 22nd, 2017 at Renmin University of China. Local organizer: Dominique Barjot, Huang Chun and Wang Jue, of Renmin University of China

3/ Tokyo, Japan, November 15th & 16th, 2017 at Waseda University. Local organizer: Yago Kazuhiko, Waseda University.

4/ Paris, France, March 29th, 2018 at Académie des Sciences d' Outre-Mer (French Academy of Overseas Sciences) with the support of the Sorbonne University and the CNRS (French National Center for Scientific Research). Local organizer: Dominique Barjot, Sorbonne University and French Academy of Overseas Sciences.

From these four preparatory conferences and the papers presented there, it is possible to distinguish three sets of nations: Western Industrialized Nations, Eastern and South Eastern Asia; Other Emerging Nations.

WESTERN INDUSTRIALIZED COUNTRIES

One of the major objectives of the Paris conference was to highlight the specificity, both macroeconomic and microeconomic, of the development patterns of the major industrial nations of North America and Western Europe.

North America : the American Way

With regards to the American Way, three approaches were retained: the link between entrepreneurship and technological innovation at the origins of the industrial development of the United States; the role of the political vision of American leaders ; the paths adopted by large multi-divisional and managerial corporations to adapt to the economic and technological changes of the second half of the 20th century. Finally, it might be interesting to question the specificities of the Canadian case.

USA: The Entrepreneurial Culture and the Mysteries of Economic Development

Louis Galambos showed that many of US entrepreneurial start-ups involved only a small degree of novelty.[25] This vision broke up with the well-known analysis of Joseph Schumpeter. [26] According to him, heroic entrepreneurs first introduced the new consumer goods, the new methods of production or transport, the new markets and the new forms of industrial organization created by the capitalist enterprise. It was the entrepreneurial culture that encouraged people to take the risk of exploring opportunities for innovation: most would fail in the long run and many would fail in the short term. This culture existed from the foundation of United States around 1800. Neither the entrepreneurial culture, not the search for new opportunities for innovation were unique to primitive America. Main factors, including immigration and change in the public sector, shaped performance and entrepreneurship culture of the young American nation, facilitated the transition to industrialization and accelerated

25 Louis Galambos, "The Entrepreneurial Culture and the Mysteries of Economic Development", in Dominique Barjot (ed), "Theory and Empirical Performance. Economic Paradigm and Performance in the Long Run (18th to 21st century)", *Revue française d'histoire économique – The French Economic History Review*, n° 11-12 (n°1-2, 2019), *op. cit.*, p. 60-80.

26 Joseph A. Schumpeter, *The theory of economic development: an inquiry into profits, capital, credit, interest, and the business cycle*, New Brunswick, New Jersey, Transaction Books, 1934.

growth. Nevertheless, two factors were essential to foster development: the existence of a vigorous and locally oriented commercial sector was necessary to provide capital; in return, this capital opened the way to a large-scale innovation process supported by a strong entrepreneurial culture.

USA: A Primacy of Politics on Economics?
Drawing on the post-1945 US experience, François David illustrated the thesis of the primacy of politics on the economy, through the American policy towards Europe.[27] In the reorganization of the world demanded by the United States since Woodrow Wilson, the economy is a means; politics, an absolute goal. In the founding years 1945-1963, the major economic and commercial projects conceived by the United States for the benefit of Western Europe have a strategic aim: to create an interdependent international society, with the rejection of stubborn sovereignty, so as to dissolve the aggressiveness of the Westphalian Nation-State. The Marshall Plan, the European and Steel Community (ECSC) and then the Common Market successively pursue this goal. About the method, the United States has been able to adapt, passing from a kind of blackmail (dollar diplomacy), to a finer diplomacy summed up as follows: neither isolationism nor open intrusiveness.

At the end of the first twenty years of the Pax Americana in Europe, the United States took away the essential: they solved the biggest international question since the Congress of Vienna, the German question. A peaceful Germany finally fits into a stable West, provided that the West includes the United States: European integration on the one hand (the Franco-German couple in reality); the American security guarantee through North Atlantic Treaty Organization (NATO), on the other hand. The definitive exit of isolationism by the United States is inherent in the integration of Germany into the peaceful game of nations. In this great game, international trade is only a means, not an end in itself.

On the method, the United States have been able to adapt, passing from a form of blackmail to dollars, to a fine diplomacy boiled down to the slogan: neither isolationism nor interference in the life of the European States. From the failure of the Marshall Plan as a catalyst for European economic integration, to the even more masterminded geo-military failure of the European Defense Community (EDC) in 1954, American conceptions of the European process espoused three principles: In any case, the United States of Europe remained the ultimate objective. On the other hand, they tolerate the emergence of European commercial competition, facilitated by generation-wide protectionism. Finally, the United States let Europeans decide for themselves the pace of their institutional progress.

27 François David, « L'Économie européenne au prisme du projet politique des États-Unis. Du Plan Marshall au Grand Dessein de Kennedy », paper presented at the Paris Preconference.

United States: the biggest multidivisional and managerial firms, a diversity of strategic choices

After the Second World War, the assertion of the American economic and technological leadership also relied heavily on the rise of the large multi-divisional and managerial enterprise. As Miyata Kenichi has clearly shown about General Electric (GE) and Westinghouse (WH) between 1946 and 2000, the model never has the monolithic character that is usually attributed to it.[28] Indeed, after World War 2, GE Company and Westinghouse Electric Corporation changed their respective business structures. It resulted of a divergence in top management behaviors arising from their respective perceptions of environment, conceptions of prospects, actions taken to pursue unrelated diversification.

More generally, the second half of the 20th Century witnessed a major change in the US economy: the passage of a rapid to a slower growth staring in 1970. Whereas large US enterprises accounted for 78% of the 100 World top firms in 1956, by 1990, their number was rechecked to only 33%. According to that, Miyata K. examined the process of divergence in corporate growth for large US enterprises in the second half of the 20th century. In this way, there exist some discussions between economic historians, around the factors of competitive success or failure between industrial firms during the years 1946 to 2000. Alfred D. Chandler emphasized the internal factors organization, that top managers chose unrelated diversification for short-term gains rather than related diversification for long-term growth.[29] Others scholars developed other explanations: changing in technology (Langlois[30]), in demand (Lamoreaux, Raff, and Temin[31]) or interaction between institutions and organizations (Douglas North[32]). More precisely, D. North found a full understanding of the long-run change that transaction costs and property rights are embedded in institutions, but also institutional choices are embedded in beliefs.

The Miyata's analysis focused on corporate strategy as a set of actor actions. In the process of change of technologies and markets, the top management of industrial enterprise make decisions regarding prospects. Managerial *visaction* (a combination of vision and action) represents the set of three management actions (perception, conception, actual action) and was used to develop explanation. Between the two firms, GE and WH, the most important differences were:

1/ GE found the way to re-growth through managing unrelated diversification beyond that of the typical industrial enterprise.

2/ WH chose to go back to pursue a vertical integration through a major business transformation to a broadcasting service from its traditional manufacturing base.

28 Miyata Kenichi, "Modern Corporate Growth after the Modern Economic Growth: A Comparative Study of General Electric and Westinghouse, 1946-2000", paper presented to the Tokyo Preconference.

29 Alfred D. Chandler, Jr., *Scale and Scope. The Dynamics of Industrial Capitalism*, Cambridge (Mass.) and London, Harvard University Press, 2004.

30 Richard N. Langlois, "The Vanishing Hand: The Changing Dynamics of Industrial Capitalism", *Industrial and Corporate Change*, 12, n° 2, 2003, p. 351-385.

31 Naomi R. Lamoreaux, Daniel M. Raff and Peter Temin, "Beyond Markets and Hierarchies : Toward a New Synthesis of American Business History", *American Historical Review*, 108, n° 2, 2003, p. 404-433.

32 Douglass C. North, *Understanding the Process of Economic Change*, Princeton , NJ, Princeton University Press, 2005.

Facing the necessity to pass of a quick to a slower growth, the focus of managerial perceptions swayed amongst existing resources and potential markets. Indeed conceptions were constrained by perceptions and result of past actions. Consequently GE realized high growth through an unrelated diversification strategy that combined manufacturing with service business. On the contrary, WH pursed corporate growth as a mass media company and returned to a vertical integration strategy that favored the most profitable and competitive business. Finally, the Miyata's analysis led to two results:

1/ to resent an evaluation of the unrelated diversification. According to the GE's case, an unrelated diversification can bring a long term high growth that related diversification cannot provide (it was also the case for Apple, Google and Amazon).

2/ to provide a new study of the process of path dependency. The comparative study of GE and WH highlights the process of defining limits to the change in business organization by applying managerial *visaction*.

The Canadian Case

Canada experienced significant economic development after 1840, making it one of the most prosperous nations in the world.[33] It owes its success to its own companies, but also to multinational firms (MNF), American and British for the most part, whose presence intensified from the late nineteenth century. Various theories have been advanced to explain Canadian success. One of them is still in vogue, that of Harold Innis and William A. MacKintosh.[34] This theory emphasizes the impact that the exploitation of natural resources has always had on the Canadian economy: a succession of staple foods has contributed to the building of the colony and, subsequently, to the nation. It began with fishing and continued with the fur trade, timber, wheat, various metals (iron and nickel in particular) and the sale of various forms of energy (including hydroelectricity and more recently oil). Extraction or production of basic products (fishing and trade in fur, wood, wheat, then iron and nickel, and finally the sale of various forms of energy (including hydroelectricity and more recently the oil) played a vital role in Canadian industrialization, but this made Canada a dependent economy, first to the British Empire, then to the United States.

There is no doubt that natural resources have always played a major role in the Canadian economy. Canadian entrepreneurs have launched their own MNCs in this sector, particularly in the mining industry. Nevertheless, the question remains: how does one explain the success of this nation given its small population and the fact that the exploitation of natural resources, as we see elsewhere, can lead to dependence and even underdevelopment? What strategies has Canada followed to avoid this pitfall? Following the example of the industrialization of the Mauricie Valley (Quebec), it is possible to attempt to characterize Canadian industrialization. While urbanized areas such as Montreal or Toronto have a very different industrial history, their businesses

33 Pierre Lanthier, "The Canadian Experience in Business: the Case of the St. Maurice Valley from 1890 to 1975", paper presented at the Paris Preconference.

34 W.T. Easterbrook, and M.H Watkins, "The Staple Approach", in *Approaches to Canadian Economic History*. Ottawa, Carleton Library Series, Carleton University Press, 1984, p. 1-98.

have managed to create niche markets for semi-finished goods, and therefore beyond the basic level.

Adam Smith is really helpful in explaining the Canadian case? In fact, the invisible hand of the market has been too often and too resolutely replaced by the very visible hand of public institutions. Public authorities intervened first as legislators, then as investors and clients. Alexander Gerschenkron's analyzes are no more relevant: the self-financing of companies was such that they did not require permanent support from large financial institutions. If there has been a succession of vertical and horizontal concentration processes or diversification, as described by AD Chandler, Canadian companies are struggling to reach and maintain the finished products, like Nortel, Blackberry and even Bombardier. One thing is certain though: while Canada's industrialization depended largely on foreign investment, it also depended on Canada's ability to absorb this investment. Canada has demonstrated its ability to outperform the basic economy. Nevertheless, given the small size of its own market, it remains difficult for this country to achieve full autonomy vis-à-vis its export markets, especially American. The ongoing debate around the renewal of NAFTA is a painful reminder of this dependence.

Western Europe: British paradigm or path dependency processes?

Although the United States is today a model of industrialization, until the 1880s, it was the United Kingdom that seemed to be the model to follow, hence the question of the British way of industrialization was a paradigm.

Belgium and the Netherlands: towards a revision of the Rostowian model of industrialization?

Today it is not very clear. Indeed, in contrast to the linear, national "rapid take-off" of industrialization as presented by Rostow (1960), Robin C. M. Philips proposed an empirically grounded account on the causes of industrialization in Belgium or the Netherlands since 1820 until present, drawing mostly from data of the Belgian and Dutch population and industry censuses.[35] Applying an updated ion of the Midelfarth-Knarvik model (2000), he argued that the same factors which can explain the location of the Industrial Revolution (factor endowments, market potential, and institutions), can be used to explain the location of industry in these countries during the subsequent phases of industrialization and de-industrialization of the 20th and 21st century. In contrast to the "rapid take-off" which Rostow (1960: 7) presented, Robin C. M. Philips evidenced that industrialization built on previous phases of proto-industrialization and did have an enduring path-dependent effect in the recent period. Rather than a national, linear presentation of industrialization or the Industrial Revolution, he defended the idea of a regional and sectoral varied dynamical process of industrialization.

35 Robin C. M. Philips, "Regional Industrial Development in Belgium and the Netherlands (1820-2010)", communication presented at the Paris Preconference.

As Marshall (1890) pointed out, agglomeration factors played a crucial role in the location of industry, as manufacturing sectors and firms tended to cluster within regions or localities over time. During the nineteenth century, high transportation costs caused many factories to cluster around pools of labor and natural resources, as such was the case for the metallurgy and machinery manufacturing companies in Hainaut and Liège in Belgium or the textiles factories in the cities of Zwolle, Ghent, or Tilburg (Mokyr 1976). Increasingly more commercial-oriented sectors started industrializing, with factories setting up business close to urban centers where a higher educated work force and a higher purchasing power was present (Philips, Foldvari, and Van Leeuwen 2017). Due to the fall of transport costs and energy prices during the second and third phase of industrialization, many labor-intensive sectors relocated, while sectors with high fixed costs or high degrees of specialization remained relatively longer in their initial place of establishment. After the 1960s – 1970s, a phase of de-industrialization took place, in which many manufacturing firms moved to other regions: first within the Low Countries, later to other countries in Europe and eventually to Southeast-Asia. In many former industrial-dominated regions, such as the Charleroi-Liège axis, the local labor market was unable to absorb this sudden increased supply of labor, increasing regional divergent patterns of unemployment and income levels. In Fine, Rostow's view (1960) of "rapid take-off" - industrialization – de-industrialization needs revision, based on the industrial history of the Low Countries.

Typologies of Industrialization: Lessons From Spain

The progress of nineteenth and twentieth century Spanish economic historiography during the last two generations has been fuelled by an aim common to all researchers: to place Spanish economic performance in a world-wide perspective.[36] Between 1968 and 1975, some scholars achieved a first success in introducing Spain in a more general framework of research. This was the case of Nicolás Sánchez-Albornoz (1968) and his discussion of "dualism";[37] Gabriel Tortella (1972 & 1973) and the role of banking in economic development, or his reinterpretation of Spanish railway building through the glasses of Albert Hirschman economic development models;[38] Josep Fontana (1971 & 1973) and the role of public finance and agrarian change on Spanish capitalist development – Prussian, French or British way? –; Jordi Nadal (1973 & 1975) and Spain in the industrial race – his thesis of the "failure of the industrial revolution" –;[39] or Santiago Roldán and José Luis García Delgado (1973) and the First World War as a "catching-up" opportunity for Spain. The shock of these contributions, mostly concentrated in only five years (1968 to 1973), echoed in subsequent research. For fifty years we have been discussing around these "grand" (at the Spanish level) themes. Some of

36 Albert Carreras, "Typologies of industrialization : Lessons from Spain ", in Dominique Barjot (ed), "Theory and Empirical Performance. Economic Paradigm and Performance in the Long Run (18th to 21st century)", *Revue française d'histoire économique – The French Economic History Review*, n° 11-12 (n°1-2, 2019), *op. cit.*, p. 82-119.

37 Nicolás Sánchez-Albornoz, ed., *The Economic Modernization of Spain, 1830-1930*, New York U.P., New York, 1987.

38 Gabriel Tortella, "Spain, 1829-1874", in Rondo Cameron ed., *Banking and Economic Development. Some Lessons of History*, Oxford U.P., Oxford, 1972, p. 91-121.

39 Jordivers Nadal, "The Failure of the Industrial Revolution in Spain, 1830-1914", in Cipolla, Carlo M. ed., *The Fontana Economic History of Europe*, vol. 4, *The Emergence of Industrial Societies*, 2, vol. 4.2, Collins, London, 1973, p. 532-626.

the most successful PhD's of the subsequent years pointed explicitly to reconsider the hypothesis established by the preceding generation. Let's remind the articles or books by Jordi Maluquer de Motes (1977), Antonio Gómez-Mendoza (1982), Leandro Prados de la Escosura (1982 and 1988), Sebastián Coll and Carles Sudrià (1987), Francisco Comín (1988) or Albert Carreras (1984 and 1991), to name only some of those explicitly framed as challenging or extending the "1973" paradigm.

The trepidation of the national debate allowed for the initial diffusion of some elements into the European economic historiography: Milward & Saul (1977), Trebilcock (1981), Pollard (1981), Berend & Ranki (1982), although in a limited way.[40] The main recollection of first hand English written material is to be found in the book edited by Nicolás Sánchez-Albornoz (1987) where many of the names cited before contributed sectorial or regional essays.[41] The most ambitious and provocative statement was put forward by César Molinas & Leandro Prados (1989) in "Was Spain Different?".[42] Up to 1995 the discussion on Spain in industrialization typologies was very active[43].

The peculiarity of Spanish experience was stressed in many of the first-generation contributions. The "assault" of the second generation has produced much more "normality" – considering Europe as the normal evolution –. This is why the Molinas & Prados paper was puzzling. To the long-standing question they addressed, the answer given by them was affirmative. The main purpose of this paper is to explore this problem in two particular ways. Firstly, trying to overview the research that has been done on Spanish economic history in the framework of the "grand" theories -or typologies- of industrialization and economic growth as a crude test of how normal was Spanish economic performance (SEP) during the last two centuries. Secondly, deriving from Spanish economic performance a few potential "lessons" for the general understanding of the diffusion of economic development. Spanish long-term economic performance provides some insights that can be useful for the reassessment of industrialization and modern economic growth. Her inability to be classified in the usual typologies – although being closer to them than was previously thought – suggests three interrelated interpretative clues that may be worth to explore: the rate of growth of protected markets as an explanatory variable of long-term economic performance, the importance of cautious trade liberalization policies and the decisiveness of a proper geopolitical location to enjoy the growth promoting impact of wealthy neighbours. In the three cases, the underlying lesson is as old as Adam Smith: "the division of labour is limited by the size of the market".

40 Alan S. Milward & Samuel B. Saul, *The Development of the Economies of Continental Europe, 1850-1914*, Allen & Unwin, London, 1977; Clive Trebilcock, *The Industrialization of the Continental Powers, 1780-1914*, Longman, London, 1981; Sidney Pollard, *Peaceful Conquest. The Industrialization of Europe, 1760-1970*, Oxford U.P., Oxford, 1981; Ivan Berend & Gyorgy Ranki, *The European Periphery and Industrialization, 1780-1914*, Cambridge U.P. & Éditions de la Maison des Sciences de l'Homme, Cambridge & Paris, 1982.

41 Nicolás Sánchez-Albornoz, ed., *The Economic Modernization of Spain, 1830-1930*, New York U.P., New York, 1987.

42 César Molinas & Leandro Prados de la Escosura, "Was Spain Different? Spanish Historical Backwardness Revisited", *Explorations in Economic History*, 26, 1989, p. 385-402.

43 Gabriel Tortella 1994, "Patterns of Economic Retardation and Recovery in South Western Europe in the XIX and XX Centuries", *Economic History Review*, 1994, p. 124; Albert Carreras, "What Can We Learn from Long-Term Spanish Economic Performance?", in Pablo Martín-Aceña & James Simpson, eds., *The Economic Development of Spain since 1870*, Edward Elgar, Aldershot, p. 24-47.

The German economic model: path dependency and continuity or creative destruction and discontinutity

Harm G. Schroter questioned the use of economic history theories to explain German economic growth from 1949 to 1990.[44] There are quite a number of socio-economic theories on economic growth. Strange: economic historians explained the economic development of Germany 1945-1990 to a large extent without refering to theory. This includes also leading mainstream economists.[45] Economic historians working on the industrial revolution have partly applied theory. Especially the theories of Gerschenkron on economic backwardness and that of Rostow / Hirschman on stages of economic growth and leading sectors were applied.[46]

Harm G. Schroter has been led to ask three main types of questions:

1 / Which theory fits best? in this case the main question is as follows: Can the economic development of West-Germany 1945-1990 be explained by theory, not theories on industrialization but on economic development? In case the call to the theory is necessary (why not think so?), the question would then become: Which theory would fit best? Path dependency and continuity (Douglas North)? Or qualitative change, creative destruction and discontinutity (Schumpeter)?

2 / What sort of change needs explaination? In this way, it is necessary to distinguish and even to choose between quantitative (path dependency) and qualitative (creative destruction) changes. Usually quantitative change needs little theoretical explanation. But quantitative change need explanation if the change goes into a negative direction or if it causes a new quality. On the contrary, Qualitative change need explanation per se.

3/ Where is explanation needed? One of the essential points is to analyze the structural changes that occurred in the structure of GDP and in the labor force between 1950 and 1990.

The main stages of the restart of German economic growth were as follows:

1/ 1945: "hour zero?". The elements of continuity seemed to prevail. This is what emerges from the following remarks: There was no "hour zero" in Germany (if that would have been the case we would need for industrialization theory, not for development theory)? Bombing terror destroyed around 45% of German dwellings, all major bridges, but only 15% of production capacity. More, how to explain over night fully equipped shops the very day after the introduction of the Deutschmark (DM) 1948?

2/ Intervention of the European Recovery Reconstruction (ERP). In 1948, the introduction of a new currency (the Deutsche Mark) caused a boost. But another decisive factor was the Berlin Blockade. Indeed, the Berlin Blockade entailed change of perception: US no longer enemy but friend. It opened the way to the Reconstruction with the help of ERP 1949-52.

44 Harm G. Schroeter, "Germany's Economic Development 1949 to 1990: Its Significance for Development Economics", communication presented at the Paris Preconference.

45 Herbert Giersch, Karl-Heinz Paqué and Holger Schmieding, *The Fading Miracle. Four Decades of Market Economy in Germany*, Cambridge, Cambridge University Press, 1992.

46 Rainer Fremdling, *Eisenbahn und deutsches Wirtschaftswachstum 1840-1879*, Dortmund, Gesellschaft fuer Wirtschaftsgeschichte, 1985.

Two examples of industries illustrated this restart. This is primarily the automotive industry. At his command, it is possible to ask the question: creative destruction or path dependency? A study shows that Volkswagen (VW) reconstructed not on German principles but on American ones, with ERP-money, advice of US-consultancies and US machinery. In this case the key to world-success was adapting to Americanization. The same question may arise in the case of the chemical industry. In reality, the restart process differed a little: Reconstruction on German principles but change to US ones during 1950, passage from coal to oil as basic energy and as raw materials, adoption of totally different proceedings. Ultimately, the path followed was the same to achieve global success: adapt to Americanization. Of course, the shock of oil crisis of 1973/74 was perceived as a great challenge. Consequently, German Government made clear by political means that to proceed as before was no longer possible (e.g. by interdiction of using cars at a couple of week-ends). Nevertheless, if the reaction during 1970s was to use of Keynes' remedy, it became different during 1980s: to adopt the Chicago school – monetarism. There were some differences in development before and after Oil-crisis: deregulation and privatization for to inject competition. The most important aims at the same time were to obtain higher rates of growth of productivity and growth of standard of living. The consequence was a rapid evelopment of labour-productivity (100 = 1995): 1960: 28; 1970: 47; 1980: 69 and 1990: 83. But, in general, there was no important change by economic shock or other policy!

In conclusion, who should be used, Schumpeter or North? There were many elements in the direction of change and discontinuity. Substantial changes have occurred (structural change from argriculture to service, clear change in economic policy), but in how things are made. *A contrario*, one can also find arguments in favor of path dependency and continuity: no change in the industrial profile of the country (always the same branches). In short, little change which things are made (product-groups, type of service).

Western Europe: the Case of France

Historiography has often emphasized the slowness of France's economic growth during the 19th century, by comparison with the new industrialized countries such as the United States or Germany, or even with the United Kingdom[47]. It was true but must be nuanced: the per capita performance of the French economy has been parallel to that of the United Kingdom; because a progressive acceleration of the French growth from 1840 to 1857 and between 1906-1907 to 1913-1914; in 1914, France benefited from its financial strength (second world largest exporter of capital). But impact of the First World War has been disastrous for the French economy (from creditor nation to debtor nation, depreciation of the franc, monetary inflation, war deaths and invalids aggravating the structural shortage of manpower). The growth of the 1920s, the fastest in Western Europe, masked profound fragilities, despite the recovery made by Poincaré, from 1926 to 1928, and the revival of the automo-

47 Dominique Barjot, "A «French Miracle»? The Economic Growth of France 1949-1969", paper presented at the Paris Preconference.

bile industry. The crisis of the 1930s, although late, continued until 1938, because acceleration of aging, decline of industrial production, regulation of foreign trade, failure of deflationary policies. More, the Popular Front's policy failed: the revival of demand and the structural reforms do not allow the resumption of production, hence the inflation. The Second World War further weakened the French economy. Three factors concurred: the state extended its hold on the economy, Inflation exploded from November 1939, above all, from 1940 to 1944, France suffered enormous German levies. From where, in 1945, France came out very diminished of the conflict: the material losses were gigantic and concerned almost the entire country. Nevertheless the French external indebtedness was not very heavy and the monetary reserves remained negligible. Under these conditions, the spectacular economic recovery of the years 1945 to 1969 could be considered a miracle.

Realities and limits of the "French miracle" of the "Thirty Glorious"

Indeed, after the WW2, production increased greatly in France : from 1949 to 1969, the GDP growth rate was + 5.1% per year on average. In this way, the use of a Cobb-Douglas function leads to interesting results. According to Jean-Jacques Carré, Paul Dubois and Edmond Malinvaud, the growth in production was due to a number of factors.[48] It resulted first of all from the increased labor efficiency. Labor resources have increased slightly: + 0.2% per year. The total population has gone from Malthusianism to the renewal of the birth rate. If the activity rate has decreased compared to 1918, the level of employment remained very high since 1949, in spite of a very limited deterioration since 1965 and the duration of work strongly grew between 1946 and 1969. At the same time, the quality of the labor force has improved because of the higher level of education. Consequently, labor productivity accelerated slowly before the war, strongly thereafter. It also resulted from the increase in the stock of productive capital due to a considerable investment effort. Indeed, the growth of productive capital was indisputable. Nevertheless, after 1945, labor and capital growths only explained a limited part of the growth of GDP. Since 1945, the growth was mainly due to a residue. It was explained by economies of scale, better management methods and the development of technical progress and measured by total factor productivity gains. The level of this one was low in 1949 but was characterized by a rapid growth from 1949 to 1966.

Five other causes conditioned, in turn, the evolution of physical factors.

1/ the French economic growth benefitted of a global demand effect, due to urgent needs: old needs, the transformation of the entrepreneurs' decision-making context, confident in the dynamism of the global expansion, a deliberate choice of economic policy given priority is to growth over stability. In return, demand catalyzed growth by creating a particularly intense call for work, hence a high immigration of foreign labor, a sustained rate of activity of the French population, an almost minimum reduction of underemployment, the maintenance of a duration of relatively long work.

48 Jean-Jacques Carré, Paul Dubois, Edmond Malinvaud, *La croissance française. Un essai d'analyse économique causale de l'après-guerre*. Paris, Seuil, 1972.

At the same time, a high demand favored innovation, optimized the use of productive equipment, stimulated professional migration. The rapid development of France's foreign trade promoted growth, thanks to a specialization of the productive system, created economies of scale and catalyzed technical progress.

2/ The need for physical capital has led to abundant savings, a positive factor. If the demand for capital increased, the savings supply has increased since the last war. For households, the distribution of resources stabilized. In addition, the permanence of the housing difficulties of the French forced them to devote a growing share of their income to financing construction. The rise in post-war prices forced households to increase their cash balances considerably in order to maintain their purchasing power. But changes in the financing of investments were not an explanatory factor for post-war investments. In fact, the role of own resources was reduced and external financing increased sharply.

3/ Total factor productivity has improved through the development of a competitive market. From 1949 to 1968, the labor market evolved in the direction of a better allocation of resources. From 1955 to 1965 the enlargement of the capital market gradually transformed the conditions affecting the distribution of financial resources. If the price control always remained the rule, the creation of the Technical Committee on Cartels and Dominant Positions in 1953, and from 1960, the opening of the borders restored a more competitive market. Probably, regional development policy has slightly accelerated growth.

4/ State action unevenly was effective. Certainly cyclical regulation was generally beneficial for growth, but France had to solve the growth / external equilibrium dilemma. Planning helped create a climate of expansion but played only a very minor role in economic policy.

In conclusion, the French growth resulted from a series of favorable factors: catching up the birth rate, shock of 1939-45, institutional reforms parallel to the efforts of instruction of the French population, reconversion of the industry, release of the demand, environment favorable. Some factors were decisive: firstly, the French gave some priority to work; secondly during the 1960s, France benefited from a modernized productive apparatus and a dynamic, coherent and efficient economic policy was conducted then.

An industry predisposed to cartels: the example of the cement industry

Cécile Coursiéras-Jaff searched to understand the evolution of the cement market especially in Europe and France during the 20th century and to show how the cartels played a major role toward this market building.[49] During the interwar period, most European cement producers began considering the advantages of building national and international agreements. Some, such as the English producers, already owned strong national agreement organizations while others, such as the French producers, only had local and periodic price-fixing organizations. The behavior of the cement

49 Cécile Coursiéras-Jaff, "The Cement Market during the 20th Century: between Cartels and Regulation", paper presented at the Rio de Janeiro Preconference.

industry differed from other heavy industry sectors. For example, unlike the steel industry, the French cement industry did not organize its national cartel during the 1920's. C. Coursiéras-Jaff explained the reasons for this particular situation which were related to the oligopolistic structure of the cement market as well as economic cycles. During the 1920's, French cement producers mostly attempted to build local organizations in order to fix selling prices. But during the 1930's, they created strong centralized cartels, initially at a national scale and then at the European scale.

The reasons for this change in behavior are to be found primarily in the effects of the economic crisis. During the after-war period, the French cement industry knew a restructuration process. This evolution led to a decrease of the cement producers' number because of an acceleration of the concentration process. The cement market already had an oligopolistic structure before World War II. Yet, some regional family companies managed to get their game. However, from 1945 to 1970, the oligopoly was reinforced around the largest companies. C. Coursiéras-Jaff demonstrated that the cement cartel succeeded in fighting the crisis. She brought to light the role of French cement producers in the European cartel, and how French and European cartels allowed not only economic alliances, but technical and commercial alliances as well.

This evolution found an explanation in the particular structure of the cement market but also because of economic and political reasons. The cement industry was a heavy industry with a low value product. Therefore, one of the key issues consisted in limiting storage and transportation costs to preserve a competitive end product cost on the market. C. Coursiéras-Jaff analyzed how each producer manages to combine investment in productivity, capacity and spatial location to remain competitive. As a matter of fact, the study of the information sharing process between producers through cartels was crucial to understand this concentration process. Moreover, the growing demand of the reconstruction imposes capacity constraints that only members of the oligopoly seemed able to assume. That is why the link between growth and investment rate highlighted to understand the race between producers to increase their production capacity. The behavior of the French public authorities was also critical: probably the French state contributed to this concentration, especially by its price limitation policy.

The European Union and the French specificity since the 1960s

In 1957, the Treaty of Rome brought together six countries, but especially two opposed economic models.[50] This difference between France and its five other partners goes back to the beginnings of the modern era. France has built over the centuries a large domestic market that it has reserved for its producers through a whole arsenal of prohibitions and customs taxes. The progress of its taxation has allowed it to have a developed administrative apparatus. Its elites have become accustomed to affirming their prestige by joining the senior civil service. On the other hand, during the same

50 Michel Hau, « L'Union Européenne. L'évolution économique des pays d'Europe occidentale et la spécificité française depuis les années 1960 », paper presented at the Paris Preconference.

period, in the weak and scattered states of the Rhine or Alps, producers had to look for outlets and the elites made the company the means to found and sustain their social preeminence. The end of the Second World War considerably amplified the opposition between the two models, France opting in 1945 for a firmly statist system, its five future partners opting instead for a return to the market economy. Subsequently, the construction of Europe inevitably led to convergence between the two models. The choice to create a customs union rather than a free trade area and the acceptance of common policies could have changed the European construction towards a geographical extension of the French economic system. But things went quite differently.

France has failed to create a European Union in its image. Its economic model has been less well adapted to globalization than that of its five partners in the Treaty of Rome. By its very operation, the French economic system, based on the expansion of domestic demand, exposed France to the increasing pressure of its partners. France has, in its own right, adopted many elements of the liberal Rhine model. After renouncing protectionism in 1958, it gave up inflation in 1983, dirigisme in 1986, planning in 1992, monetary sovereignty in 1999 and stimulation by public spending in 2018. The social and political crises that have marked and continue to punctuate this development cannot make us lose sight of this heavy trend, which has emerged over the past six decades. They only show that the temporality of cultural facts obeys at slower rates than economic facts. The way the French apprehend their relationship to the rest of the world has probably not evolved as quickly as their unconscious consumer behavior attracted by free trade and sa attached to the euro.

Globalization and emergence: Eastern Europe

Central Europe offers several examples of small countries that have been successful in industrialization process.

Central Europe : national competitive advantages for small countries

Concerning the Hungary's industrialization process, Mária Hidvégi applies the Michael Porter school methodologies, as "the double diamond" in the case of the state-backed path of industrialization in small open economies.[51] It focuses on the example of Two Hungarian companies on the world market 1867-1989.[52] Indeed Alexander Gerschenkron's concept of backwardness implies an accelerated catch-up process facilitated by the government. In this scheme, governments facilitate and subsidize the transfer of new technologies as well as the establishment of new industries and institutions necessary for long-term growth. The state-backed path of industrialization may begin with infant industry protection (List 1840); Government intervention in the economy can be extended to new areas. In the footsteps of Gerschenkron, the extent of developmental delay, economic efficiency and, in part, the size of the country have been considered in economic and commercial history as factors deter-

51 Michael E. Porter, *Competitive Strategy*, Free Press, New York, 1980; *Competitive Advantage*, Free Press, New York, 1985; *The Competitive Advantage of Nations*, Free Press, New York, 1990, 1998.

52 Mária Hidvégi, "The Double Diamond and the State-backed Path of Industrialization in Small Open Economies: Two Hungarian Companies on the World Market 1867-1989", communication presented to the Paris Preconference.

mining how and to what extent the state can active and beneficial role in economic development (Kuznets 1960, Wu 2011, Müller und Myllintaus 2008). It is possible to speak of a developmental state, as in South America. The link with sources of national competitiveness (Porter 1990) is less well studied, as is the different importance of multinational activity for countries of different size in this respect.

The generalized double diamond approach has applied Michael Porter's interpretive scheme to small open economies incorporating national and international variables into the analysis of the determinants of national competitive advantages for countries outside Europe (Rugman al., 1995)[53]; (Moon et al., 1998)[54]. An analysis examines how the means and extent of state intervention in industrialization have influenced the multinational activities of the Hungarian national champions in the long run. Emphasis is placed on the efforts of these companies to overcome the constraints of their small open economy and late industrialization by promoting their competitiveness through better integration into the world economy. It thus becomes possible to describe some of the factors that are useful in applying the theory of state-backed path of industrialization to small open and late industrialized countries in the analysis of the entrepreneurial contribution to the performance of national economies in the long run. Hungary provides a good example in terms of fundamental changes in the political and economic system, but also constant efforts to catch up with the precursors of industrialization. If, at the macroeconomic level, there are country specific advantages, the microeconomic level emphasizes the concept of firm specific advantages. These elements have been common features of Hungary and many emerging and developing countries outside Europe.

An economic renaissance of Russia?

Today, as on the eve of the First World War, Russia is an emerging nation.[55] In 2015, at parity of purchasing power, as in 1914, Russia was ranked sixth world economic power. From 1892 until 1914, Russia experienced a spectacular take-off, based on rapid industrialization and an influx of foreign capital. It was the result of a national economic development strategy, which identified with Witte and Stolypin, two outstanding statesmen. If it was accompanied by a rapid worsening of social and geographical inequalities, this development was a major attraction for French capitalists and entrepreneurs. At the starting point were important economic and intellectual exchanges. These were flows on the one hand of goods, services and capital, and on the other hand transfers in the fields of technology, science and law, but whose influence was exerted unevenly across the regions of the country.

53 A.M. Rugman and J.R. D' Cruz , "The "Double Diamond" Model of International Competiveness: The Canadian Experience", *Management International Review*, 33 (2), 1993, p. 17-39.
54 H.C. Moon, A.M. Rugman and A. Verbeke, "A Generalized Double Diamond Approach to the Global Competitiveness of Korea and Singapore", *International Business Review* 7, 1998, p. 135-150.
55 Dominique Barjot, « Introduction », in Thierry Claeys and Francine-Dominique Liechtenhan (eds.), « Economic, Financial and Technological Relations between the Russia and the West at the Dawn of First World War. Les relations économiques, financières et technologiques entre la Russie et l'Occident à l'aube de la Première Guerre mondiale », *Revue française d'histoire économique – The French Economic History Review*, n° 7-8 (n°1-2), avril-octobre 2017, p. 14-32.

Russian industry relied heavily on Western European technologies throughout the period of modern economic growth.[56] Thanks to the contribution of the foreign organizational and technological experience, the Russian Empire conquered the fifth place among the main industrial nations of the world. At the beginning of the 20th century, technology transfer took place on a large scale and deeply affected the advanced branches of industry. The independence of economic development was achieved through a cautious and sustainable policy of technology adoption by a number of Russian entrepreneurs. The microeconomic approach reveals the mechanisms of the process. The leaders of Morozov have achieved their technological renovation through a systematic modernization day by day. The list of potential suppliers was very long. In general Morozov's trading strategies corresponded, on the one hand, to the commercial interests of foreign firms, essential suppliers of modern equipment for the flourishing Russian textile industry. On the other hand, they fully met the requirements of the growth of the company. At the same time, the country has made enormous efforts to accelerate the development of secondary and higher technical and technical education, the leading provider of national specialist cadres to the industry. In addition, Russian entrepreneurs have done their best to replace foreign specialists with highly qualified engineers, graduates of local universities.

The problem of the Russian economy today remains largely the same as at the time. Faced with the scale of Western sanctions, this economy has experienced a further slowdown in 2015 and 2016. This situation reflects unstable growth. Sustained between 2000 and 2008, the pace of GDP growth fell from 7.8% in 2009, to 4.5% in 2010, and then to decline steadily until 2015. In 2017, a slight recovery seems to have operated. It is based on a few positive indicators: an unemployment rate of 5.5%, but at the cost of a very flexible job; inflation dropped to 5.6%, but probably higher for the end consumer; encouraging signs of import substitution. In fact, Russia has achieved some success in the construction of aircraft and missiles, the pharmaceutical industry and radio electronics. Today, nearly 80% of the cars marketed in Russia benefit from a local assembly, from 65% of parts manufactured in the country. In addition, between 2014 and 2016, the share of medicines produced in Russia increased from 24 to 30%. But the most important progress seems to concern the agricultural and food industries (meat processing and dairy products), which are not very innovative sectors. Indeed, Russia seems to be sacrificing its R & D expenditure. As a result, the competitiveness of Russian products is deteriorating as wages remain too high in relation to productivity. Because the real incomes of Russians are decreasing, 14% of the country's inhabitants are now below the poverty line. Finally, foreign investment fell from 2013 to 2017. Because the country remains, as on the eve of the First World War, too dependent on the export of raw materials, the dynamism of the Russian economy remains suspended in the oil and gas cycle.

56 Irina Potkina, "The Nikolskaya Mill Partnership and the West European Firms: Some Aspects of Technological Transfer" in Thierry Claeys et Francine-Dominique Liechtenhan (eds.), "Economic, Financial and Technological Relations between the Russia and the West at the Dawn of First World War", *op. cit.*, p. 34-48.

UC Rusal, in aluminum, provides a good example of global challenger.[57] But to understand the emergence of this world leader in the aluminum industry, we must take into account the upheavals that have occurred for forty years and internationally in this industry. These upheavals were as follows: a shift in other geographic production, a decrease in the degree of concentration and integration of the industry; the emergence of new consumption centers, the development of new markets and the increasing competition of substitutes, including recycled metal; a real of the downward trend in the real price of the gray metal, new factors pushing up production costs and therefore prices, under the pressure of BRICS growth demand, the depreciation of the US dollar, the appreciation of the yuan and the dominant role of China; a change in the market imbalance adjustment mechanism, higher price volatility and increased investment demand, since the entry of aluminum into the London Metals Exchange (LME).

It is in this context that Rusal became in a few years the leader of aluminum production. Its history can be attributed to the origins of the Russian aluminum industry, and then to its rise in the Soviet era. The deep crisis experienced by this industry during the years was born, at the initiative of a few oligarchs and with the support of the Putinian regime, a vast group of factories, centered on Siberia, and able to evolve into a competitive multinational. Rusal was the second largest aluminum producer in the world until spring 2018. Its industrial base was built partly thanks to French technologies (Pechiney since the eve of the first world war). Since the US blacklisted Rusal on April 6, 2018, the largest metal producer outside China has lost more than half of its value in Hong Kong. Sanctions make it extremely difficult for Rusal to do business in dollars. Thus, it is very difficult to predict the future of the business.

Indeed, as many studies have shown, foreign capital played a very positive role in the economic development of Russia from the beginning of the second half of the nineteenth century.[58] It took the form of external loans (debt capital), direct investments in stock companies and entrepreneurial capital. Thanks to capital transfers, Russia has also benefited from the transfer of technology. The machine tool industry of the Soviet industry had insufficient capacity to produce special machines and automatic lines for mass production. The industry lacked experience in managing automobile production at the scale provided for in the long-term transportation plan. French and Italian car manufacturers (Renault, Fiat) were selected to provide technical assistance to the Soviet car industry. The results of Western technology transfer on the efficiency and productivity of the Russian economy have been rather positive. European manufacturers have largely contributed to the development of Russian industry. The success of today's Russian industry is largely due to the transfer of Western and especially French technologies, as shown by the case of the construction of the Renault car plant in Moscow. In addition, over the years, Total has established strong partnerships with leading Russian companies in the oil and gas sector. Since

57 Dominique Barjot, « Rusal : l'émergence d'un challenger. Premiers résultats », in Patrick Fridenson & Florence Hachez-Leroy (eds.), *L'aluminium, matière à création XIX*e*-XXI*e *siècles*, Tours, Presses universitaires François Rabelais, 2017, p. 273-307.
58 Boris Vinogradov, "Russia in the 19th Century, Russia Today, the Permanence of Technology Transfer", paper presented to the Paris Preconference.

2015, Russia has become the largest contributor to Total's global hydrocarbon production and most of its contribution is gas.

EASTERN AND SOUTH EASTERN ASIA: ASIAN MODEL OR NATIONAL PATH DEPENDANCY?

The considerable economic weight achieved today by China and India reflects the rise of Asia in the global economy. Indeed, if one thinks in terms of gross domestic product and purchasing power parity, the hierarchy of economic powers is very much modified for the benefit of Asia. Four Asian nations are in the top ten: China (1), India (3), Japan (4) and Indonesia (7); then come South Korea (14), Thailand (19) and Taiwan (20). This rise of Asia appears general. Nevertheless, in the medium and long term, this rise in Asia continues to rest on three main groups of countries, whose originality of the development model has been well highlighted by economists (WW Rostow, S. Kuznets A. Gerschenkron, R. Prebisch, P. A. Krugman[59], D. Senghaas, etc.):

1. Three economically dominant powers, one of which could be considered as a model by its precocity and the exemplary nature of its economic growth, Japan (hence, among others, the success of the famous theory of development "in wild goose flight" formulated by Kaname Akamatsu, in the 1930s[60]) and the other two, China and India, identify with the rise of the BRICS (Brazil, Russia, India, China and South Africa) in the global economy;

2. The "Four Dragons": These are four countries in the Far East that have experienced strong industrial growth since the 1960s, namely South Korea, Hong Kong, Singapore and Taiwan.

3. New Asian Tigers (or New Exporting Countries or "Tiger Babies") often referred to as Tiger Club Economics, according to Goldman Sachs. These are Indonesia, Malaysia, the Philippines, Thailand and Vietnam.

There could be no question during the two pre-conferences held in Asia to study all these countries. Nevertheless, it was possible to come back to the Japanese experience, whose pioneering nature deserves to be recalled, to open the door to a Chinese historiography still too well known and, without neglecting the importance of international trade flows, compare their specific development pathways with those followed by South Korea, Vietnam and, of course, India.

59 Paul R. Krugman with Masahisa Fujita and Anthony Venables, *The Spatial Economy – Cities, Regions and International Trade*, Cambridge (Mass.), MIT Press, 1999.

60 Kiyoshi Kojima, "The "Flying Geese" Model of Asian Economic Development: Origin, Theoretical Extensions, and Regional Policy Implications", *Journal of Asian Economics*, 11, 2000, p. 375-401.

Japan: pioneer but in a specific way?

As with Great Britain, today's historiography, without calling into question the pioneering nature of Japanese industrialization, tends more and more to emphasize the original character of the path followed by this country. This specificity of the Japanese way is clear from the work presented at the Tokyo pre-conference. These focused on three major themes: the role of entrepreneurship in the take-off of the Meiji era (and today) ; the respective role of technological change in the industrialization of the same Meiji period, both in the railways (technology transfers) and in the textile industry[61] (links between technological change and organizational change) ; the role of economic policies and their designers as an explanatory factor of the Japanese miracle from the 1950s to the 1990s.

At the origin of modern Japanese entrepreneurship

Shibusawa Eiichi was one the most representative figures of the Japanese capitalism of the Meiji era.[62] Called the "founder of Japanese capitalism, he was a Confucian equivalent of the Max Weber's model. However, Shibusawa's career was at first a pragmatic driven action, as a result of the Franck Michelin's study about relations between. Akita Prefecture and Shibusawa Eiichi. The Shibusawa's impact on the development of the capitalist economy in Japan in general and in Tohoku region in particular remains difficult to assess. Shibusawa did not have a huge investment power, but he had unique expertise in financial techniques: he was instrumental in launching and developing the banking systems across Japan. But with the intensification of military intervention on the continent and the transition to protectionism in many countries, Japan began to abandon free trade and to give a growing role to the state in economic development. Consequently, Shibusawa agreed that the state should play the leading role and became a supporter of the economic colonization of Taiwan and Korea. According to the renewed competitiveness of its industry, Japan remains today the third (or the fourth, in terms of purchasing power parity) world economic power. It was demonstrated by a comparison between Kodak and Fuji film (Yuzawa Takeshi).[63] In the 1960s and early 1970s, Kodak was the world's largest film maker. But Kodak failed to adapt to "the digital revolution". On the contrary, Fuji film is again a very profitable business.

Technology Transfers, Technical Change and Organizational Change in Meiji Japan

While the role of entrepreneurs has been essential, the decisive importance of technology transfer must also be stressed. In this respect, the railways are an excellent field of observation, as shown by Nakamura Naofumi's research.[64] The main purpose of

61 Tetsuji Okazaki, « Disentangling the Effects of Technical and Organizational Changes in the Rise of the Factory: The Case of the Japanese Fabric Industry 1905-1914 », *CRJE Discussion Papers*, July 2017, paper presented to the Tokyo Preconference.

62 Franck Michelin, "Shibusawa Eiichi and the Rise of the Capitalist Economy in Northern Japan. A Research Project", in Dominique Barjot (ed), "Theory and Empirical Performance. Economic Paradigm and Performance in the Long Run (18th to 21st century)", *Revue française d'histoire économique – The French Economic History Review*, n° 11-12 (n°1-2, 2019), *op. cit.*, p. 190-202.

63 Yuzawa Takeshi, "The Digital Revolution and Business Behavior. The case of Kodak us Fuji film", in Dominique Barjot (ed.), « L'ascension économique de l'Asie », *Entreprises & Histoire*, n° 90, 2018/1, p. 37-50.

64 Nakamura Naofumi, "Diversification and Convergence : Development of the Locomotive Technology in Meiji Japan", ISS Discussion Paper Series F – 180, June 2016, paper presented to the Tokyo Preconference.

Nakamura's article was to clarify the process of developing railway technology in Japan during the Meiji era (1868-1912) while emphasizing the role of railway engineers and their technical imitation. The process of developing railway technology in Japan can be divided into four stages: (1) transfer of railway systems from the United Kingdom by the Japanese Government during the period 1870-1880; (2) acquisition of railway materials, from the United States and Germany, and diversification of technology, during the 1890s; (3)) standardization and convergence of technology through the merging and nationalization of rail networks in the 1900s; and (4) the development of an original technology by the state railways during the 1910s.

In the first stage, rail technology was transferred to Japan in two ways: hiring foreigners or general contracts. The first method was promoted by the British for the railways at Honshu. The second was encouraged by the United States in Hokkaido. The hiring of foreigners has had a greater influence on the development of Japanese railway technology. However, this second method should not be neglected. Indeed it allowed the formation of Soichiro Matsumoto and Seichiro Hirai, engineers who played a central role in the Imperial Railways during the 1890s and 1900s, and the subsequent diversification. However, at the beginning of the Meiji era, the influence of foreign Honshu and British employees, who had a monopoly on the supply of railway equipment, was extremely strong and dominant.

In Stage 2, locomotive supply countries diversified very rapidly. The growing prosperity of the railway companies and the increased technological independence of Japanese engineers led in the 1880s and 1890s to a diversification of railway technologies. This diversification took place against a background of intensifying international competition in the global locomotive market. It became possible to optimally purchase railway materials from around the world. In Japan, competitive bidding and limited competitive practice were introduced in the 1890s, resulting in the creation of a competitive system for the purchase of equipment. At the same time, since each railway company bought locomotives independently, there were many locomotives in Japan with a wide variety of specifications. In addition, efforts were made to make copies using various locomotives from different countries as models, which led to the accumulation of technological skills in the manufacture of rolling stock.

In a third stage (stage 3), the lack of uniform standards between the different companies appeared as a growing problem due to the need to standardize facilities. Following the promulgation of the Railway Operations Law in 1900, various regulations were adopted to standardize rails, couplers and rolling stock. This movement towards standardization was accelerated with the nationalization of 1906-07. In step 4, a manufacturing section was established within the Railway Agency. Its business was growing along with that of private rolling-stock manufacturers in order to manufacture locomotives in Japan. Different models of locomotives were ordered from Europe and the United States. A specifically Japanese know-how was thus acquired, taking advantage of the inspection system. By 1914, Japan had thus developed an independent locomotive design and manufacturing capability, which ultimately led to the emergence of Japanese locomotive mass production. In the end, it is clear that the imitation of a wide variety of foreign models and the training of Japanese engineers in both state and private companies have enabled Japanese industry to know-how equivalent to that of the major Western industrial powers. In other words, the diversification of technology and the concomitant accumulation of experiences have been the keys to the development of an original technology.

The sources of the "Japanese economic miracle" revisited

Much has been written about the Japanese economic miracle, but still not enough about his intellectual origins and especially about the origins of economic policies that accompanied and encouraged him. This is to say all the interest of the works of Yago Kazuhiko. Japan achieved impressive high economic growth from the end of the 1950s until the beginning of the 1970s. Japan's economic growth after WWII was driven by continuous plans, of which the most famous was the Doubling National Income Plan (1961-1970)[65]. Yago K. tries to reconstruct the visions proposed and debated among the Japanese officials involved in the process of making of these plans. He also refer to another actor, the Organization for Economic Cooperation and Development (OECD), especially the Working Group 2 for the Economic Policy Committee (WP2) standing under the Ministerial Council of the OECD. The OECD Ministerial Council, soon after its foundation in 1961, set up a growth target for member countries to achieve between 1960 and 1970s: "a growth of 50 per cent in the real gross national product". Japan, upon entering the OECD in 1964, would participate in this growth target as a forerunner of economic upsurge. The Yago's hypothesis is that the plans elaborated during the 1950s and the 1960s under the fixed-rate exchange rate system might have been more prudent, in terms of the target and the view of the future society, than the real outcome which we know today from hindsight. Viewing Japan's growth plan and practice from the OECD point of view (and *vice versa*), Yago K. is paying special attention to the theoretical and political division witnessed by the Japanese authorities, which was also echoed in the OECD view.

A second Yago's paper searched to present an alternative view on Japanese growth, referring to contemporary debates in the OECD in order to review how contemporaries understood productivity, with updated historiography[66]. Viewing the notion of productivity from the OECD archives, the followings have been discovered: The notion of productivity was imperfect, and the Japanese view has been constrained to a contemporary context, in particular the foreign reserves. However, the above understandings and misunderstandings occasionally enabled Japanese high growth. The "backwardness" of the rural population first supplied cheap labor, with strong propensity for saving, and finally turned into a vast market for household goods. The role played by the government was essential in introducing foreign technologies, but one of the important backdrops was the capital movement regulation, which suggested the licensing and trade of intellectual properties instead of direct investment.

65 Yago Kazuhiko, "Convergence and Divergence over the Growth Paradigm: The OECD Working Party 2 and the Japanese "Doubling National Income Plan", *Revue économique, op. cit.*, 2020/4, Vol. 71, p. 697-713.
66 Yago Kazuhiko, "The "black box" of Japanese growth (1945-1973): the origins of productivity", original chapter.

The fruits of this economic growth have allowed Japan to become a huge donor of foreign aid, mainly to developing countries in Asia[67]. What were the thoughts and paradigm which supported the evolution of Japanese aid, in relation to the country's high-speed growth? Yago K. aims to give answers to the above question from historical perspectives, focusing on how the "insiders" watched the issues, depending upon two series of archives: The Development Assistance Committee (DAC) of the Organization for Economic Cooperation and Development (OECD), and the External Development Cooperation Council (EDCC) of Japan. The Japanese Government aimed to join the DAC and operate aid in order to ensure the export and resource markets for Japanese growth. On the other hand, Japan sooner or later succeeded in pushing its high-speed growth without taking care of the aid-tied market. The Japanese "growth paradigm" in relation to aid changed with a certain time-lag and continuity, together with deep strategic thinking and inconsistent fear of facing a new phase of growth.

Awakening of Chinese economic power

With the reforms introduced in China by Deng Xiaoping, starting in 1979, China has made giant strides in the path of self-sustained economic growth. She caught up, then passed Japan, imposing itself as another Asian model. But the challenge of modernization is not fully addressed. How to reform the economy, politics and culture of a traditional Chinese society and how to change the relationship between the three aspects accordingly? These questions dictate the path that China takes to become a modern nation. Huang Chun and Wang Jue showed that the strategy used by China to learn from the modern Western world was to promote the modernization of economic, political and cultural capacity through industrial modernization.[68] Centered around this goal, the learning of Western institutions and ideology has been and necessarily remains adaptive, reforming and inclusive. From the point of view of the development of China's own culture, the challenge of modernizing China lies in the question of successfully integrating the traditions of Chinese culture with modern Western culture to create a new form of culture.

To the research of the specificity of the Chinese model of development

Chinese economic history is changing today. A whole generation of young researchers have embarked on original research. Research focuses on the history of financial and commercial institutions as well as scientific and technological developments. In traditional China, there was a delicate relationship between the official economy and non-governmental economy[69]. The former lacks necessary concern for the

67 Yago Kazuhiko, "Japanese Aid and Economic Growth during the 1960s and Early 1970s", in Dominique Barjot (ed), "Theory and Empirical Performance. Economic Paradigm and Performance in the Long Run (18th to 21st century)", *Revue française d'histoire économique – The French Economic History Review*, n° 11-12 (n°1-2, 2019), *op. cit.*, p. 204-224.

68 Huang Chun and Wang Jue, "China's Path to Become a Modern Nation: Industrialization, Learning Strategy and System Choice", in Dominique Barjot (ed.), "Economic development, financing and business strategies (19th-21st century)". « Développement économique, financement et stratégies d'entreprises XIXe-XXIe siècle) », *Revue française d'histoire économique – The French Economic History Review*, n° 9-10 (n°1 et n° 2, janvier et septembre 2018), p. 38-59.

69 Sun Rui and Wang Qing "Chinese Model and the Choice of Development Path: A Perspective from Economic History", in Dominique Barjot (ed), "Theory and Empirical Performance. Economic Paradigm and Performance in the Long Run (18th to 21st century)", *Revue française d'histoire économique – The French Economic History Review*, n° 11-12 (n°1-2, 2019), *op. cit.*, p. 182-189.

latter, but gives the latter sufficient space for free development in practice. On the road to modernization, facing with the threat of Western powers, China has be experienced a large-scale national remodeling, as well as the transformation of the role of the government, forming the so-called "Chinese Model". From the perspective of economic history, China's reform and opening up in the last 40 years has freed the private economy again, which seems to be a kind of return to Chinese traditions.

For instance, Sun Rui realized a study of the traditional Chinese communal organization and the State transition.[70] This paper focus on the local commercial management in Hu Nan Province during 1787 to 1909 of China. The research is the 269 regulations, including 2636 clauses, 133 industries as Chinese traditional ways. There was a commercial autonomy in these regulations. And the core industry interests was noticed and kept in each one of them, which was the most important things instead of religions. Procedural justice could be insist on election and interior finance management. There also had rules about supervising the top directors. They must be responsible for their association. The associations has great marketing authority that made the transaction regulations as well as the punishments. The local government's influence was important but not the essential. They provide a better understanding of a traditional system set up around 1500 and in place until 1945. These regulations concern the regulation of markets and the management of guilds. They show the management autonomy these guilds benefited.

A major theme: setting up the technology transfer and transport development

A good example of spectacular modernization concerns rail transport. Through a massive investment in high-speed trains, China has gone from a phase of catching-up to another, based on innovation.[71] The history of high-speed rail development can be divided into three periods: a period of exploration based on independent research and development, from 1992 to 2003, a phase of massive introduction of foreign technology, from 2004 to 2007, finally, since that date, a new period of self-dependent innovation. As a result, the Chinese high-speed train (TGV) industry has seen an increase in mileage (19,000 kilometers in 2015, 30,000 in 2020) and technological innovations. In the case of China, the state could be defined as an entrepreneur.

The development of the Chinese HSR was led by the State Council, in close coordination with the National Commission for Development and Reform, the Ministry of Science and Technology, the Ministry of Finance and other departments and local governments. In the process of introducing technology as a leader, the former Ministry of Railways (MOR) exercised administrative and managerial functions both as a representative of the state and as an active enterprise. He was both strategist and executor. He was the legislator of all negotiations and contracts. Managing the introduction of technology, he financed R & D, created the market, guided public

70 Sun Rui, "What is the Local Governmental Management in Economy? A View on the Commercial Association during the Late Qing Dynasty in China?", paper presented to the Beijing and Tokyo Preconferences.
71 Wang Jue and Wang Qing, "China's High-speed Rail. From Technological Catching-up to Innovation", paper presented to the Tokyo Preconference.

opinion. The MOR was responsible for the investments and the financing, but also for the drafting of plans and the implementation of unified standards, tenders, the construction and the approval of all works, purchase and management of vehicles and other accessories. In the beginning, the development period of HSR was deeply rooted in the planned economy. As a result, there was a series of defects. The loosening of credit constraints and excessive debt, the inadequacy and wastage of resources, the lack of technical maturity existed in the old MOR. However, its effectiveness and its implementation capacity should not be neglected.

A recent but impressive rise in power : the Chinese Construction Industry
After the declaration of the foundation of The People's Republic of China in 1949 by Mao Zedong, the construction industry suffered a serious "draw back" because of the dreadful influence of the newly acquired state ideology on the economy[72]. After decades of under usage, the renewal of this long since stagnant industry only came with the arrival of a new leader: Deng Xiaoping, whose reforms were to propel China to a whole new economic rank. The reforms among the public enterprises consisted of altering the planned economic system, giving more freedom to the construction enterprises, and research for more financial resources through the stock market. However, in spite of numerous economic reforms the legacies of an outdated economic system have remained considerable. Faced with China's entry into the World Trade Organization (hereafter WTO) since 2001, not only does the construction industry, still on its way to reform, have to fight against powerful rivals from all over the world, but also has to pass through national borders with the purpose of making profits on a larger scale of the international market. In 2007 according to the statistics of the WTO, China was listed as the third biggest country in terms of output just after the USA and Japan. Also China and India, with expenses on construction growing annually by more than 8%, the two countries both stand out as being the two biggest markets in the construction industry in the world.

The recently founded Asia Infrastructure Investment Bank (hereafter AIIB) which aims at exporting the exceeding capitals from China to support the construction of infrastructures, including railways, roads, bridges, ports and airports throughout Asia since November 2014, is largely depending on the construction industry. At the same time, China Railway Group Limited and China Railway Construction Corporation Limited the two biggest construction companies in China. These two companies are also the two biggest world-wide in term of capital. Alongside a third company, China State Construction, whose power is rapidly growing, is about to take the third place.

Generally speaking, Chinese construction industry on one hand made remarkable progress in the overseas markets, mostly in developing countries. Their success is often marked by landmark buildings such as highways, hospitals and irrigation systems where the local governments are not capable of constructing these kinds of

72 Zhou Xiaolan, "The International Activities of the Chinese Construction Industry under the Context of China's Entry into the WTO. The Case of China Railway Group Limited"?, paper presented to the session Multinationals from emerging and developing countries: historical roots [S10080], XVIIth World Economic History Congress 2015 Kyoto, Japan, 3-7 August 2015.

works. On the other hand, they still have difficulties in breaking through the markets in developed countries where the sanction of laws and contracts prevail over the governmental power. The case of "China Railway Group Limited" might be a perfect case for demonstrating the embarrassing situation of the construction industry in China nowadays. The eventual success of the industry in the international stage might rely on the deeper optimization on the structure of the state-owned groups, especially a better management of their branches, on the improvement of their Research and Development sector and on their consciousness of the legal systems in foreign countries if they still have intention to share the markets in Europe and North America.

New industrializing nations in Asia

The paths of industrialization are not limited to Japanese and Chinese models. At the margins of China, South Korea, the largest of the "four dragons", and Vietnam, one of the "Asian tigers", offer two interesting examples, with very different trajectories. Above all, a new economic giant emerged: India, with its large companies, some of them multinational. In its development, it appealed to foreign capital. There are interested European countries, like Germany.

South Korea

With Taiwan, South Korea is therefore one of the best illustrations of the theories of Rostow, who carried out several consulting and assistance missions in the 1960s. Firstly, recent South Korean historiography tends to reassess the role of the Korean business community in the economic boom of the early 20th century. It is true that the Japanese forced the country's entry into modernity[73], but there were also real Korean capitalists, particularly in the rice trade and packaging industry. The Kim merchants were a family of brokers [gaekju] operating in the Dongmak area of Seoul, right by the Han River. Hong Sung Chan, Lee Jong Hwa and Kim Mi Lim have documented the establishment and operation of the of the Dongil Rice Mill of the Kim family, which used a petrol or electric motor, transmission gears and systems that had been in operation since 1910[74]. Rice preparation was a manufacturing industry that attracted many Korean investors during the Hanmal and early colonial periods. Using the Kim family's account books, it is possible to reconstruct the space and facilities of the Dongil Rice Mill, the operations of purchasing and processing raw materials (unshelled rice and brown unpolished rice), those of selling products (brown rice or white rice), to study the evolution of employment and the level such as the evolution of wages, banking transactions and use of capital, and the daily operations carried out in the 1910s. Thus it is possible to clearly show the transformation of Korean traders and brokers into a bourgeoisie and the conversion of commercial capital into industrial

73 Dominique Barjot, Rang-Ri Park-Barjot, « La société coréenne face à l'impérialisme japonais (1875-1945) : entre exploitation économique, modernisation forcée et assimilation », in Jean-François Klein, Claire Laux, *Les sociétés coloniales à l'âge des empires : Afrique, Antilles, Asie (années 1850-années 1950)*, Ellipses, 2012, chapitre 7, p. 96-104.

74 Hong Sung Chan, Lee Jong Hwa and Kim Mi Lim, "From Grain Merchants to Millers:The Kims of Seoul and the Origins of Korean Capitalism", *Revue économique*, *op. cit.*, 2020/5, Vol. 71, p. 895-909.

capital. In other words, it is possible to highlight and demonstrate the internal origins and long-term continuity of Korean capitalism.

More, after the economic take-off of Japan, South Korea knew another "Miracle", in spite of a heavy inheritance (the "Hermit Kingdom" of the 19th century, the Japanese Occupation and the Korean War).[75] From 1960s, the country benefitted of a rapid economic development, based on the growth of exports, and, with a certain delay, of the internal market of mass consumption. From the point of view of the dominant historiography the most important factors of success were the American aid and the cooperation between the State and the big conglomerates (or *chaebols*). That is not false but must be qualified. The various experiences of steel industry, shipbuilding and automobile industry clearly moves in this way; on the contrary, the case of electronics brings to relativize the importance of this connection, as shows it the examples of LG and Samsung: two models of growth coexisted.

The South Korean economic success largely resulted of a remarkable mobilizing of human capital.[76] It was the case only from 1961, because the Nation operated a strategic reorientation to a new model of industrialization, under the impulse of President Park Chung-Hee. From a macroeconomic point of view, the success of this model based on exports largely resulted of three factors: there existed powerful industrial and financial Korean groups; the strategy of exports always remained profitable; the government led a voluntarist economic policy. Nevertheless, if South Korea today is a developed country, a determining factor of this success lives in the mobilization of human capital. Probably, the neo-confucianism constituted an accelerator of the progress. At the same time, Korea benefited and today benefits of an already scientific and cultural heritage. Even if it today is discussed, both the school and University system seem successful. Above all, South Korea supplies a massif effort of research and development.

Micro-economically speaking, South Korea benefitted of positive effects of international specialization, as Shipbuilding is offering a good example.[77] In 2011, shipbuilding was the four post of South Korea exports (10%), playing the role of a leading sector. Form the early 2000s, South Korea became the world leader before Japan. But since 2009, Korean Shipbuilders must resist to the Chinese competition, thanks to a highly skilled workforce and an excellent strategic positioning. Nevertheless, nothing would have been possible without the emergence, in South Korea, of Posco, an Asian leader of the steel industry.[78] If South Korea today remains the fifth world producer, the

75 Dominique Barjot and Park Rang-Ri, "The Korean "Miracle" between the State and the Chaebols", paper presented to the Beijing Preconference.

76 Park-Barjot Rang-Ri & Parc Jimmyn, « Le capital humain : facteur clé du modèle coréen de développement », in *Outre-Terre,* n° 39, numéro spécial « Corée du Nord, Corée du Sud : la guerre sans la guerre », 2014, p. 74-90.

77 Dominique Barjot and Park Rang-Ri, « L'industrie des constructions navales : un secteur stratégique pour le take-off économique de la Corée du Sud (1945-environs de 2000) », in Dominique Barjot (dir.), « Les entreprises et entrepreneurs d'Asie », *Entreprises et Histoire,* n° 90, avril 2018, p. 51-75.

78 Dominique Barjot and Park Rang-Ri, « L'émergence d'un leader asiatique de la sidérurgie : Posco (1968-2010 », in Barthel (Charles), Kharaba (Ivan) & Mioche (Philippe) (dir. /eds.), *Les mutations de la sidérurgie mondiale du XXe siècle à nos jours. The Transformation of the World Steel Industry from the 20th Century to the Present,* Bruxelles, P.I.E. Peter Lang, 2014, p. 299-319.

dynamism of the Korean steel industry based mainly on Posco, the fifth company in the world. Founded by the Korean State in 1968, Posco knew a fast development during the 1980. Under the Park Tae-Joon's impulse, Posco became number one in terms of productivity, founded Postech (Pohang University of Science and Technology). Offering an example of successful privatization, Posco constituted a key factor of the Korean economic recovery after the crisis of 1997. Today Posco remains the most profitable steel company in the world.

At the same time, South Korea realized a successful breakthrough in the electronics, thanks to LG (or Lucky Goldstar) or Samsung.[79] The LG Electronics success was the result of a growth pattern founded on exports, associating a vigorous innovation of product and an efficient strategy of globalization. Consequently, LG acceded to the mature markets (North America, Germany, Poland) and conquered emergent countries market (China, India, Brazil, Turkey, Russia) and reinforced its position on the Korean market facing Samsung Electronics. Nevertheless, Samsung today remains the most important Korean Group. Indeed Samsung benefitted of the strong heritage of the founder Lee Byung-Chull, and the specific action of his son and successor, Lee Kun-Hee. Lee B.C. developed an original philosophy, based on Confucian ethics, but pragmatically applied, and adapted by Lee K.H. After the financial crisis of 1997-98, this one relaunched the Samsung Group, thanks a striking opening in technology. Consequently the Samsung's profitability increased.

Today, the Korean model seems both threatened, but also relaunched.[80] If the international economic crisis of 2008-2011 pulled a crisis of Chaebol, as in the LG's example, more largely, three major threats remains; the relations with North Korea, the rise of international competition (loses of competitiveness facing China, Japan, Taiwan and Indonesia) and specific South Korean societal problems (accelerated ageing, rate of suicides). But South Korea always benefits of strong assets: a good quality of life, an absolute priority given to new technologies (Samsung, nuclear sector), a voluntarist choice in favor of the "green growth", the growing strength of the cultural Korean Model (Hallyu).

Vietnam

Vietnam belongs to the group of "Asian Tigers", but like China, Indonesia or Malaysia, surmounted quite well the financial crisis of 1997-98.[81] The regularity of its growth raises questions about the relevant model(s) of interpretation: model « in flight of the wild goose » (Akamatsu), Rostow's, Kuznets's, Perroux or evolutionnist models. Densely populated and marked by history, Vietnam established his national inte-

79 Dominique Barjot and Park Rang-Ri, « Samsung. Le modèle de croissance entre exemplarité et originalité (1938-2007) », in Dominique Barjot (ed.), "Economic development, financing and business strategies (19th-21st century)", *op. cit.*, p. 78-111; Park Rang-Ri, *Samsung. L'œuvre d'un entrepreneur hors pair, Byung Chull Lee* (*Samsung. The work of an extraordinary entrepreneur, Byung Chull Lee*), Paris, Economica, 2008.

80 Dominique Barjot, « Corée du Sud : entre risques et opportunités d'investissement », *Sécurité et stratégie*, juin-septembre 2013, p. 66-76.

81 Dominique Barjot, "Vietnam: The Rise of a New Industrialized Nation", paper presented to the Tokyo Preconference ; Dominique Barjot et Jean-François Klein (eds.), *De l'Indochine coloniale au Việt Nam actuel*, Paris, Académie des Sciences d'Outre-Mer, Éditions Magellan, 2017, 816 p. See in particular Dominique Barjot, « Introduction », p. 42-69.

gration on a walk to the South and an assimilation of the high lands. In spite of an unachieved demographic transition the population remained young and feminized. At the same time, the Vietnamese culture, marked by the Confucian influence, around original language and writing. In Vietnam, the end of a system of centralized economy and the decisive influence of the Southern opened the way to a premature transition towards a free market characterized at the same time by the call for foreign aid, the rise of informal activities and the progressive, but unfinished privatization of the State sector. Indeed between 1954 and 1975, the Democratic Republic of Vietnam (in the North) knew the war economy with a growing Soviet aid. The reunification of 1975 changed the situation. If in the South, the inheritance was heavy, in the North, the discovery of the South shook the spirits, in a context marked by the stop of Chinese aid, a decreasing Soviet aid and an explosion of black market. It became a necessity to save the national economy.

Largely accelerated by the geopolitical context (entry in the Comecon, fall of the Khmer regime, conflict with People's Republic of China), the consequence was a profound change.[82] In December 1980, was adopted the strategy of *Đổi mới* (change to make of the new), which recognized the market economy, encouraged the individual initiative, rehabilited the business without abandoning the socialist frame. The success was undeniable: reinstatement in the circuits in the international trade (ASEAN) construction of infrastructures, liberalization of the land market, agricultural diversification, State regulation of the foreign capital flows, development of domestic private activities, decline of the State economic role. In spite of the 1997-98 financial crisis, Vietnam fully integrated into Asian Trade (APEC, WTO, border agreement with China) and engaged a depth reform of its business system (public limited companies introduction of VAT, insertion into outsourcing networks).

From 1986, Vietnam experienced a high growth rate of GDP (per capita, GDP tripled from 2002 to 2010).[83] Consequently Vietnam became one of the Asian economics most open to the international exchanges. Facing persisting macroeconomic imbalances (inflation, government indebtedness, unemployment), the Vietnam State imposed strict measure (reform of the banking system). Nevertheless, the economy remained highly dependent on agriculture (second world exporter for rice and coffee) and raw materials (petrol and natural gas, coal), because an industry insufficiently diversified (textiles, agri-food products, electronic components). But, the Vietnamese economy became more and more attractive for foreign capitals, especially because the growth was drives by leading industrial sectors (textiles, oil industry, shipbuilding, automotive, electronic components), but also by tourism and telecommunication. Consequently, exports provided two thirds of GDP. Benefitting from the low relative cost of its workforce, Vietnam exported more and more. At the same time, foreign direct investment grew, mostly becoming of Japan, Singapore, South Korea, China and Russia.

82 Marie-Sybille de Vienne, *L'Économie du Việt Nam (1955-1995). Bilan et prospective*, Paris, CHEAM, 1994.
83 Emmanuelle Paquet, *Réforme et transformation du système économique vietnamien, 1979-2002*, Paris, L'Harmattan, 2004.

If today, Vietnam remain an emerging economy, remaining behind the other "Asian Tigers" in terms of GDP by capita, Vietnam, apart from Indonesia, is the one with the highest growth potential, because a lot of decisive assets, an efficient labor market, a strong innovation capacity, a gradual economic opening, generation of leading sectors favoring a spectacular take-off, a position of preferred subcontractor for Japanese and South Korean industries (Samsung). Consequently Vietnam is verifying several western theories: Rostow (take-off, leading sectors), Kuznets (large reallocation of productivity sectors), Perroux (pole of development of the Ho Chi Minh City), Porter (clusters of Hanoi, Haiphong, Da-Nang) and evolutionism (path dependency).

India

Japan, China and even South Korea have become important exporters not only of goods and services, but also of capital: so in Vietnam. In the case of China, this surge in capital exports has been spectacular, to the point where we now speak of "Chinafrica" as we did in the case of Francafrique. Other Western countries have also chosen the path of capital exports to accompany and consolidate in the long term a development strategy based on exports of capital goods and sustainable consumption. This was the case of Federal Germany after the Second World War. The two decades after the Second World War were commonly analyzed as a phase of rebuilding the global economy and a prelude to the second wave of globalization of the 1970s. Julian Faust studied German societies and their re-internationalization after World War II in India as actors in these globalization processes leading to a closer integration of the developing economy into world trade and value chains. [84] He focused on the objectives and expectations of these actors in the micro-perspective of foreign companies in India. He sought to understand how these commercial actors used the industrialization policies of a newly independent country like India or were hindered by them.

Indeed, the association with development policies and programs has been used as a strategy to gain a foothold in the Indian market. Indeed, India, according to the model of import-substitution-industrialization (ISI) had become a more closed market to foreigners. J. Faust adopted the hypothesis of a coalition of interests between German companies and government in the early years of international development policy. It shows how companies were able to use their origin and reputation. India was an excellent example of the formal and informal way in which German firms dealt with the non-tariff barriers and restrictions imposed on foreign investors in India, which had adopted rigorous ISI strategy.

Indeed, many big players in German industry like Beyer had established business ties with India before the war. With the change in the political and economic system and the prospect of strong growth in India's population, they expected the country to become one of the largest markets in Asia in the future. The main objective during the period of investigation was the Indian domestic market. Despite the five-year

84 Julian Faust, "Expectations and Strategies of the German India during Decolonisation and Import Substitution-Industrialisation", Paper presented to the Beijing Preconference.

plans and economic planning in general, the big German industry has not abandoned the market. Instead, German manufacturers have developed strategies to deal with growing market regulation and entry barriers such as production and import licensing. Along with other western and eastern foreign companies, companies like Bayer and Bosch were competing to set up the first joint venture production units and their industry. Indeed, the Indian government only granted the necessary production capacity to one or very few companies. This, after the market was closed to other competitors, created profit opportunities.

The protection of the fledgling industry, the need for know-how and foreign capital from India to industrialize the country without completely offsetting its balance of payments allowed foreign companies to intervene. Bosch and Bayer were able to build relationships in India for their products. By not considering industrial projects primarily as commercial and for-profit, they demonstrated their goodwill, their technical know-how and their commercial expertise with the result of helping India in this way. They saved their real investment against stronger regulation, bureaucracy and pressure on their joint ventures to become a minority. Bayer and Bosch managed to gain a foothold and prosper in India because they offered products and expertise in areas critical to the advancement of the Indian economy: basic chemicals, agrochemicals, diesel engines and solutions for commercial vehicles and transport. With such offers and investments in products strategically offering a growing market and political support for German development aid: for example Bosch's investment in the MICO joint venture, from 1959 until the 1980s, has provided a regular dividend to the German parent company.

German participation in the planned industrialization of India was actively promoted until the mid-sixties. Companies such as Bayer and Bosch have positioned themselves as Germans. This label was an advantage over other competitors in other countries, despite the Nazi regime that had just ended in 1945. With the political and economic goal of attaining both countries, the technical know-how and the expertise of the United States, Soviet Union, United Kingdom and other European countries. The political imperative was to cut ties with the former German foreign policy. This was the more so, as the framework of the West Germany economy was less contested than the image of American capitalism within India's "Socialist Pattern of Society" outspoken by its first Prime Minister.

For a long time, India thus seemed to offer a model of a third party, favouring a socialist economy, based on the search for import substitution, but without going as far as the communist totalitarianism adopted in the Soviet Union and then in China. Nevertheless, in the 1990s, the country liberalised its economy and embarked on a path of development that was better integrated into the world economy. The reforms undertaken by India since 1991 had a positive effect on its economy. They stimulated the liberalization of trade, especially with the rest of the world. Can we postulate that India evolved from a planned economy to free market, or from A. Gerschenkron's to

A. Smith's vision?[85] The analysis of the structures and strategies of the top 20 Indian companies in 2016-2017, following A.D. Chandler's approach, enables us to formulate some hypotheses. We can effectively see that the reforms favoured the modernization and expansion of old enterprises dealing with sectors associated with the second industrial revolution over the creation of technologically advanced firms. Moreover, these reforms didn't put aside SOEs nor even the financial participation of the state in the private sector. To be sure, the mass consumption of technologically sophisticated products took off only fifteen years ago in India. The Indian enterprises followed the trend carefully, even if some ran the risk of diversifying their activities. At the same time, however, they opened themselves to managerial practices, they modernized and internationalized themselves while hiring cheap labour. If free market has more weight today, the evolution has been slower than expected; but it is speeding up. The big companies will go along, but that doesn't mean they will free themselves from the state's interferences.

OTHER EMERGING NATIONS

If Asia is par excellence the emerging continent, especially the Far East and the Indian subcontinent, other major regions of the world see the commitment and even affirmation of new industrialized nations. This is particularly the case in Latin America. Once again, macroeconomic approaches developed in the context of nations, and microeconomics, essentially business history, are enriching each other, as in the case of cooperation and competition in Brazil. The consequence is a revision, by some Latin American historians, of the theories generally applied to explain the specificities of economic development, particularly in Argentina and Brazil. However, other regions of the world are looking for ways to grow: French-speaking Africa, for example. Some nations have even been able to emerge, but with unequal final success, as reference models for the countries of the South, such as Egypt, then South Africa, while Australia finally managed to reach the highest world's levels of development.

Latin America

Since the Second World War, the nations of Latin America have become highly industrialized, not without tensions and crises, notably because of excessive inequalities of income and wealth. From this point of view, Peru provides a good observatory of the contradictions inherent in Latin American development. Colombia too, where the work of the World Bank has been decisive. In these countries, one of the major challenges has been the formation of human capital, as the Brazilian example reveals. Moreover, as in all emerging countries, one of the keys to industrialization has been the emergence of global players, including Mexico's Cemex, the world's fourth largest cement company, but the leader in terms of profitability, and Brazil's Vale in iron ore are emblematic examples.

85 Pierre Lanthier, "From Gerschenkron back to Smith? The Case of Indian Big Business Today", in Dominique Barjot (ed), "Theory and Empirical Performance. Economic Paradigm and Performance in the Long Run (18th to 21st century)", *Revue française d'histoire économique – The French Economic History Review*, n° 11-12 (n°1-2, 2019), *op. cit.*, p. 162-181.

The macroeconomic approach: Peru and Colombia

Getsiva Cayo-Durand questioned the economic models advocated by the Peruvian governments during the 1950s and 1960s.[86] While after the Second World War, most Latin American countries adopted protectionist policies, Peru preferred become a firm supporter of liberalism. In the multilateral system, governments wanted to achieve the take-off of the Peruvian economy by following the concepts of W.W. Rostow. Nevertheless, the thought of R. Prebisch gradually settled. Protectionist policies were implemented in the early sixties. The country was then looking for its model of economic development.

Indeed, since the crisis of 1930, two models of development have clashed in Latin America: the first-export model (guided by liberalism) and the industrialization by import substitution (ISI). Taking into account the internal and external conditions of development, Getsiva Cayo-Durand showed that the Peruvian governments have not favored a single model of development. The influence of the first-export model has been interpreted as an "outward-looking" model, and that of the ISI model "inward". The latter model did not first impose itself as an ideology, but rather as a necessity. Although the theory of dependence developed by the Argentine economist Raúl Prebisch was one of the most commonly adopted at the time, it was not a general rule. Argentina, Brazil, Mexico, Chile, Colombia and Uruguay offer classic examples of "inward" Latin American countries. In contrast, Peru remained more of a supporter of the "outward" model. It was not until the 1960s for the impact of Prebisch's thought to become effective.

What was the economic policy advocated in Peru during the 1950s and 1960s? What were the development models implemented and what were their results? To answer these questions, G. Cayo-Durand gave an approach to the Peruvian economy in two stages: first, a review of Peruvian economic policy under the prism of Rostow; then an analysis under that of Prebisch. It was able to show the ambitions of the models adopted by governments but taking into account their limits and their contradictions. It shows that the policies implemented by the Peruvian governments led by liberalism or the ISI were contrasted, but not totally opposed. Since the late 1950s, protectionist policies have been implemented, revealing the limits of the "outward" trend. These two economic strategies managed to cohabit together without causing a major break.

Under the government of the civilians as well as under that of the military, of right or left, the country never gave up its project of industrialization. However, no development program has been conducted in the long term. Taking into account the local and international situation, the implementation of "outward-looking", "inward" or "mixed models" models did not guarantee success because of the lack of continuity in policies. adopted. The take-off of the Peruvian economy has been delayed or even blocked by problems of endogenous and exogenous nature: On the one hand, politi-

86 Getsiva Cayo Durand de Geist, « Le développement économique péruvien durant les années 1950 et 1960 : distinguer deux modèles ? », paper presented to the Paris Preconference.

cal instability, corruption, economic dualism, conflicts between social classes, rapid and uneven demographic growth, strong geographical constraints and on the other hand, the increased dependency of the commercial (terms of trade) and financial (investment, credit) sectors. As a result, all these factors did not favor the take-off. In reality, however, successive Peruvian governments adopted a mixed model. A "third way" to the Peruvian has emerged to achieve an economic takeoff.

For her part, Elisa Grandi worked to study the work of the World Bank in Colombia from the start of the first missions to 1966.[87] Born out of the Bretton Woods agreements in 1944, the World Bank played a pioneering role in setting up development assistance programs. Rather than trying to evaluate the effectiveness of development loans financed by international agencies, the goal of E. Grandi was to analyze how these missions worked concretely, in order to understand how the policies of the World Bank evolved. Specifically E. Grandi reveals how World Bank's early missions in Columbia influenced its policies toward underdeveloped countries and which actors and practices contributed to this evolution. Focusing on the work of the World Bank between 1949 and 1954, E. Grandi describes the emergence and institutionalization of a dual process that concerned both international development consulting practices and the management of international credits by Colombian actors.

The World Bank's general inquiry mission to Colombia, launched in 1949, initiated this process. Led by New Deal economist Lauchlin Currie, this mission was the first to undertake a comprehensive study of the country's conditions, to put in place a development program to address all sectors of the economy. As a result, E. Grandi focused on the Colombian missions, to discover the networks set up by his advisers and how their networks were involved in the mission. The result was a dataset of some 1500 letters, in which more than 900 actors appeared. The network analysis of these actors, combined with a study of the microstructure of World Bank missions, provides new insights into the World Bank's early policies. It sheds light on the role of some local actors in the decision-making process regarding loan approval and orientation. It shows the impact of the World Bank's first missions on Colombian economic institutions, particularly with regard to the planning agencies created to manage international financial assistance.

Elisa Grandi reveals why the World Bank's global study mission was instrumental in steering World Bank lending in the country and how the relative position of the individuals involved in the negotiations influenced the process, the characteristics and the aftermath. The specificity of early intervention by the World Bank and the special relationship developed by Colombian elites with international lending organizations in the 1920s and 1930s allowed local staff to access international credit directly through their operations. direct management and loan. The social and relational capital that some actors acquired during the mission has also influenced the repayment of loans.

87 Elisa Grandi, "Networks of Experts and Political Actors in the World Bank's Early Programs: Loans Programs in Columbia and their Overall Effects on Aid to Development (1940-1960)", paper presented to the Paris Preconference.

Therefore, the design of the development program and the decision making took place during and before the settlement of the organizational procedures. Personal relationships have played a fundamental role in the emergence and affirmation of these procedures.

The microeconomic approach: Cemex and Vale

The microeconomic approach is no less fruitful, especially for the study of leading multinational firms like Cemex in Mexico.[88] Cemex was the world's fifth largest cement production capacity in 2008 and the fourth largest in terms of turnover. But Cemex remains number 1 in Latin America, ahead of Holcim and Lafarge. Above all, the Group was and is today the world leader in ready-mix concrete. In 2008, Cemex remained a Mexican group headquartered in Mexico City with a secondary office in New York, and all directors remained Mexican. Cemex is an archetypal example of the rise of emerging global companies. This huge company founded in 1906 was a symbol of the success of capitalism in Monterrey and Mexico City. Originally, the family Zambrano was a trading house operating from the mid-nineteenth century. It had developed after the war with the United States, in 1846-1847, which had established the Rio Bravo line. This family established in Monterrey, between 1890 and 1910, with the families Garza, Ferrara, Madero, Meiz, Milmo and Sada, well studied by Mario Cerutti [89]. The central idea is that in 1982 there was a decisive economic crisis, which led to intense restructuring and internationalization.

Consequently, Cemex became an original model, characterized by five elements. He was at the same time the world leader in white cement and trading, had the most advanced information and communication technology in the cement industry, was very creative in financial solutions, and the lowest cost of its sector. Cemex also appeared as the first global enterprise in Mexico. After having taken over the national market between 1982 and 1989, and achieved its international breakthrough, the group had established itself in culturally well-known areas: the United States, Spain and South America (1989-1994). He had broken into the trading market from 1992 to 2000, before joining the global firm (1997-2003). Its original trading system made it the direct competitor of Lafarge and Holderbank (then Holcim). Thus, it explained that Cemex had gone from the periphery to the center, demonstrating the incredible capacity of this entrepreneurial firm to adapt to the modes of organization of contemporary business.

The model, however, remained both dynamic and fragile. In 2009-2010, the Cemex group experienced a very serious financial crisis. However, he managed to overmatch it by adapting its operations to the new market dynamics. In 2016, the group maintained

88 Dominique Barjot, "Cemex or the Rise of a Mexican Multinational", paper presented to the Paris, Preconference ; Dominique Barjot, "Introduction", in Dominique Barjot (ed.), "Globalization, national patterns of development and strategies of firms (19th-21st centuries) – Mondialisation, modèles nationaux de développement et stratégies d'entreprises (XIXe-XXIe siècles)", *Revue française d'histoire économique – The French Economic History Review*, n°1, May 2015, p. 14-27.

89 Cerutti Mario, *Proprietarios, Empresarios y Empresa en et Norte de Mexico,* Siglo Veintiuno Editores, Mexico, 2000 ; Marichal Carlos y Cerutti Mario, *Historia de las Grandes Empresas en Mexico, 1850-1930,* Uniidad Autonoma de Nuevo Léon & Fundo de Cultura Economica, Mexico, 1997.

its positions in its three dominant markets, but by reorienting its activity towards cement, the most profitable segment in the sector and by renouncing its diversification activities. In addition, Cemex strengthened its positions in the United States, Latin America and the Caribbean, as well as in Asia, Oceania, the Middle East and Africa, to the detriment of Europe and, above all, Mexico. In this regard, the major operation was the 2007 acquisition of the Australian group Rinker, through which Cemex increased its breakthrough in the United States, the integration of this group ending in 2009, under financially difficult conditions. Nevertheless, the risk had paid off: in the 2010s, Cemex thus became the North American leader in the cement industry. In 2016, the group remained largely in the hands of the Zembrano family. More, if the group faces severe international competition, Cemex remains nevertheless the fourth world cement group. Furthermore, Cemex took it on all its main European competitors in terms of profitability. Today, in spite of its small size, Cemex appears largely competitive with its major European and Chinese competitors.

The internationalization of companies in developing countries is a novelty of contemporary globalization. The Brazilian mining company Vale is a good example of what the Boston Consulting Group calls the Global Challengers.[90] The Companhia Vale Rio Doce was created by the nationalization and incorporation of two existing companies in 1942. The Western allies needed iron ore especially for the arms industries. For Brazil, it was an opportunity to penetrate successful developed markets. Yet, at the end of the war in 1945, Britain and the United States gave up their purchase option, leaving Vale without a guaranteed market. High sea freight costs have made it difficult for Vale to compete with companies closer to the consumer markets of Europe, the United States and Asia. In the 1960s, the CEO, Elieser Batista, wanted to supply the Japanese steel industry, heavily damaged by the Second World War and under reconstruction. Batista made his bet, thanks to the use of large multipurpose ships that transported minerals to Asia and brought oil from the Persian Gulf to Brazil. In doing so, Vale was able to compete with Australian miners, much closer to Japan, combining productivity gains and economies of scale. In the 1970s, Vale became the world's largest producer of iron ore.

After privatization in 1997, the company's main goal was to maximize value for its shareholders. As a result, in 2001, the company implemented a multi-year strategic plan to transform Vale into a global player. The plan sets out clear principles: maximizing margins, becoming a global multi-product. At that time, Vale was by far the mining leader in Brazil, but its potential for product diversification was limited. The international presence of society remained very modest. From 2001, Vale diversified its portfolio by investing in thermal and coking coal, copper, cobalt, platinum group metals and nutrient fertilizers. These opportunistic acquisitions were partially financed by disposals of non-core activities such as pulp and paper. But iron ore remains its main product. Gradually, the idea of buying a big North American miner

90 Hildete de Moraes Vodopives, "Becoming a Multinational Mining Company: the Case of Vale (Brazil)", paper presented to the Paris Preconference.

took shape. Canada is a major mining country, with high quality assets and a skilled workforce. The ideal candidate could be one of the major Canadian companies, such as Alcan, Noranda or Inco. The acquisition of Inco truly marked the starting point of Vale's internationalization. Following this transaction, Vale became one of the three largest diversified mining companies in the world, with BHP Billiton and Rio Tinto. These Latin American multinationals are, however, of recent constitution. This is why it remains topical to question the specific role of economic elites and foreign multinationals.

Rethinking the theories of economic development for South America? Argentina and Brazil

Norma Silvana Lanciotti, Martín Schorr and Gustavo García Zanotti proposed to evaluate the influence of economic development theories on the economic performance of two Latin American countries by analyzing business elites and the role of foreign firms in two different periods of economic growth: the period of industrialization led by the State (1945-1973) and the emergency of the new global economy (1990-2016)[91]. After reviewing the main arguments of neoclassical and critical theories, they examine the evolution of the largest companies in Argentina and Brazil to identify the changes in the sectoral distribution of the activities controlled by the largest companies, their export share and the presence of foreign multinationals. They find that in the first period, economic policies incorporated elements from different theories, both neoclassical and critical, articulating the entry of foreign capital with state coordination and public investment during bottlenecks. On the contrary, economic policies initiated in the 1990s were based exclusively on neoclassical approaches that propose trade liberalization and the promotion of foreign private investment. As a result, foreign firms searched rents in public utilities and in natural resources, and involved "foreignization" and "de-industrialization".

Since the 1990s, Latin American economies have moved towards development models that make a greater contribution to the market economy and competition: this has been the case in Brazil. The introduction of antitrust schemes has paved the way for better monitoring of mergers[92]. The legal provisions adopted have revealed their importance for achieving significant results, particularly in the energy and mineral resources sectors (oil[93], electricity[94], iron[95] and cement[96]), but not only (the case of

91 Norma Silvana Lanciotti, Martín Schorr and Gustavo García Zanotti, "When theories don't fit: Rethinking the theories of economic development for South America. Argentina and Brazil 1945-2015", in Dominique Barjot (ed), "Theory and Empirical Performance. Economic Paradigm and Performance in the Long Run (18th to 21st century)", *Revue française d'histoire économique – The French Economic History Review*, n° 11-12 (n°1-2, 2019), *op. cit.*, p. 120-118.

92 Luiz Carlos Delorme Prado & Hildete de Moraes Vodopives, « Éditorial : Régulation et développement sectoriel en perspective historique : le cas du Brésil », in Luiz Carlos Delorme Prado & Hildete de Moraes Vodopives (eds.), « Concurrence et régulation au Brésil », *Entreprises & Histoire*, n° 99/2020, p. 5-20. This special issue is based on papers presented at the Rio de Janeiro conference in preparation for the 18th WEHC in Boston (29 July - 3 August 2018).

93 Camilla Pires-Alves, Marcelo Colomer, Luiz Carlos Delorme Prado and Marcos Lyra, "The Market of Liquefied Petroleum Gas in Brazil: a Brief Structural, Institutional-historical Perspective", *Entreprises & Histoire*, n° 99/2020, *op. cit.*, p. 21-34; Giorgio Romano Schutte, « La réglementation pétrolière au Brésil : quelle trajectoire ? », *Ibidem*, p. 35-52.

94 Claude Ferraz, Les difficultés des réformes des marches électriques : le Brésil, de l'essor industriel à la transition énergétique » », *Ibidem*, p. 53-65.

95 Hildete de Moraes Vodopives, "Mining Going Global in the 2000s: Vale Leaps Forward", *Ibid.*, p. 66-78.

96 Dominique Barjot, « L'ascension des entreprises cimentières brésiliennes : l'exemple du groupe Votorantim », *Ibid.*, p. 79-106.

video streaming[97] and the book industry[98]). The Brazilian experience in state reform in public administration resulted in the creation of a new set of regulatory agencies administered with the rationality of a Weberian bureaucracy[99]. Several of the directors and commissioners of those agencies, although have been appointed by political reason, were career civil servants. The system was not free from problems – some directors, mainly in the smaller agencies, where not qualified and were the product of clientelism and political influence of pressure groups. But in these cases, the presence of the press and other kinds of checks and balances reduces the ability of harmful actions of these directors. Finally, the *de facto* autonomy of the agencies was not as large as was planned in the original project, but this is certainly not incompatible with a rational bureaucracy – as far as there was democratic control of public policy. Therefore, the technocratic project to create regulatory agencies very similar to the USA model were not successful. It was not possible to make a complete separation of political and regulatory powers. But the state was modernized and the quality of public managers have improved. The state intervention was not as active as was in the developmentalist period – but the state did not became so small as was intended in the 1990s neoliberal projects. The state role changes, but less than was projected. It can be found evidences of changes and continuities in this history. Last, but not at least, Brazilian experiences shows that institutions and institutional models are strongly path dependent.

Globalization and emergence: French-speaking Africa

If Latin America has seen the affirmation of powerful emerging economies such as Brazil, Mexico or Colombia for example, the phenomenon has become global. It also French-speaking Africa.

Algeria and oil: curse of raw materials or instrument of national independence?

Marta Musso studied the economic history of independent Algeria. In particular, it has focused on the economic policies adopted by its governments during the first fifty years of its independence and the oil and gas industry.[100] The Algerian hydrocarbon industry is closely linked to the independence process. It is more precisely to analyze, taking Algeria as a case study, the evolution of the concept of oil curse. Until the 1970s, oil appeared to be the best tool for solving the problem of capital formation in newly independent countries. It was also an opportunity to promote industrialization through the abundance of a cheap energy source, making potential companies competitive with Western companies. Finally, oil was seen as a diplomatic tool in the negotiations with Europe, a means of pressure against the largest importing area in

97 Luiz Carlos Delorme Prado et Diandra Rocha, "Streaming Video on Demand Platforms and Competition Policy: The Brazilian Case", *Ibid.*, p. 107-125.

98 Fabio Sá Earp, « La crise de la filière du livre au Brésil (2006-2018) », *Ibid.*, p. 126-136.

99 Luiz Carlos Delorme Prado, "Two Decades of Economic Reforms: The Institutions of Regulation in Brazil 1991-2011", in Dominique Barjot (ed.), "Theory and Empirical Performance. Economic Paradigm and Performance in the Long Run (18th to 21st century)", *Revue française d'histoire économique – The French Economic History Review*, n° 11-12 (n°1-2, 2019), *op. cit.*, p. 140-161.

100 Marta Musso, "Oil and Development in Algeria (1956-2000)", communication to the Paris Preconference.

the world. The oil companies, unsurprisingly, have also supported the theory of oil as an instrument of development.

The industry has emerged both as a beneficiary of international development, because of the opportunity to expand its market, and as a development promoter, because of the contribution of capital provided by revenues. Oil, the fastest growing energy industry of the post-war period, was directly related to development; oil consumption was related to transportation, mass motorization, domestic heating and the use of plastics and other petrochemicals, namely fertilizers, for industrial agriculture. The higher is the oil consumption, the higher is the level of economic development of a country. Countries that do not depend on oil imports are therefore considered as candidates for faster development. Gradually, this optimistic view of oil as an instrument of development has given way to oil as a major explanation for the economic failures caused by decolonization. Then the question has slipped from an economic or politico-economic dimension to a mainly political perspective, analyzing the relations between the democracy industry in many producing countries, hence the success of notions like "Rentier States", "oil regimes" and "oil wars". Finally, a critique of the literature on the "resource curse" has emerged in recent years.

Algeria has rarely been the subject of studies devoted to the oil curse. However, this is a particularly interesting case. Large oil and gas reserves were discovered by French companies at the beginning of what would become the Algerian war of independence, which had a significant impact on the negotiations between Algeria and France during the conflict and since. The acquisition of control over oil resources has become a major goal for Algerian governments. Oil was considered by them as the resource opening the way for economic growth, economic independence from France and a reduction of the development gap with Europe. At the same time, European development aid projects in North Africa in the 1950s and 1960s suggest the drafting of a kind of European "Marshall Plan" for the development of North Africa. There is therefore a close link between the construction of the state and the development of the Sonatrach, biggest company benefitting of a State monopoly.

Very often, the nationalization of the oil industry has been considered as one of the reasons why oil has become a curse rather than a blessing for the economy of the producing country. However, there was no reason to believe that if Algeria had allowed French or American companies to operate without intervention, or if it had agreed to make the Sahara an international hub for oil, the overall development of the country would have been very different. On the contrary, thanks to the nationalization of the oil industry, Algeria was able to regain control of its oil in the same way that France had regained control of the Sahara: a mixed system with the widest possible participation in the oil industry. State furnished a massive effort to develop local technology and skills. There is no evidence that, had the oil industry been left in foreign hands, the political and economic development of Algeria would have resulted in a more democratic and integrative state.

Tunisia: a resistible association with the EEC?

The question of the cooperation between Tunisia and the European Economic Community (EEC) was worked by dynamics multiple divergences of interests, problem of the security, dynamic and changing reality within the EEC, multiplicity of the points of view as for the forms possible partnerships, and, above all, the inescapable face-to-face character with France, especially for everything related to agricultural policy, diplomatic or geostrategic issues.[101] This situation was linked to the diversity and divergence of intra-European (Europe of the Six) and interregional (Maghreb-Europe, etc.) interests, as the gap widened between North and South. This long process of "intergovernmentalization" sanctioned third countries, especially those which, thanks to historical links, depended on relations with Europe. The first half of the 1970s, which coincided with major international crises, but also with the consolidation of the EEC institutions, saw the advent of a comprehensive Mediterranean policy. Tunisia was one of the main beneficiaries, but the rules of the game remained mainly defined by the European partner. Because the formation of a united (and powerful) Europe required protectionist forms of the Common Agricultural Policy (CAP) type, no country, with the exception of the Netherlands, intended to subject its farmers to competition in world markets. Although Tunisia enjoyed the support of most of the Six when launching its association project with the EEC, tensions with France caused huge losses in terms of synergies. The emerging Europe, on the other hand, was of unusual institutional complexity. With markets increasingly globalized since the 1960s, there was already a high mobility of capital and, therefore, real opportunities for Tunisia. But Tunisian diplomatic action focused on the demand for institutional aid and much less on the supply of market opportunity as a growth factor for European companies.

Senegal and Ivory Coast, two opposite development models

Senegal and Ivory Coast were the two privileged colonies of the former French colonial power in West Africa.[102] After the Second World War, in the process of decolonization, their leaders in these territories, respectively Léopold Sédar Senghor and Félix Houphouët-Boigny, condemned colonial policies. They contributed to the creation of the African Democratic Union (Rassemblement Démocratique Africain or RDA) in 1946 in Bamako. The RDA was the party of the French colonies of Africa that were to provide 29 African deputies representing French West Africa (AOF). While Senghor created the Senegalese Democratic Bloc (Bloc Démocratique Sénégalais or BDS), Houphouet-Boigny founded the Democrat Party of Ivory Coast (Parti Démocrate de Côte-d'Ivoire or PDCI), which are local branches of the RDA. Thanks to these political parties and their activism, the two leaders successively held posts of deputy and then minister, within the framework of the French Union and the Community. These experiences also gave them the opportunity to be in the forefront of the negotiations that led to independence and to have some political legitimacy. Similarly, Léopold

101 Mohamed Sassi, "The North-South Negotiations in the Sixties: The Case of Tunisia with the EEC", paper presented to the Paris Preconference.

102 Joseph Diouf, "Western Africa: "Compared models of Development: Léopold Senghor Sédar Senegal and Côte d'Ivoire of Houphouët-Boigny", paper presented to the Paris Preconference.

Sédar Senghor and Félix Houphouët-Boigny did not want immediate independence and are strong supporters of maintaining the link with the former colonial power. In addition, they weigh all their weight to endorse and sign the cooperation agreements that preceded the accession of their country to sovereignty. Thus, the first became President of the Republic of Senegal while the second was elevated to the presidency of the Ivory Coast.

However, the two men had different visions of the development of their country and also had inherited colonization of economic structures different. As a result, the two countries had different and opposite development trajectories in form and substance. Léopold Sédar Senghor defended and theorized a development model based on African socialism. He advocated a complete break with the colonial legacy but both rejected Marxist-Leninist socialism and the Western capitalist model in a cold war context. In addition, Senghor designed and implemented an endogenous development theory. As for Felix Houphouet-Boigny, he chose the liberalism inherited from the colonial "development" policy and inscribed Ivory Coast in the Western camp. In addition, cash crops remained the pillars of development. Indeed, while shrubs, especially cocoa and coffee, were the main wealth of Côte d'Ivoire, Senegal based its development on groundnut monoculture. However, if these cultures had made the wealth of these two countries as evidenced by the "Ivorian miracle", it nevertheless led to bankruptcy in the late seventies.

The case of the Franc Zone: escaping Mundell's Trilemma

According to Olivier Feiertag, the Franc Zone offered a case study to deal with an area corresponding to an optimal currency.[103] This Zone knew her Golden Age in the 1960s, while she was still very influenced by the influence of the Colonial Pact. According to the Mundell's analysis concerning the role of money in the industrialization process (1961), various arguments made it possible to speak about the optimal currency area. Indeed, Franc Zone was heterogeneous; At the same time, the Monetary unification did not always aim to transaction costs, but to accelerate a good circulation of production factors. In fact, it was organized in three zones; French West Africa, French Equatorial Africa, Madagascar. But was it not the continuation, by another way, of colonialism?

This explains the reluctant economic integration of the Franc Zone. In 1962, the West African Monetary Union was created to promote intra-zone trade. The History of the Franc Zone shows that three phases followed:

1 / The golden age of the 1960s. This golden age ended in the 1980s, particularly because of the heterogeneity of the African development models. Indeed, Ivory Coast and Cameroon's advance on other countries was growing more and more.

103 Olivier Feiertag, "History of the Development of the Franc zone (1939-1944), Does the Theory of Optimal Currency to be applied to Franc?", communication to the Tokyo Preconference and « La zone Franc de 1945 à nos jours : échapper au triangle d'incompatibilté de Mundell », in Marie-Claude Esposito and Olivier Feiertag (eds.), « Histoire financière, histoire globale », *Revue française d'histoire économique – The French Economic History Review*, n° 14 (n°2 - 2020), p . 39-49.

2 / If a change occurred in the 1980s, it was primarily because of the African Debt Crisis. Indeed the end of the commodity boom provoked an asymmetrical shock.

3 / The result was the devaluation of the CFA franc in 1994. It corresponded to the real turning point of globalization.

In the end, the optimal currency model applied well to the franc zone in the 1960s, but no longer in the 1980s and 1990s. The illusion of homogeneity dissipated. The franc zone was certainly a victim of national rivalries, but also of the progress of Pan-Africanism. More fundamentally, the move to the global market could only reduce the power of the franc zone.

Development models and path dependency: Egypt, South Africa and Australia

Clearly, there are multiple paths of development, because the product of specific conditions and experiences, according to a logic of path dependency. This is what the examples of Egypt, South Africa and Australia show.

Egypt

Under the leadership of Muhammad Ali, Egypt experienced significant economic development in the 19th century, supported by European capital[104]. The latter contribute to the economic opening of the country and to its modernization in terms of equipment, but associated with political domination, they also generate violent tensions. The link between economic openness and colonial domination that developed at the end of the 19th century had strong implications for 20th century economic models. Successive regimes are faced with the difficulty of finding a path of economic development that can both rely on the necessary external financing while being at the service of national reform.

Indeed, during the last two centuries, foreign capital invested in Egypt has played an ambivalent role: it has favoured the integration of the country into the world economy, but, associated with the colonial practices of the European powers, it has also provoked a reaction of withdrawal and isolation of the national economy on itself. The process of Egypt's integration into the world economy, which began in the 19th century, slowed down during the period of decolonisation and Nasserism. It was then clearly reactivated in the last quarter of the 20th century by Presidents Anwar el-Sadat and Hosni Mubarak. After the parenthesis of the Muslim Brotherhood from June 2011 to June 2013, it is again pursued by President Sissi since his accession to power in 2014. The latter encourages foreign capital to invest massively in the country with the creation of partnerships or free zones. But this process is more difficult to achieve than during the colonial period because of the strong political and economic instability in the region. The economy is still hampered by the traumas of the 19th century, which contribute

104 Caroline Piquet, « L'Égypte : réalité et limites d'une voie nationale de développement », original chapter. See also : Caroline Piquet, *La Compagnie du canal de Suez. Une concession française en Égypte (1888-1956)*, Paris, PUPS, 2008 ; *Histoire du canal de Suez*, Perrin, Paris, 2009 ; John Waterbury, *The Egypt of Nasser and Sadat: the Political Economy of the two Regimes*, Princeton, Princeton University Press, 1983; Louis Blin, *L'économie égyptienne, Libéralisation et insertion dans le marché mondial*, Paris, L'Harmattan, 1993.

to maintaining the logic of a dirigist system where the state remains perceived as a bulwark against economic globalisation threatening national sovereignty.

South Africa

Industrialisation in South Africa followed the resource determined by forward and backward linkages as in the Rostowian model.[105] From the nineteenth century agro-industries established the initial foundation of Schumpeterian entrepreneurial changes to agrarian life. The transition into industrialisation occurred within the Polanyian state intervention in the market to drive industrial development. The context of the mineral- agrarian economy determined a state mitigation of the high cost structure of the economy. Geographical location, factors of production (labour, capital) and policy directives determined a market intervention. Import-substitution as strategic policy option as proposed by Prebisch, was followed, but the state refrained from full socialism or central market planning. The industrialisation of the South African economy gained momentum since the 1920 under protectionist state industrial policies. Powerful business groups, corporate entrepreneurs, especially from the mining sector, collaborated with state protectionism. The Gerschenkronian latecomer effect indeed played itself out in South African industrialisation, but local human capital developed innovative technology locally to enhance the industrialisation process. The specific trajectory of South African industrialisation reflects the establishment of a near first-world industrial base, grounded in a mix of scare factors of production (capital, entrepreneurship, skilled labour) and abundant factors of production (unskilled labour, natural resources). Weberian traits of the Protestant work ethic is a significant driver of economic, and specifically industrial development in South Africa. The specific context of a European minority population controlling the economic policy, eventually impacted negatively on the modernisation and progress of the industrial sector in South Africa by the end of the twentieth century.

Australia

According to Martin Shanahan, the factors influencing Australia's economic development have been the subject of much recent analysis and discussion by national economic historians.[106] Attempts to explain Australia's economic development, however, are not especially new, however. Ever since Europeans first transported people and capital to the continent in 1788 and began shaping the land and its inhabitants to conform to their own aspirations, commentators have mused on the factors that allowed the non-indigenous to reach the highest living standards in the world within a century of occupation. The transition from penal colony to nation was all the more remarkable considering that for virtually all of the 19th century, the six isolated

105 Grietjie Verhoef, "South in Africa, metropolitan in culture: industrial development trajectory of South Africa", in Dominique Barjot (ed), "Theory and Empirical Performance. Economic Paradigm and Performance in the Long Run (18th to 21st century)", *Revue française d'histoire économique – The French Economic History Review*, n° 11-12 (n°1-2, 2019), *op. cit.*, p. 244-259; "The South African economy in the twentieth century" in Pretorius F (ed.), *A History of South Africa. From the distant past to the present day*, Pretoria, Protea Book House, 2014, p. 448-477.

106 Martin Shanahan, "Australia's industrial development: The importance of importing capital and ideas", in "Theory and Empirical Performance. Economic Paradigm and Performance in the Long Run (18th to 21st century)", *Revue française d'histoire économique – The French Economic History Review, Ibidem.*, p. 226-242.

colonies were not only settled around the edge of the world's largest island continent, they were also on the distant periphery of the North Atlantic trade world. While the rich resources of the country provided much of the basis for economic advance, this was not the only element contributing to growth. As McLean has recently highlighted, the factors that contributed to Australia's rapid rise in living standards, and which helped sustain a high level of prosperity for another century, were many and varied, often combining at different times and in different ways in response to opportunities and threats.[107]

At least one explanation for economic analysists' tendency toward narrative and description rather than theory, was the composition of elements influencing the country's economy. In the space of a little over 200 years, the continent was transformed from one 'outside' any contact with capitalism, to a modern, industrialized economy strongly connected to international markets. While land was abundant, capital (financial, real and human), and labour were not. Learning what could develop with this mix of factors while also compensating (and importing) the factors that were required, took time and effort. Although manufacturing began in the 19th century to sustain local needs, industrialisation of the economy only occurred from the middle of the 20th century. This timing places Australia's period of modern development closer to the advances in certain South-East Asian nations than in the industrial revolution of Europe. Australia's combination of endowments and challenges differed from those that faced European nations over the same period. Despite this, and despite the geographical distance, Australia's ties with Europe are such that its economic development is best examined through a (modified) European frame of reference. In recent years, the range of factors that have been studied to explain economic development, have expanded significantly. While previous theories included a range of elements as die as capital accumulation, population growth, aggregate demand, international trade, and technological change, there are now many more.[108] Elements that have recently been identified as important include human capital and knowledge creation; the interdependence of countries' growth rates; inequality; geography; the role of economic and political institutions.[109]

The central motivation for the Shanahan's study was to respond to the question: Can European development theories adequately explain Australia's industrialisation experience? The simple answer is no.

1/ Australia is not Europe. Over the past two centuries, it has evolved from as a series of disconnected colonies with a handful of European settlers, through periods of exploration, economic expansion and integration in ways not followed by the countries of Europe. There was no single trajectory of development in the Australian experience. Unlike the European case, for example, extensive as well as intensive deve-

107 Ian W. McLean, *Why Australia Prospered. The shifting sources of economic growth*, Princeton University Press, Princeton, 2013.
108 Mark Setterfield (ed) *Handbook of Alternative Theories of Economic Growth*, Edward Elgar, Cheltenham (UK), 2010.
109 Elhanan Helpman, *The Mystery of Economic Growth*, Harvard University Press, Harvard, 2009.

lopment occurred simultaneously for many decades, as immigrants both expanded the country's economic base and intensified their investment to exploit it. The country was the recipient, rather than supplier, of migrants and capital. Despite being involved in European wars, it did not suffer the same level of physical destruction that many there endured.

2/ The abundance and relative price of many natural resources in Australia differed (and for many resources, continues to differ) from those existing in Europe. This provided Australians with different opportunities and incentives. The consequence in both the 19th and 20th century was an economy more focused on natural resource exploitation than industrial intensification. None-the-less, industrial intensification did occur, albeit later and on a smaller scale than in Europe; a development that helped support the economy through periods of commodity prices volatility.

3/ Australian political, legal and market institutions were based first on the English structures, and then gradually modified for local challenges. Thus, while emerging from a common base (much of which remains) there has been the opportunity to change the trajectory of these in ways that have impacted on growth. For example, the almost century long period of protectionist policies appears to not only have been fortuitous in its timing (facilitating infant industry growth and attracting international business behind the tariff barrier), many of its formal structures were dismantled when the system was assessed to be a check on growth, while also leaving a legacy of institutions and attitudes that maintain elements of market constraint. As a large continent with a small population, scattered markets and large distances, government's role in facilitating development was established relatively early; a legacy that remains comparatively strong. This is a path of institutional development that differs from those of many European countries.

4/ Australia's development was also fortuitously timed. In the 19th century, falling transportation costs accompanying the need for basic commodities aligned with many of resources that Australia had in relative abundance, or could develop at a comparatively lower cost. In the 20th century technological change accompanied by a second large surge of immigrants created the markets and knowledge accumulation for continued development. Australia benefited significantly from the technological innovations of the North Atlantic economies, while focusing its own efforts on technological challenges relevant to local problems. The capital, technology and economy built by earlier generations was sufficiently robust to be a foundation for continued development.

5/ Finally, Australia's linkages with the rest of the world have been many, not just through trade openness, or even its adoption of economic and political institutions initiated overseas, but also through its acceptance of overseas finance and international businesses. The result has been an economy and a society with multiple layers of integration with the rest of the world. As a nation open to the world even the personal and familial links of its population are of a kind unlike that which occurs in many

European nations. While such interconnections can work to the country's advantage or disadvantage, depending on one's perspective and the issue at hand, on balance, they have served Australia and its economic development well. Over generations these linkages have gravitated away from one country (the UK) or one region (Europe) and increasingly included in Asian and the American networks. This range of people, ideas and institutions have been the most valuable of the nation's imports and allowed it to develop and maintain one of the world's highest standards of living.

Conclusion

From this vast collective work come three main conclusions:

1 / The contract initially fixed, namely the confrontation of the models of interpretation of the phenomena of industrialization conceived by Western thinkers with the reality of the national ways of industrialization, was only imperfectly fulfilled. Indeed, the study of these phenomena implies the control of an important statistical apparatus, but also the realization of numerous calculations and the reading of a huge mass of scientific works pertaining to the economic history, but also and especially of the disciplines which are related to him. The consequence is that the process involves long-term, difficult work in the short three-year interval between each international congress of economic history. Nevertheless, it has been possible to make a useful comparative review and a no less useful inventory of the research carried out on the subject. The latter probably reflects quite well the different degrees of progress of the questions and methods of economic history and their renewal.

2 / In general, theoretical models of Western origin, whether macro- or microeconomic, are useful and even indispensable, because they are the basis of possible typologies, but also likely to provide explanatory models.

2.1 / Some models appear more relevant than others. Such is the case of the Rostow, Kuznets and Gerschenkron analyzes in the macroeconomic field. In their major axes, they have been largely confirmed by history: the advantage of delay is a reality, but also the superiority of development models based on exports of goods and services and imports of technology and technology know-how; in terms of technology, the relevance of Schumpeterian or Neo-Schumpeterian approaches, but provided however not to oppose them systematically to monetarist approaches. As far as regional economic development is concerned, Michael Porter's cluster vision offers the advantage of providing more explanatory elements than the growth pole theory and of applying to a number of cases much larger than the A. Marshall's industrial districts.

2.2 / But the complexity of historical phenomena often leads to the combination of approaches:

A / Thus the neoclassical analyzes of economic growth remain relevant. Not only do they permit simple comparisons between industrialized or developing nations, but they also provide the broad categories necessary to measure the respective importance of the factors of economic development.

B / They are not incompatible with the approaches often adopted today in terms of learning by doing and path dependency, but also with the specific contributions of industrial microeconomics and management sciences.

C / In this respect, evolutionary theories offer particularly useful perspectives, as they also place a premium on technological and scientific evolution, the specific role of human capital, without closing the door to more quantitative and statistical approaches taking into account monetary and financial phenomena.

D / They are also entirely compatible with taking into account the effects of competitiveness to which Michael Porter attaches all importance. Both the path dependency and the Porter's analyzes have the advantage of being able to pass without difficulty from the micro level to the macro without modifying a better sensitivity as part of the reasoning.

3 / Under these conditions, are the Western models, the real ones, not those of stylized facts and theory, so specific that they cannot be compared to those of emerging industrialized countries of today? In this regard, some remarks can be made:

3-1 / As Western studies on the phenomena of industrialization in the West have shown, it is clear that there is no paradigmatic model, that of Great Britain (England, Scotland and Wales), which would have been reproduced by the continental countries and North America.

A/ Some even defend today the idea that Britain was rather an exception. In fact, if there is proximity between it and Belgium, the case of France is largely at odds with British development. This disparity is found in the next generation, that of the United States and Germany, or that of the latecomers such as Italy and, to a certain extent, Russia.

B/ Nevertheless, these disparities in the development model have never excluded vigorous transfers of technology and know-how, driven in particular by trade and services. Moreover, what differs in a clear way at the macroeconomic level, differs or sometimes opposes at the microeconomic level: that of the regions (Wallonia, Nord-Pas-de-Calais, the Ruhr, or even Silesia, are not without points in common with non-British countries), but also companies (similarity of functioning in the nineteenth century, between British and French companies in the textile industry).

3-2 / This remark also applies to Asia, where the Japanese model has often been used as a reference, especially to the "Four Dragons" from the 1970s to 2000, but also, to a certain extent, to the "Asian Tigers" from Southeast Asia. Certainly, these pathways of industrialization adopted in China or Vietnam have little to do with that of Japan. The same is true of Hong Kong, Singapore and Taiwan, where Chinese influence has always dominated. The similarities are even smaller if one looks at the Indian subcontinent. Nevertheless, if we go beyond the big aggregates of the economy to look at the regions, the companies and, more broadly, the actors, then some elements of comparison emerge: the importance of industrial conglomerates or, in the East Asian countries, the influence of Confucianism, often compared to that of Calvinism in the West, or the role of minorities (in India, Bombay, Malaysia).

3-3 / Even if the news would have the tendency to make it believe, there is not *a priori* countries definitively barred in the cause to industrialization and development. This shows the Latin American example.

A/ Although for a long time dominated by the economic and financial interests of Western Europe and then of the United States, Latin America opened the way to industrial growth. This is the case of Brazil, thanks to the appearance of industrial giants, first with public capital, and then become multinational through privatization. The adoption of pro-competitive provisions has been a key factor in easing economic blockages. But, it would be inaccurate to downplay the role of families, individual entrepreneurs and their business networks, as in Mexico especially around Monterrey.

B/ Brazil and Mexico are not the only examples of industrial take-off, with their successes, failures and fragilities still great. Today we are well aware of Colombia's spectacular breakthrough, which has drawn American and World Bank lessons from an original development, but also from Chile, Peru and, presumably, Paraguay. Remains the case of Argentina, which could have been a southern Canada, but which nevertheless benefits from the dynamic printed by Mercosur. Certainly, in Europe, as in Asia (with ASEAN for example), but also in North America (NAFTA) and South (Andean Pact), the integration efforts have encouraged the acceleration of the phenomena of industrialization.

3.4 / In the rest of the world too, industrialization is progressing.

A / Such is the case of Russia, again, as on the eve of the First World War, one of the major emerging powers (third of the BRICS behind China and India, but almost equivalent to Germany in purchasing power parity). It also gave birth to powerful multinationals (Gazprom, Rusal), developed technological skills and benefited from foreign investments (especially Western European) on its soil. The same goes for Turkey, which continues its slow economic rise, thanks to the dynamism of its entrepreneurs and the support provided by the state.

B / Although the idea of a commodity curse should not be ruled out, the example of the United Arab Emirates, well after that of Canada, shows that there are original ways of development capable of generating self-sustaining growth, conditional on sustained and increased global economic integration. In a way, it's a message to Africa. Indeed, if it is important, as in Algeria that the oil resources are in the hands of the State, this cannot be enough if one does not seek, like Tunisia, the way of the international economic integration.

C / Thus, the small African countries and even the largest ones (Ethiopia), worn today by their internal dynamism, could, like Cameroon, Senegal or Ivory Coast, find the way sustainable development. If it was impossible, their high-level graduates would have to flee the country in a large number and the current War Trade would plunge the world economy into a deep depression, which would hit the weakest economies, as in the 1930s.

Introduction

Dans quelle mesure les théories européennes sur l'industrialisation sont-elles valables d'un point de vue mondial ?

Dominique Barjot
Sorbonne Université, Renmin National University
et Académie des Sciences d'Outre-Mer

Introduction

Notre monde s'est mondialisé[1]. Aujourd'hui, la croissance impressionnante de la Chine et, plus généralement, des BRICS (Brésil, Russie, Inde, Chine, Afrique du Sud) et du MIST (Mexique, Indonésie, Corée du Sud, Turquie) constitue une bonne illustration de la profonde mutation de ce monde en voie de mondialisation. Le développement spectaculaire des « Global Challengers » - c'est-à-dire les 100 entreprises « perturbant l'ordre économique mondial » (Boston Consulting Group) - démontre la poursuite de la mutation rapide de l'économie mondiale[2]. Ces « Global Challengers » viennent de pays tardivement industrialisés comme la Chine (Huawei, Xiaomi, Lenovo, China Communications Construction, etc.), le Brésil (Petrobras, Votorantim, Natura), l'Inde (Mittal, Tata Group), la Russie (Gazprom, Rusal, Severstal) ou l'Afrique du Sud (Bidvest, Sappi, Sasol), mais aussi de plus en plus d'autres pays comme le Mexique (Cemex ou Bimbo) ou l'Égypte (El Seweby Electric). Parce que l'émergence de nouvelles puissances économiques a été un moteur fondamental du développement humain, l'importance de ces phénomènes constitue aujourd'hui une question très passionnante pour les historiens de l'économie.

1 Dominique Barjot, Harm G. Schroeter (dir.), « La circulation de l'information et des connaissances », *Entreprises et Histoire*, juin 2014, n° 75.

2 The New Global Challengers – BCG, https://www.bcg.com/documents/file14801.pdf; Global Challengers Lead Digital Business Revolution - The Boston Consulting Group - BCG, https://www.bcg.com/.../17may2018-global-challenges-business-revolution.

Cela constitue une raison majeure de notre projet mondial.[3]

Questions scientifiques : remise en question des théories traditionnelles
Le projet combine la dimension macroéconomique avec la dimension microéconomique. La principale question est la suivante : dans quelle mesure ces théories traditionnelles peuvent-elles être appliquées de manière significative aux pays non européens ? L'approche utilisée est celle des acteurs économiques : les entreprises et leur environnement. En effet, le point de vue microéconomique n'a pas encore systématiquement appliqué dans une perspective comparative.

Théories classiques de l'industrialisation et du développement
Les théories traditionnelles du développement économique mondial, en particulier l'industrialisation, relèvent d'une conception axée sur l'Europe occidentale. Parmi celles-ci, mentionnons les théories d'Alexander Gerschenkron[4], de Walt Wittman Rostow[5], de Raymond Aron[6], de Paul Bairoch[7], de Karl Polanyi[8] et même de Karl Marx[9]. Elles ont fait de l'Europe et de ses ramifications un point de référence général en matière de réussite et de développement. Aussi, les théories ultérieures, comme celle de Dieter Senghaas[10] ou la théorie des dépendances (Eduardo Galeano[11] et autres), des structuralistes (Raoul Prebisch[12]) et du développement inégal (Samir Amin[13], Paul Bairoch et même François Perroux[14]) ont placé l'Europe et ses institutions au centre de leur analyse et de leur explication. Toutes ces approches revendiquent une validité générale, voire mondiale. L'idée de base de la session organisée à Boston était d'évaluer dans quelle mesure ces théories sont utiles pour expliquer l'industrialisation de l'Asie de l'Est et du Sud-Est ou de l'Amérique du Sud et, aujourd'hui peut-être, de l'Afrique, surtout du point de vue de leurs acteurs. Par conséquent, ont été examinés les acteurs institutionnels, tels que les entreprises industrielles, les banques et les

3 Harm G. Schroeter, "Foreword: Theory and Empirical Performance Or: did development theories hold their promise?", in Dominique Barjot (ed.), "Theory and Empirical Performance. Economic Paradigm and Performance in the Long Run (18th to 21st century)", *Revue française d'histoire économique – The French Economic History Review*, n° 11-12 (n°1-2, 2019), p. 6-9.

4 Alexander Gerschenkron, *Economic backwardness in historical perspective, a book of essays*, Cambridge, Massachusetts: Belknap Press of Harvard University Press, 1962.

5 Walt Whitman Rostow, *The Stages of Economic Growth: A Non-Communist Manifesto*. Cambridge University Press, 1960.

6 Raymond Aron, *Dix-huit leçons sur la société industrielle*, Paris: Gallimard, 1963; *Eighteen Lectures on Industrial Society*, London: Weidenfeld & Nicolson, 1967.

7 Paul Bairoch, *Economics and World History: Myths and Paradoxe*, Chicago, University of Chicago Press, 1993.

8 Karl Polanyi, *The Great Transformation: The Political and Economic Origins of Our Time*, 2nd ed. Foreword by Joseph E. Stiglitz; introduction by Fred Block. Boston: Beacon Press, 2001.

9 Karl Marx, *Le Capital (livre I)*, Paris, Garnier-Flammarion, 1969.

10 Dieter Senghaas (ed.), *Imperialismus und strukturelle Gewalt*, Frankfurt: Suhrkamp Verlag 1972 (7th edition. 1987); (ed.), *Peripherer Kapitalismus. Analysen über Abhängigkeit und Unterentwicklung*, Frankfurt: Suhrkamp Verlag 1974 (2nd edition. 1977); (ed.) *Kapitalistische Weltökonomie. Kontroen über ihren Ursprung und ihre Entwicklungsdynamik*, Frankfurt: Suhrkamp Verlag 1979 (2nd edition. 1982).

11 Eduardo Galeano, *Open Veins of Latin America: Five Centuries of the Pillage of a Continent*, (25th anniversary ed.). Monthly Review Press, 2010.

12 Raúl Prebisch, *The Economic Development of Latin America and Its Principal Problems* (New York: United Nations, 1950); Raúl Prebisch, Change and Development: Latin America's Great Task, Inter-American Development Bank, 1970.

13 Samir Amin, *L'accumulation à l'échelle mondiale*, Éditions Anthropos, Paris 1970. Translated and published as *Accumulation on a world scale*, Abe Books, Paris, 1970.

14 *François Perroux, œuvres complètes*, 6 tomes, Presses universitaires de Grenoble, 1993 ; François Perroux, *L'Économie du XXe siècle*, Presses universitaires de Grenoble, 1961.

institutions financières, les ménages, les administrations publiques ou privées dans leur environnement économique, social et politique.

Quatre bonnes raisons de réexaminer ces théories :
Il existe quatre raisons de réexaminer les théories traditionnelles sur le développement du monde.

1/ Il semble utile de mobiliser les acquis récents de la *business history* et de la recherche microéconomique sur les entreprises, l'État et les consommateurs. L'objectif est d'évaluer le rôle des entreprises, grandes et petites, dans la dynamique de croissance des pays industrialisés et émergents, en explorant leurs performances, leurs stratégies et leurs types d'organisation, ainsi que les implications sociales, culturelles et environnementales de leur comportement en tant qu'acteurs.

2/ Parce qu'il concerne fondamentalement le comportement des acteurs économiques, le projet s'apparente à une étude de la prise de décision. Il comprend la prise en compte d'un point de vue macroéconomique ainsi que celle des agents institutionnels de la comptabilité nationale et de l'action microéconomique à l'arrière-plan des théories mentionnées ci-dessus. Il a été demandé aux contributeurs d'évaluer en priorité les actions du comportement des agents individuels au sens néoclassique : entreprises industrielles, banques et institutions financières, ménages, administrations publiques ou privées.

3/ La question de l'émergence de la mondialisation porte sur de nombreuses questions fondamentales : la croissance de la consommation de masse et l'américanisation ; les politiques publiques, conjoncturelles et structurelles ; les politiques d'investissement des entreprises et, plus largement, les décisions opérationnelles et stratégiques (selon la célèbre distinction de Ansoff[15]), en tenant compte des coûts de transaction (Ronald Coase[16], Oliver Williamson[17]) ; l'interaction des réseaux et/ou des techniques sociales, les dynamiques spatiales (districts industriels, systèmes productifs locaux et clusters) ; la dépendance de sentier ou *path dependency* (telle que décrite par Arrows[18] ou, surtout, Nelson et Winter[19]).

4/ En même temps, la contribution spécifique des historiens peut également être rendue fructueuse, comme les approches concernant la proto-industrialisation (Mendels[20], Kriedtke, Medick & Schlumbohm[21]). L'idée est de tester les théories européennes traditionnelles pour évaluer dans quelle mesure elles peuvent être appliquées de manière fructueuse en Asie, en Afrique ou en Amérique latine. L'approche est également une réflexion sur une mode récente dans l'écriture de l'histoire. De

15 H. Igor Ansoff, *Corporate strategy: an analytic approach to business policy for growth and expansion*, New York, McGraw-Hill, 1965.

16 Ronald Coase, "The Nature of the Firm", *Economica*, 4 (16), 1937, p. 386-405.

17 Oliver Williamson, *Markets and Hierarchies: Analysis and Antitrust Implications*, 1975; *The Economic Institutions of Capitalism*, 1985; (co-edited with Sidney Winter), *The Nature of the Firm: Origins, Evolution, and Development*, 1991.

18 Kenneth J. Arrow, "The economic implications of learning by doing", *The Review of Economic Studies*. Oxford Journals, 29 (3), June 1962, p. 155-73.

19 Richard R. Nelson, Sydney G. Winter, *An Evolutionary Theory of Economic Change*, Cambridge (Mas.), Harvard University Press, 1982.

20 Franklin F. Mendels, *Industrialization and population pressure in eighteenth-century Flanders.*, Front Cover, University of Wisconsin-Madison, 1970.

21 Peter Kriedte, Hans Medick, Jurgen Schlumbohm, *In Industrialization before Industrialization*, Cambridge, Cambridge University Press, 1981.

nombreux auteurs tentent de promouvoir une vision biaisée non européenne (*History of the World* édité par Iriye et Osterhammel[22]). Le changement est basé sur le simple aspect moral selon lequel les moins puissants ont également un droit égal à l'histoire. Ce changement moral repose-t-il également sur un fondement théorique ? Si la théorie européenne n'est pas assez bonne pour expliquer le reste du monde, l'approche morale à la mode est nécessaire. Sinon, c'est toujours bien, mais beaucoup moins important et urgent.

Objectifs scientifiques et organisationnels

Ces questions ont conduit à la définition d'objectifs à la fois scientifiques et organisationnels.

Les objectifs scientifiques

Dans ce contexte, deux questions sont importantes dans notre approche : le travail se concentre sur les réussites, sans inclure la recherche d'excuses comme le fait l'école californienne (Kenneth Pomeranz et al. [23]) ; l'approche est centrée sur la *business history* : comment des entreprises individuelles ont développé leur sentier de croissance spécifique dans les conditions et l'environnement particuliers de leur pays. L'idée de la session est de tester le point de vue traditionnel : les théories européennes sont-elles suffisantes pour refléter le succès industriel en Asie, en Amérique du Sud ou sur d'autres continents ? En effet, la question fondamentale est de savoir si le paradigme économique correspond au succès ou à l'échec. Trois grands types de cas ont été présentés :

- Cas 1 - Adam Smith et la concurrence ouverte : monde anglo-saxon, Danemark, Norvège, États d'Amérique latine
- Cas 2 - Friedrich List et l'idée de protection temporaire de l'« industrie naissante » : Allemagne, Suède, Finlande, Chine, Italie, Hongrie
- Cas 3 - Voie soutenue par l'État : France, Japon, Corée du Sud, Russie, Espagne), Afrique du Sud, Turquie et États du Golfe, États d'Amérique latine.

Du point de vue des acteurs, les contributions ont combiné les approches microéconomique et macroéconomique : le changement ne peut s'expliquer sans les acteurs, tandis que les mouvements des acteurs ne peuvent s'expliquer sans leur environnement. Le projet n'exclut ni les approches spatiales (économie régionale, géographie économique, sinon géostratégie), ni celles de la sociologie (structures sociales et mobilité, sociologie de l'action), ni d'autres relevant de l'histoire des sciences et des technologies ou de la démographie historique. Les approches ont tenu compte des approches microéconomiques. L'objectif était de mieux comprendre le rôle des entreprises et des autres acteurs, tels que les autorités publiques, dans l'émergence de l'économie moderne (par opposition à l'économie traditionnelle, selon Arthur B.

22 Emily S. Rosenberg, Akira Iriye, Jürgen Osterhammel (eds), *A History of the W*orld by joint publication of Harvard University Press and C. H. Beck, 2014.

23 Kenneth Pomeranz, *The Great Divergence: China, Europe, and the Making of the Modern World Economy*. Princeton, Princeton University Press, 2000.

Lewis[24]). Dans cette perspective, aucune approche traitant de l'histoire des entreprises n'est à exclure : microéconomie de l'entreprise ; économie et histoire de l'innovation ; sociologie des organisations ; psychologie sociale ; histoire du travail ; anthropologie des entrepreneurs, des travailleurs et des consommateurs.

Questions d'organisation

Afin de mener à bien le projet, il a été décidé de mettre en place un schéma organisationnel impliquant la tenue de quatre conférences préparatoires pour une session finale qui se tiendra à Boston, dans le cadre du WEG 2018. Ces quatre conférences préparatoires étaient les suivantes :

1/ Rio de Janeiro, Brésil, les 17 et 18 août 2017 à l'Université fédérale de Rio de Janeiro. Organisateur local : Luiz Carlo Delorme Prado, Professeur, IE-UFRJ, Institut d'économie, Université fédérale de Rio de Janeiro ;

2/ Pékin, Chine, 21 et 22 octobre 2017 à l'Université de Renmin en Chine. Organisateur local : Dominique Barjot, Huang Chun et Wang Jue, de Renmin University of China ;

3/ Tokyo, Japon, 15 et 16 novembre 2017 à l'Université Waseda. Organisateur local : Yago Kazuhiko, Université Waseda ;

4/ Paris, France, 29 mars 2018 à l'Académie des Sciences d'Outre-Mer avec le soutien de la Sorbonne université et du CNRS. Organisateur local : Dominique Barjot, Université de la Sorbonne et Académie française des sciences d'outre-mer.

À partir de ces quatre conférences préparatoires et des communications qui y ont été présentées, il est possible de distinguer trois ensembles de nations : les nations occidentales industrialisées, l'Asie de l'Est et du Sud-Est ; les autres nations émergentes.

PAYS INDUSTRIALISÉS OCCIDENTAUX

L'un des principaux objectifs de la conférence de Paris était de souligner la spécificité, tant macroéconomique que microéconomique, des modes de développement des grandes nations industrielles d'Amérique du Nord et d'Europe occidentale.

Amérique du Nord : l'American Way

En ce qui concerne l'American Way, trois approches ont été retenues : le lien entre l'esprit d'entreprise et l'innovation technologique à l'origine du développement industriel des États-Unis ; le rôle de la vision politique des dirigeants américains ; les voies adoptées par les grandes entreprises multi-divisionnaires et managériales pour s'adapter aux changements économiques et technologiques de la seconde moitié du XXe siècle. Enfin, il pourrait être intéressant de s'interroger sur les spécificités du cas canadien.

24 William Arthur Lewis, *The Theory of Economic Growth*, London, Taylor and Francis, 2003.

États-Unis : la culture entrepreneuriale et les mystères du développement économique

Louis Galambos montre que beaucoup de jeunes entreprises américaines n'impliquaient qu'un faible degré de nouveauté[25]. Cette vision rompt avec l'analyse bien connue de Joseph Schumpeter[26]. Selon lui, les entrepreneurs héroïques ont d'abord introduit les nouveaux biens de consommation, les nouvelles méthodes de production ou de transport, les nouveaux marchés et les nouvelles formes d'organisation industrielle créées par l'entreprise capitaliste. C'est la culture entrepreneuriale qui a encouragé les gens à prendre le risque d'explorer les possibilités d'innovation : la plupart échoueraient à long terme et beaucoup échoueraient à court terme. Cette culture a existé dès la fondation des États-Unis vers 1800. Ni la culture entrepreneuriale, ni la recherche de nouvelles opportunités d'innovation n'ont été propres à l'Amérique primitive. Les principaux facteurs, notamment l'immigration et les changements dans le secteur public, ont façonné les performances et la culture entrepreneuriale de la jeune nation américaine, ont facilité la transition vers l'industrialisation et ont accéléré la croissance. Néanmoins, deux facteurs ont été essentiels pour favoriser le développement : l'existence d'un secteur commercial vigoureux et orienté localement a été nécessaire pour fournir des capitaux ; en retour, ces capitaux ont ouvert la voie à un processus d'innovation à grande échelle soutenu par une forte culture entrepreneuriale.

États-Unis : une primauté de la politique sur l'économie ?

En s'appuyant sur l'expérience américaine post-1945, François David illustre la thèse de la primauté du politique sur l'économie, à travers la politique américaine vis-à-vis de l'Europe[27]. Dans la réorganisation du monde exigée par les États-Unis depuis Woodrow Wilson, l'économie est un moyen ; la politique, une finalité absolue. Dans les années fondatrices 1945-1963, les grands projets économiques et commerciaux conçus par les États-Unis au profit de l'Europe occidentale ont un but stratégique : créer une société internationale interdépendante, avec le rejet de la souveraineté obstinée, afin de dissoudre l'agressivité de l'État-nation westphalien. Le plan Marshall, la Communauté européenne et sidérurgique (CECA) puis le Marché commun poursuivent successivement cet objectif. Sur le plan de la méthode, les États-Unis ont su s'adapter, passant d'une sorte de chantage (diplomatie du dollar) à une diplomatie plus fine qui se résume ainsi : ni isolationnisme, ni intrusion ouverte.

Au terme des vingt premières années de la *Pax Americana* en Europe, les États-Unis ont emporté l'essentiel : ils ont résolu la plus grande question internationale depuis le Congrès de Vienne, la question allemande. Une Allemagne pacifique s'intègre enfin dans un Occident stable, à condition que l'Occident comprenne les États-Unis :

25 Louis Galambos, "The Entrepreneurial Culture and the Mysteries of Economic Development", in Dominique Barjot (ed), "Theory and Empirical Performance. Economic Paradigm and Performance in the Long Run (18th to 21st century)", *Revue française d'histoire économique – The French Economic History Review*, n° 11-12 (n°1-2, 2019), *op. cit.*, p. 60-80.

26 Joseph A. Schumpeter, *The theory of economic development: an inquiry into profits, capital, credit, interest, and the business cycle*, New Brunswick, New Jersey, Transaction Books, 1934.

27 François David, « L'Économie européenne au prisme du projet politique des États-Unis. Du Plan Marshall au Grand Dessein de Kennedy », communication présentée à la Préconférence de Paris.

l'intégration européenne d'une part (le couple franco-allemand en réalité) ; la garantie de sécurité américaine par l'Organisation du traité de l'Atlantique Nord (OTAN), d'autre part. La sortie définitive de l'isolationnisme des États-Unis est inhérente à l'intégration de l'Allemagne dans le jeu pacifique des nations. Dans ce grand jeu, le commerce international n'est qu'un moyen et non une fin en soi.

Sur la méthode, les États-Unis ont su s'adapter, passant d'une forme de chantage aux dollars à une belle diplomatie réduite au slogan : ni isolationnisme, ni ingérence dans la vie des États européens. De l'échec du plan Marshall en tant que catalyseur de l'intégration économique européenne à l'échec géo-militaire encore plus retentissant de la Communauté européenne de défense (CED) en 1954, les conceptions américaines du processus européen ont épousé trois principes. En tout état de cause, les États-Unis d'Europe restent l'objectif ultime. D'autre part, ils tolèrent l'émergence d'une concurrence commerciale européenne, facilitée par un protectionnisme à l'échelle d'une génération. Enfin, les États-Unis laissent les Européens décider eux-mêmes du rythme de leurs progrès institutionnels.

États-Unis : les très grandes entreprises multidivisionnaires et managériales, une diversité de choix stratégiques

Après la Seconde Guerre mondiale, l'affirmation du leadership économique et technologique américain s'est fortement appuyée sur la montée en puissance de la grande entreprise multidivisionnelle et managériale. Comme Miyata Kenichi l'a clairement montré à propos de General Electric (GE) et Westinghouse (WH) entre 1946 et 2000, le modèle n'a jamais eu le caractère monolithique qu'on lui attribue habituellement[28]. En effet, après la deuxième guerre mondiale, la GE Company et la Westinghouse Electric Corporation ont modifié leurs structures commerciales respectives. Cela résulte d'une divergence dans les comportements des cadres supérieurs découlant de leurs perceptions respectives de l'environnement, de leurs conceptions des perspectives, des mesures prises pour poursuivre une diversification sans rapport avec l'activité principale.

Plus généralement, la seconde moitié du XXe siècle a été marquée par un changement majeur dans l'économie américaine : le passage d'une croissance rapide à une croissance plus lente à partir de 1970. Alors que les grandes entreprises américaines représentaient 78% des 100 premières entreprises mondiales en 1956, leur nombre est passé à 33% seulement en 1990. Partant de là, Miyata K. examine le processus de divergence de la croissance des grandes entreprises américaines dans la seconde moitié du 20e siècle. Ainsi, il existe des débats entre historiens de l'économie, autour des facteurs de succès ou d'échec de la concurrence entre les entreprises industrielles au cours des années 1946 à 2000. Alfred D. Chandler a mis l'accent sur l'organisation des facteurs internes, à savoir que les cadres supérieurs ont choisi une diversification non liée pour assurer des gains à court terme plutôt qu'une diversification liée

28 Miyata Kenichi, "Modern Corporate Growth after the Modern Economic Growth: A Comparative Study of General Electric and Westinghouse, 1946-2000", communication présentée à la Préconférence de Tokyo.

favorisant la croissance à long terme[29]. D'autres chercheurs ont développé d'autres explications : l'évolution de la technologie (Langlois[30]), de la demande (Lamoreaux, Raff et Temin[31]) ou l'interaction entre les institutions et les organisations (Douglas North[32]). Plus précisément, D. North a fourni une intepprétation complète du changement à long terme, à savoir que les coûts de transaction et les droits de propriété sont ancrés dans les institutions, mais que les choix institutionnels le sont également dans les croyances.

L'analyse de Miyata se concentre sur la stratégie d'entreprise en tant qu'ensemble d'actions des acteurs. Dans le processus de changement des technologies et des marchés, la direction générale des entreprises industrielles prend des décisions concernant les perspectives. La vision managériale (une combinaison de vision et d'action) combine l'ensemble des trois actions de gestion (perception, conception, action réelle) et est utilisée pour argumenter l'explication. Entre les deux entreprises, GE et WH, les différences les plus importantes sont les suivantes :

1/ GE a trouvé la voie de la croissance en gérant une diversification non liée à celle de l'entreprise industrielle initiale.

2/ WH a choisi de revenir en arrière pour poursuivre une intégration verticale par une transformation commerciale majeure en un service de radiodiffusion à partir de sa base manufacturière traditionnelle.

Face à la nécessité de passer d'une croissance rapide à une croissance plus lente, les perceptions des gestionnaires ont évolué en fonction des ressources existantes et des marchés potentiels. En effet, les conceptions étaient limitées par les perceptions et les résultats des actions passées. En conséquence, GE a obtenu une croissance forte grâce à une stratégie de diversification sans rapport avec le marché et qui a combiné la fabrication et les services. Au contraire, WH a poursuivi sa croissance en tant que société de médias et est revenue à une stratégie d'intégration verticale qui a favorisé les activités les plus rentables et les plus compétitives. Enfin, l'analyse de Miyata aboutit à deux résultats :

1/ un réexamen de l'évaluation de la diversification sans lien avec le secteur. Selon le cas de GE, une diversification non liée peut apporter une croissance élevée à long terme que la diversification liée ne peut pas fournir (c'était également le cas pour Apple, Google et Amazon).

2/ une nouvelle étude du processus de dépendance à l'égard de la filière. L'étude comparative de la GE et de la WH met en évidence le processus de définition des limites au changement d'organisation des entreprises en appliquant la vision managériale.

29 Alfred D. Chandler, Jr., *Scale and Scope. The Dynamics of Industrial Capitalism*, Cambridge (Mass.) and London, Harvard University Press, 2004.

30 Richard N. Langlois, "The Vanishing Hand: The Changing Dynamics of Industrial Capitalism", *Industrial and Corporate Change*, 12, n° 2, 2003, p. 351-385.

31 Naomi R. Lamoreaux, Daniel M. Raff and Peter Temin, "Beyond Markets and Hierarchies : Toward a New Synthesis of American Business History", *American Historical Review*, 108, n° 2, 2003, p. 404-433.

32 Douglass C. North, *Understanding the Process of Economic Change*, Princeton , NJ, Princeton University Press, 2005.

Le cas canadien

Le Canada a connu un développement économique important après 1840, qui en a fait l'une des nations les plus prospères du monde[33]. Il doit son succès à ses propres entreprises, mais aussi à des multinationales (FMN), américaines et britanniques pour la plupart, dont la présence s'est intensifiée à partir de la fin du XIXe siècle. Diverses théories ont été avancées pour expliquer le succès du Canada. L'une d'entre elles est toujours en vogue, celle d'Harold Innis et de William A. MacKintosh[34]. Cette théorie souligne l'impact que l'exploitation des ressources naturelles a toujours eu sur l'économie canadienne : une succession de produits de base a contribué à la construction de la colonie et, par la suite, à celle de la nation. Elle a commencé avec la pêche et s'est poursuivie avec le commerce des fourrures, du bois, du blé, de divers métaux (fer et nickel notamment) et la vente de diverses formes d'énergie (dont l'hydroélectricité et plus récemment le pétrole). L'extraction ou la production de produits de base (pêche et commerce des fourrures, du bois, du blé, puis du fer et du nickel, et enfin la vente de diverses formes d'énergie (dont l'hydroélectricité et plus récemment le pétrole) a joué un rôle essentiel dans l'industrialisation du Canada, mais cela a fait du Canada une économie dépendante, d'abord de l'Empire britannique, puis des États-Unis.

Il ne fait aucun doute que les ressources naturelles ont toujours joué un rôle majeur dans l'économie canadienne. Les entrepreneurs canadiens ont lancé leurs propres multinationales dans ce secteur, en particulier dans l'industrie minière. Néanmoins, la question demeure : comment expliquer le succès de cette nation étant donné sa faible population et le fait que l'exploitation des ressources naturelles, comme on le voit ailleurs, peut conduire à la dépendance et même au sous-développement ? Quelles stratégies le Canada a-t-il suivies pour éviter cet écueil ? À partir de l'exemple de l'industrialisation de la vallée de la Mauricie (Québec), il est possible de caractériser l'industrialisation canadienne. Si des zones urbanisées comme Montréal ou Toronto ont une histoire industrielle très différente, leurs entreprises ont réussi à créer des marchés de niche pour les produits semi-finis, au-delà des productions de base.

Adam Smith est vraiment utile pour expliquer le cas canadien ? En fait, la main invisible du marché a été trop souvent et trop résolument remplacée par la main très visible des institutions publiques. Les pouvoirs publics sont intervenus d'abord en tant que législateurs, puis en tant qu'investisseurs et clients. Les analyses d'Alexander Gerschenkron ne sont pas plus pertinentes : l'autofinancement des entreprises était tel qu'elles n'avaient pas besoin du soutien permanent des grandes institutions financières. S'il y a eu une succession de processus de concentration ou de diversification verticale et horizontale, comme le décrit A. D. Chandler, les entreprises canadiennes ont du mal à atteindre et à conserver les produits finis, comme Nortel, Blackberry et même Bombardier. Une chose est sûre cependant : si l'industrialisation du Canada dépend en grande partie des investissements étrangers, elle dépend aussi de la capacité

33 Pierre Lanthier, "The Canadian Experience in Business: the Case of the St. Maurice Valley from 1890 to 1975", communication présentée à la Préconférence de Paris.

34 W.T. Easterbrook, and M.H Watkins, "The Staple Approach", in *Approaches to Canadian Economic History*. Ottawa, Carleton Library Series, Carleton University Press, 1984, p. 1-98.

du Canada à absorber ces investissements. Le Canada a démontré sa capacité à surpasser l'économie de base. Néanmoins, étant donné la petite taille de son propre marché, il reste difficile pour ce pays d'atteindre une autonomie totale vis-à-vis de ses marchés d'exportation, notamment américain. Le débat en cours sur le renouvellement de l'ALENA est un rappel douloureux de cette dépendance.

Europe occidentale : paradigme britannique ou processus de dépendance à la voie ?

Bien que les États-Unis soient aujourd'hui la référence en matière d'industrialisation, jusqu'aux années 1880, c'est le Royaume-Uni qui semblait être le modèle à suivre, d'où la question du mode d'industrialisation britannique comme paradigme.

Belgique et Pays-Bas : vers une révision du modèle d'industrialisation de Rostow ?

Aujourd'hui, ce n'est pas si clair. En effet, contrairement au «décollage rapide» linéaire et national de l'industrialisation tel que présenté par Rostow (1960), Robin C. M. Philips propose un schéma empirique explicatif des causes de l'industrialisation en Belgique et aux Pays-Bas depuis 1820 jusqu'à nos jours, en s'appuyant principalement sur les données des recensements de la population et de l'industrie belges et néerlandais[35]. Appliquant une version actualisée du modèle Midelfarth-Knarvik (2000), il a fait valoir que les mêmes facteurs qui peuvent expliquer la localisation de la révolution industrielle (dotations en facteurs, potentiel du marché et institutions), peuvent être utilisés pour expliquer celle de l'industrie dans ces pays au cours des phases ultérieures d'industrialisation et de désindustrialisation du XXe et XXIe siècle. Contrairement au décollage rapide présenté par Rostow (1960 : 7), Robin C. M. Philips a démontré que l'industrialisation s'est appuyée sur les phases précédentes de proto-industrialisation et qu'elle a eu un effet durable dépendant du chemin parcouru au cours de la période récente. Plutôt qu'une présentation nationale et linéaire de l'industrialisation ou de la révolution industrielle, il a défendu l'idée d'un processus dynamique d'industrialisation à la fois varié, régional et sectoriel.

Comme l'a souligné Marshall (1890), les facteurs d'agglomération ont joué un rôle crucial dans la localisation de l'industrie, car les secteurs et les entreprises manufacturières ont eu tendance à se regrouper au fil du temps au sein des régions ou des localités. Au cours du XIXe siècle, les coûts de transport élevés ont amené de nombreuses usines à se regrouper autour de bassins de main-d'œuvre et de ressources naturelles, comme ce fut le cas pour les entreprises de métallurgie et de fabrication de machines dans le Hainaut et à Liège en Belgique ou les usines textiles des villes de Zwolle, Gand ou Tilburg (Mokyr 1976). Des secteurs de plus en plus orientés vers le commerce ont commencé à s'industrialiser, avec des usines s'installant à proximité des centres urbains où une main-d'œuvre plus qualifiée et un pouvoir d'achat plus élevé étaient présents (Philips, Foldvari, et Van Leeuwen 2017). En raison de la chute des

35 Robin C. M. Philips, "Regional Industrial Development in Belgium and the Netherlands (1820-2010)", communication présentée à la Préconférence de Paris.

coûts de transport et des prix de l'énergie durant les deuxième et troisième phases de l'industrialisation, de nombreux secteurs à forte intensité de main-d'œuvre se sont délocalisés, tandis que les secteurs à coûts fixes élevés ou à haut degré de spécialisation sont restés relativement plus longtemps sur leur lieu d'établissement initial. Après les années 1960-1970, une phase de désindustrialisation a eu lieu, au cours de laquelle de nombreuses entreprises manufacturières se sont déplacées vers d'autres régions : d'abord dans les Pays-Bas, puis dans d'autres pays d'Europe et enfin en Asie du Sud-Est. Dans de nombreuses régions anciennement dominées par l'industrie, comme l'axe Charleroi-Liège, le marché du travail local n'a pas pu absorber cette soudaine augmentation de l'offre de main-d'œuvre, ce qui a accentué les divergences régionales en matière de chômage et de niveaux de revenus. *In fine*, le point de vue de Rostow (1960) sur le décollage rapide, l'industrialisation et la désindustrialisation, doit être révisé, sur la base de l'histoire industrielle des Pays-Bas.

Typologies de l'industrialisation : Les leçons de l'Espagne

Les progrès de l'historiographie économique espagnole des XIXe et XXe siècles au cours des deux dernières générations ont été alimentés par un objectif commun à tous les chercheurs : situer les performances économiques espagnoles dans une perspective mondiale[36]. Entre 1968 et 1975, certains chercheurs ont réussi pour la première fois à introduire l'Espagne dans un cadre de recherche plus général. Ce fut le cas de Nicolás Sánchez-Albornoz (1968) et sa discussion du « dualisme »[37] ; de Gabriel Tortella (1972 & 1973) à propos du rôle de la banque dans le développement économique[38] ou de sa réinterprétation de la construction ferroviaire espagnole à travers la vision des modèles de développement économique d'Albert Hirschman ; de Josep Fontana (1971 et 1973) s'agissant du rôle des finances publiques et du changement agraire sur le développement capitaliste espagnol - à la prussienne, à la française ou à la britannique ? – ; de Jordi Nadal (1973 & 1975) et de l'Espagne dans la course industrielle – sa thèse de « l'échec de la révolution industrielle » –[39] ; ou de Santiago Roldán et José Luis García Delgado (1973) et la Première Guerre mondiale comme une occasion de « rattrapage » pour l'Espagne. Le choc de ces contributions, pour la plupart concentrées en seulement cinq ans (1968 à 1973), a trouvé un écho dans les recherches ultérieures. Depuis cinquante ans, l'on discute autour de ces « grands » thèmes (au niveau espagnol). Certains des doctorats les plus brillants des années suivantes ont explicitement indiqué qu'il fallait reconsidérer l'hypothèse établie par la génération précédente. Rappelons les articles ou les livres de Jordi Maluquer de Motes (1977), Antonio Gómez-Mendoza (1982), Leandro Prados de la Escosura (1982 et 1988), Sebastián Coll et Carles Sudrià (1987), Francisco Comín (1988) ou Albert

36 Albert Carreras, "Typologies of industrialization : Lessons from Spain ", in Dominique Barjot (ed), "Theory and Empirical Performance. Economic Paradigm and Performance in the Long Run (18th to 21st century)", *Revue française d'histoire économique – The French Economic History Review*, n° 11-12 (n°1-2, 2019), *op. cit.*, p. 82-119.

37 Nicolás Sánchez-Albornoz, ed., *The Economic Modernization of Spain, 1830-1930*, New York, New York U.P., 1987.

38 Gabriel Tortella, "Spain, 1829-1874", in Rondo Cameron ed., *Banking and Economic Development. Some Lessons of History*, New York, Oxford U.P., 1972, p. 91-121.

39 Jordi Nadal, "The Failure of the Industrial Revolution in Spain, 1830-1914", in Cipolla, Carlo M. ed., *The Fontana Economic History of Europe*, vol. 4, *The Emergence of Industrial Societies*, 2, vol. 4.2, London, Collins, 1973, p. 532-626.

Carreras (1984 et 1991), pour ne citer que quelques-uns de ceux qui ont explicitement remis en cause ou étendu le paradigme de « 1973 ».

L'agitation du débat national a permis la diffusion initiale de certains éléments présents dans l'historiographie économique européenne : Milward & Saul (1977), Trebilcock (1981), Pollard (1981), Berend & Ranki (1982), mais de façon limitée[40]. Le principal témoignage d'écrits de première main en anglais se trouve dans le livre édité par Nicolás Sánchez-Albornoz (1987) où de nombreux noms cités auparavant ont contribué à des essais sectoriels ou régionaux[41]. La déclaration la plus ambitieuse et la plus provocante a été faite par César Molinas & Leandro Prados (1989) dans « L'Espagne était-elle différente »[42] ? Jusqu'en 1995, la discussion sur la place de l'Espagne dans les typologies d'industrialisation a été très active[43].

La particularité de l'expérience espagnole a été soulignée dans de nombreuses contributions de la première génération. L'« assaut » mené par la deuxième génération a produit beaucoup plus de « normalité » – en considérant l'Europe comme l'évolution normale. C'est pourquoi l'article de Molinas & Prados a été déroutant. À la question qu'ils ont posée, la réponse qu'ils ont donnée est affirmative. L'objectif principal d'A. Carreras est d'explorer ce problème de deux manières particulières. Tout d'abord, il tente de passer en revue les recherches effectuées sur l'histoire économique espagnole dans le cadre des « grandes » théories – ou typologies – de l'industrialisation et de la croissance économique, afin de déterminer dans quelle mesure les performances économiques espagnoles (SEP) ont été normales au cours des deux derniers siècles. Deuxièmement, il s'agit pour lui de tirer des performances économiques espagnoles quelques « leçons » potentielles pour la compréhension générale de la diffusion du développement économique. Les performances économiques à long terme de l'Espagne fournissent quelques indications qui peuvent être utiles pour la réévaluation de l'industrialisation et de la croissance économique moderne. Son incapacité à être classée dans les typologies habituelles – bien qu'elle en soit plus proche qu'on ne le pensait auparavant – suggère trois indices interprétatifs interdépendants qui pourraient valoir la peine d'être explorés : le taux de croissance des marchés protégés comme variable explicative des performances économiques à long terme, l'importance de politiques prudentes de libéralisation du commerce et le caractère décisif d'une situation géopolitique appropriée pour bénéficier de l'impact stimulant de la croissance de voisins riches. Dans les trois cas, la leçon sous-jacente est aussi vieille qu'Adam Smith : « la division du travail est limitée par la taille du marché ».

40 Alan S. Milward & Samuel B. Saul, *The Development of the Economies of Continental Europe, 1850-1914*, Allen & Unwin, London, 1977; Clive Trebilcock, *The Industrialization of the Continental Powers, 1780-1914*, Longman, London, 1981; Sidney Pollard, *Peaceful Conquest. The Industrialization of Europe, 1760-1970*, Oxford U.P., Oxford, 1981; Ivan Berend & Gyorgy Ranki, *The European Periphery and Industrialization, 1780-1914*, Cambridge & Paris, Cambridge U.P. & Éditions de la Maison des Sciences de l'Homme, 1982.

41 Nicolás Sánchez-Albornoz, ed., *The Economic Modernization of Spain, 1830-1930*, New York, New York U.P., 1987.

42 César Molinas & Leandro Prados de la Escosura, "Was Spain Different? Spanish Historical Backwardness Revisited", *Explorations in Economic History*, 26, 1989, p. 385-402.

43 Gabriel Tortella 1994, "Patterns of Economic Retardation and Recovery in South Western Europe in the XIX and XX Centuries", *Economic History Review*, 1994, p. 124; Albert Carreras, "What Can We Learn from Long-Term Spanish Economic Performance?", in Pablo Martín-Aceña & James Simpson, eds., *The Economic Development of Spain since 1870*, Aldershot, Edward Elgar, p. 24-47.

Le modèle économique allemand : dépendance et continuité du sentier ou destruction créative et discontinuité

Harm G. Schroeter s'interroge sur l'utilisation des théories de l'histoire économique pour expliquer la croissance économique allemande de 1949 à 1990[44]. Il existe un grand nombre de théories socio-économiques sur la croissance économique. Fait étrange, les historiens économistes ont expliqué le développement économique de l'Allemagne de 1945 à 1990 dans une large mesure sans se référer à la théorie. Cela inclut également les principaux économistes classiques[45]. Les historiens économiques qui travaillent sur la révolution industrielle ont en partie appliqué la théorie. En particulier, les théories de Gerschenkron sur le retard économique et celle de Rostow / Hirschman sur les étapes de la croissance économique et les secteurs moteurs ont été utilisées[46].

Harm G. Schroeter pose trois grands types de questions :

1 / quelle théorie convient le mieux ? Dans ce cas, la question principale est la suivante : Le développement économique de l'Allemagne de l'Ouest de 1945 à 1990 peut-il être expliqué par la théorie, non par des théories sur l'industrialisation, mais sur le développement économique ? Au cas où l'appel à la théorie serait nécessaire (pourquoi ne pas le penser ?), la question deviendrait alors : quelle théorie conviendrait le mieux ? La *path dependency* et la continuité des voies de développement (Douglas North) ? Ou le changement qualitatif, la destruction créative et la discontinuité (Schumpeter) ?

2 / Quel type de changement doit être expliqué ? De cette façon, il est nécessaire de distinguer et même de choisir entre les changements quantitatif (*path dependency*) et le qualitatif (destruction créative). En général, les changements quantitatifs ne nécessitent que peu d'explications théoriques. Mais le changement quantitatif a besoin d'une explication si le changement va dans une direction négative ou s'il engendre une nouvelle qualité de croissance. Au contraire, le changement qualitatif a besoin d'une explication en soi.

3/ Où l'explication est-elle nécessaire ? Un des points essentiels est d'analyser les changements structurels qui se sont produits dans la structure du PIB et de la population active entre 1950 et 1990.

Les étapes principales du redémarrage de la croissance économique de l'Allemagne ont été les suivantes :

1/ 1945 : "année zéro". Les éléments de continuité semblent prévaloir. C'est ce qui ressort des remarques suivantes : il n'y a pas eu d'"année zéro" en Allemagne (si tel avait été le cas, nous aurions eu besoin d'une théorie de l'industrialisation, non d'une théorie du développement) ? Les bombardements et les combats ont détruit environ 45 % des habitations allemandes, tous les grands ponts, mais seulement 15 % de la

44 Harm G. Schroeter, "Germany's Economic Development 1949 to 1990: Its Significance for Development Economics", communication présentée à la Préconférence de Paris.

45 Herbert Giersch, Karl-Heinz Paqué and Holger Schmieding, *The Fading Miracle. Four Decades of Market Economy in Germany*, Cambridge, Cambridge University Press, 1992.

46 Rainer Fremdling, *Eisenbahn und deutsches Wirtschaftswachstum 1840-1879*, Dortmund, 1985.

capacité de production. De plus, comment expliquer que des ateliers entièrement équipés aient été ouverts du jour au lendemain dès l'introduction du Deutsche Mark (DM) en 1948 ?

2/ Intervention de l'European Recovery Reconstruction (ERP). En 1948, l'introduction d'une nouvelle monnaie a donné un coup de fouet. Mais un autre facteur décisif a été le blocus de Berlin. En effet, le blocus de Berlin a entraîné un changement de perception : les États-Unis ne sont plus des ennemis, mais des amis. Il a ouvert la voie à la Reconstruction avec l'aide de l'ERP 1949-52.

Deux exemples d'industries illustrent ce redémarrage. Il s'agit d'abord de l'industrie automobile. À son propos, on peut se poser la question : destruction créative ou *path dependency* ? Une étude montre que Volkswagen (VW) a reconstruit non pas sur des principes allemands, mais sur des principes américains, avec l'argent de l'ERP, les conseils de consultants américains et des machines américaines. Dans ce cas, la clé du succès mondial a été l'adaptation à l'américanisation. La même question peut se poser dans le cas de l'industrie chimique. En réalité, le processus de redémarrage a été un peu différent : reconstruction sur des principes allemands mais passage à des principes américains en 1950, passage du charbon au pétrole comme énergie de base et comme matière première, adoption de procédures totalement différentes. En fin de compte, la voie suivie a été la même pour aboutir à un succès mondial : s'adapter à l'américanisation. Bien sûr, le choc de la crise pétrolière de 1973/74 a été perçu comme un grand défi. Le gouvernement allemand a alors clairement indiqué par des moyens politiques qu'il n'était plus possible de procéder comme avant (par exemple, en interdisant l'utilisation des voitures pendant les week-ends). Néanmoins, si la réaction dans les années 1970 a été d'utiliser le remède de Keynes, il en a été autrement dans les années 1980 : le recours au monétarisme de l'école de Chicago . Il y a donc eu quelques différences dans le développement avant et après la crise du pétrole : déréglementation et privatisation pour injecter de la concurrence. Les objectifs les plus importants étaient en même temps d'obtenir des taux de croissance plus élevés de la productivité et de la croissance du niveau de vie. La conséquence a été un développement rapide de la productivité du travail (sur une base 100 en 1995) : 1960 : 28 ; 1970 : 47 ; 1980 : 69 et 1990 : 83. Mais, en général, il n'y a pas eu de changement important dû à un choc économique ou à une autre politique !

En conclusion, qui doit être utilisé, Schumpeter ou North ? De nombreux éléments vont dans le sens du changement et de la discontinuité. Des changements substantiels ont eu lieu (changement structurel de l'agriculture au service, changement clair de la politique économique), mais dans la façon dont les choses sont faites. *A contrario*, on peut aussi trouver des arguments en faveur de la dépendance et de la continuité du cheminement : pas de changement dans le profil industriel du pays (toujours les mêmes branches). En bref, peu de changement dans la manière dont les choses sont produites (groupes de produits, type de services).

Europe occidentale : le cas de la France

L'historiographie a souvent souligné la lenteur de la croissance économique de la France au XIXe siècle, en comparaison avec les nouveaux pays industrialisés comme les États-Unis ou l'Allemagne, ou encore avec le Royaume-Uni[47]. C'était vrai mais il faut nuancer : la performance par habitant de l'économie française a été parallèle à celle du Royaume-Uni, du fait d'une accélération progressive de la croissance française de 1840 à 1857 et entre 1906-1907 à 1913-1914 ; en 1914, la France a bénéficié de sa puissance financière (deuxième exportateur mondial de capitaux). Mais les conséquences de la Première Guerre mondiale ont été désastreuses pour l'économie française (passage de nation créancière à nation débitrice, dépréciation du franc, inflation monétaire, morts de guerre et invalides aggravant la pénurie structurelle de main-d'œuvre). La croissance des années 1920, la plus rapide d'Europe occidentale, a masqué de profondes fragilités, malgré la reprise opérée par Poincaré, de 1926 à 1928, et la relance de l'industrie automobile. La crise des années 1930, bien que tardive, s'est poursuivie jusqu'en 1938, en raison de l'accélération du vieillissement, du déclin de la production industrielle, de la régulation du commerce extérieur, de l'échec des politiques déflationnistes. De plus, la politique du Front Populaire a échoué : la relance de la demande et les réformes structurelles n'ont pas permis pas la reprise de la production, d'où l'inflation. La Seconde Guerre mondiale affaiblit encore l'économie française. Trois facteurs se conjuguent : l'État étend son emprise sur l'économie, l'inflation explose à partir de novembre 1939, et surtout, de 1940 à 1944, la France subit les énormes prélèvements allemands. D'où, en 1945, la France sort très diminuée du conflit : les pertes matérielles sont gigantesques et concernent presque tout le pays. Néanmoins l'endettement extérieur français n'est pas très lourd et les réserves monétaires restent négligeables. Dans ces conditions, la spectaculaire reprise économique des années 1945 à 1969 peut être considérée comme un miracle.

Réalités et limites du « miracle français » des « Trente Glorieuses »

En effet, après la seconde guerre mondiale, la production augmente fortement en France : de 1949 à 1969, le taux de croissance du PIB est de + 5,1% par an en moyenne. Ainsi, l'utilisation d'une fonction Cobb-Douglas conduit à des résultats intéressants. Selon Jean-Jacques Carré, Paul Dubois et Edmond Malinvaud, la croissance de la production est due à un certain nombre de facteurs[48]. Elle résulte tout d'abord de l'augmentation de l'efficacité du travail. Les ressources en main-d'œuvre ont légèrement augmenté : + 0,2 % par an. La population totale est passée du malthusianisme au renouvellement de la natalité. Si le taux d'activité a diminué par rapport à 1918, le niveau de l'emploi est resté très élevé depuis 1949, malgré une détérioration très limitée à partir de 1965 et la durée du travail a fortement augmenté entre 1946 et 1969. Dans le même temps, la qualité de la main-d'œuvre s'est améliorée grâce à un niveau d'éducation plus élevé. Par conséquent, la productivité du travail s'est lentement accélérée avant la guerre, beaucoup plus après. La croissance du PIB également de

47 Dominique Barjot, "A «French Miracle»? The Economic Growth of France 1949-1969", communication présentée à la Préconférence de Paris.

48 Jean-Jacques Carré, Paul Dubois, Edmond Malinvaud, *La croissance française. Un essai d'analyse économique causale de l'après-guerre*. Paris, Seuil, 1972.

l'augmentation du stock de capital productif due à un effort d'investissement considérable. En effet, la croissance du capital productif était incontestable. Néanmoins, après 1945, les croissances du travail et du capital n'ont expliqué qu'une partie limitée de la croissance du PIB. Depuis 1945, la croissance est principalement due à un résidu. Il s'explique par les économies d'échelle, l'amélioration des méthodes de gestion et le développement du progrès technique et se mesure par les gains de productivité totale des facteurs. Le niveau de celle-ci était faible en 1949, mais elle a été caractérisé par une croissance rapide de 1949 à 1966.

Cinq autres causes ont conditionné, à leur tour, l'évolution des facteurs physiques.

1/ la croissance économique française a bénéficié d'un effet de demande globale, en raison de l'urgence des besoins : besoins anciens, transformation du contexte décisionnel des entrepreneurs, confiance dans le dynamisme de l'expansion mondiale, choix délibéré d'une politique économique privilégiant la croissance par rapport à la stabilité. En retour, la demande a catalysé la croissance en créant un appel au travail particulièrement intense, d'où une forte immigration de main-d'œuvre étrangère, un taux d'activité soutenu de la population française, une réduction quasi minimale du sous-emploi, le maintien d'une durée de travail relativement longue. Dans le même temps, une forte demande a favorisé l'innovation, optimisé l'utilisation des équipements productifs, stimulé la migration professionnelle. Le développement rapide du commerce extérieur de la France a favorisé la croissance, grâce à une spécialisation du système productif, a créé des économies d'échelle et a catalysé le progrès technique.

2/ Le besoin de capital physique a conduit à une épargne abondante, facteur positif. Si la demande de capital a augmenté, l'offre d'épargne s'est accrue depuis la dernière guerre. Pour les ménages, la répartition des ressources s'est stabilisée. De plus, la permanence des difficultés de logement des Français les a contraint à consacrer une part croissante de leurs revenus au financement de la construction. La hausse des prix de l'après-guerre a obligé les ménages à augmenter considérablement leur trésorerie afin de maintenir leur pouvoir d'achat. Mais l'évolution du financement des investissements n'a pas été un facteur explicatif des investissements de l'après-guerre. En fait, le rôle des ressources propres a été réduit et le financement extérieur a fortement augmenté.

3/ La productivité totale des facteurs s'est améliorée grâce au développement d'un marché concurrentiel. De 1949 à 1968, le marché du travail a évolué dans le sens d'une meilleure allocation des ressources. De 1955 à 1965, l'élargissement du marché des capitaux a progressivement transformé les conditions affectant la répartition des ressources financières. Si le contrôle des prix est toujours resté la règle, la création du Comité technique sur les ententes et les abus de position dominante en 1953, et à partir de 1960, l'ouverture des frontières ont rétabli un marché plus compétitif. Probablement, la politique de développement régional a légèrement accéléré la croissance.

4/ L'action de l'État, inégalement répartie, a été efficace. Certes, la régulation conjoncturelle a été généralement bénéfique pour la croissance, mais la France a dû résoudre le dilemme croissance / équilibre extérieur. La planification a contribué à créer un climat d'expansion mais n'a joué qu'un rôle très mineur dans la politique économique.

En conclusion, la croissance française résulte d'une série de facteurs favorables : rattrapage de la natalité, choc de 1939-45, réformes institutionnelles parallèles aux efforts d'instruction de la population française, reconversion de l'industrie, libération de la demande, environnement favorable. Certains facteurs ont été décisifs : d'une part, les Français ont donné une certaine priorité au travail ; d'autre part, au cours des années 1960, la France a bénéficié d'un appareil productif modernisé et d'une politique économique dynamique, cohérente et efficace.

Une industrie prédisposée aux cartels : l'exemple de l'industrie du ciment
Cécile Coursiéras-Jaff a cherché à comprendre l'évolution du marché du ciment, en particulier en Europe et en France, au cours du XXe siècle et à montrer comment les cartels ont joué un rôle majeur dans la construction de ce marché[49]. Pendant l'entre-deux-guerres, la plupart des producteurs européens de ciment ont commencé à réfléchir aux avantages de la mise en place d'accords nationaux et internationaux. Certains, comme les producteurs anglais, possédaient déjà de solides traditions d'accords nationaux, tandis que d'autres, comme les producteurs français, ne disposaient que d'organisations locales et périodiques de fixation des prix. Le comportement de l'industrie du ciment différait de celui des autres secteurs de l'industrie lourde. Par exemple, contrairement à l'industrie sidérurgique, l'industrie française du ciment n'a pas organisé de cartel national au cours des années 1920. C. Coursiéras-Jaff explique les raisons de cette situation particulière qui sont liées à la structure oligopolistique du marché du ciment ainsi qu'aux cycles économiques. Au cours des années 1920, les producteurs français de ciment ont surtout tenté de mettre en place des organisations locales afin de fixer les prix de vente. Mais dans les années 1930, ils ont créé de puissants cartels centralisés, d'abord à l'échelle nationale, puis à l'échelle européenne.

Les raisons de ce changement de comportement se trouvent principalement dans les effets de la crise économique. Dans l'après-guerre, l'industrie française du ciment a connu un processus de restructuration. Cette évolution a conduit à une diminution du nombre de producteurs de ciment en raison d'une accélération du processus de concentration. Le marché du ciment avait déjà une structure oligopolistique avant la Seconde Guerre mondiale. Certes, certaines entreprises familiales régionales ont réussi à s'imposer. Cependant, de 1945 à 1970, l'oligopole s'est renforcé autour des plus grandes entreprises. C. Coursiéras-Jaff a démontré que le cartel du ciment a réussi à combattre la crise. Elle a mis en lumière le rôle des producteurs français de ciment dans le cartel européen et comment les cartels français et européens ont permis non seulement des alliances économiques, mais aussi des alliances techniques et commerciales.

49 Cécile Coursiéras-Jaff, "The Cement Market during the 20th Century: between Cartels and Regulation", communication présentée à la Préconférence de Rio de Janeiro.

Cette évolution a trouvé une explication dans la structure particulière du marché du ciment mais aussi pour des raisons économiques et politiques. L'industrie du ciment était une industrie lourde avec un produit de faible valeur. Par conséquent, l'une des questions clés consistait à limiter les coûts de stockage et de transport afin de préserver un coût de produit final compétitif sur le marché. C. Coursiéras-Jaff a analysé comment chaque producteur parvient à combiner les investissements en matière de productivité, de capacité et de localisation spatiale pour rester compétitif. En fait, l'étude du processus de partage de l'information entre les producteurs par le biais des cartels a été cruciale pour comprendre ce processus de concentration. En outre, la demande croissante de la reconstruction a imposé des contraintes de capacité que seuls les membres de l'oligopole semblaient pouvoir assumer. C'est pourquoi le lien entre la croissance et le taux d'investissement a été mis en évidence pour comprendre la course entre producteurs pour augmenter leur capacité de production. Le comportement des pouvoirs publics français a également été critiqué : l'État français a probablement contribué à cette concentration, notamment par sa politique de limitation des prix.

L'Union européenne et la spécificité française depuis les années 1960
En 1957, le traité de Rome a réuni six pays, mais surtout deux modèles économiques opposés[50]. Cette différence entre la France et ses cinq autres partenaires remonte aux débuts de l'ère moderne. La France a construit au fil des siècles un grand marché intérieur qu'elle a réservé à ses producteurs grâce à tout un arsenal d'interdictions et de taxes douanières. Les progrès de sa fiscalité lui ont permis de disposer d'un appareil administratif développé. Ses élites ont pris l'habitude d'affirmer leur prestige en rejoignant la haute fonction publique. En revanche, à la même époque, dans les États faibles et dispersés du Rhin ou de l'arc alpin, les producteurs ont dû chercher des débouchés et les élites ont fait de l'entreprise le moyen de fonder et de maintenir leur prééminence sociale. La fin de la Seconde Guerre mondiale a considérablement amplifié l'opposition entre les deux modèles, la France ayant fait le choix en 1945 d'un système résolument étatique, ses cinq futurs partenaires optant plutôt pour un retour à l'économie de marché. Par la suite, la construction européenne a inévitablement conduit à une convergence entre les deux modèles. Le choix de créer une union douanière plutôt qu'une zone de libre-échange et l'acceptation de politiques communes auraient pu faire évoluer la construction européenne vers une extension géographique du système économique français. Mais les choses se sont passées tout autrement.

La France n'a pas réussi à créer une Union européenne à son image. Son modèle économique a été moins bien adapté à la mondialisation que celui de ses cinq partenaires du traité de Rome. Par son fonctionnement même, le système économique français, basé sur l'expansion de la demande intérieure, a exposé la France à la pression croissante de ses partenaires. La France, à son tour, a adopté de nombreux éléments du modèle libéral rhénan. Après avoir renoncé au protectionnisme en 1958, elle a renoncé à l'inflation en 1983, au dirigisme en 1986, à la planification en 1992, à la souveraineté

50 Michel Hau, « L'Union Européenne. L'évolution économique des pays d'Europe occidentale et la spécificité française depuis les années 1960 », communication présentée à la Préconférence de Paris.

monétaire en 1999 et à la stimulation par les dépenses publiques en 2018. Les crises sociales et politiques qui ont marqué et qui continuent de ponctuer cette évolution ne peuvent faire perdre de vue cette tendance lourde, qui s'est dessinée au cours des six dernières décennies. Elles montrent seulement que la temporalité des faits culturels obéit à un rythme plus lent que celui des faits économiques. La manière dont les Français appréhendent leur relation au reste du monde n'a probablement pas évolué aussi vite que leur comportement inconscient de consommateurs attirés par le libre-échange et les épargnants attachés à l'euro.

Mondialisation et émergence : Europe de l'Est

L'Europe centrale offre plusieurs exemples de petits pays qui ont réussi leur processus d'industrialisation.

Europe centrale : avantages compétitifs nationaux pour les petits pays

En ce qui concerne le processus d'industrialisation de la Hongrie, Mária Hidvégi applique les méthodologies de l'école de Michael Porter, comme « le double diamant » dans le cas du *process* d'industrialisation soutenue par l'État dans les petites économies ouvertes[51]. Elle se concentre sur l'exemple de deux entreprises hongroises sur le marché mondial 1867-1989[52]. En effet, le concept de retard d'Alexander Gerschenkron implique un processus de rattrapage accéléré facilité par le gouvernement. Dans ce schéma, les gouvernements facilitent et subventionnent le transfert de nouvelles technologies ainsi que la création de nouvelles industries et institutions nécessaires à la croissance à long terme. La voie de l'industrialisation soutenue par l'État peut commencer par la protection des industries naissantes (List 1840) ; l'intervention du gouvernement dans l'économie peut être étendue à de nouveaux domaines. Sur les traces de Gerschenkron, l'ampleur du retard de développement, l'efficacité économique et, en partie, la taille du pays ont été considérées dans l'histoire économique et commerciale comme des facteurs déterminant comment et dans quelle mesure l'État peut jouer un rôle actif et bénéfique dans le développement économique (Kuznets 1960, Wu 2011, Müller und Myllintaus 2008). Il est possible de parler d'un État développeur, comme en Amérique du Sud. Le lien avec les sources de la compétitivité nationale (Porter 1990) est moins bien étudié, tout comme l'importance différente de l'activité multinationale pour des pays de taille différente.

L'approche généralisée du double losange a appliqué le schéma interprétatif de Michael Porter aux petites économies ouvertes en intégrant des variables nationales et internationales dans l'analyse des déterminants des avantages compétitifs nationaux pour les pays hors Europe (Rugman al., 1995)[53] ; (Moon et al., 1998)[54].

51 Michael E. Porter, *Competitive Strategy*, Free Press, New York, 1980; *Competitive Advantage*, Free Press, New York, 1985; *The Competitive Advantage of Nations*, New York, Free Press, 1990, 1998.

52 Mária Hidvégi, "The Double Diamond and the State-backed Path of Industrialization in Small Open Economies: Two Hungarian Companies on the World Market 1867-1989", communication présentée à la Préconférence de Paris.

53 A.M. Rugman and J.R. D' Cruz , "The "Double Diamond" Model of International Competiveness: The Canadian Experience", *Management International Review*, 33 (2), 1993, p. 17-39.

54 H.C. Moon, A.M. Rugman and A. Verbeke, "A Generalized Double Diamond Approach to the Global Competitiveness of Korea and Singapore", *International Business Review* 7, 1998, p. 135-150.

L'analyse examine comment les moyens et l'étendue de l'intervention de l'État dans l'industrialisation ont influencé les activités multinationales des champions nationaux hongrois à long terme. L'accent a été mis sur les efforts de ces entreprises pour surmonter les contraintes de leur petite économie ouverte et de leur industrialisation tardive en favorisant leur compétitivité par une meilleure intégration dans l'économie mondiale. Il devient ainsi possible de décrire certains des facteurs utiles pour appliquer la théorie de la voie de l'industrialisation soutenue par l'État aux petits pays ouverts et à l'industrialisation tardive dans l'analyse de la contribution des entreprises aux performances des économies nationales à long terme. La Hongrie offre un bon exemple en termes de changements fondamentaux du système politique et économique, mais aussi d'efforts constants pour rattraper les précurseurs de l'industrialisation. Si, au niveau macroéconomique, il existe des avantages spécifiques à chaque pays, le niveau microéconomique met l'accent sur le concept d'avantages spécifiques aux entreprises. Ces éléments ont été des caractéristiques communes à la Hongrie et à de nombreux pays émergents et en développement en dehors de l'Europe.

Une renaissance économique de la Russie ?

Aujourd'hui, comme à la veille de la Première Guerre mondiale, la Russie est une nation émergente[55]. En 2015, à parité de pouvoir d'achat, comme en 1914, la Russie est classée sixième puissance économique mondiale. De 1892 à 1914, la Russie a connu un décollage spectaculaire, basé sur une industrialisation rapide et un afflux de capitaux étrangers. Il est le résultat d'une stratégie nationale de développement économique, qui s'identifie à Witte et Stolypine, deux hommes d'État remarquables. S'il s'est accompagné d'une aggravation rapide des inégalités sociales et géographiques, ce développement a constitué un attrait majeur pour les capitalistes et les entrepreneurs français. Au point de départ, d'importants échanges économiques et intellectuels ont eu lieu. Il s'agissait d'une part de flux de biens, de services et de capitaux, et d'autre part de transferts dans les domaines de la technologie, de la science et du droit, mais dont l'influence s'exerçait de manière inégale selon les régions du pays.

L'industrie russe s'est fortement appuyée sur les technologies d'Europe occidentale pendant toute la période de croissance économique moderne[56]. Grâce à l'apport de l'expérience organisationnelle et technologique étrangère, l'Empire russe a conquis la cinquième place parmi les principales nations industrielles du monde. Au début du XXe siècle, le transfert de technologie s'est effectué à grande échelle et a profondément affecté les branches avancées de l'industrie. L'indépendance du développement économique a été obtenue grâce à une politique prudente et durable d'adoption des technologies par un certain nombre d'entrepreneurs russes. L'approche microéconomique révèle les mécanismes du processus. Les dirigeants de Morozov ont réalisé

55 Dominique Barjot, « Introduction », in Thierry Claeys and Francine-Dominique Liechtenhan (eds.), « Economic, Financial and Technological Relations between the Russia and the West at the Dawn of First World War. Les relations économiques, financières et technologiques entre la Russie et l'Occident à l'aube de la Première Guerre mondiale », *Revue française d'histoire économique – The French Economic History Review*, n° 7-8 (n°1-2), avril-octobre 2017, p. 14-32.

56 Irina Potkina, "The Nikolskaya Mill Partnership and the West European Firms: Some Aspects of Technological Transfer" in Thierry Claeys et Francine-Dominique Liechtenhan (eds.), "Economic, Financial and Technological Relations between the Russia and the West at the Dawn of First World War", *op. cit.*, p. 34-48.

leur rénovation technologique grâce à une modernisation systématique jour après jour. La liste des fournisseurs potentiels était très longue. En général, les stratégies commerciales de Morozov correspondaient, d'une part, aux intérêts commerciaux des entreprises étrangères, fournisseurs essentiels d'équipements modernes pour l'industrie textile russe florissante. D'autre part, elles répondaient pleinement aux exigences de la croissance de l'entreprise. En même temps, le pays a fait d'énormes efforts pour accélérer le développement de l'enseignement secondaire et supérieur technique et technique, premier fournisseur de cadres nationaux spécialisés pour l'industrie. En outre, les entrepreneurs russes ont fait de leur mieux pour remplacer les spécialistes étrangers par des ingénieurs hautement qualifiés, diplômés des uniités locales .

Le problème de l'économie russe aujourd'hui reste largement le même qu'à l'époque. Face à l'ampleur des sanctions occidentales, cette économie a connu un nouveau ralentissement en 2015 et 2016. Cette situation reflète une croissance instable. Soutenu entre 2000 et 2008, le rythme de croissance du PIB est passé de 7,8 % en 2009 à 4,5 % en 2010, puis a diminué régulièrement jusqu'en 2015. En 2017, une légère reprise semble s'être opérée. Elle repose sur quelques indicateurs positifs : un taux de chômage de 5,5 %, mais au prix d'un emploi très flexible ; une inflation tombée à 5,6 %, mais probablement plus élevée pour le consommateur final ; des signes encourageants de substitution des importations. En fait, la Russie a obtenu quelques succès dans la construction d'avions et de missiles, dans l'industrie pharmaceutique et dans l'électronique radio. Aujourd'hui, près de 80 % des voitures commercialisées en Russie bénéficient d'un assemblage local, à partir de 65 % des pièces fabriquées dans le pays. En outre, entre 2014 et 2016, la part des médicaments produits en Russie est passée de 24 à 30 %. Mais les progrès les plus importants semblent concerner les industries agricoles et alimentaires (transformation de la viande et produits laitiers), qui sont des secteurs peu innovants. En effet, la Russie semble sacrifier ses dépenses de R & D. En conséquence, la compétitivité des produits russes se dégrade car les salaires restent trop élevés par rapport à la productivité. Les revenus réels des Russes étant en baisse, 14 % des habitants du pays se trouvent désormais en dessous du seuil de pauvreté. Enfin, les investissements étrangers ont diminué de 2013 à 2017. Parce que le pays reste, comme à la veille de la première guerre mondiale, trop dépendant de l'exportation de matières premières, le dynamisme de l'économie russe demeure suspendu au cycle du pétrole et du gaz.

UC Rusal, dans l'aluminium, constitue un bon exemple de challenger mondial[57]. Mais pour comprendre l'émergence de ce leader mondial de l'industrie de l'aluminium, il faut prendre en compte les bouleversements qui se sont produits depuis quarante ans et au niveau international dans cette industrie. Ces bouleversements ont été les suivants : un déplacement des autres productions géographiques, une diminution du degré de concentration et d'intégration de l'industrie ; l'émergence de nouveaux centres de consommation, le développement de nouveaux marchés et la concurrence

57 Dominique Barjot, « Rusal : l'émergence d'un challenger. Premiers résultats », in Patrick Fridenson & Florence Hachez-Leroy (eds.), *L'aluminium, matière à création XIXe-XXIe siècles*, Tours, Presses universitaires François Rabelais, 2017, p. 273-307.

croissante des produits de substitution, y compris le métal recyclé ; un renversement de la tendance à la baisse du prix réel du métal gris, de nouveaux facteurs poussant à la hausse les coûts de production et donc les prix, sous la pression de la demande de croissance des BRICS, de la dépréciation du dollar américain, de l'appréciation du yuan et du rôle dominant de la Chine ; un changement du mécanisme d'ajustement du déséquilibre du marché, une plus grande volatilité des prix et une demande accrue d'investissements, depuis l'entrée de l'aluminium à la Bourse des métaux de Londres (LME).

C'est dans ce contexte que Rusal est devenu en quelques années le leader de la production d'aluminium. Son histoire peut être attribuée aux origines de l'industrie de l'aluminium russe, puis à son essor à l'époque soviétique. La crise profonde qu'a connue cette industrie au cours des années est née, à l'initiative de quelques oligarques et avec le soutien du régime poutinien, d'un vaste groupe d'usines, centrées sur la Sibérie, et capables d'évoluer vers une multinationale compétitive. Jusqu'au printemps 2018, Rusal était le deuxième producteur d'aluminium au monde. Sa base industrielle a été construite en partie grâce aux technologies françaises (Pechiney depuis la veille de la première guerre mondiale). Depuis que les États-Unis ont mis Rusal sur la liste noire le 6 avril 2018, le plus grand producteur de métal hors de Chine a perdu plus de la moitié de sa valeur à Hong Kong. Les sanctions font qu'il est extrêmement difficile pour Rusal de faire des affaires en dollars. Il est donc très difficile de prédire l'avenir de l'entreprise.

En effet, comme l'ont montré de nombreuses études, les capitaux étrangers ont joué un rôle très positif dans le développement économique de la Russie dès le début de la seconde moitié du XIXe siècle[58]. Ils ont pris la forme de prêts extérieurs (capital d'emprunt), d'investissements directs dans des sociétés par actions et de capital d'entreprise. Grâce aux transferts de capitaux, la Russie a également bénéficié du transfert de technologie. L'industrie des machines-outils de l'industrie soviétique n'avait pas la capacité suffisante pour produire des machines spéciales et des lignes automatiques pour la production de masse. L'industrie manquait d'expérience dans la gestion de la production automobile à l'échelle prévue dans le plan de transport à long terme. Des constructeurs automobiles français et italiens (Renault, Fiat) ont été sélectionnés pour fournir une assistance technique à l'industrie automobile soviétique. Les résultats du transfert de technologies occidentales sur l'efficacité et la productivité de l'économie russe ont été plutôt positifs. Les constructeurs européens ont largement contribué au développement de l'industrie russe. Le succès de l'industrie russe actuelle est largement dû au transfert de technologies occidentales et surtout françaises, comme le montre le cas de la construction de l'usine automobile Renault à Moscou. En outre, au fil des ans, Total a établi des partenariats solides avec des entreprises russes de premier plan dans le secteur du pétrole et du gaz. Depuis 2015,

58 Boris Vinogradov, "Russia in the 19th Century, Russia Today, the Permanence of Technology Transfer", communication présentée à la Préconférence de Paris.

la Russie est devenue le premier contributeur à la production mondiale d'hydrocarbures de Total et l'essentiel de sa contribution est le gaz.

ASIE DE L'EST ET DU SUD-EST : MODÈLE ASIATIQUE OU "NATIONAL PATH DEPENDANCY" ?

Le poids économique considérable atteint aujourd'hui par la Chine et l'Inde reflète la montée de l'Asie dans l'économie mondiale. En effet, si l'on pense en termes de produit intérieur brut et de parité de pouvoir d'achat, la hiérarchie des puissances économiques est très modifiée au profit de l'Asie. Quatre nations asiatiques figurent parmi les dix premières : la Chine (1), l'Inde (3), le Japon (4) et l'Indonésie (7) ; viennent ensuite la Corée du Sud (14), la Thaïlande (19) et Taiwan (20). Cette progression de l'Asie semble générale. Néanmoins, à moyen et long terme, cette montée en puissance de l'Asie continue de reposer sur trois grands groupes de pays, dont l'originalité du modèle de développement a été bien mise en évidence par les économistes (WW Rostow, S. Kuznets A. Gerschenkron, R. Prebisch, P. A. Krugman[59], D. Senghaas, etc.) :

1. Trois puissances économiques dominantes, dont l'une pourrait être considérée comme un modèle par sa précocité et le caractère exemplaire de sa croissance économique, le Japon (d'où, entre autres, le succès de la célèbre théorie du développement «en vol d'oie sauvage», formulée par Kaname Akamatsu, dans les années 1930[60]) et les deux autres, la Chine et l'Inde, s'identifient à la montée des BRICS (Brésil, Russie, Inde, Chine et Afrique du Sud) dans l'économie mondiale ;

2. Les « quatre dragons » : il s'agit de quatre pays d'Extrême-Orient qui ont connu une forte croissance industrielle depuis les années 1960, à savoir la Corée du Sud, Hong Kong, Singapour et Taïwan.

3. Les nouveaux tigres asiatiques (ou nouveaux pays exportateurs ou « Tiger Babies »), souvent appelés « Tiger Club Economics », selon Goldman Sachs. Il s'agit de l'Indonésie, de la Malaisie, des Philippines, de la Thaïlande et du Vietnam.

Il n'a pas été question, lors des deux pré-conférences organisées en Asie, d'étudier tous ces pays. Néanmoins, il a été possible de revenir sur l'expérience japonaise, dont le caractère pionnier mérite d'être rappelé, d'ouvrir la porte à une historiographie chinoise encore trop connue et, sans négliger l'importance des flux commerciaux internationaux, de comparer les trajectoires de développement spécifiques du Japon et de la Chine avec celles suivies par la Corée du Sud, le Vietnam et, bien sûr, l'Inde.

Le Japon : pionnier, mais de manière spécifique ?

Comme pour la Grande-Bretagne, l'historiographie actuelle, sans remettre en cause le caractère pionnier de l'industrialisation japonaise, tend de plus en plus à souligner le caractère original de la voie suivie par ce pays. Cette spécificité de la voie japonaise ressort des travaux présentés lors de la pré-conférence de Tokyo. Ceux-ci s'articulent

59 Paul R. Krugman with Masahisa Fujita and Anthony Venables, *The Spatial Economy – Cities, Regions and International Trade*, Cambridge (Mass.), MIT Press, 1999.

60 Kiyoshi Kojima, "The "Flying Geese" Model of Asian Economic Development: Origin, Theoretical Extensions, and Regional Policy Implications", *Journal of Asian Economics*, 11 (2000), p. 375-401.

autour de trois grands thèmes : le rôle de l'entrepreneuriat dans le décollage de l'ère Meiji (et aujourd'hui) ; le rôle respectif du changement technologique dans l'industrialisation de la même période Meiji, tant dans les chemins de fer (transferts de technologie) que dans l'industrie textile[61] (liens entre changement technologique et changement organisationnel, rôle des politiques économiques et de leurs concepteurs comme facteur explicatif du miracle japonais des années 1950 aux années 1990.

À l'origine de l'esprit d'entreprise japonais moderne

Shibusawa Eiichi est l'une des figures les plus représentatives du capitalisme japonais de l'ère Meiji[62]. Appelé le « fondateur du capitalisme japonais », il est l'équivalent confucéen du modèle de Max Weber. Cependant, la carrière de Shibusawa a d'abord été une action pragmatique, suite à l'étude de Franck Michelin sur les relations entre les deux pays. la préfecture d'Akita et Shibusawa Eiichi. L'impact de Shibusawa sur le développement de l'économie capitaliste au Japon en général et dans la région de Tohoku en particulier reste difficile à évaluer. Shibusawa n'avait pas un énorme pouvoir d'investissement, mais il possédait une expertise unique en matière de techniques financières : il a joué un rôle déterminant dans le lancement et le développement des systèmes bancaires dans tout le Japon. Mais avec l'intensification de l'intervention militaire sur le continent et le passage au protectionnisme dans de nombreux pays, le Japon a commencé à abandonner le libre-échange et à donner un rôle croissant à l'État dans le développement économique. En conséquence, Shibusawa a accepté que l'État joue le rôle principal et est devenu un partisan de la colonisation économique de Taïwan et de la Corée. Grâce à la compétitivité renouvelée de son industrie, le Japon reste aujourd'hui la troisième (ou la quatrième, en termes de parité de pouvoir d'achat) puissance économique mondiale. C'est ce que démontre une comparaison entre Kodak et Fuji Film (Yuzawa Takeshi) [63]. Dans les années 1960 et au début des années 1970, Kodak était le plus grand réalisateur de films au monde. Mais Kodak n'a pas su s'adapter à la «révolution numérique». Au contraire, le film Fuji est à nouveau une activité très rentable.

Transferts de technologie, changements techniques et organisationnels au Japon Meiji

Si le rôle des entrepreneurs a été essentiel, l'importance décisive du transfert de technologie doit également être soulignée. À cet égard, les chemins de fer constituent un excellent champ d'observation, comme le montrent les recherches de Nakamura Naofumi[64]. L'objectif principal de la contribution de Nakamura est de clarifier le processus de développement de la technologie ferroviaire au Japon pendant l'ère Meiji (1868-1912) tout en soulignant le rôle des ingénieurs des chemins de fer et leur

61 Tetsuji Okazaki, « Disentangling the Effects of Technical and Organizational Changes in the Rise of the Factory: The Case of the Japanese Fabric Industry 1905-1914 », *CRJE Discussion Papers*, July 2017, communication présentée à la Préconférence de Tokyo.

62 Franck Michelin, "Shibusawa Eiichi and the Rise of the Capitalist Economy in Northern Japan. A Research Project", in Dominique Barjot (ed), "Theory and Empirical Performance. Economic Paradigm and Performance in the Long Run (18th to 21st century)", *Revue française d'histoire économique – The French Economic History Review*, n° 11-12 (n°1-2, 2019), *op. cit.*, p. 190-202.

63 Yuzawa Takeshi, "The Digital Revolution and Business Behavior. The case of Kodak us Fuji film", in Dominique Barjot (ed.), « L'ascension économique de l'Asie », *Entreprises & Histoire*, n° 90, 2018/1, p. 37-50.

64 Nakamura Naofumi, "Diversification and Convergence : Development of the Locomotive Technology in Meiji Japan", ISS Discussion Paper Series F – 180, June 2016, communication présentée à la Préconférence de Tokyo.

imitation technique. Le processus de développement de la technologie ferroviaire au Japon peut être divisé en quatre étapes : (1) le transfert des systèmes ferroviaires du Royaume-Uni par le gouvernement japonais au cours de la période 1870-1880 ; (2) l'acquisition de matériel ferroviaire, en provenance des États-Unis et de l'Allemagne, et la diversification de la technologie, au cours des années 1890 ; (3) la normalisation et la convergence de la technologie par la fusion et la nationalisation des réseaux ferroviaires dans les années 1900 ; et (4) le développement d'une technologie originale par les chemins de fer d'État au cours des années 1910.

Dans un premier temps, la technologie ferroviaire a été transférée au Japon de deux manières : par l'embauche d'étrangers ou par des contrats généraux. La première méthode a été promue par les Britanniques pour les chemins de fer de Honshu. La seconde a été encouragée par les États-Unis à Hokkaido. L'embauche d'étrangers a eu une plus grande influence sur le développement de la technologie ferroviaire japonaise. Cependant, la deuxième méthode ne doit pas être négligée. Elle a permis la formation de Soichiro Matsumoto et de Seichiro Hirai, des ingénieurs qui ont joué un rôle central dans les chemins de fer impériaux dans les années 1890 et 1900 et la diversification qui s'en est suivie. Cependant, au début de l'ère Meiji, l'influence des employés étrangers Honshu et britanniques, qui ont le monopole de la fourniture de matériel ferroviaire, est extrêmement forte et dominante.

Au cours de la deuxième étape, les pays fournisseurs de locomotives se sont très rapidement diversifiés. La prospérité croissante des compagnies de chemin de fer et l'indépendance technologique accrue des ingénieurs japonais ont conduit dans les années 1880 et 1890 à une diversification des technologies ferroviaires. Cette diversification a eu lieu dans un contexte d'intensification de la concurrence internationale sur le marché mondial des locomotives. Il est devenu possible d'acheter de façon optimale du matériel ferroviaire du monde entier. Au Japon, les appels d'offres et la pratique de la concurrence limitée ont été introduits dans les années 1890, ce qui a entraîné la création d'un système concurrentiel pour l'achat de matériel. En même temps, comme chaque compagnie ferroviaire achète des locomotives indépendamment, il existe au Japon de nombreuses locomotives aux spécifications très variées. En outre, des efforts ont été faits pour réaliser des copies en utilisant comme modèles diverses locomotives de différents pays, ce qui a conduit à l'accumulation de compétences technologiques dans la fabrication du matériel roulant.

Dans une troisième étape (étape 3), l'absence de normes uniformes entre les différentes entreprises est apparue comme un problème croissant en raison de la nécessité de normaliser les installations. Après la promulgation de la loi sur l'exploitation ferroviaire en 1900, divers règlements ont été adoptés pour normaliser les rails, les coupleurs et le matériel roulant. Ce mouvement de normalisation s'est accéléré avec la nationalisation de 1906-07. Au cours de l'étape 4, une section de fabrication a été créée au sein de l'Agence des chemins de fer. Ses activités se développent en même temps que celles des fabricants privés de matériel roulant afin de fabriquer des locomotives au Japon. Différents modèles de locomotives sont commandés en Europe et aux États-Unis. Un savoir-faire spécifiquement japonais est ainsi acquis, en profitant du système d'inspection. En 1914, le Japon a ainsi développé une capacité indépendante de conception et de fabrication de locomotives, ce qui a finalement conduit à l'émergence d'une production de masse de locomotives japonaises. En fin de compte, il est clair que l'imitation d'une grande variété de modèles étrangers et la formation d'ingénieurs japonais dans des entreprises publiques et privées ont permis à l'industrie japonaise d'acquérir un savoir-faire équivalent à celui des grandes puissances industrielles occidentales. En d'autres termes, la diversification de la technologie et l'accumulation concomitante d'expériences ont été les clés du développement d'une technologie originale.

Les sources du «miracle économique japonais» revisitées

On a beaucoup écrit sur le miracle économique japonais, mais pas encore assez sur ses origines intellectuelles et surtout sur les origines des politiques économiques qui l'ont accompagné et encouragé. C'est dire tout l'intérêt des travaux de Yago Kazuhiko. Le Japon a connu une croissance économique impressionnante de la fin des années 1950 au début des années 1970. La croissance économique du Japon après la Seconde Guerre mondiale a été alimentée par des plans continus, dont le plus célèbre est le plan de doublement du revenu national (1961-1970)[65]. Yago K. tente de reconstituer les visions proposées et débattues par les responsables japonais impliqués dans le processus d'élaboration de ces plans. Il fait également référence à un autre acteur, l'Organisation pour la coopération et le développement économique (OCDE), en particulier le groupe de travail 2 du Comité de politique économique (WP2) qui relève du Conseil ministériel de l'OCDE. Le Conseil ministériel de l'OCDE, peu après sa création en 1961, a fixé un objectif de croissance à atteindre par les pays membres entre 1960 et 1970 : « une croissance de 50 % du produit national brut réel ». Le Japon, lors de son entrée dans l'OCDE en 1964, doit participer à cet objectif de croissance en tant que précurseur de la reprise économique. L'hypothèse avancée est que les plans élaborés au cours des années 1950 et 1960 dans le cadre du système de taux de change fixes auraient pu être plus prudents, en termes d'objectif et de vision de la société future, que le résultat réel que nous connaissons aujourd'hui avec le recul. En examinant le plan de croissance et la pratique du Japon du point de vue de l'OCDE (et *vice versa*), Yago K. accorde une attention particulière à la division théorique et politique dont ont été témoins les autorités japonaises, et qui a également trouvé un écho dans le point de vue de l'OCDE.

Un deuxième article de Yago K. a cherché à présenter une vision alternative de la croissance japonaise, en se référant aux débats contemporains au sein de l'OCDE afin de revoir la façon dont les contemporains comprenaient la productivité, avec une historiographie actualisée[66]. En examinant la notion de productivité à partir des archives de l'OCDE, il a mis en lumière les éléments suivants : la notion de productivité était imparfaite et le point de vue japonais s'est limité au contexte contemporain, en

65 Yago Kazuhiko, "Convergence and Divergence over the Growth Paradigm: The OECD Working Party 2 and the Japanese "Doubling National Income Plan", *Revue économique, op. cit.*, 2020/4, Vol. 71, p. 697-713.
66 Yago Kazuhiko, "The "black box" of Japanese growth (1945-1973): the origins of productivity", chapitre original.

particulier les réserves de change. Toutefois, les interprétations et les malentendus susmentionnés ont parfois permis au Japon de connaître une forte croissance. Le «retard» dû à l'importance de la population rurale a d'abord fourni une main-d'œuvre bon marché, avec une forte propension à l'épargne, et s'est finalement transformé en un vaste marché pour les biens ménagers. Le rôle joué par le gouvernement a été essentiel dans l'introduction des technologies étrangères, mais l'un des arrière-plans importants a été la réglementation des mouvements de capitaux, qui a suggéré l'octroi de licences et le commerce de la propriété intellectuelle au lieu de l'investissement direct.

Les fruits de cette croissance économique ont permis au Japon de devenir un grand donateur d'aide étrangère, principalement aux pays en développement d'Asie[67]. Quelles sont les réflexions et le paradigme qui ont soutenu l'évolution de l'aide japonaise, en relation avec la croissance rapide du pays ? Yago K. cherche à répondre à la question ci-dessus dans une perspective historique, en se concentrant sur la façon dont les « initiés » ont observé les problèmes, en fonction de deux séries d'archives : le Comité d'aide au développement (CAD) de l'Organisation de coopération et de développement économiques (OCDE) et le Conseil de coopération au développement extérieur (CCDE) du Japon. Le gouvernement japonais avait l'intention de rejoindre le CAD et de gérer l'aide afin de garantir les marchés d'exportation et de ressources pour la croissance japonaise. D'autre part le Japon a tôt ou tard réussi à pousser sa croissance à grande vitesse sans s'occuper du marché lié à l'aide. Le « paradigme de la croissance » japonais en matière d'aide a changé avec un certain décalage et dans une certaine continuité, sous l'effet conjugué d'une réflexion stratégique profonde et d'une crainte incohérente d'affronter une nouvelle phase de croissance.

L'éveil de la puissance économique chinoise

Avec les réformes introduites en Chine par Deng Xiaoping, à partir de 1979, la Chine a fait des pas de géant sur la voie d'une croissance économique autonome. Elle a rattrapé son retard, puis dépassé le Japon, s'imposant comme un autre modèle asiatique. Mais le défi de la modernisation n'est pas totalement relevé. Comment réformer l'économie, la politique et la culture d'une société chinoise traditionnelle et comment modifier en conséquence les relations entre ces trois aspects ? Ces questions dictent le chemin que la Chine a dû emprunter pour devenir une nation moderne. Huang Chun et Wang Jue ont montré que la stratégie utilisée par la Chine pour apprendre du monde occidental moderne consistait à promouvoir la modernisation des capacités économiques, politiques et culturelles par le biais de la modernisation industrielle[68]. Centré autour de cet objectif, l'apprentissage des institutions et de l'idéologie occidentales a été et reste nécessairement adaptatif, réformateur et inclusif. Du point de vue du développement

67 Yago Kazuhiko, "Japanese Aid and Economic Growth during the 1960s and Early 1970s", in Dominique Barjot (ed.), "Theory and Empirical Performance. Economic Paradigm and Performance in the Long Run (18th to 21st century)", *Revue française d'histoire économique – The French Economic History Review*, n° 11-12 (n°1-2, 2019), *op. cit.*, p. 204-224.

68 Huang Chun and Wang Jue, "China's Path to Become a Modern Nation: Industrialization, Learning Strategy and System Choice", in Dominique Barjot (ed.), "Economic development, financing and business strategies (19th-21st century)". « Développement économique, financement et stratégies d'entreprises XIXe-XXIe siècles) », *Revue française d'histoire économique – The French Economic History Review*, n° 9-10 (n°1 et n° 2, janvier et septembre 2018), p. 38-59.

de la propre culture de la Chine, le défi de la modernisation de la Chine réside dans la question de l'intégration réussie des traditions de la culture chinoise avec la culture occidentale moderne pour créer une nouvelle forme de culture.

À la recherche de la spécificité du modèle de développement chinois

L'histoire économique chinoise est en train de changer aujourd'hui. Toute une génération de jeunes chercheurs s'est lancée dans des recherches originales. La recherche se concentre sur l'histoire des institutions financières et commerciales ainsi que sur les développements scientifiques et technologiques. Dans la Chine traditionnelle, il existait une relation délicate entre l'économie officielle et l'économie non gouvernementale[69]. La première ne se préoccupe pas nécessairement de la seconde, mais laisse à cette dernière suffisamment de place pour un libre développement dans la pratique. Sur la voie de la modernisation, face à la menace des puissances occidentales, la Chine a connu un remodelage national à grande échelle, ainsi que la transformation du rôle du gouvernement, formant ce qu'on appelle le «modèle chinois». Du point de vue de l'histoire économique, la réforme et l'ouverture de la Chine au cours des quarante dernières années ont permis de libérer à nouveau l'économie privée, ce qui semble être une sorte de retour aux traditions chinoises.

Par exemple, Sun Rui a réalisé une étude sur l'organisation communale traditionnelle chinoise et la transition de l'État[70]. Cet article se concentre sur la gestion commerciale locale dans la province de Hu Nan entre 1787 et 1909 en Chine. La recherche porte sur 269 règlements, comportant 2636 clauses, et 133 industries comme moyens traditionnels chinois. Ces réglementations étaient dotées d'une autonomie commerciale. Et les intérêts fondamentaux de l'industrie étaient fixés et conservés dans chacun d'eux, ce qui était le plus important, plus que les religions. La justice procédurale pouvait insister sur l'élection des gérants et la gestion des finances intérieures. Il y avait aussi des règles concernant le contrôle des directeurs principaux. Ils devaient être responsables de leur association. Les associations ont une grande autorité de commercialisation qui a fait les règlements de transaction ainsi que les sanctions. L'influence du gouvernement local était importante mais pas essentielle. Elles permettent de mieux comprendre un système traditionnel mis en place vers 1500 et en vigueur jusqu'en 1945. Ces réglementations concernent la régulation des marchés et la gestion des guildes. Ils montrent l'autonomie de gestion dont bénéficiaient ces guildes.

Un thème majeur : la mise en place du transfert de technologie et le développement des transports

Un bon exemple de modernisation spectaculaire concerne le transport ferroviaire. Grâce à un investissement massif dans les trains à grande vitesse, la Chine est passée

69 Sun Rui and Wang Qing "Chinese Model and the Choice of Development Path: A Perspective from Economic History" , in Dominique Barjot (ed), "Theory and Empirical Performance. Economic Paradigm and Performance in the Long Run (18th to 21st century)", *Revue française d'histoire économique – The French Economic History Review*, n° 11-12 (n°1-2, 2019), *op. cit.*, p. 182-189.

70 Sun Rui, "What is the Local Governmental Management in Economy? A View on the Commercial Association during the Late Qing Dynasty in China?", communication présentée aux Préconférence de Pékin et Tokyo.

d'une phase de rattrapage à une autre, fondée sur l'innovation[71]. L'histoire du développement des trains à grande vitesse peut être divisée en trois périodes : une période d'exploration basée sur une recherche et un développement indépendants, de 1992 à 2003 ; une phase d'introduction massive de technologies étrangères, de 2004 à 2007 ; enfin, depuis cette date, une nouvelle période d'innovation autonome. En conséquence, l'industrie chinoise des trains à grande vitesse (TGV) a connu une augmentation du kilométrage (19 000 kilomètres en 2015, 30 000 en 2020) et des innovations technologiques. Dans le cas de la Chine, l'État pourrait être défini comme un entrepreneur.

Le développement du HSR chinois a été mené par le Conseil d'État, en étroite coordination avec la Commission nationale pour le développement et la réforme, le ministère de la science et de la technologie, le ministère des finances et d'autres départements et gouvernements locaux. Dans le processus d'introduction de la technologie en tant que leader, l'ancien ministère des chemins de fer (MOR) a exercé des fonctions administratives et de gestion à la fois comme représentant de l'État et comme entreprise active. Il était à la fois stratège et exécutant. Il était le législateur de toutes les négociations et de tous les contrats. Gérant l'introduction de la technologie, il a financé la R & D, créé le marché, guidé l'opinion publique. Il était responsable des investissements et du financement, mais aussi de l'élaboration des plans et de la mise en œuvre des normes unifiées, des appels d'offres, de la construction et de l'approbation de tous les travaux, de l'achat et de la gestion des véhicules et autres accessoires. Au début, la période de développement de la grande vitesse était profondément ancrée dans l'économie planifiée. En conséquence, il y avait une série de défauts. L'assouplissement des contraintes de crédit et l'endettement excessif, l'insuffisance et le gaspillage des ressources, le manque de maturité technique existaient dans l'ancien MOR. Toutefois, son efficacité et sa capacité de mise en œuvre ne doivent pas être négligées.

Une montée en puissance récente mais impressionnante : l'industrie chinoise de la construction

Après la déclaration de la fondation de la République populaire de Chine en 1949 par Mao Zedong, l'industrie de la construction a subi un sérieux « recul » en raison de l'influence terrible de la nouvelle idéologie d'État sur l'économie[72]. Après des décennies de sous-utilisation, le renouveau de cette industrie depuis longtemps stagnante n'est venu qu'avec l'arrivée d'un nouveau dirigeant : Deng Xiaoping, dont les réformes devaient propulser la Chine à un tout nouveau rang économique. Les réformes des entreprises publiques ont consisté à modifier le système économique planifié, à donner plus de liberté aux entreprises de construction et à rechercher plus de ressources financières par le biais du marché boursier. Cependant, malgré les nombreuses réformes économiques, l'héritage d'un système économique dépassé

71 Wang Jue and Wang Qing, "China's High-speed Rail. From Technological Catching-up to Innovation", communication présentée à la Préconférence de Tokyo.
72 Zhou Xiaolan, "The International Activities of the Chinese Construction Industry under the Context of China's Entry into the WTO. The Case of China Railway Group Limited"?, paper presented to the session Multinationals from emerging and developing countries: historical roots [S10080], XVIIth World Economic History Congress 2015 Kyoto, Japan, 3-7 August 2015.

est resté considérable. Face à l'entrée de la Chine dans l'Organisation mondiale du commerce (ci-après OMC) depuis 2001, non seulement l'industrie de la construction, encore en cours de réforme, doit se battre contre de puissants rivaux du monde entier, mais encore elle doit aussi franchir les frontières nationales dans le but de réaliser des profits à plus grande échelle sur le marché international. En 2007, selon les statistiques de l'OMC, la Chine était le troisième pays le plus important en termes de production, juste après les États-Unis et le Japon ; de même s'agissant de la Chine et de l'Inde, dont les dépenses de construction augmentent chaque année de plus de 8 %, ces deux pays se distinguent comme étant les deux plus grands marchés de l'industrie de la construction dans le monde.

La Banque d'investissement pour les infrastructures en Asie (Asia Infrastructure Investment Bank, ci-après AIIB), récemment créée, qui vise à exporter de Chine les capitaux excédentaires pour soutenir la construction d'infrastructures, notamment de chemins de fer, de routes, de ponts, de ports et d'aéroports dans toute l'Asie depuis novembre 2014, dépend largement de l'industrie de la construction. Dans le même temps, China Railway Group Limited et China Railway Construction Corporation Limited sont les deux plus grandes entreprises de construction en Chine. Ces deux entreprises sont également les deux plus grandes entreprises mondiales en termes de capital. À leurs côtés, une troisième entreprise, China State Construction, dont la puissance est en pleine croissance, a pris la troisième place.

D'une manière générale, l'industrie chinoise de la construction a fait des progrès remarquables sur les marchés étrangers, principalement dans les pays en développement. Le succès des entreprises est souvent marqué par des bâtiments emblématiques tels que des autoroutes, des hôpitaux et des systèmes d'irrigation pour lesquels les gouvernements locaux ne sont pas capables de construire ce genre d'ouvrages. D'autre part, elles ont encore des difficultés à percer les marchés des pays développés où la sanction des lois et des contrats prévaut sur le pouvoir gouvernemental. Le cas de « China Railway Group Limited » pourrait être un cas parfait pour démontrer la situation embarrassante de l'industrie de la construction en Chine aujourd'hui. Le succès éventuel de l'industrie sur la scène internationale pourrait reposer sur une optimisation plus profonde de la structure des groupes d'État, en particulier une meilleure gestion de leurs filiales, sur l'amélioration de leur secteur de recherche et développement et sur leur connaissance des systèmes juridiques des pays étrangers s'ils ont toujours l'intention de partager les marchés en Europe et en Amérique du Nord.

Les nouveaux pays industrialisés en Asie

Les voies de l'industrialisation ne se limitent pas aux modèles japonais et chinois. En marge de la Chine, la Corée du Sud, le plus grand des «quatre dragons», et le Vietnam, un des « tigres asiatiques », offrent deux exemples intéressants, aux trajectoires très différentes. Surtout, un nouveau géant économique est apparu : l'Inde, avec ses grandes entreprises, dont certaines sont multinationales. Dans son développement, elle a fait appel aux capitaux étrangers. Certains pays européens, comme l'Allemagne, s'y intéressent.

Corée du Sud

Avec Taiwan, la Corée du Sud est donc l'une des meilleures illustrations des théories de Rostow, qui y a effectué plusieurs missions de conseil et d'assistance dans les années 1960. Tout d'abord, l'historiographie récente de la Corée du Sud tend à réévaluer le rôle de la communauté des affaires coréenne dans le boom économique du début du XXe siècle. Il est vrai que les Japonais ont forcé l'entrée du pays dans la modernité[73], mais il y avait aussi de véritables capitalistes coréens, notamment dans le commerce du riz et l'industrie de l'emballage. Les marchands Kim étaient une famille de courtiers [gaekju] opérant dans la zone de Dongmak à Séoul, tout près du fleuve Han. Hong Sung Chan, Lee Jong Hwa et Kim Mi Lim ont documenté l'établissement et le fonctionnement de la rizerie Dongil de la famille Kim, qui utilisait un moteur à essence ou électrique, des engrenages de transmission et des systèmes qui fonctionnaient depuis 1910[74]. La préparation du riz était une industrie manufacturière qui a attiré de nombreux investisseurs coréens pendant la période Hanmal et le début de la période coloniale. En utilisant les livres de comptes de la famille Kim, il est possible de reconstituer l'espace et les installations de la rizerie de Dongil, les opérations d'achat et de transformation des matières premières (riz non décortiqué et riz brun non poli), celles de vente des produits (riz brun ou riz blanc), d'étudier l'évolution de l'emploi et le niveau comme l'évolution des salaires, des transactions bancaires et de l'utilisation du capital, et les opérations quotidiennes effectuées dans les années 1910. Ainsi, il est possible de montrer clairement la transformation des commerçants et des courtiers coréens en une bourgeoisie et la conversion du capital commercial en capital industriel. En d'autres termes, il est possible de mettre en évidence et de démontrer les origines internes et la continuité à long terme du capitalisme coréen.

Plus encore, après le décollage économique du Japon, la Corée du Sud a connu un autre « miracle », malgré un lourd héritage (le « Royaume hermite » du XIXe siècle, l'occupation japonaise et la guerre de Corée)[75]. À partir des années 1960, le pays a bénéficié d'un développement économique rapide, basé sur la croissance des exportations, et, avec un certain retard, du marché intérieur de la consommation de masse. Du point de vue de l'historiographie dominante, les facteurs de succès les plus importants ont été l'aide américaine et la coopération entre l'État et les grands conglomérats (ou *chaebols*). Cela n'est pas faux, mais doit être nuancé. Les différentes expériences de la sidérurgie, de la construction navale et de l'industrie automobile vont clairement dans ce sens ; au contraire, le cas de l'électronique amène à relativiser l'importance de ce lien, comme le montrent les exemples de LG et de Samsung. Ainsi deux modèles de croissance ont coexisté.

73 Dominique Barjot, Rang-Ri Park-Barjot, « La société coréenne face à l'impérialisme japonais (1875-1945) : entre exploitation économique, modernisation forcée et assimilation », in Jean-François Klein, Claire Laux, *Les sociétés coloniales à l'âge des empires : Afrique, Antilles, Asie (années 1850-années 1950)*, Ellipses, 2012, chapitre 7, p. 96-104.

74 Hong Sung Chan, Lee Jong Hwa and Kim Mi Lim, "From Grain Merchants to Millers:The Kims of Seoul and the Origins of Korean Capitalism", *Revue économique*, *op. cit.*, 2020/5, Vol. 71, p. 895-909.

75 Dominique Barjot and Park Rang-Ri, "The Korean "Miracle" between the State and the Chaebols", communication présentée à la Préconférence de Pékin.

La réussite économique de la Corée du Sud est en grande partie due à une remarquable mobilisation du capital humain[76]. Ce n'est le cas qu'à partir de 1961 : la nation opère alors une réorientation stratégique vers un nouveau modèle d'industrialisation, sous l'impulsion du président Park Chung-Hee. D'un point de vue macro-économique, le succès de ce modèle basé sur les exportations est largement dû à trois facteurs : il existait de puissants groupes industriels et financiers coréens ; la stratégie des exportations est toujours restée rentable ; le gouvernement a mené une politique économique volontariste. Néanmoins, si la Corée du Sud est aujourd'hui un pays développé, un facteur déterminant de cette réussite réside dans la mobilisation du capital humain. Probablement, le néoconfucianisme a constitué un accélérateur du progrès. En même temps, la Corée a bénéficié et bénéficie aujourd'hui d'un patrimoine scientifique et culturel déjà bien établi. Même si l'on en discute aujourd'hui, le système scolaire et universitaire semble avoir réussi. Surtout, la Corée du Sud fournit un effort massif de recherche et de développement.

Sur le plan micro-économique, la Corée du Sud a bénéficié des effets positifs de la spécialisation internationale, comme le montre l'exemple de la construction navale[77]. En 2011, la construction navale était le quatrième poste d'exportation de la Corée du Sud (10 %), jouant le rôle d'un secteur moteur. Dès le début des années 2000, la Corée du Sud est devenue le leader mondial avant le Japon. Mais depuis 2009, les constructeurs navals coréens doivent résister à la concurrence chinoise, grâce à une main-d'œuvre hautement qualifiée et à un excellent positionnement stratégique. Néanmoins, rien n'aurait été possible sans l'émergence, en Corée du Sud, de Posco, un leader asiatique de l'industrie sidérurgique[78]. Si la Corée du Sud reste aujourd'hui le cinquième producteur mondial, le dynamisme de l'industrie sidérurgique coréenne repose principalement sur Posco, la cinquième entreprise au monde. Fondée par l'État coréen en 1968, Posco a connu un développement rapide au cours des années 1980. Sous l'impulsion de Park Tae-Joon, Posco est devenue numéro un en termes de productivité et a fondé Postech (Université des sciences et des technologies de Pohang). Offrant un exemple de privatisation réussie, Posco a constitué un facteur clé de la reprise économique coréenne après la crise de 1997. Aujourd'hui, Posco reste l'entreprise sidérurgique la plus rentable au monde.

Dans le même temps, la Corée du Sud a réalisé une percée réussie dans le domaine de l'électronique, grâce à LG (ou Lucky Goldstar) et Samsung[79]. Le succès de LG Electronics est le résultat d'un modèle de croissance fondé sur les exportations, asso-

76 Park-Barjot Rang-Ri & Parc Jimmyn, « Le capital humain : facteur clé du modèle coréen de développement », in *Outre-Terre*, n° 39, numéro spécial « Corée du Nord, Corée du Sud : la guerre sans la guerre », 2014, p. 74-90.

77 Dominique Barjot and Park Rang-Ri, « L'industrie des constructions navales : un secteur stratégique pour le take-off économique de la Corée du Sud (1945-environs de 2000 », in Dominique Barjot (dir.), « Les entreprises et entrepreneurs d'Asie », *Entreprises et Histoire*, n° 90, avril 2018, p. 51-75.

78 Dominique Barjot and Park Rang-Ri, « L'émergence d'un leader asiatique de la sidérurgie : Posco (1968-2010 », in Barthel (Charles), Kharaba (Ivan) & Mioche (Philippe) (dir. /eds.), *Les mutations de la sidérurgie mondiale du XXe siècle à nos jours. The Transformation of the World Steel Industry from the 20th Century to the Present*, Bruxelles, P.I.E. Peter Lang, 2014, p. 299-319.

79 Dominique Barjot and Park Rang-Ri, « Samsung. Le modèle de croissance entre exemplarité et originalité (1938-2007) », in Dominique Barjot (ed.), "Economic development, financing and business strategies (19th-21st century)", *op. cit.*, p. 78-111; Park Rang-Ri, *Samsung. L'œuvre d'un entrepreneur hors pair, Byung Chull Lee* (*Samsung. The work of an extraordinary entrepreneur, Byung Chull Lee*), Paris, Economica, 2008.

ciant une vigoureuse innovation de produit et une stratégie efficace de mondialisation. Ainsi, LG a accédé aux marchés matures (Amérique du Nord, Allemagne, Pologne), a conquis le marché des pays émergents (Chine, Inde, Brésil, Turquie, Russie) et a renforcé sa position sur le marché coréen face à Samsung Electronics. Néanmoins, Samsung reste aujourd'hui le groupe coréen le plus important. En effet, Samsung a bénéficié du fort héritage du fondateur Lee Byung-Chull, et de l'action spécifique de son fils et successeur, Lee Kun-Hee. Lee B.C. a développé une philosophie originale, basée sur l'éthique confucéenne, mais appliquée de manière pragmatique, et adaptée par Lee K.H. Après la crise financière de 1997-98, celle-ci a relancé le groupe Samsung, grâce à une ouverture technologique marquante. En conséquence, la rentabilité de Samsung s'est accrue.

Aujourd'hui, le modèle coréen semble à la fois menacé, mais aussi relancé[80]. Si la crise économique internationale de 2008-2011 a entraîné une crise des chaebols, comme dans l'exemple de LG, plus largement, trois menaces majeures demeurent : les relations avec la Corée du Nord, la montée de la concurrence internationale (pertes de compétitivité face à la Chine, au Japon, à Taiwan et à l'Indonésie) et les problèmes sociétaux spécifiques à la Corée du Sud (vieillissement accéléré, taux de suicides). Mais la Corée du Sud bénéficie toujours d'atouts forts : une bonne qualité de vie, une priorité absolue donnée aux nouvelles technologies (Samsung, secteur nucléaire), un choix volontariste en faveur de la «croissance verte», la force croissante du modèle culturel coréen (Hallyu).

Vietnam

Le Vietnam fait partie du groupe des « Tigres asiatiques », mais comme la Chine, l'Indonésie ou la Malaisie, il a assez bien surmonté la crise financière de 1997-98[81]. La régularité de sa croissance soulève des questions sur le ou les modèles d'interprétation pertinents : modèle «en vol de l'oie sauvage» (Akamatsu), modèles de Rostow, Kuznets, Perroux ou évolutionnistes. Densément peuplé et marqué par l'histoire, le Vietnam a établi son intégration nationale sur une marche vers le Sud et une assimilation des hautes terres. Malgré une transition démographique inachevée, la population est restée jeune et féminisée. En même temps, la culture vietnamienne, marquée par l'influence confucéenne, s'est développée autour d'une langue et d'une écriture originales. Au Vietnam, la fin d'un système d'économie centralisée et l'influence décisive du Sud ont ouvert la voie à une transition prématurée vers un marché libre caractérisé à la fois par l'appel à l'aide étrangère, la montée des activités informelles et la privatisation progressive, mais inachevée du secteur de l'État. En effet, entre 1954 et 1975, la République démocratique du Vietnam (au Nord) a connu l'économie de guerre avec une aide soviétique croissante. La réunification de 1975 a changé la situation. Si au Sud, l'héritage était lourd, au Nord, la découverte du Sud a secoué les esprits, dans

80 Dominique Barjot, « Corée du Sud : entre risques et opportunités d'investissement », *Sécurité et stratégie*, juin-septembre 2013, p. 66-76.

81 Dominique Barjot, "Vietnam: The Rise of a New Industrialized Nation", communication présentée à la Préconférence de Tokyo ; Dominique Barjot et Jean-François Klein (eds.), *De l'Indochine coloniale au Viêt Nam actuel*, Paris, Académie des Sciences d'Outre-Mer, Éditions Magellan, 2017, 816 p. See in particular Dominique Barjot, « Introduction », p. 42-69.

un contexte marqué par l'arrêt de l'aide chinoise, une diminution de l'aide soviétique et une explosion du marché noir. Il y avait nécessité de sauver l'économie nationale.

Largement accélérée par le contexte géopolitique (entrée dans le Comecon, chute du régime khmer, conflit avec la République populaire de Chine), la conséquence en a été un changement profond[82]. En décembre 1980, est adoptée la stratégie du Đổi mới (changement pour faire du neuf), qui reconnaît l'économie de marché, encourage l'initiative individuelle, réhabilite l'entreprise sans abandonner le cadre socialiste. Le succès est indéniable : réintégration dans les circuits du commerce international (ASEAN), construction d'infrastructures, libéralisation du marché foncier, diversification agricole, régulation par l'État des flux de capitaux étrangers, développement des activités privées intérieures, déclin du rôle économique de l'État. Malgré la crise financière de 1997-98, le Vietnam s'est pleinement intégré dans le commerce asiatique (APEC, OMC, accord frontalier avec la Chine) et a engagé une réforme en profondeur de son système d'entreprise (introduction de la TVA pour les sociétés anonymes, insertion dans les réseaux d'externalisation).

À partir de 1986, le Vietnam a connu un taux de croissance élevé du PIB (par habitant, le PIB a triplé de 2002 à 2010)[83]. En conséquence, le Vietnam est devenu l'une des économies asiatiques les plus ouvertes aux échanges internationaux. Face à la persistance des déséquilibres macroéconomiques (inflation, dette publique, chômage), l'État vietnamien a imposé des mesures strictes (réforme du système bancaire). Néanmoins, l'économie reste très dépendante de l'agriculture (deuxième exportateur mondial de riz et de café) et des matières premières (pétrole et gaz naturel, charbon), car une industrie insuffisamment diversifiée (textile, produits agroalimentaires, composants électroniques). Mais, l'économie vietnamienne est devenue de plus en plus attractive pour les capitaux étrangers, notamment parce que la croissance était tirée par les secteurs industriels de pointe (textile, industrie pétrolière, construction navale, automobile, composants électroniques), mais aussi par le tourisme et les télécommunications. En conséquence, les exportations ont fourni les deux tiers du PIB. Bénéficiant du faible coût relatif de sa main-d'œuvre, le Vietnam exporte de plus en plus. Dans le même temps, les investissements étrangers directs ont augmenté, principalement en provenance du Japon, de Singapour, de la Corée du Sud, de la Chine et de la Russie.

Si aujourd'hui, le Vietnam reste une économie émergente, en restant derrière les autres « Tigres asiatiques » en termes de PIB par habitant, on peut dire qu'à l'exception de l'Indonésie, le Vietnam est celui qui a le plus fort potentiel de croissance, car il dispose de nombreux atouts décisifs, d'un marché du travail efficace, d'une forte capacité d'innovation, d'une ouverture économique progressive, d'une génération de secteurs de pointe favorisant un décollage spectaculaire, d'une position de sous-traitant privilégié pour les industries japonaises et sud-coréennes (Samsung). En conséquence, le Vietnam vérifie plusieurs théories occidentales : celles de Rostow (décollage, secteurs

82 Marie-Sybille de Vienne, *L'Économie du Việt Nam (1955-1995). Bilan et prospective*, Paris, CHEAM, 1994.
83 Emmanuelle Paquet, *Réforme et transformation du système économique vietnamien, 1979-2002*, Paris, L'Harmattan, 2004.

de pointe), de Kuznets (large réallocation des secteurs de productivité), de Perroux (pôle de développement de Ho Chi Minh Ville), de Porter (pôles de Hanoi, Haiphong, Da-Nang) et évolutionnisme (dépendance de sentier ou *path dependency*).

Inde

Le Japon, la Chine et même la Corée du Sud sont devenus d'importants exportateurs non seulement de biens et de services, mais aussi de capitaux : c'est le cas du Vietnam. Dans le cas de la Chine, cette poussée des exportations de capitaux a été spectaculaire, au point que nous parlons maintenant de « Chinafrica » comme nous l'avons fait dans le cas de Francafrique. D'autres pays occidentaux ont également choisi la voie des exportations de capitaux pour accompagner et consolider à long terme une stratégie de développement basée sur l'exportation de biens d'équipement et la consommation durable. Ce fut le cas de l'Allemagne fédérale après la Seconde Guerre mondiale. Les deux décennies qui ont suivi la Seconde Guerre mondiale ont été communément analysées comme une phase de reconstruction de l'économie mondiale et un prélude à la deuxième vague de mondialisation des années 1970. Julian Faust a étudié les sociétés allemandes et leur ré-internationalisation après la Seconde Guerre mondiale en Inde en tant qu'acteurs de ces processus de mondialisation conduisant à une intégration plus étroite de l'économie en développement dans le commerce mondial et les chaînes de valeur[84]. Il s'est concentré sur les objectifs et les attentes de ces acteurs dans la micro-perspective des sociétés étrangères en Inde. Il a cherché à comprendre comment ces acteurs commerciaux ont utilisé les politiques d'industrialisation d'un pays nouvellement indépendant comme l'Inde ou ont été entravés par celles-ci.

En effet, l'association avec les politiques et programmes de développement a été utilisée comme stratégie pour prendre pied sur le marché indien. En effet, l'Inde, selon le modèle de l'import-substitution-industrialisation (ISI) était devenue un marché plus fermé aux étrangers. J. Faust a adopté l'hypothèse d'une coalition d'intérêts entre les entreprises allemandes et le gouvernement dans les premières années de la politique de développement international. Il montre comment les entreprises ont pu utiliser leur origine et leur réputation. L'Inde fournit un excellent exemple de la manière formelle et informelle dont les entreprises allemandes ont fait face aux barrières non tarifaires et aux restrictions imposées aux investisseurs étrangers en Inde, qui avait adopté une stratégie rigoureuse en matière d'ISI.

En effet, de nombreux grands acteurs de l'industrie allemande comme Beyer avaient établi des liens commerciaux avec l'Inde avant la guerre. Avec le changement de système politique et économique et la perspective d'une forte croissance de la population indienne, ils s'attendaient à ce que le pays devienne l'un des plus grands marchés d'Asie à l'avenir. L'objectif principal au cours de la période d'enquête était le marché intérieur indien. Malgré les plans quinquennaux et la planification économique en général, la grande industrie allemande n'a pas abandonné le marché. Au contraire, les

84 Julian Faust, "Expectations and Strategies of the German India during Decolonisation and Import Substitution-Industrialisation", communication présentée à la Préconférence de Pékin.

fabricants allemands ont développé des stratégies pour faire face à la réglementation croissante du marché et aux barrières à l'entrée telles que la production et les licences d'importation. Avec d'autres entreprises étrangères occidentales et orientales, des sociétés comme Bayer et Bosch étaient en concurrence pour créer les premières unités de production en *joint-venture* et leur industrie. En effet, le gouvernement indien n'a accordé la capacité de production nécessaire qu'à une seule ou à un très petit nombre d'entreprises. Ceci, après que le marché ait été fermé aux autres concurrents, a créé des opportunités de profit.

La protection de l'industrie naissante, le besoin de savoir-faire et de capitaux étrangers en provenance de l'Inde pour industrialiser le pays sans compenser complètement sa balance des paiements ont permis aux entreprises étrangères d'intervenir. Bosch et Bayer ont pu établir des relations en Inde pour leurs produits. En ne considérant pas les projets industriels comme étant principalement commerciaux et à but lucratif, ils ont démontré leur bonne volonté, leur savoir-faire technique et leur expertise commerciale, ce qui a permis d'aider l'Inde de cette manière. Ils ont sauvé leur véritable investissement en contrepartie d'une réglementation plus stricte, de la bureaucratie et de la pression exercée sur leurs entreprises communes pour qu'elles deviennent minoritaires. Bayer et Bosch ont réussi à prendre pied et à prospérer en Inde parce qu'ils ont offert des produits et une expertise dans des domaines essentiels au progrès de l'économie indienne : produits chimiques de base, produits agrochimiques, moteurs diesel et solutions pour les véhicules commerciaux et les transports. Avec de telles offres et des investissements dans des produits offrant stratégiquement un marché en croissance et un soutien politique à l'aide au développement allemande : par exemple, l'investissement de Bosch dans la coentreprise MICO, de 1959 aux années 1980, a permis de verser un dividende régulier à la société mère allemande.

La participation allemande à l'industrialisation planifiée de l'Inde a été activement encouragée jusqu'au milieu des années soixante. Des entreprises telles que Bayer et Bosch se sont positionnées en tant qu'allemandes. Ce label constituait un avantage par rapport à d'autres concurrents dans d'autres pays, malgré le régime nazi qui venait de prendre fin en 1945, avec l'objectif politique et économique d'atteindre dans les deux pays le savoir-faire technique et l'expertise des États-Unis, de l'Union soviétique, du Royaume-Uni et des autres pays européens. L'impératif politique était de couper les liens avec l'ancienne politique étrangère allemande, d'autant plus que le cadre de l'économie ouest-allemande était moins contesté que l'image du capitalisme américain au sein du « Socialist Pattern of Society » de l'Inde évoquée par son premier Premier ministre.

Pendant longtemps, l'Inde a donc semblé offrir un modèle de tierce partie, privilégiant une économie socialiste, basée sur la recherche d'une substitution des importations, mais sans aller jusqu'au totalitarisme communiste adopté en Union soviétique puis en Chine. Néanmoins, dans les années 1990, le pays a libéralisé son économie et s'est engagé dans une voie de développement mieux intégrée à l'économie mondiale. Les réformes entreprises par l'Inde depuis 1991 ont eu un effet positif sur son économie.

Elles ont stimulé la libéralisation des échanges, notamment avec le reste du monde. Peut-on postuler que l'Inde est passée d'une économie planifiée à un marché libre, ou de la vision d'A. Gerschenkron à celle d'A. Smith [85]? L'analyse des structures et des stratégies des 20 premières entreprises indiennes en 2016-2017, selon l'approche de A.D. Chandler, permet de formuler quelques hypothèses. En effet, il est possible constater que les réformes ont favorisé la modernisation et l'expansion des anciennes entreprises traitant de secteurs associés à la seconde révolution industrielle plutôt que la création d'entreprises technologiquement avancées. De plus, ces réformes n'ont pas mis de côté les entreprises d'État, ni même la participation financière de l'État dans le secteur privé. Il est certain que la consommation de masse de produits technologiquement sophistiqués a pris son envol il y a seulement quinze ans en Inde. Les entreprises indiennes ont suivi la tendance avec attention, même si certaines ont pris le risque de diversifier leurs activités. Mais en même temps, elles se sont ouvertes aux pratiques managériales, elles se sont modernisées et internationalisées tout en embauchant une main-d'œuvre bon marché. Si le marché libre a aujourd'hui plus de poids, l'évolution a été plus lente que prévue ; mais elle s'accélère. Les grandes entreprises suivront, mais cela ne signifie pas qu'elles se libéreront des interférences de l'État.

AUTRES NATIONS ÉMERGENTES

Si l'Asie est le continent émergent par excellence, en particulier l'Extrême-Orient et le sous-continent indien, d'autres grandes régions du monde voient l'engagement, voire l'affirmation, de nouvelles nations industrialisées. C'est notamment le cas de l'Amérique latine. Une fois de plus, les approches macroéconomiques développées dans le cadre des nations et la microéconomie, essentiellement la *busines history*, s'enrichissent mutuellement, comme en matière de coopération et de concurrence au Brésil. La conséquence est une révision, par certains historiens latino-américains, des théories généralement appliquées pour expliquer les spécificités du développement économique, notamment en Argentine et au Brésil. Cependant, d'autres régions du monde cherchent des moyens de se développer : l'Afrique francophone, par exemple. Certaines nations ont même pu émerger, mais avec un succès final inégal, comme modèles de référence pour les pays du Sud, comme l'Égypte, puis l'Afrique du Sud, tandis que l'Australie a finalement réussi à atteindre les niveaux de développement du monde industriel avancé.

Amérique latine

Depuis la Seconde Guerre mondiale, les nations d'Amérique latine se sont fortement industrialisées, non sans tensions et crises, notamment en raison des inégalités excessives de revenus et de richesses. De ce point de vue, le Pérou constitue un bon observatoire des contradictions inhérentes au développement de l'Amérique latine. La Colombie aussi, où le travail de la Banque mondiale a été décisif. Dans ces pays, l'un

85 Pierre Lanthier, "From Gerschenkron back to Smith? The Case of Indian Big Business Today", in Dominique Barjot (ed), "Theory and Empirical Performance. Economic Paradigm and Performance in the Long Run (18th to 21st century)", *Revue française d'histoire économique – The French Economic History Review*, n° 11-12 (n°1-2, 2019), *op. cit.*, p. 162-181.

des défis majeurs a été la formation du capital humain, comme le montre l'exemple brésilien. Par ailleurs, comme dans tous les pays émergents, l'une des clés de l'industrialisation a été l'émergence d'acteurs mondiaux, dont le Mexicain Cemex, quatrième cimentier mondial, mais leader en termes de rentabilité, et le Brésilien Vale dans le domaine du minerai de fer constituent des exemples emblématiques.

L'approche macroéconomique : Pérou et Colombie

Getsiva Cayo-Durand a remis en question les modèles économiques prônés par les gouvernements péruviens dans les années 1950 et 1960[86]. Alors qu'après la Seconde Guerre mondiale, la plupart des pays d'Amérique latine ont adopté des politiques protectionnistes, le Pérou a préféré devenir un fervent partisan du libéralisme. Dans le système multilatéral, les gouvernements ont voulu réaliser le décollage de l'économie péruvienne en suivant les concepts de W.W. Rostow. Néanmoins, la pensée de R. Prebisch s'est peu à peu installée. Des politiques protectionnistes ont été mises en œuvre au début des années soixante. Le pays cherchait alors son modèle de développement économique.

En effet, depuis la crise de 1930, deux modèles de développement se sont affrontés en Amérique latine : le modèle de la priorité aux exportations (inspiré par le libéralisme) et l'industrialisation par substitution des importations (ISI). Tenant compte des conditions internes et externes du développement, Getsiva Cayo-Durand montre que les gouvernements péruviens n'ont pas favorisé un modèle unique de développement. L'influence du modèle de priorité aux exportations a été interprétée comme un modèle « tourné vers l'extérieur », et celle du modèle ISI comme un modèle « tourné vers l'intérieur ». Ce dernier modèle ne s'est pas d'abord imposé comme une idéologie, mais plutôt comme une nécessité. Bien que la théorie de la dépendance développée par l'économiste argentin Raúl Prebisch ait été l'une des plus communément adoptées à l'époque, elle ne constituait pas une règle générale. L'Argentine, le Brésil, le Mexique, le Chili, la Colombie et l'Uruguay offrent des exemples classiques de pays latino-américains « tournés vers l'intérieur ». En revanche, le Pérou est resté plus favorable au modèle « extérieur ». Ce n'est que dans les années 1960 que l'impact de la pensée de Prebisch y a été effectif.

Quelle était la politique économique préconisée au Pérou dans les années 1950 et 1960 ? Quels ont été les modèles de développement mis en œuvre et quels ont été leurs résultats ? Pour répondre à ces questions, G. Cayo-Durand se livre une approche de l'économie péruvienne en deux temps : d'abord un réexamen de la politique économique péruvienne sous le prisme de Rostow ; ensuite une analyse sous celui de Prebisch. Elle met en lumière les ambitions des modèles adoptés par les gouvernements, mais en tenant compte de leurs limites et de leurs contradictions. Elle montre que les politiques mises en œuvre par les gouvernements péruviens motivées par le libéralisme ou l'ISI étaient contrastées, mais pas totalement opposées. Depuis la fin

86 Getsiva Cayo Durand de Geist, « Le développement économique péruvien durant les années 1950 et 1960 : distinguer deux modèles ? », communication présentée à la Préconférence de Paris.

des années 1950, des politiques protectionnistes ont été mises en œuvre, révélant les limites de la tendance «vers l'extérieur». Ces deux stratégies économiques ont réussi à cohabiter sans provoquer de rupture majeure.

Sous le gouvernement des civils comme sous celui des militaires, de droite ou de gauche, le pays n'a jamais renoncé à son projet d'industrialisation. Cependant, aucun programme de développement n'a été mené sur le long terme. Compte tenu de la situation locale et internationale, la mise en œuvre de modèles « tournés vers l'extérieur », « tournés vers l'intérieur » ou « mixtes » n'a pas garanti le succès en raison du manque de continuité des politiques adoptées. Le décollage de l'économie péruvienne a été retardé, voire bloqué, par des problèmes de nature endogène et exogène : d'une part, l'instabilité politique, la corruption, le dualisme économique, les conflits entre les classes sociales, la croissance démographique rapide et inégale, les fortes contraintes géographiques et, d'autre part, la dépendance accrue des secteurs commercial (termes de l'échange) et financier (investissement, crédit). En conséquence, tous ces facteurs n'ont pas favorisé le décollage. Cependant, les gouvernements péruviens successifs ont adopté un modèle mixte. Une « troisième voie » péruvienne a émergé pour réaliser un décollage économique.

Pour sa part, Elisa Grandi s'est attachée à étudier le travail de la Banque mondiale en Colombie depuis le début des premières missions jusqu'en 1966[87]. Née des accords de Bretton Woods en 1944, la Banque mondiale a joué un rôle pionnier dans la mise en place de programmes d'aide au développement. Plutôt que d'essayer d'évaluer l'efficacité des prêts au développement financés par les agences internationales, l'objectif d'E. Grandi a été d'analyser le fonctionnement concret de ces missions, afin de comprendre comment les politiques de la Banque mondiale ont évolué. Plus précisément, E. Grandi révèle comment les premières missions de la Banque mondiale en Colombie ont influencé ses politiques en les pays sous-développés et quels acteurs et pratiques ont contribué à cette évolution. En se concentrant sur le travail de la Banque mondiale entre 1949 et 1954, E. Grandi décrit l'émergence et l'institutionnalisation d'un double processus qui concernait à la fois les pratiques de conseil en développement international et la gestion des crédits internationaux par les acteurs colombiens.

La mission d'enquête générale de la Banque mondiale en Colombie, lancée en 1949, a initié ce processus. Dirigée par Lauchlin Currie, économiste du New Deal, cette mission a été la première à entreprendre une étude complète des conditions du pays, afin de mettre en place un programme de développement pour tous les secteurs de l'économie. En conséquence, E. Grandi s'est concentrée sur les missions colombiennes, pour découvrir les réseaux mis en place par ses conseillers et comment leurs réseaux ont été impliqués dans la mission. Le résultat a été un ensemble de données de quelque 1500 lettres, dans lesquelles plus de 900 acteurs sont apparus. L'analyse des réseaux de ces acteurs, combinée à une étude de la microstructure des missions de la Banque

87 Elisa Grandi, "Networks of Experts and Political Actors in the World Bank's Early Programs: Loans Programs in Columbia and their Overall Effects on Aid to Development (1940-1960)", communication présentée à la Préconférence de Paris.

mondiale, fournit de nouvelles informations sur les premières politiques de la Banque mondiale. Elle met en lumière le rôle de certains acteurs locaux dans le processus de décision concernant l'approbation et l'orientation des prêts. Elle montre l'impact des premières missions de la Banque mondiale sur les institutions économiques colombiennes, notamment en ce qui concerne les agences de planification créées pour gérer l'aide financière internationale.

Elisa Grandi révèle pourquoi la mission d'étude mondiale de la Banque mondiale a joué un rôle déterminant s'agissant de l'orientation des prêts de la Banque mondiale dans le pays et comment la position relative des personnes impliquées dans les négociations a influencé le processus, les caractéristiques et les conséquences. La spécificité de l'intervention précoce de la Banque mondiale et la relation spéciale développée par les élites colombiennes avec les organismes de prêt internationaux dans les années 1920 et 1930 ont permis au personnel local d'accéder directement au crédit international par le biais de leurs opérations. gestion directe et prêt. Le capital social et relationnel que certains acteurs ont acquis au cours de la mission a également influencé le remboursement des prêts. Par conséquent, la conception du programme de développement et la prise de décision ont eu lieu pendant et avant la mise en place des procédures organisationnelles. Les relations personnelles ont joué un rôle fondamental dans l'émergence et l'affirmation de ces procédures.

L'approche microéconomique : Cemex et Vale

L'approche microéconomique n'est pas moins fructueuse, surtout pour l'étude des grandes multinationales comme Cemex au Mexique[88]. Cemex était la cinquième capacité de production de ciment au monde en 2008 et la quatrième entreprise mondiale en termes de chiffre d'affaires. Mais Cemex reste le numéro 1 en Amérique latine, devant Holcim et Lafarge. Surtout, le groupe est aujourd'hui le leader mondial du béton prêt à l'emploi. En 2008, Cemex est demeuré un groupe mexicain dont le siège social se trouve à Mexico, avec un bureau secondaire à New York, et tous les directeurs sont restés mexicains. Cemex constitue un exemple archétypal de la montée en puissance des entreprises mondiales émergentes. Cette entreprise fondée en 1906 constitue un symbole du succès du capitalisme à Monterrey et à Mexico. À l'origine, se trouve la famille Zambrano, une maison de commerce opérant depuis le milieu du XIXe siècle. Elle s'était développée après la guerre avec les États-Unis, en 1846-1847, qui avaient établi la ligne du Rio Bravo. Cette famille s'est établie à Monterrey, entre 1890 et 1910, avec les familles Garza, Ferrara, Madero, Meiz, Milmo et Sada, bien étudiées par Mario Cerutti[89]. L'idée centrale est qu'en 1982, il y a eu une crise économique décisive, qui a conduit à une restructuration et une internationalisation intenses.

88 Dominique Barjot, "Cemex or the Rise of a Mexican Multinational", communication présentée à la Préconférence de Paris ; Dominique Barjot, "Introduction", in Dominique Barjot (ed.), "Globalization, national patterns of development and strategies of firms (19th-21st centuries) – Mondialisation, modèles nationaux de développement et stratégies d'entreprises (XIXe-XXIe siècles)", *Revue française d'histoire économique – The French Economic History Review*, n°1, May 2015, p. 14-27.

89 Cerutti Mario, *Proprietarios, Empresarios y Empresa en et Norte de Mexico,* Siglo Veintiuno Editores, Mexico, 2000 ; Marichal Carlos y Cerutti Mario, *Historia de las Grandes Empresas en Mexico, 1850-1930,* Uniidad Autonoma de Nuevo Léon & Fundo de Cultura Economica, Mexico Universidad, 1997.

Par conséquent, Cemex est devenu un modèle original, caractérisé par cinq éléments. Il apparaît à la fois comme le leader mondial du ciment blanc et du négoce, dispose des technologies de l'information et de la communication les plus avancées dans l'industrie du ciment, est très créatif en matière de solutions financières, et bénéficie des coûts les plus bas de son secteur. Cemex s'est également imposée comme la première véritable multinationale du Mexique. Après avoir pris le leadership sur le marché national entre 1982 et 1989 et réalisé sa percée internationale, le groupe s'est établi dans des zones culturellement connues : les États-Unis, l'Espagne et l'Amérique du Sud (1989-1994). Il a fait son entrée sur le marché du négoce de 1992 à 2000, avant de devenir une entreprise mondiale (1997-2003). Son système de négociation original en fait alors le concurrent direct de Lafarge et de Holderbank (alors Holcim). Ainsi, Cemex est passé de la périphérie au centre, démontrant l'incroyable capacité de cette firme entrepreneuriale à s'adapter aux modes d'organisation des entreprises contemporaines.

Le modèle, cependant, reste à la fois dynamique et fragile. En 2009-2010, le groupe Cemex a connu une très grave crise financière. Il a cependant réussi à la dépasser en adaptant ses opérations à la nouvelle dynamique du marché. En 2016, le groupe a maintenu ses positions sur ses trois marchés dominants, mais en réorientant son activité vers le ciment, le segment le plus rentable du secteur, et en renonçant à ses activités de diversification. En outre, Cemex a renforcé ses positions aux États-Unis, en Amérique latine et dans les Caraïbes, ainsi qu'en Asie, en Océanie, au Moyen-Orient et en Afrique, au détriment de l'Europe et surtout du Mexique. À cet égard, l'opération majeure a été l'acquisition en 2007 du groupe australien Rinker, grâce à laquelle Cemex a accru sa percée aux États-Unis, l'intégration de ce groupe s'achevant en 2009, dans des conditions financières difficiles. Néanmoins, le risque a porté ses fruits : dans les années 2010, Cemex est ainsi devenu le leader nord-américain de l'industrie du ciment. En 2016, le groupe reste largement entre les mains de la famille Zembrano. En outre, si le groupe est confronté à une concurrence internationale sévère, il demeure néanmoins le quatrième groupe cimentier mondial. De plus, Cemex l'a emporté sur tous ses principaux concurrents européens en termes de rentabilité. Aujourd'hui, en dépit de sa plus petite taille, Cemex reste largement compétitif par rapport à ses principaux concurrents européens et chinois.

L'internationalisation des entreprises dans les pays en développement est une nouveauté de la mondialisation contemporaine. La société minière brésilienne Vale offre un bon exemple de ce que le Boston Consulting Group appelle les « Global Challengers »[90]. La Companhia Vale Rio Doce a été créée par la nationalisation et l'incorporation de deux sociétés existantes en 1942. Les alliés occidentaux avaient besoin de minerai de fer, en particulier pour les industries de l'armement. Pour le Brésil, c'était l'occasion de pénétrer avec succès les marchés développés. Pourtant, à la fin de la guerre en 1945, la Grande-Bretagne et les États-Unis ont renoncé à leur

90 Hildete de Moraes Vodopives, "Becoming a Multinational Mining Company: the Case of Vale (Brazil)", communication présentée à la Préconférence de Paris.

option d'achat, laissant Vale sans marché garanti. Les coûts élevés du fret maritime ont rendu difficile pour Vale de concurrencer les entreprises plus proches des marchés de consommation de l'Europe, des États-Unis et de l'Asie. Dans les années 1960, le PDG, Elieser Batista, a voulu approvisionner l'industrie sidérurgique japonaise, fortement endommagée par la Seconde Guerre mondiale et en reconstruction. Batista a fait un pari, grâce à l'utilisation de grands navires polyvalents qui transportaient des minerais en Asie et apportaient du pétrole du Golfe Persique au Brésil. Ce faisant, Vale a pu concurrencer les mineurs australiens, beaucoup plus proches du Japon, en combinant gains de productivité et économies d'échelle. Dans les années 1970, Vale est devenu le plus grand producteur mondial de minerai de fer.

Après sa privatisation en 1997, l'objectif principal de la société est de maximiser la valeur pour ses actionnaires. En conséquence, en 2001, la société met en œuvre un plan stratégique pluriannuel visant à transformer Vale en un acteur mondial. Ce plan énonce des principes clairs : maximiser les marges, devenir un multiproduit mondial. À cette époque, Vale est de loin le leader de l'industrie minière au Brésil, mais son potentiel de diversification des produits reste limité. La présence internationale de la société demeure très modeste. À partir de 2001, Vale diversifie son portefeuille en investissant dans le charbon thermique et cokéfiable, le cuivre, le cobalt, les métaux du groupe du platine et les engrais nutritifs. Ces acquisitions opportunistes sont partiellement financées par des cessions d'activités non essentielles telles que la pâte à papier et le papier. Mais le minerai de fer reste son principal produit. Peu à peu, l'idée d'acheter un grand mineur nord-américain prend forme. Le Canada est un grand pays minier, avec des actifs de grande qualité et une main-d'œuvre qualifiée. Le candidat idéal pourrait être l'une des grandes entreprises canadiennes, comme Alcan, Noranda ou Inco. L'acquisition d'Inco marque véritablement le point de départ de l'internationalisation de Vale. À la suite de cette transaction, Vale devient l'une des trois plus grandes sociétés minières diversifiées au monde, avec BHP Billiton et Rio Tinto. Ces multinationales latino-américaines sont cependant de constitution récente. C'est pourquoi il reste d'actualité de s'interroger sur le rôle spécifique des élites économiques et des multinationales étrangères.

Repenser les théories du développement économique pour l'Amérique du Sud ? l'Argentine et le Brésil

Norma Silvana Lanciotti, Martín Schorr et Gustavo García Zanotti ont proposé d'évaluer l'influence des théories du développement économique sur les performances économiques de deux pays d'Amérique latine. Il s'agit d'analyser le rôle des élites commerciales et des entreprises étrangères dans deux périodes différentes de croissance économique : la période d'industrialisation menée par l'État (1945-1973) et l'urgence de la nouvelle économie mondiale (1990-2016)[91]. Après avoir passé en revue les principaux arguments des théories néoclassiques et critiques, ils examinent l'évo-

91 Norma Silvana Lanciotti, Martín Schorr and Gustavo García Zanotti, "When theories don't fit: Rethinking the theories of economic development for South America. Argentina and Brazil 1945-2015", in Dominique Barjot (ed), "Theory and Empirical Performance. Economic Paradigm and Performance in the Long Run (18th to 21st century)", *Revue française d'histoire économique – The French Economic History Review*, n° 11-12 (n°1-2, 2019), *op. cit.*, p. 120-118.

lution des plus grandes entreprises en Argentine et au Brésil afin d'identifier les changements dans la répartition sectorielle des activités contrôlées par les plus grandes entreprises, leur part à l'exportation et la présence de multinationales étrangères. Ils constatent que, dans la première période, les politiques économiques ont incorporé des éléments de différentes théories, à la fois néoclassiques et critiques, articulant l'entrée de capitaux étrangers avec la coordination de l'État et l'investissement public lors des goulets d'étranglement. Au contraire, les politiques économiques initiées dans les années 1990 se sont exclusivement basées sur des approches néoclassiques qui proposent la libéralisation du commerce et la promotion des investissements privés étrangers. En conséquence, les entreprises étrangères ont cherché des rentes dans les services publics et dans les ressources naturelles, et se sont lancées dans l'appel à l'étranger et la « désindustrialisation ».

Depuis les années 1990, les économies latino-américaines ont évolué vers des modèles de développement qui contribuent davantage à l'économie de marché et à la concurrence : c'est le cas du Brésil. L'introduction de régimes antitrust a ouvert la voie à un meilleur contrôle des fusions[92]. Les dispositions juridiques adoptées ont révélé leur importance pour obtenir des résultats significatifs, en particulier dans les secteurs de l'énergie et des ressources minérales (pétrole[93], électricité[94], fer[95] et ciment[96]), mais pas seulement (cas de la vidéo et du streaming[97] ainsi que de l'industrie du livre[98]). L'expérience brésilienne en matière de réforme de l'administration publique a abouti à la création d'un nouvel ensemble d'agences de régulation administrées avec la rationalité d'une bureaucratie wébérienne[99]. Plusieurs des directeurs et des commissaires de ces agences, bien qu'ils aient été nommés pour des raisons politiques, étaient des fonctionnaires de carrière. Le système n'était pas exempt de problèmes – certains directeurs, principalement dans les petites agences, n'étaient pas qualifiés et étaient le produit du clientélisme et de l'influence politique de groupes de pression. Mais dans ces cas, la présence de la presse et d'autres types de contrôles et d'équilibres réduisent la possibilité d'actions préjudiciables de ces directeurs. Enfin, l'autonomie de fait des agences n'était pas aussi importante que ce qui était prévu dans le projet initial, mais cela n'est certainement pas incompatible avec une bureaucratie rationnelle, dans la mesure où il existe un contrôle démocratique de la politique publique. Par conséquent,

92 Luiz Carlos Delorme Prado & Hildete de Moraes Vodopives, « Éditorial : Régulation et développement sectoriel en perspective historique : le cas du Brésil », in Luiz Carlos Delorme Prado & Hildete de Moraes Vodopives (eds.), « Concurrence et régulation au Brésil », *Entreprises & Histoire*, n° 99/2020, p. 5-20. Ce numéro spécial est basé sur les articles présentés à la conférence de Rio de Janeiro organisée en préparation du 18e WEHC à Boston (29 juillet - 3 août 2018)

93 Camilla Pires-Alves, Marcelo Colomer, Luiz Carlos Delorme Prado and Marcos Lyra, "The Market of Liquefied Petroleum Gas in Brazil" : a Brief Structural, Institutional -historical Perspective", *Entreprises & Histoire*, n° 99/2020, *op. cit.*, p. 21-34; Giorgio Romano Schutte, « La réglementation pétrolière au Brésil : quelle trajectoire ? », *Ibidem*, p. 35-52.

94 Claude Ferraz, « Les difficultés des réformes des marches électriques : le Brésil, de l'essor industriel à la transition énergétique », *Ibidem*, p. 53-65.

95 Hildete de Moraes Vodopives, "Mining Going Global in the 2000s: Vale Leaps Forward", *Ibid.*, p. 66-78.

96 Dominique Barjot, « L'ascension des entreprises cimentières brésiliennes : l'exemple du groupe Votorantim », *Ibid.*, p. 79-106.

97 Luiz Carlos Delorme Prado et Diandra Rocha, "Streaming Video on Demand Platforms and Competition Policy: The Brazilian Case", *Ibid.*, p. 107-125.

98 Fabio Sá Earp, « La crise de la filière du livre au Brésil (2006-2018) », *Ibid.*, p. 126-136.

99 Luiz Carlos Delorme Prado, "Two Decades of Economic Reforms: The Institutions of Regulation in Brazil 1991-2011", in Dominique Barjot (ed.), "Theory and Empirical Performance. Economic Paradigm and Performance in the Long Run (18th to 21st century)", *Revue française d'histoire économique – The French Economic History Review*, n° 11-12 (n°1-2, 2019), *op. cit.*, p. 140-161.

le projet technocratique de création d'agences de régulation très similaires au modèle américain n'a pas abouti. Il n'a pas été possible de procéder à une séparation complète des pouvoirs politiques et réglementaires. Mais l'État a été modernisé et la qualité des gestionnaires publics s'est améliorée. L'intervention de l'État n'a pas été aussi active qu'à l'époque développementaliste, mais l'État ne s'est pas autant réduit que ce qui était prévu dans les projets néolibéraux des années 1990. Le rôle de l'État change, mais moins que ce qui a été prévu. On peut trouver des preuves de changements et de continuités dans cette histoire. Enfin, l'expérience brésilienne montre que les institutions et les modèles institutionnels sont fortement dépendants du sentier parcouru.

Mondialisation et émergence : l'Afrique francophone

Si l'Amérique latine a vu l'affirmation de puissantes économies émergentes comme le Brésil, le Mexique ou la Colombie par exemple, le phénomène est devenu mondial. C'est aussi le cas de l'Afrique francophone.

L'Algérie et le pétrole : malédiction des matières premières ou instrument de l'indépendance nationale ?

Marta Musso a étudié l'histoire économique de l'Algérie indépendante[100]. Elle s'est notamment intéressée aux politiques économiques adoptées par ses gouvernements au cours des cinquante premières années de son indépendance et à l'industrie pétrolière et gazière. L'industrie algérienne des hydrocarbures est étroitement liée au processus d'indépendance. Il s'agit plus précisément d'analyser, en prenant l'Algérie comme cas d'étude, l'évolution du concept de malédiction du pétrole. Jusqu'aux années 1970, le pétrole est apparu comme le meilleur outil pour résoudre le problème de la formation de capital dans les pays nouvellement indépendants. C'était également une opportunité de promouvoir l'industrialisation par l'abondance d'une source d'énergie bon marché, rendant les entreprises potentielles compétitives par rapport aux entreprises occidentales. Enfin, le pétrole était considéré comme un outil diplomatique dans les négociations avec l'Europe, un moyen de pression contre la plus grande zone importatrice du monde. Les compagnies pétrolières, sans surprise, ont également soutenu la théorie du pétrole comme instrument de développement.

L'industrie est apparue à la fois comme un bénéficiaire du développement international, en raison de la possibilité d'élargir son marché, et comme un promoteur du développement, en raison de l'apport de capitaux fournis par les revenus. Le pétrole et l'industrie énergétique qui a connu la croissance la plus rapide de l'après-guerre, étaient directement liées au développement ; la consommation de pétrole était liée au transport, à la motorisation de masse, au chauffage domestique et à l'utilisation de plastiques et d'autres produits pétrochimiques, notamment les engrais, pour l'agriculture industrielle. Par conséquent, plus la consommation de pétrole est élevée, plus le niveau de développement économique d'un pays est élevé. Les pays qui ne dépendent pas des importations de pétrole sont donc considérés comme des candidats à un développement plus rapide. Peu à peu, cette vision optimiste du pétrole comme

100 Marta Musso, "Oil and development in Algeria (1956-2000)", communication présentée à la Préconférence de Paris.

instrument de développement a fait place au pétrole comme explication majeure des échecs économiques causés par la décolonisation. Puis la question a glissé d'une dimension économique ou politico-économique à une perspective principalement politique, analysant les relations entre l'industrie de la démocratie dans de nombreux pays producteurs, d'où le succès de notions telles que « États rentiers », « régimes pétroliers » et « guerres du pétrole ». Enfin, une critique de la littérature sur la « malédiction des ressources » a émergé ces dernières années.

L'Algérie a rarement fait l'objet d'études consacrées à la malédiction du pétrole. Cependant, il s'agit d'un cas particulièrement intéressant. D'importantes réserves de pétrole et de gaz ont été découvertes par des sociétés françaises au début de ce qui allait devenir la guerre d'indépendance de l'Algérie. Cela a eu un impact significatif sur les négociations entre l'Algérie et la France pendant le conflit et depuis. L'acquisition du contrôle des ressources pétrolières est devenue un objectif majeur pour les gouvernements algériens. Le pétrole a été considéré par eux comme la ressource ouvrant la voie à la croissance économique, à l'indépendance économique vis-à-vis de la France et à la réduction de l'écart de développement avec l'Europe. En même temps, les projets européens d'aide au développement en Afrique du Nord dans les années 1950 et 1960 suggèrent l'élaboration d'une sorte de « plan Marshall » européen pour le développement de l'Afrique du Nord. Il existe donc un lien étroit entre la construction de l'État et le développement de la Sonatrach, la plus grande entreprise bénéficiant d'un monopole d'État.

Très souvent, la nationalisation de l'industrie pétrolière a été considérée comme l'une des raisons pour lesquelles le pétrole est devenu une malédiction plutôt qu'une bénédiction pour l'économie du pays producteur. Cependant, il n'y avait aucune raison de croire que si l'Algérie avait permis aux compagnies françaises ou américaines d'opérer sans intervention, ou si elle avait accepté de faire du Sahara une plaque tournante internationale pour le pétrole, le développement global du pays aurait été très différent. Au contraire, grâce à la nationalisation de l'industrie pétrolière, l'Algérie a pu reprendre le contrôle de son pétrole de la même manière que la France avait repris le contrôle du Sahara : un système mixte avec la participation la plus large possible dans l'industrie pétrolière. L'État a fourni un effort massif pour développer la technologie et les compétences locales. Rien ne prouve que, si l'industrie pétrolière avait été laissée entre des mains étrangères, le développement politique et économique de l'Algérie aurait abouti à un État plus démocratique et plus intégrateur.

Tunisie : une association résistible avec la CEE ?

La question de la coopération entre la Tunisie et la Communauté économique européenne (CEE) a été travaillée par une dynamique complexe : multiples divergences d'intérêts, problème de la sécurité, réalité dynamique et changeante au sein de la CEE, multiplicité des points de vue quant aux formes de partenariats possibles, et, surtout, caractère incontournable du face à face avec la France, notamment pour tout ce qui concerne la politique agricole, les questions diplomatiques ou géostratégiques[101]. Cette situation est liée à la diversité et à la divergence des intérêts intra-européens (Europe des Six) et interrégionaux (Maghreb-Europe, etc.), le fossé entre le Nord et le Sud se creusant. Ce long processus d'« intergouvernementalisation » a sanctionné les pays tiers, en particulier ceux qui, en raison de liens historiques, dépendaient des relations avec l'Europe. La première moitié des années 1970, qui a coïncidé avec des crises internationales majeures, mais aussi avec la consolidation des institutions de la CEE, a vu l'avènement d'une politique méditerranéenne globale. La Tunisie en a été l'un des principaux bénéficiaires, mais les règles du jeu sont restées essentiellement définies par le partenaire européen. La formation d'une Europe unie (et puissante) nécessitant des formes protectionnistes du type de la Politique agricole commune (PAC), aucun pays, à l'exception des Pays-Bas, n'avait l'intention de soumettre ses agriculteurs à la concurrence sur les marchés mondiaux. Bien que la Tunisie ait bénéficié du soutien de la plupart des Six lors du lancement de son projet d'association avec la CEE, les tensions avec la France ont causé d'énormes pertes en termes de synergies. L'Europe émergente, en revanche, était d'une complexité institutionnelle inhabituelle. Avec des marchés de plus en plus mondialisés depuis les années 1960, il y avait déjà une grande mobilité des capitaux et, par conséquent, de réelles opportunités pour la Tunisie. Mais l'action diplomatique tunisienne s'est concentrée sur la demande d'aide institutionnelle et beaucoup moins sur l'offre d'opportunités de marché comme facteur de croissance pour les entreprises européennes.

Le Sénégal et la Côte d'Ivoire, deux modèles de développement opposés

Le Sénégal et la Côte d'Ivoire étaient les deux colonies privilégiées de l'ancienne puissance coloniale française en Afrique de l'Ouest[102]. Après la Seconde Guerre mondiale, en voie de décolonisation, leurs dirigeants dans ces territoires, respectivement Léopold Sédar Senghor et Félix Houphouët-Boigny, ont condamné les politiques coloniales. Ils ont contribué à la création du Rassemblement Démocratique Africain (RDA) en 1946 à Bamako. Le RDA était le parti des colonies françaises d'Afrique qui devait fournir 29 députés africains représentant l'Afrique occidentale française (AOF). Tandis que Senghor créait le Bloc Démocratique Sénégalais (BDS), Houphouët-Boigny fondait le Parti Démocrate de Côte-d'Ivoire (PDCI), qui sont des branches locales du RDA. Grâce à ces partis politiques et à leur militantisme, les deux dirigeants ont occupé successivement les postes de député puis de ministre, dans le cadre de l'Union française et de la Communauté. Ces expériences leur ont également donné l'occasion d'être à l'avant-garde des négociations qui ont conduit à l'indépendance et d'avoir une certaine légitimité politique. De même, Léopold Sédar Senghor et Félix Houphouët-Boigny n'ont pas voulu d'une indépendance immédiate et sont de fervents partisans du maintien du lien avec l'ancienne puissance coloniale. En outre, ils ont pesé de tout leur poids pour approuver et signer les accords de coopération qui ont précédé l'accession de leur pays à la souveraineté. Ainsi, le premier

101 Mohamed Sassi, "The North-South Negotiations in the Sixties: The Case of Tunisia with the EEC", communication présentée à la Préconférence de Paris.

102 Joseph Diouf, "Western Africa: "Compared models of Development: Léopold Senghor Sédar Senegal and Côte d'Ivoire of Houphouët-Boigny", communication présentée à la Préconférence de Paris.

est devenu président de la République du Sénégal tandis que le second a été élevé à la présidence de la Côte d'Ivoire.

Cependant, les deux hommes avaient des visions différentes du développement de leur pays et avaient également hérité de la colonisation de structures économiques différentes. En conséquence, les deux pays ont eu des trajectoires de développement différentes et opposées dans la forme et le fond. Léopold Sédar Senghor défend et théorise un modèle de développement basé sur le socialisme africain. Il prône une rupture totale avec l'héritage colonial, mais tous deux rejettent le socialisme marxiste-léniniste et le modèle capitaliste occidental dans un contexte de guerre froide. En outre, Senghor conçoit et met en œuvre une théorie du développement endogène. Quant à Félix Houphouët-Boigny, il choisit le libéralisme hérité de la politique coloniale de développement et inscrit la Côte d'Ivoire dans le camp occidental. De plus, les cultures de rente restent les piliers du développement. En effet, si les arbustes, notamment le cacao et le café, sont la principale richesse de la Côte d'Ivoire, le Sénégal fonde son développement sur la monoculture de l'arachide. Cependant, si ces cultures ont fait la richesse de ces deux pays comme en témoigne le « miracle ivoirien », celui-ci a néanmoins conduit à la faillite à la fin des années 1970.

Le cas de la zone franc : échapper au trilemme de Mundell

Selon Olivier Feiertag, la zone franc offre une étude de cas pour traiter d'une zone correspondant à une monnaie optimale[103]. Cette zone a connu son âge d'or dans les années 1960, alors qu'elle était encore très influencée par l'influence du Pacte colonial. Selon l'analyse de Mundell concernant le rôle de la monnaie dans le processus d'industrialisation (1961), différents arguments ont permis de parler d'une zone monétaire optimale. En effet, la zone franc était hétérogène ; en même temps, l'unification monétaire ne visait pas toujours les coûts de transaction, mais l'accélération d'une bonne circulation des facteurs de production. En fait, elle était organisée en trois zones : Afrique occidentale française, Afrique équatoriale française, Madagascar. Mais n'était-ce pas la continuation, par un autre biais, du colonialisme ?

Cela explique la réticence de la zone franc à s'intégrer économiquement. En 1962, l'Union monétaire ouest-africaine a été créée pour promouvoir le commerce intra-zone. L'histoire de la zone franc montre que trois phases se sont succédées :

1 / L'âge d'or des années 1960. Cet âge d'or s'est achevé dans les années 1980, notamment en raison de l'hétérogénéité des modèles de développement africains. En effet, l'avance de la Côte d'Ivoire et du Cameroun sur les autres pays s'accentue de plus en plus

2 / Si un changement s'est produit dans les années 1980, c'est principalement en raison de la crise de la dette africaine. En effet, la fin du boom des matières premières a provoqué un choc asymétrique

103 Olivier Feiertag, "History of the Development of the Franc zone (1939-1944), Does the Theory of Optimal Currency to be applied to Franc?", communication à la préconférence de Tokyo et « La zone Franc de 1945 à nos jours : échapper au triangle d'incompatibilté de Mundell », in Marie-Claude Esposito and Olivier Feiertag (eds.), « Histoire financière, histoire globale », *Revue française d'histoire économique – The French Economic History Review*, n° 14 (n°2 - 2020), p. 39-49.

3 / Le résultat en a été la dévaluation du franc CFA en 1994. Elle correspond au véritable tournant de la mondialisation.

Finalement, le modèle monétaire optimal s'est bien appliqué à la zone franc dans les années 1960, mais plus dans les années 1980 et 1990. L'illusion d'homogénéité s'est dissipée. La zone franc a certes été victime des rivalités nationales, mais aussi des progrès du panafricanisme. Plus fondamentalement, le passage au marché mondial ne pouvait que réduire la puissance de la zone franc.

Modèles de développement et dépendance de sentier : Égypte, Afrique du Sud et Australie

Il est clair qu'il existe de multiples voies de développement, car elles sont le produit de conditions et d'expériences spécifiques, selon une logique de dépendance des voies. C'est ce que montrent les exemples de l'Égypte, de l'Afrique du Sud et de l'Australie.

Égypte

Sous la direction de Muhammad Ali, l'Égypte a connu un développement économique important au XIXe siècle, soutenu par les capitaux européens[104]. Ces derniers contribuent à l'ouverture économique du pays et à sa modernisation en termes d'équipements, mais associés à la domination politique, ils engendrent également de violentes tensions. Le lien entre l'ouverture économique et la domination coloniale qui s'est développée à la fin du XIXe siècle a eu de fortes implications sur les modèles économiques du XXe siècle. Les régimes successifs sont confrontés à la difficulté de trouver une voie de développement économique qui puisse s'appuyer sur les financements extérieurs nécessaires tout en étant au service des réformes nationales.

En effet, au cours des deux derniers siècles, le capital étranger investi en Égypte a joué un rôle ambivalent : il a favorisé l'intégration du pays dans l'économie mondiale, mais, associé aux pratiques coloniales des puissances européennes, il a également provoqué une réaction de repli et d'isolement de l'économie nationale sur elle-même. Le processus d'intégration de l'Égypte dans l'économie mondiale, qui a débuté au XIXe siècle, s'est ralenti pendant la période de décolonisation et de nassérisme. Il a ensuite été clairement réactivé dans le dernier quart du XXe siècle par les présidents Anouar el-Sadate et Hosni Moubarak. Après la parenthèse des Frères musulmans de juin 2011 à juin 2013, elle est à nouveau poursuivie par le président Sissi depuis son accession au pouvoir en 2014. Ce dernier encourage les capitaux étrangers à investir massivement dans le pays avec la création de partenariats ou de zones franches. Mais ce processus est plus difficile à réaliser que pendant la période coloniale en raison de la forte instabilité politique et économique de la région. L'économie est encore entravée par les traumatismes du XIXe siècle, qui contribuent à maintenir la logique d'un

104 Caroline Piquet, « L'Égypte : réalité et limites d'une voie nationale de développement », chapitre original. Voir aussi : Caroline Piquet, *La Compagnie du canal de Suez. Une concession française en Égypte (1888-1956)*, Paris, PUPS, 2008 ; *Histoire du canal de Suez*, Paris, Perrin, 2009 ; John Waterbury, *The Egypt of Nasser and Sadat: the Political Economy of the two Regimes*, Princeton, Princeton University Press, 1983; Louis Blin, *L'économie égyptienne, Libéralisation et insertion dans le marché mondial*, Paris, L'Harmattan, 1993.

système dirigiste où l'État reste perçu comme un rempart contre la mondialisation économique menaçant la souveraineté nationale.

Afrique du Sud

L'industrialisation en Afrique du Sud répond assez largement au modèle de Rostow[105]. À partir du XIXe siècle, les agro-industries ont posé les bases initiales des changements entrepreneuriaux schumpétériens dans la vie agraire. La transition vers l'industrialisation s'est faite dans le cadre de l'intervention de l'État polanyien sur le marché en vue de stimuler le développement industriel. Le contexte spécifique de l'économie minérale et agraire a permis l'atténuation par l'État de la structure des coûts élevés caractérisant l'économie. La situation géographique, les facteurs de production (travail, capital) et les directives politiques ont orienté l'intervention sur le marché. La substitution des importations comme option politique stratégique, telle que proposée par Prebisch, a été appliquée, mais l'État s'est abstenu de pratiquer le socialisme intégral ou la planification centrale du marché. L'industrialisation de l'économie sud-africaine s'est accélérée depuis les années 1920 sous l'effet des politiques industrielles protectionnistes de l'État. De puissants groupes d'entreprises, des chefs d'entreprise, notamment du secteur minier, ont coopéré avec le protectionnisme d'État. L'effet Gerschenkronian de retard a joué dans l'industrialisation sud-africaine, mais le capital humain local a développé des technologies innovantes sur place permettant d'améliorer le processus d'industrialisation. La trajectoire spécifique de l'industrialisation sud-africaine reflète la mise en place d'une base industrielle proche du monde de la première industrialisation et fondée sur un mélange de facteurs de production rares (capital, esprit d'entreprise, main-d'œuvre qualifiée) et de facteurs de production abondants (main-d'œuvre non qualifiée, ressources naturelles). Les traits weberiens de l'éthique protestante du travail constituent un moteur important du développement économique, et plus particulièrement industriel, en Afrique du Sud. Le contexte spécifique d'une population minoritaire européenne contrôlant la politique économique a finalement eu un impact négatif sur la modernisation et le progrès du secteur industriel en Afrique du Sud à la fin du XXe siècle.

Australie

Selon Martin Shanahan, les facteurs qui influencent le développement économique de l'Australie ont fait l'objet de nombreuses analyses et discussions récentes de la part des historiens économiques nationaux[106]. Les tentatives d'explication du développement économique de l'Australie ne sont cependant pas particulièrement nouvelles. Depuis que les Européens ont transporté pour la première fois des personnes et des capitaux sur le continent en 1788 et ont commencé à façonner la terre et ses habitants pour

105 Grietjie Verhoef, "South in Africa, metropolitan in culture: industrial development trajectory of South Africa", in Dominique Barjot (ed), "Theory and Empirical Performance. Economic Paradigm and Performance in the Long Run (18th to 21st century)", *Revue française d'histoire économique – The French Economic History Review*, n° 11-12 (n°1-2, 2019), *op. cit.*, p. 244-259; 'The South African economy in the twentieth century' in Pretorius F (ed.), *A History of South Africa. From the distant past to the present day*, Pretoria, Protea Book House, 2014, p. 448-477.

106 Martin Shanahan, "Australia's industrial development: The importance of importing capital and ideas", in "Theory and Empirical Performance. Economic Paradigm and Performance in the Long Run (18th to 21st century)", *Revue française d'histoire économique – The French Economic History Review, Ibidem.*, p. 226-242.

qu'ils se conforment à leurs propres aspirations, les commentateurs se sont penchés sur les facteurs qui ont permis aux non-indigènes d'atteindre les niveaux de vie les plus élevés au monde en un siècle d'occupation. La transition de colonie pénale à véritable nation a été d'autant plus remarquable que pendant la quasi-totalité du XIXe siècle, les six colonies isolées n'étaient pas seulement installées en bordure du plus grand continent insulaire du monde, mais elles se trouvaient également à la lointaine périphérie du monde commercial de l'Atlantique Nord. Si les riches ressources du pays ont constitué la base du progrès économique, ce n'est pas le seul élément qui a contribué à la croissance. Comme McLean l'a récemment souligné, les facteurs qui ont contribué à l'augmentation rapide du niveau de vie en Australie et qui ont permis de maintenir un niveau élevé de prospérité pendant un autre siècle étaient nombreux et variés, se combinant souvent à des moments différents et de différentes manières en réponse aux opportunités et aux menaces[107].

Il existe au moins une moins une explication de la tendance des analystes économiques à privilégier la narration et la description plutôt que la théorie : la composition des éléments qui influencent l'économie du pays. En un peu plus de deux cent ans, le continent est passé d'un contact extérieur avec le capitalisme à une économie moderne, industrialisée et fortement liée aux marchés internationaux. Si la terre était abondante, le capital (financier, réel et humain) et le travail ne l'étaient pas. Apprendre ce qui pouvait se développer avec ce mélange de facteurs tout en compensant (et en important) les facteurs nécessaires, a pris du temps et des efforts. Bien que la fabrication ait commencé au XIXe siècle pour répondre aux besoins locaux, l'industrialisation de l'économie n'a eu lieu qu'à partir du milieu du XXe siècle. Cette période situe la période de développement moderne de l'Australie plus près des avancées de certaines nations du sud-est asiatique que de la révolution industrielle de l'Europe. La combinaison de dotations et de défis spécifiques à l'Australie diffère de celle à laquelle les nations européennes ont été confrontées au cours de la même période. En dépit de cela et malgré la distance géographique, les liens de l'Australie avec l'Europe sont tels que son développement économique est mieux examiné à travers un cadre de référence européen (modifié). Ces dernières années, l'éventail des facteurs qui ont été étudiés pour expliquer le développement économique s'est considérablement élargi. Alors que les théories précédentes incluaient une série d'éléments aussi divers que l'accumulation de capital, la croissance démographique, la demande globale, le commerce international et le changement technologique, il y en a maintenant beaucoup plus[108]. Parmi les éléments récemment identifiés comme importants figurent le capital humain et la création de connaissances ; l'interdépendance des taux de croissance des pays ; l'inégalité ; la géographie ; le rôle des institutions économiques et politiques[109].

107 Ian W. McLean, *Why Australia Prospered. The shifting sources of economic growth*, Princeton, Princeton University Press, 2013.
108 Mark Setterfield (ed) *Handbook of Alternative Theories of Economic Growth*, Cheltenham (UK), Edward Elgar, 2010.
109 Elhanan Helpman, *The Mystery of Economic Growth*, Harvard, Harvard University Press, 2009.

La motivation centrale de l'étude du Shanahan est de répondre à la question : les théories européennes du développement peuvent-elles expliquer de manière adéquate l'expérience d'industrialisation de l'Australie ? La réponse est simple : non.

1/ L'Australie n'est pas l'Europe. Au cours des deux derniers siècles, elle est passée d'une série de colonies déconnectées avec une poignée de colons européens à des périodes d'exploration, d'expansion économique et d'intégration d'une manière qui n'a pas été suivie par les pays d'Europe. L'expérience australienne n'a pas suivi une trajectoire de développement unique. Contrairement au cas européen, par exemple, un développement aussi bien extensif qu'intensif s'est produit simultanément pendant de nombreuses décennies, les immigrants ayant à la fois élargi la base économique du pays et intensifié leurs investissements pour l'exploiter. Le pays était le destinataire, plutôt que le fournisseur, des migrants et des capitaux. Bien qu'il ait été impliqué dans les guerres européennes, il n'a pas subi le même niveau de destruction physique que beaucoup d'autres pays.

2/ L'abondance et le prix relatif de nombreuses ressources naturelles en Australie différaient (et pour de nombreuses ressources, continuent à différer) de celles existant en Europe. Les Australiens ont donc bénéficié de possibilités et d'incitations différentes. La conséquence, tant au XIXe qu'au XXe siècle, a été une économie plus axée sur l'exploitation des ressources naturelles que sur l'intensification industrielle. Néanmoins, l'intensification industrielle s'est produite, bien que plus tard et à une échelle plus réduite qu'en Europe, ce qui a contribué à soutenir l'économie pendant les périodes de volatilité du prix des matières premières.

3/ Les institutions politiques, juridiques et de marché australiennes ont d'abord été basées sur les structures anglaises, puis progressivement modifiées pour répondre aux défis locaux. Ainsi, tout en émergeant d'une base commune (dont une grande partie subsiste), il a été possible de modifier la trajectoire de celles-ci de manière à influer sur la croissance. Par exemple, la période de près d'un siècle de politiques protectionnistes semble non seulement avoir été fortuite dans son calendrier (facilitant la croissance des industries naissantes et attirant les entreprises internationales derrière la barrière tarifaire), mais beaucoup de ses structures formelles ont été démantelées lorsque le système a été évalué comme un frein à la croissance, tout en laissant un héritage d'institutions et d'attitudes qui maintiennent des éléments de contrainte du marché. En tant que grand continent avec une petite population, des marchés dispersés et de grandes distances, le rôle du gouvernement dans la facilitation du développement a été établi relativement tôt ; un héritage qui reste relativement fort. Il s'agit d'une voie de développement institutionnel qui diffère de celle de nombreux pays européens.

4/ Le développement de l'Australie a également été fortuitement programmé. Au XIXe siècle, la baisse des coûts de transport accompagnant le besoin de produits de base s'est alignée sur de nombreuses ressources dont l'Australie disposait en relative abondance, ou qu'elle pouvait développer à un coût comparativement moindre. Au XXe siècle, le changement technologique accompagné d'une deuxième grande vague d'immigrants a créé les marchés et l'accumulation de connaissances nécessaires à la poursuite du développement. L'Australie a largement bénéficié des innovations technologiques des économies de l'Atlantique Nord, tout en concentrant ses propres efforts sur les défis technologiques pertinents pour les problèmes locaux. Le capital, la technologie et l'économie construits par les générations précédentes étaient suffisamment robustes pour constituer une base pour la poursuite du développement.

5/ Enfin, les liens de l'Australie ont été nombreux avec le reste du monde, non seulement par l'ouverture commerciale ou même par l'adoption d'institutions économiques et politiques initiées à l'étranger, mais aussi par son acceptation de la finance et des entreprises internationales. Il en a résulté une économie et une société avec de multiples couches d'intégration avec le reste du monde. En tant que nation ouverte sur le monde, même les liens personnels et familiaux de sa population sont d'un type différent de ceux qui existent dans de nombreuses nations européennes. Bien que ces interconnexions puissent être à l'avantage ou au détriment du pays, selon le point de vue de chacun et la question en jeu, dans l'ensemble, elles ont bien servi l'Australie et son développement économique. Au fil des générations, ces liens se sont éloignés d'un pays (le Royaume-Uni) ou d'une région (l'Europe) et ont de plus en plus orientés vers l'Asie et les Amériques. Cet éventail de personnes, d'idées et d'institutions a été la plus précieuse des importations de la nation et lui a permis de développer et de maintenir l'un des niveaux de vie les plus élevés au monde.

Conclusion

De ce vaste travail collectif se dégagent trois conclusions principales :

1 / Le contrat initialement fixé, à savoir la confrontation des modèles d'interprétation des phénomènes d'industrialisation conçus par les penseurs occidentaux avec la réalité des modes nationaux d'industrialisation, n'a été qu'imparfaitement rempli. En effet, l'étude de ces phénomènes implique la maîtrise d'un important appareil statistique, mais aussi la réalisation de nombreux calculs et la lecture d'une masse énorme de travaux scientifiques relevant de l'histoire économique, mais aussi et surtout des disciplines qui lui sont liées. La conséquence est que le processus implique un travail long et difficile dans le court intervalle de trois ans entre chaque congrès international d'histoire économique. Néanmoins, il a été possible de faire un utile bilan comparatif et un inventaire non moins utile des recherches menées sur le sujet. Ce dernier reflète probablement assez bien les différents degrés d'avancement des questions et des méthodes de l'histoire économique et leur renouvellement.

2 / En général, les modèles théoriques d'origine occidentale, qu'ils soient macro ou microéconomiques, sont utiles, voire indispensables, car ils sont à la base des typologies possibles, mais aussi susceptibles de fournir des modèles explicatifs.

2.1 / Certains modèles apparaissent plus pertinents que d'autres. C'est le cas des analyses de Rostow, Kuznets et Gerschenkron dans le domaine macro-économique. Dans leurs grands axes, ils ont été largement confirmés par l'histoire : l'avantage du retard est une réalité, mais aussi la supériorité des modèles de développement basés sur les exportations de biens et de services et les importations de technologie et de savoir-faire ; sur le plan technologique, la pertinence des approches schumpétériennes ou néo-schumpétériennes, mais à condition toutefois de ne pas les opposer systématiquement aux approches monétaristes. En ce qui concerne le développement économique régional, la vision des *clusters* de Michael Porter présente l'avantage de fournir des éléments plus explicatifs que la théorie des pôles de croissance et de s'appliquer à un nombre de cas beaucoup plus vastes que les districts industriels de A. Marshall.

2.2 / Mais la complexité des phénomènes historiques conduit souvent à la combinaison d'approches :

A / Ainsi, les analyses néoclassiques de la croissance économique restent pertinentes. Non seulement elles permettent des comparaisons simples entre pays industrialisés ou en développement, mais elles fournissent également les grandes catégories nécessaires pour mesurer l'importance respective des facteurs de développement économique.

B / Elles ne sont pas incompatibles avec les approches souvent adoptées aujourd'hui en termes d'apprentissage par la pratique et de dépendance de sentier, mais aussi avec les apports spécifiques de la microéconomie industrielle et des sciences de la gestion.

C / À cet égard, les théories évolutionnistes offrent des perspectives particulièrement utiles, car elles mettent également en avant l'évolution technologique et scientifique, le rôle spécifique du capital humain, sans pour autant fermer la porte à des approches plus quantitatives et statistiques ainsi qu'à la prise en compte des phénomènes monétaires et financiers.

D / Elles sont également tout à fait compatibles avec la prise en compte des effets de la compétitivité à laquelle Michael Porter attache toute son importance. Tant la dépendance de trajectoire que les analyses de Porter ont l'avantage de pouvoir passer sans difficulté du niveau micro au niveau macro sans modifier une meilleure sensibilité dans le cadre du raisonnement.

3 / Dans ces conditions, les modèles occidentaux, les vrais, ne sont-ils pas ceux des faits et des théories stylisées, si spécifiques qu'ils ne peuvent être comparés à ceux des pays industrialisés émergents d'aujourd'hui ? À cet égard, quelques remarques peuvent être faites :

3-1 / Comme l'ont montré les études occidentales sur les phénomènes d'industrialisation en Occident, il est clair qu'il n'existe pas de modèle paradigmatique, celui de la Grande-Bretagne (Angleterre, Écosse et Pays de Galles), qui aurait été reproduit par les pays continentaux et l'Amérique du Nord.

A/ Certains défendent même aujourd'hui l'idée que la Grande-Bretagne était plutôt une exception. En fait, s'il existe une proximité entre elle et la Belgique, le cas de la France est largement en contradiction avec le développement britannique. Cette disparité se retrouve dans la génération suivante, celle des États-Unis et de l'Allemagne, ou celle des retardataires comme l'Italie et, dans une certaine mesure, la Russie.

B/ Néanmoins, ces disparités dans le modèle de développement n'ont jamais exclu de vigoureux transferts de technologie et de savoir-faire, tirés notamment par le commerce et les services. Par ailleurs, ce qui diffère de manière évidente au niveau macroéconomique, diffère ou parfois s'oppose au niveau microéconomique : celui des régions (la Wallonie, le Nord-Pas-de-Calais, la Ruhr, ou encore la Silésie, ne sont pas sans points communs avec les pays non britanniques), mais aussi celui des entreprises (similitude de fonctionnement, au XIXe siècle, entre les entreprises britanniques et françaises dans l'industrie textile).

3-2 / Cette remarque s'applique également à l'Asie, où le modèle japonais a souvent servi de référence, notamment aux « Quatre Dragons » des années 1970 à 2000, mais aussi, dans une certaine mesure, aux « Tigres asiatiques » de l'Asie du Sud-Est. Certes, ces voies d'industrialisation adoptées en Chine ou au Vietnam n'ont pas beaucoup à voir avec celle du Japon. Il en va de même pour Hong Kong, Singapour et Taïwan, où l'influence chinoise a toujours dominé. Les similitudes sont encore plus faibles si l'on regarde le sous-continent indien. Néanmoins, si l'on dépasse les grands agrégats de l'économie pour regarder les régions, les entreprises et, plus largement, les acteurs, alors certains éléments de comparaison apparaissent : l'importance des conglomérats industriels ou, dans les pays d'Asie de l'Est, l'influence du confucianisme, souvent comparée à celle du calvinisme en Occident, ou encore le rôle des minorités (en Inde, à Bombay, en Malaisie).

3-3 / Même si la nouvelle aurait tendance à le faire croire, il n'y a pas *a priori* de pays définitivement écartés dans la cause de l'industrialisation et du développement. C'est l'exemple de l'Amérique latine.

A/ Bien que longtemps dominée par les intérêts économiques et financiers de l'Europe occidentale puis des États-Unis, l'Amérique latine a ouvert la voie à la croissance industrielle. C'est le cas du Brésil, grâce à l'apparition de géants industriels, d'abord à capital public, puis devenus multinationaux par le biais de la privatisation. L'adoption de dispositions pro-concurrentielles a été un facteur clé dans l'assouplissement des blocages économiques. Mais il serait inexact de minimiser le rôle des familles, des entrepreneurs individuels et de leurs réseaux d'entreprises, comme au Mexique, notamment autour de Monterrey.

B/ Le Brésil et le Mexique ne sont pas les seuls exemples de décollage industriel, avec leurs succès, leurs échecs et leurs fragilités encore importants. Aujourd'hui, nous sommes bien conscients de la percée spectaculaire de la Colombie, qui a tiré les leçons d'un développement original pour les États-Unis et la Banque mondiale, mais aussi pour le Chili, le Pérou et, vraisemblablement, le Paraguay. Reste le cas de l'Argentine, qui aurait pu être un Canada méridional, mais qui bénéficie néanmoins de la dynamique imprimée par le Mercosur. Certes, en Europe, comme en Asie (avec l'ASEAN par exemple), mais aussi en Amérique du Nord (ALENA) et du Sud (Pacte andin), les efforts d'intégration ont favorisé l'accélération des phénomènes d'industrialisation.

3.4 / Dans le reste du monde aussi, l'industrialisation progresse.

A / Tel est le cas de la Russie, là encore, comme à la veille de la Première Guerre mondiale, une des grandes puissances émergentes (troisième des BRICS derrière la Chine et l'Inde, mais presque équivalente à l'Allemagne en parité de pouvoir d'achat). Elle a également donné naissance à de puissantes multinationales (Gazprom, Rusal), développé des compétences technologiques et bénéficié d'investissements étrangers (notamment d'Europe occidentale) sur son sol. Il en va de même pour la Turquie, qui poursuit sa lente ascension économique, grâce au dynamisme de ses entrepreneurs et au soutien de l'État.

B / Bien que l'idée d'une malédiction des marchandises ne soit pas à exclure, l'exemple des Émirats Arabes Unis, bien après celui du Canada, montre qu'il existe des voies originales de développement capables de générer une croissance auto-entretenue, conditionnée par une intégration économique mondiale soutenue et accrue. D'une certaine manière, c'est un message pour l'Afrique. En effet, s'il est important, comme en Algérie que les ressources pétrolières soient entre les mains de l'État, cela ne peut suffire si l'on ne cherche pas, comme la Tunisie, la voie de l'intégration économique internationale.

C/ Ainsi, les petits pays africains et même les plus grands (Éthiopie), portés aujourd'hui par leur dynamisme interne, pourraient, comme le Cameroun, le Sénégal ou la Côte d'Ivoire, trouver la voie du développement durable. Si cela s'avérait impossible, leurs diplômés de haut niveau devraient fuir le pays en grand nombre et le commerce de guerre actuel plongerait l'économie mondiale dans une profonde dépression, qui frapperait les économies les plus faibles, comme dans les années 1930.

PARTIE 1

Pays occidentaux industrialisés

PART 1

Western industrialized countries

L'économie Européenne au prisme du projet politique des États-Unis

Du plan Marshall au Grand Dessein de Kennedy

François David
Université du Littoral, Côte d'Opale.

Nous illustrerons ici la thèse du primat du politique sur l'économie, à travers le cas précis de la politique américaine en l'Europe, après 1945. Dans la réorganisation du monde par les États-Unis, l'économie est un moyen ; la politique, une fin. Si l'Amérique peut se définir, entre autres, comme un *Business*, c'est un *Business* au service d'un ordre politique. Dans les années fondatrices 1945-1963, presque tous les grands projets économiques et commerciaux pensés par les États-Unis au profit de l'Europe occidentale procèdent d'une vision stratégique : créer un monde interdépendant, avec des partages de compétences, voire des abandons de souveraineté, de façon à diluer, puis dissoudre l'agressivité belligène de l'État-nation westphalien. Les 14 points de Wilson forment le point de départ historique et idéologique de cette transformation du monde et de l'Europe à partir de 1945, en particulier les 2e et 3e points (libre-échange, liberté de commerce maritime) ; et le point 14, avec la Société des nations, dont les principes posent une base théorique vers des entités ou bien interétatiques, ou bien supranationales tels que nous les connaissons à partir de la CED, de la CECA et bien entendu des traités de Rome de 1957. À partir de 1945, pour de longues décennies, sinon jusqu'à aujourd'hui, le projet américain pour l'Europe se résume ainsi :

D'abord, le « doux commerce » de Montesquieu : la compétition économique poursuit la guerre par d'autres moyens. Aux conflits interétatiques succéderait l'affrontement des entreprises privées, sans restrictions douanières. L'intensification des échanges commerciaux, la circulation des marchands et des citoyens, puis celle des idées abaisseraient nécessairement les tensions interétatiques. Notons tout de suite, que le respect du libre-échange économique s'avère sinusoïdal chez les États-Unis aux XXe-XXIe s. La lutte contre le protectionnisme est certainement le moins intangible des 14 points appliqués par les successeurs de Wilson, dès lors que des concurrents sérieux émergent ou qu'une crise perturbe le marché intérieur. On se souvient de la terrible loi Smoot-Hawley de 1930 qui exclut l'importation de 20 000 produits, dans le contexte naissant de la grande dépression. En 1948, encore, le Congrès exclut de ratifier l'institutionnalisation du GATT à travers l'Organisation internationale du commerce, mort-née, jusqu'aux accords de Marrakech fondateurs de l'Organisation mondiale du Commerce en 1994. En réalité, sur le long XXe siècle, les États-Unis ne renoncent jamais à appliquer le libre-échange au reste de la planète. Ce qui peut être mauvais pour l'Amérique, à l'occasion, reste bon pour les autres.

Ensuite, le projet américain pour l'Europe se caractérise par la promotion des partages de compétences économiques, militaires et économiques vers des « agences » supranationales. Dans cette optique, l'État-nation se voit désigné comme le responsable des guerres européennes, en particulier entre la France et l'Allemagne depuis 1870. Celles-ci doivent s'effacer progressivement devant un futur gouvernement européen fédéral, dont l'essence régalienne consistera à gérer l'économie des pays membres et non à devenir une nouvelle puissance géomilitaire mondiale capable de défier la posture mondiale des États-Unis (*Cf.* le refus de l'« Europe puissance » à partir des années 1970).

Enfin, le wilsonisme procède de la paix démocratique de Kant : « les démocraties ne guerroient pas entre elles » devient après 1945 « les fédérations démocratiques ne se font pas la guerre » (*Cf.* le Grand Dessein de Kennedy). Après 1945, les gouvernements américains décident fermement de reprendre le grand projet wilsonien là où le refus du Sénat de ratifier le Traité de Versailles l'avait sèchement interrompu en 1920 (*Cf.* la théorie de la « grande parenthèse » de Jean Baechler[1]). Durant cette période créatrice Truman-Eisenhower-Kennedy, s'impose l'équation : *Containment* = reconstruction et modernisation économique = intégration européenne. Ces trois démarches consubstantielles visent à assurer la paix sur le vieux continent, avant de constituer un bloc occidental fondé sur les mêmes valeurs libérales (en y ajoutant le Japon et, un jour peut-être, la Chine). Ajoutons un paramètre macro-économique supplémentaire :

1 Jean Baechler, *La grande parenthèse, 1914-1991. Essai sur un accident de l'histoire*, Paris, Calmann Lévy, 1993.

Les administrations Roosevelt-Truman tirent les leçons de Wilson à Paris en 1919, laquelle ne proposa aucune relance des circuits commerciaux et bancaires européens en manque de capitaux et de clients à l'exportation. En bonne logique, un tel plan aurait dû s'associer aussi à un plan de relance de l'économie américaine (*Cf.* les *farmers* surendettés du Middle West et les manufactures de la ceinture industrielle en quête de débouchés[2]). Après le V-Day, on comprend enfin la nécessité de lier l'économie américaine au retour définitif de la prospérité européenne de l'après-Dépression, et vice versa. On garde à l'esprit la possibilité qu'à une nouvelle croissance vigoureuse, du type *roaring twenties*, puisse succéder une autre dépression interminable. Dans les espérances les plus folles, personne n'imagine alors les « trente glorieuses ». Beaucoup redoutent (le général-président Eisenhower en tête, ainsi que son secrétaire au Trésor Humphrey) que la surchauffe de l'économie de guerre en 1942-1945 masque artificiellement les causes structurelles de la crise des années 1930. La guerre finie, le marasme antérieur pourrait très vite ressurgir.

Nous allons donc réexaminer les grands projets économiques américains pour l'Europe d'après-guerre à l'aune du politique et de la géopolitique : le plan Marshall, la CECA, ainsi que les prémices de la CEE. Nous finirons par le Grand Dessein de Kennedy pour mieux souligner sa modernité actuelle. En effet, l'Union européenne d'aujourd'hui, tout comme l'hypothétique TAFTA, descendent en ligne directe des cadres de pensée et d'action posés par les États-Unis en 1945-1963. En trois générations, les États-Unis néo-wilsoniens atteignent leur objectif d'une Europe démocratique en paix, accrochée aux principes américains (malgré les dénégations parfois des intéressés) par le puissant ressort de l'économie libérale.

1/ L'OBJECTIF PREMIER DU PLAN MARSHALL : REGROUPER L'EUROPE DE L'OUEST POLITIQUEMENT, D'ABORD PAR LE VOLET ÉCONOMIQUE

Sur le strict plan de l'efficacité, l'*European Recovery Program* reste une énigme et laisse ouvert l'hypothèse d'un redémarrage économique endogène des économies européennes. Hors de l'aide massive apportée à l'allié britannique, le plan Marshall reformule avant tout la question allemande – l'enjeu contemporain le plus massif de tous. Auparavant, en 1946-1948, les Anglo-Saxons ont déjà refusé à la France l'internationalisation de la Ruhr (à laquelle l'URSS aurait participé…), puis lui ont imposé la fusion économique des trois zones. Dès lors, les États-Unis exigent de la France l'égalité des droits avec son ancien bourreau. L'économie sert de levier.

Certes – c'est l'aspect le plus éclatant – le plan Marshall amorce un dispositif de redressement financier, commercial et industriel indispensable à la survie matérielle mais aussi morale du vieux continent. Deuxièmement, l'ERP ne veut pas simplement restaurer, mais aussi moderniser les technologies et les esprits. Les Européens ne

2 Denise Artaud, *La question des dettes interalliées et la reconstruction de l'Europe (1917-1929)*, Lille, Champion, 1978.

connaîtraient pas le capitalisme authentique. Ils ignoreraient les vraies lois du marché et redouteraient l'ouverture à la concurrence internationale. Aussi, les producteurs européens gagneraient-ils beaucoup à s'imprégner des méthodes américaines de gestion, de production et d'organisation du travail. C'est le sens des « missions de productivité », étudiées en profondeur par Dominique Barjot, lesquelles envoient des ingénieurs, des hommes d'affaires et des syndicalistes outre-Atlantique, pour se familiariser avec les procédés industriels et de *management*, supposés avoir fait leurs preuves[3]. Troisièmement, enfin (mais le plus important), le plan Marshall, veut catalyser les énergies européennes, vers des institutions communes et supranationales, prélude, peut-être un jour, à un État unique.

1.1/ European Recovery Program et Pacte atlantique : restauration économique, défense et intégration européenne

En 1947-1950, la classe politique américaine ne redoute pas une guerre imminente. Selon elle, la force principale de Moscou dépend moins de ses 80 divisions sur le pied de guerre, que de son idéologie. La France et l'Italie pourraient sombrer de l'intérieur, sans qu'un seul coup de feu soit tiré, grâce à un mélange de crainte et de séduction[4]. Le futur engagement militaire des États-Unis doit faciliter le plan Marshall qui doit lui-même accélérer l'unité entre les États européens. Le plan Marshall et le traité de l'Atlantique Nord connaissent donc deux développements identiques, avec un décalage d'un an[5]. Dans les deux cas, on observe :

Premièrement, deux déclarations d'intention lancent le processus : le discours du secrétaire d'Etat Marshall à Harvard, le 5 juin 1947 ; d'autre part, le vote par le Sénat de la résolution Vandenberg qui autorise le président américain à participer à des alliances défensives régionales. Voté le 11 juin 1948, ce texte bipartisan cherche à rassurer les Européens, en leur montrant que les États-Unis ne restent pas indifférents à leur situation militaire, contrairement à 1914 et à 1939[6]. Deuxièmement, les États-Unis invitent les Européens à définir un programme commun économique puis militaire. Dans son discours du 5 juin 1947, à Harvard, le secrétaire d'Etat Marshall incite les Européens à se transformer économiquement, c'est-à-dire en fait politiquement : « Un accord devra être réalisé par les pays de l'Europe sur leurs besoins actuels ». Ceux-ci devront dresser une liste de leurs besoins, sur le court et le long terme, et organiser entre eux leur redressement : « C'est là l'affaire des Européens. L'initiative, doit, à mon avis, venir de l'Europe ».

3 Dominique Barjot & Christophe Réveillard (dir.). *L'américanisation de l'Europe occidentale au XX*[e] *siècle – Mythe et réalité*. Paris, Presses de l'Université de Paris-Sorbonne, 2001.

4 Mémorandum de George Kennan, directeur du *Policy Planning Staff*, 16 mai 1947, National Archives and Records Administration, département d'État, Maryland (ci-après NARA, DOS), Policy Planning Staff Files.

5 *North Atlantic Treaty. Hearings Before the Committee On Foreign Relations.United States Senate. Eighty-First Congress. First Session*. (2e partie : *Private Witnesses*). Washington, 1955, publié en 1972.

6 *The Vandenberg Resolution and the North Atlantic Treaty. Hearings Held in Executive Session before the Committee on Foreign Relations. United States Senate. 80th Congress, Second Session, on S. Res. 239, reaffirming the policy of the United States to achieve international peace and security through the United Nations and indicating certain objectives to be pursued.* Mai-juin 1948, publié en 1973.

Comme l'écrit avec lucidité l'ambassadeur italien à Paris (P. Quaroni) à son ministre, « la décision est entre les mains du Congrès, qui représente l'opinion de l'homme de la rue américain et celui-ci est conscient des destructions européennes, mais il est aussi convaincu que l'Europe ne pourra jamais se relever si elle continue sur la voie qu'elle a suivie jusqu'ici : tous ces petits *États*, séparés par des barrières douanières, par des monnaies qu'ils défendent par des restrictions oppressives, par des querelles territoriales petites et futiles, politiques et de prestige, ces *États* ne pourront jamais se relever s'ils ne décident pas de faire place nette de tout le passé, de créer un espace européen, pareil à l'espace américain, à l'intérieur duquel l'argent, les hommes, les produits puissent circuler en ne suivant d'autre loi que celle de la libre initiative et du profit économique »[7]. En bout de course, nous identifions ici les valeurs de l'Union européenne actuelle (*Cf.* Schengen, le marché unique et l'espoir vain de créer un *demos* européen par le dénominateur commun de l'EURO).

Toutefois, la coopération européenne appelée de ses vœux par George Marshall, suffira-t-elle à encadrer la nouvelle Allemagne et à placer son dynamisme technique et économique au service de l'unité européenne ? Pour les anciennes victimes du *Reich*, la réponse est vitale. Le plan Marshall est un pari dangereux. Traiter les nations libérées et leur ancien dominateur sur un pied d'égalité, trente mois à peine après la fin du conflit, suscite des risques sérieux pour la stabilité politique du continent européen, à terme. Pour les Américains, toutefois, sans pressions morales, économiques ou psychologiques, jamais les Européens ne consentiront à se fédérer.

De fait, l'Europe occidentale est beaucoup plus soucieuse d'efficacité à court terme que d'harmonie fusionnelle. La France plaide un « protectionnisme transitoire », le temps pour elle de redevenir compétitive. De façon générale, les responsables européens essaient de convaincre leurs interlocuteurs américains qu'il faut d'abord sauver l'économie du vieux continent avant de réformer ses structures politiques – et non l'inverse. Sous la pression des États-Unis, une Conférence de coopération économique européenne se réunit, le 12 juillet 1947. Elle réunit à Paris, les seize États ayant accepté le plan Marshall : la Belgique, le Danemark, la France, la Grèce, l'Irlande, l'Islande, l'Italie, le Luxembourg, les Pays-Bas, le Royaume-Uni, la Suède, la Suisse (avec le Liechtenstein). La Norvège accepte de participer contrairement à la Finlande qui poursuit sa politique de stricte neutralité vis-à-vis de son voisin envahissant[8].

Las pour les vues américaines, les Seize s'entendent seulement sur la forme, en créant un *Comité de coopération économique européen*, qui préfigure en théorie seulement la future agence supranationale chargée de gérer la répartition et la finalité des fonds américains (*Cf. infra*, l'OECE). Sur le fond, la conférence échoue : les nations concernées veulent bien de l'aide américaine, mais la marche vers l'unité politique et économique ne les intéresse pas. Les Européens envoient uniquement des listes d'achats à

7 Cité par Bruna Bagnato dans « *Le plan Marshall et l'union douanière italo-française* » dans *Le plan Marshall et le relèvement économique de l'Europe*, Comité pour l'histoire économique et financière de la France, 1993, p. 390.

8 Circulaire de Robert Murphy aux ambassadeurs accrédités auprès des pays participant à la Conférence pour la coopération économique européenne, 7 septembre 1947, NARA, DOS, Central Files, 840.50 Recovery/9–747.

Washington. Rien n'indique qu'ils songent à stabiliser leurs finances intérieures, ni à adopter le libre-échange, ni à opérer une distinction sérieuse entre les importations de ravitaillement et les achats d'équipements. Bien pis, aucune agence européenne ne se profile, pour administrer le plan Marshall[9].

1.2/ L'OECE, bref laboratoire des États-Unis d'Europe

En fait, dès le départ, on n'ose pas donner à l'OECE un caractère supranational. On préfère encore le modèle de l'inter-gouvernementalité : un secrétaire général la préside et rend des comptes au Conseil de l'OECE, composé des représentants des États membres (qui en réfèrent à leurs gouvernements), dont de fortes personnalités qui conservent leurs attaches nationales (les Belges Paul-Henri Spaak et Paul Van Zeeland, le néerlandais Dirk Stikker, le Britannique Anthony Eden). Si l'histoire était logique et déterministe, l'Union européenne telle qu'elle se développe aujourd'hui, devrait descendre en ligne directe de l'OECE instituée le 16 avril 1948, devenue finalement OCDE, laquelle a du mal aujourd'hui à s'imposer comme un acteur puissant et efficace des relations économiques internationales. La CECA, et la CEE dériveront d'une autre branche de l'histoire européenne.

Dans les faits, l'interlocuteur américain de l'OECE, l'*Economic Cooperation Administration* (ECA) garde la haute main à travers des accords strictement bilatéraux, inspirés d'une gestion « businesslike ». De fait, au moment où Paul G. Hoffman prend la direction du plan Marshall et celui où l'OECE s'installe, l'administration Truman et le Congrès ont tacitement renoncé à user de leur position de force extraordinaire pour imposer une union douanière et financière, une autorité européenne supranationale et une division géographique du travail. Pourquoi cet échec ? L'unité européenne se révèle un projet trop idéaliste pour s'imposer tant que les considérations matérielles les plus prosaïques conditionnent les esprits. En 1947-1948, la priorité reste de revigorer un continent menacé par l'hégémonie soviétique et tout aussi inquiet d'un éventuel revanchisme allemand.

Aussi, la nouvelle administration Eisenhower (1953-1961) considère-t-elle son arrivée au pouvoir comme la dernière chance de fédérer l'Europe, pourvu que les États-Unis se montrent moins pusillanimes et exercent enfin les pressions adéquates. La Communauté européenne de défense devient alors pendant 18 mois le vecteur principal des projets fédéralistes américains, défendus avec passion par le secrétaire d'Etat John Foster Dulles. Nous ne pouvons pas nous étendre ici sur cet épisode aussi pénible pour l'amitié franco-américaine qu'essentiel à la genèse de l'Europe politique. Signalons néanmoins deux points cruciaux. Sur le fond, l'armée fédérale européenne devait annuler l'antagonisme franco-allemand (disparition des armées nationales, les forces armées européennes obéissant au SACEUR américain et à un Commissaire européen supra-étatique). Sur la forme, l'administration Eisenhower-Dulles exerça les pressions médiatico-politiques les plus extrêmes pour contraindre

9 Mémorandum de William T. Philipps (*International Resources Division*) au secrétaire d'État adjoint pour les Affaires économiques (Paul Nitze), 4 mars 1948, NARA, DOS, Central Files 840.50 Recovery/3–448.

les députés français à ratifier le traité d'armée européenne. À l'arrivée, l'alliance des gaullistes et des communistes ajoutée à certains députés centristes vint à bout d'un projet échevelé dangereux pour la survie du continent européen. À l'arrivée, la CED est un projet initialement militaire qui se transforme en projet purement politique, d'essence fédéraliste. Nous retrouvons cette analogie avec le plan Marshall, un projet humanitaire et économique aussitôt transmué en projet stratégique. Cela apparaît même pire à l'arrivée puisque contrairement à l'économie, le militaire reste jusqu'à aujourd'hui le domaine le plus régalien et le plus réfractaire à une fusion fédérale. Dès lors, la stratégie européenne des États-Unis se modifie en profondeur.

En effet, le regard et l'action des États-Unis sur l'Europe évoluent radicalement après l'échec parlementaire ultime de la CED, en décidant à l'automne 1954 de réactiver le pacte de Bruxelles de 1948, en créant l'unique institution européenne compétente en matière de défense jusqu'au traité de Lisbonne de 2008 : l'Union de l'Europe Occidentale. La République Fédérale Allemande entrant enfin sur un pied d'égalité dans l'OTAN, les dirigeants américains constatent malgré tout qu'une partie de leur programme se réalise. Aux conférences de Londres (septembre 1954), puis de Paris (octobre 1954), la délégation américaine n'y dit presque rien, sinon – acte capital – confirmer l'engagement militaire des États-Unis en Europe (déclaration solennelle du président Eisenhower)[10]. Et nous tenons là, la clé des États-Unis en Europe : isolationnisme et ingérence sont les deux pôles, les deux tentations entre lesquelles l'action de l'Amérique s'inscrit. L'absence de garantie américaine a permis l'agression allemande en 1914 et 1939. Un excès de zèle peut provoquer un rejet européen, face à un projet trop « Made in America ».

2/ REGAIN DE L'EUROPE ÉCONOMIQUE : ENGOUEMENT DE L'AMÉRIQUE POUR LA CECA – LA SUPRANATIONALITÉ DE LA CEE EN QUESTION

2.1/ Le prêt symbolique à la CECA ($ 100 millions) : primat de l'Europe supra-étatique sur les progrès industriels (1953-1954)

En 1953, la CECA – la sœur de la CED en matière industrielle, et comme elle la fille de Jean Monnet – est par contre signée, ratifiée et mise en application. Tout reste à faire cependant pour asseoir le prestige et le pouvoir de la Haute Autorité du charbon et de l'acier vis-à-vis du Conseil européen des gouvernements, que Jean Monnet veut reléguer à un rôle consultatif. La CECA, en tant qu'organisation supranationale, doit prouver son indépendance vis-à-vis des États souverains[11]. Comme souvent en matière constitutionnelle, les questions financières servent de support à une souveraineté naissante. La CECA lève notamment des taxes (50 millions $ en 1953). Selon le schéma

10 Déclaration Eisenhower, Tg. n° 3175-88 de Washington, signé Basdevant, 5 mars 1955, MAE, *Quai d'Orsay*, série *Service des pactes 1947-1970*, boîte n° 111, sous-dossier «*Union de l'Europe Occidentale, novembre 1954-décembre 1956*».

11 «*Monnet's Views on European Union*», compte-rendu d'une conversation entre Jean Monnet, Franz Ezel et Dirk Spierenberg (membres de la Haute Autorité) et des représentants du département d'État, du Trésor et du *Mutual Security Assistance* (future *Foreign Operations Administration*, FOA), Washington, 4 juin 1953, NARA, DOS, PPS files, lot 64 D 563, "Europe, 1952-53".

keynésien majoritairement en vogue, elle doit aussi amplifier son action par le levier de la dette publique, en empruntant.

Du côté de l'administration républicaine hostile au *New Deal*, personne n'est pas dupe. Vue du Potomac et non du Rhin, la CECA ressemble tout de même beaucoup à ces superstructures dirigistes héritées du *New Deal*, comme la Tennessey Valley Authority. Par ailleurs, au cœur de ce schéma compliqué et spécieux, l'administration Eisenhower est *a priori* acquise à la liberté du *Big Business*. Elle considère donc d'abord avec suspicion toute idée de régulation institutionnelle imposée à la bonne marche des affaires, surtout si on demande au contribuable américain de la financer. Au-delà de la rentabilité espérée, le but de l'administration Eisenhower est de faire reconnaître la Haute Autorité comme une institution au-dessus des États européens, capable de dialoguer d'égale à égale avec les États-Unis en s'endettant auprès d'eux. Sous l'impulsion de J. Monnet, et comme pour la CED, Washington transforme le moyen (produire 20 millions de tonnes de coke en plus et passer de 40 à 52 millions de tonnes d'acier) en fin absolue (l'Europe supranationale).

En 1953-1954, l'administration Eisenhower place toute son énergie au service des idées de Jean Monnet. En février 1953, le secrétaire d'État Foster Dulles commence son voyage inaugural en Europe par une escale spéciale au siège de la Haute Autorité, à Luxembourg. Il veut ainsi montrer à la face de l'Europe que la CECA est l'héritière et la dépositaire d'anciennes fonctions gouvernementales souveraines. De même, Dulles s'engage auprès de son ami français à nommer un ambassadeur américain auprès de la CECA, autre que celui nommé auprès de l'OTAN ou de l'OCDE, celles-ci n'étant pas des organisations supranationales[12]. Dans cet esprit, les 3 et 4 juin 1953, Eisenhower et Dulles invitent Jean Monnet en visite officielle à Washington en lui accordant le protocole des chefs de gouvernements, et en le logeant à Blair House. Une campagne de presse téléguidée précède son séjour[13].

2.2/ Des centaines de millions de dollars pour subventionner les concurrents européens des sidérurgistes américains ?

Le plus dur commence. Car entre les deux principaux ministres, le secrétaire d'État Dulles et le secrétaire au Trésor Humphrey, commence une lutte où le premier incarne une diplomatie idéaliste, et le second la composante technico-réaliste du parti au pouvoir. Dès le départ, le secrétaire d'État soutient l'ampleur de l'emprunt initialement souhaité par J. Monnet : 500 millions $[14]. Cette somme formidable équivaut à 5% du déficit budgétaire américain de l'exercice 1954, à un moment où l'administration réduit autant que possible l'aide civile et militaire aux alliés (Indochine exceptée). Pour sa part, le secrétaire au Trésor, George Humphrey, dans une lettre à Foster Dulles

12 Accord entre les deux hommes, rappelé dans la lettre de J. Monnet à J.F. Dulles du 1er décembre 1954, NARA, DOS, 850.33/12-154.

13 *"Farewell to the Past"*, interview donnée à *Newsweek*, 16/2/1953. Dans le même numéro, un portrait : *"Monnet, Europe's Number 1 Man of Ideas and Hope"*, p. 42-43.

14 *"Position to be Taken on a Proposal for au US Loan to the High Authority of the Coal and Steel Community"*, note du directeur du secrétariat exécutif du département d'Etat (Scott) au secrétaire d'Etat par intérim (Bedell Smith), 7 décembre 1953, NARA, DOS, Central Files, 850.33/12-753.

critique l'insistance de Jean Monnet à traiter uniquement avec l'État américain pour des motifs de prestige politique, alors que la Banque mondiale conviendrait mieux[15]. Sur le fond, Humphrey se fait aussi le porte-parole des intérêts sidérurgiques américains en proie à une crise structurelle. La fiscalité des États-Unis doit-elle encourager la concurrence des producteurs rivaux ?

Le 9 janvier, le département d'État apprend que le Trésor, le bureau du Budget et la *Foreign Operations Administration* écartent d'aller au-delà de $ 100 millions. Et comme le Congrès refuse aussi d'augmenter le budget de l'aide à l'étranger, les diplomates contraignent le Pentagone à verser les 100 millions de dollars, intégralement à partir de son budget, par définition destiné aux dépenses militaires. À l'arrivée, en soutenant la CECA, les États-Unis renoncent à certaines situations dominantes, dans l'intérêt de l'unité européenne[16]. L'Amérique tolère que l'Europe des Six se montre protectionniste à ses débuts. Elle renonce à sa rente de situation sidérurgique depuis 1945 et relève le défi d'une l'émulation qu'elle aura elle-même suscitée. Mais dans l'esprit de tous, une fois l'équilibre rétabli, on en reviendrait de toute façon au *Business as usual*, c'est-à-dire à une concurrence impitoyable, tempérée par le droit international... d'inspiration américaine...

2.3/ La CEE ? Favoriser un concurrent durant une génération

Contre toute attente, les États-Unis s'impliquent peu dans la CEE naissante. Il s'agit pour eux d'une solution confédérale (sans voir bizarrement les pouvoirs supranationaux de la Commission européenne) et non fédérale, malgré des champs nouveaux de coopération jamais abordés jusqu'à présent comme la Politique agricole commune. Pour autant, l'administration Eisenhower ferme à nouveau les yeux devant un Marché commun beaucoup plus intergouvernemental que supranational, à condition qu'il serve de deuxième étape, après la CECA, vers une fédération. L'administration comprend que si on empêche le Tarif Extérieur Commun d'exister, on casse l'intégration économique de l'Europe et, à terme, son unification politique[17]. Par conséquent, l'Amérique accepte de se heurter provisoirement à des barrières douanières préjudiciables. C'est dans cette optique associant encore et toujours l'économie aux problématiques sécuritaires, que l'administration Kennedy suivante tente l'expérience du « Grand Dessein ».

3/ DU « GRAND DESSEIN » DE KENNEDY AU *BUSINESS AS USUAL*

De fait, la nouvelle génération arrivant au pouvoir embrasse enfin du regard les premiers arpents de la terre promise. Néanmoins, celle-ci ne ruisselle pas de miel ni

15 Lettre de H. Humphrey à J.F. Dulles, 8 décembre 1953, NARA, DOS, Central Files, 850.33/12-853.

16 Lettre de J.F. Dulles à H. Macmillan, ministre britannique des Affaires étrangères ; 10 décembre 1955, Central Files, 840.1901/12-1055, NARA, DOS, Central Files, 394.41/4-2861.

17 Lettre du conseiller économique du président Eisenhower – Clarence B. Randall – à J.F. Dulles, 4 octobre 1956, Eisenhower Library (Abilene, Kansas), Ann Whitman File, Eisenhower Diaries.

de lait. Les présidences Kennedy-Johnson découvrent ce qu'elles savaient : l'Amérique a provoqué l'émergence d'un concurrent économique sérieux et compétitif, avec la création d'un marché commun et – demain, qui sait ? – d'un rival politique. L'Europe représente tout de même 30% des exportations industrielles US et 40% des exportations agricoles US[18]. En réalité, le contexte a profondément évolué depuis le plan Marshall et le pacte atlantique de 1949. Dans les années 1960, les États-Unis poussent leur politique dans deux directions. La première orientation consiste à éviter une troisième force capable de s'immiscer dans le face-à-face américano-soviétique. Il s'agit en particulier de limiter la capacité de nuisance de la France gaullienne et de ne pas la laisser organiser l'Europe sous sa prédominance. La seconde perspective consiste à empêcher l'Europe de perpétuer son protectionnisme et de nuire aux exportations américaines, lors des négociations du Kennedy Round.

Pour atteindre ces deux objectifs, le jour de la fête nationale, le 4 juillet 1962, Kennedy prononce un discours aussi célèbre que symbolique à Philadelphie, à l'occasion du 175e anniversaire de la constitution : il y proclame que « les États-Unis sont prêts à une déclaration d'interdépendance (...) et prêts à discuter avec une Europe unie les moyens et la méthode de former un partenariat atlantique concret ». Il est difficile, aujourd'hui encore, d'assigner un contenu exact au projet du jeune président. Il s'agirait de créer une unité politique entre deux fédérations sœurs qui formeraient alors les « deux piliers » du monde libre. Toutefois, on constate derechef une imbrication du stratégico-politique, de la sécurité et de l'économie. De fait, les dirigeants américains échouent à dissimuler, malgré une rhétorique idéaliste, que leurs projets cherchent à institutionnaliser la direction américaine du monde occidental[19].

Chronologiquement, en effet, le « Grand Dessein » se concrétise en premier par un volet militaire, avec le projet de Force multilatérale : des équipages multinationaux manieraient les sous-marins nucléaires de l'OTAN. L'idée n'a aucune chance de séduire de Gaulle, puisque les États-Unis garderaient un droit de veto sur l'emploi des missiles Polaris. Sur le plan commercial, ensuite, le « Grand Dessein » se traduit par le vote du *Trade Expansion Act*, qui autorise le président à réduire les droits de douane de moitié en cinq ans, voire à les éliminer entièrement, dans certains secteurs, en échange de l'ouverture de la Communauté économique européenne aux importations américaines[20]. Le *Dillon Round* (1960-1961) aboutira à un abaissement tarifaire de 6,5% en moyenne entre la CEE et les États-Unis tandis que le *Kennedy Round* (1964-1967) réduira les tarifs industriels de 35%, sans conclure sur les produits agricoles. Sur le

18 *US Concern at the Rejection of the US Agricultural Package by the EEC Representatives at GATT XXIV:6 Negotiations*, conversation entre George W. Ball, sous-secrétaire d'État aux Affaires économiques et Louis Scheyven, ambassadeur de Belgique, 28 avril 1961, NARA, DOS, Central files, Central Files, 394.41/4-2861.

19 Conation de Gaulle-Kennedy, Elysée, 2 juin 1961, *Foreign Relations of the United States*, 1961-1963, vol. XIII, Washington, USGPO, 1994, doc. n° 11. « Nous ne pouvons pas échapper à la conclusion qu'un seul gouvernement se propose de dénier à la Grande-Bretagne l'entrée dans le marché commun à cause d'une relation historique entre celle-ci et les États-Unis, et selon un calcul pour éliminer la présence américaine en Europe et l'interdépendance transatlantique. Cela contredit directement les principes élémentaires régissant la défense de l'Europe occidentale et celle des États-Unis, à savoir l'indivisibilité et la vitalité d'une Alliance qui dépend de la confiance mutuelle des deux côtés de l'Atlantique ». Télégramme pour la mission américaine auprès des communautés européennes, 28 janvier 1963, NARA, DOS, Central Files, 375.42/1–2863.

20 Geir Lundestad, *« Empire » by Integration. The United States and European Integration, 1945-1997*, Oxford University Press, 1997, chap. 2 : "*European Unity and Atlantic Partnership*", p. 32-75.

reste, le général de Gaulle fera avorter les beaux principes unanimistes kennedyens, en tête l'entrée du Royaume-Uni dans la CEE.

Là encore, l'Amérique soutient cette dernière au nom de ses objectifs géopolitiques : « Notre objectif politique à propos de l'élargissement de la CEE (Royaume-Uni et Danemark) consiste à donner une consistance ferme au noyau dur des principales puissances européennes selon des principes communs fondamentaux au sein d'une union économique vouée aux mêmes objectifs politiques. Notre position sur les négociations entre la CEE et l'AELE a pour but de donner à la Grande-Bretagne un levier pour négocier séparément [du Commonwealth] en vue d'une communauté européenne forte et cohérente »[21]. Toutefois, celle-ci ne se révèle pas nécessairement neutre en termes de balance commerciale. Elle finit même par leur apparaître contraire, comme l'avoue Kennedy, en privé : « J'ai des inquiétudes sur l'impact économique sur les États-Unis d'une éventuelle entrée de l'Angleterre dans le Marché commun (...) Bien sûr, jusqu'à présent, notre position a consisté à encourager l'expansion de la CEE pour des raisons politiques (...) Pour autant, si cela doit entraîner des conséquences graves sur nous, nous nous retrouverions avec de graves décisions à prendre »[22]. Pourtant, à l'arrivée Whitehall ne trouvera jamais de meilleur allié en la circonstance qu'auprès de Washington.

En face, de Gaulle défendra vigoureusement le principe d'un Tarif extérieur commun aux membres de la CEE, que les Américains qualifient désormais de « mur douanier ». Il y trouvera aussi un argument puissant contre Londres, pour contrer la vieille préférence impériale du Commonwealth. Dès 1962, éclate la première guerre commerciale avec la Communauté économique européenne à propos des produits chimiques de base[23]. Dans les faits, l'opposition entre le Grand Dessein de Kennedy et l'Europe gaullienne, est le prologue d'un affrontement économique, appelé à devenir la règle dans les relations américano-européennes. Pour les États-Unis, c'est une chose d'avoir anticipé cette concurrence, c'en est une tout autre de la vivre et d'en subir les conséquences concrètes.

*

Au terme des vingt premières années de la *Pax americana* en Europe, les États-Unis ont emporté l'essentiel : ils ont résolu la plus grande question internationale depuis le congrès de Vienne, la question allemande. Une Allemagne pacifique s'insère enfin dans un Occident stable, à condition que l'Occident inclue les États-Unis : l'intégration européenne d'une part (le couple franco-allemand en réalité) ; la garantie de sécurité américaine à travers l'OTAN, d'autre part. La sortie définitive de l'isolationnisme par les États-Unis est inhérente à l'intégration de l'Allemagne dans le jeu pacifique des

21 Télégramme circulaire envoyé aux ambassades américaines en Europe, 27 octobre 1961, NARA, DOS, Central Files, 375.800/10-2761.

22 Mémorandum présidentiel pour le sous-secrétaire d'État George Ball, 21 août 1961, NARA, DOS, NSAMs : Lot 72 D 316.

23 *Current Economic Developments*, juin 1962, NARA, DOS, E/CBA/REP Files: FRC 72 A 6248.

nations. Dans ce grand jeu, le commerce international n'est qu'un moyen, pas une fin en soi.

Sur la méthode, les États-Unis ont su s'adapter, passant d'une forme de chantage à coups de dollars, à une diplomatie fine se résumant au slogan : ni isolationnisme, ni ingérence dans la vie des États-Européens. A partir de l'échec du plan Marshall comme catalyseur de l'intégration économique européenne, puis de l'échec géo-militaire encore plus magistral de la CED en 1954, les conceptions américaines sur le processus européen épousent trois principes : d'un côté, la création des États-Unis d'Europe demeure le souhait ultime. D'un autre côté, ils tolèrent l'émergence d'une concurrence commerciale européenne, facilitée par un protectionnisme à l'échelle d'une génération. Enfin, les États-Unis laissent les Européens décider eux-mêmes du rythme de leurs progrès institutionnels. « *It's politics stupid* »

Modern Corporate Growth after the Modern Economic Growth: A Comparative Study of General Electric and Westinghouse Electric 1946-2000

Kenichi Miyata
Meiji University, Japan

Introduction

In this chapter, I focus on the historical change of the corporate growth and strategy of the U.S. modern industrial enterprise during the second half of twentieth century: often called the period of shifting from the modern economic growth through industrialization to through de-industrialization. The period witnessed a major change in the U.S. economy and business enterprises. Industrial sectors which took the significant role to the modern economic growth as Kuznets emphasized moved to another form of manufacturing from the 1970s as Cohen and Zysman stressed[1]. It involved a shift to the reconstruction of the leading U.S. enterprises and adjusting from a prolonged period of rapid economic growth to one of slower growth, starting in 1970[2].

In the process of change, U.S. enterprises declined in dominance, not only internationally but also in domestic markets[3]. Whereas they accounted for 78 out of the top 100 firms in 1956, by 1990 the number was reduced to only 33 of the top 100 global

1 Simon Kuznets, *Modern Economic Growth* (New Haven: Yale University Press, 1966), p.492; Stephen S. Cohen and John Zysman, *Manufacturing Matters* (New York: Basic Books, 1987), p. 260.

2 Louis Galambos, "The U.S. Corporate Economy in the Twentieth Century," in Stanley L. Engerman and Robert E. Gallman (eds), *The Cambridge Economic History of the United States Vol. III*, 2000, p. 959; Robert J. Gordon, *The Rise and Fall of American Growth* (Princeton: Princeton University Press, 2016), p. 7-8.

3 Louis Galambos and Joseph Pratt, *The Rise of Corporate Commonwealth* (New York: Basic Books, 1988), p. 201.

mining and manufacturing firms[4]. However, the decline was uneven amongst them. While a number of large U.S. enterprises were dropped from the top 200 list by 1997, 28 enterprises with histories going back to 1880 continued to remain in the ranking from 1917 to 1997[5]. This raises the question of why some of the larger U.S. industrial enterprises sustained growth in an economic environment of change while others were in decline.

The divergence of corporate growth amongst the U.S. enterprises has been a topic of discussion in business history. The debates to date have focused on the fundamental factors of competitive success or failure between industrial enterprises in the second half of twentieth century. Alfred Chandler, the renowned business historian of the American modern business enterprise, emphasized the internal factors of the organization, that top managers chose unrelated diversification for short-term gains rather than related diversification for long-term health and growth, while others emphasized external factors such as the large industrial organization not adapting itself to changes in the supply side and new technologies, such as the internet following the modularization of production instead of vertically integrated organization, or changes in demand side of individuated markets with long-term informal relations replacing managerial hierarchy[6].

One of the reasons for this discrepancy in the argument seems to come from the different premise on the perspective for economic growth. As he partially relied on Kuznets' data, Chandler takes a close stance of the perspective on Kuznets' modern economic growth and discusses the corporate modern growth, while others argue with based on another form of technology and market gradually emerged from the 1970s[7]. Another reason is that each side discusses own story with citing the different enterprises. For instance, when they refer to PC industry which is a new and vital industry in the post war period, Chandler mentions to IBM while others use Dell as its example[8]. It leads to the ambiguity regarding the rise and fall of the modern industrial enterprise in the period.

Nitin Nohria et al., on the other hand, examine the point as corporate transformations undertaken by a number of U.S. industrial enterprises listed on the *Fortune* 100. They reveal the different changes between them and propose four types of transformation[9]. Although their study provides the historical insights of the decades regarding the divergence of corporate growth, the scope focuses on the period between 1974 and

4 Leslie Hannah and Kazuo Wada, *Miezaru te no hangyaku* [Delusions of Durable Dominance or the Invisible Hand Strikes Back] (Tokyo: Yuhikaku, 2001), p. 58.

5 Francisco Louçã and Sandro Mendonça, "Steady Change," *Industrial and Corporate Change*, Vol.11, No. 4, 2002, p. 818.

6 Alfred D. Chandler, Jr., "The Enduring Logic of Industrial Success." *Harvard Business Review* Vol. 90, No. 2, 1990, p. 130-140 ; Richard N. Langlois, "The Vanishing Hand," *Industrial and Corporate Change*, Vol. 12, No. 2, 2003, p. 351-385 ; Naomi R. Lamoreaux, Daniel M Raff, and Peter Temin, "Beyond Markets and Hierarchies," *American Historical Review*, Vol. 108, No. 2, 2003, p. 404-433. It could be another word for the difference between Langlois and Lamoreaux et al. as "in the end there are markets" in the former and "in the beginning there were markets" in the latter.

7 Alfred D. Chandler, Jr., *Scale and Scope* (Cambridge: Belknap Press of Harvard University Press, 1990), p. 3-8.

8 Examining the history of the computer industry in his later books firstly published in 2001, Chandler discusses Dell and other computer firms too. See Alfred D. Chandler, Jr., *Inventing the Electronic Century* (Cambridge: Harvard University Press, 2005).

9 Nitin Nohria, Davis Dyer and Frederick Dalzell, *Changing Fortunes* (New York: John Wiley & Sons, 2002), p. 259.

2000 through relatively quantitative approach, which leave the question of the linkage from an industrial to a post-industrial economy on corporate growth.

To understand the detail process of divergent between the U.S. modern industrial enterprise during the period, my approach takes comparative case studies; General Electric Company (hereafter GE) and Westinghouse Electric Corporation (hereafter WH), as derived from historical data and documents[10]. Both enterprises were rivals of the typical modern industrial enterprises that were centered in the electrical and electronics industry, thus providing for similar business structures that helps reduce the bias of dissimilarity in the comparative research. In addition, these two enterprises are symbolic examples of U.S. enterprises that took contrasting transformation paths toward the end of the century[11].

My analysis of GE and WH focuses on corporate strategy. Douglass North emphasized the intentionality of the players (or organizations) to understanding the process of economic institutional change, because economic change is for the most part a deliberate process shaped by the perceptions of the actors regarding the consequences of their actions[12]. This suggests that it should examine the corporate strategy as the perceptions of the actors to understand this economic change and divergent of corporate growth in the U.S. in the latter half of the century.

I probe the corporate strategy as a set of actor actions. In the process of change to technologies and markets, the top management of industrial enterprises make decisions regarding prospects. Decision-making or corporate strategy is a classic topic in business history and other related fields, such as management studies and economics. From a number of studies on decision-making, at least three basic actions can be derived for the process of decision-making to behaviour. Specifically, what top management perceives from the external environment, what they see as prospects or conceptions for the future, and what they take in terms of actual actions. Managerial visaction (a combination of vision and action) represents the set of three top management actions (perception, conception, actual action), and is hereafter used to facilitate explanation. To empirically examine the disparity between business enterprises from an action-based perspective, the framework of visaction is a means of consolidating a variety of historical documents and materials for this purpose. Although some theoretical discussions provide more detail on analytical frameworks, difficulties can arise in an empirical examination of historical documents. Moreover, a looser framework can sometimes help in drawing in more historical dynamics over the long-term scope.

10 The historical materials for this study are collected by the author at the miSci Archives, Schenectady, NY, and the Library and Archives of the Heinz History Center, Pittsburgh, PA.

11 Nitin Nohria, Davis Dyer and Frederick Dalzell, *Changing Fortunes, op. cit*, p. 3-26.

12 Douglass C. North, *Understanding the Process of Economic Change* (Princeton: Princeton University Press, 2005), p. viii-ix.

1/ A BUSINESS HISTORY OF GE AND WH FROM 1946 TO 2000[13]

1.1/ Divergence of Business Competitiveness

GE and WH gradually extended their gap in differences after the Second World War. Although GE, on average, was already twice the size of WH in terms of sales and market share as shown in the Figure 1 and 2, both firms dominated the conventional steam turbine market in the U.S. during the postwar period. However, while they increasingly progressed their expansions and diversification of businesses, such as embedding in the military and social industrial complex, their relative business competitiveness began to diversify in their traditional core business, conventional steam turbines, although their total profitability converged in the late 1960s when confronted by foreign competitors, as shown in Figure 3.

FIGURE 1 **NET SALES ($ MILLION) FOR GE AND WH AND THE RESULTING GAP (WH/GE %), 1946-1970.**

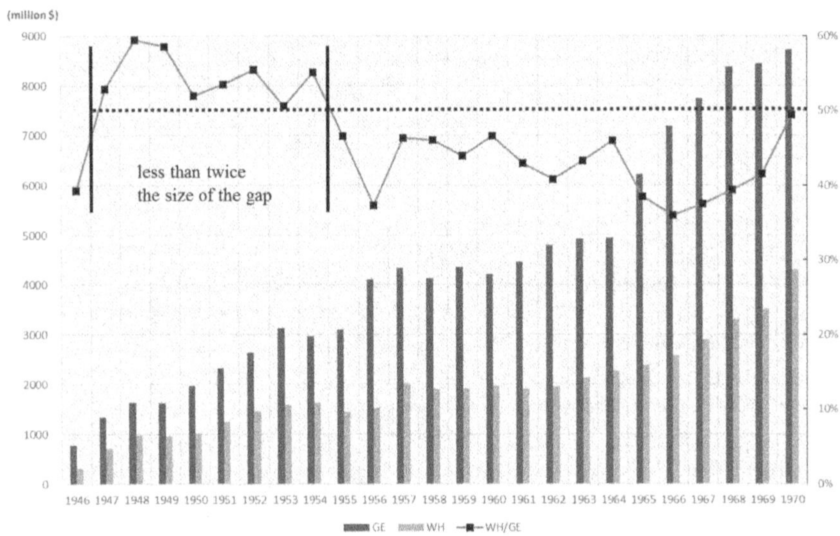

Source: Compilation of data from GE, *Annual Report*, various years and WH, *Annual Report*, various years.

These corporate performances were the result that GE and WH pursued mostly the same visaction from 1946 to 1958. They were more or less obligated to diversify into military products, partly because it was perceived to be a public responsibility at the time. This led both firms to become embedded into parts of the military-industrial complex. In the expansion of military business, GE took the lead converting the steam turbine business to produce large custom-designed products, which required more human resources to build. Consequently, under a similar diversification strategy, the size of firm and its availability of business resources became factors of competition

13 The references on this case study are omitted due to page limits. For the completed references, see Kenichi Miyata, "Corporate Transformation, Diversification, and Managerial Perception: A Comparative Study of General Electric Company and Westinghouse Electric Corporation," PhD diss., Meiji University, 2016.

in the conventional steam turbine industry. While GE had access to sufficient human resources for both its military and turbine businesses, WH was challenged by a shortage of engineers as more engineers were required than they were able to secure. Subsequently WH experienced a decline in profitability in the turbine business and, by 1960, had also left the jet engine business. While the two enlarged the gap in their military and turbine businesses, they still shared a number of similarities.

After appeasing a huge demand for steam turbines, the top managements of both firms shared perceptions of the external environment and had similar conceptions of the future, but each took their own actions on diversification between 1959 and 1970. Both firms found potential business in education, health and community development, which appeared to have the support of the government's new social welfare program. Although they both entered into these markets, WH demonstrated a stronger commitment through the purchase of new businesses, while GE also established these businesses while it was expanding its international business.

FIGURE 2 **MARKET SHARE OF CONVENTIONAL TURBINE GENERATOR ORDERS, 1946-1970.**

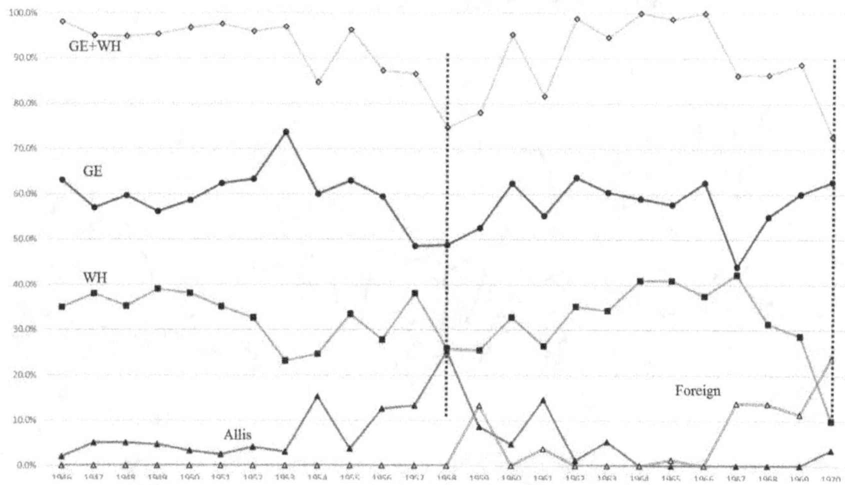

Original source: Tabulation of Electrical Equipment Antitrust Actions data, filed at S.D.N.Y.

Source: Compilation of data from Ralph G. Sultan, *Pricing in the Electrical Oligopoly, Vol. 2* (Boston, MA: Division of Research, 1974): table 13.2., p. 228.

Note: Orders by the U.S. utility and industrial organizations (aggregate kw. basis)

When they started to become embedded in the social-industrial complex, in addition to the military-industrial complex, the turbine business had entry into a new industrial environment. The U.S. electric utilities gradually began awarding contracts to foreign firms and also sought new products, such as gas turbine and nuclear power in addition to much larger steam turbines. GE was able to respond to the demand and maintain competitiveness for these products. Being successful in attaining almost the same market share in nuclear power as GE, WH was unable to manage massive orders of other turbines. Furthermore, its product quality and customer reputation was in decline in the late 1960s due to product technological issues. As a result, foreign competitors such as Brown Boveri and Parsons started to displace WH on new orders. A major reason of this problem was an inadequate investment in the turbine business, other than for nuclear power. Even though WH saw its competitiveness decline in its traditional business, WH still managed to improve corporate performance through diversification, while GE, by 1970, was seeing its profitability decline through diversification (see Figure 3).

1.2/ Divergence of Financial Standings

The next decade, the 1970s, saw a divergence between the two firms in terms of their respective financial standings. Both firms relied on strategic planning to try to maximize corporate performance in a stagnant economy. The top managements of GE and WH eventually took different managerial visaction in the 1970s. Particularly after the first oil crisis in 1973, the respective top managements took different approaches to get through the national economic decline while also being concerned with double-digit inflation.

FIGURE 3 **OPERATING PROFIT AND NET PROFIT TO SALES, 1947-1980.**

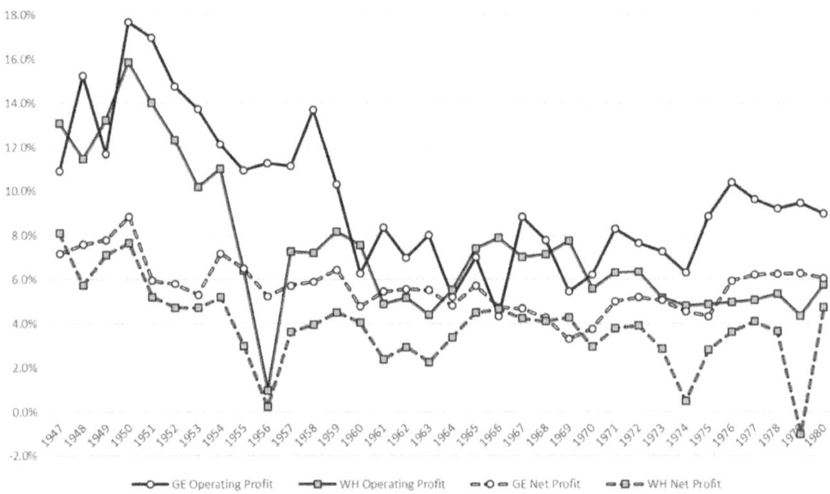

Source: Compilation of data from GE, *Annual Report*, various years and WH, *Annual Report*, various years.

GE top management, under CEO Reginald Jones, saw the most significant influence of the first oil crisis on the economic system to be galloping inflation, and began seeking a cure for inflation while divesting unprofitable businesses. For that reason, GE merged with Utah International in 1976, the largest acquisition at the time, as a valuable hedge against worldwide inflation. Although it was a diversification into an unrelated business line, natural resources, GE proceeded on the basis that it would improve profitability, as Figure 3 presents. In addition, their internal studies on countermeasure to inflation resulted in the launch of a management education program in 1979, called COIN (Effectively Coping with Inflation).

While reinforcing its financial standing, GE embarked on multiple responses to cope with the energy crisis. GE did not focus on a particular technology, such as nuclear energy, but instead provided full-line power equipment and infrastructures. GE, in particular, received numerous orders for gas turbine after electric utilities became concerned over nuclear regulations, technological developments and uncertainty over the supply of uranium and plutonium treatment.

WH, on the other hand, attempted to cope with the energy crisis and rampant inflation by focusing on nuclear power and transforming back into an electrical equipment firm. Their logic was that the main long-term solution to the energy problem was to have more installations of nuclear power, which would use uranium as a possible candidate to substitute oil. In addition, nuclear energy would lead to a decline in the cost of electric energy, contributing to a slowdown in the rate of inflation because electricity was a basic driver for economic growth. The reason for emphasizing nuclear power was actually due to the decline of WH competitiveness in other turbine products, such as conventional steam turbines and gas turbines.

When they focused on the generation, transmission, distribution and efficient utilization of energy, however, WH had to face unforeseen expenditures that emerged from its core businesses of steam turbines and nuclear power. WH faced a lawsuit from utilities due to problems with steam turbines and responded by repairing a number of its steam and gas turbines that had been installed since the late 1960s. To make matters worse, WH encountered a huge problem in the nuclear power business in the middle of the 1970s. From 1975 to 1979, WH had to defend against 17 lawsuits launched by 27 public utility customers, this because WH was unable to supply uranium at the guaranteed price stated in its contracts, due to a rapid rise in the price of uranium that was caused by the formation of an international cartel of uranium production companies. As a consequence, the settlements from the legal actions generated $493 million in losses. The problem related to the supply price for uranium, in particular, worsened its financial standing, extending the gap between them by the end of the 1970s. WH was, undoubtedly, facing a much harder financial position in the late 1970s than GE. By 1980, the gap had grown in financial standing as well as in lines of business and competitiveness in turbine products.

1.3/ Divergence of Corporate Transformation

Entering 1980, GE and WH had more dissimilarities than what they had in common. Even though they both competed in the power system business and had financial and other service businesses, their portfolio of other businesses resulted in extending the gap in financial standings even more than was the case prior to 1970. Nevertheless, what the top managements of GE and WH sought for corporate growth was somewhat similar. Contrary to the 1970s, GE and WH had perceived and conceived in a similar manner since 1980, but the actions taken were dissimilar, mainly because they were significantly different firms.

During the first half of the 1980s, GE and WH commenced the process of restructuring their business portfolios in the face of fierce competition with foreign firms. Even though both entered the factory automation business and sold off electrical appliances, there were increasingly more differences due to their divergence in business operations. GE took a "No.1 or No.2" strategy under new CEO Jack Welch and executed its restructuring through a series of large scale M&A. GE obtained software services, insurance companies and disposed of its natural resources businesses. Meanwhile, WH was also acquiring and divesting businesses though with a far less volume of M&A. WH acquired nuclear service, beverage bottling, broadcasting, and divested some of its broadcasting and businesses in the educational division.

The last half of 1980s was a business growth period for both GE and WH, centered on M&A and boosted by an international relaxation of monetary restrictions that resulted in the development and expansion of the global financial market. Both companies rode this wave. GE expanded their financial service subsidiaries through M&A, and merged RCA and other businesses to strengthen its holdings in lines such as medical equipment, plastics and locomotives. GE parted with parts of its RCA business, NBC being the exception, and business related to factory automation and TV manufacturing. WH mergers, on the other hand, focused mainly on broadcasting, furniture, nuclear service, real estate, and business related to residential construction, while it divested elevator, transmission and distribution equipment businesses. Perceiving financial services as vital source of profit, WH took an internal growth strategy for its financial business whereas GE pursued an external growth strategy.

The more global competition increased in the 1980s, the more the existing business portfolio, a reflection of past decisions, became the basis for corporate growth. Under this restructuring, the common business for GE and WH, steam turbines, contributed to an expansion of the gap in business competitiveness. GE maintained its competitiveness and leading firm position, including for the new product (i.e. combined cycle gas turbine), while WH relied on foreign firms of its strategic alliance as one of followers. Although WH was still a leading firm in nuclear power, the demand for nuclear power in the 1970s was lower than anticipated and worsened after the Three Mile Island accident in 1979. The low competitiveness eventually led WH to split its power system business.

The divergence of corporate growth became the turning point when both had to pay for huge losses in their financial businesses. GE was capable of absorbing the loss and then went onto rapidly expand the business for significant profit, with its strong financial standing due to an abundance of internal funds attained through higher corporate growth. WH could not cover the huge loss, having to sell a number of businesses to cover the loss. And the gap in operated businesses and financial standings resulted in different corporate transformations by the end of the century. GE was successful in combining manufacturing, services and financial businesses while WH focused on another traditional radio business from the 1920s, broadcasting, and turned itself into a large media company, known as the CBS Corporation. Hence, the divergence in corporate transformation can be seen as a result of a long road of managerial visaction influences and to changes in the socioeconomic environment surrounding their business enterprises.

To sum up, the result of the expanding gap between the two firms led to rather contrasting corporate transformations in the late 1990s. The gap, itself, was the consequence of an accumulation of top management actions taken over five decades. More precisely, it was determined by the interrelation between path dependency, as an accumulation of past top management actions, and corporate strategy, as a reflection of top management actions taken in each period. While the growth in sales and profit was attributed to diversification, existing business competitiveness in steam turbines, for example, was also affected by the distribution of business resources. In other words, the different diversification strategies were a result of differences in managerial visaction, and this led to an expanded gap between GE and WH.

2/ TRANSITION TO NEO-MODERN CORPORATE GROWTH

What does the history of these two corporate transformations tell us? It indicates to us the change from the modern corporate growth to neo-modern corporate growth along with the economic change during the second half of twentieth century. It designates the distinction of modern and neo-modern corporate growth through arraying the two diversification strategies. The history of the two firms leads one to separate diversifications in two categories, related diversification and unrelated diversification[14]. One can assume it would be management perceptions that would lead to the decisions on which category to pursue or divest. As these diversifications are based on top management perceptions of the socio-economic environment, it is managerial perception that gives legitimacy to any proposed diversification.

There are two possible reasons that may have influenced top management decisions on diversification. The first one would be internal reasons, such as the need to weigh available resources across the business portfolio. When top management perceived that they could utilize their existing resources, they entered new business. The second reason is external, such as entering into complementary markets. The decision to launch a new business is made when they see a link can be made to its existing business, as complementary products. Charting the GE and WH diversification paths between 1946 and 2000, the intersection of the axes can be depicted on the basis of four factors, as shown in Figure 4. The horizontal axis indicates the diversification, which is divided into related and unrelated diversifications. The vertical axis considers managerial perception, reflecting which factor top management more emphasizes to legitimate its diversification into new business.

14 Although the distinction between 'related' or 'unrelated' is ambiguous, it is used here as a sense of previous studies with based on SIC code.

In the 1940s, the top managements of GE and WH legitimized the need for related diversification such as electrical appliances and television. They stressed the linkage to markets with existing business under the benign circle of electric power between heavy electric machinery and home electrical equipment. They were also diversified into national defense business, as an aftereffect to the war. Partly in response to demands from the government, they both expanded their defense business over the next decade so that it led them to steer away from related diversification, but not to return to the unrelated business seen in the 1960s. At the end of the decade, although GE also expanded its existing and international businesses, both firms are situated at the lower right on the Figure 4, when they began highly diversifying their business by expanding the logic of the benign circle.

Their manner of diversification diverged after the 1960s. WH top management recognized a disintegration of the benign circle in the early 1970s. Facing a severe cash crisis, WH began disposing a number of unprofitable businesses, both related and unrelated businesses. WH continued to operate both related and unrelated businesses as long as they were profitable, although the logic that legitimated the diversification was already gone. When WH began restructuring its business structure in the 1980s through M&A, the same profitability of business policy used in the 1970s continued, so they expanded to low-technology businesses such as furniture. Hence, WH's diversification of the 1970s and 1980s is plotted on the center of the grid due to its unsuitability to any category on the matrix.

In the 1990s, however, WH took the path of becoming a media company through M&A&D, drawing from one of its traditional business lines, broadcasting. Because WH could not afford to hold onto its variety of business lines after the failure of its financial business, top management concentrated its resources on the most profitable businesses in the portfolio. By the end of the century, WH proceeded on related diversification in media and disposed of other manufacturing and services businesses. WH seemed to follow the logic of managerial enterprise, as emphasized by Chandler, but was implementing in a non-industrial business[15].

FIGURE 4 **CHARACTERISTICS OF DIVERSIFICATION FOR POSTWAR GE AND WH.**

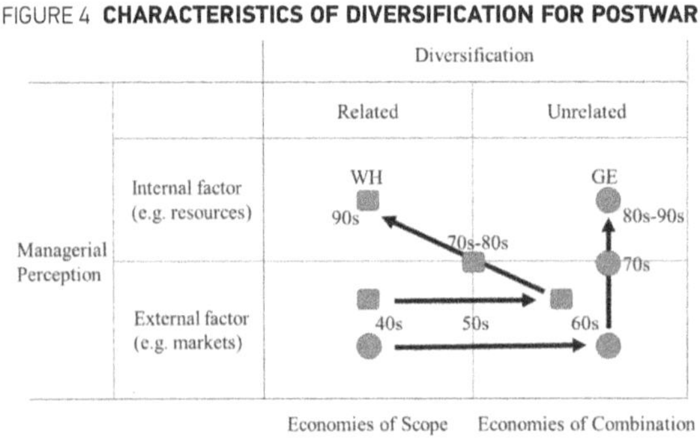

Source: Author.

15 Alfred D. Chandler, Jr., "The Enduring Logic of Industrial Success." art. cit., p. 131-32.

GE, on the other hand, took a different path. Although they sold a number of businesses acquired in the 1960s, GE top management diversified into the natural resource business through its merger with Utah. This unrelated diversification was motivated by other factors, such as profitability and inflation. Therefore the GE of the 1970s is plotted in the unrelated diversification category, but neither internal nor external categories on managerial perception.

Over next two decades, GE advanced on a new unrelated diversification phase. Like WH, GE dismissed the logic of the benign circle by divesting the related businesses to their power system business, such as large transformer, air-conditioning, small appliances, consumer electronics and so on. Concurrently, GE top management began disposing of whatever business that did not follow the criteria: No. 1 or No. 2 in growth market, higher-margin and higher-growth, high pricing power, and consistent income growth. Subsequently, they left businesses such as natural resources, semiconductors, and even profitable defense business. The result of restructuring left GE remaining to be an unrelated diversified firm, which operated from power system, medical equipment, to broadcasting and financial service businesses. However, despite this unrelated diversification, the GE of the 1980s, in terms of managerial perception, differed from the previous GE.

GE top management not only selected the business on the basis of the above criteria, attention was also paid to the integration of the business through sharing corporate value and information. Instead of a highly hierarchical organization, GE top management controlled the businesses and coordinated its organization by modifying its governance system in headquarters[16]. To integrate unrelated businesses, GE developed the system called the Operating System, which centralized the corporate reporting structure through the development of new governance channels and information sharing systems for employees. Through the revised corporate headquarter system, GE set sights to becoming an integrated diversified company.

Thus GE top management selected businesses that had something in common, in terms of speed of growth, competitive environment, and the sharing ideas or values. GE consequently took a different path from that of WH, and is placed at the lower right in the Figure 4. In a sense, GE did not follow the logic of managerial enterprise, but developed another logic for corporate growth through unrelated diversification with combination of industrial and service businesses.

The left side of Figure 4 is the world of logic that Chandler emphasized for the achievement of corporate growth. A firm located on the upper left in Figure 4 is able to realize corporate growth through diversifying into the forward or backward businesses that are related to its existing business, well known as vertical integration[17]. Top management took on diversification to control materials and outlets for its product.

16 William Ocasio and John Joseph, "Rise and Fall, or Transformation?," *Long Range Planning* Vol. 41, No. 3, 2008, p. 248-272.
17 Alfred D. Chandler, Jr., "The Enduring Logic of Industrial Success." art. cit., p. 133.

Thus, the fundamental determination to enter a business was based on internal factors, such as resources and core business. Since vertical integration usually responded to narrow opportunities, top management pursued further growth by moving into related product markets or by moving abroad[18].

The lower left on Figure 4 reflects such a world of logic for corporate growth, through diversifying into related product markets. It is true that diversification is based on the cost advantages arising from economies of scope, but firms begin diversifying when top management perceives an opportunity in the market[19]. The emphasis on this managerial perception in diversification is different from the one in vertical integration because it focuses more on external factor, such as markets. In any case, the left side of Figure 4 is what Chandler insisted to be the logic for corporate growth, especially as a managerial enterprise. As a consequence of diversification, the industrial enterprises adopted a multidivisional structure to solve administrative overload[20].

The right side of the figure is the world of neo-modern corporate growth where Chandler had negative comments for growth, as the tangled logic of diversification[21]. In the case of GE and WH, a valid reason for the over-diversification would be an expansion of the logic of related diversification, such as the benign cycle. They identified new ways of providing their products, a system product, and saw the opportunities.

WH was more committed to this approach and accordingly expanded their business. Managerial perception in this segment of the grid, therefore, also emphasizes external factors. I call this lower right segment systemization to distinguish it from diversification, where GE and WH tried to provide a system of products by combining a number of products. The foundation of the systemization strategy is based on the economies of selling a system with combined products, which can be called economies of combination. However, GE and WH were unable to achieve corporate growth under this new strategy, and declined in profitability.

By solving the problem GE was able to advance to the upper right segment on the Figure 4. As already described, GE was able to achieve high growth by selecting its business under common criteria and integrating the businesses though the sharing of ideas, best practices, information and corporate values. In other words, GE's top management perception was more concentrated on internal factors when they selected businesses. As a consequence, GE's business portfolio was still an unrelated diversification but with high growth.

Behind this high growth, GE realized another form of economies of combination. GE did not go for the demand side of economies of combination, which is accomplished in the 1960s by combining each product demanded into one system of product

18 *Ibid*, p. 133.

19 David J. Teece, "Economies of Scope and the Scope of the Enterprise," *Journal of Economic Behavior & Organization* Vol. 1, No. 3, 1980, p. 233-34.

20 Alfred D. Chandler, Jr., *Scale and Scope, op. cit*, p. 43.

21 Alfred D. Chandler, Jr., "The Enduring Logic of Industrial Success." art. cit., p. 139.

demand, but instead focused on the supply side of economies of combination. Thus GE regrowth was accomplished through a new type of integration. GE and WH got away from the modern corporate growth through related diversification and M-form in industrial business. GE went to unrelated diversification, combining with industrial and service, while WH sought related diversification in non-industrial business. Another form of growth emerged behind the divergence of two enterprises.

Conclusion

GE and WH provide new insight on the divergence of the U.S. modern industrial enterprises during the second half of twentieth century. It is the historical production of managerial visaction, a set of top management behaviors arising from their respective perceptions of environment, conceptions of prospects and actions taken to manage diversification, in response to economic change.

The story of GE and WH suggests at least two points to divergence of the industrial enterprises. First, the transition during the 1970s from the peak of the modern economic growth to another type of economic growth was the turning point toward the divergence. The other is that both enterprises manage to pursue corporate growth on the basis of a historical path of corporate strategy. It led to find the neo-modern corporate growth toward the end of the century, which sustains the features of the modern enterprises but archives to corporate growth through different strategies of the modern industrial enterprises.

This understanding is true to the divergence of GE and WH, but unsure to other industrial enterprises. In fact it is accepted a possible interpretation of the case study is that it may have been considerably influenced by the huge growth of GE late in the century. Admittedly, gaining insight to the general tendencies of corporate changes amongst U.S. firms during the period would be much improved if analyzed at the macro and mezzo level. In addition, the case study was basically examined in terms of corporate strategy. But organizational structures or organizing systems greatly influence corporate growth and divergence too. It would be a future study to take multiple case studies in terms of actions and organizing. It may contribute to a deepened understanding of the process of economic change.

The Canadian experience in business: the case of the St. Maurice Valley from 1890 to 1975

Pierre Lanthier
Université du Québec à Trois-Rivières /
Centre interuniversitaire d'études québécoises

Introduction

Canada has known an important economic development after 1840, making it one of the most prosperous nations in the world. It owed its success to its own enterprises, but also to multinational firms (MNF), mostly American and British, whose presence intensified from the end of the 19th century onwards. Various theories have been applied to explain the Canadian success. One in particular did and still does attract scholars, even more so that it has been conceived by two Canadian historians during the Interwar period, Harold Innis and William A. MacKintosh. It is called the "Staple theory"[1]. This theory put emphasis on the impact natural resources always had on the Canadian economy: a succession of staples helped to build up the colony and, afterwards, the nation. It began with fisheries and went on with the commerce of fur, wood, wheat, various metals (iron and nickel especially) and the selling of die forms of energy such as hydroelectricity and, more recently, oil. The exploitation of these staples represented an essential part of Western industrialization and urbanization, and benefitted the Canadian economy as well. However, the theory goes, it also made Canada a dependent economy towards the British Empire and later the United States.

1 For more information on this theory, one may consult: Easterbrook, W.T. and Watkins, M.H. (1984) «The Staple Approach». In *Approaches to Canadian Economic History*. Ottawa: Carleton Library Series, Carleton University Press, p. 1-98.

There is no doubt that natural resources have always played a major role in Canada's economy. Canadian entrepreneurs have launched their own MNFs in this sector, and particularly in the mining industry. Nevertheless, the question remains: how can we explain this nation's success considering its small population and the fact that exploiting natural resources, as seen elsewhere, can lead to dependency and even underdevelopment? How did Canada avoid this pitfall? Should we invoke other theories, such as those of Adam Smith, Alexander Gerschenkron and Alfred D. Chandler? With the example of the Mauricie region (Québec)[2], we will put forward some hypotheses and we will conclude by examining Canada's industrialization in the light of the theories mentioned above.

1/ GENERAL CONSIDERATIONS ABOUT THE CANADIAN ECONOMY

Before dealing with the Mauricie case, it is appropriate to present a broad outline of the Canadian economy before 1900.

1.1/ The colonial market

Since they set foot in Canada, the French and the British developed its territory according to their needs. The staple economy, as described in the introduction, had its roots in colonialism. Cod fishing around Newfoundland and Labrador, and later fur trade and lumbering, which encouraged the French to penetrate in the heart of the North American continent, were crucial to New France and, under the British authority, to the Province of Québec. They contributed to enriching many merchants in Québec City and in Montréal as well as landlords settled along the St. Lawrence River.[3] In conformity with the staple theory, a strong east-west tie linked together British North America before and more so after the American Revolution. By the end of the 18th century and throughout the 19th century, the British reinforced the east-west axis with infrastructural works opening the Great Lakes to navigation towards Britain and Europe. They built canals, especially around Montréal, and widen them afterwards to accommodate bigger ships.[4] After 1860, they added a transcontinental railway linking the Prairies and the Pacific Coast to Central and Maritime Canada. These investments bore fruit. Before World War I, Montréal became the most serious competitor to New York as an Atlantic harbour and as an exporter of staples such as wheat in Europe.

2 This region is named after the St. Maurice River and is located north of the St. Lawrence River, halfway between Montréal and Québec City.

3 Dechêne, Louise, *Habitants et marchands de Montréal au XVIIe siècle*, Paris, 1974, Plon (collection « Civilisations et mentalités »); Innis, Harold A., *Staples, markets, and cultural change : selected essays*, Montréal, McGill-Queen's University Press, 1995; Tulchinsky, Gerald, *The river barons: Montreal businessmen and the growth of industry and transportation, 1837-53*, Toronto, University of Toronto Press, 1977.

4 Faucher, Albert, *Québec en Amérique au XIXe siècle. Essai sur les caractères économiques de la Laurentie*, Montréal, Fides, 1973.

The colonial market stimulated smaller staple industries in the Eastern provinces as well. In Québec, for instance, sawmills and cheese factories exported their production to the UK. Cape Breton (Nova Scotia) extracted iron for the British market. Small towns like Sherbrooke and Merritton made their appearance in the wake of the staple industry.[5] The east-west axis has been extended into the 20th century with the mining of non-ferrous metal in the Northern part of Ontario and Québec and also with the production of aluminium in the Saguenay-Lac-Saint-Jean area. Before 1950, their market was primarily European.[6] However, another customer grew up after 1880: the United States.

1.2/ The continental market

By the middle of the 19th century, reciprocity agreements between Canada and the United States allowed the possibility for Canadian enterprises to do business south of the border. Consequently, in addition to the British Empire, a second market, closer to home, was offered to Canadians. For the Americans, exporting to Canada was not vital, considering the smallness of this country's population. Nevertheless, Canada attracted the Americans for two reasons: the abundance and, with proper investment, the availability of its natural resources; and the possibility, through Canada, to have access to the British Empire market. Consequently, Ontario and Québec became hosts to many American companies.

This phenomenon coincides with the advent of the second industrialization and a strong urbanization throughout the West. These two processes stimulated a growing demand for natural resources. However, the Canadian authorities considered essential that the natural resources should not just be exported. Both the Federal and the ten Provincial governments adopted a series of laws and rules encouraging the transformation, or, at least, the partial transformation of natural resources in Canada.[7] This has been particularly the case with the pulp and paper industry. In 1910, the Government of Québec forbade the export of wood originating from the Crown lands. The Americans didn't object. In 1913, they even facilitated the import of newsprint since the demand for that product was too huge for the American industry alone. Meanwhile, the Canadian municipalities took an active part in stimulating the coming of big business (including multinational firms) into their territory. Many even offered a 20-year tax break with a possible renewal. Actually, a sustained competition occurred among towns before 1914 to attract investors.

Multinational firms (MNF) began multiplying during that period in Canada. The majority of them came from the US. The others were British and, to a lesser extent,

5 Kesteman, Jean-Pierre, *Histoire de Sherbrooke*, tome 1 : *De l'âge de l'eau à l'ère de la vapeur (1802-1866)*, Sherbrooke, Les éditions G.G.C., 2000; Taylor, Robert R., "Merritton, Ontario: The Rise and Decline of an Industrial Corridor (ca. 1845-1939)", in *Scientia Canadiensis*, 1990, vol. XIV-1-2 (38/39), p. 90-130.

6 Dow, Alexander, "The markets for Canadian base metals, 1900-50", paper presented to the Canadian Historical Association Annual Conference, Montréal, May 1985; Campbell, Duncan C., *Mission mondiale. Histoire d'Alcan*, volume I: *Jusqu'à 1950*, s.l., Ontario Publishing Company Ltd, 1985.

7 McCalla, Douglas, "Canadian Capitalism in a "Borderless World": A Business History Perspective", in *Area Studies Tsukuba*, vol. 14, 1996.

European. Many of them invested not only in plants but also in setting up towns for the workers. These were known as company towns. They appeared in remote areas where the natural resources could be extracted or exploited. However, many MNFs settled in urban areas to produce semi-finished and finished products. This was the case with the car industry, especially in the Province of Ontario.[8]

The arrival of American MNFs had a major impact on the Canadian economy. So far, this economy was east-west integrated, as we have seen earlier. From now on, a north-south axis over the Canada-US border would arise. After World War II, it tended to replace the east-west link, since the Commonwealth market was diminishing in volume. Newsprint produced in Québec, for instance, was meant for the New York and New England markets. This north-south axis, far from killing the staple economy, actually reinforced it, but at the expense of an economic national integration. One could have expected a proper Canadian market replacing the imperial one. It happened, but only to a point. At best, Canada generated local markets imperfectly related to each other. Such a vast country with so little population couldn't do better.

Can we deduce that Canada's economy was henceforth dominated by foreign companies, and especially by American ones? It would be tempting to make such an assertion. However, research has shown that Canadian entrepreneurs did participate to the second industrialization as well. In the northern part of Ontario, Canadians were competing with Americans in the mining business.[9] In Québec, French Canadian launched companies in the pulp and paper industry, in electricity generation and distribution, and in shipbuilding.[10] Many of these entrepreneurs created SMEs that would become large enterprises afterwards. Even if the average size of the Canadian companies increased after 1890,[11] SMEs multiplied and many owed their existence to subcontracting from big businesses or to the availability of labour surplus generated by the presence of large companies in the vicinity.[12]

Moreover, if MNFs intervened strongly in the Canadian economy, many of them have been Canadianized from the financial as well as the managerial points of view. Local entrepreneurs did not react passively to the presence of foreign companies, be they British or American. The Mauricie industrialization illustrates this situation well.

8 Wilkins, Mira and Frank Ernest Hill, *American business abroad: Ford on six continents*, Detroit, Wayne State University Press, 1964.

9 Dow, Alexander, "Finance and Foreign Control in Canadian Base Metal Mining, 1918-55", in *Economic History Review*, 2nd series, vol. 37 no 1, February 1984, p. 54-67.

10 Girard, Camil and Normand Perron, *Histoire du Saguenay – Lac-Saint-Jean*, Québec, IQRC, 1989 (collection *Les régions du Québec*, no. 2); Pelletier, Jean-Marie, Ghislain Michaud and Jacques Lavoie, « La petite histoire de l'électricité dans le Bas-Saint-Laurent : Le résultat d'une volonté sans concession », *Revue d'histoire du Bas-Saint-Laurent*, vol. 3, no 2, novembre 1976, p. 3-10 ; Tremblay, Yves, *Histoire sociale et technique de l'électrification au Bas-Saint-Laurent, 1888-1963*, doctoral dissertation, Université Laval, Département d'histoire, 1993 (Pro Quest Dissertation Publishing); Ouellet-Riendeau, Chloé, « ‹ Les Princes de Sorel ' : analyse du rôle de la famille Simard dans le développement de la ville de Sorel (1909-1965) », M.A. dissertation, University of Sherbrooke, 2017; Paul Larocque et Richard Saindon, *Jules-A. Brillant. Bâtisseur d'empires*, Québec, Septentrion, 2019.

11 Altman, Morris, « The Evolution of Plant Size in Canadian Manufacturing, 1870-1910 », in *Canadian Historical Review*, vol. 74 no 4, 1994, p. 557-585.

12 Many SMEs employed female workers being either the wives or daughters of male workers hired by a big company in the vicinity.

2/ THE INDUSTRIALIZATION OF THE MAURICIE[13]

The Mauricie region is a valley north of Trois-Rivières longing the St. Maurice River. In the 19th century, this area was known for its abundant forest exploited by local sawmills, a small iron work factory and falls attracting tourism. It was agriculturally poor and consequently its population wasn't numerous. Nevertheless, during the decades following 1880, new cities made their appearance besides and north of Trois-Rivières: Cap-de-La-Madeleine, Shawinigan, Grand-Mère, La Tuque and, in the Interwar period, two villages became cities, Louiseville and Saint-Tite. All of them were or became company towns. Even Trois-Rivières welcomed major companies. On the eve of the 1930 Depression, the Mauricie area was considered as one of the biggest industrialized areas of Canada. How can we explain this sudden economic surge?

2.1/ The first years

Contrary to regions like Saguenay-Lac-Saint-Jean and Abitibi[14], the Mauricie area has not been industrialized by well-established MNFs. The companies which settled in the Mauricie before 1910 were all new or recently created. Their entrepreneurs were mostly young and ambitious. The majority did not come from rich families. However, they already had contact with financial circles from Montréal and elsewhere in America and Europe. In spite of his modest origins, John E. Aldred, was head of the Boston Puritan Trust before becoming CEO of the Shawinigan Water and Power Company Limited (SWPC). Hubert Biermans, who created the Belgo Canadian Pulp & Paper in 1900, was the son of a barber in the Netherlands: after eleven years managing colonial projects in Algeria and in Congo, he became the representative of the Belgian Banque d'Outremer in Shawinigan.[15] Thomas L. Willson, who launched the Shawinigan Carbide Company in 1898, came from a small business family in Ontario. His passion for chemistry and his political contacts with the Laurier government helped him to get into business. However, he sold his interest in the Shawinigan company in order to create a bigger concern in the Saguenay-Lac-Saint-Jean area. Unfortunately, his project didn't work and he ruined himself.[16] The Brown family owned only a small paper mill in Berlin (New Hampshire) when they created a pulp factory in La Tuque in 1907.[17] These men did not emerge from rich families; their main assets were useful connections.

13 This section relies on the following works : Lanthier, Pierre and Alain Gamelin, *L'industrialisation de la Mauricie; dossier statistique et chronologique, 1870-1975*, Trois-Rivières, Publication du Groupe de recherche sur la Mauricie (cahier no 6), 1981; Lanthier, Pierre, « Stratégie industrielle et développement régional: le cas de la Mauricie au XXe siècle », in *Revue d'histoire de l'Amérique française*, juin 1983, vol. 37 no 1, p. 3-19; Brouillette, Normand, *Le développement industriel d'une région du proche hinterland québécois : la Mauricie, 1900-1975*, Montréal, thèse de doctorat, Université McGill, 1983; Bellavance, Claude, Normand Brouillette and Pierre Lanthier, « Financement et industrie en Mauricie, 1900-1950 », in *Revue d'histoire de l'Amérique française*, vol. 40, no 1, été 1986, p. 29-50; Hardy, René and Normand Séguin, *Histoire de la Mauricie*, Québec, Institut québécois de recherche sur la culture, 2004; Hardy, René and Normand Séguin, *Forêt et société en Mauricie : la formation d'une région*, Québec, Septentrion, 2011.

14 About these two regions, one may consult: Camil Girard and Normand Perron, *op. cit.*; Massell, David, *Amassing Power. J.B. Duke and the Saguenay River, 1897-1927*, Montréal and Kingston, McGill – Queen's University Press, 2000; Gourd, Benoît-Beaudry, *Les régions du Québec, histoire en bref : L'Abitibi-Témiscamingue*, Québec, Presses de l'Université Laval, 2007.

15 Vermeirre, André, *Hubert Biermans : du Congo à Shawinigan*, Québec, Septentrion, 2001.

16 Massell, *op.cit.*

17 Nadeau-Paradis, Sandra, « La petite bourgeoisie de La Tuque et son rôle dans l'exercice du pouvoir local (1907-1939)», M. A., Université du Québec à Trois-Rivières, 2015.

This generation of businessmen showed an interest not only in their companies, but also in the region and its cities as well. They made a point, especially in the case of Aldred, to develop the urban infrastructure and also impose a set of municipal rules eradicating slums and promoting public spaces such as parks and sports centres.[18] Initially, the availability of capital was minimal. At best, these companies had contact with financial institutions, especially broking houses that could lend them short-term financing. Issuing bonds proved to be difficult, since these companies were new. But the owning of heavy machinery for some firms, the concession of vast woodland and even the implementation of severe rules on municipalities so that the land they own would increase in value helped the companies to obtain loans. This permitted the firms to get into production and generate substantial self-financing during the following years.

The first company to establish itself in the region was the Laurentide Pulp Company in the future municipality of Grand-Mère in 1882-87. This company was run by German-American investors. It has been sold to an American-Canadian group led by Bank of Montréal and by Canadian Pacific Railways. In 1907, the company became entirely Canadian.[19] Nevertheless, the most serious developer of the Mauricie was the SWPC, created in 1898 by American businessmen with the help of Montréal financiers. [20] The company's ambition was to produce electricity from the Shawinigan falls. It was an ambitious and costly project; it was also technically uncertain: reaching Montréal with a 100 km line was still risky.[21] This project took time to materialize. This is why, in the short term, SWPC invited energy-consuming companies to build plants in the Shawinigan area. In 1898, Thomas Willson, with the financial support of SWPC, set up a carbide plant in Shawinigan. Two years later, he agreed to buy 5 000 HP from SWPC. In 1899, the Pittsburgh Reduction Company[22] built a plant in Shawinigan and bought 5 000 HP in the shape of hydraulic energy. This company gave its Shawinigan assets to a subsidiary in 1902, the Northern Aluminum Co Ltd. In 1900, the Banque d'Outremer, with the insistence of Biermans, signed a contract with SWPC for the furnishing of hydraulic power for a pulp and paper plant in Shawinigan.

These initial successes convinced SWPC to incite more companies to establish in the Mauricie. After World War I, the company institutionalized this policy with the inauguration of a department whose mission was to attract investment in the Mauricie. In 1921, its engineers conceived a high-capacity electrical boiler to replace coal boiler. This innovation provided a persuasive argument for companies to set up in Trois-Rivières and Shawinigan.

18 Fortier, Robert (dir.), *Villes industrielles planifiées*, Montréal, CCA-Boréal, 1996.

19 One can wonder whether the 1907 crisis in the US incited the Americans to sell their interests in the Canadian company.

20 On this company, see Bellavance, Claude, *Shawinigan Water and Power 1898-1963. Formation et déclin d'un groupe industriel au Québec*, Montréal, Boréal, 1994.

21 At that time, California was building such a line. See Hughes, Thomas P., *Networks of Power. Electrification in Western Society, 1880-1930*, Baltimore, The Johns Hopkins University Press, 1983.

22 This company became the Aluminum Company of America (ALCOA) in 1907.

The SWPC's policy bore fruit. Companies opened or expanded plants in the Mauricie. This was the case in Trois-Rivières with the Canadian Iron Foundry Company in 1908. It also stimulated a British entrepreneur, C.R. Whitehead, to associate himself with two Canadian investors, Rodolphe Forget and J.N. Greenshields, to launch a textile factory in 1907, Wabasso Cotton Company, and a pulp & paper firm in 1911, Wayagamack Pulp & Paper Company, both in Trois-Rivières. In La Tuque, the Brown Corporation, a New Hampshire venture, built a pulp plant in 1904-07. Many companies came during and after World War I: International Paper[23], St. Lawrence Paper Mills Limited, Canadian Carborundum, Dupont, C.I.L., Westinghouse, Reynolds Aluminum, etc.
The industrial dynamism of the Mauricie area was such that some journalists and politicians, on the eve of the Great Depression, did not hesitate to say that the region should be considered as the "future Ruhr of Canada".[24] Hereafter, the St. Maurice Valley had the capacity to attract companies that were not necessarily exploiting natural resources, and many of them were well-established multinational firms. The SWPC developmental strategy was vital for the region. However, there is another factor to be taken into consideration: the companies' strategies, which evolved with time. They took place over two distinct periods: 1910-1940 and 1940-1973.

2.2/ Strategies from 1910 to 1940

Before the Second World War, the strategies of the Maurician enterprises consisted of two successive policies. Firstly, vertical integration in order to go beyond the strict exploitation of natural resources and to embrace the transformation phase; and secondly, horizontal concentration so to reinforce the companies' position within the transformation level.

The first step was achieved by most before 1925. The pulp and paper sector displayed the strongest example of vertical integration. In their early days, companies like Laurentide and Belgo produced only pulp. Laurentide added newsprint in 1902 and Belgo in 1906. Wayagamack made both pulp and kraft paper since its creation; it added newsprint in 1926. Among the pulp and paper enterprises in Mauricie, only the Brown Company in La Tuque failed to perform vertical integration since 75% of the pulp produced in this town was transformed in the company's plant in Berlin (New Hampshire), the remaining being sold elsewhere in Canada and in Europe.

The SWPC is an interesting case since the company combined horizontal and vertical integration. The company gradually bought most of the small power stations in existence in the Mauricie and the neighbouring regions. At the same time, it made sure that one of its important customers in Shawinigan would survive and develop its assets in this city or nearby. In 1908-09, SWPC took control of Shawinigan Carbide. This company had plants in Shawinigan, Merritton and Ottawa and produced acetylene gas for lighting. It launched a subsidiary in 1903, Continental Heat & Light Company,

23 In 1916, International Paper created the Canadian International Paper Company (CIP) and built a giant pulp and paper plant in Trois-Rivières. With the coming of this company, the Mauricie became the biggest pulp and paper producer in the world.
24 Verrette, René, *Les idéologies de développement régional. Le cas de la Mauricie, 1850-1950*, Québec, Les Presses de l'Université Laval, 1999.

to manufacture and install lamps using acetylene gas. Electrical lighting made this process obsolete and Shawinigan Carbide lacked capital to reconvert into new activities. By taking control of the company, SWPC provided new funds and spurred Shawinigan Carbide to do research in order to widen the acetylene market. In 1911, it replaced Shawinigan Carbide by a new company, Canada Carbide Company, which inherited the former's assets and subsidiaries. The new firm, however, closed down the Ottawa plant.

Canada Carbide would make its most significant vertical integration during World War I. Upon the request of the Imperial Munitions Board and with the collaboration of McGill University, it did research on magnesium and came out with metallic magnesium. Then Canada Carbide created the Shawinigan Electro-Metals Company for a daily production of 400 pounds of metallic magnesium. At the same time, the SWPC set up two more subsidiaries specializing in ferro-silicium, electrodes and a new product, acetone, and a third subsidiary in Baltimore. The Canadian companies created during the war merged with Canada Carbide in 1927 to become the Shawinigan Chemicals Limited. The following year, the group added a new subsidiary, Shawinigan Stainless Steel and Alloys Limited, which became a division of Shawinigan Chemicals in 1929. The SWPC / Shawinigan Chemicals team constituted an interesting case of vertical integration that finally resulted in diversification.

So far, the cases studied underwent vertical integration without attaining the level of the finished product. Wabasso Cotton tried to reach it. In 1910, it launched a spinning mill in Shawinigan and three subsidiaries in cloth making: Diamond Whitehead in Trois-Rivières (underwear, shirts and coats), Shawinigan Knitting (knitted clothes), and Oxford Knittings in Woodstock (Ontario) (hosiery and knitting products). In 1912-13, Wabasso doubled its production capacity in Trois-Rivières. And in the 1920s, it made further improvements and enlargements, notably by setting up a printing and dyeing division. The three firms, however, disappeared during the same decade. Vertical integration towards finished products, so it seems, was excessive. One may wonder why.

One possible answer would be that reaching the finished product level meant investing in marketing strategies. For companies with heavy equipment and away from densely populated areas, such an investment represented a risk. SMEs were more efficient in Canada than the subsidiaries of Wabasso in marketing clothes. Northern Aluminum also created an aluminium utensil factory in Ontario, but the results were far from being successful.

Another explanation is to be found in the impact of World War I on the companies' strategies. With the increase demand for semi-finished products, the war stimulated the horizontal concentration above all, and this strategy persisted during the Interwar period. The end of the war left companies with overcapacity production, subjecting them to harsh competition. Vertical integration was not the solution anymore.[25] Agreements and horizontal concentration, notably through mergers, became the roads to follow.[26] This was particularly the case with the pulp and paper industry. From 1926 to 1931, four pulp and paper companies in the Mauricie merged with another one in the Saguenay-Lac-Saint-Jean region to form the Consolidated Paper Corporation Ltd.[27] In 1925, CIP absorbed Riordon Company Limited and its five plants in Québec and Ontario, and from 1928 to 1931 it would take the control of many more companies throughout North America.

The Northern Aluminum Company also shared the ambition of growing significantly. After two modest vertical integration in 1913 and in 1915, the company considered to erect an enormous hydroelectric complex in the Saguenay-Lac-Saint-Jean area and set up the biggest aluminium smelter in the world close to a city it would also create, Arvida. For that purpose, Alcoa transferred its international assets to the company that replaced Northern Aluminum, Aluminium Canada Limited (Alcan). SWPC followed the trend. The company erected more power stations along the St. Maurice River. It also took financial and technical control of the power stations owned by the Laurentide and by the Brown pulp and paper companies, and absorbed competitors in Québec City and in the St. François River area.

Vertical integration followed by horizontal concentration was decisive for the Mauricie. Vertical integration favoured the region. Horizontal concentration benefitted the region as well but also exceeded its boundary. When the Great Depression erupted, the Mauricie companies put a halt to their expansion, waiting for business resumption. World War II provided this opportunity for some of them.

2.3/ Strategies from 1940 to 1973

The 1930s were difficult for the Mauricie industry. The companies that underwent horizontal concentration had to spend over rationalization and internal reorganization of the plants. The Crisis made these reforms inefficient and costly. Consolidated Paper and Wabasso stopped investing until 1945. SWPC slowed down the construction of new power stations. World War II, however, with its massive and urgent requests caused Alcan and Shawinigan Chemicals to add plants in the Mauricie. Alcan built a second smelter in Shawinigan and another one in La Tuque. Shawinigan Chemicals set up three plants in Shawinigan, Cap-de-la-Madeleine and near the St. Maurice village.[28] But as in 1918, overproduction threatened these companies at the end of the war. Alcan's plant in La Tuque and "Singapore" did not survive the war.

25 Actually, instead of pursuing vertical integration, the companies preferred to invite customers to settle in the Mauricie. Many well-known MNFs such as Dupont and CIL set up plants in Shawinigan.

26 Barjot, Dominique (dir.), *International Cartels Revisited/Vues nouvelles sur les cartels internationaux (1880-1980),* Centre de recherche d'histoire quantitative (Université de Caen- C.N.R.S.), 1994.

27 Charland, Jean-Pierre, *Les pâtes et papiers au Québec, 1880-1980 : technologies, travail et travailleurs,* Québec, Institut québécois de recherche sur la culture, 1990.

28 The last plant was constructed in the countryside because of the dangerous nature of its production: explosives. The plant was nicknamed "Singapore", most probably as an allusion to the bombing of this city by the Japanese on December 8, 1941.

After 1945, only a few companies kept practising horizontal concentration. SWPC went on with the absorption of competitors and the construction of three power stations from 1949 to 1958. In 1954, CIP bought the plant of the Brown Corporation in La Tuque. And Alcan inaugurated a new smelter in Kitimat (British Columbia) in 1951. All in all, with the exception of SWPC, these horizontal concentrations were accompanying or preceding a more decisive process: vertical integration and diversification. This time, the Mauricie region did not profit from this new strategic phase.

A new generation of business leaders were emerging. They were generally less preoccupied by regional development and more by the companies' profitability. The adoption of new technologies or the intent of getting closer to the finished product level let them invest elsewhere than the Mauricie. It would be less expensive to produce finished products close to densely urbanized areas in Canada and the US than in remote and less populated places like the Mauricie. The development of mass consumption was then a general phenomenon in all the Western countries and appealed to a new generation of businessmen, mostly graduated from universities and business schools. This trend asked for new strategies.
Alcan offers a typical case of this orientation. After the building of the Kitimat-Kemano complex, which fulfilled the demands generated by the Korean War, this group faced overproduction once the war was over. By 1957, it decided to invest in the diversification of aluminium applications and to expand all over the world. From 1959 to 1975, Alcan invested C$ 835 million in transformation, ranging from parts for cars up to the prefabricated houses, not to mention aluminium foils, licence plates, soft drink containers, etc. In 1976, Alcan had 27 plants, 4 subsidiaries and 1 joint venture dealing with transformation in Canada alone, half of them in Ontario. Moreover, the group invested abroad to such an extent that it became the most important Canadian MNF.[29]

Pulp and paper companies also diversified by adding to their traditional products carton, paper bags, toilet paper and, in the case of CIP, plywood and Masonite board. They favoured the Province of Ontario and the Montréal area to build new plants. At the same time, both Consolidated Paper and CIP erected 6 pulp and paper plants outside the Mauricie in order to be closer to new forest concessions.

The Canadian Iron Foundry Company followed a similar path with the acquisition of subsidiaries in electrical material, frameworks, pipes (including those made in cement and in plastic), industrial material, etc. These subsidiaries were located, once again, in Ontario and in Montréal. In the 1950s, the Whitehead family sold Wabasso Cotton to an Ontarian group, Woods, specializing in camping material. This change led Wabasso to add thick canvas and twill to its production. However, the growing imports from developing countries after 1960 constituted a threat to Wabasso. The company's response was to specialize in denim, bedsheets and tinctured cotton

29 Barjot, Dominique et Philippe Petitpas, « Alcan et Pechiney : une comparaison des processus d'internationalisation de deux multinationales du secteur de l'aluminium durant les années 1950 et 1960. Premiers résultats. », dans *Cahiers d'histoire de l'aluminium / Journal for the History of Aluminium*, no 52-53, December 2014, p. 107-139.

thread; moreover, it created a division for terry towel in Dunville (Ontario) after the absorption of Dominion Fabrics.

Shawinigan Chemicals went into vertical integration with the creation of Canadian Resins in 1941 (for war purpose, then for developing various applications of synthetic resins) and with the acquisition of McArthur Chemicals in 1958 (pharmaceutical and cosmetic products). More importantly, however, the company decided to invest in petrochemistry in association with B.A. Oil Company in 1951. The joint venture built plants in the US and in the suburb of Montréal. It was deemed that investing in petrochemistry would be more advantageous than in classical chemistry. This decision meant the slow withdrawal of chemistry from Shawinigan, in spite of adding new lines of production in the 1950s like sodium cyanide and sulphuric acid. The SWPC / Shawinigan Chemicals team bet on the cohabitation of hydroelectricity with petrochemistry. However, in 1963, SWPC was nationalized and its assets transferred to Hydro-Québec. A few years later, the chemical branch was sold to Gulf Canada. The group ceased to exist.

This phase of vertical integration left behind the Mauricie Valley. New companies settling in the region were small in comparison with their predecessors. Many have blamed the workers' militancy during the 1950s, especially in Shawinigan, while others deplored the nationalization of electricity a decade later. It seems to us, as we have just seen, that the decision to invest outside the Mauricie results primarily from new strategic orientations in conformity with the mass consumption market.

3/ FACTORS EXPLAINING THE INDUSTRIALIZATION OF THE MAURICIE

It is possible to identify six factors that contributed to the industrialization of the Mauricie region. The first one is the role played by the governments and the municipalities. The adoption of laws and rules demanding minimal transformation of natural resources in Canada along with municipal tax exemptions proved to be beneficial. However, it is interesting to note that the public institutions remained neutral concerning the nationality of the companies. Whether they were Canadian or not didn't seem to preoccupy the pubic authorities. What mattered was that these companies would create jobs and wealth in Canada.

A second factor to be taken into consideration is the presence of a business class not only in Montréal and Toronto, but also in smaller-size cities like Halifax and Québec City. Canadian businessmen did participate to the launching of many companies in the Mauricie. In a city like Montréal, business families were in close contact with financial centres like London and New York. However, one should not exaggerate the role played by these families. The Mauricie experience has shown that many of the companies owned their existence to entrepreneurs not originating from big families. For instance, such an influential director as Alcan's Ray Powell, active during and after

World War II, came from rural US.[30] These business leaders, nevertheless, associated themselves with Montréal investors. A large part of them even lived in this city, where they eventually integrated the ruling class.

A third factor not to be neglected: Canada provided these companies with educated engineers and technicians. Ontario and Québec had universities and business schools, some of them being prestigious internationally. McGill University, in particular, regularly supplied Shawinigan Chemicals' laboratories with scholars and students.[31] Many company towns did not hesitate to open technical schools to form their own workers. In Shawinigan, SWPC inaugurated such a school before 1914.[32] Actually, this contributed to the coming up of an educated generation of entrepreneurs after 1930 and ultimately to the Canadianization of the MNFs.

The fourth factor consists of the impact of war on the Canadian economy during the 20th century. Major investments were made during the two World Wars and the Korean War. Substantial orders came not only from the Canadian government but from the British and the American governments as well. Canada Carbide would have never been able to become Shawinigan Chemicals without World War I. Alcan received a decisive impulse from World War II. The sudden and massive participation of the public authorities was, however, a mixed blessing. If, on the short and medium terms, it provoked a boost to the companies, it also gave them production capacities that pushed them to make questionable decisions once the war was over.

The fifth factor is the capacity of the Canadian firms to generate self-financing.[33] With the exception of SWPC, whose assets required investment far superior to the other companies in the Mauricie, self-financing reached a significant portion of the total investment. In 1948-50, it represented 68% of the total financing of the Consolidated Paper and 79% of the Wabasso Cotton.[34] Self-financing gave greater autonomy in relation to the financial market and more freedom in the planning of their strategies.

Strategies represent the sixth factor. After an initial vertical integration which helped them to settle firmly in the semi-finished production level, the Mauricie companies expanded horizontally thanks to new construction or acquisition of existing assets. This niche in the semi-finished products is certainly decisive in explaining the success of the Mauricie industrialization. By contrast, the period after 1945, with its new wave of vertical integration and diversification, neglected the region since it pushed the companies to invest in more urbanized areas of Canada and the US. In a way, the region should have depended less on its business leaders for its economic

30 Lanthier, Pierre, « Les hauts dirigeants du groupe Alcan, 1940-2000. Une première enquête ». *Cahiers d'histoire de l'aluminium*, no 52-53 (décembre 2014), p. 89-105.

31 Langford, Martha Whitney, *Shawinigan Chemicals Limited : history of a Canadian scientific innovator*, Montréal, doctoral dissertation, Université de Montréal, 1987.

32 Larochelle, Fabien, *Shawinigan depuis 75 ans*, Shawinigan, Hôtel de Ville de Shawinigan, 1976; Charland, Jean-Pierre, *L'enseignement spécialisé au Québec : 1867 à 1982*, Québec, Institut québécois de recherche sur la culture, 1982.

33 Drummond, Ian M., « Banks and Banking in Canada and Australia, 1870-1914 : Capital Mobilization, Capital Imports, and the Ownership of the Banking Institutions », in Rondo Cameron and V.I. Bovykin (eds), *International Banking 1870-1914*, New York and London, Oxford University Press, 1991, p. 189-213.

34 Bellavance, Brouillette, Lanthier, *op. cit.*

future and diversify its industrial outlet. However, it is difficult for company towns to become free from their designers. These towns need population and institutions to be met in big cities only. On the other hand, this new wave of vertical integration and diversification didn't benefit the companies either. By the mid-1970s and more so during the recent decades, many tried to come back to the semi-finished product level. Alcan, Consolidated Paper gave up on diversification and gave priority to horizontal concentration.[35]

Concluding Remarks

How can we characterize the Canadian industrialization as seen through the case of the Mauricie? Above all, one must be careful not to generalize this example. Urbanized areas like Montréal or Toronto have a very different industrial history. Nevertheless, can we postulate that the middle-sided and company towns made the staple theory relevant? It would be more accurate to advance that their companies did manage to create niches in the semi-finished products level, thus, beyond the staple level.
Could we invoke Adam Smith to explain the Canadian case? Actually, not really. The invisible hand of the market has been too often and too decisively replaced by the very visible hand of the public institutions. Public authorities intervened first as legislators, then as investors and customers. Are the theories of Alexander Gerschenkron more accurate? No. The self-financing of the companies was such that they didn't require a permanent support from big financial institutions.

What about A.D. Chandler's ideas? After all, there had been a succession of vertical, horizontal and vertical/diversification processes, as described by the American business historian. The problem, however, remains with the difficulty the Canadian enterprises have to reach and maintain themselves in the finished products level. Today, this problem still affects Canadian companies that have developed in high technology, such as Nortel, Blackberry and even Bombardier. Their products provided them success initially, but these companies went into serious difficulties afterwards.

One thing is sure: if the industrialization of Canada depended in large part on foreign investment, it also relied on Canada's capacity to absorb this investment; in other words, to Canadianize the foreign presence on its territory. Canada has shown its ability to overpass the staple economy. Nonetheless, considering the modest size of its own market, it remains hard for this country to achieve total autonomy regarding its export markets, and especially the American one. The recent negotiations to renew NAFTA are a painful reminder of this dependency.

35 Lanthier, Pierre, « Les récents aspects de la multinationalisation d'Alcan, 1998-2017 : la fin d'un héritage? ». *Cahiers d'histoire de l'aluminium*, no 60-61 (2018), p. 44-67 ; Ricard, Jonathan, *L'intégration d'une usine régionale à l'intérieur des grandes sociétés internationales : le cas de la Belgo (1967-2007)*, mémoire de maîtrise en Études québécoises, Université du Québec à Trois-Rivières, 2013.

Germany's economic development 1950-1990 its significance for development economics[1]

Harm Schröter
Emeritus Professor of Modern Economic History
University of Bergen

Introduction

The majority of contributions in this volume deal with the economic development of emerging countries and the relationship to development economics. Why then include a discussion of one of world's most developed countries? In 1945 the German economy was characterized by widespread destruction and general collapse; the country's efforts to re-construct its former economic position can be seen as paralleling those of emerging countries such as Brazil. Thus this contribution considers key aspects of Germany's recent economic history from the standpoint of their significance for theories of economic development. We do not retell the well-known story of what happened when, but rather search for factors of explanation behind why things happened as they did.[2] Two issues must be mentioned at the outset: 1) In 1949 two German states embodying very different political economies emerged from the wreckage of the defeated German Reich. One of them, capitalist West Germany, became a remarkable economic success, whereas the other, communist East Germany (GDR), became a failure that saved itself from financial, economic and political collapse only by joining West Germany in 1990 (henceforth simply "Germany"). 2) Few of today's historians adhere to philosophically consistent theories of historical development such as Marxism. Most now follow a theoretical eclecticism that draws on sociological, economic, political, even anthropological theories and uses those theoretical insights which seem to be helpful in answering specific questions. This is our approach.

1 I thank the participants of the symposia, mentioned in the introduction of this volume, for their advice and critique, and especially of our Colleague William Hubbard, who also turned my outcast into real English.

2 There were of course many problems, set-backs, and clear wrong decisions. But limited in space, this contribution focuses on factors of success only.

The German economy's rapid development from rubble to riches after 1945 was by no means predictable given the widespread war-related devastation. Yet by 1950 GDP per capita in Germany had reached 80 per cent of the West European average, prompting the term 'economic miracle'; it pulled level in 1955 and was 15 per cent above in 1990.[3] Already in the 1970s the country had regained its pre-war position as one of the world's five leading economies. As in most other countries German economic growth between 1950 and 1990 came in two distinct phases: a period of very rapid secular growth between 1950 and 1973, often called the Golden Age, followed by a second period of slower, or "normal", growth. Since the reunification of the two Germanies in 1990 redefined the entire country, we end our discussion with that year. During the first phase Germany's growth of GDP averaged 6 per cent annually (unmatched before or since); during the second phase it declined but still exceeded the European average (2.2% vs 2.0%). During the Golden Age real wages quadrupled in Germany, enabling the emergence of a mass consumption society. – How can all this be explained? Most historians have described the development but have not asked the obvious question: "How did this come about?". Or, like Alfred D. Chandler, they have addressed it in a rather speculative way.[4]

Because Germany was already an industrial economy in 1945, theories on industrialization, which have been assessed in other contributions in this volume, cannot logically apply as explanations for this development. Nor are the various theories of economic growth useful, as they do not match the historical data. Even modern ones such as *Endogenous Growth Theory* or *Unified Growth Theory* have been criticised by Nobel-Prize winner Paul Krugman for their lack of empirical evidence.[5] But here we look for reasons in a historical, empirical case. Other economic theories, such as input-output analysis, do not include soft factors such as recreation, trust, motivation for work and so on, which we found very important if not decisive. – How can we otherwise explain Germany's overtaking of the British economy, which had much stronger starting situation after WWII? – It seems that *New Institutional Economics* offers the best approach, especially if two sides of it are taken together: Joseph Schumpeter's suggestion of entrepreneurial innovation causing *creative destruction* and Douglas North's emphasis on long-term, incremental change constituting a *path dependency*. Using these insights we will pursue the traditional agenda of historians and examine factors of discontinuity and continuity.[6] A rupture or discontinuity we define as a qualitatively new development even if its time span stretched over several years. By contrast a continuity is a development with roots going back decades. The central question is which major factors prevailed in the development of the German economy between 1950 and 1990? Of course, all factors of continuity contained

3 Also for the following figures: Angus Maddison, *Monitoring the World Economy, 1820-1992* (Geneva, 1995).

4 Herbert Giersch, Karl-Heinz Paqué, Holger Schmieding, *The Fading Miracle. Four Decades of Market Economy in Germany*, Cambridge, Cambridge University Press, 1992; Tamás Vonyó, *The economic consequences of the war: West Germany's growth miracle after 1945*, Cambridge: Cambridge University Press, 2018); Alfred D. Chandler, *Scale and Scope, The dynamics of industrial capitalism* (Cambridge: Cambridge University Press 1990).

5 Paul Krugman, "The New Growth Fizzle" in: *New York Times* (August 18, 2013).

6 Dominique Barjot, "Theories reconsidered. To what extent are European development theories on industrialization valid from a world point of view?" in: *Revue française d'Histoire Économique*, Vol. 2019 I-II., p. 12-58.

elements of change and all factors of discontinuity elements of persistence. We have allocated issues or events to one or the other factor category depending on which characteristics dominated.

1/ FACTORS OF RUPTURE AND DISCONTINUITY

History is usually dominated by continuity. But we start instead with a discussion of ruptures and discontinuities, for WWII ended with the collapse and unconditional surrender of the German Reich, and the thesis of a *Stunde Null* (Zero Hour) was widely propagated in the immediate post-war years. In a strict economic sense this thesis has been discredited. Allied strategic bombing did indeed destroy all major bridges and severely damage 45 per cent of residential dwellings, yet only 15 per cent of manufacturing industry was incapacitated. However, a modern economy is more than buildings, machines, transport and communications; it requires institutions that establish and administer the rules of proper economic behaviour. In short, it needs a state, and the German Reich ceased to exist in May 1945. The Allies divided the country into four zones of occupation, each governed by its separate military administration (British, American, French and Russian), whose authority was absolute and covered everything, including production, transport and distribution of goods. All German activities – political, social, cultural or economic – had to be approved by the respective military administration. The emerging Cold War from 1947 opened gradually for the re-establishment of German institutions. This culminated in the foundation of separate West and East German states in 1948. The political division, which also entailed the loss of the German Reich's Eastern territories to Poland and the Soviet Union, marked unquestionably a major discontinuity in the country's economic history. The rupture's impact was greatly amplified by a massive population resettlement as a consequence of the evacuation and expulsion of Germans from parts of Central and Eastern Europe. The four zones of occupied Germany, which had an estimated population of 53 million in 1946, had to accommodate some 12 million such refugees between 1945 and 1950.

The constitutional and organizational framework of the new Germany reinforced the territorial discontinuity. It asserted a democratic federalism that rejected the Third Reich's centralization. In the new German federal republic of 1949 no member state (*Land*) represented more than 25 per cent of inhabitants or GNP, and several member states acquired new names or boundaries or both. Discontinuities, often involving market or political liberalisation, occurred also in the economy. The control of market competition by legally binding cartels, a central characteristic of Germany since the 1880s, was prohibited. Until its dissolution in 1945 the German Reich's central bank was controlled directly by the German government. In 1948 a new independent central bank was established by the Western Allied powers for the introduction of the new DM currency. Before being outlawed in the Third Reich, German trade unions were organized according to political party affiliation; after 1945 they were rebuilt according to branches of industry or economic activity. The rebuilding of the German economy after 1945 also gave rise to innovative start-up companies focused on new products or business methods. Some, such as Adolf Würth GmbH[7], have become world leaders in their field; others, such as Nixdorf Computer or the mail order firm Neckermann, first prospered then faded. Collectively, these start-ups illustrate Schumpeter's theory of economic development by creative renewal.

The Marshall Plan (European Recovery Plan (ERP), 1948–52) was also a major factor of discontinuity. The financial aid dispensed was astonishing for the time: Germany received 1,413 billion USD, the UK 3,443 USD, and France 2,806 USD.[8] The Marshall Plan helped Germany with access to strategic goods such as oil and wheat, but its strict economic stimulus was much smaller than in other European states. Instead other effects were decisive: Politically, the ERP guaranteed that the US (especially its military) would stay in Europe (especially in Germany) and not abandon it to a Soviet takeover. Psychologically, this meant for Germans that it would be worthwhile to work and to invest, because the feared westward march of "the Russians" would be blocked, thereby preventing a nationalization of property and means of production in the Western zones of occupation. Participation in the ERP was understood as a signal that Germany would not remain an outcast forever, if its government and population cooperative with the Western Allies. In June 1948, shortly after the formal start of the ERP, the Soviets reacted to the Allies' unilateral introduction of DM with a total blockade of West Berlin. The US and the UK answered with an airlift to supply West Berlin. Thereafter most Germans perceived the Western Allies no longer as foreign military occupiers but as a guarantors of their personal freedom. Thus, the ERP had a profound impact on Germany, but above all politically and psychologically. "Work", diligent hard work, was the path Germans chose to cover up the sense of loss and guilt in the immediate post-war years as well as to give themselves hope for a better material life and perhaps a respected place in Europe in the future.

The ERP unleashed a wave of Americanization that initiated a bundle of discontinuities. America and its way of doing things became the model for German business. The car industry reorganized its production following American advice and using American machines. The chemical industry dropped coal as its basic raw material in favour of petroleum, a rupture that entailed a whole new type of chemistry and was a demonstration of trust in the US as guarantor of oil supplies (Germany has coal but no oil).[9] In general German big business adopted American management principles and reorganized its internal structure from the traditional unitary company to a multidivisional firm.[10] The change was the key to establishing real mass production and mass distribution, which until then had been little known in Germany. At the same time US consultants pushed for German enterprises to shift from product orientation to market orientation. That entailed the adoption of advertising and market research,

7 Würth, founded in 1945, represents today the world champion in trading screws, bolts, etc.

8 Gerd Hardach, *Der Marshall-Plan. Auslandshilfe und Wiederaufbau in Westdeutschland 1948-1952* (München: dtv, 1994), p. 244.

9 Raymond Stokes, *Opting for oil; the political economy of technological change in West German chemical industry, 1945-1961* (Cambridge: Cambridge University Press, 1994).

10 Alfred D. Chandler, *Strategy and Structure: Chapters in the History of the Industrial Enterprise* (Cambridge: MIT Press, 1962).

both of which were designed along American patterns. Perhaps the most visible aspect of Americanization was the introduction of self-service in the distribution of goods. The wave of Americanization was strongest in the 1950s and ebbed in the 1960s, but by then adaptations of American-style methods and concepts had set in train many changes for both German producers and German consumers.[11]

The very prosperity of the thirty-year Golden Age provoked many discontinuities in Germany's economic development. Similarly large and consistent growth rates in both GNP and real wages were never again achieved. The demand for labour was great. To 1950 the demand was partly met by the influx of refugees, thereafter by the politically influenced emigration of East Germans until the building of the Berlin Wall in August 1961. However, the economy's thirst for labour asked for new sources of labour. Soon workers were imported from southern Europe (especially Italy, Greece and Yugoslavia) and Turkey. Though many of these so-called *Gastarbeiter* returned to their home countries after some time, in the end this migration caused a net population growth of several million people and created a multicultural society. The Golden Age also brought about a qualitative improvement of dwellings, infrastructure, a quantitative and qualitative change in demand and consumption on a scale never before experienced. The great rise in living standards in the end caused the emergence of a society of waste. In reaction to overdrawn consumption and waste a new perception of the natural environment emerged. The oil-price crisis that ended the Golden Age in 1973/74 encouraged popular support for the reduction of the country's "environmental footprint". Since then ecological questions have become an important part of German political discourse both locally and nationally. Support for these issues deepened considerately in the last quarter of the twentieth century, leading to the country's 2011 decision to close down nuclear generated power by 2022. The political ruptures of the 1940s also promoted discontinuities in regional development. There were several historical major economic regions in 1937 Germany: the Ruhr basin in the West, Saxony south of Berlin, Upper Silesia in the East, and the metropolitan areas of Berlin and Hamburg. The post-war settlement transferred Upper Silesia to Poland; between 1945 and 1990 Saxony was part of communist GDR, while Berlin was split in two with its western half an enclave. South Germany, especially Bavaria, was traditionally largely agrarian with only pockets of industrial activity. After 1945, however, the South managed not only to develop these industrial centres, but also succeeded in attracting East German enterprises that wanted to escape expropriation and nationalisation. For instance, in 1946 Zeiss, a world-leading optical company, moved from its historic base in Jena to a small town in south-western Germany. The electrotechnical conglomerate, Siemens, moved its headquarters from Berlin to Munich. In the 1950s a large part of internal German financial aid for regional development went to the South; 20 years later the newly prosperous South generated state revenue that supported aid to crisis-ridden, economically depressed regions in the North and Northwest. The reason for the geographic reversal of flows of state

11 Harm Schröter, *Americanization of the European Economy. A compact survey of American economic influence in Europe since the 1880s* (Springer: Dordrecht, 2005).

financial aid was deep structural change in the German, European and world economy from the mid-1970s. Heavy industry (coal, iron, steel), the traditional strength of the Ruhr region, turned from an asset to a liability. The same rupture happened to North German ship-building. Of course, northern Germany also had examples of continuously prosperous enterprises, such as Volkswagen (VW) in Wolfsburg with one of the world's biggest car plants, but VW's economic weight did not match the combined resources of Mercedes, Porsche and BMW in Stuttgart and Munich. These regional economic and political discontinuities also affected the location of major financial institutions: after the new German central bank was established in Frankfurt/Main, the city definitively replaced Berlin as the country's financial centre.

The post-1945 economic rupture with the widest-reaching consequences was perhaps the sectoral transformation of production and employment: the decline of the primary and secondary sectors of agriculture and industry and the growth of the tertiary sector of services. Although this secular structural shift happened in all OECD countries, the German path deviated considerably from the norm. As Table 1 shows, primary sector employment (agriculture and forestry) in Germany fell fast (faster than in Italy or France), while employment in the country's secondary sector (industry, mining and construction) showed much more resilience than found in other economies of comparable size.[12]

Thus, between 1950 and 1990 Germany experienced several deep-going ruptures and discontinuities, several of which profoundly changed its economy and society. Apart from those mentioned here, there are additional ones, which however are intertwined with continuity. We will deal with them in section 3.

TABLE 1 **EMPLOYMENT BY ECONOMIC SECTOR, GERMANY 1950–2019**

Year	Employed in millions	primary (%)	secondary (%)	tertiary (%)
1950	19 570	24,6	42,9	32,5
1960	26 063	13,7	47,9	38,3
1970	26 589	8,4	46,5	45,1
1980	27 420	5,1	41,1	53,8
1990	30 409	3,5	36,6	59,9
2000	39 971	1,9	28,4	69,7
2010	41 048	1,6	24,4	74
2020	44 920	1,3	23,8	75

Source: Statistisches Bundesamt, Destatis 2022

https://www.destatis.de/DE/Themen/Wirtschaft/Konjunkturindikatoren/Lange-Reihen/Arbeitsmarkt/lrerw13a.html

primary sector: agriculture, fishery; secondary sector: industry, mining, construction; tertiary sector: services

12 Size of secondary sector in 1992: USA: 23.3%; France: 28.1%; UK: 26.2%; Germany: 37.8% (Maddison, *op. cit.*, p. 39).

2/ FACTORS OF CONTINUITY

In the immediate post-war years the occupying Allies changed everything in German politics, much in German culture (especially media), yet very little in the (West) German economy. Many intermediary institutions, such as chambers of commerce, continued unchanged. Though a few Nazi managers were removed, personnel, regulations and structures remained unchanged except for de-cartelization and the division of a few very large firms into separate entities. However, many of these break-ups were reed within two decades. For example, Thyssen reassembled the parts of Vereinigte Stahlwerke, and Deutsche Bank reunited its regional branches. The exception was IG Farben: the three main successors – Bayer, BASF and Hoechst – agreed that they would fare better independently. Large parts of the economy from agriculture to chimneysweeps, allocation of pharmacies or rail- and air traffic remained regulated on unchanged lines. For firms membership in chambers of commerce remained mandatory. Savings banks with their small-people clientele stayed state-backed. Most public utilities were publicly owned, and the ten federal states as well as the central state owned a sizable part of the national economy. Larger steps in deregulation did not occur before 1990.

In *Scale and Scope* Alfred Chandler characterized the German economy of the period 1870 to 1970 as "cooperative". A key example is managerial co-determination. In a couple of firms workers' commissions were introduced even before 1914. The German revolution of 1918/19 established works councils, which were set aside by the Nazi regime in 1934, then reintroduced by the Allies. In 1951 co-determination was established in heavy industry and in 1976 in all firms with more than 2000 employees. The result has been cooperation between capital and labour. Even when bitter decisions need to be taken, such as reduction of employment or even closure of plants, workers' representatives are usually informed about the necessity and, if convinced, cooperate. Their aim is to avoid a worse scenario and to obtain a high compensation. Sometimes they come up with better suggestions for saving employment, and occasionally management accepts them.[13] Co-determination has turned out to be the key for industrial peace and cooperation.

Another field of strategic cooperation between firms, craftsmen chambers, and labour unions with a long tradition is the system of dual education for young adults. It is based historically on apprenticeships supervised by guilds. Practical work in the respective firm is supplemented by theory, taught at schools outside the enterprise. The system is supervised by craftsmen chambers, which, after a standardized test, award a personal certificate of competency in the specific craft: painting, lath operation, and so on. That makes it easy for employers to find workers with a specific accredited skill as well as for workers to find a job in their field of qualification. The system undoubtedly explains why Germany has usually had the lowest rates of youth unemployment in Europe.

13 For instance, Siemens intended to close its plant in Görlitz, but reed its decision after constructive suggestions by labour.

Also other parts of the state-run system of education have long focused on the acquisition of technical skills and knowledge. After primary school children attended one of three different schools for secondary education. One of them (*Mittelschule*) is designed for more technical or vocational education, while the others emphasize mainly basic and theoretical education. Thereafter come technical colleges that again offer primarily practical education for, for example, future engineers, in contrast to the more theoretically oriented instruction given in universities. The German educational system has thus traditionally provided a large and wide variety of certified practical or technical educated graduates, who can fill the economy's need for skilled labour.

Family firms have been so important for so long that the German word *Mittelstand* (small and medium-sized business) has entered the English language. Though the phenomenon as such is widespread also in other states as the UK (*Brittelstand*), France, and Italy, it was the German word which became known – why? In contrast to the USA, in Germany it is not big business but family-owned business which above all stands for economic success. Often they are export-oriented and focused on supplying niches, such as Vulkan.[14] Among the advantages of the Mittelstand count a highly educated workforce and a special cooperation between owners and workers. Often they mutually understand – or even know – each other not as "investor" or "workforce" but as personally known individuals including their family background.

In that sense the Mittelstand also represents two other long-term characteristics of the German economy: its focus on products for long-term use, such as investment goods or durables, and its concentration on medium-high technology. According to OECD statistics machine-building, metal-working, chemicals, electronics, and all activities related to car production are over-represented in Germany. At the same time German industry excelled in medium-high technology rather than high technology.[15] For instance, the UK has more Nobel laureates than Germany, but German firms have been more successful in making products based on advance technical solutions. In both cases price competition is often not as tough as with consumer goods, because characteristics such as high quality, precision, longevity, guaranteed date of delivery or service play a more important role than prices. From the start of industrialization until today durable capital goods have been over-represented in the German portfolio of production.

In contrast to the rest of Europe, a majority of Germans have always lived in rented flats. While in France or the UK about 60 per cent dwelled in their own homes and 40 per cent in rented flats, in Germany the ratio was the other way round (40:60). And while in other states the share of the self-owned lodgings has increased over time, there has been little change in Germany. The reasons are: 1) a lack of capital the 1950s, 2) the traditionally important role of housing cooperatives, 3) state allocation of subsidies to investors, who in turn were obliged to keep rents low for a defined

14 Vulkan, founded in 1889, is world champion in ship's couplings.

15 High technology requires more than 7% R&D-costs of turnover; medium-high tech only 2,5-7% (Alexander Loschky, *Reviewing the nomenclature for high-technology trade*, (Brussel: ECJRC, without year), p. 8.

period, 4) a scheme by which the state paid a certain amount of the rent if the tenant needs it (*Wohngeld*), and 5) tax policy which did not encourage investment in one's own accommodation. Together these factors resulted in Germans, in spite of their higher income during the last years of our period, possessing on average much less capital wealth than their homologues, for instance, in France, Italy or Spain. This characteristic holds true today.

Although the critical concept, *Deutschland* AG (Germany Inc.), emerged in the 1960s, it expresses a well-known factor of continuity. This strange expression stands for a habit of cooperation between German big business, banks and the state that has roots in the *Gründerjahre* of industrialization. Its underlying attitude is something as "only limited competition is good", and mergers are all right if both parts agreed to it. Hostile takeover bids of large firms were uncommon. For example, in 1990 Pirelli's bid for Continental was stopped by a combined front of German banks, the regional government, and Continental's employees. However, this was the last major action of *Deutschland* AG. During the 1990s it fell apart under the impact of new American ideas such as shareholder value. That new approach of investment, solely financially oriented, has no roots in Germany and is, in a strict sense, unconstitutional. The first successful international hostile bid was Vodafone's takeover of Mannesmann in 2000. Such transactions belong to a new phase that began after Germany's reunification in 1990 when the country's business practices were swept into a new wave of Americanization.[16]

Finally, we have to mention that German society has traditionally had an exceptional degree of cohesion and collective trust, which is surpassed by only a few countries like the Scandinavian ones. This means, for instance, that government changes on the basis of honest elections, that taxes are (usually) paid, and that the most trusted institution is the police (in second place are doctors). Bribing is not unknown, but the country traditionally counts among the top ten of the world's least corrupt countries. Usually there is much initial trust between actors, and collaboration is considered to be a good idea. Though the country's tradition of economic cooperation has been weakened somewhat by Americanization, Alfred Chandler's general characteristic of a broad economic cooperation as a major issue, characteristic, and value of the German economy is valid still.

3/ DISCONTINUITY AND CONTINUITY INTERTWINED

In a couple of issues discontinuity and continuity are so intertwined that we cannot decide clearly which they belong to. One of them is the currency Deutschmark (DM) introduced in 1948. The DM started as a soft currency, but over the years it became one of the world's hardest, periodically re-valuing upwards against other currencies. In reaction to the oil-price shock in 1973/74, most other developed countries inflated their currency in order to help exports, but Germany did not. That hurt exports in the

16 Harm Schröter, *Americanization, op. cit.*

short run, but helped in the medium term, as firms were forced to improve their international competitiveness. The population unanimously supported the hard currency policy. Thus, initially forced to their luck by the USA, Germans became extremely happy with their currency, which became an item of national pride and identity with more widespread support than any other national achievement. Germans were not overjoyed when the Euro replaced the DM in 1999, but they accepted the change as the price to be paid to Europe for their country's reunification.

After WWII all German foreign investment was nationalized by the respective host country. Before 1914 Germany owned substantial amounts of foreign investment, but during WWI these assets were confiscated - which happened again during WWII. These actions represents a double discontinuity. During the 1950s affected German companies complained more about the forfeit of trademarks than about the capital lost. Like other confiscated assets the Allies had sold them to private enterprise. For instance the Bayer-cross, trademark of the pharmaceutical company Bayer, was owned by its non-German competitors. The same happened to the cosmetic brand NIVEA as well as to others. In nearly all cases these companies used their first earned foreign exchange to buy back their trademarks. This process was mostly finished during the 1960s, but in the case of NIVEA the last owner was not ready to sell before the 1980s. From 1958 the central bank allowed unrestricted investment abroad, and slowly foreign direct investment (FDI) resumed. It grew from year to year and by 1990 reached annually ca. 100 000 billion €. As always portfolio investment was larger, both into and out of the country. In consequence during the 1970s Germany became a net capital exporter. Towards the end of the 1980s its net balance increased to 25 000 billion € per year.[17]
Thus, while there was a clear discontinuity in the early post-war years, the country gradually recovered its traditional position as an important net exporter of capital. With regard to the German welfare state, however, we argue historically the other way round as in the previous two paragraphs: here we start with a long-term continuity in the start, but a massive deepening and widening of the state's welfare provision gave it a new quality and therefore a strong degree of discontinuity. Germany was one of the first countries to establish state-supervised welfare. In the early 1880s it introduced insurance legislation covering old age, accidents, and sickness. Membership was compulsory for industrial workers, but non-insured persons (self-employed, agricultural workers and so on) were not covered. Unemployment insurance was introduced in 1929. These schemes were not only maintained, but gradually expanded from the 1950s. Then unemployment insurance covered all, while the length of assistance was extended from a few weeks to one year, and the percentage received in relation to the previous wage was considerably increased. Pensions were coupled to the average wage causing an automatic annual increase. Other parts of welfare were organized directly by the state and covered all persons independent of any insurance enrolment. The biggest group is called "social benefits". Law defines their extent as covering a

17 Because of its different character FDI usually is not balanced counting inward FDI against outward FDI. During the 1980s inward FDI into Germany stood at ca. 50 000 billion €.

low standard of living on the one hand and on the other a guarantee of participation of social life at a non-discriminating level. The entire sector of education, from kindergarten to University, is state-financed and without fees. There are many more examples. In consequence, the state's social spending grew enormously. Expenditures in health insurance increased from 2 million DM in 1950 to 25 billion DM in 1970 and 130 billion DM in 1990; the outlay for social benefits grew from 2 million DM to 4 billion DM in 1970 and 27 billion DM in 1990.[18] Whereas the German welfare state in 1950 amounted to little more than a repair shop for the sick and the needy, in 1990 it provided assistance against nearly all the ills of social life. Therefore we argue that the amount of change in the state welfare provision represented a qualitative discontinuity – especially during the 1960s and 70s.

Conclusion: exception, chance, or grand design – is there something which can be transferred?

Our discussion (of exclusive factors of success) has showed that German economic development between 1950 and 1990 was characterized by factors of discontinuity as well as of continuity. For issues that could not be definitively assigned to either category, we constructed a mixed group. At the same time, on close examination we find that nearly all factors considered exhibited aspects of both, rupture and continuity. Thus, the question of what was more important, continuity or change, cannot be decided clearly as both aspects worked together in forming the final result. The question of "grand design" can be excluded; there was no master plan covering these decades, neither at government- nor at company-level. "Chance", such as the new states founded under Allied occupation or Americanization, was more related to discontinuity. "Exception" seems to be more related to continuity, simply because we find similar breaks also in the other leading European countries, but with a different outcome. However, when we weigh the factors of discontinuity against those of continuity, a conclusion that discontinuous factors were somewhat more prominent in stimulating post-war German development, especially during the Golden Age, is very plausible.

Finally, in addressing the main question of this volume, the theoretical explanation of development or non-development, what potential for positive transfer does the German case offer? Two answers may be acceptable.
1) To promote knowledge economic theory has to include in a better way the soft skills based on cultural factors. In the German case soft skills played a decisive role.
2) In order to promote economic development, investment is necessary, not only in manufacturing or financial facilities, but also in educational institutions, agencies encouraging societal trust and cohesion, and good governance at all levels. The most important area of investment here is probably education. The long-term winners in economic development since 1950 have not been the expected favourites of the time, namely those emerging countries which were spared war destruction such as Brazil, Mexico, India or Pakistan, but rather those that were devastated by WWII: Japan,

18 German Statistical Yearbook, several editions (current values).

Korea, Singapore, and Taiwan. In contrast to the first-named non-starters, the last-named four countries traditionally valued education exceptionally highly.

A "French Miracle"? The Economic Growth of France 1949-1969

Dominique Barjot
Emeritus Professor of Modern Economic History
Sorbonne University

Introduction

Firstly, historiography has often emphasised the slow economic growth of France during the 19th century in comparison with newly industrialised countries such as the United States or Germany, or even the United Kingdom. This was a reality, but one that needs to be qualified.[1] Indeed, the French population grew much less during the 19th century than that of these three large countries. As a result, the per capita performance of the French economy paralleled that of the United Kingdom. Moreover, French growth has been very contrasted. Five periods can be distinguished:

(1) gradual acceleration from 1815 to 1840;

(2) sustained pace (+3.8 to 4.5% annual GDP growth from 1840 to 1857);

(3) a marked decline in the 1860s and 1870s;

(4) prolonged economic depression from 1882-1883 to 1905-1906;

(5) sustained growth (+4.3 to 4.5% annual GDP growth from 1906-1907 to 1913-1914).

In the first place, historiography has often insisted on the slowness of the French growth. In addition, in 1914, France benefited from its financial power. As the world's second largest exporter of capital, France benefited from the power of its deposit banks (Crédit Lyonnais, Société Générale, Banque Nationale de Crédit Industriel or BNCI) and business banks (Paribas, Banque de l'Union Parisienne or BUP).

1 Dominique Barjot, *L'Économie française au XIXe siècle*, Paris, Nathan, 1995 ; François Caron, *Histoire économique de la France XIXe-XXe siècle*, Paris, Armande Colin, 1995.

TABLE 1 **AVERAGE ANNUAL GROWTH RATES IN FRANCE AND SOME OTHER COUNTRIES** (in %)

Périodes	France	Germany	U.S.A.	Italy	United Kingdom
Total Production					
1856-1929	1.7	-	4.2	2.1	1.0
1929-1963	2.1	-	3.0	2.7	2.1
1943-1963	4.6	7.8	3.8	5.8	2.6
Production per capita					
1856-1929	1.5	1.3	2.1	1.3	0.5
1929-1963	1.7	2.1	1.7	2.0	1.6
1943-1963	3.7	6.1	2.1	5.1	2.1

Source: National Studies of the Social Science of Research Council Project[2]

Secondly, France was very much marked by the experience of the years 1914 to 1939. The primary reason for this is the impact of the First World War.[3] It was disastrous for the French economy. The conflict led to the ruin of France's monetary and financial power. It went from being a credit nation to a debtor nation, suffering from the massive depreciation of the franc and monetary inflation. The war was accompanied by enormous human losses (deaths, but also war invalids) aggravating the structural shortage of labour, already marked since the 1880s. On the other hand, the war accelerated the processes of industrialisation, particularly in the mechanical and chemical industries.

In contrast, economic growth in the 1920s was the fastest in Western Europe.[4] But it masks deep-seated weaknesses. Indeed, until 1926, exports were boosted by inflation. Moreover, these years saw the persistence of protectionism and low birth rates, despite the recovery achieved by Poincaré, from 1926 to 1928, and the revival of the industry, particularly in the automobile sector).[5] As for the crisis of the 1930s, although late, it continued until 1938.[6] This seriousness tended to lead to a convergence of causes: acceleration of the ageing of the population, decline in industrial production, regression of foreign trade, failure of deflation policies, the policy of the Popular Front failed: the revival of demand and structural reforms did not allow the resumption of production, hence inflation.

The Second World War further weakened the French economy.[7] Three factors contributed to this:

2 Jean-Jacques Carré, Paul Dubois, Edmond Malinvaud, *La Croissance française. Un essai d'analyse économique causale de l'après-guerre*. Paris, Seuil, 1972, p. 34.

3 François Caron, *Histoire économique de la France XIXe-XXe siècle, op. cit.*, chapitres 10, p. 171-182 et 11, p. 183-193 ; Richard F. Kuisel, *Le capitalisme et l'État en France : Modernisation et dirigisme en France au XXe siècle*, NRF, Gallimard, 1981.

4 François Caron, *Histoire économique de la France XIXe-XXe siècle, op. cit.*, chapitres 10, p. 171-182 et 11, p. 183-193.

5 Michel-Pierre Chélini, *Histoire du Franc au XXe siècle*, Paris, Picard, 2002, chapitre 3, p. 86-118.

6 François Caron, *Histoire économique de la France XIXe-XXe siècle, op. cit.*, chapitre 11, p. 193-203 ; Alain Leménorel, *Nouvelle histoire économique de la France contemporaine. 3 - L'économie libérale à l'épreuve 1914-1948*, p. 30-42.

7 François Caron, *Histoire économique de la France XIXe-XXe siècle, op. cit.*, chapitre 11, p. 193-238.

1/ the State extended its control over the economy (1938 law on the organisation of the nation in wartime, distribution of the shortage from 1940, support for unprofitable production since 1941, control of non-industrial professions);

2/ Inflation exploded from November 1939 onwards;

3/ above all, from 1940 to 1944, France was subject to enormous German levies (requisitions, occupation costs, unbalanced clearing).

The consequence was that in 1945, France came out of the conflict in a much weaker position.[8] In fact, despite less human losses than in 1914-1918, the material losses were enormous and concerned almost the whole country. On the other hand, France's foreign debt was not very heavy: monetary reserves, although insufficient, were not negligible.[9] Under these conditions, the spectacular economic recovery of the years 1945 to 1969 could be considered a miracle (part 1), but with its limitations and setbacks (part 2).

1/ THE FRENCH ECONOMIC GROWTH OF THE "THIRTY GLORIOUS YEARS" AND ITS FACTORS (1945-1969)

A recourse to neo-classical approaches makes it possible to shed light on the factors explaining French growth in the years 1945-1969.[10] They were well exposed by Lionel Stoleru in his 1978 book, *L'équilibre et la croissance* économique.[11]

1.1/ Strong growth in production in France from 1945 to 1969

In fact, production in France increased significantly from 1945 to 1969.[12] At least since 1949, thanks to the national accounts, the Gross Domestic Product is the best known global economic indicator. Although it is difficult to measure growth for statistical and conceptual reasons, however, from 1949 to 1969 and expressed in constant francs (or in volume), the GDP growth rate was +5.1% per year on average. This growth went through four phases (1945-51, 1951-57, 1957-63, 1963-69), but was accompanied by strong intersectoral disparities. In fact, from 1949 to 1969, again in constant francs, the respective growth rates of the added value of the branches were as follows: agriculture, +3.0%; industry, +5.6%; building and public works (construction industry), +6.3; productive services, +5.0%. Above all, growth was a new phenomenon, due to its continuous nature over a long period of time, contrasting with the strong fluctuations of the other phases of rapid growth in French economic history, namely 1840-1856, 1907-1913 or 1919-1929. This explains the huge growth differential between the three subsequent seventeen-year periods:

8 *Ibidem*, chapitre 12, p. 238-260.

9 Michel-Pierre Chélini, *Histoire du Franc au XXe siècle, op. cit.*, p. 154-181.

10 Jean-Jacques Carré, Paul Dubois, Edmond Malinvaud, *La Croissance Française. Un essai d'analyse économique causale de l'après-guerre., op. cit.*; *Abrégé de la croissance française*, Paris, Le Seuil, 1973.

11 Lionel Stoleru, *L'équilibre et la croissance économique. Gérer la croissance douce*, Paris, Dunod, 1978.

12 Jean-Jacques Carré, Paul Dubois, Edmond Malinvaud, *La Croissance française. Un essai d'analyse économique causale de l'après-guerre, op. cit.*, chapitre 1, p. 19-50.

TABLE 2 **INTER-PERIOD GROWTH DIFFERENTIALS FOR FRENCH GROSS DOMESTIC PRODUCTION**
from 1896 to 1964 (in % and in constant francs)

Periods	GDP growth in seventeen years
1896-1913	+ 38 %
1920-1937	+ 45 %
1947-1964	+ 159 %

Source: Lionel Stoleru, *L'équilibre et la croissance économique. Gérer la croissance douce*, Paris, Dunod, 1978, p. 378.

1.2/ A necessary recourse to econometric models: the Cobb-Douglas function

Measuring this growth involves the use of econometric models.[13] The Cobb-Douglas function has been used most often for this purpose: it was used by Edward F. Denison and Jean-Pierre Poullier to compare the growth rates of Western Europe and the United States from 1955 to 1962,[14] and then used by Jean-Jacques Carré, Paul Dubois and Edmond Malinvaud to study French economic growth from 1949 to 1969.[15] As Lionel Stoleru shows, the method consists of three stages. The first consists in identifying the main factors of growth: rate of increase of the active population, demographic structure of the total population, working hours, quality of work (measured both by productivity by age, gender distribution, level of education, % of agricultural and non-agricultural labour force), capital accumulation.

The second step is the establishment of a series of labour force activities. This co three distinct aspects: an index of the quantity of labour mobilised for production (population employed in total branches, overall activity rate and annual hours worked); an index of the quality of this same labour (i.e. its distribution by age, gender and education level); and a measure of the impact of agricultural migration (with two hypotheses of agricultural productivity, low and high).

The third and final stage requires the establishment of a series of capital. It also involves distinguishing between a capital quantity index (measured from a series of gross investments) and a quality index (taking into account the rejuvenation of equipment and the resulting increase in productivity). To obtain the value of capital in service, it is therefore not sufficient to know not only the series of investments, but also the rate of depreciation of equipment, hence the need to use tax statistics, insurance values and information on the life expectancy of equipment.

Under these conditions, the use of a Cobb-Douglas function leads to interesting results. The Cobb-Douglas function is formulated as follows:
Y = A.Lα K1-α

13 Lionel Stoleru, *L'équilibre et la croissance économique. Gérer la croissance douce*, Paris, Dunod, 1978, chapitre XI, p. 369-388.
14 Edward F. Denison et Jean-Pierre Poullier, *Why Growth Rates Differ*, Washington, The Brookings Institution, 1967, *passim*.
15 Jean-Jacques Carré, Paul Dubois, Edmond Malinvaud, *La Croissance française. Un essai d'analyse économique causale de l'après-guerre, op. cit.*

where Y = national income
L = the labour factor
K = the capital factor
from which one can draw that :

$$\frac{\Delta Y}{Y} = \frac{\Delta Y}{A} + \alpha\frac{\Delta Y}{L} + (1\text{-}\alpha)\frac{\Delta Y}{K}$$

The following findings emerge from its application to the case of France:

1/ Even if the ideal equality between wages and marginal productivity was far from being achieved, French growth in the years 1949-1969 was mainly the result of an improvement in the quality of the means of production (+2.6% residual and +1.8% quality of capital for 5.1% GDP growth).

2/ As a result, in France, the coefficient of capital (value of capital used/value of the production obtained from this capital) was generally lower than abroad.

2/ Moreover, the rejuvenation effect of capital has been more important than the accumulation effect of this same capital .

4/ Finally, it is clear that the French economy of the years 1949 to 1969 had increasing returns (due to economies of scale effects), able to compensate for the weak expansion of its means of production by a better way of using them, but that French growth remained fragile.

1.3/ In search of the factors behind France's economic growth (1949-1969)

J.J. Carré, P. Dubois and E. Malinvaud sought to analyse the economic factors of France's economic growth between 1949 and 1969.[16]

TABLE 3 **ANALYSIS OF THE GROWTH OF THE FRENCH GROSS DOMESTIC PRODUCTION** (average annual growth in % by year 1951-1969)

GDP	+5.0
Employment in the productive branches (peoples by year)	0
Working hours	-0.1
Work quality (age, education, intensity)	+0.4
Work migrations	+0.6
Net capital (in volume)	+1.1
Decrease in age of capital	+0.4
Demand intensity	+0.1
Economics of scale	+0.7
Technical progress	+1.8

Source : J. J. Carré, P. Dubois, E. Malinvaud, *La Croissance Française*, Le Seuil, 1971, p. 223.

According to them, there were a number of factors behind the growth in production at that time. First, it was the result of increased labour efficiency.[17]

16 Jean-Jacques Carré, Paul Dubois, Edmond Malinvaud, *Abrégé de la croissance française, op. cit.*
17 Jean-Jacques Carré, Paul Dubois, Edmond Malinvaud, *La Croissance française. Un essai d'analyse économique causale de l'après-guerre, op. cit.*, chapitre 3, p. 107-142.

TABLE 4 **LABOUR PRODUCTIVITY GROWTH IN FRANCE AND SOME OTHER COUNTRIES** (average annual growth rates (%)

Production per man/hour	France	Germany	U.S.A.	United Kingdom
1856-1929	2.1	1.8	2.1	1.1
1929-1963	2.4	2.7	2.5	1.3
1943-1963	4.5	6.0	6.9	2.1

Source: National Studies of the Social Science of Research Council Project[18]

In fact, labour resources have grown only slightly: +0.2% per year.[19] Even if the total population went from Malthusianism to a renewed birth rate, the effect on the labour market was not felt until the second half of the 1960s. Indeed, the evolution of labour resources is a function of the evolution of total availability of labour (the activity rate has decreased compared to 1918), of the level of employment, which has been very high since 1949, but which deteriorated from 1965 onwards, of working hours (reduced in 1919 and 1936, but increased from 1950 onwards, to become, with 38.8 hours of work per week, one of the longest of all OECD countries). In addition, the quality of the labour force has improved as a result of higher educational attainment. As for labour productivity, it accelerated slowly before the war and rapidly afterwards.

It was also the result of the increase in the stock of productive capital itself, carried by a considerable investment effort.[20]

TABLE 5 **SHARE OF THE GROSS INVESTMENTS IN THE GLOBAL GNP OF THE WESTERN EUROPEAN COUNTRIES 1950-1971** (in %, average annual by period)

	1950-1960	1961-1971
Belgium	16.5	21.0
France	19.1	24.6
FRG	24.0	26.0
Italy	20.8	20.4
Netherlands	24.2	25.6
Great Britain	15.4	18.3
USA	19.1	16.8

Source: OECD[21].

18 *Ibidem*, p. 115.

19 *Ibid.*, p. 51-105. See also: Olivier Marchand et Claude Thélot, *Deux siècles de travail en France*, Paris, INSEE, Études, 1991; *Le Travail en France 1800-2000*, Paris, Nathan, 1997.

20 Jacques Mairesse, *L'évaluation du capital fixe productif : méthodes et résultats*, Paris, INSEE, 1972 ; Alain Cotta, *Inflation et croissance en France depuis 1962*, Paris, Presses universitaires de France (PUF), 1974.

21 Dominique Barjot, « Tendances d'ensemble 1945-1970 », in Barjot (Dominique) (ed.), *Industrialisation et sociétés en Europe occidentale du début des années 1880 à la fin des années 1960. France, Allemagne-RFA, Royaume-Uni et Benelux*, Paris, CNED-SEDES, 1997, p. 332.

The latter was divided into three groups (productive, housing and civil administrations, the latter two more dynamic).[22] The investment effort, which was high from 1949 onwards, increased irregularly until 1969. Over the long period, investment in equipment developed faster than investment in building and public works. After correcting for demographic trends, France did much better than the United States or the United Kingdom.

TABLE 6 **GROSS FIXED CAPITAL INVESTMENT RATE IN VARIOUS COUNTRIES** (in %)[23]

Dates	France (1)	U.S.A. (1)	United Kingdom (1)	Italy (1)	France (2)	U.S.A. (2)	United Kingdom (2)	Italy (2)
1900	14	18	9	10	13	10	6	9
1929	17	18	9	19	17	-	9	18
1950	15	18	18	18	15	14	14	18
1960	18	17	18	23	18	13	13	17

(1) In relation to GNP

(2) After adjusting for labour force growth.

Source: National Studies of the Social Science of Research Council Project

The growth of productive capital, although difficult to measure, was unquestionable.[24] Even if the capital in housing and administration grew faster, however, unless one eliminates the productive capital in construction. Despite its acceleration after 1945, it explained only part of the labour productivity gains.

Since 1945, growth was mainly due to a residual.[25] But what did this residue consist of? It was explained by economies of scale, management methods and the development of technical progress. The gradual reorganisation of production structures increased the efficiency of the production system by making use of economies of scale. Agriculture in particular had been transformed: agricultural migration had accelerated and farm sizes had increased, especially since 1955. As for industry, it had modernised: crafts had almost disappeared and the concentration of companies had increased.[26] Between 1955 and 1964, the number of enterprises decreased, but the trend towards concentration was more pronounced for medium-sized enterprises than for larger ones until 1965). Thus, total factor productivity measures the combined effects of different physical factors. Total factor productivity grew much less rapidly than labour productivity from 1913 to 1949: while its level was low in 1949, it grew rapidly from 1949 to 1966. A major reason was that the quality of physical factors had improved: the quality of labour rose gradually while productive capital was rejuvenated and modernized.

22 Jean-Jacques Carré, Paul Dubois, Edmond Malinvaud, *La Croissance française. Un essai d'analyse économique causale de l'après-guerre, op. cit.*, chapitre 4, p. 143-166.
23 *Ibidem*, p. 163.
24 *Ibidem*, chapter 5, p. 167-212.
25 *Ibid.*, chapters 6, p. 213-236, et 7, p. 237-290.
26 Christian Stoffaes, « La restructuration industrielle, 1945-1990 », in Maurice Lévy-Leboyer & Jean-Claude Casanova, (dir.), *Entre l'État et le marché. L'économie française des années 1880 à nos jours*, Paris, NRF, Gallimard, 1991, p. 445-472.

The evolution of physical factors has been conditioned, in turn, by other causes. In the first place, there has been a global demand effect.[27] Indeed, demand pressure was high from 1951 to 1968, due to global expansion, the urgency of needs, whether old (obsolete or worn-out equipment, housing, education and hospitals) or new (household capital goods...), the transformation of the decision-making context for entrepreneurs, confident in the dynamism of global expansion and the prospects of the Plan, and a deliberate choice of economic policy. Indeed, priority was given to growth over stability.[28]

This demand has been a catalyst for growth. It has created a particularly intense demand for labour,[29] resulting in an acceleration of labour reallocations from the agricultural sector to industry and services, especially construction and public works:[30]

TABLE 7 **SHARE OF AGRICULTURAL WORKERS IN THE TOTAL WORKING POPULATION**
(in % of the total)

	1950	1973
United Kingdom	5.0	2.9
France	33.0	12.2
Italy	41.0	17.4

Source: OECD.

It also resulted in high immigration of foreign labour, which exceeded 10% of the total labour force in the early 1970s.

TABLE 8 **SHARE OF IMMIGRANTS IN THE TOTAL POPULATION AND THE WORKING POPULATION OF THE COUNTRIES OF THE EEC AT THE JANUARY 1973, THE 1ST**

	% of the total population	% of the working population
Belgium	8.0	16.9
France	7.0	10.8
Germany (FRG)	4.6	10.9
Italy	0.3	0.3
Luxembourg	26.4	35.1
Netherlands	1.5	3.1
United Kingdom	4.6	7.2
Total	4.1	7.2

Source : H. Van der Wee, *Histoire économique mondiale*, Bruxelles, Duculot, 1990, p. 128.

27 *Ibid.*, chapter 8, p. 293-342.

28 Alain Cotta, *Inflation et croissance en France depuis 1962*, Paris, PUF, 1974 ; Jean-Pierre Mockers, *L'Inflation en France (1945-1975)*, Paris, Cujas, 1976.

29 Jean-Jacques Carré, Paul Dubois, Edmond Malinvaud, *La Croissance française. Un essai d'analyse économique causale de l'après-guerre, op. cit.*, chapitre 8, p. 330-335 ; Jean-Charles Asselain, « L'ouverture à la concurrence internationale », in Maurice Lévy-Leboyer & Jean-Claude Casanova, (dir.), *Entre l'État et le marché. L'économie française des années 1880 à nos jours, op. cit.*, p. 413-424.

30 Dominique Barjot, « Les industries d'équipement et de la construction 1950-1980 », in Maurice Lévy-Leboyer (dir.), *Histoire de la France industrielle*, tome 2. *Les trente glorieuses*, Paris, Larousse, 1996, p. 412-433.

This same demand led to a sustained activity rate of the French population, an almost minimal reduction in underemployment, the maintenance of a relatively long working time (with a later downward trend than abroad). It had a positive effect on productivity. It is clear that high demand favoured innovation, optimised the use of productive equipment and stimulated professional migration.

The rapid development of France's foreign trade has favoured growth.[31] France's foreign trade developed until 1929, but the crisis of the 1930s brought it to an abrupt halt. The increase in the volume of trade did not correspond to a return to a normal mode of development. In 1969, exports were multiplied by 3.6 and imports by 4.2. The rapid growth of foreign trade was evidence of a specialisation of the productive system, but was accompanied by a structural deficit that was growing in the long term.[32] In contrast, the acceleration of trade stimulated demand, created economies of scale and catalysed technical progress.

Secondly, growth was fuelled by abundant savings.[33] The need for physical capital generated abundant savings, a positive factor for long-term economic development. While the demand for capital has increased since the Second World War, the supply of savings has also increased. For households, the distribution of resources stabilised (increase in the number of employees and social transfers). In addition, the permanent housing difficulties of the French forced them to devote an increasing part of their income to the financing of construction. The post-war rise in prices forced households to significantly increase their cash holdings in order to maintain their purchasing power. On the other hand, changes in the financing of investments were not a factor in explaining post-war investments.[34] In fact, the role of own resources diminished and external financing increased sharply.

Third, total factor productivity has improved as a result of the development of a competitive market.[35] At the beginning of the 1950s, France lived under a mixed economy regime. From 1949 to 1968, the labour market evolved towards a better allocation of resources. In addition, from 1955 to 1965 the expansion of the capital market gradually transformed the conditions affecting the distribution of financial resources among the various applicants. Although quotas had disappeared in 1950, price control was still the rule.[36] The creation of the Technical Commission on Cartels and Dominant Positions (Commission technique des ententes et des positions dominantes) in 1953 and, from 1960 onwards, the opening of borders helped to re-establish

31 Jean-Jacques Carré, Paul Dubois, Edmond Malinvaud, *La Croissance française. Un essai d'analyse économique causale de l'après-guerre, op. cit.*, chapter 12, p. 493-520 ; René Girault, "Les relations économiques avec l'extérieur (1945-1975), mutations et permanences », chapter 6, in Ernest Labrousse et Fernand Braudel, *Histoire économique et sociale de la France*, tome 4, vol. 3, PUF, 1982, p. 1379-1423.

32 Jean-Claude Casanova, « Les échanges extérieurs : un équilibre précaire », in Maurice Lévy-Leboyer & Jean-Claude Casanova, (dir.), *Entre l'État et le marché. L'économie française des années 1880 à nos jours, op. cit.*, p. 545-572.

33 Jean-Jacques Carré, Paul Dubois, Edmond Malinvaud, *La Croissance française. Un essai d'analyse économique causale de l'après-guerre, op. cit.*, chapter 9, p. 343-388.

34 *Ibidem*, chapter 10, p. 389-435.

35 *Ibid.*, chapter 13, p. 521-565.

36 Michel-Pierre Chélini, *Inflation, État et opinion en France de 1944 à 1952*, Paris, CHEFF, 1998.

a more competitive market. As for regional development policy, it is likely that it slightly accelerated growth.[37]

State action was unevenly effective.[38] Economic regulation was on the whole beneficial to growth. The impact of inflation on growth appears to have been low, although it was higher than elsewhere. This would not be the case in the 1970s and 1980s.[39] On the other hand, inflation most often explained economic policy: throughout the period, France, like the United Kingdom and unlike Germany, had to resolve the growth/external balance dilemma. Planning undoubtedly contributed to the development of the role of economic information, but, as is well known, the effect quickly tended to fade away after 1973-74.[40] In fact, the Plan's forecasts contributed above all to changing the behaviour of companies: in fact, especially during the 4th and 5th Plans, the economic projections were approximately achieved. As a result, the Plan's forecasts helped to create a climate of expansion. Planning had only a very secondary role in economic policy: it only conditioned public investment from the Fourth Plan onwards, but introduced a new type of State-enterprise relationship. Moreover, planning improved economic techniques (development of the Physical-Financial Model or FIFI and D.M.S.) and information circuits.

2/ THE LONG-TERM CONSEQUENCES OF FRENCH GROWTH: REALITIES AND LIMITS OF THE MIRACLE

France's spectacular performance in terms of economic growth was, however, accompanied by a widening income gap.

2.1/ A growth that generates growing inequalities

One of the keys to sustained long-term growth lies in an optimal distribution of the fruits of growth. These inequalities were interregional,[41] but also social.[42] However, income inequalities increased in France between 1952 and 1969, but to a more modest extent than has often been said. Indeed, the wage disparity between a worker and a senior manager appears to be an injustice when it exceeds a reasonable amount. In this respect, the gap increased from 1 to 4 to 1 to 6 between 1952 and 1969, a relatively small increase in the disparity. As for the range of income is more difficult to measure,

37 Pierre Caro, Olivier Dard, Jean-Claude Daumas (eds.), *La politique d'aménagement du territoire : racines, logiques et résultats*, Presses universitaires de Rennes, 2002.

38 Jean-Jacques Carré, Paul Dubois, Edmond Malinvaud, *La Croissance française. Un essai d'analyse économique causale de l'après-guerre, op. cit.*, chapter 11, p. 437-492.

39 Michel Hau & Félix Torres, *Le virage manqué. 1974-1984 : ces dix années où la France a décroché*, Paris, Les Belles Lettres, 2020. Voir en particulier, chapter 2, p. 33-68.

40 Jean-Jacques Carré, Paul Dubois, Edmond Malinvaud, *La Croissance française. Un essai d'analyse économique causale de l'après-guerre, op. cit.*, chapter 14, p. 567-609. On planning, see in particular: Henry Rousso (ed.), *De Monnet à Massé*, Paris, Éd. du CNRS, 1986 ; (ed.), *La Planification en crise (1965-1985)*, Paris, Éd. du CNRS, 1987.

41 François Caron, « Les évolutions régionales », in Ernest Labrousse et Fernand Braudel, *Histoire économique et sociale de la France*, tome 4, vol. 3, PUF, 1982, p. 1321-1378 ; Maurice Parodi, « Le mirage du développement économique équilibré », chapter 9, *L'économie et la société française depuis 1945*, Paris, Armand Colin, p. 159-174.

42 Maurice Parodi, « Le partage des fruits de la croissance », chapter 12, *Ibidem*, p. 246-277.

because only declared tax revenues are available. With regard to tax income: social inequalities did not stem primarily from disparities between branches or from hierarchical disparities according to qualification, but rather from disparities by nature of activity (between employees, traders, self-employed and liberal professions). Moreover, social transfer mechanisms (family benefits, income tax) had only a limited effect on reducing income inequalities.

During the 1960s, the concept of surplus productivity formed the basis of an income policy (as formulated by Pierre Massé, Planning Commissioner from 1959 to 1966).[43] According to this analysis, there is no possible wage increase without a surplus to distribute. This surplus is measured by the formula: [44]

$= p \,.\, \Delta P - g \,.\, \Delta N$

surplus

where $p \,.\, \Delta P$ = unit price of labour increase in employment

Its use can be broken down as follows:

Use of the surplus:[45]

$= - P \,.\, \Delta p + N. \,\Delta W + \Delta.\varpi$

où $- P \,.\, \Delta p$

= lower product prices, to the benefit of the consumer

$+ N. \,\Delta W$

= wage increase in favour of employees

$+ \Delta.\varpi$

= increase in profit for the entrepreneur or the company.

This results in different distribution assumptions (income triangle). The first is the equilibrium distribution: in this case, prices remain stable; the second, much less realistic, postulates that all earnings go to employees, at the expense of profits, but with stable prices; the third is that wages increase too quickly, causing prices to rise.

The results were only measured for 1949-1963 (by P. Massé, Louis-André Vincent, L. Stoléru).[46] They are as follows :

1/ in the agricultural and food industries, from 1949 to 1963, a decrease in the mass of profits and taxes allowed a redistribution to the benefit of consumers and wages. Nevertheless, the surplus to be distributed was much smaller from 1956 to 1963 than from 1949 to 1956.

2/ for all branches, from 1956 to 1963, it appears that the discriminating factor was more the size of productivity gains than the way in which they were distributed, that the rate of growth of wages was rarely equal to that of profits and taxes, that wages and profits profited less quickly than the surplus, because relative prices fell, except in services and construction, and finally, that there was a tendency to equalize wage growth between branches.

43 Pierre Massé, Pierre Bernard, *Les dividendes du progrès*, Paris, Le Seuil, 1969.

44 Pierre Massé, Pierre Bernard, « Surplus, fonction de production et coefficient de capital », *Ibidem*, p. 133-135.

45 « Le Surplus et la productivité globale des facteurs », *Ibid.*, p. 136-139.

46 Louis-André Vincent, « Productivité et prix relatifs dans quinze branches de l'économie française (1949-1963) », in *Études et conjoncture*, février 1966, p. 17-84 ; Christian Sautter, *Fresque historique du système productif*, n°141 des Collections de l'INSEE, série E, n° 27, octobre 1974.

2.2/ In the 1960s, economic policies were undoubtedly more effective.

Moreover, it seems that part of the acceleration of growth in the 1960s can be explained by the greater effectiveness of French economic policies.[47] From 1945 to 1958, economic policies were imposed from outside by a brutal economic situation. Three cycles followed one another:

1/ 1945-1950.[48] A late, but energetic stabilisation aimed at dealing with unstable and unbalanced growth. France first underwent a hyper-inflationary reconstruction (1945-1947). It was marked by radical structural reforms (nationalization,[49] modernisation plan[50]), but also by the failure to fight inflation (Pleven, a supporter of a simple tax levy on the money supply and supported by De Gaulle, won out over Mendès-France, in favour of drastic deflation as in Belgium) and devaluation, resulting in a huge trade imbalance. Then a strong stabilisation (René Mayer Plan of 1948[51]) was imposed, which paved the way for an undeniable economic recovery.

2/ 1951-1953.[52] With the Korean War, there was a new inflationary boom which was finally resolved by means of a second drastic stabilisation. Governments were increasingly unable to cope with the internal and external economic crisis (1951-52). The recovery was the work of Antoine Pinay). It was accompanied by falling prices, but at the cost of a strong recession.

3/ 1954-1958.[53] The French economy was struggling to adapt to an increasingly unfavourable economic climate. However, in 1954-1955, Edgar Faure had achieved "expansion in stability" (without inflation). In 1956-1957, on the contrary, the socialist government of G. Mollet failed to overcome a deep crisis at home and abroad. On the other hand, in 1958, a recovery began, under the impetus of Félix Gaillard and, above all, with the return to power of General de Gaulle.[54]

From 1958 to 1969, on the contrary, a gradual loosening of cyclical constraints was accompanied by an incomplete regularisation of growth.[55] Between 1958 and 1962, there was a brilliant, but still fragile, economic recovery. Based on a logic of true prices and open borders, the policy of the Debré government resorted to radical measures (devaluation and total convertibility of the franc, Interim Plan, reform of agricultural markets). Pursued by Georges Pompidou, this policy accelerated growth while restoring France's international credit position. Between 1963 and 1965, overheating led to the stabilisation plan. During these years, the rise in prices was the result of

47 André de Lattre et Daniel Deguen, *Politiques économiques de la France*, Paris, Cours de l'Institut d'Études politiques de Paris, 1973-74.

48 François Caron, *Histoire économique de la France XIXe-XXe siècle, op. cit.*, chapter 12, p. 203-238.

49 Dominique Barjot , « Les nationalisations de la Libération », in Christian Stoffaes (dir..), *Psychanalyse de l'antilibéralisme. Les Français ont-ils raison d'avoir peur ?*, Paris, Éditions Saint-Simon, IDHI, 2006, p. 146-156.

50 Henry Rousso (dir.), *De Monnet à Massé, op. cit.*

51 François Caron, « Le plan Mayer : un retour aux réalités : trois personnalités de l'après-guerre face à l'action (1945-1946) », *Histoire économie & société (HES)*, 1982, 1-3, p. 423-437

52 François Caron, *Histoire économique de la France XIXe-XXe siècle, op. cit.*, chapter 12, p. 203-238 ; Jean-François Eck, *Histoire de l'économie française de la crise de 1929 à l'Euro*, chapter 2, Paris, Armand Colin, 2009, p. 39-73.

53 François Caron, *Ibidem*, chapter 12, p. 203-238 ; Jean-François Eck, *Histoire de l'économie française de la crise de 1929 à l'Euro, op. cit.*, p. 39-73.

54 Michel-Pierre Chélini, *Histoire du franc, op. cit.*, chapter 6, p. 182-214.

55 François Caron, *Histoire économique de la France XIXe-XXe siècle, op. cit.*, chapter 14, p. 261-288.

a faster increase in wages than in productivity. This is why, in September 1963, the Valéry Giscard d'Estaing stabilisation plan applied brutal anti-inflationary measures consisting of price freezes, credit control and increased budgetary rigour. Continued until 1966, the plan nevertheless produced mixed results (internal and external debt reduction, balance of payments surplus, but slower growth). Finally, between 1966 and 1969, the economic recovery was slowed down by the crisis of 1968-1969. The replacement of V. Giscard d'Estaing by Michel Debré in the Economy and Finance Department revealed a willingness to revive (solution to investments, banking reform, revival of the Common Agricultural Policy, liberalisation of intra- and extra-European trade). But the crisis of May 1968 weakened the French economy, with the revival of wage inflation in addition to the monetary crises of August and November 1968. This led to the loss of almost all foreign exchange reserves. However, the devaluation of August 1969 allowed a spectacular recovery of the economy.[56]

This recovery was reflected in particular in the evolution of the country's final balance of payments:[57]

TABLE 9 **EVOLUTION OF THE FRENCH BALANCE OF PAYMENTS 1968-1972 (BILLIONS FRANCS)**[58]

	1968	1969	1970	1971	1972
Balance of Trade	+0.4	-4.3	+1.8	+6.1	+6.5
Balance of Service	+0.1	+1.8	+3.0	+3.7	+2.8
Free Allowances (FEOGA, Euratom, FED, etc.)	-4.7	-5.1	-4.4	-6.9	-7.8
Balance on Current Accounts	-4.2	-7.6	+0.4	+2.9	+1.5
Capitals of Residents	-5.3	-4.2	-5.1	-6.8	-7.7
Capital of Non-residents	+1.5	+3.4	+8.5	+7.9	+8.2
Banking Sector	-1.7	0	-1.8	-0.1	-3.7
Public Sector	-0.3	-0.7	-1.0	-1.0	-0.2
Long Term Capitals	-5.8	-1.5	+0.6	0	-3.4
Short Term Capital (including errors and omissions)	- 8.0	-2.5	+8.8	+14.9	+10.0
Variation of Assets and Liabilities of the Public Sector	-18.0	-6.6	+9.7	+17.9	+8.0

Source: Banque de France (Bank of France)

The devaluation allowed, from 1970 onwards, the re-establishment of a significant trade surplus, while the balance of services strengthened its own surplus (exports of major works and engineering, receipts from tourism in particular). The resulting surplus in the current account balance allowed a restoration of confidence in international financial circles, hence the strong increase in the inflow of foreign capital, parti-

56 Michel-Pierre Chélini, *Histoire du franc, op. cit.*, chapter 8, p. 249-285.
57 Philippe Meunier, « Les relations économiques et financières de la France avec l'extérieur », in Jean-Pierre Pagé (ed.), *Profil économique de la France au seuil des années 1980*, Paris, La Documentation française, 1981, p. 351-389.
58 Philippe Meunier, « Les relations économiques et financières de la France avec l'extérieur », in Jean-Pierre Pagé, (ed.), *ibidem*, p. 384.

cularly American,[59] but also the increase in French investments abroad, for example in the Soviet Union and in the countries of Eastern Europe[60] and Latin America.[61]

2.3/ France: an accelerated process of catching up with the major Western economies

France has benefited from an accelerated catch-up process with the major competing Western economies. The analysis of the factors of growth (Edward F. Denison and Jean-Pierre Poullier, *Why Growth Rates differ?*, Washington, The Brookings Institution, 1967) has made it possible to compare the performances of the major nations.

TABLE 10 **ANNUAL GROWTH RATES OF THE NATIONAL PRODUCT AND ITS EXPLANATORY FACTORS (1955-1965)**

	France	Federal Republic of Germany	United Kingdom	United States of America	Italy
National Income	+ 5.03	+ 5.39	+ 2.27	+ 2.67	+ 5.71
Labour	+ 0.44	+ 0.94	+ 0.35	+ 0.97	+ 0.68
Capital	+ 0.84	+ 1.57	+ 0.80	+ 0.73	+ 0.80
Reallocation of resources	+ 0.98	+ 0.76	+ 0.11	+ 0.25	+ 1.60
Economies of scale	+ 1.00	+ 1.25	+ 0.43	+ 0.30	+ 1.40
Cyclical irregularities	- 0.07		- 0.29	- 0.40	- 0.07
Residue	+ 1.84	+ 0.87	+ 0.87	+ 0.76	+ 1.30

Source: E. Denison and J. P. Poullier, *Why Growth Rates differed from Washington*, The Brooking Institution, 1967

E. Denison and J.P. Poullier proposed a method. It can be defined as follows: it involves weighting the various factors of growth by the weight of each in national income, and then determining the contribution of this factor to the growth rate. There are four groups of factors: labour (level of the active population, working hours, age and gender structure, structure of professional qualifications, agricultural migration); capital (levels of productive investment, in housing and abroad); size factors (increasing returns, price structure, opening of borders); residual factors (or residual or share of the growth rate of national income that cannot be explained by that of the factors of production).

59 Dominique Barjot, « La France et les investissements directs américains (1945-1973) » ("France and American Direct Investment (1945-1973)"), text publishing in *French Historical Studies*, 2022.

60 Dominique Barjot & Rang-Ri Park-Barjot, « Transferts de technologie entre France et URSS du milieu des années 1960 à celui des années 1970 : entre coopération scientifique et technique, choix des politiques étrangères et montages financiers à long et moyen termes», in Alexandre Tchoubarian & Francine-Dominique Liechtenhan, Sophie Cœuré et Olga Okouneva (eds.), *Les Français dans la vie intellectuelle et scientifique en URSS au XXe siècle*, Moscou, Institut d'histoire unielle de l'Académie des sciences de Russie, 2014, p. 101-116.

61 Dominique Barjot & Getsiva Cayo-Durand, « Les échanges économiques entre la France et l'Amérique latine pendant la présidence du Général de Gaulle : une première approche», in Maurice Vaïsse (ed.), *De Gaulle et l'Amérique latine*, Rennes, Presses universitaires de Rennes, 2014, p. 177-195.

TABLE 11 **AVERAGE ANNUAL GROWTH RATES** (in %)

	France	Federal Republic of Germany	United Kingdom	United States of America	Italy
1955-1962	+ 5.0	+ 5.4	+ 2.3	+ 2.7	+ 5.7
1962-1967	+ 4.9	+ 3.4	+ 2.9	+ 4.9	+ 4.5

Source: E. Denison and J. P. Poullier, *Why Growth Rates differed from Washington,* The Brooking Institution, 1967

For France, the results lead to the following conclusions concerning the period 1955-1962: firstly, with a virtually constant working population, France was at a disadvantage compared with other countries, hence the need for longer working hours; secondly, the age pyramid and the gender distribution of the population were relatively favourable to France; thirdly, the improvement in qualification levels remained within the European average, lagging far behind the United States; fourthly, agricultural migration to high-productivity sectors made a strong contribution to French growth; fifthly, the contribution of productive fixed capital was significantly lower than in Germany, but higher than in the United States and the United Kingdom; sixthly, the effects of trade liberalisation on economies of scale were equivalent in France, Germany, the United Kingdom and Italy and very little higher than in the United States; seventhly and last, overall, the opening of borders benefited Italy, Germany and France most.

In the years 1955 to 1962, France was in an intermediate position.[62] Compared to the United States, France benefited from its technological gap (accumulation of invention and imitation).[63] Germany prevailed over France, thanks to an increase in its activity rate and a higher investment effort. In contrast, the United Kingdom lost ground to France due to lower working hours, productive investment and productivity gains. Finally, Italy has benefited over France through greater agricultural migration, economies of scale and a higher activity rate.

During the period 1962-67, a rebalancing took place (well highlighted by Lionel Stoléru[64]). First of all, France best maintained the pace of its growth. While the United States almost joined France in its growth rate, the United Kingdom accelerated its growth somewhat without catching up with any of its major Western competitors, while the Federal Republic of Germany and Italy lost ground. There were specific reasons for this development: the American catch-up was due to a strong expansion of the working population and productive investment; the stagnation of West German investment allowed France to catch up; the Italian dropout was the result of a slowdown in agricultural migration and a reduction in working hours. Finally,

62 Jean-Pierre Mockers, *Croissances économiques comparées : Allemagne, France, Royaume-Uni 1950-1967,* Paris, Dunod, 1969 ; Michel Hau, *France-Allemagne : la difficile convergence,* Paris, Peter Lang, 2015.

63 Bernard Guibert *et alii, La mutation industrielle de la France. Du traité de Rome à la crise pétrolière,* Les Collection de l'INSEE, E31--32, tomes I et II, Paris, Institut national de la statistique et des sciences économiques, 1975.

64 Lionel Stoleru, *L'impératif Industriel,* Paris, Le Seuil, 1969.

between 1955 and 1967, only the Federal Republic of Germany experienced higher growth than France, despite an unfavourable trend in the activity rate, thanks to high working hours, strong productivity gains and a catch-up in housing and wages that was possible without surpluses to distribute.

Conclusions

In short, between 1945 and 1969, French growth was the result of a series of favourable factors: catching up with the birth rate, the 1939-45 shock, institutional reforms parallel to the educational efforts of the French population, industrial conversion, a decrease in demand and a favourable environment.[65] Certain factors were particularly decisive. Firstly, the French gave a certain priority to work. Moreover, in the 1960s, France benefited from a modernised productive apparatus and a dynamic, coherent and relatively efficient economic policy. As a result, in the 1960s, France was a particularly dynamic economy, engaged in a strong catching-up process, even though it had lost ground overall since the last third of the 19th century:

TABLE 12 **AVERAGE ANNUAL GROWTH RATES OF THE GNP** (1870-1970, in %)

	1870-1913	1913-1950	1950-1960	1960-1970
Belgium	2.7	1.0	2.9	4.9
France	1.6	0.7	4.6	5.8
Germany	2.9	1.2	7.8	4.8
Italy	1.4	1.3	5.8	5.7
Netherlands	2.2	2.1	4.7	5.1
United Kingdom	2.2	1.7	2.7	2.8
USA	4.3	2.9	3.2	4.3

Source: A. Maddison, "Performance in Europe", *The Fontana Economic History Europe*, vol. 5, London, Collins-Fontana, 1976, p. 502 and sq.; *Economic Growth in the West. Comparative Experience in Europe and North America*, London, Allen & Unwin, 1969, p. 28 & 30.

The consequences have been globally favourable for the global integration of the French economy. Indeed, like Germany and Italy, it had increased its share of world exports:

TABLE 13 **GEOGRAPHICAL DISTRIBUTION OF THE WORLD EXPORTS OF MANUFACTURED PRODUCTS** (in %)

	1963	1973
USA	17.2 (1)	12.6 (2)
Japan	6.0 (5)	9.9 (3)
France	7.0 (4)	7.3 (4)
Federal Republic of Germany	15.5 (2)	17.0 (1)
Italy	4.7 (6)	5.3 (6)
United Kingdom	11.1 (3)	7.0 (5)

Source : OECD.

65 Dominique Barjot, « Tendances d'ensemble 1945-1970 », in Dominique Barjot (ed.), *Industrialisation et sociétés en Europe occidentale du début des années 1880 à la fin des années 1960. France, Allemagne-RFA, Royaume-Uni et Benelux*, Paris, CNED-SEDES, 1997, p. 309-347.

It owed this largely to the development of trade within the Common Market of the Six:

TABLE 14 **EVOLUTION OF THE PART OF THE INTERNAL EXCHANGES WITHIN THE TOTAL EXPORTS OF THE ECC COUNTRIES FROM 1958 TO 1969** (in %)

	1958	1969
UEBL (Belgium + Luxembourg)	45	68
Netherlands	42	60
France	22	48
Italy	24	43
FRG	27	40
EEC	32	48

Source: EEC.

With a 26% increase in the European Union's share of trade, France was ahead of the Benelux countries (UEBL: +23%, Netherlands: +18%), Italy (+19%) and Federal Germany (+13%).

It had also made an increased effort in favour of the education system, even surpassing Germany in the 1960s, but was able to match the performance of the United States, the Netherlands and the United Kingdom.

TABLE 15 **SHARE OF THE EDUCATION EXPENDITURES IN THE GNP** (1955-1964, in % of the total)

	1955	1960	1964
USA	4.1	5.3	6.2
Belgium (a)	3.0	4.5	4.3
France	2.9	3.4	4.3
FRG	2.9	3.0	3.4
Italy	3.3	4.5	5.4 (b)
Netherlands	3.6	4.7	5.7
United Kingdom	3.5	4.1	4.9

Only public expenditures.

Private expenditures: estimation on the basic of the dates of 1960.

Source: OECD

But this progress did not make it possible to make up for France's relative backwardness in research and development:

TABLE 16 **GROSS EXPENDITURES OF R&D SHARED BY ORIGINS** in % of the GNP 1963-1973

	Expenditures of the private and foreign firms				Public and National Resources			
	1963	1967	1971	1973	1963	1967	1971	1973
France	?	0.3	0.4	0.5	?	0.3	0.3	0.3
FRG	0.8	1.	1.0	1.2	0.7	0.7	0.7	0.9
Italy	0.4	0.4	0.5	0.5	0.3	0.3	0.4	0.4
Japan	0.9	0.9	1.1	1.2	0.4	0.4	0.4	0.5
Netherlands	1.1	1.3	1.3	1.2	0.8	0.8	0.8	0.8
United Kingdom	1.0	1.1	1.1	?	1.3	1.3	1.2	?
USA	0.9	1.1	1.1	1.0	1.9	2.1	1.7	1.6

Source: OECD.

In 1973, on the eve of a major economic crisis, France appeared to be lagging behind all the major industrial nations, including behind Italy, not only because of the weakness of private sector R&D, but also because of the weakness of public funding. This was undoubtedly one of the great weaknesses of the French productive system.

The cement market during the 20th century: between cartels and regulation

Cécile Coursiéras-Jaff
Sorbonne Université and Institut Catholique de Paris

Introduction

During the interwar period, most European producers began considering the assets of building national and international agreements. Some, such as the English or German producers already owned strong national agreement organizations while others, as the French producers only had local and periodic price-fixing organizations[1]. The evolution of the French cement cartel in Europe during the interwar-period had almost never been studied before[2]. The behavior of the French cement industry differs from other heavy industry sectors[3]. Unlike the steel industry, the cement industry did not organize its national cartel during the 1920's[4]. Its evolution is also unique compared to its European neighbors. The reasons for this particular situation are related to the oligopolistic structure of the cement market as well as to the economic cycles but also to the individual strategies implemented by the French cement companies. The economic crisis of the 1930's caused a disruption of the cement market.

During the after-war period, the French cement industry knew a restructuration process. This evolution led to a decrease of the cement producers' number because

1 Louis Reid, « La lutte pour l'indépendance de l'industrie du ciment », quoted from *The Economist* in *Bulletins de la Fédération des Chambres syndicales des fabricants de Chaux et ciments de France,* mai 1929.

2 However, a study on Spanish cement already exists : Mendoza Antonio Gómez « La formacion de un cartel en el primer tercio del siglo XX : la industria del cemento portland », *Revista de Historia Economica,* Mai 1987, vol.5, Issue 2, p. 325-361.

3 Gilles Montant, « Analyse du cartel charbonnier du Nord-Pas-de Calais sur la période 1925-1935 », *Histoire économie et société,* 2001, 20e année, n°4, p. 471-488.

4 Dominique Barjot, (ed.), *International Cartels Revisited. Vues nouvelles sur les cartels internationaux, 1880-1980,* Caen, Éditions du Lys, 1994.

of an acceleration of the concentration process. The cement market already had an oligopolistic structure before World War II. Yet, some regional family companies managed to get their game. However, from 1945 to 1971, the oligopoly was reinforced around the largest companies.

This evolution finds an explanation in the particular structure of the cement market but also because of economic and political reasons. The cement industry is a heavy industry with a low value product. Therefore, one of the key issues consists in limiting storage and transportation costs to preserve a competitive end product cost on the market. The study of the information sharing process between producers is also crucial to understand this concentration process. Moreover, the growing demand of the reconstruction imposed capacity constraints that only members of the oligopoly seemed able to assume.

What is the link between the structures of the cement industry and the producers' concentration degree? What strategies did use the members of the oligopoly to fight their competitors? We'll try to answer these questions by stressing the link between growth and investment rate. This point is essential to understand the race between producers to increase their production capacity. The behavior of the French public authorities is also critical: did the French state contribute to this concentration, especially by its price limitation policy that replaced the official cartel institution since 1945?

After the war, the concentration process of the cement industry fell into two parts. From 1945 to the 1960's, the reconstruction allowed the cement producers with the largest investment capacities to improve their production process. At the same time, the price limitation policy reduced the firm's investment capacities. The gap was widening between family companies with local sales and national firms directed by managers, following strategic expansion policies and turning to foreign.

During the 1960's, the family companies almost completely disappeared and the competition between the members of the oligopoly was reinforced. The French cement market was on its way to maturation. The demand stayed stable and the flexibility became narrow. Each producer had to manage to combine investment in productivity, capacity and spatial location to remain competitive. Each of the four members of the oligopoly, Lafarge, Ciments français, Vicat and Poliet et Chausson, needed to expand its production capacities at the same level as its competitors. At this time the strategic efficiency of the firm became a decisive factor to maintain its position in the oligopoly. In the beginning of the seventies, the French oligopoly tightened around three companies and then, had to face the new challenges of internationalization.

In order to present this points, the first part of the paper will deal with a global introduction concerning the edification of the French cement oligopoly before the second World War, its global issues and actors. The second part will be dedicated to the after war period. The limitation price policy and the slowdown of the cement market during the 1950's seemed to favor the oligopoly members and led the cement producers to find new strategies to remain competitive. Finally the last part will explain how the growing demand of the 1960's brought a reorganization inside the oligopoly.

1/ THE CEMENT MARKET: TOWARD THE CONSTITUTION OF AN OLIGOPOLY

The cement market issues led most producers to focus on regional market. Even if the commercial competition is most of the time local because of transportation costs, cement commercial expansion enabled cement companies to grow and to fight each other to increase their national market shares[5]. During the 1920's the huge demand of the reconstruction allowed the expansion of the cement industry. Some producers, anticipating this demand by building news plants to increase their capacity, became quickly powerful on the cement market. These producers are those constituting the French oligopoly since the 1930's.

1.1/ The general characteristics of the cement market

Next to a pre-existent binder market, a cement market gradually appeared during the 19th century. In 1817, the French engineer Louis Vicat discovered the hydraulicity of the lime and worked out the artificial cement that we call today cement. Cement is a blend of clay, limestone and coal with varying proportions depending on their characteristics. Cement and lime shared the binder market during the 19th century before cement slowly substituted to lime. The cement industry is a heavy industry with a very simple production process. Four phases are necessary: extracting, calcinating, drying and shipping. The technological progression was very slow. Indeed, between 1817 and the end of the 1880's, there were no major process or manufacturing innovation[6].

The First World War triggered the domination of artificial cement on the binder market. After the war, the reconstruction generated new needs and artificial cement overcame lime at this time. Beforehand, some technical innovations had been necessary for this commercial takeoff: the use of gas ovens and the progressive substitution of straight kilns by rotary kilns, which were more productive and ensured to a good cement quality. The generalization of rotary kilns during the 1900's contributed to unify French cement production by reducing the differences of quality and price between producers[7]. Indeed, before the growth of the cement industry, the prices of cement were not at all stable and this instability lasted during the second half of the 19th century. As the production reached its technical maturity, when the product's characteristics and the manufacturing methods got fixed, the average price evolution remained steady at a higher level. This price evolution led cement companies to fix

5 Bertrand Collomb, « L'industrie européenne du ciment au XXème siècle », *Entreprises et Histoires*, n°3, mai 1993, p. 97-111.

6 Syndicat national des fabricants de ciments et de chaux (France), *L'industrie cimentière française*, Paris, 1979.

7 Alain Desdevises, «Le ciment, matériau de construction: histoire et développement», *Culture et technique*, n°26, Ministère de l'Équipement, du Logement et des Transports, 1992, p. 51-57.

new competitive strategies[8]. The characteristics and technical standards of cement hardly evolved since the beginning although different kinds of quality or dosage exist, depending on the usage that is made of the material. We will consider that cement is a simple product. Manufacturing costs are hardly the same from one concurrent to another: 40% for fuel, 15% for raw materials, 15% for labor, 15% for maintenance and overhead costs and finally 15% for packing and depreciation[9]. Producing cement is not expensive. On an other hand, it's a low value product. Therefore, one of the key issues in its production consists in limiting storage and transportation costs to preserve a competitive end product cost on the market. For this particular reason, before setting up a cement factory, downstream and upstream factors has to be considered. Distances between the quarry and the kilns or fuel accessibility played a key role as an asset or a weakness in the competitor's balance of power inside the market[10].

1.2/ Local market and spatial competition

Because of these constraints, the cement market is a local market inside which a natural balance gradually settled between production and distribution capacities. This structure is suitable for "spatial competition" as defined by the economists Scotchmer and Thiss[11]. In this model, each company is comparatively spatially separated from its competitors and has almost a monopoly in its distribution area. Assuming that during good economic conjunctions, we find mainly the same prices among competitors as mentioned above, a tacit consensus to respect "preferential market areas"[12] seems to prevail. These "preferential market areas" are divided between producers to maximize their profits. In this particular situation, which is roughly one of the cement industry situation up to the end of the 1870s, the ideas of branch, market or total request were very vague or hardly existed. There was no interdependency between two producers, and therefore no agreement between competitors. These "preferential market areas" could be destabilized if the market became unsteady and led a company to overproduction or if the profit share increased more slowly than the producer's number. Each seller, observing the weakening of his own situation, would have to engage a new dynamic competition different from the spatial one. This situation appeared during the 1880s, when the Great Depression (1873-1896) began to reach the cement industry. As the cement industry depends on the construction cycles, it experienced with a slight delay the general downturn of the French economy and then, of the building and public works sector of the beginning 1870s[13]. The resulting reduced demand, sometimes very changing within the market area, inflamed competition between producers and reduced individual profits. So each company began to plan the conquest of new markets to balance the losses inside their preferential market areas.[14]

8 Jacques Reynaud, *Les investissement dans l'industrie des chaux et ciments*, Verneuil-sur-Avre, Dierville- Harmonic, 1965.

9 *Ibidem.*

10 Bertrand Collomb, « L'industrie européenne du ciment au XXème siècle », *op. cit.*

11 Suzanne Scotchmer, Jean-François Thisse, «Les implications de l'espace pour la concurrence», *Revue économique*, Vol. 44, n° 4, 1993, p. 653-669.

12 *Ibidem.*

13 Yasuo Gonjo, « Le plan Freycinet 1878-1882: un aspect de la Grande dépression économique en France », *Revue historique*, juillet 1972.

14 Suzanne Scotchmer, Jean-François Thisse., art. cit.

Having stronger expansion means, the largest companies tried to eliminate their competitors or at least to reduce their market share by a mergers and acquisitions offensive policy. This policy led already to a process of market concentration. Thus, Lafarge began to purchase its closest competitors as Les chaux et ciments du Teil, de Cruas et de Meysse in Ardèche and la Société des Portland Méridionaux between 1887 and 1900. M&A process enabled companies to increase their production capacities and opportunities without increasing total supply on the market and therefore the oupply risks when economic growth slows down. Thus, an oligopolistic market was gradually set up since the late nineteenth century. This development was mainly based on the fact that, because of the first concentration, there were only few companies trying to sell most of their production in their own areas. The new situation did not introduce any disruption in the mentioned above spatial competition principles but it reinforced the interdependency between the companies on the market. Already in the 1920's the cement producers were aware of this interdependency. That's why they were especially vigilant concerning their competitor's actions.

This attitude is typical inside a oligopolistic market, as explained by Alain Jeunemaître and Hervé Dumez[15]. Inside a oligopolistic market, the mimetic phenomenon becomes an element of the corporate strategies. Inside industries involving advanced technology, the mimetic phenomenon generally leads to a virtuous cycle of positive externalities, by a technology-lock lowering production costs and stimulating demand. Yet, in the cement industry, demand does not depend on costs and the technological potential is reduced. Thus, the lasting effects of lowering costs remains very small and tend to emphasize the risks of overproduction or overcapacity in case of an economic downturn. The crisis of 1930 led to this situation and pushed the producers to organize themselves at national scale to share the market according to their production capacity. A struggle for influence began in which the leading producers exercised their power on the more modest firms.

1.3/ An already existing oligopoly during the 1930's

The construction of the cement market took place in the first third of the 20[Th] and was marked by the rapid appearance of large cement producers. In 1910, the major cement producers are already Lafarge, Ciments Français, Poliet et Chausson and Vicat, the members of the oligopoly of the 1960's[16]. The urgency of the reconstruction and the rise of new demands after the First World War modified the cement industry. First of all, productive capacities of the cement industry were insufficient because of the boom of the demand and of the M&A policy applied before the war. Indeed this growth strategy enabled the cement companies to increase their production capacity while minimizing the risks related to demand, but did not contribute to increase the overall production capacity of the market. The artificial cement sector was particularly weakened by a weak production capacity. Each company tried to increase its facilities

15 Hervé Dumez, Alain Jeunemaître, « Rôle et statut de l'économiste dans les affaires de concurrence. Leçon tirées de l'histoire américain de l'industrie cimentière», *Revue économique,* 6/2001 (Vol. 52), p. 1279-1299.

16 Dominique Barjot, « Lafarge : l'ascension d'une multinationale à la française (1833-2005) », *Relations internationales* 2005/4, n° 124, p. 51-67.

as fast as possible, in the best conditions and manufacturing costs. Four mechanisms were used to achieve this goal: the pursuit of mergers and acquisitions, equity investments in various subsidiaries, the establishment of new factories and the renovation of older units to reinforce their productivity[17].

Despite the produced tonnage collapsed during the First World War, new capitals were invested by the firms that produced cement in France or in the Colonies after 1913.[18] In the beginning 1920's, several French companies stood out on the cement market. Les Établissements Poliet et Chausson, La Société des Ciments Français et des Portland de Boulogne sur Mer[19], La société anonyme des ciments Vicat, la Société des Chaux et Ciments Lafarge et du Teil et la Société Anonyme des Ciments Romain Boyer were at this time the most successful firms. The cement industry became the subject of growing investments. The firms that made the most important investments in the previous decade dominated the market.

TABLE N°1 **CAPITAL INVESTMENT IN THE CEMENT INDUSTRY IN 1913**

Firms	Capital investment (Francs)
Établissements Poliet et Chausson	39 710 000
Compagnie nouvelle des ciments Portland du Boulonnais	4 900 000
Société anonyme des ciments Vicat	8 949 000
Société Lafarge et du Teil	18 427 000
Société anonyme des Ciments Romain Boyer	4 025 000
TOTAL	76 011 000

Sources : Arch. hist. du Crédit Lyonnais, DEEF 59896/1, Industrie du ciment en France, étude économique et statistique, 1921

Cement producers that emerged during the nineteenth century such as Ciments Français, Lafarge, or Vicat resisted with varying success to the war production halt. In the North, the Société des Ciments Français et des Portland de Boulogne sur Mer, better known as the Ciments Français encountered a steady growth since its inception in 1861. Its sale exceeded 400 000 tons in 1913[20]. Because of their age and their strong position in the south of France, Vicat and Lafarge[21] maintained their rank. However, for the new building materials company, Les Établissements Poliet et Chausson, the First World War acted as a springboard. The company, founded in 1899 in the Paris Region, made significant investments between 1913 and the end of the war. Its success is due to the increase of its mergers and acquisitions[22] and its huge plants building

17 Aurore Cartier, *Lafarge, de l'entreprise familiale à la multinationale (1880-1947)*, Thèse de l'École des Chartes, supervisor: Dominique Barjot, mars 2011.

18 Cécile Coursiéras, C. *Poliet et Chausson, Essor et consolidation d'une entreprise française cimentière française de 1901 à 1933*, Mémoire de Master 2 d'Histoire sous la direction de Dominique Barjot, Juin 2010, Université Paris Sorbonne (Paris IV).

19 The Compagnie nouvelle des Ciments Portland du Boulonnais was the former name for the company Les Ciments Français.

20 Cécile Coursiéras, *Poliet et Chausson, Essor et consolidation d'une entreprise française cimentière française de 1901 à 1933*, op.cit.

21 Founded in 1833

22 During 1916, *Poliet et Chausson* takes over *La Métalline society* and the *Société Anonyme des Ciments et Chaux hydrauliques de Beffes* in 1917.

program during the war including the 200 000 tons capacity Gargenville cement factory built in 1917[23].

Between 1933 and 1938, the underconsumption crisis introduced three new elements on the cement market : a concentration process, the use of a trade union as a national lobby by the cement producers and the edification of regional counters to establish price agreements. The concentration process was characterized by merger and acquisition policies or acquisition of stake from the most important cement firms toward the others. The cement producers organized themselves in official cartels through the Trade Union Federation of Chambers of Lime and Cement Manufacturers *(*Fédération des Chambres Syndicales des Fabricants de Chaux et Ciments de France *or* FCSFCCF) and inside regional cartels. This cartels replaced the old regional counters, mostly developed in the 1920's and then felt into disuse. This counters were usually based on joint ventures. In the Southeast, a limited company, the Southeastern Association of artificial Cement called ASECA[24] was created in October 1932. In 1933, an agreement was also signed in the Southwest with the constitution of CIMSUDOUEST. Again, this group of French building materials companies is created to reach an agreement on sale in the Southwest. However, the market concentration and the national importance taken by many companies quickly revealed the limits of a disparate set of regional agreements.

To be truly effective, the industry needed a central organization, capable of uniting various agreements. Taking CIMSUDOUEST as an example, other organizations were formed. At this time, their goal was to serve at regional scale the national cement cartel set up in March 1934 for four years. This cartel brought together four regional groups from the East, Southeast, Southwest and Northwest of France and a group from Algeria in a federate Union with headquarters in Paris. This counters formed in Mai and July 1934 are the Union des Groupements des fabricants de liants hydrauliques (UG), the Association Centre Nord-Ouest des ciments artificiels (ACENO) and the Association des Ciments Algériens (CIMAL). They aimed mainly to the regulation of the most popular artificial products.

Between 1933 and 1937, the agreements between the cement producers generalized the setting of a similar destination price for all the producers. In 1937, the producers became free to set their prices. Thus, a system of taxation was set : the expenses had to be shared between the different unions on a prorata based on the true references of anterior buyback tonnages or on an estimation of the not yet produced tonnages. This distribution planned between April 1st 1934 and March 31th 1938, was interesting because it highlighted the leader firms in every union. Within the ACENO for example, the biggest investors were by far Poliet et Chausson with 24 % of the capital, followed by other almost equivalent firms like Ciments Français, Ciments Lafarge, Société Lambert et Frères, Ciments d'Origny and the Ciments La Loisne.

23 Crédit Agricole-Crédit Lyonnais Archives. DEEF 38768 : Assemblée générale des actionnaires de 1919.
24 Association Sud-Est du Ciment Artificiel (ASECA).

The ASECA was clearly dominated by Lafarge which owns 34 % of the interests and which also shares at 22 % the interests of CIMSUDOUEST with its competitors Poliet et Chausson and Ciments Français.

Finally, Lafarge and the Société Villeneuve shared the control on the CIMAL with each one possessing 25 % of the investments. This, even though a hypothetical distribution of the Holding society stocks, at least helped to reveal the amount of the investments and the control that each oligopoly member exercised on the different union and thus on the cartel. Even if, regarding the parent companies, Poliet remained the major shareholder of the holding with 18 % of the investments, against 13% for Lafarge and 12,7 % for the Ciments Français. On the other hand, considering the funded companies, Lafarge comes in the lead with an indirect control of more than 20 % of the capital[25]. Moreover, from 1937, every change of the official prices mercurial were scrutinized by the public authorities[26]. Under the Vichy regime, economic organisation committees were set by the work charter of October 4th 1941. This state's control established during the German occupation remained after the war as a price control institution.

During the 1930's, the economic crisis led the cement producers to create an official cartel and paradoxically strengthened the most powerful cement producers by controlling the others through the cartel. Lafarge, Ciments Français and Poliet et Chausson were during the 1930's the cement producers that invested and produced the most. At this time, Vicat was lagging, partly because is settlement region, the southeastern France, was the same as Lafarge. In the beginning 1960's, Vicat became really a member of the oligopoly.

2/ A TWO TIER INDUSTRY (1945-1962)

Between 1945 and 1962, with the price limitation of the reconstruction, the gap becomes larger between the members of the oligopoly and the local producers. After the war, the cement industry was put in the dock because of the closeness of a certain number of its producers with the Vichy government and the German occupant. If the reconstruction needs allowed them to escape their nationalization, thus, the French state set a price limitation policy that strengthened the oligopoly. Indeed, the context of inflation established an investment discrimination between the largest producers and the regional cementers. This fact led the cement market to a material and financial concentration. The concentration process went with a gathering of the production means within the oligopoly firms themselves.[27] Their reorganizations were crucial for them to stay among the top sellers. For the majority of cement producers, this reorganization turned family firms into managerial companies.

25 Cécile Coursiéras and Aurore Cartier, "Running with the wolves or fighting the crises? The roles of large french firms in the european cement cartels during the interwar period", EBHA Conference, Athens, 2011.

26 Jacques Reynaud, *Les investissement dans l'industrie des chaux et ciments*, Verneuil-sur-Avre, Dierville-Harmonic, 1965, p. 27.

27 François Mader, « Un exemple de restructuration industrielle : l'oligopole du ciment en France entre 1962 et 1972 », *Revue d'économie industrielle.* Vol 4. 2e trimestre 1978. p. 96-116.

2.1/ After the war, a troubled price limited industry

The necessity to rebuild the country after the Second World War would be useful to the cement producers[28]. Indeed, the most influential cement producers were put on the dock for collaborating with the German occupant during the Second World War and after the Liberation, the new government that led a nationalization policy was wandering to nationalize the cement industry[29]. Poliet et Chausson's members of the board of directors were accused of collaboration. Henri Chausson the son of the founder of Poliet et Chausson, that became the C.E.O. during the war, was struck by national indignity and had to submit his resignation as the major part of the members of the board of directors. As far as Ciments Français is concerned, the firm was put under investigation, which led to an almost complete renewal of its directors. Vicat had also to face the resignation of its C.E.O., Joseph Merceron-Vicat, a member of the National Council of Vichy and director of the new Nazi Europe. But the company remained under family control and he came back as C.E.O.in 1953. Finally, Lafarge was sequestered in September 1944 because the firm was accused to supply concrete to the German Todt Organization[30]. The action was decided by the prefect of the Ardeche region, at the initiative of the Communist Party. It is part of a broader perspective: the nationalization of the cement industry. But this nationalization failed. The escrow remained limited to the plant of Teil, and was over in June 1946. Indeed, the cement industry was one of the most important priority of the government for the reconstruction. In 1948, the cement production was at the same level as it was in 1932, a record year[31].

TABLE N° 2 **THE MAJOR CEMENT FIRMS IN 1948 : SHARE CAPITAL AND MARKET CAPITALISATION IN MILLIONS FRANCS**

	Share capital	Market capitalisation
Poliet et Chausson	1121	2100
Lafarge	476,5	1800
Ciments Français	180	1200
Lambert Frères	165	1150

Source: Dominique Barjot, «Travaux publics et biens intermédiaires, 1900- 1950 », in Maurice Lévy-Leboyer (sous la dir. de), *Histoire de la France industrielle*, t. 23 : « 1900-1950. L'âge de la technique », Paris, Larousse, 1996, p. 300.

Even if the producers escaped the nationalization, the public authorities would carefully control the cement prices. After August 1946, the starting prices were set at national scale. In July 1947, regional starting prices were established. They were justified by the plants' location, according to the remoteness of coal supply center and of the centers of production of slag cement as well as differences in costs of

28 Dominique Barjot, « Lafarge : l'ascension d'une multinationale à la française (1833-2005) », *Relations internationales* 2005/4, n° 124, p. 51-67.

29 Dominique Barjot, « Travaux publics et biens intermédiaires 1900-1950 », in Maurice Lévy-Leboyer (dir.), *Histoire de la France industrielle*, tome 2. *Les trente glorieuses*, Paris, Larousse, 1996, p. 296-319.

30 Rémy Desquesnes, « L'Organisation Todt en France », *in* « Stratégies industrielle sous l'occupation », *op. cit.*, p. 535-550 ; *Atlantikwall et Südwall. La défense allemande et le littoral français (1941-1944)*, thèse de doctorat d'Etat, Université de Caen, 1987, 2 vol.

31 Dominique Barjot, « Travaux publics et biens intermédiaires 1900-1950 », *op. cit*, p. 296-319.

quarrying[32]. Thus, five geographic areas were created: the North, the Western France and Paris Basin, the East and Centre, the Southwest and Southeast[33]. During the 1950's the competition became stronger. The producers had to adjust their prices to take account of the similar price policy applied with the nearest plant where the cement was used. According to Bernard Collomb, this is a dark period for the French cement profession[34]. Indeed, from 1938 to 1953, the price of cement was multiplied by 20 when all industrial products were multiplied by 32 in average. Small local cement producers survived at the cost of the non-modernization of theirs plants and the members of the oligopoly were beginning to turn to foreign sector, and especially Lafarge to North America[35].

Did the State knowingly promote the oligopoly members by limiting the cement price? François Mader asked the question, adding that, being a sheltered industry because of its transportation costs that prevented any international business, the necessity for the cement industry to have a few numbers of producers reaching an European scale was not as crucial as in others industry sectors[36]. Jean Pierre Angelier also pointed out in his studies that the limitation price established by the French government allowed the industry to develop and favoured the concentration process around the oligopoly[37]. During the 1950s, the French cement industry reached the stage of technical maturity on the production process. Financial constraints due to the cost of equipment and investments required to follow the growth of the market have led to the emergence of large national groups that coexisted with local cement relied on rents situation[38].

2.2/ An investment discrimination

After the war, we may distinguish two groups, each representing the half part of the production. On one hand he three larger cement firms : Lafarge, Ciments Français and Poliet et Chausson that were able to massively invest, and on an other hand, the other regional producers. Their profits prevented them to invest and stay competitive on the market. The production capacity of the three larger firms is between 2,7 millions tons and 4,5 millions tons. They owned several plants at national scale. On the contrary the other cement producers usually owned only one plant with a production capacity between 200 000 and 1 200 000 tons. They were mostly regional firms with local and familial interests.[39] In 1947, the major cement producers invested as massively as possible. This major investment would allow them already in 1954, to increase their dividends and to attract new shareholders[40]. If we examine the investment of Lafarge, Ciments Français and Poliet et Chausson between 1955 and 1962, we may distinguish a higher investment rate for Lafarge mostly related to its internationalization. On the

32 Jacques Reynaud, *op. cit.*, p. 27.

33 François Mader, « Un exemple de restructuration industrielle : l'oligopole du ciment en France entre 1962 et 1972 », *op. cit.*

34 Bertrand Collomb, *op. cit.*

35 Lafarge already begun its internationalization during the 1920's with the Lafarge Aluminous Cement Company in the United Kingdom. See Dominique Barjot, « Lafarge : l'ascension d'une multinationale à la française (1833-2005) », art. cit.

36 François Mader, art. cit.

37 Jean-Pierre Angelier, *Étude sur l'évolution de la concentration dans l'industrie du ciment en France (1978)*, *op. cit.*, p. 124.

38 *Ibidem.*

39 Mader F., *op. cit.*

40 BNP-Paribas Archives. IND 1700. Poliet et Chausson, note générale de présentation et de synthèse.1968.

other side, the investment part of Poliet et Chausson is a bit lower, this delay is related to the managing problems of the firms [41]. The chart below compares the investments of the three larger firms.

CHART N°1 **THE OLIGOPOLY MEMBERS' INVESTMENT (1955-1962)** in per cent of fixed capital

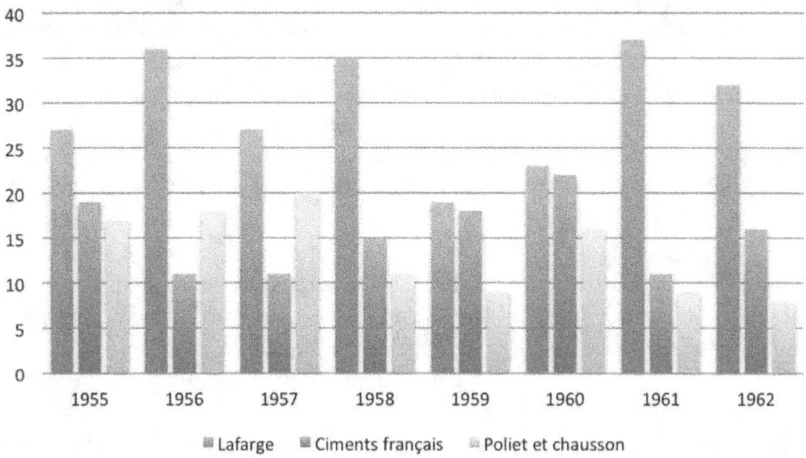

Source: Jacques Reynaud, *Les investissements dans l'industrie des chaux et ciments,* Université de Paris, 1965, p. 54.

For the smaller firms, the investment is lower. Indeed, for a medium-size firm, a new kiln represented a burden for the treasury. The following years, this firm would only realize the required renewal changes. This fact is reinforced by the price limitation, as already mentioned. Eventually, the investment policy, by allowing the larger firms to quickly answer the market demand, enlarged the gap between the members of the oligopoly and the local cement producers. Yet, the oligopoly itself has to face a lot of mutations.

2.3/ Inside the oligopoly : mutation and competition

During the 1950's the cement industry evolved and changed. The members of the oligopoly achieved their mutation from family firms to managerial companies. They were also influenced by new American management methods. This evolution is partly due to the necessity to call new shareholders to sustain the growing investment needs and stay competitive. Lafarge exemplified this mutations. Indeed, in 1947, the family firm cannot find a successor to Jean de Waubert inside the family Pavin de Lafarge. The firm had to call new men: Alfred François as a chief executive and Marcel Demonque, graduate of the École des Mines engineering school, as a managing director. He quickly became the real leader of the firm. He was attached to the paternal and catholic values

41 Cécile Coursiéras-Jaff « Poliet et Chausson. A French ciment firm facing the Banks » in Dominique Barjot (ed.), « L'industrie de la construction au XXe siècle : une comparaison internationale vue sous l'angle de l'entreprise », *Revue française d'histoire économique* n°1, 2014, p. 40-56.

of the firm but at the same time, he introduced new American management methods[42], especially through the American consulting firm Mc Kinsey.

Poliet et Chausson left also the family hands in 1947. After 1945, the brother in law of Henri Chausson, Raoul Kern, who was a man of consensus, became the chief executive. For health reasons, he had to resign in 1947 to let the presidency to Pierre Gillet, member of the board of directors since the 1920's. The man did not encountered the same successes as Marcel Demonque. Indeed, during these years, the board of directors 'difficulties to face the staff's claims undermined the firm. Under these conditions, it was difficult for many technicians of value to do their job and the company suffered the resignation of prominent collaborators as M.M. Caillette, commercial director, Lecoeur, staff chief, and Lofficier, technical director. They left Poliet et Chausson for Lafarge[43].

The case of Vicat is an exception. The firm stayed in the family fold thanks to André Merceron-Vicat, the son of Joseph Merceron Vicat. The man is the main architect of the successes of the sixties of the firm. He was an Engineer from the Special School of Public Works and has climbed the ladder of the internal hierarchy: in the 1950s, he was technical director, with Maurice Bouchayer, CEO and husband of Denise Merceron-Vicat, sister of André, and then succeeded him. He was the leader of the investment programs conducted from 1952 to 1960 and by 1959, he introduced a new manufacturing process, the way "semi-dry" in its factories. He succeeded to his father as a CEO in 1960 and allowed Vicat to enter the French cement oligopoly during the 1960's.

This managerial evolution is followed by a new strategic policy. The agreements, the mimetic phenomenon, and the M&A policies are not new in the cement oligopolistic situation. They were already used during the 1930's. However, the acquisition of minority stake of the capital of other members of the oligopoly is relatively new. The case of Poliet et Chausson in 1954, controlled by the financial group CGIFE allowed this situation. After a lot of negotiations, the cement firms Lafarge and Lambert Frères and the financial group CGIFE[44] entered the board of directors. Various agreements of primary importance for the future of the company were signed between the group and its shareholders. The convention of the 29 July 1954 between the shareholders and Poliet consolidated the position of Pierre Gillet as Chairman and set the distribution of participation between the shareholders. CGIFE owned 5, 67%, Lafarge 5, 23%, Lambert 4, 26% and the Banque de Paris et des Pays Bas (BPPB) 2,84. By foreseeing a financial advisor from BPPB to assist the board of director. BPPB became also the first bank for Poliet et Chausson.

42 Lee Jung-yeon, *Poliet et Chausson : l'ascension d'une multinationale à la française durant les Trente Glorieuses : Lafarge (1946-1974)*, mémoire de maîtrise d'histoire, Université de Paris IV - Sorbonne, supervisor D. Barjot, septembre 2004.

43 Gaston Bourgeois, *Souvenirs de Poliet et Chausson*, Édition de la Revue Moderne, Paris, 1973.

44 Compagnie générale industrielle pour la France et l'étranger.

However a confidential agreement between CGIFE and Lafarge signed the 10 December of 1956 darkens the future of Poliet et Chausson. A conciliation agreement between the two signatories had to be hold for all Poliet et Chausson new investments which should be "harmonized" with those of Lafarge. Even more, the CGIFE promised to prevent Poliet et Chausson's projects that could undermine the position of Lafarge in specific areas. A coordinating committee between CGIFE and Lafarge had to study the outline of Poliet et Chausson industrial policy. From this time, Lafarge was aware of any new plant and prevented Poliet et Chausson the access to attractive markets. Then, the company was confined to traditional areas of action and its industrial policy limited to the only renovation of existing units. With its most serious competitors in its board of directors, the future of the company was seriously burdened and had dramatic financial, industrial and commercial consequences[45]. This agreement shows how important are the strategic decision to stay competitive in the oligopoly.

3/THE IMPORTANCE OF STRATEGY IN A CONCENTRATION PROCESS (1962-1972)

During the 1960s, several changes on the cement market led to an intense competition and promoted a concentration process in the oligopoly. This oligopoly eventually tightens around three firms in the beginning 1970's.

3.1/ An evolving market

Between 1962 and 1972, we may notice three kinds of changes in the cement market : a quick production increase, an important technical evolution and a slight price increase of cement[46]. Since 1963, the expansion pace of the construction industry and the cement industry, which depends on the construction one, were higher than the expansion pace of the whole industry. It is above all the necessity to follow a very quick demand increase that led a sector restructuration. Some producers have not been able to invest enough, while others increased their production capacity through the acquisition of other companies. Between 1962 and 1972, the average growth in production is of 6% per year (chart n° 2).

The technical evolution of the cement industry is of major importance to understand the concentration process. Between 1962 and 1972, the fuel oil part moved from 25 to 85% in the energy consumption. This raise introduced the necessity to invest in new adequate amenities. This new installations were too expansive for the average cement plants. The development of a new cement manufacturing dry method, by far less expensive than the wet method, led also the cement producers to expansive investments in new kilns. This method allowed to save 22% of the total energy and ensured a decisive advantage to those who made the investment. Moreover, another technical

45 Cécile Coursiéras-Jaff « Poliet et Chausson. A French ciment firm facing the Banks » in Dominique Barjot (ed.), « L'industrie de la construction au XXe siècle : une comparaison internationale vue sous l'angle de l'entreprise », *Revue française d'histoire économique*, art. cit.

46 François Mader, *op. cit.*

discrimination that weighted heavily in the balance was that the cement industry has increasing returns. The biggest plants are the most profitable. The average size of a cement plant turned from a capacity of 140 000 tons in 1961 to 570 000 tons in 1971. Trough 63 plants in 1971, 10 had a one million tons capacity.

CHART N°2 **THE OLIGOPOLY MEMBERS' INVESTMENT**

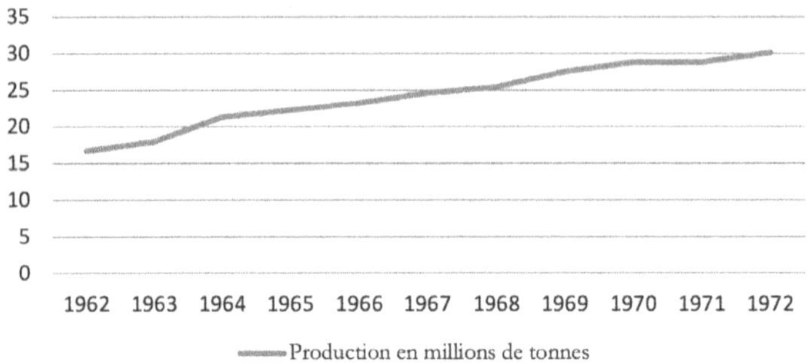

Source: François Mader, « Un exemple de restructuration industrielle : l'oligopole du ciment en France entre 1962 et 1972 », *Revue d'économie industrielle*, Vol 4, 2e trimestre 1978, p. 96-116

All this technical facts pushed the cement producers to increase the capacity of their already existing and well located plants. The cement price evolution is also lighting. This price raised of 17% between 1959 and 1965 which is a very slight raise according to the inflation. In 1966, the cement producers signed an agreement with the government but the average raising was of 2,7% per year between 1965 and 1969. In the beginning of the 1970's the price increase were more important: 6,4% in 1970 and 7,4% in 1971. They followed strong energy, carriage and payroll increases. This price limitation reduced the cash flow available to invest for the firms and allowed only the oligopoly members to borrow and to make large industrial investments.

3.2/ A consolidation of the oligopoly

During the 1960's, the French cement oligopoly experienced a quick concentration of its production and capital. To stay competitive, the oligopoly members relied on new acquisitions and cash flow increases and reached a greater capital autonomy. The number of cement producers constantly decreased since the 1930's. Indeed, in 1930, there were 48 firms and 77 plants, after the crisis, in 1938, 35 firms and 60 plants and in 1964, only 28 firms and 60 plants[47]. During the 1960's this concentration process speeded up. 24 firms were counted in 1968 and only 18 in 1971[48]. This phenomenon is more obvious when we differentiate the firms by size.

47 Jacques Reynaud, *op. cit.*

48 Jean-Pierre Angelier, *Étude sur l'évolution de la concentration dans l'industrie du ciment en France (Série-Evolution de la concentration et de la concurrence, n°13)*, Commission des Communautés Européennes, Brussels, 1978, p. 37.

TABLE N°3 THE CEMENT FIRMS CLASSIFIED BY TURNOVER (EXCLUDING TAXES)

	1968	1969	1970	1971	1972
Less than 100 millions	20	16	11	12	12
100 to 200 millions	1	2	2	1	1
More than 200 millions	3	3	4	3	3

Source: Jean-Pierre Angelier, *Étude sur l'évolution de la concentration dans l'industrie du ciment en France, Série-Évolution de la concentration et de la concurrence, n°13,* Commission des Communautés Européennes, Brussels, p. 38.

The production became also more concentrated. Indeed, in 1964, nine firms assumed 70% of the French production: next to Lafarge, Poliet et Chausson, Ciments Français and Vicat, we find Ciments d'Origny, Ciments de Loisne, Lambert Frères, Ciments de Marseille and Ciments de Rombas.[49] In 1971, after the purchase of the cement business of Poliet et Chausson by Ciments Français, 86% of the production came from the three members of the oligopoly: Lafarge, Ciments Français and Vicat. The concentration process is at this time over. To achieve this process, the main oligopoly members followed a strategy of horizontal external absorption, competing to take over surviving independents as noticed by Jean-Pierre Angelier[50]. Taking the example of Lafarge, he showed that the firm followed a strategy of centralization of cement capital[51]. During the 1960's, the firm is controlling 4 subsidiaries and acquisitions in 110 other firms around the world. In 1968, the firm of the Ciments Lafarge-Lambert is created equally between Lafarge and Lambert Frères. The company included all the cement assets from Lambert. In 1969, Lafarge absorbed one of their subsidiary, the Ciments de Villeneuve and the important firm the Ciments de Marseille et d'Outre-Mer. They also took the control of the Ciments du Sud-Ouest. In 1970 they finally took the control of Ciments Lafarge-Lambert that was renamed Ciments de la Seine and absorbed this subsidiary in 1971.

The Ciments Français, owning 17 subsidiaries, followed the same strategy. In 1968, they absorbed the family firm Les Établissements de Klopstein. In 1970, the Ciments de Rombas became a holding and let his cement business to Ciments Français, taking at the same time a minority stake in the firm. In 1971, Poliet et Chausson did the same thing. It allowed Ciments Français to get the acquisitions of Poliet et Chausson in the Ciments de l'Adour (45%) and the Ciments de la Loire (50%). Eventually, Vicat, owning 26 subsidiaries also followed a strategy of external horizontal absorption. In 1969, they absorbed their subsidiary the Ciments de Xeuilly and in 1970 the Ciments de la Porte and the Ciments de Voreppe. They were then able to control the Rhone-Alpes market. In 1971, Vicat took the majority stake of the Ciments de Pont-à-Vendin in the northern France and absorbed this subsidiary in 1973.

This external horizontal absorption process has to be linked with a new evolution of the cement producers' capital during the 1960's. The cement industry reached an

49 François Mader, art. cit.

50 Jean-Pierre Angelier, *Étude sur l'évolution de la concentration dans l'industrie du ciment en France, op. cit.,* p. 37.

51 Michel Aglietta, *Régulation et Crise du capitalisme ; l'expérience des Etats-Unis.* Paris, Calmann-Lévy, 1976, p. 189-190.

overall stronger capital autonomy during the late 1960's and the beginning 1970's. This trend is the opposite of the previous period. Indeed, during the 1950's, the cement producers, needing a strong financial support to invest, were turning to new shareholders. During the 1960's, the members of the oligopoly relied on their own flow. Lafarge had always kept a strict financial independency. Vicat on the other hand, partly lost his financial in 1969, when the German cement firm Heidelberg took a 12% sharing against its sharing in Ciments de Xeuilly. In 1973, the sharing of Heidelberg cement raised 20%. As far as Ciments Français is concerned, its capital is probably the less independent one: Paribas is its major shareholder through the Poliet S.A. holding. The strengthening of their production, capital and financial independency increased the power of the cement leaders. Yet, being a member of the oligopoly is not a guarantee to survive as proved by the end of Poliet et Chausson as a cement producers. So how the cement firms did fight inside the oligopoly?

3.3/ The struggle inside the oligopoly

Inside a national mature cement market, the competition between producers took a particular form. If the price competition did not exist, the regional implantation was crucial and partly related to the industrial competition. Otherwise, during the market expansion, each producer carefully observed investments of its competitors to reach their expansion strategy. As mentioned in the most part of the oligopoly members meeting reports, Lafarge, Ciments Français and Vicat intended to develop faster than the average growth estimated by the Planning commission. In 1963, the planning commission predicted at least 5,5% of growth each years between 1966 and 1970. Poliet et Chausson was the only one aiming only to maintain its market share and eventually did not reached its modest objectives[52].

As already mentioned, there were local market areas in the cement industry. Because of the transportation costs, the competition existed between the plants of a same region more than between the firms. Actual price wars were uncommon. The last sustained one appears to have occurred in the Paris Region in the period 1967-69, reflecting a structural output surplus in the Nord. Some smaller companies there joined to create Norcim, a joint marketing organisation aimed at the Paris market. This price war was reportedly painful, in a period when the French government imposed maximum prices[53]. If the prices could not be a weapon for commercial competition, other weapons as credit for customers or advertisement were used, but they were not decisive[54]. The credit to customers was in fact among the uses inside the cement market and as far as advertisement is concerned, some joint discount operations were led towards the public works sector. It may have an impact on the demand increase but not as much as the technical evolution impact. However, the regional implantation was decisive. Some departments as the Nord Pas-de-Calais were marked by an intense competition between 2 or 3 plants that did not managed to sell all their production.

52 François Mader, art. cit.

53 John Martin, "Location and Corporate Structure: The Case of the French Cement Industry", *Research Papers in Environmental and Spatial Analysis*, n°54, May 1999.

54 François Mader, art. cit.

They had to sell them far from the plant at low cost. Others firms were located in areas with a slow increasing demand as Poliet et Chausson in the center. Eventually, some areas as Normandie and Massif central had very few cement plants. With the increasing demand, the cement producers wanted to create new plants in this regions during the 1960's. In 1966 Poliet et Chausson et Chausson wanted to build a cement plant with a 350 000 tons capacity in Clermont Ferrand while Vicat intended to build a plant in Vichy with the same capacity.

We already mentioned that the technical progresses were decisive for the industrial competition between cement producers: they allowed the firms to lower their costs and make a higher profit to increase their production capacity by investing. François Mader brought out the link between industrial competition and regional implantation. Indeed, the technical innovation led to build new cement plants in new areas without any cement plants or with competitors cement plants. To avoid a fruitless competition at regional scale, the oligopoly members, preferred, rather than compete head on, to co-ordinate their investment plans. In three cases in the late Sixties, the construction of completely new works was undertaken by a pair of major companies setting up a subsidiary under joint ownership.

This case drive us to mention the mutual reactions triggered by the oligopoly members new investment. As already explained by Dumez and Jeunemaître, inside an oligopolistic market, the mimetic phenomenon becomes an element of the corporate strategies[55]. During the expansion market of the 1960's, each producer had to combine productivity and capacity investment and spatial implantation. By comparing the investment rate of the firms and their rate of growth, François Mader highlighted the competition between the members of the oligopoly. His figures brought out that Lafarge was the main target for the others firms. Lafarge, Vicat and Ciments Français fought together without really worrying about Poliet et Chausson during the 1960, indeed, as already mentioned, the secret agreement signed by Lafarge prevented any concurrency from Poliet et Chausson. In 1971, the winner on the French market seemed to be Ciments Français as showed on this table.

TABLE N°4 **AVERAGE RELATIVE PERFORMANCE OF THE FIRMS INSIDE THE OLIGOPOLY FROM 1962 TO 1972.**

Relative performance	Poliet et Chausson	Lafarge	Ciments Français	Vicat
Poliet et Chausson	1	1,48	2,15	0,81
Lafarge	0,59	1	0,79	2,35
Ciments français	2,03	3,24	1	4,70
Vicat	2,73	5,48	2,41	1

Source: Mader F., *op. cit.*

55 Hervé Dumez, Alain Jeunemaître, « Rôle et statut de l'économiste dans les affaires de concurrence. Leçons tirées de l'histoire américaine de l'industrie cimentière », *op. cit.*

Moreover, Ciments Français is the firm that enlarged the most its market share during the sixties as depicted by graph n°3.

GRAPH N°3 **THE OLIGOPOLY MARKET SHARE BETWEEN 1962 AND 1972**

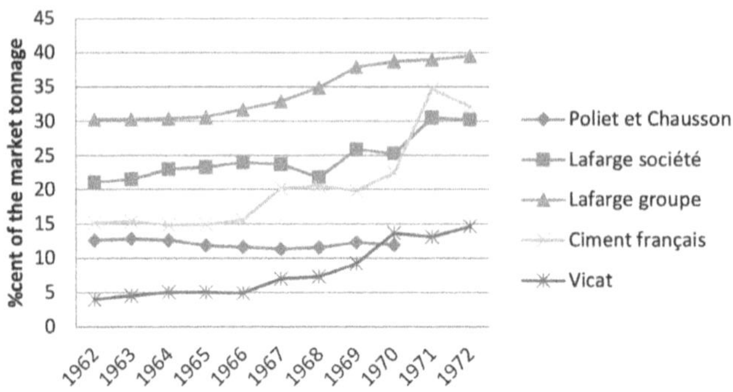

Source: *Mader F., op. cit.*

During this period, each firm used its own strategy to fight its competitors. Lafarge used mostly the external absorption during the sixties whereas the other firms used external absorption only during period of quick growth[56]. This fact enlightens the planned development strategy of Lafarge. That firm was indeed a precursor for new American management methods and internationalization.

Conclusion

The prosperity of the 1920's reinforced the cement oligopoly. The offensive agreements reached by producers allowed them to continue a merger and acquisition policy and in that way to share the market. But the context of economic growth also encouraged individual expansion strategies. The producers perceived the construction of a national organization as a strain. Because of that situation, the crisis led them at first to fight each other and to tire out in a useless dumping policy. After they finally constituted regional unions, the cement producers went further by using the Trade Union Federation of Chambers of Lime and Cement Manufacturers (FCSFCCF) as a political pressure organism to the state and created a central control institution of regional unions. This institution, the Commission Financière des Ciments, must be considered as the starting point of an official national cartel. The economic recession of the 1930's so progressively led to the constitution of a national cartel in the cement industry. This cartel paved the way to the setting up of economic organisation committees under the Vichy regime by the work charter of October 4th 1941. This state's control established during the German occupation remained after the war as a price control institution.

A real internationalisation of the cement industry happened after the Second World War. Those who managed the most successfully their internationalization were

56 François Mader, *op. cit.*

mostly European firms like Holderbank, Lafarge or Blue Circle. We can explain these successes partly by the cartel organization experienced by the European cement industry before the war. The oligopolistic structure of the French cement industry came out reinforced by the economic growth of the after-war period in spite of the new European laws against cartels. The concentration process of the French cement industry between 1945 and 1975 finds an explanation in the structure of the cement industry and is reinforced by the political and economic context of the period. Producing low cost intermediate goods in very expansive amenities with local constraints, the cement producers were organized in cartels since the 1930's. Indeed, because of the demand's rigidity and the local constraints, the commercial competition between them was not useful. Yet, since the 1930's, the production capacity and the regional implantation were of primary importance to dominate the national cartel. That's why the oligopoly members of the after war period were already the most important producers during the interwar period. If Lafarge, Poliet et Chausson, Vicat and Ciments Français had some problems with the Public authorities after 1945, the limitation price policies paradoxically reinforced them relatively to the regional firms. They were able to invest and increase their production, profit and market shares. Their financial power allowed them to buy the smaller firm and to achieve a concentration of the market around them.

This concentration is firstly marked by a structural change of the firms. During the 1950's, the cement producers, who were mostly family firms, became managerial companies influenced by the new American management methods. At this time, they discovered the importance of establishing a strategy. During the 1960's, the French market reached its maturity: the oligopoly members had more and more limited expansion prospects. Competition became fierce between them and led to the disappearance of one member. Indeed, Poliet et Chausson did not react quickly enough to its competitor's new investment programs and its cement sector was finally bought by Ciments Français. Lafarge, Ciments Français and Vicat fought together mostly through industrial competition and takeo. In 1971, the three producers represented more than 90% of the production. The cement market restructuring process was completed and the competition then moved to the foreign implantations.

L'Union Européenne :

L'évolution économique des pays d'Europe occidentale et la spécificité française depuis les années 1960

Michel Hau

Professeur émérite,
Université de Strasbourg et Institut universitaire de France

En 1957, le traité de Rome réunit six pays, mais aussi deux modèles économiques opposés, celui de la France et celui de ses cinq partenaires. Le premier visait à l'autosuffisance, le commerce extérieur étant perçu comme une variable d'ajustement et comme un élément de puissance internationale parmi d'autres. Le second concevait le commerce extérieur comme une nécessité vitale, l'exportation de produits fabriqués permettant de compenser l'insuffisance des ressources locales. Cette différence remontait aux débuts de l'ère moderne. La France avait constitué au cours des siècles un vaste marché intérieur qu'elle avait réservé à ses producteurs grâce à tout un arsenal de prohibitions et de taxes douanières. Les progrès de sa fiscalité lui avaient permis de se doter d'un appareil administratif étoffé. Une partie de ses élites avait pris l'habitude d'affirmer son prestige en intégrant la haute fonction publique. À l'inverse, durant la même période, dans les États faibles et dispersés des bords du Rhin ou du piémont des Alpes, les producteurs n'avaient pu trouver des débouchés qu'à l'extérieur et les élites avaient fait de l'entreprise le moyen exclusif de fonder et de pérenniser leur prééminence sociale.

La fin de la seconde guerre mondiale avait amplifié l'opposition entre les deux modèles, la France optant en 1945 pour un système fermement dirigiste, ses cinq futurs partenaires optant au contraire pour un retour à l'économie de marché. Par la suite, la construction européenne allait inévitablement provoquer une convergence entre les deux modèles. Le choix de réaliser une union douanière plutôt qu'un espace de libre-échange et l'acceptation de politiques communes auraient pu faire évoluer la construction européenne vers une extension géographique du système économique français. Mais, comme nous allons le voir, les choses se passèrent tout autrement, créant en France et en Europe des tensions et des malentendus qui ne sont pas près de se dissiper.

1. LE MODÈLE FRANÇAIS ÉCONOMIQUE ET SOCIAL FRANÇAIS D'APRÈS-GUERRE

La victoire allemande de 1940, puis la victoire soviétique de 1945 semblèrent démontrer la supériorité des économies planifiées. La nationalisation des secteurs-clés et la prise en main par l'État du développement industriel reposèrent en 1945 sur un consensus étendu. La gauche voyait dans les circonstances de la Libération l'occasion d'exproprier la classe capitaliste et les grands commis de l'État ne cachaient pas leur mépris pour un patronat qu'ils taxaient de frilosité. Les postulats anticapitalistes du parti communiste et de la gauche rejoignaient ceux des jeunes hauts fonctionnaires qui rêvaient, grâce aux nationalisations et à la planification, de prendre en main la modernisation du pays.

1.1/ L'aspiration des hauts fonctionnaires français à remplacer les patrons

Des alourdissements successifs de la fiscalité[1] limitèrent les possibilités d'autofinancement des entreprises privées. Les investissements contrôlés par l'État, donnèrent la priorité à quelques secteurs clés, l'énergie, la recherche nucléaire, l'aéronautique et le transport ferroviaire, créant pour l'industrie française, dans ces domaines, des positions fortes pour les décennies postérieures, mais freinant d'autant le développement des autres branches.

Les gouvernements français multiplièrent au fil des ans les dispositifs d'aide, qui permettaient aux hauts fonctionnaires de contrôler la gestion des entreprises du secteur privé[2]. Le refus de laisser une plus grande capacité financière aux entreprises durant les années de l'après-guerre peut s'interpréter comme un manque de confiance dans les capacités de décision des industriels. On a parfois qualifié le capitalisme français de « capitalisme de guichet ».

Toute la politique économique était censée s'inscrire dans un plan où les objectifs de production des diverses branches d'activité nationales étaient calculés en fonction d'une matrice de coefficients techniques et d'un taux de croissance global de la demande finale. Ce plan, non contraignant, constituait une vaste étude de marché dans l'hypothèse d'un développement économique autocentré. Le poste des échanges extérieurs intervenait comme une simple variable d'ajustement.

1 L'impôt sur les sociétés fut progressivement alourdi : de 24% des bénéfices en 1948 il fut porté, par hausses successives, à 50% en 1958. Il fallut attendre 1959 pour que l'amortissement dégressif sur les investissements des entreprises réduisît un peu cette ponction. À partir de 1948, l'impôt cédulaire é jusque-là par les salariés fut mis à la charge des entreprises, ce qui représenta une nouvelle taxe de 5% sur les salaires. À partir de 1953, elles durent également acquitter un prélèvement de 1% sur leur masse salariale pour financer l'effort de construction. À partir de 1959, les entreprises furent largement mises à contribution pour la mise en place d'un système d'assurance-chômage, la cotisation des employeurs étant supérieure à celle des assurés.

2 En 2013, le rapport Queyranne mentionnait 660 dispositifs d'aides émanant de l'État auxquels s'ajoutaient ceux mis en place par 25 agences régionales, 53 agences départementales et 32 agences intercommunales. Jean-Jack Queyranne, *Pour des aides simples et efficaces au service de la compétitivité*, La Documentation française, juin 2013.

1.2/ Une sécurité sociale financée principalement par les entreprises

Il revient à l'historien de rappeler à l'économiste le contexte politique dans lequel s'est formé le modèle social français. Les institutions qui furent créées à cette époque ont été fondées sur un compromis, unique dans le monde occidental, entre les deux grandes forces de la Résistance française, les gaullistes et les communistes.

Du côté du chef du Gouvernement provisoire, la préoccupation principale était de réserver tous les moyens de l'armée française à la lutte contre l'Allemagne et de maintenir l'unité de la Résistance pour obtenir une autonomie par rapport aux États-Unis. Du côté du parti communiste, le choix fut de gagner un maximum d'avantages en vue de progrès futurs, quitte à accepter en octobre 1944 la dissolution de ses organisations combattantes[3]. Le 14 octobre, 30 communistes officiels furent nommés à l'Assemblée nationale consultative. Ambroise Croizat, ancien secrétaire général de la fédération des métaux CGT et député communiste de 1936 à 1939, avait déjà reçu dès 1943 à Alger la présidence de la commission du Travail de l'Assemblée consultative et fut confirmé dans ce poste, avant de devenir ministre du Travail en novembre 1945. Dans le gouvernement formé le 13 novembre 1945, le parti communiste obtint, à la grande déception des socialistes, tous les ministères économiques ainsi que le ministère de la Santé.[4]

Le programme du Conseil National de la Résistance, adopté le 15 mars 1944, prévoyait un plan complet de Sécurité Sociale « visant à assurer à tous les citoyens des moyens d'existence dans tous les cas où ils sont incapables de se les procurer par le travail »[5]. Dans les différents pays d'Europe occidentale, les équipes qui préparaient l'après-guerre projetaient, dans des termes similaires, un développement de l'État Providence. Mais les modalités de la mise en œuvre de ces réformes furent spécifiques à la France. Lors des débats d'avant-guerre sur les assurances sociales, le parti communiste et la CGTU s'étaient fortement opposés au principe d'une cotisation ouvrière : ils soutenaient que c'était au patronat de financer la reproduction et l'entretien de la force de travail[6]. Cette conviction resta fortement ancrée chez les communistes. Les circonstances historiques leur donnèrent l'occasion de faire prévaloir leurs vues. Le projet communiste était de prolonger le combat contre l'occupant par une lutte contre le capitalisme. Dans le climat de règlement de comptes qui prévalait au moment de la Libération, gaullistes et communistes s'accordèrent sur le mythe d'un peuple tout entier résistant trahi par un patronat collaborationniste[7]. Le système de sécurité

3 Les Francs-Tireurs-Partisans furent intégrés sur engagement individuel dans l'armée française à partir du 27 septembre 1944. Le 24 octobre, une ordonnance autorisa l'amnistie des condamnations pour désertion prononcées par les tribunaux militaires avant le 17 juin 1940. Les Milices Patriotiques, devenues depuis peu les Gardes Civiques, furent dissoutes par décret le 28 octobre. Le 6 novembre, un décret autorisa le retour de Maurice Thorez.

4 Charles Tillon reçut le ministère de l'Armement, Ambroise Croizat celui du Travail, Marcel Paul celui de la Production industrielle et François Billoux celui de la Santé, puis celui de l'Économie nationale. Quant à Maurice Thorez, il fut nommé ministre d'État chargé de la fonction publique.

5 Conseil National de la Résistance, *Les jours heureux*, 1944. Philip Nord, *Le New Deal français*, Paris, Perrin, 2016.

6 Depuis 1930, un système d'assurances sociales obligatoires (maladie, invalidité, décès, maternité retraite) existait pour les salariés modestes. Il était financé par des prélèvements correspondant à 8% de la masse salariale, partagés à égalité entre les employeurs et les salariés. Ce financement était insuffisant et les prestations ne couvraient qu'une faible partie des risques. À ce dispositif s'ajoutaient les assurances contre les accidents du travail et les allocations familiales, financées entièrement par les employeurs.

7 Éric Jabbari, *Pierre Laroque and the Welfare State in Postwar France*, Oxford University Press, 2012, p. 109.

sociale visa à récompenser le premier en punissant le second. Encore aujourd'hui, dans l'imaginaire de la gauche, la Sécurité Sociale apparaît comme une conquête ouvrière réalisée aux dépens du patronat au terme d'une insurrection victorieuse[8].

La part payée par les employeurs pour alimenter les caisses d'assurance maladie et vieillesse fut fixée à un niveau plus élevé que celle pesant sur les assurés[9]. Il s'y ajouta des prélèvements nouveaux pour le financement des comités d'hygiène et sécurité, de la médecine du travail et des comités d'entreprise. Le modèle social français put être d'autant plus généreux qu'il ne pesait pas principalement sur la masse des assurés ni sur celle des contribuables. Les conseils d'administration des caisses furent, au début, composés pour les trois quarts, de représentants des syndicats. Le budget de la Sécurité Sociale fut soustrait au vote du Parlement jusqu'en 1996.

Dans l'économie fermée d'après-guerre, la cherté des produits français causée par ces charges supplémentaires était compensée par les taxes qui frappaient les marchandises importées. Mais il n'en alla plus de même à partir du moment où la France commença à abaisser ses droits de douane. Financer les prestations sociales en taxant fortement la production et le travail réduisait les capacités de modernisation et d'innovation des entreprises. Jusqu'à nos jours, leur taux de marge dépassa rarement 30%, alors que chez les entreprises allemandes, il oscillait en permanence autour de 40%.

1.3/ La priorité donnée à la consommation après 1974

Dans le cadre commercial fermé qui fut celui de la France jusqu'en 1959, l'expansion se fonda sur la demande intérieure, avec une forte croissance des investissements publics et de la consommation des ménages. Pour préparer l'industrie française à la suppression complète des droits de douane au sein de la CEE fixée au 1er juillet 1968, le Ve Plan (1966-1970) préconisa de freiner la hausse de la consommation pour accélérer celle de l'investissement. La crise de 1968 obligea les gouvernements français à y renoncer.

Jacques Chaban-Delmas, devenu Premier ministre en juin 1969, lança une politique de hausse des prestations, sous le slogan de la «nouvelle société». Pour financer ces nouvelles avancées de l'État Providence sans alourdir les prélèvements sur les revenus des personnes physiques ou sur la consommation, les hauts fonctionnaires de la Direction du Budget firent, comme à l'habitude, peser l'essentiel de ces charges nouvelles sur les entreprises. Le 3 janvier 1970, la « contribution sociale de solidarité des sociétés » fut créée pour financer les régimes de protection sociale des non-salariés. L'année suivante, le gouvernement ajouta un prélèvement supplémentaire pour financer les transports en commun, le « versement transport », ainsi qu'un autre prélèvement supplémentaire pour financer la formation continue. Les retraites furent

8 Michel Dreyfus, Michèle Ruffat, Vincent Viet, Bruno Vallat, *Se protéger, être protégé : une histoire des assurances sociales en France*, Presses universitaires de Rennes, 2006, p. 264.

9 Les ordonnances d'octobre 1945 portèrent le prélèvement sur la masse salariale des entreprises à 16%. Ce prélèvement fut réparti en taxant plus lourdement les entreprises (à raison de 10% de la masse salariale) que les salariés (6%). Les allocations familiales, déjà entièrement à la charge des employeurs depuis les années Trente, furent fortement relevées.

substantiellement augmentées, par la loi du 31 décembre 1971, grâce à une hausse de la cotisation employeur[10].

Après la mort du président Georges Pompidou, la priorité donnée à la consommation fut renforcée. Celle-ci se développa dès lors plus vite que l'investissement. Fortement marqué par son expérience de mai 1968, le nouveau Premier ministre, Jacques Chirac, s'était convaincu que l'on pouvait acheter la stabilité politique en reportant à plus tard le rétablissement des grands équilibres économiques. En juillet 1974, les caisses d'allocations familiales créèrent l'allocation de rentrée scolaire. En juin 1975, l'allocation pour adulte handicapé vit le jour[11]. En juillet 1976, l'« allocation de parent isolé » ajouta, à l'aide versée pour le décès d'un parent, celle versée pour une séparation[12]. Le développement des prestations sociales se déconnecta brusquement, à partir de 1974, de la croissance du Produit Intérieur Brut. Leur rythme de croissance resta presque inchangé alors que la croissance économique fléchissait. Aux alourdissements de cotisations sociales s'ajoutèrent ceux de la fiscalité. En juillet 1975, pour accroître les ressources des collectivités locales, la patente, rebaptisée « taxe professionnelle », fut significativement augmentée et frappa particulièrement les entreprises industrielles[13].

Entre 1976 et 1981, Raymond Barre essaya de contenir la poussée de la demande intérieure pour tenter rétablir l'équilibre des comptes publics et celui de la balance des paiements courants. Mais le gouvernement de Pierre Mauroy qui lui succéda prit le contre-pied. Il fallut attendre juin 1982 pour que quelques mesures correctrices fussent prises, comme la désindexation des salaires sur les prix.

La majorité des experts gouvernementaux français et des médias continuèrent longtemps à penser que la stimulation du marché intérieur pouvait mieux dynamiser la croissance que l'effort de compétitivité. L'argument de la «fragilité des marchés extérieurs» resta un thème récurrent des discours officiels et des médias, même lorsque le marché intérieur français devint ouvert à tous les vents de la concurrence étrangère. En matière monétaire, les élites intellectuelles françaises prônèrent la poursuite d'une gestion keynésienne pour soutenir la demande intérieure, comme si la France était encore une économie fermée[14].

10 *Cf.* Conseil d'orientation des retraites, *Document* n° 11, janvier 2009, p. 6.

11 Cette nouvelle prestation fut versée par le canal des caisses d'allocations familiales Ce n'est que plus tard, à partir de 1982, que son montant fut pris en charge par l'État.

12 Versée initialement par les caisses d'allocations familiales, l'allocation de parent isolé ne fut prise en charge par l'État qu'à partir de 1999.

13 Il fallut attendre 2003 pour que les salaires ne fussent plus un élément d'imposition à la taxe professionnelle. *Cf.* Sophie Deligiannis, *Le plafonnement de la taxe professionnelle*, mém. Master2 Recherche Droit public, Université de Strasbourg, 2009.

14 Raymond Courbis, *La détermination de l'équilibre général en économie concurrencée*, Paris, Éd. du CNRS, 1971, p. 49.

2/ LE CHOIX DE L'ÉCONOMIE DE MARCHÉ CHEZ LES CINQ AUTRES PAYS FONDATEURS DU MARCHÉ COMMUN

Dans les cinq autres pays fondateurs de la Communauté économique européenne, l'après-guerre vit au contraire l'accession au pouvoir de gouvernements fermement partisans de l'économie de marché, en réaction contre les expériences fasciste et nazie d'économie dirigée. À côté du modèle planificateur et protectionniste français, se mit ainsi en place un modèle rhénan, caractérisé par le recentrage de l'économie sur l'entreprise, par le choix de l'exportation pour combattre le chômage et par la limitation de la hausse des prix intérieurs. Sur ce dernier point, le modèle libéral rhénan s'écartait du modèle libéral anglo-saxon. Les États-Unis et le Royaume-Uni pensaient pouvoir pratiquer une politique d'expansion monétaire grâce au statut de devises internationales de la livre et du dollar, mais les pays de l'axe rhénan ne pouvaient préserver la stabilité du taux de change de leur monnaie que par une gestion rigoureuse de l'émission.

2.1/ Des majorités indépendantes du parti communiste

Les forces antinazies et antifascistes qui arrivèrent au pouvoir en 1945 chez les cinq partenaires de la France furent centrées sur fortes majorités démocrates-chrétiennes. Sur le plan politique, elles n'étaient pas disposées à faire des concessions aux communistes. Elles craignaient beaucoup l'Union Soviétique et s'en remettaient sans restriction à la protection américaine. En Allemagne, le parti communiste, affaibli par la persécution nazie, avait peu d'adhérents et le parti social-démocrate refusa, dans les zones occidentales, de fusionner avec lui. En Belgique et au Luxembourg, les communistes participèrent aux coalitions gouvernementales jusqu'en 1947, mais ils n'obtinrent pas de ministères économiques.

L'Italie possédait, comme la France, un parti communiste puissant, mais d'un moindre poids électoral[15]. Le démocrate-chrétien Alcide de Gasperi, chef du dernier gouvernement du Royaume d'Italie et des premiers gouvernements de la République Italienne, s'appuya fortement sur les Américains. Il attribua au communiste Mauro Scoccimaro le ministère des Finances, mais confia le ministère du Travail et de la Prévoyance sociale à un socialiste. Dès février 1947, il remplaça Scoccimaro par un démocrate-chrétien. En mai 1947, il confia un ministère du budget (*ministerio del bilancio*) à un partisan convaincu du libéralisme économique, le professeur Luigi Einaudi.

2.2/ L'entreprise, pivot du système économique chez les Cinq

La majorité des économistes allemands étaient préparés au nouvel ordre international libéral préconisé par les Américains. Un courant de pensée développé dès le lendemain de la Première Guerre mondiale par les économistes de l'université de Fribourg-en-Brisgau considérait les mécanismes de marché comme plus efficaces

15 Aux élections de la constituante italienne en juin 1946, le PCI n'obtint que 18,7% des suffrages exprimés contre 37,2% pour la démocratie chrétienne. Aux élections à la première constituante française, le PCF avait obtenu 26,2% des suffrages exprimés contre 23,9% pour le MRP.

que ceux de l'économie administrée. Ils prônaient un équilibre entre une économie concurrentielle et une société solidaire. Ils avaient fait connaître leurs idées avec une revue, *Ordo*. Leur succès en Allemagne après 1945 dut beaucoup à la constatation des dysfonctionnements de l'économie dirigée sous le régime nazi. Ludwig Erhard, professeur d'Économie Politique à Francfort, était leur chef de file. Son programme de réformes fut adopté par les chrétiens-démocrates[16], à quelques semaines des élections législatives d'août 1949, qui permirent au parti CDU de former une coalition gouvernementale avec les libéraux. La République Fédérale fut celui des grands pays d'Europe qui libéralisa le plus tôt et le plus complètement son économie.

L'entreprise redevint le pivot du système économique allemand et tout fut fait pour lui laisser la plus large autonomie financière. Les régimes d'assurance obligatoire hérités de la législation bismarckienne continuèrent à peser autant sur les salariés que sur les employeurs et les allocations familiales, rétablies en 1954, furent prises en charge par l'État fédéral. L'impôt sur les sociétés fut allégé par un régime d'amortissement accéléré et par des déductions sur les bénéfices non distribués. Les fonds propres dont pouvaient disposer les entreprises allemandes pour l'investissement se renforcèrent et celles-ci purent autofinancer d'ambitieux projets de développement.

En Belgique, aux Pays-Bas et au Luxembourg, la tendance prédominante était, depuis le XIXe siècle, l'ouverture aux échanges. En 1948, ces trois pays mirent en vigueur un accord d'union douanière et ils fixèrent un tarif extérieur commun très bas. Soucieux de maintenir la compétitivité des entreprises, leurs gouvernements développèrent la sécurité sociale en complétant les cotisations sociales par des financements de l'État. Le système de protection sociale adopté par l'Italie après 1945 ne porta pas non plus la marque des conceptions communistes. Dans une Italie en proie à un chômage endémique au sortir de la guerre, les gouvernants se montrèrent très tôt soucieux de la compétitivité des entreprises. Le système de sécurité sociale de l'Italie fut le moins généreux des six futurs pays fondateurs de la Communauté Économique Européenne et il fut financé en partie par des contributions budgétaires.

2.3/ Ouverture aux échanges et rejet du keynésianisme

Les pays du Bénélux et l'Allemagne écartèrent très tôt le recours aux politiques de déficit budgétaire et d'expansion monétaire : dans l'économie ouverte qui s'annonçait, une stimulation de la demande risquait de faire tourner surtout les usines étrangères. Leurs gouvernants étaient attachés aux principes de stabilité monétaire prônés alors par les Américains. Même en Italie, où la gestion monétaire fut au départ plus souple, l'inflation décéléra remarquablement à partir de 1958 et se maintint à un niveau très bas jusqu'en 1969. Toutefois, dans les années qui suivirent, les autorités, confrontées à de vives tensions sociales, choisirent, comme en France, de pratiquer une politique

16 Le programme économique de la CDU fut présenté en juillet 1949 à Düsseldorf par un groupe de membres présidé par Franz Etzel, lui-même en contact étroit avec Ludwig Erhard.

d'expansion monétaire et laissèrent même progresser la dette publique de façon encore plus poussée[17].

2.4/ L'orientation libérale des Pères de l'Europe

La création du Marché Commun résulta de la rencontre entre les gouvernants de cette Europe libérale et deux dirigeants français très proches d'eux, mais tout à fait atypiques dans leur milieu, Robert Schuman et Jean Monnet. Né citoyen allemand en Lorraine annexée et catholique pratiquant, Robert Schuman était nettement éloigné de la classe politique française. Le Mouvement Républicain Populaire, auquel il était affilié, avait une assise électorale plus étroite que les autres gouvernants démocrates-chrétiens d'Europe occidentale. Robert Schuman avait, comme député, voté les pleins pouvoirs au maréchal Pétain en juillet 1940, et pouvait être à ce titre facilement critiqué par ses adversaires. Il ne fut que brièvement président du conseil des ministres (de novembre 1947 à juillet 1948, puis deux jours seulement, en septembre 1948). Ses homologues démocrates-chrétiens, Konrad Adenauer et Alcide de Gasperi, furent au contraire chefs de gouvernement respectivement de 1949 à 1963 et de 1945 à 1953.

Quant à Jean Monnet, c'était quelqu'un d'encore plus atypique dans le paysage français. Il n'avait pas son baccalauréat, dans un pays qui avait la religion du diplôme et dont le personnel politique était souvent issu des grandes écoles. Il n'avait pas fait carrière dans la fonction publique française ni dans la politique et avait au contraire exercé des fonctions importantes hors de France (fonctionnaire interallié responsable de la coordination des ressources, secrétaire adjoint de la SDN, coprésident de la Bancamerica, coordonnateur des efforts de guerre américain et britannique). Sa nomination comme commissaire au Plan entre 1946 était due en grande partie à sa capacité à négocier des prêts américains dont la France avait un impérieux besoin.

Pour des raisons de politique extérieure, Robert Schuman fut maintenu au poste de ministre des Affaires étrangères de 1947 à 1952. C'est comme ministre des Affaires étrangères qu'il proposa, le 9 mai 1950, après avoir travaillé dans le plus grand secret avec Jean Monnet, de placer les productions française et allemande de charbon et d'acier sous une autorité supranationale, dans un marché commun auquel pourraient s'adjoindre d'autres pays d'Europe. Les opposants à un tel plan, nombreux dans la classe politico-administrative française, furent pris de court. Les gouvernements démocrates-chrétiens d'Allemagne, d'Italie et des pays du Bénélux étaient, à l'inverse, prédisposés à adhérer très vite à un tel plan.

La Haute Autorité instituée par le traité de 1951 fut dotée d'un pouvoir de tutelle et de contrôle sur l'ensemble des entreprises du secteur charbonnier et sidérurgique. Mais, des deux doctrines qui s'affrontaient, la planification et le libéralisme, c'est tout de suite vers la seconde que pencha cette première institution européenne. Ses membres, parmi lesquels ceux originaires du Bénélux étaient fortement représentés,

17 Jacques Le Cacheux, «L'économie italienne, du miracle à la banalité dans l'Europe», *Vingtième Siècle Revue d'Histoire*, n° 100, 2008/4, p. 131-135.

consacrèrent l'essentiel de leur action à éliminer les discriminations dans les transports et à faire respecter l'interdiction de conclure des ententes[18].
Le même parti pris libéral inspira après 1957 la Commission de la Communauté Économique Européenne. L'essentiel de son action s'exerça en faveur du respect de la concurrence et de l'ouverture des frontières à l'intérieur du Marché Commun. Les tentatives de relance en faveur de politiques industrielles communes menées ensuite par Georges Pompidou en 1969 à la conférence de La Haye, puis en 1972 à la conférence de Paris, ne reçurent qu'un accueil poli. Les seuls grands projets industriels qui furent réalisés dans un cadre européen, Airbus, Ariane et l'usine d'enrichissement d'uranium du Tricastin, furent ceux qui avaient déjà été engagés par la France[19].

Par esprit internationaliste, les socialistes français soutinrent la construction européenne dès l'origine. Ils étaient habités par le souvenir de Jean Jaurès, assassiné pour avoir soutenu la cause de la paix en Europe. Guy Mollet, alors président du conseil au moment des négociations de Messine, voyait dans des états unis d'Europe une première étape vers les états unis du monde et il était pressé d'aboutir. Il ne tint aucun compte du mémorandum de l'administration française qui posait l'harmonisation des fiscalités comme un préalable à l'union douanière et il accepta comme base des négociations le rapport du socialiste belge Paul Henri Spaak, qui préconisait la création du marché commun sans plus attendre[20].

La construction européenne fut donc lancée par une minorité d'hommes politiques animés de fortes convictions chrétiennes et internationalistes sans que l'ensemble de la classe politico-administrative française[21], les partenaires sociaux et les médias eussent pris la mesure de ce qu'elle impliquait. Par la suite, tout se passa comme si les Français avaient pensé que les accords signés seraient différés ou atténués. Non seulement ils furent appliqués sans délai, mais encore les mesures de désarmement douanier furent, en l'espace de trois décennies, élargies au monde entier.

Dès l'origine, le Marché Commun fut conçu comme destiné à s'ouvrir sur le reste du monde. Pour être compatible avec l'accord général sur les tarifs douaniers et le commerce (GATT), qui stipulait que tous les signataires se consentiraient mutuellement le traitement de la nation la plus favorisée, le traité de Rome comportait une possibilité de baisse du tarif extérieur commun dans son article 110. Les convictions libre-échangistes des gouvernants des cinq partenaires de la France les portaient dès le départ à recevoir avec bienveillance les demandes de réduction du tarif extérieur commun qui ne manqueraient pas d'être formulées par les pays tiers. En 1957, les négociateurs français se souciaient avant tout des risques que la concurrence de l'industrie allemande faisait peser sur l'industrie française. Ils ne

18 Dirk Spierenburg et Raymond Poidevin, *Histoire de la Haute Autorité de la Communauté européenne du charbon et de l'acier. Une expérience supranationale*, Bruxelles, Bruylant, 1993, p. 111 à 172 et 680 à 699.

19 Bernard Esambert, «Une politique industrielle pour l'Europe», *Espoir*, n° 178, 2014, p. 41-58.

20 Mathieu Fulla, *Les socialistes français et l'économie (1944-1981) : une histoire économique du politique*, Paris, Sciences Po les Presses, 2016, p. 106.

21 La majorité des décideurs français étaient hostiles à la création de la CEE. *Cf.* Laurent Warlouzet, *Quelle Europe économique pour la France? La France et le Marché Commun industriel, 1956-1969*, thèse Paris Sorbonne, 2007, chap. 1 et 11.

prêtèrent guère d'attention à des dispositions qui portaient en germe un élargissement de la concurrence au monde entier. Mais ils venaient sans le savoir de mettre le doigt dans un engrenage, celui d'une évolution, vers une soumission aux vues libre-échangistes des pays anglo-saxons soutenus par l'Allemagne fédérale et le Bénélux. Le premier président de la commission européenne, Walter Hallstein, était lui-même un chaud partisan de l'ouverture des frontières.

Après la conclusion du traité de Rome, les chambres de commerce allemandes s'étaient montrées tout de suite favorables à l'inclusion de l'Europe des Six dans la grande zone de libre-échange européenne proposée dès juillet 1956 au Conseil de l'OECE par les Britanniques[22]. Le ministre allemand de l'Économie Ludwig Erhard était totalement acquis à cette idée, de même que les gouvernements des pays du Bénélux. Le gouvernement français s'y opposait au contraire. L'affaire fut réglée entre Konrad Adenauer et le général de Gaulle, au cours de leurs entretiens de Colombey-les-Deux-Églises et de Bad Kreuznach à l'automne 1958. Le gouvernement français s'engagea à réaliser le décontingentement de 90% des importations dans le cadre de l'OECE et à effectuer sans délai les premières baisses tarifaires prévues dans le cadre de la CEE. Il accepta également le principe d'une baisse limitée du tarif extérieur commun sur les produits industriels dans une future négociation du GATT réclamée par les États-Unis[23]. En échange, le gouvernement allemand se rallia à la position française de refus d'inclusion dans une zone de libre-échange, ce qui contraignit le Royaume-Uni à se contenter de la promesse de baisses futures du tarif extérieur commun dans le cadre du GATT.

Le gouvernement français réserva dès lors tous ses efforts diplomatiques à la protection de l'agriculture. Il refusa le passage de l'unanimité à la majorité qualifiée pour les questions douanières, allant jusqu'à paralyser le fonctionnement de la CEE entre le 30 juin 1965 et le 29 janvier 1966. Il obtint gain de cause, du moins pour deux décennies. Mais, dans le cadre d'un marchandage discret avec le gouvernement allemand, il accepta de fortes baisses du tarif extérieur commun concernant les produits industriels dans le cadre des négociations du *Kennedy Round*.

À partir de 1973, les élargissements successifs de l'Europe n'affaiblirent nullement l'inspiration libre-échangiste initiale des pères de l'Europe, bien au contraire. Cette année vit l'entrée de la Grande-Bretagne, champion historique du libre-échange. Les adhésions, en 1981, de la Grèce, puis en 1986, de l'Espagne et du Portugal ne représentèrent pas le contrepoids espéré par Paris. L'adhésion, en 1995, de l'Autriche, de la Suède et de la Finlande renforça encore le camp libéral. Enfin, l'adhésion

22 Martial Libera, *Diplomatie patronale aux frontières. Les relations des chambres de commerce frontalières françaises avec leurs homologues allemandes (1945-milieu des années 1980)*, Genève, Droz, 2020.

23 C'est Walter Hallstein qui, en mars 1958, avait proposé de poser le problème de la baisse du tarif extérieur commun dans le cadre du GATT et non plus dans celui de l'OECE. Cela permettait à la fois de ne pas fermer la porte à une baisse du tarif extérieur commun et de débuter sans plus tarder un désarmement douanier dans le cadre de l'Europe des Six, dès janvier 1959. En octobre 1958, les Américains s'étaient ralliés à cette perspective, qui allait conduire aux négociations du *Dillon Round*. Cf. Laurent Warlouzet, *Le choix de la CEE par la France. L'Europe économique en débat, de Mendès-France à de Gaulle (1955-1969)*, Paris, Comité pour l'histoire économique et financière de la France, 2011, p. 21-100.

ultérieure des pays d'Europe Centrale et Orientale à partir de 2003 ruina les espoirs de ceux qui croyaient que le système d'économie mixte français offrirait une solution intermédiaire aux pays sortis du communisme. Ces derniers optèrent tout de suite pour le modèle le plus libéral et tirèrent un parti maximum de leurs bas coûts salariaux pour conquérir les marchés extérieurs.

La baisse des droits de douane vis-à-vis des pays tiers fut menée avec une rapidité défiant toutes les prévisions. Les accords du *Dillon round* (1960) et du *Kennedy Round* (1967) furent suivis de l'accord de 1971 sur le système de préférences généralisé en faveur des exportations des pays en voie de développement, puis en 1979 d'un nouvel accord de baisse tarifaire, celui du *Tokyo Round*, qui, en outre, ouvrit les appels d'offres pour les achats publics à l'ensemble des producteurs mondiaux. Enfin, l'accord concluant les négociations de l'*Uruguay Round* réduisit en 1994 le tarif extérieur commun de l'Union Européenne jusqu'au niveau moyen de 4% *ad valorem*, plus symbolique que réel. Même la politique agricole commune fut progressivement démantelée, avec les abaissements successifs des prix de soutien à partir de 1992.

On pourra s'étonner que l'entrée de la France dans un monde de libre-échange ait si peu fait l'objet de grands débats publics. Les élites syndicales et administratives continuèrent à penser la France comme un espace préservé de la concurrence extérieure. Les experts qui conseillaient les hommes politiques répugnaient à imaginer un monde où la croissance dépendrait de plus en plus de décisions prises sans eux par des millions de chefs d'entreprises anonymes. Enfin, les diplomates ne tenaient pas avouer l'ampleur de leurs concessions dans les négociations internationales. La société française entra ainsi, sans en avoir pris conscience, dans l'âge de l'économie ouverte.

3/ LA CRISE DU MODÈLE FRANÇAIS

3.1/ L'épuisement des avantages de la politique industrielle centralisée

La politique industrielle à la française fonctionna assez bien, tant que l'État disposa de tous les leviers pour organiser l'industrie : contrôle du crédit, définition des normes techniques, monopoles détenus par quelques grandes entreprises publiques, grands contrats conclus de gré à gré avec l'État français ou avec des États étrangers. Le budget de l'État français offrait encore des ressources suffisantes pour financer d'ambitieux programmes de recherche et le succès couronna souvent ces efforts dans les secteurs du ferroviaire, de l'énergie ou de l'aéronautique.

Mais la gestion par l'État de grands programmes technologiques ne tarda pas à révéler certaines faiblesses. La recherche appliquée, en grande partie entre les mains d'agences gouvernementales, resta trop éloignée des marchés. Les sociétés publiques ne se dotèrent pas des réseaux de prospection et de maintenance internationaux qui permettaient de connaître les besoins quotidiens du grand public des consommateurs ou des professionnels du monde entier.

À partir des années 1970, dans toutes les industries de pointe, les besoins de financement dépassèrent de plus en plus les capacités financières de l'État français, notamment dans le secteur aérospatial, celui de l'électronique et celui de l'informatique. Il fallut, de plus en plus, s'orienter vers la coopération internationale. À la longue, même les industries de la défense sortirent de la sphère régalienne, car la diminution des budgets militaires obligea les grands groupes d'armements à contracter de plus en plus souvent avec des sous-traitants étrangers.

Enfin, à l'inverse des quelques branches privilégiées par l'État, le reste de l'industrie française souffrit d'un manque permanent de ressources pour l'investissement et la recherche-développement. Faute de bureaux d'études suffisamment étoffés, trop d'entreprises françaises durent, à partir des années 1960, se cantonner dans des spécialisations fondées sur les baisses de coûts de fabrication et les économies d'échelle. Elles parvinrent moins bien que leurs concurrentes européennes à conquérir une compétitivité hors prix et furent de plus en plus soumises à la concurrence de pays à moindres coûts salariaux.

3.2/ De la désindustrialisation à l'aggravation du déficit commercial

En 1974, la France comptait près de 40% de travailleurs de l'industrie (bâtiment-travaux publics inclus) dans sa population active occupée. Au recensement de 2016, la France ne comptait déjà plus que 20% d'actifs dans ce secteur. En quatre décennies, elle avait perdu la moitié de sa population industrielle quand l'Allemagne n'en avait perdu que le quart[24]

Moins affectée par la désindustrialisation, l'Italie devint la deuxième puissance industrielle européenne, devant la France et la Grande-Bretagne.

TABLEAU 1 **VALEUR AJOUTÉE DE L'INDUSTRIE EN 2011 (€)**

	Valeur ajoutée de l'industrie par habitant (€)	Valeur ajoutée de l'industrie (M €)
Irlande	8 137	37,2
Allemagne	6 171	495,4
Autriche	6 059	50,8
Suède	5 773	54,5
Belgique	4 203	46,4
Pays-Bas	4 117	68,7
Italie	3 706	220,1
République Tchèque	3 209	33,7
Espagne	2 865	133,9
France	2 778	181,5

24 Entre 1974 et 2012, les effectifs industriels de l'Allemagne Fédérale sont passés de 10 290 000 à 7 840 000 (-24%). L'adjonction de l'ancienne RDA en 1990 ne s'est traduite que très temporairement par une hausse des effectifs occupés dans l'industrie : plus de la moitié des emplois dans ces industries ont été détruits dans les mois qui ont suivi.

	Valeur ajoutée de l'industrie par habitant (€)	Valeur ajoutée de l'industrie (M €)
Royaume-Uni	2 679	169,5
Portugal	1 830	19,3
Pologne	1 534	58,3
Grèce	1 667	18,5
Allemagne+ Italie+ Bénélux	*4962*	*830,6*

Source: Karl Brenke, « Production industrielle : comparaison France-Allemagne », *Regards sur l'économie allemande*, n° 106, oct. 2012.

Après 1974, la croissance buta de plus en plus sur la hausse des importations en raison de la trop faible capacité de l'appareil industriel français à répondre à une demande accrue par rapport à ses homologues étrangers[25]. Grâce à un meilleur maintien de sa production manufacturière, l'Italie réussit à préserver l'équilibre de ses échanges et sortit de la crise des *subprimes* avec un important excédent commercial alors que la France ne parvenait plus à résorber un déficit considérable de sa balance des biens et services (voir figure 1).

Le déficit commercial persistant fut une cause majeure de ralentissement de la croissance et d'aggravation du chômage en France. Le seul excédent durable qui fut enregistré (de 1991 à 2004) fut lié au choc de la demande intérieure allemande causé par la réunification. Ce que le commerce extérieur n'apportait pas pour l'emploi, les gouvernements successifs le compensèrent partiellement par la création d'emplois publics dont le nombre augmenta fortement à partir de 1974. Mais cette hausse fut financée par la fiscalité. Dans ce jeu à somme nulle, ce qui était gagné par l'emploi public était soustrait à l'emploi du secteur marchand, avec un grand perdant : le solde de la balance commerciale. En fin de compte, c'est la croissance économique elle-même qui se retrouva toujours davantage bridée par la contrainte extérieure.

3.3/ Un ralentissement de la croissance du PIB par habitant de plus en plus prononcé

Si l'on compare le PIB par habitant de la France par rapport à celui de ses cinq partenaires du Marché Commun, on peut constater qu'après un redressement significatif durant les années 1960, , la France perdit beaucoup de terrain par rapport à eux entre 1983 et 1997 (cf. figure 4).

25 *Ibid.*, p. 151 et 156.

FIGURE 1 **ÉVOLUTION DU SOLDE DE LA BALANCE DES BIENS ET SERVICES DE LA FRANCE ET DE L'ITALIE (1950-2016)**

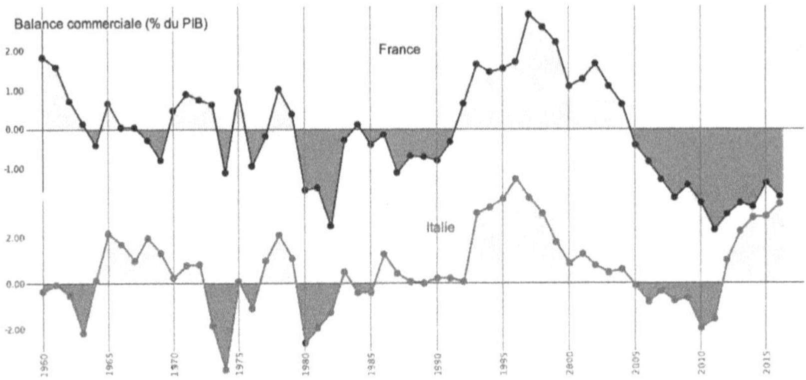

Source : Perspective monde, Université de Sherbrooke.

FIGURE 2 **ÉVOLUTION DE LA BALANCE DES BIENS ET SERVICES DE L'ALLEMAGNE**

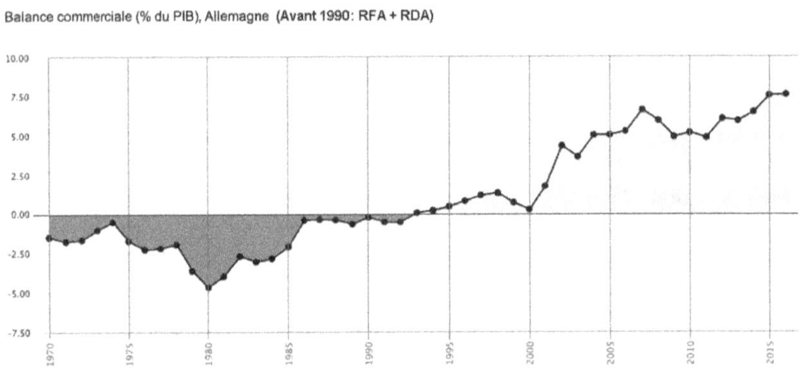

Source : Perspective monde, Université de Sherbrooke.

FIGURE 3 **SOLDE DE LA BALANCE DES BIENS ET SERVICES DE LA BELGIQUE ET DES PAYS-BAS (1960-2016)**

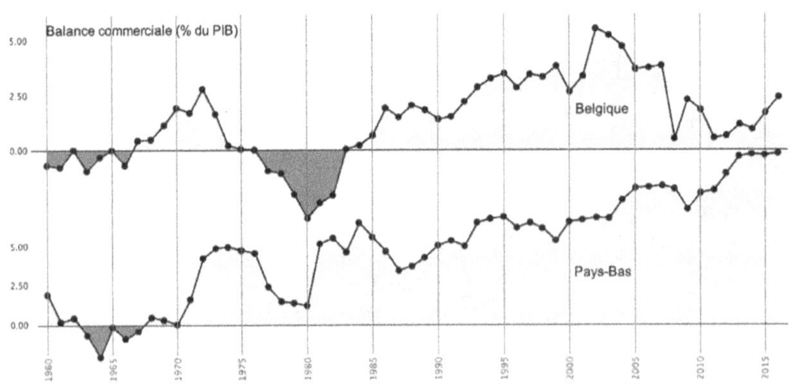

Source : Perspective monde, Université de Sherbrooke.

FIGURE 4 **PIB PAR HABITANT DE LA FRANCE RAPPORTÉ À CELUI DE SES CINQ PARTENAIRES DE L'EUROPE DES SIX (1950-2014)**

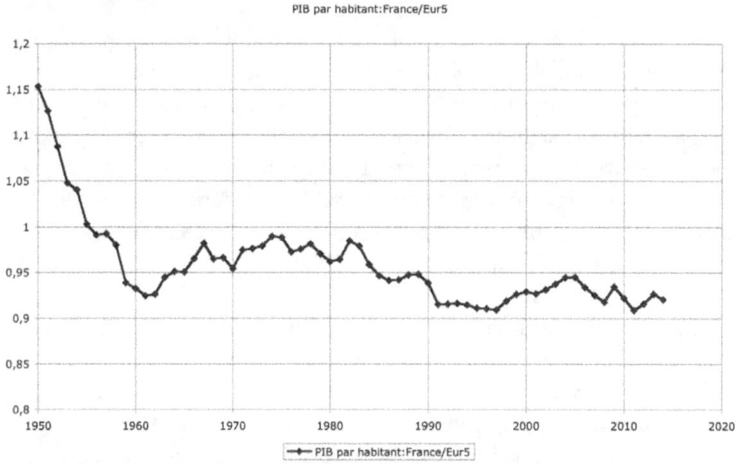

Source: Penn World Tables 9.0. Real GDP at constant national prices, Mil. of 2011 US$. Feenstra Robert C., Robert Inklaar and Marcel P. Timmer (2015), "The next Generation of the Penn World Table", *American Economic Review*, 105 (10), 3150-3182

Si l'on élargit la comparaison à l'ensemble de l'Europe occidentale, le redressement de l'économie britannique et les fortes croissances de l'Irlande et des pays de la péninsule ibérique font apparaître plus ample encore le décrochage de l'économie française (cf. figure 5). Encore nettement supérieur à la moyenne ouest-européenne jusqu'au milieu des années 1980, le PIB par habitant de la France lui devint inférieur après 2005.

FIGURE 5 **PIB PAR HABITANT DE LA FRANCE RAPPORTÉ À CELUI DE L'EUROPE OCCIDENTALE (1950-2014)**

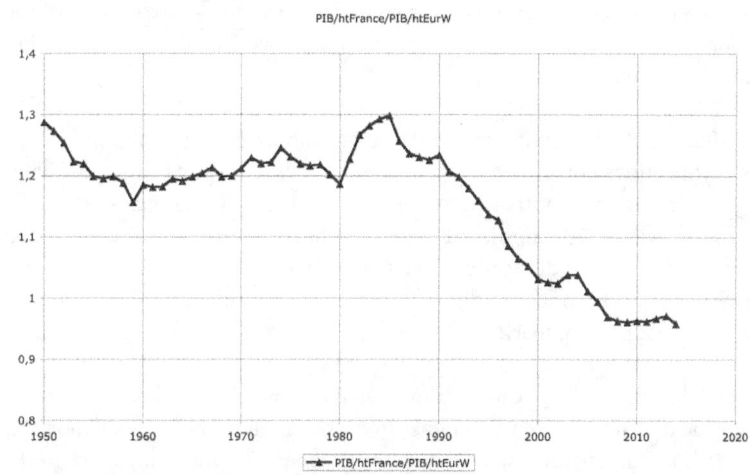

Source: Maddison Project database, ion 2018. Bolt, Jutta, Robert Inklaar, Hermann de Jong and Ian Lutten van Zanden (2018), "Rebasing 'Maddison': new income comparisons and the shape of long-run economic development", *Maddison Project Working Paper*, nr 10, www.ggdc.net/maddison.

4/ LA FRANCE, À MARCHE FORCÉE LE MODÈLE LIBÉRAL

Par son fonctionnement même, le modèle français se condamnait à être remplacé progressivement par le modèle libéral. Stimuler la croissance par la demande intérieure aux dépens de la compétitivité des entreprises entraîna un déficit de la balance commerciale qui affaiblit à partir de 1969 la monnaie nationale et obligea à demander la coopération des nations à monnaie forte. La stagnation du secteur marchand limita la matière imposable et mit les comptes publics en déficit à partir de 1975. L'accumulation de la dette publique en France et dans les pays d'Europe du Sud finit par ébranler le système financier international en 2009.

En théorie, le modèle suivi par les pays de l'axe rhénan, qui visait à stimuler la croissance grâce aux excédents de la balance commerciale, aurait dû rencontrer lui aussi une limite, celle de la hausse du taux de change de la monnaie. Mais cette limite recula sans cesse, grâce à la montée en gamme des productions. De Milan à Rotterdam, le développement d'industries à haute valeur ajoutée apporta de substantiels suppléments d'emplois et de revenus aux salariés. L'Allemagne et les Pays-Bas réussirent à faire baisser leurs taux de chômage tout en accédant à une position de créancier international. La France se trouva donc progressivement dans rapport de négociation dissymétrique avec ses partenaires européens, d'abord dans le domaine de la coopération monétaire, puis, à partir du moment où exista une monnaie unique, dans celui de la régulation du marché des dettes souveraines.

4.1/ La marche vers l'orthodoxie monétaire (1969-1986)

En décembre 1969, la France, affaiblie par les grèves et les hausses salariales de mai 1968, demanda au sommet européen de La Haye la création d'un mécanisme européen de soutien des monnaies. Le comité d'experts dirigé par le ministre luxembourgeois des finances Pierre Werner proposa en contrepartie la mise en place d'une instance supranationale indépendante en octobre 1970. Il se heurta alors à un refus indigné du président Pompidou.

L'accord de Bâle de 1972 se contenta d'instituer une limite étroite de fluctuation des monnaies européennes entre elles (le « Serpent ») sous la responsabilité de chaque pays. En gage de bonne volonté, le gouvernement français limita plus strictement, par la loi du 3 janvier 1973, la possibilité de faire financer le déficit du budget par des avances de la Banque de France. Mais la France dut, en mars 1976, quitter définitivement l'accord monétaire dit du «Serpent». Le franc subit alors une nette dépréciation par rapport au mark.

Après le remplacement de Jacques Chirac par Raymond Barre, des négociations reprirent en vue d'un nouvel accord monétaire européen. Au cours des discussions qui, en juillet 1978, instituèrent le Système monétaire européen, les Allemands acceptèrent des marges de fluctuation un peu plus larges et un système conçu, une fois encore, sans autorité supranationale. Mais, ils obtinrent en septembre 1978 au sommet d'Aix-la-Chapelle la contrainte du respect des parités bilatérales, ce qui revenait à faire de la monnaie la plus stable la vraie référence monétaire.

Après la mise en œuvre du programme commun de la gauche en France, le système monétaire européen fut secoué de crises successives, marquées par trois dévaluations du franc en 18 mois et plusieurs réévaluations du mark et du florin. C'est en mars 1983, lors de la troisième dévaluation du franc, accompagnée d'une réévaluation du mark, qu'intervint le tournant majeur. L'Allemagne n'avait accepté cette nouvelle réévaluation de sa monnaie que contre un engagement ferme de modération de la hausse de la dépense publique française. Le gouvernement Mauroy dut se résoudre à augmenter de 1% le prélèvement sur le revenu imposable, à réviser en hausse les tarifs publics, et à alourdir les taxes sur les carburants. À compter de ce moment, le taux d'inflation de l'économie française tendit à se rapprocher de celui de l'Allemagne.

Le choix de la « rigueur » ouvrit la voie à une politique du franc fort, posée par l'Allemagne comme préalable à une coopération monétaire plus poussée. Mis une nouvelle fois en difficulté par une nouvelle fragilité du franc à l'automne 1985, le gouvernement français accepta, dans les négociations du traité de 1986 sur l'Acte Unique, l'élargissement des compétences communautaires aux questions monétaires.

L'Allemagne présidant le Conseil européen durant le premier semestre 1988, le ministre des Affaires étrangères allemand Hans Dietrich Genscher proposa que l'espace monétaire européen fût régi par une banque centrale indépendante des gouvernements nationaux. Au Conseil européen de Hanovre, en juin 1988, les chefs d'État et de gouvernement adoptèrent ce principe. Après la chute du Mur de Berlin, le président français François Mitterrand et le président du conseil italien Giulio Andreotti accélérèrent le processus, croyant pouvoir échanger la réunification de l'Allemagne contre la fin du mark et de la rigueur monétaire qu'il faisait peser sur l'Europe. Mais le chancelier Helmut Kohl fit admettre que le seul objectif assigné à la Banque centrale européenne serait d'éviter l'inflation.

4.2/ Le recentrage sur l'entreprise (de 1986 à nos jours)

Le 17 février 1986, le nouveau traité, dit « de l'Acte Unique », modifia le traité de Rome. La France accepta de remplacer la règle de l'unanimité par celle de la majorité qualifiée pour tout ce qui avait trait au marché intérieur. Le gouvernement Fabius renonça ainsi au droit de veto de la France pour ce qui concernait le niveau du tarif extérieur commun, la circulation des biens et services, celle des personnes et, surtout, la circulation des capitaux. Il s'engagea aussi à limiter de plus en plus strictement l'intervention économique de l'État en faveur des entreprises, le tout sous le contrôle vigilant de la Commission de Bruxelles.

Avec le gouvernement Chirac de 1986, l'orientation libérale se confirma. Treize grands groupes furent privatisés. Désormais, le but affiché par le gouvernement fut moins de promouvoir une politique industrielle que d'établir un environnement favorable au déploiement des initiatives des entreprises. Par l'ordonnance du 1er décembre 1986, le contrôle des prix fut définitivement supprimé, quatre décennies après l'Allemagne. Il en alla de même pour l'encadrement du crédit. En 1992, le projet de XIe plan fut abandonné et le Commissariat général au Plan fut transformé en 2006 en un organisme de prévision à moyen terme.

La facilité des dévaluations ayant disparu, le souci de compétitivité des entreprises regagna un peu de terrain dans la classe politico-administrative française. Les rapports d'experts qui se succédèrent à partir de 1990 préconisèrent tous de transférer une partie des charges pesant sur le coût du travail vers les dépenses des consommateurs et les revenus des personnes physiques[26].

La recherche de nouvelles sources de financement pour la protection sociale s'amorça avec la création, sous le gouvernement Rocard, en 1990, de la contribution sociale généralisée (CSG), perçue sur les revenus des personnes physiques. En 1993, des baisses de cotisations sociales furent décidées pour les bas et moyens salaires[27]. En novembre 2012, le gouvernement augmenta la TVA et accorda aux entreprises le « crédit d'impôt compétitivité emploi » (CICE), consistant à leur rembourser les charges perçues sur les salaires inférieurs à 2,5 SMIC. En décembre 2013, il accorda, par le « pacte de responsabilité », un abaissement de la charge correspondant au financement des allocations familiales.

En 2017, la loi El Khomri rendit possible la conclusion de conventions collectives dans le cadre de l'entreprise, en dérogation aux accords de branche. Cette loi prenait acte du fait que la concurrence entre les entreprises avait cessé de s'inscrire dans le cadre délimité par les frontières nationales. En 2018, une réforme du code du Travail conduite par Muriel Pénicaud plafonna les indemnités prudhommales de licenciement. Ces diverses mesures visaient à redonner un peu plus de moyens financiers aux entreprises pour mieux résister aux crises.

4.3/ La renonciation au moteur de la dépense publique (de 1992 à nos jours)

La stabilité de l'euro pouvait donner la tentation à des gouvernements de développer leurs emprunts en profitant des bas taux d'intérêt résultant de la confiance dans la monnaie unique. Les négociateurs du traité de Maastricht signé en 1992 avaient bien anticipé ce risque et ils y avaient fait figurer l'engagement de ne pas dépasser 3% du PIB pour le déficit budgétaire ni 60% pour le niveau d'endettement. Le traité excluait également toute possibilité d'une aide communautaire pour renflouer les finances d'un État impécunieux. En 1997, le traité d'Amsterdam mit en place une procédure

26 Les rapports Charpin (1992), de la Martinière-Demarolle (1996) et Malinvaud (2001) furent suivis des rapports Attali (2007), Besson (2007), Estrosi (2010) et Gallois (2012). Cf. Jacques Attali, *300 décisions pour changer la France*, Paris, La Documentation Française, 2008. Eric Besson, « TVA sociale », travail coordonné par Olivier Passet, Secrétariat d'état chargé de la prospective et de l'évaluation des politiques publiques, 2007. Ministère de l'Industrie, *États-généraux de l'industrie. Bilan de la concertation. Rapport final*, 1er février 2010. Louis Gallois, *Pacte pour la compétitivité de l'industrie française*, 5 nov. 2012.

27 En juillet 1993, le nouveau Premier ministre, Édouard Balladur exonéra de cotisations sociales les salaires jusqu'à 1,1 SMIC, puis à 50 % jusqu'à 1,2 SMIC, avec extension progressive jusqu'à 1,6 SMIC.

de sanction pour déficit excessif. Un État qui ne respecterait pas les recommandations de la Commission pouvait, au terme d'une procédure longue et complexe, se voir contraint de payer une amende.

Mais avec la crise des *subprimes*, le déficit des dépenses publiques repartit de plus belle dans plusieurs pays, dont la France. En avril 2009, le Conseil européen enclencha une procédure de déficit excessif contre l'Espagne, la France, la Grèce et l'Irlande. L'affaire aurait pu fort bien se perdre dans les méandres de la procédure, quand soudain, en novembre 2009, la révélation de l'ampleur du déficit grec provoqua une panique financière. La rigueur que ne parvenaient pas à obtenir les instances européennes, les marchés l'imposèrent brutalement.

Devant la menace de banqueroute de la Grèce, la position de l'Allemagne consista à accepter une solidarité accrue, en échange de la soumission de ses partenaires à une discipline budgétaire plus stricte, contrôlée par la Commission européenne et la Cour européenne. Berlin accepta, en mai 2010, la création d'un dispositif commun de prêts aux États européens surendettés, le « Fonds européen de stabilisation financière » pour une durée de trois ans, mais obtint en contrepartie que son activation fût accompagnée d'une véritable mise sous surveillance des gouvernements aidés [28]. Les mouvements spéculatifs ayant continué, l'Allemagne accepta, le 2 février 2012, de pérenniser le dispositif d'aide aux pays surendettés, qui prit alors le nom de « Mécanisme Européen de Stabilité ».

Mais elle posa une nouvelle condition : seuls les États ayant fait un pas supplémentaire sur la voie de la rigueur budgétaire pouvaient en bénéficier. Cet engagement fut concrétisé par la signature d'un nouveau traité, appelé officiellement « Traité sur la stabilité, la coordination et la gouvernance » et, plus couramment, « pacte budgétaire européen », signé à Bruxelles le 2 mars 2012. Il posa la « règle d'or » que le déficit structurel ne devrait pas dépasser 0,5% du PIB. Deux nouveaux règlements, connus sous l'expression de *Two pack* , obligèrent les gouvernements de la zone Euro à transmettre leur projet de budget à la Commission avant le 15 octobre de chaque année. La Commission délivrerait alors une sorte de bon à voter pour les Parlements nationaux après s'être assurée que chaque État avait bien traduit dans sa loi de finances ses recommandations antérieures. La France se plia aux règles imposées par les traités. Elle ramena en 2018 le déficit de ses comptes publics au-dessous du seuil fixé à Maastricht.

En 2020, la crise du coronavirus sembla tout remettre en question. Au mois de mai, l'Allemagne accepta pour la première fois la mutualisation d'une partie des dettes. Tournant historique ou simple assouplissement provisoire motivé par une crise exceptionnelle? Nous penchons pour la seconde hypothèse. Le Bundestag vota cette mesure à une faible majorité et quatre pays d'Europe du Nord, les « frugaux »,

28 Le 7 septembre 2010, les ministres des Finances de l'Union Européenne décidèrent la mise en place d'une procédure dite du « Semestre européen » consistant à faire examiner les projets de budgets nationaux par les instances européennes avant leur adoption par les parlements nationaux.

manifestèrent leurs réticences. Les concessions faites par l'Allemagne à la solidarité européenne n'iront probablement pas jusqu'à la pousser à remettre en question des principes qui ont fondé ses succès économiques d'après-guerre.

Conclusion

Au vu de l'évolution des soixante dernières années, le moins qu'on puisse dire est que la France n'a pas réussi à créer une Union Européenne à son image. Son modèle économique s'est avéré moins bien adapté à la mondialisation que celui de ses cinq partenaires du traité de Rome. Par son fonctionnement même, le système économique français, fondé sur l'expansion de la demande intérieure, l'a exposé à subir la pression croissante de ses partenaires. La France a dû, à son corps défendant, adopter des éléments du modèle libéral rhénan. Après avoir renoncé au protectionnisme en 1958, elle a renoncé à l'inflation en 1983, au dirigisme en 1986, à la planification en 1992 et à la souveraineté monétaire en 1999. Les crises sociales et politiques qui ont jalonné et jalonnent encore cette évolution ne doivent pas faire perdre de vue cette tendance lourde, qui s'est révélée au cours des six décennies écoulées.

The double diamond and the state-backed path of industrialization in small, open economies:

Two Hungarian companies on the world market 1867-1989

Mária Hidvégi[1]
University of Konstanz

Introduction

Alexander Gerschenkron's concept of backwardness implies a government-facilitated process of accelerated catch-up: Governments facilitate and subsidize the transfer of new technologies as well as the establishment of new industries and new institutions required for long-term growth.[2] The state-backed path of industrialization may start with a protection of infant industries.[3] Following in the footsteps of Gerschenkron, the extent of the development gap, economic efficiency and in part the size of the country have been considered in economic and business history as factors determining how and to what extent the state can play an active and beneficial role in economic development.[4] Less well studied is the link to sources of national competitiveness[5] and the different importance of multinational activity for countries of different size in this respect. The generalized double diamond approach applied Porter's framework

1 Mária Hidvégi is a historian of Tungsram Group.

2 Alexander Gerschenkron, *Economic backwardness in historical perspective. A book of essays*. Cambridge, Mass.: Belknap Press of Harvard University Press, 1962.

3 Friedrich List, *The National System of Political Economy*. New York: Kelley, 1966.

4 i.e. E[dward] A. G. Robinson (ed): *Economic consequences of the size of nations. Proceedings of a conference held by the International Economic Association*. London: Macmillan, 1960; Margrit Müller and Timo Myllintaus (eds), *Pathbreakers. Small European countries responding to globalisation and deglobalisation*. Bern: Peter Lang, 2008; Harry X. Wu, "Rethinking China's Path of Industrialization", *UNU - Wider Working Paper* (2011), 76.

5 Michael C. Porter, *Nationale Wettbewerbsvorteile*. Wien: Wirtschaftsverlag Carl Ueberreuter, 1993.

to small open economies incorporating both domestic and international variables into the analysis of the determinants of national competitive advantages, and for countries outside Europe as well.[6] The goal of the present article is to depict some factors that may be useful to apply within the theory of state-backed path of industrialization to small, late industrializing countries in the analysis of entrepreneurial contribution to national economies' performance on the long run.

Hungary provides a good case study as fundamental shifts in the political and economic regime and a constant strive for catching up with the forerunners of industrialization have been characteristics shared with many of the emerging countries outside Europe. After the WWI and the dissolution of the Austro-Hungarian Monarchy, the Hungarian Kingdom ceased to be the constituting part of a European Great Power. Striving for the revision of the territorial decisions of the Trianonpeace treaty, Hungary drifted towards Nazi Germany and lost the WWII. 1949-1989 the People's Republic of Hungary was part of the Soviet hegemonic block. The small open economy suffered under the dissolution of the economic unit of the Austro-Hungarian Monarchy.[7] The integration into the COMECON (Council of Mutual Economic Assistance) did not offer a solution for the shortage of capital and only a partial one for the loss of the pre-1914 market.

During these main phases of hegemonic constellations, a state-backed industrialization was followed, up to its extreme version through the planned economy. Managerial freedom and therefore, the chance to follow successful paths of development of multinational companies from small countries[8] have varied considerably during these phases just as the form and extent of state intervention into the economy did – both for ideological reasons and for the limits of the state budget.[9] Two large Hungarian companies, the United Incandescent and Electrical Ltd., from 1984 called Tungsram Ltd.(!), and Ganz & Co. Electrical, Machine-building, Wagon and Shipbuilding Ltd. (hereafter Ganz & Co. or Ganz) exemplify business answers to these changes.
The paper is centered around the following questions:
a) How did the means and the extent of state intervention into industrialization influence national champions' multinational activities on the long run?
b) How did national champions contribute to the performance of the national economy on the long run?

6 H. Chang Moon, Alan M. Rugman, and Alain Verbeke, "The generalized double diamond approach to international competitiveness", in Alan M. Rugman, Julien van den Broec and Alain Verbeke (eds): *Beyond the diamond*. Emerald Group Publishing Ltd., Bingley, 1995, p. 97-114; H. Chang Moon, Alain Rugman and Alain Verbeke, "A generalized double diamond approach to the global competitiveness of Korea and Singapore", in *International Business Review*, Vol. 7, No. 2. 1998, p. 135-150.

7 György Ránki, "The great powers and the economic reorganization of the Danube valley after World War I.", in *Acta Historica* Vol. 27, No. 1-2, 1983, p. 63-97.

8 Schröter, Harm G., *Aufstieg der Kleinen. Multinationale Unternehmen aus fünf kleinen Staaten vor 1914*. Berlin: Duncker & Humblot, 1993.

9 E.g. Ágnes Pogány, "Kormányzati gazdaságpolitika a két világháború közötti Magyarországon", in Levente Püski and Tibor Valuch (eds), *Mérlegen a XX. századivers magyar történelem. Értelmezések és értékelések*. Debrecen: Jelenkortörténeti Műhely, III. 1956-os Intézet – Debreceni Egyetem Történelmi Intézet Új és Legújabbkori Magyar Történelmi Tanszéke, 2002, p. 49-58.

1/ INDUSTRIAL DEVELOPMENT IN SMALL, OPEN ECONOMIES: THEORETICAL BACKGROUND

The concept of the developmental state had been studied by many scholars trying to identify key elements and characteristics of state support to industrialization. One common denominator is the state's ability to profit from opportunities of globalization or of international economic relations, to put it in more general terms, shelter vulnerable groups from competition, promote the country's competitiveness, and promote gradual development adjusted to local institutions.[10] Flexibility and quick learning and implementation, key advantages of small countries, are seminal factors in realizing these goals.[11]

Michael Porter's *diamond model* analyzed a nation's or its specific industries' international competitiveness along four, interrelated components of the domestic market: 1) factor conditions 2) demand conditions 3) firm strategy, structure and rivalry and 4) related and supporting industries, including chance and the role of government as exogenous factors. The diamond model assumes that successful companies contribute to the establishment of innovative sectors, which in turn stimulate the creation of national competitiveness, that is a context for business activity favorable for the development of companies to compete in the international arena.

The model was first applied to small, open economies by extending it to a *double diamond*.[12] The term expresses that especially managers in small countries build upon both their domestic market base and that of the relevant larger region's or country's diamond to become globally competitive. The *generalized double diamond model* explicitly incorporates multinational activities into the analysis of competitiveness, operationalizes it and incorporates the government not as an exogenous factor but as a variable heavily influencing all four key variables of national competitiveness. This model reflects the developmental context of companies and industries of small open economies more truly as it takes the complex network of international interdependencies into account, for example governments' from small countries have to develop country-specific advantages based on both local and foreign based MNEs' activities.[13]

This chapter argues through the example of both selected firms emphasize that governments may efficiently support the development of firms' competitiveness in small, catching-up economies by supporting firms' internationalization, their flexibility to respond to changes of the relevant international diamond construction and encouraging the development of technological solutions based on the (generalizable)

10 Mihály Simai, "A "láthatatlan kéz", az állam és a globalizáció", in *Közgazdaság* Vol. 1, No. 1, 2006, pp. 47-62; Dani Rodrik, *One Economics, Many Recipes: Globalization, Institutions and Economic Growth*. Princeton, NJ: Princeton University Press, 2007.

11 Simon Kuznets, "Economic growth of small nations", in Robinson 1960, p. 14-32; Peter J. Katzenstein, *Small states in world markets. Industrial policy in Europe.* New York: Cornell University Press, 1985.

12 Alan M. Rugman and Joseph R. D'Cruz, "The Double Diamond Model of International Competitiveness: The Canadian Experience", in: *Management International Review*, Special Issue 1993/2, p. 17-39.

13 Daniel van den Bulcke, Alain Verbeke and.Wenlong Yuan (eds), *Handbook on small nations in the global economy. The contribution of Multinational Enterprises to National Economic Success.* Cheltenham/Northhampton, MA: Edward Elgar, 2009.

needs of the home market. In turn, firms' growing competitiveness, support the development of country-specific advantages but cannot substitute these or compensate for them in the long run.

2/ 1867-1914 HUNGARY AS PART OF THE AUSTRO-HUNGARIAN MONARCHY

2.1/ How did the electro-technical industry become a rapidly growing branch in pre-1914 Hungary?

Hungary was a late-comer in industrialization; well into the 19th century it was still a predominantely agrarian country. However, partly enabled by a compromise with the Habsburg dynasty in 1867 Hungary embraced the opportunities of the second industrial revolution. The customs union of the dual monarchy and the autonomous economic policy of the Hungarian government provided for the development of country-specific advantages. A similar legal environment to that of Cisleithania (the Austrian half of the monarchy), the proven commitment of the Hungarian government to the monetary union and to service debts, the great commercial banks operating in both halves of the Monarchy and the improvement of the human capital basis made Hungary an attractive place for investment. Inward FDI supported market integration by building the backbone of its transport and communication network, inducing the development of machine-building, too. From the 1880s, railways were mostly built by local firms; railway rolling stock found markets abroad as well. Railways diminished transport costs and integrated large rural areas into the economy contributing to the success of an export-led agriculture and the rapid development of the leading industry of the 1880s, the milling industry[14]. The large common market, geographical diversity and significant coal deposits drove technological development towards power generation based both on coal and water. The re-articulated pre-1848-concept of Hungary bridging East and West, agrarian and industrializing countries conceptually supported market building for industrial export on the Balkan and the Middle East, 'the Hungarian Orient'.

The government expreimented with various means to support industrialization in spite of direct competition from Austria, specified in a series of laws (No. XVIV/1881, No. XIII/1890, No. XLIX/1899, No. III/1907). At public investments, local producers were favored more and more consequently. Subsidies and tax cuts helped introduce new products and substantially enlarge production capacities. The organization of vocational training and the tariff policy of the Hungarian State Railways became two further main pillars of this system. Additionally, companies could receive subsidies for building houses for employees and workers, supporting migration from rural areas and for developing industrial centres. Knowledge transfer was encouraged through stipulating the share of foreign staff in companies enjoying state subsidies.

14 György Kövér, *Iparosodás agrárországban. Magyarország gazdaságtörténete 1848-1914*. Budapest: Gondolat Kiadó, 1982; Iván T. Berend and György Ránki: *The European periphery and industrialization, 1780-1914*. Cambridge: Cambridge University Press, 1982.

The Commercial Museum, a national export office and exhibitor of export goods assisted market building especially in 'the Hungarian Orient'.[15] The rapid development of Budapest as administrative, commercial and industrial centre, the growth of the population employed in industry from 10 to 17% and the development of GDP/capita from 66 to 77% of that in Austria demonstrated economic growth 1867-1914.[16]

2.2/ The emergence of national champions - Developing competitive advantages

The national champion of the pre-war era was Ganz & Co. The first machine-building company of Hungary was founded in 1844 by a Swiss immigrant, Abraham Ganz who first produced high-quality cast iron tires for railway carriages. Company growth was fueled by railway construction all over Europe. Andreas Mechwart from Bavaria took over management after Ganz's death and successfully opened new markets both at home and abroad by applying the cast iron technology for rolling mills. By the late 1880s, Budapest became second after Minneapolis in milling capacity thanks in part to that innovation. Mechwart realized the strategic potential of the electro-technical industry. He employed a small team of brilliant young people from 1878 who patented a substantial innovation on the AC-system in 1882 and applied this technology particularly efficiently for hydroelectric power plants.

Though the start was definitely supported by the profit generated by and the network of sales and engineering offices set up by the machine building department of Ganz & Co., the electro-technical department quickly grew to the first large electro-technical company of the Austro-Hungarian Monarchy and was capable to compete with AEG and Siemens within the Monarchy and abroad. Ganz' most important foreign market was Italy which proved more ready to experiment with risky new technology at main railway lines than the Monarchy, exemplified by the first mainline railway electrification (Valtellina railway in Northern Italy). Though a financial loss for Ganz, this electrification system was a great step in technological development. Westinghouse bought the technology, took over the Ganz team, and built made good business in Italy. Mostly inspired by Ganz' ability to compete on foreign markets and its impressive presence at the world exhibition in Turin in 1911, the leading Hungarian expert on exhibitions claimed that his country belonged to the leaders in the electro-technical industry.[17]

From the subsidiary of a Viennese electrical company, founded by Béla Bernáth Egger from Óbuda (today Budapest), emerged the United Incandescent and Electrical Ltd. 1896 is reckoned as its founding date, the name United Incandescent was taken

15 László Varga, „Az állami ipartámogatás a dualizmus időszakában a századforduló után", in *Századok* Vol. 112, No. 4., 1978, p. 662-703; László Varga, „Állami ipartámogatás a dualizmus korában (1880-1900)", in *Történelmi Szemle* Vol. 23, No. 2, 1983, p. 196-226; Adolf Strausz, „Keleti kereskedelmünk és egy magyar kereskedelmi museum", in *Nemzetgazdasági Szemle* Vol. 9, No. 4, 1883, p. 234-267.

16 Béla Tomka, *Gazdasági növekedés, fogyasztás és életminőség. Magyarország nemzetközi összehasonlításban 1918-tól napjainkig*. Budapest: Akadémiai Kiadó Zrt. 2011.

17 Mária Hidvégi, *Anschluss an den Weltmarkt. Ungarns elektrotechnische Leitunternehmen 1867-1949*. Göttingen: Vandenhoeck & Ruprecht, 2016, p. 13.

on in 1906, and the company was soon called 'Tungsram' due to its successful trademark created from the English and German expression for tungsten, it was the United Incandescent that first used this metal in an efficient way as the glowing file of incandescent lamps. As supplier of modern telephone systems (license from Western Electric Co., Chicago, 1899) and railroad safety equipment (license from Westinghouse Co., London, 1899) Tungsram grew fast thanks to large public investments in the transport and communication infrastructure in Hungary and Southern Eastern Europe. The dynamic growth and strong market presence of Tungsram was reflected in its becoming founding member of the first international light bulb cartel in 1902, which controlled the market of coal filament light bulbs in Europe until 1913, and much more in Tungsram's market share of 11 %, at par with Philips, and coming third after AEG and Siemens which held 25% each. The cartel stabilized the market. Participation in it was lucrative as long as coal filament lamps dominated the market. Furthermore, Tungsram learnt 'the rules of the game', i.e., how to protect its interests within cartels and organize market presence as a cartel member.

Beyond state support to company growth, during the ascent of both companies access to Vienna, the commercial and financial center of the Monarchy was another crucial growth factor for both companies as a source of capital, advanced management methods and technological information. The socially and economically more advanced market of the Austrian half of the monarchy prompted Hungarian companies' investments into new marketing methods. Serving the Austrian market in turn was important for establishing their reputation as quality good producers.

3/ 1919-1939 HUNGARY - FOSTERING COMPETITIVE ADVANTAGES

3.1/ A small, open economy

After the WWI and the dissolution of the Austro-Hungarian Monarchy, Hungary ceased to be the constituting part of a European Great Power, lost around 2/3 of the territory of the Hungarian Kingdom and became a small, open economy. The costs of a new state, reparation payments and uncertainty until their final sum was determined in 1929 and less favorable terms of capital import compared to pre-1914 restrained public investments. The commitment to the gold standard and foreign debt service resulted in high taxes restraining the growth of the home market. Political tensions with the neighboring countries presented further obstacles to export at times of protectionism and diminishing volume of world trade. The Great Depression exacerbated the intertwining banking, currency, fiscal, and foreign debt crises.[18] The fertile soil, relatively low production costs, internal political stability, a strive for re-establishing stable international economic relations, and all-time high educational investments

18 Ágnes Pogány, "Financial Crises during the Great Depression. The Hungarian Financial Crisis in a Central-European Context.", *MTA-ELTE Crises History Research Group. Working Papers in Crisis History* No. 1., 2014 http://valsagtortenet.elte.hu/upload/new_folder/WP_1.pdf

could hardly compensate for these constraints, but still provided opportunities for growth.

As some contemporaries admitted at the eve of the Great Depression, the government did not have a plan for structural adjustment to the fundamental change in political power and market characteristics[19]. Economic and trade policy mainly strived for import substitution. However much the size of the home market and financial constraints restricted the room for manoeuvre though, quite a few missed opportunities to improve competitiveness by state support to industry could be identified such as using cartels to initiate coordinated rationalization or using public investments to initiate coordinated specialization or 'enlarging' the market by standardization.[20]

3.2/ How did the state support the development of firm specific advantages?

Tungsram was one of the few Hungarian companies that successfully surmounted the difficulties of the territorial and political changes and reacted to rapid technological development and obstacles to export by specialization in vacuum-technological mass products building a full vertical production line and FDI in various countries, and participation in the transnational networks of production, marketing and technological expertise of the leaders of the industry was key to formerly is! As part of these networks the excellent but small Tungsram R&D-team was able to keep pace with the development in production techniques, to participate in development of innovative goods and Tungsram had a say in setting the rules to be applied on its main markets. Tungsram became the third largest light bulb and radio valve producer in continental Europe, started to build up the technological basis for TV-valve production and was able to meet army demand for radar development during WWII.

The government supported Tungsram's growth by tax cuts for taking up new production lines on the Hungarian market (radio valves), via reference projects (radio tower in Lakitelek, built in 1933 by Standard Electrical Ltd., the former mechanical department of Tungsram) and diplomatic support to the integration of Tungsram into the radio valve cartel with Telefunken and Philips. Revisionist politics however, endangered access to the Yugoslav and Romanian market; the control over these was crucial for Tungsram's global position. At the eve of WWII, the so-called Jewish laws deteriorated Tungsram's market position at home and abroad.[21]

Ganz & Co. electrified the Budapest-Hegyeshalom railway, the connection to Vienna, based on its own new technology and financed by British credit, in co-operation with British companies. This costly technological development did not pay out (again), as electrification was not carried on due to financial constraints. Ganz struggled to keep

19 E.g. Gustáv Gratz, "Das Wirtschaftsprogramm der ungarischen Regierung", in: Gratz, Gustav (ed.): *Ungarisches Wirtschaftsjahrbuch Jg. V: 1929*, Budapest: Buchhandlung R. Gergely, 1929, p. 11-26.

20 Mária Hidvégi, "Crises and responses: Government policies and the Machine-Building Cartels in Hungary, 1919-1949", in *Enterprise and Society* Vol. 20, No. 1, March 2019, p. 89-131.

21 Hidvégi 2016, p. 159-250.

up with the financial, managerial and technological requirements of the large-scale electrification projects of the interwar era.

In contrast, Ganz rail cars equipped with reliable Diesel engines constructed by György Jendrassik provide a textbook case of a successful attempt to double the national diamond. Motorization of the railways with such cars offered a viable solution to a vital problem of Hungarian transport policy by making passenger transport profitable in scarcely populated regions; modernization of steam traction, railway electrification or a shift to road transport were only partial alternatives due to the dire financial state of the country resp. of rural population. The Hungarian State Railways placed orders to Ganz & Co. for different types of cars, stimulating product development and created an excellent rail car service that served as a model for foreign railway companies. Ganz started to accumulate expert knowledge about the introduction of rail cars in different countries, assessing traffic needs, developing cars adjusted to local geographical conditions and service requirements, and organizing car maintenance.

The transnational organizational infrastructure and the access to capital necessary for a company from a small and poor country for global business was being built up in form of a license and cartel agreement with well-established British engineering companies. Market entry was facilitated by General Electric. The drive of pre-WWII Argentina for industrialization and loosening ties to the former colonizer made this country an ideal stepping-stone for marketing rail cars in other scarcely populated countries with challenging climate and geographical conditions. The Hungarian government supported that by renegotiating the terms of bilateral trade relations to South American countries and by the intervention of the National Bank at the governor of the Bank of England for pre-financing Ganz' deliveries to Argentina. Local production of some components and cooperation with a US-American producer were contemplated to overcome disruptions in deliveries from Hungary while the cooperation of the Argentine State Railways and British investors of Argentine railway companies in financing large-scale motorization was to guarantee political and financial support. However, internal management problems questioned the plans of doubling the national diamond with that of Argentina, and Hungary's entry into the WWII frustrated Ganz' ambitions once and for all.[22]

4/ 1949-1989 HUNGARY IN THE SOVIET BLOCK: FIRMS' COMPETITIVE ADVANTAGES AND STATE CONTROL

During WWII, around 10% of the population was lost, around 40% of national wealth was destroyed, the transport and communication infrastructure was severely impaired. International political isolation and reparation payments and the transfer of German participation in large firms into Soviet ownership accelerated reorienting trade

22 István Szécsey, Az Árpádtól a Hargitáig. *A Ganz gyorssínautóbusz, motorkocsi és motorvonat gyártásának aranykora.* Budapest: Magyar Államvasutak Zrt., 2006; Mária Hidvégi, "A Ganz-Jendrassik dízel motorkocsik Argentinában", in *AETAS* Vol. 29, No. 4, 2014, p. 45-64.

towards the Soviet Union. Despite initial democratic political development Hungary was integrated into the socialist block. In the 1950s, Hungary was to be transformed into 'a land of iron and steel' setting the destructive path for an energy-dependent, distorted industrial development. From 1953, attempts toward a strategic, selective industrial development focusing on knowledge intensive products and using local raw material lay at the heart of a series of reforms (1956, 1964, 1968, 1973, 1980s). Methods of planning and control changed moving from direct control over companies to the implementation of central plans through the control of output, prices and investment capital. However, basic principles of economic coordination and hegemonic relations remained unchanged and path dependency weighed heavily: problems arising from low productivity, outdated production structure and high energy consumption in industry, and growing indebtedness mounted.[23]

The state's influence on firm strategy, structure and rivalry manifested in breaking up vertical company structures and subsequent frequent reorganizations of companies, frequently changing developmental goals (influenced considerably by the COMECON) and the state's direct or indirect control over price building, investment capital, the terms of access to foreign markets and other key elements of companies' strategic planning. Ganz & Co. was split up into six factories, among them the electrical factory, called from 1964 Ganz Electrical Works, and the wagon and machine building factory, merged in 1959 with the Royal Hungarian Iron and Steel Works and Machine-Building Factory into Ganz – MÁVAG (1959-1987) and Klement Gottwald Electrical Factory (1953-1964) resp. Ganz Electrical Works (1964-1990). The electrical department had to hand over the production of various machines Ganz used to mass produce to other companies. This reduced Ganz' financial stability as the other pillar of heavy-current electrical machinery, supplying equipment for power plants, is a highly volatile business with long development and production phases, especially on a small market. Furthermore, Ganz Electrical Works were allocated investment capital only for mastering technological leaps in the development of equipment for power plants like increasing the capacity of generators, not however for constant R&D or developing complementary products. This all but prevented Ganz' capability from delivering complete technological solutions, specialization in small and medium capacity power plants and profiting from R&D investments. Reference works on the home market are crucial for producers' financial stability, R&D-capability and image; volatile and insufficient financial investment, inconsistent preference for the domestic to producer, paired with frequently changing priorities in national energy management (fuel type, level of autarchy, co-ordination with transport development) made long-term planning and market building for heavy-current electrical machinery-building difficult.[24]

23 János Honvári, *XX. századi magyar gazdaságtörténet*. Budapest: Aula Kiadó, 2006.

24 János Král, *Energiahordozóink és a hazai vízerőhasznosítás*. Budapest: Magyar Hidrológiai Társaság, 1959, p. 145-166; Éva Tárnok, "Az önálló műszaki fejlődés határai. Gyártás és fejlesztés egy hagyományos licenckapcsolat megszakadása után", in Márton Tardos (ed), *Vállalati magatartás - vállalati környezet*. Budapest: Közgazdasági és Jogi Könyvkiadó, 1980, p. 359-391; Pál Valentiny, "Az állam szerepe az erősáramú termékek piacának befolyásolásában", in: *Ibid*, p. 331-357.

The ambitious Diesel program provides another telling story. Based on the know-how developed by Ganz & Co. in the 1930s, economic policy defined highly ambitious R&D goals concerning Diesel rolling stock development and allocated considerable resources to this end in the 1950s. Interesting is why these ambitious goals failed.
a) Development goals were too ambitious and were modified too often for the small R&D team to meet them: The number of the rail car engine types to be developed was
b) significantly raised in a short time. Engines for road vehicles had to be developed as well though some key components worked at low efficiency in such engines. Under political pressure, some prototypes were sold to foreign railway companies directly from the construction office, , resulting in costly reparations and causing serious damage to Ganz' goodwill.
c) The whole program was put in danger when the question of allocation of Diesel rolling stock production among the COMECON-countries came to the fore. Though Hungary did not have to give up this branch of production, economies of scale and sales prices, therefore return on R&D were considerably reduced by the GDR and Czechoslovakia taking up production. The Soviet Union became the by far the most important market for Hungarian rolling stock; low prices and restricted demand for technological development of this market did not however, foster quality improvements at Ganz-MÁVAG.
d) The Ganz development team was long held in the dark about the possibility to buy licenses from Western-Europe for specific categories of engines; that resulted in splashing resources for unnecessary R&D, as it proved.
e) Under the pressure of saving hard currency import, Hungarian products of inferior quality had to replace a few components from capitalist sources even in case of quite low individual value such as sealings, considerably decreasing the quality of the final product.
f) Ganz' reputation and export earnings were inflicted by policy decisions on not allocating resources to spare parts production.[25]
Under such circumstances, strategic investment into knowledge production, production processes and foreign market presence was extremely difficult.

The state's influence on the development of related and supporting industries started with the nationalization of all companies with a workforce of over 10 people. Coordinative problems arose from frequently changing allocation of the production of various goods, or ever new mergers to guarantee quality and timely delivery. It is no wonder that no reliable, dynamic supporting industries emerged around the key companies such as Ganz. They could not rely on component delivery of good quality from other Central Eastern European countries either due to similar economic structures and the secondary importance of intraregional economic relations compared to each county's urge in meeting Soviet demand and earning convertible currencies.

25 Interviews with István Horányi and Ferenc Somogyi, former employees of Ganz MÁVAG and various documents from Ganz Company Historical Collection and Hungarian National Archives.

The decline of Tungsram's competitiveness in the late 1940s and 1950s exemplified consequences of the Cold War and the introduction of the Soviet-type planned economy, especially the state's influence on industrial R&D. In the interwar years an excellent, if relatively small research laboratory was able to focus on niche developments thanks to first-hand market information through Tungsram's global sales and production network and its being part of the transnational knowledge production and distribution network of the leaders of the lighting and telecommunication industry. The practical nationalization of Tungsram cut these ties. Excellent researchers died in the war or emigrated to escape prison; many members of the research team had to work in newly established national research centers. Tungsram only got back the right for direct export and import in the late 1950s. In absence of direct market information until then, cut off from the networks of the market leaders and to some extent due to COCOM-regulations, investments into replicative and redundant R&D rose in all production segments while sales opportunities were naturally restricted.

Tungsram regained competitiveness in light-source production from the late 1960s, demonstrated by halogen car lamp development and Tungsram's being the only COMECON producer that could buy cutting-edge Western production technology. From 1951 Tungsram built up a new production line, the design and construction of vacuum-technological machinery. As Hungary gained the right to produce such machines for the whole COMECON, this production line got a unique chance to grow. The USSR can, though with reservations, be called the foreign part of Tungsram's double diamond in that respect due to ambiguous incentives for technological development and asymmetric power relations in price building. At the beginning of the 1980s, the 'Government Program for Development of Microelectronics' provided an example for ambiguous state support: It distorted Tungsram's viable strategy for R&D and mass production of semi-conductors supported by Telefunken and Fairchild-licenses and Tungsram's machine-building capacity.

Thus, Tungsram was indeed a third-world multinational with a 6-7% market share in the Western European light source market, delivered lamps to the most demanding market (car lamps), supplied mostly socialist and developing countries with vacuum-technological production equipment and turn-key factories, developed capabilities to design and produce industrial robots and made considerable advances in keeping pace with the rapid development in the information and telecommunication industry. However, similarly to Ganz & Co., Tungsram exemplified János Kornai's finding on the socialist economy as being capable to perform well but working considerably below efficiency.[26]

26 Kornai, János, *A hiány*. Budapest: Közgazdasági és Jogi Könyvkiadó, 1980.

5/ FINDINGS: STATE SUPPORT AND ENTREPRENEURIAL CONTRIBUTION TO NATIONAL COMPETITIVENESS

Let us note some factors and implications this case study may offer for applying theories of the state-backed path of industrialization combined with the generalized double diamond model for emerging countries' strategies today. The very experience of Tungsram and Ganz in the planned economy, especially in contrast to pre-1949, leads to the conclusion of the necessity of more planning in coordinating the state's support to industry. A plea for more planning means not direct management at arm's length. Instead, it was a careful selection of the means to support industry that proved decisive just, as well as a right balance between consistency and flexibility concerning strategic decisions on national energy management, the development of the transport and communication infrastructure and key elements of the legal and economic framework the companies operated in.

Tensions in intraregional political relations in the interwar era and the Cold War era restricted or redirected multinational activities and greatly influenced the direction and terms of doubling the national diamond, especially regarding the foreign diamond's potential to induce technological development at the companies in the home country. Entrepreneurial freedom for (early) internationalization, gradual competence building via licenses and joint ventures, and removing obstacles to incremental technological development (such as policy constraints on the allocation of firms' investment funds or distorted prices or inter-company relations misleading R&D) seem to provide better long-term results in enhancing firms' and industries' competitiveness at lower costs for the national economy than the heroic national development programs seen both at Tungsram and Ganz.

Governments may support firms' efforts to turn scarce resources of the home market into competitive advantages exemplified here by the Hungarian government's support to Ganz & Co.'s diesel rail car business in the 1930s. The Ganz rail cars exemplified how the scarcity of natural and financial resources induced technological development which found its foreign diamond. Especially in case of small home markets and strategic, complex, capital and knowledge intensive product and service development the state's intervention in the interest of the local producer in form of reference works for export markets proved important for company growth and ultimately for the competitiveness of the specific industry.

Difficulties in meeting the goals of the Diesel program of the 1950s demonstrated in turn that especially in case of scarce resources (for example human capital) special care must be taken of their allocation and best possible use; force, fear, impossible goals and splashing resources wastefully are rarely useful means to these ends just as the wrong kind of economy may cause serious problems. Throughout the whole time period, investments into human capital both by the state and the companies paid out best; indeed, a well-trained and quickly learning, disciplined and relatively cheap human capital pool proved to be the most constant country-specific advantage of these companies, the basis for entering ever new fields of activity and keeping pace with technological development.

The role of these firms in Hungarian industrialization was not restricted to their contribution to infrastructure building, the introduction of advanced management methods, earning foreign currencies or attempts to influence economic policy making. National champions' involvement into the knowledge production and distribution networks of the leaders of high-tech industry leaders provide an opportunity for disseminating knowledge to the home economy. For example, Tungsram was co-founder and the main sponsor of the Lighting Technology Station (1927) and founded the chair for Nuclear Physics at the Technological University in Budapest (1937), which benefited from close cooperation with and the transnational contacts of Tungsram Research Laboratory. Successful doubling of the diamond may induce market entry of other companies from the home country and FDI to the home country due to reputation gain and established connections, thereby contribute to the development of the industrial base of their country and upgrade the terms of integration of the national economy or specific industries in the world economy.

Thus, in case of small countries with hegemonically restricted room for maneuver a flexible, competent developmental state and efficient knowledge management on company and national level are key to building synergies between the local diamond and that of key foreign markets.

Russia in the 19th century, Russia today: the permanence of technology transfer

Boris Vinogradov
Sorbonne University

Today, as before World War I Russia is an emerging country. As shown by numerous studies foreign capital played a very positive role in the economic evolution of Russia from the beginning of the second half of the 19th century onwards. It took the form of external loans (loan capital), direct investments in joint-stock enterprises, and entrepreneurial capital. Through capital transfers, Russia also benefited from technology transfer. For example, the Russian telegraphic or railway systems would never have been created without the import of knowledge, technologies, technical equipment and specialists from Western Europe[1]. This also applies to other economic sectors, in particular the promotion of raw materials and the development of heavy industry[2]. This paper aims at showing how much the Russian economy and the Russian industry are linked to Western industry, the French one in particular.

1/ TSARIST RUSSIA - THE TAKE-OFF STAGE : 1860-1917

I will start with Tsarist Russia before the 1917 revolution. Before World War I, there was a vast movement to liberalize economic, technological and cultural ex-

1 See the fundamental reflections of F. Benjamin Schenk, « Das Zarenreich als Transitraum zwischen Europa und Asien. Russische Visionen und westliche Wahrnehmungen um die Jahrhundertwende », in: Martin Aust (ed.*), Globalisierung imperial und sozialistisch : Russland und die Sowjetunion in der Globalgeschichte 1851-1991,* Frankfurt a. M. 2013, p. 41-63. Roland Cvetkovski, *Modernisierung durch Beschleunigung, Raum und Mobilität im Zarenreich,* Frankfurt, Campus Verlag, 2006.

2 Hans-Heinrich Nolte, « Eisen und Stahl im Zarenreich und in der Sowjetunion », in *Ebenda*, p. 274-301.

changes between Russia and the West[3]. I will analyze two significant cases: mining and armament. In the economic history of Russia of the second half of the 19th century there were clearly two tendencies. The first one was growth from "below": peasants (both serfs and state) created small firms, from which large industrial enterprises could grow later on. This was typical for the textile industry, which actually developed without government assistance.-

The second trend was growth from the "top": the state stimulated the development of certain branches of production to solve the current and long term economic problems of the country that were responsible for its lagging behind Western countries. Took place in the mining industry. In 1869, for example, the government proposed John Hughes, a British engineer, to build a metallurgical plant in underexploited territories formerly called New Russia. The settlement Yusovka (now Donetsk) emerged in that way. John Hughes founded a metallurgical giant that became the first enterprise in the Southern areas and gave birth to a new economic region with solid foreign investment. The greater role of the state was the second fundamental characteristics of the Russian industrialization process. In comparison with Great Britain, Belgium and France the delayed capitalist development gave the Russian Empire very important advantages: the newcomer benefited from the organizational and technological experience of the pioneers of industrialization. The most energetic and enterprising Russian merchants made use of that unique historical opportunity.

The industrial revolution as one of the essential components of the Industrial Revolution passed through several stages in Russia during the 19th century. The first phase of this long-term process was associated with the transition from cottage industry to large-scale machine production. The history of the cotton manufacturing may serve as the best illustration of the process of technological changes in the Russian industry. A key role in the supply of equipment was played by enterprising foreign go-getters who had become intermediaries between Western manufacturers and Russian factories. Intermediaries were necessary due to many obstacles which prevented at that time the establishment of direct relations between Russian companies and the producers of Western machines. Firstly, there was no direct dialogue between foreign equipment suppliers and Russian companies. Secondly, foreign companies were reluctant and did not provide long-term loans to Russian entrepreneurs. Hence, the emergence of special offices that established links with foreign suppliers of equipment and raw materials and provided loans to Russian entrepreneurs. Ludwig Knop became such an intermediary at the right time.

Russian industry greatly relied on West European technologies during the whole period of Modern Economic Growth. Due to foreign organizational and technological experience, the Russian Empire ranked fifth among the leading industrial states of the world. By the beginning of the 20th century multifaceted, wide-scale technological

3 Kerstin Susanne Jobst et Francine-Dominique Liechtenhahn, « Avant-propos », *Revue française d'histoire économique – The French Economic History Review*, n° 7, février 2018, p. 6-10.

transfers had a strong impact on the advanced branches of industry. In many respects, the independence of economic development was achieved owing to prudent and sustainable policy in the sphere of technological adoption conducted by the famous Russian entrepreneurs[4].

19th century Russia, like in Western Europe, coal became essential : railway locomotives and iron furnaces of the iron and steel industry (which supplied railways) were more and more in need of coal. Like on other continents, solid mineral fuels (coal, lignite and peat) were extracted at shallow depths by peasants deprived of fuels. The first available estimate of their volume, reports an annual production of 2,400 tons between 1796 and 1800 for the Russian Empire[5]. In the first two decades of the 19th century, the extraction of coal grew slowly, by 7 to 10 %[6].

This growth was initially based on the Donbas basin (Donets), whose exploitation did not begin until the prospection commissioned by Peter the Great in 1721, followed by the development of the iron and steel industry linked to shipbuilding and the manufacturing of guns following the annexation of Crimea to Russia at the end of the century. The six mines operated by Russian contractors during the nineteenth century were sold to the British company Azov Coal Company before the First World War. Meanwhile, other foreigners had joined: John Hughes, a French pioneer in the steel industry obtained a concession to exploit coal in 1871.

With rare exceptions, foreigners and not Russians make cross made the young coal industry outgrow one million tons, almost 60% of coal production was controlled by foreign firms[7]. Russia also developed a policy for the formation of human capital during the second half of the 19th century; it materialised with the creation of technical colleges to train the workforce for the textile industry and heavy industry, and then railways, construction, mechanical engineering and the chemical industry, so that Russia became the world leader for technical education together with the United States just before World War I. Thanks to this investment in human capital, it could substitute foreign specialists, notably British, by Russian specialists during the last decade of the 19th century[8].

As regards technology transfers in the military industry, we will study cooperation between Schneider-Creusot, the major French weapons manufacturer and the Russian metallurgical plant Putiloff[9]. From the end of the 19th century to the First World War, Schneider-Creusot, a major French steelworks, which then became a major

4 Irina Potkina, « The Nikolskaya Mill Partnership and the West European Firms: some aspects of technological transfer », *Revue française d'Histoire* économique – *The French Economic History Review*, n° 7, February 2018, p. 34-48.

5 Jean-Marie Martin-Amouroux, « L'énergie en Russie avant 1917 », *Encyclopédie de l'énergie*, url : http://encyclopedie-energie.org/articles/l-%C3%A9nergie-en-russie-avant-1917#_ftn20

6 *Ibidem.*

7 Anatoly Sudoplatov, *L'industrie houillère de l'URSS*. Moscou : Éditions en langues étrangères, 1958, 161 p.

8 Elena Alekseeva, "Diffusion of Western technological innovations in the Russian Empire in the late 19th - early 20th centuries)", *Revue française d'Histoire* économique – *The French Economic History Review*, n° 7, February 2018, p. 72-84.

9 Claude Beaud, « De l'expansion internationale à la multinationale Schneider en Russie (1896-1914) », *Histoire, Économie et Société*, 1985, n° 4, p. 575-602.

arms manufacturer, experienced a first phase of international expansion. It was in Russia on the eve of the revolution that a truly organized and coherent multinational organization was formed which was to play a very important role until the October 1917 revolution.

The establishment in Russia was in two successive phases linked to the rhythm of the economic development of Russia and the extension of the French influence in this country. A first phase took place at the end of the 19th century and was limited to two disappointing performances: Volga-Vichera and Paratoff. Expansion in this country resumed from 1907 onwards and Schneider organized around Poutiloff a whole network of warehouses creating a war material manufacturing site as consistent as the one in France around Schneider Establishments.

Since the late nineteenth century, the firm Creusot had expanded strongly, and its technical efforts and manufacturing were increasingly artillery oriented. As for Russia, after the decline of the first years of the twentieth century, it was experiencing an accelerated economic recovery that attracted foreign capital, especially French; the recovery was particularly stimulated by the growing importance of government orders related to rearmament programs[10]. State arsenals were sometimes plundered like that of Perm, and could not meet the needs; private factories, such as Poutiloff's, were better equipped but could only respond to orders with the technical assistance of a world-renowned foreign firm such as Creusot. In order to allow the manufacture of Schneider system equipment, the firm of Creusot put at the disposal of the Poutiloff Company all its inventions and subsequent improvements; to facilitate technological transfers, both firms exchanged engineers and foremen. At the request of the Russian company, Schneider built for the Russian Government all types of equipment to rearm Russian artillery.

In compensation, Schneider was to receive a fee of 8% of the price of equipment on the understanding that the total amount could not be less than 100 000 F per year. Ammunition was excluded from the contract, and Creusot retained the freedom to respond directly to requests for proposals and supplies of equipment in case the Russian Government, "by way of derogation from the imperial ukases", decided to have these supplies produced abroad[11]. Schneider obtained an important order of 122 guns of 42". In May-June 1910, the mission of the technical director of Creusot Husson at Poutiloff came back with a report showing that Poutiloff factories could be an interesting base of intervention. In particular the Russian firm would need strong support for the installation of the manufacture of heavy guns, in order to meet the demands of the War Ministry and the Navy and its new rearmament program. In this context, a capital increase of at least 7 million rubles was to be considered and Schneider would be asked to provide an industrial site that would be paid by various electrical and mechanical products. The visit of the factories showed that the tools

10 *Ibidem.*
11 Claude Beaud, « De l'expansion internationale à la multinationale Schneider en Russie (1896-1914) », *Histoire, Économie et société*, 1985, n° 4, p. 577.

– especially for the boring of two cylinders at a time – presented interesting points and required a study by a foreman of Creusot.

Above all, the report showed strong competition between the major artillery systems; there were agreements with "the French confrères", as evidenced by the agreement of 9 May 1911 with Saint-Chamond for research and the sharing of artillery and ammunition supplies for foreign countries[12]. The Schneider material was of good quality, especially the 42" gun adopted unanimously by the Artillery Committee, and the Russian government, especially the Grand Duke Serge, relied on the Poutiloff factories for the rearming programs giving more and more preference to the Schneider system. A new agreement signed on 14 February 1913 provided Schneider's technical collaboration for the installation of workshops at Poutiloff to manufacture machine guns of any calibre. Moreover, following negotiations in Vienna, another agreement was concluded on 24 February 1913 between Schneider, Skoda, Poutiloff and Newsky, this agreement allowing both Creusot and Skoda to give Newsky Company their assistance to manufacture molded and forged steels, including cannon elements necessary for Poutiloff's artillery manufactures.

Since 1909, Schneider had been interested in introducing its system of automobile manufacturing into Russia, but not capable to sign a technical contract with Poutiloff. In spring 1913, the issue was again on the agenda and studied by a mission of the engineer-builder Brillié. He had an interview with Colonel Secretof on the types of military equipment presented at the exhibition ; the conclusion was that this equipment was of "good quality", except for the current truck engines which lacked power, were "out of date" and had to be replaced by modern engines of 25 and 40 hp. Brillie's note on the upcoming auto show in St. Petersburg, like Racouza's on the automotive business in Russia, showed that the civil and military auto markets were growing and had a bright future; but Germany was the main supplier, and Russian manufacture was extremely small. Like Brillié Racouza after his visit at Newsky workshops, considered that these workshops would be most suitable for the manufacture of military or civilian trucks.

On the eve of the First World War, Schneider was in Russia at the head of a coherent network of complementary dependencies. However, as a result of never ending negotiations, the building that had been painfully planned was still a mere construction site; delays had accumulated and many projects would not be completed as a result of the brutal circumstances. There is no doubt that the Russian companies grouped around Poutiloff played an important role during the war thanks to the Schneider mission, but Russia at war was not able to benefit from an arsenal as powerful as the one that Schneider could have developed since 1911[13]. The result of the cooperation between Schneider and the Russian Empire was that many artillery components held by the Russian Empire were either made at the Schneider Electric plants or manufactured by Russian enterprises under the license of Schneider Electric.

12 *Ibid*, p. 579.

13 Claude Beaud, « De l'expansion internationale à la multinationale Schneider en Russie (1896-1914) », *Histoire, Économie et société*, 1985, n° 4, p. 580.

Many historical sources of the time prove the existence of permanent contacts between Russian and European engineers, scientists and professionals. These connections stimulated domestic scientific and technical ideas, enabled Russian specialists to conduct their research at an advanced international level and introduced new technological solutions into Russia and abroad. The analysis of publications proves that the "transfers" of innovations were in fact a much wider process that included dissemination, use, adaptation and their ree impact on European countries, that is a full-scale diffusion of technologies.

2/ SOVIET RUSSIA, CONTINUOUS TRANSFER

The aluminum industry was at the time an example of permanent transfer of technology into Russia. This Soviet industry suffered from a lack of skilled labor. It struggled to complete the process of aluminum processing. It also experienced difficulties in moving from applied research to mass production of sufficient quality products on a large scale. In this context, the Soviet aluminum industry had to rely on turnkey factories in order to gain strength.

It is well known that the Soviets were familiar with French aluminum technologies.[14] Since the First World War, Russia had contacts with Aluminium Français (AF) to cover its needs. After the 1917 Revolution, AF quickly reestablished contact. Russia tried to set up an aluminum industry: it created, in August 1931, Soyouzalumin, which included bauxite mines, alumina and bauxite plants. Alais, Froges et Camargue (AFC), the main member company of the AF and future Pechiney, signed a technical assistance contract on 20 January 1930 with the Russian government. It allowed the rapid construction of industrial complex of the Volkhov and Dnieper. The cooperation ended in an friendly break in April 1933.

Contacts with the USSR resumed after the Second World War, even before the merger of Pechiney-Ugine-Kuhlmann (PUK). Becoming Pechiney,[15] AFC Company was interested in the USSR between 1965 and 1969 through its joint subsidiary with Saint-Gobain[16] As for Ugine seems, it seems to have been interested in the USSR in 1963. On 28 December 1971, between Pechiney and Ugine Kuhlmann was completed[17]. One of the impulses of the strategy of the new group was to develop technical assistance abroad: PUK signed a contract with Metallurgimport on 31 May 1973 to

14 Réné Bonfils, « Pechiney au pays des Soviets. Le contrat russe de 1930 », in *Cahiers d'histoire de l'aluminium*, n° 23, hiver 1998, p. 29-50.

15 L'assemblée générale extraordinaire du 25 septembre 1950 adopte la dénomination « Pechiney-Compagnie de Produits Chimiques et Électrométallurgiques ». Elle se substitue à la raison sociale antérieure, à savoir « Compagnie des Produits Chimiques et Électrométallurgiques Alais Froges et Camargue ».

16 Pechiney-Saint-Gobain.

17 Pechiney Ugine Kuhlmann, *exercice 1971, rapport d'activité*, p. 7. Voir aussi M. Beaud, P. Danjou, J. David, *Une multinationale française*, Paris, Le Seuil, 1975.

build an Anodes plant of Tajikistan of very large capacity[18]. This policy continued until the end of the 1970s in the form of license agreements or the setting up of factories[19].

The automotive industry is another good example of Western technology transfer in Russia. The most important project during the Eighth Five-Year Plan was the construction of a huge new passenger car plant, the Volga Automobile Plant (VAZ). The value of Soviet purchases of Western machinery and equipment for VAZ exceeded $550 million. Because passenger car production had been a low priority for the Soviet automotive industry, industry officials were keenly interested in the latest Western developments in both production technologies and product designs. The Soviet machine tool industry had insufficient capacity to produce special machines and automatic lines for mass production, and the automotive industry was unable to design and put into production passenger cars that met contemporary world standards. Perhaps most important, the industry lacked experience in managing the production of automobiles on the scale considered in the long-term transportation plan.

Soviet officials, after a considerable research and long negotiations with a number of Western firms, selected the Italian automobile manufacturer Fiat to provide technical assistance to VAZ. Fiat's involvement began in 1965 with the signing of a protocol for scientific and technical cooperation with the Soviet State Committee for Science and Technology. The protocol provided a framework for discussions between Fiat and Soviet automotive officials that led to the signing of a contract on 15 August 1966. The contract provided Fiat assistance in designing a passenger car and ~~in~~ building a production facility with an annual capacity of 660,000 vehicles. Fiat agreed to serve as a general consultant for the project: it provided designs for the production process, indicating which machinery and equipment should be purchased in the West, and trained Soviet specialists in the operation of the machinery and equipment. Fiat also sold the manufacturing rights for the Fiat-124, a contemporary car that was the prototype for the vehicles produced at VAZ, and agreed to assist in adapting the vehicle to Soviet operating conditions. Finally, Fiat supervised the assembly and installation of all imported equipment and assured its successful operation.

Fiat was accorded a more significant role than is usual in Soviet acquisitions of Western technology. Fiat was involved in every phase of the technology transfer process, from initial planning of the project to startup. Its active participation is illustrated by the enormous (by Soviet standards) exchange of personnel between Fiat and the Soviet automotive industry. About 2 500 Western specialists, including 1 500 from Fiat and others from subcontractors, traveled to VAZ. At the same time, about 2 500 Soviet technicians and managers went to Italy to be trained at Fiat production facilities. Perhaps the most important contribution of Fiat was extensive training of top management of VAZ in the organization and management of mass production of passenger cars. Almost all of the managers of the functional administrations of the

18 PUK, *rapport sur l'exercice 1973*, p. 10-11.
19 *Ibid.*, p. 6.

general board of directors of VAZ were sent to Fiat headquarters in Turin to work on the organization of production, automatic information Processing Systems and production management.

While VAZ was the major recipient of Western automotive technology during the Eighth Five-Year Plan, other Soviet automotive firms also benefited. Particularly remarkable was the assistance of the French firm Renault in modernization and expansion of the Moscow Lenin Komsomol Passenger Car Plant (AZLK), which produces the Moskvitch, and in the conversion of the Izhevsk Machinebuilding Plant to production of the Moskvitch. Renault signed an agreement in 1966 to assist in production engineering and the selection of foreign equipment for the Moskvitch plants. The value of equipment supplied to the plants was about 700 million francs ($142 million at the 1966 exchange rate). The cars produced at the modernized plants were primarily designed by Soviet specialists. To support VAZ and other automotive plants, the Soviet Union also imported Western technology to construct new, or modernize existing vendor plants supplying the automotive industry. Among the new vendor plants built in the early 1970s with Western assistance there were a rubber fittings plant at Balakovo, built with the assistance of Pirelli of Italy; plants for making oil and air filters and upholstery materials, purchased from Japanese firms; a plant for car seats purchased from West Germany; a plant for oil seals at Kursk; and an anti-friction bearing plant at Vologda.

The French and Italian car manufacturers have largely contributed to the development of the Soviet car industry. For example, Renault's support helped tripling or even quadrupling the production of cars in the USSR.

3/ POST-SOVIET RUSSIA: A RETURN TO A MARKET ECONOMY, NEW HORIZONS FOR ECONOMIC COOPERATION

Russia in the 1990s was characterized by intense outflows of capital and direct investment inflows that were almost non-existent. The main causes of this dynamics were economic and political instability and a race for liquidity among all Russian players, who preferred to re-export export earnings. The crisis of 1998 announced a new period characterized by a restoration of external balances: a high current account surplus (thanks to the export of raw materials) and an increase in foreign exchange reserves. This means that a significant part of the cumulative current account surpluses since the financial crisis have been "recycled" into the internal economy and therefore the cash economy is working better today than in the 1990s.[20]

To show the process of technology transfer in post-Soviet Russia, we will discuss the construction of the Renault car factory in Moscow. Renault is the first French car

20 Emma Ménascé, Yves Zlotowski, « Un retour des capitaux en Russie ? », *Le Courrier des pays de l'Est*, 2005/3 (n° 1049), p. 54-67, url : https://www.cairn.info/revue-le-courrier-des-pays-de-l-est-2005-3-page-54.htm

company producing cars in post-Soviet Russia. In the early 1990s, the technological level of the Russian car industry was quite low compared to Western car manufacturers. Hence the desire of the Russian federal government to develop the national automobile market and stimulate negotiations between foreign investors and Russian builders for the creation of local production units.

The Moscow Mayor's office is a major partner of Renault in Russia. This partnership arose from the convergence of the interests of both parties. On the one hand, the Moscow city government wanted to participate in the development of the Russian automobile industry and develop industrial activity in the city of Moscow, and on the other hand, as part of its development strategy Renault was eager to enter Russia by bringing a solid industrial and commercial experience gained in the different countries where the Group was based. The will of both the Moscow city government and Renault to create a joint industrial and commercial society was manifested by the signing of a letter of intent on 1 November 1997 and a framework agreement on 2 July 1998.

Shared equally between the two partners (Renault and the Moscow Mayor's office) the amount of the projects of the Renault plant in Russia was worth 350 million dollars. Funding was spread over the first five years of operation. The plant was operational in 2005 and could assemble up to 60,000 vehicles per year from 2007. The idea was to create an activity that could serve as a showcase of Renault's know-how in Russia and could have a strong synergy with future dealers in terms of business methods. Renault developed its network in the western part of Russia as a first step. However, the development, in the long run concerned all the territory of Russia.

In 2014, according to the results of Ernst & Young study[21], total investment in infrastructure projects in Russia over the period of 2009 through 2030 is expected to reach USD 969 billions[22]. However, legislative reforms and more transparent decision-making are required to facilitate growth. Another example of fruitful cooperation and technology transfer with post-soviet Russia are the projects of Total, a French oil and gas company. The importance of its oil and gas reserves makes Russia an attractive country for foreign investors. International oil companies have shown a strong interest in Russia since the collapse of the Soviet Union, reinforced by the spectacular rebound in production in the 2000s[23].

Total has been present in Russia since 1991 with a number of business ventures operating in the segments of Exploration & Production. The structure of the Russian oil industry has changed significantly in relation to the centralized, hierarchical and administered organization of the Ministry of Petroleum of the Soviet Union[24]. Russia affirms its willingness to enter international hydrocarbon markets more strongly, while

21 *The road to 2030: a survey of infrastructure development in Russia*, EY Study, 2014, https://www.infrapppworld.com/report/the-road-to-2030-a-survey-of-infrastructure-development-in-russia-e-y, accessed on 12 April 2018.
22 EY's estimate based on data from open sources (mass media, white papers on government strategy and federal programs).
23 Catherine Locatelli, « Pétrole russe et investisseurs étrangers. Des intérêts divergents », *Le Courrier des pays de l'Est*, n° 1045, 2004/5, p. 64-76.
24 *Ibidem.*

emphasizing the need to invest heavily in the oil sector, both in terms of modernization and exploration. Both objectives could be seen as a relative convergence of interests between the Russian state and Western oil companies[25]. Throughout the years, Total has established strong partnerships with leading Russian companies in the Oil & Gas sector. Since 2015 Russia has become the leading contributor to Total's global production of hydrocarbons and most of the contribution is gas. Total's production in Russia comes from its 18.9% share in Novatek, Russia's No 1 private gas producer, from the onshore Kharyaga field located in the Nenets Autonomous District and from the Termokarstovoye field operated by Terneftegas, a joint venture between Novatek (51%) and Total (49%).

And since 2011, Total has been largely involved in the Yamal LNG project. This is an integrated project encompassing natural gas production, liquefaction and shipping. The Project involves building a liquefied natural gas (LNG) plant with an output capacity of around 16.5 million tons per year, using the South Tambey Field as a resource base. The field's proven and probable reserves are estimated at 926 billion cubic meters. Extensive transportation infrastructure was built in the scope of the Project, including a seaport and an airport. The project was completed on time despite significant headwinds caused by U.S. sanctions, which blocked technology transfer and made the financing of the investment extremely difficult. As is well known, since 2014, the transfer of technologies to Russia has been complicated by U.S. and European sanctions that prohibit the transfer of dual-use technologies. This can obviously affect several sectors of the civil industry.

In 2016, Total invested $ 50 million (45.6 million Euros) in the construction of the lubricants plant for the Russian market; it is located in Vorsino 200 km south from Moscow, will produce 40,000 tons of lubricants annually from 2018, and 75,000 tons in the future, if sales continue to grow. "Total Vostok", Total's Russian lubricants division, plans to locate there the production of its brands Quartz and Rubia (motor oils), Azolla and Equivis (hydraulic oils), and the industrial oils Seriola and Carter[26]. According to the same Ernst & Young survey[27], 325 infrastructure projects have been announced for implementation in Russia till 2030. Half of them (51%) are planned to be carried out over from 2015 to 2020. At present, 59 projects have been completed, 189 are in progress and another 77 will be implemented in the future.

Conclusion

The given examples show us that the success of today's Russian industry is largely due to the transfer of Western and especially French technologies, as shown by the case of the company Rusal which was second aluminum producer in the world until the spring of 2018. It is an international company with Russian capital and leadership, whose industrial base was constructed ~~on~~ thanks to French technologies. Since the U.S. blacklisted Rusal on April 6 2018, the largest producer of the metal outside China

25 *Ibid.*
26 Emmanuel Grynszpan, « Total poursuit discrètement ses investissements en Russie », *La Tribune*, 19/10/2016.
27 *The road to 2030: a survey of infrastructure development in Russia*, EY Study, 2014.

has lost more than half its value in Hong Kong. The sanctions will make it exceedingly difficult for Rusal to do business in dollars. Thus, it is very difficult to predict the future of the company...

In fact, Russia has achieved a success in the construction of aircraft and missiles, the pharmaceutical industry and radio electronics. Today, nearly 80% of the cars constructed in Russia benefit from a local assembly line, with 65% being manufactured in the country. After two years of recession, triggered by a sharp drop in global commodity prices as well as sanctions imposed by Western countries against Moscow, Russia registered impressive progress ranking 35 among the 190 economies measured in this year's *World Bank Doing Business Report*[28]. This success was largely secured by foreign technologies and investments. Through technology transfer, Russia has been able to create its modern industry.

28 World Bank, *Doing Business Report*, 2018.

PARTIE 2

Asie de l'Est et du Sud-Est : modèle asiatique ou dépendance nationale de sentier

PART 2

Eastern and South eastern Asia: Asian model or national path dependancy

The "black box" of Japanese growth (1945-1973): the origins of productivity

Kazuhiko Yago
Waseda University

Introduction: how they understood and misunderstood productivity?

Japan experienced rapid economic growth, coupled with a steady catch-up of labor productivity from the late 1950s to early 1970s: annual GNP growth surpassed 10% almost every year during the 1960s, and the per capita GDP growth recorded average 7.6% annual increase during the 1950s and 9.3% during the 1960s.[1] Japanese growth originally started outside the Western industrial core, and despite being interrupted by the devastation of total war, was indeed the "greatest success of the twentieth century".[2] The Japanese case also provided a model of growth for following Asian emerging economies, including China, together with a model of decline for ageing societies in the near future for the West.

A huge amount of literature on the origins of Japanese growth has been cumulated: classical views emphasize the culture-specific performance of the Japanese economy, represented by government-led industrial policy and collaborative industrial

1 Data available at following websites: Long term economic statistics of Japan, Ministry of Cabinet, https://www5.cao.go.jp/j-j/wp/wp-je12/h10_data01.html; Angus Maddison Project Database, Groningen Growth and Development Centre, https://www.rug.nl/ggdc/historicaldevelopment/maddison/

2 Robert Allen, *Global Economic History: A Very Short Introduction,* Oxford University Press, Oxford, 2011, p. 6.

relations;[3] Cold War historians underline the impact of American aid,[4] while global history studies have put the Japanese experience in an Asian context.[5] Recent works of Kyoji Fukao propose a solid statistical ground for Japanese economic development.[6]

Our chapter aims to synthesize the above views, focusing on one issue: the origins of productivity rise in Japanese growth. Starting with this question, we shall refer to contemporary debates in the international arena, i.e., the Organization for Economic Cooperation and Development (OECD), in order to review how contemporaries understood and misunderstood productivity. Government officials, national and international, as well as academics and the public during the period of growth, tried to identify what was happening to productivity. Their notions were sometimes successful, sometimes not. On the other hand, today's historians, with data and archives which were not available to their contemporaries, interpret the issue from an actual viewpoint, from a period in which productivity growth has already come to an end. This chapter aims to present an alternative view on Japanese growth coupling the above contemporary notions with updated historiography.

Why look at the OECD? The OECD was an international institution founded in 1961 to cope with the growth target of the industrial West and proposed unique views on growth.[7] Our chapter pays special attention to two of the Working Parties belonging to the Economic Policy Committee of the OECD, namely the Working Party 2 (WP2) and the Working Party 3 (WP3). The task of the WP2 was to work on "Policies for the Promotion of Economic Growth". Surnamed the "sacred chamber" of growth, the WP2 gathered specialists in economic policy representing the agencies of member countries to discuss growth policy and productivity.[8] As for the WP3, which aimed to promote "better international payments equilibrium", it was a control tower of the international monetary system, garnering high-level information through powerful representatives of Financial Ministries and the Central Banks of the member countries.[9] The contemporary views represented by these international forums, together with the member countries' reactions, are still yet to be studied in detail. In other words, we would "historicize" the data and thinking on productivity and growth in the context of international policy coordination.

3 Ronald Dore, *British Factory - Japanese Factory, The Origins of National Diversity in Industrial Relations,* Allen and Unwin, London, 1973; Michel Albert, *Capitalisme contre Capitalisme,* Paris, Seuil, 1991.

4 Jennifer Miller, *Cold War Democracy, The United States and Japan,* Cambridge, Harvard University Press, 2019.

5 Kaoru Sugihara, ed., *Japan, China and the Growth of the Asian International Economy, 1850-1949 (Japanese Studies in Economic and Social History, vol.1),* Oxford, Oxford University Press, 2005; Jean-Pascal Bassino and Pierre van der Eng, "Asia's 'little divergence' in the twentieth century: evidence from PPP-based direct estimates of GDP per capita, 1913-69", *Economic History Review,* vol. 73, no.1, 2020, p. 185-208.

6 Kyoji Fukao and Paul Saumik, "Baumol, Engel, and beyond: accounting for a century of structural transformation in Japan, 1885-1985", *Economic History Review,* vol.73, no.3, 2020; Kyoji Fukao, *Sekai Keizaishi karamita Nihon no Seichou to Teitai, 1868-2018 [The Japanese Growth and Stagnation from the Global Economic History Perspectives, 1868-2018],* Tokyo, Iwanami Shoten, 2020.

7 Matthieu Leimgruber and Matthias Schmelzer, eds., *The OECD and the International Political Economy Since 1948,* London, Palgrave, 2017.

8 Matthias Schmelzer, *The Hegemony of Growth, The OECD and the making of the economic growth paradigm,* Cambridge, Cambridge University Press, 2016.

9 Kazuhiko Yago, "The Crisis Managers of the International Monetary System? The Rise and Fall of OECD Working Party 3, 1961-1980," in Leimgruber and Schmelzer, eds., *The OECD and the International Political Economy Since 1948, op. cit.,* p. 185-208.

Why productivity? Several viewpoints guided our study. First of all, by definition, economic growth derives from productivity of labor and capital, together with total factor productivity.[10] The latter total factor productivity, often called "Solow's residual", represents progress in technology. Econometrics studies make fine calculations of productivity, but where this productivity comes from is still hidden in the "black box" of history. Thinking about productivity thus provides a junction of economics and historical viewpoints. More specifically, concerning Japan in particular, labor productivity was fairly low compared to the its OECD peers. The Japanese GDP per capita, which approximates labor productivity, was about 20% of that of the United States in 1950;[11] it was in 1990 that Japan caught up the OECD average; soon Japanese labor productivity decreased, falling lower than the OECD average.[12] In other words, the rapid growth of labor productivity did not trigger Japanese GDP growth. Instead, labor productivity followed the gross increase of national income, which leads us to think of the role played by total factor productivity.

To approach the above questions regarding various categories of productivity, Section 1 presents the notion of the issue, in the international and national arena; Section 2 approaches the change which took place in the background of understanding on productivity. Section 3 takes up residual factors composing total factor productivity, focusing on investment.

1/ HOW THEY UNDERSTOOD LABOR PRODUCTIVITY: CONTEMPORARY VIEWS

Soon after the OECD set its growth target in 1961, of the "50% growth in 10 years", the WP2 defined the productivity as follows in a footnote of a report: "Throughout this paper "productivity" is used to mean output per year per person employed". In those days, the most known economics in terms of growth and productivity was that of the Cobb-Douglas type, and the "endogenous growth theory" to identify the role of innovation was yet to come.[13] The productivity which the WP2 stated was "therefore the product of changes in output per man-hour (which is perhaps the best approximation to labour efficiency) and changes in the length of the working year". The same report referred to "productivity" in a deliberate manner: "If the change in employment over the decade of the 60s is treated as a datum, productivity is the factor subject to policy influence. But the extent to which it can be influenced by policy, the types of policy which are applicable and the magnitude of the response to be expected from

10 Michael Haynes, *Productivity*, New Castle, Agenda Publishing, 2020.

11 Fukao, *Sekai Keizaishi karamita Nihon no Seichou to Teitai, [The Japanese Growth and Stagnation from the Global Economic History Perspective], op.cit.*, p. 8.

12 OECD National Accounts Database.

13 Robert Solow played an important role in drafting the OECD's growth target. For the theoretical background and institutional outcome of this issue, see Schmelzer, *Hegemony of Growth, op. cit.*, p. 174-180.

the various policy instruments are all very imperfectly understood".[14] It was on this "imperfect" understanding which stood the OECD growth target.

An early report of the WP2 established in 1962, giving a projection of "Final Demand" for the year 1970, expressed their thinking on productivity. Following the 10-year plan of growth presented by the OECD as a whole, the WP2 worked out a 10-year projection of GNP running from 1960 to 1970 to satisfy the "50% goal". In this projection, curiously, the GNP growth rate was supposed to be the sum of the rate of increase of employment and that of productivity: for example, in the case of the United States, employment growth of 1.9% in 10 years plus productivity growth of 2.7% made 4.6% GNP growth, which correspond to an index of 157 in 1970 compared to that of 100 for the year 1960. Another point to which the WP2 paid attention was the share of investment over GNP: in the case of the United States, it was projected to be 10.5% per 10 years. These understandings of productivity derived, as the WP2 report says, from the "framework of the Standardized System of National Accounts".[15] According to the framework of the period, as shown above, productivity was an important element of GNP growth, but coupled with the employment factor. In other words, full employment in Keynesian terms was essential to reach the growth target.

With labor productivity thus taken up as a focus to define productivity in general, the Japanese "backwardness" of productivity was highlighted in the country reports. It was in 1964 that Japan obtained full membership of the OECD, and by that time, GNP growth of the Japanese economy was recorded as the highest among OECD peers. On the other hand, labor productivity was among the lowest of the members. The WP2 record in 1965 reveals the contemporary notion on Japanese productivity, especially the self-consciousness of the low labor productivity on the Japanese side: in this record of a "country reply", the Japanese agency presented the "Doubling National Income Plan" (1961-1970) corresponding to the OECD target, and also the "Mid-term Economic Plan" adopted in January 1965. This Mid-term plan, consisted of five main goals, the third one related to productivity: "Modernization of the low-productivity sectors, i.e., agriculture, small business, and distribution". However, the "structural change" to cope with these low-productivity sectors stood on a motive slightly different from OECD peers: since the low-productivity sectors "employ a large proportion of the now limited labor force, an increase in productivity in these fields is desired to release manpower required by the growing modern sectors such as a manufacturing".[16] While the OECD core member noticed productivity in relation to employment, the Japanese awareness of the issue was one of self-criticism of the structural "backwardness" in productivity, but without fear of unemployment. The above difference of notion, although not made clear in this epoch, established a starting point to forming the uniqueness of Japanese growth during the 1960s.

14 OECD Historical Archives (OECD-HA), CPE/WP2(62)2, "Implementation of the resolution of the First ministerial Council, (Note by the Secretariat)", Paris, 10th January 1962.
15 OECD-HA, CPE/WP2(62)11, "Projection for Final Demand for 1970, (Note by the Secretariat)", Paris, 30th May 1962.
16 OECD-HA, CPE/WP2(65)1/21, "Mid-term Report on Progress to Aid Prospects for the Fifty Per Cent GNP Growth Target, Country Replies – Japan (Note by the Secretariat)", Paris, 2nd July 1965.

The above notion of labor productivity, in the particular historical context of the 1960s, stood upon certain "fear". The archival records of the OECD committees reveal the fear: unemployment on the OECD side, economic and social backwardness on the Japanese side.

First, the OECD side: it was natural that rising productivity could cut off employment. Though not so serious as the 1970s, the OECD countries during the 1960s already faced a certain level of unemployment in the course of their growth. How to raise productivity without bringing about too much unemployment was thus a major fear shared among the members. One theoretical framework, adopted in the OECD, explained this fear and tried to propose an answer. It was Okun's law, presented by the American economist Arthur Okun (1928-1980). Okun's method aimed to estimate "the growth of potential output by relating actual output to the rate of unemployment".[17] One of the theoretical origins of "potential growth rate", Okun's method highlights the unemployment rate, relating other factors such as labor force participation rate, average hours worked per worker, as well as man-hour productivity changes. The method was expressed in a quite primitive equation: $y = a - kx$ (y represents percentage change in real GNP, x expresses quarterly change in the unemployment rate, and k shows the sensitivity of y to x). If $k = 3$, this meant "that a decline in the rate of unemployment of one percentage point is associated with an increase in G.N.P. of three percent". The crucial coefficient k was to be calculated by the function composed of the level of potential and actual output as well as the actual and fixed (target) rate of unemployment.[18] An important point here is that according to Okun's view, the potential (and the ideal) growth was "full employment growth".

Second, the Japanese side: While the WP2 was paying attention to unemployment, Japan represented an exceptional case: In Japan, along with Italy, with a high proportion of self-employed and unpaid family working forces, "little relationship is found between the two variables", i.e., the rate of unemployment the GNP growth. According to the WP2 analysis, it was "the pressures of demand" which intervened in Okun's equation in Japan. In fact, Japan did not share the fear of unemployment held by the large OECD member countries. The rate of unemployment was lower than 2% throughout the 1960s and 1970s.[19] Rapid economic growth prepared sufficient workplaces for the flow of population from the rural sector into manufacturing, as referred to above, and lead to wage increases. As an exceptional case of Okun's law, Japanese GNP growth continued while unemployment stayed low and unchanged. The Japanese fear, shared among government officials and the public, stayed on the other side of unemployment which represented the odd side of the coin, i.e., backwardness. In the above cited "country reply", the Japanese representative noted: "The need to moder-

17 OECD-HA, CPE/WP2(66)1, "Economic Growth, 1960-70, A Mid-Term Review of Progress towards the O.E.C.D. Growth Target", Paris, 25th March 1966.

18 For the methodology, the OECD referred to a following article: Arthur Okun, "Potential G.N.P.: its Measurement and Significance", *1962 Proceedings of the American Statistical Association.*

19 Japanese Government Statistics cited in Kazue Enoki, "'Kanzen Koyou' Seisau to Roudou Shijou no Hennyou" "['Full Employment' Policy and the Transformation of Labor Market]", in Haruto Takeda, ed., *Koudo Seichouki no Nihon Keizai [Japanese Economy during the High-Growth Period],* Tokyo, Yuhikaku, 2011, p. 207.

nize industrial structure for Japan is urgent, considering the shift to an open-door economy and the shortage of labor". What is meant by "modernization of industrial structure"? It was above all an increase in the productivity of low-productivity sectors, i.e., agriculture, small business and distribution. The aim of the "modernization" was to "release manpower required by growing modern sectors such as manufacturing" from these retarded sectors.[20] The term "dual structure" has been widely recognized among the public to indicate discrepancies of productivity between large firms and small and medium-sized firms and also between agriculture and manufacturing.[21] The above notion of productivity, however, would change in the course of economic growth during the 1960s. Along with the change witnessed in economic and social circumstances, the Japanese authorities would overcome their former notions and fears.

2/ CHANGING SCENES OF PRODUCTIVITY: OVERCOMING THE FOREIGN RESERVES CONSTRAINT

After the start of 50% growth target policies in 1961, and particularly after Japan's accession to the OECD, the situation surrounding the productivity notion changed over time. The change has been significantly observed in the priority among several growth politics. The OECD in its early days put priority on price stability as a prerequisite for productivity growth, as stated in a communique as follows:

> "Price stability is of the highest importance in order to assure to the population the full benefit of economic growth and to maintain equilibrium in international payments. Excess demand should, therefore, be prevented and efforts made to improve productivity and labour mobility. The gains through higher productivity should be fairly distributed, and increases in the level of money should be kept generally in line with increases in productivity, which alone provide the means to a durable increase in the standard of living".[22]

A year later, in 1963, the WP2, unlike the above public communique, quietly posed a question in the note addressed to the committee: "If growth is accepted as an avowed aim, it must be given sufficient weight in comparison with other aims of economic policy (price stability, equilibrium in the foreign balance, etc.). How does this weight make itself felt in the counsels of the Government?".[23] The question itself reveals the fact that during the 1960s, economic growth and increased productivity was not self-sufficient, as it was in a later period. Growth and productivity were important, but other goals such as price stability also mattered. This culture in growth politics

20 OECD-HA, CPE/WP2(65)1/21, "Mid-term Report on Progress to Aid Prospects for the Fifty Per Cent GNP Growth Target", op.cit.

21 A classical view on the Dual Structure finds in Miyazawa Ken'ichi, "Dual Structure of the Japanese Economy and its Growth Pattern", in Kazuo Sato, ed., *Industry and Business in Japan*, Abingdon, Routledge, 1980, p. 14-33.

22 OECD-HA, CPE/WP2(62)2, "Press Communique" (issued as OECD/C(61)54 dated 20th November 1961), Paris, 18th January 1962.

23 OECD-HA, CPE/WP2(63)8, "Economic Growth and Policy (Note by the Secretariat)", Paris, 28th June 1963.

in general and in macroeconomic policy in particular, formed a background for the "fears" to face productivity.

The Japanese government shared the above concern of the OECD over excess demand. The mainstream thinking in the consecutive conservative governments during the 1960s was to avoid excess demand, which might lead to inflation, balance of payments deficits and income disparities.[24] In front of OECD peers, the Japanese representative declared "to take appropriate fiscal and monetary policy so as not to cause excess demand". The government also noticed that the rate of growth compatible with the above price stability "is estimated to be around 8% per annum, somewhat lower compared with the average of 10% for the past ten years" [25]. Here in this statement, we can observe a higher priority being placed on price stability rather than the growth target. The fear of excess demand was supported by another fear, over the foreign reserves. The Japanese economy during the 1960s was under the foreign reserve constraint known as "the ceiling of foreign exchange reserve": the growth of the domestic economy led to the increase in imports, which absorbed the weak stock of Japanese foreign reserves at the time. The growth was supposed to be limited by the size of the foreign exchange reserve, to be controlled by "stop-and-go" cyclical management policy.[26]

However, the foreign reserves began to increase after 1968 and continued to increase during the 1970s. The cheap yen was justified to cover low productivity, but growth remained stable after the strong revaluation following the Nixon Shock. In the theoretical debate, a Japanese economist Osamu Shimomura (1910–89) challenged the government view of price stability and foreign reserves policy, standing upon the Harrod-Domar growth model. In the end, Japanese high-speed growth overall certified victory for the view presented by this expansionist economist.[27] On the other hand, the official government view to put priority on foreign exchange reserves was maintained with the capital movement restriction up to the end of the 1970s. The cheap yen policy, to keep the yen rate as stipulated by the Bretton Woods Agreement despite strong exports, was justified partly by the rise in Official Development Aid. The government policy to keep a huge amount of foreign reserves, reluctant to open door to the capital movement, would pave the way to pushing up Japan as one of the "locomotives" of Western growth after the Oil Shock.[28]

24 Kazuhiko Yago, "Convergence and Divergence over the Growth Paradigm: The OECD Working Party 2 and the Japanese "Doubling National Income Plan" (1961-70)", in *Revue Economique*, vol. 71, no.4, 2020, p. 697-713.

25 OECD-HA, CPE/WP2(65)1/21, "A Mid-Term Review of Progress towards the O.E.C.D. Growth Target", *op. cit.*

26 Shinji Takagi, *Conquering the Fear of Freedom, Japanese Exchange Rate Policy since 1945*, Oxford University Press, Oxford, 2015. The government view on this cyclical scarcity of foreign exchange reserve is expressed in an official history of Japanese Ministry of Finances. Okurashou Zaiseishi Shitsu [Financial History Division of the Ministry of Finances] ed., *Showa Zaisei Shi [Financial History of the Showa Period], 1952-1971*, vol.1, 2000, p. 210-213 et *passim*.

27 Yago, "Convergence and Divergence over the Growth Paradigm", *op. cit.*

28 Kazuhiko Yago, "Before the "locomotive" runs: The impact of the 1973-74 oil shock on Japan and the international financial system", in *Financial History Review*, published online November 2020.

Why and how did the scene surrounding Japanese productivity change in such a short period? Several historical studies present us with new findings, which the contemporaries could not know.
First of all, the demographic factor: the shift in population from the agricultural sector to more productive manufacturing was most visible and effective in Japan compared to OECD peers. In fact, agricultural employment as a percentage of total employment in Japan was 42.4% in 1950 (the same index was 12.2% for the US, 27.0% for France, and 5.4% for the UK). Fourteen years later, in 1964, Japan still recorded the highest figure among OECD members, i.e., 26.8%, but the percentage decline was the fastest among its peers (the index was 6.9% for the US, 18.3% for France and 3.7% for the UK), demonstrating the highest index in terms of the effects of an employment shift on the total GNP per person.[29] Secondly, financial outcome: the young labor force moving from the countryside to urban areas soon formed a thick mass of salaried workers saving their wages into banks and postal savings. Exceptionally high rates of household savings, continuing from the pre-WWII period, supported the financial system of the period and sustained the lending capacity of banks to industry. The effect of high savings was also positive in avoiding inflation, which could otherwise threaten price stability.[30]

Thirdly, demand factor: the above emerging class of workers soon established their family in urban areas. Unlike their rural homeland, this mass of population formed a single-marriage small family, with strong demand for household electric goods like refrigerators, washing machines, and later, televisions.[31] One of the exceptional features of Japanese growth resides in this domestic demand of manufactured goods, produced by the Japanese firms and supplied to the domestic market, fueled by the demographic trend. By the end of 1960, the WP3 report was already aware of this trend. Despite the image of an export great power, the WP3 report described the Japanese economy, rightly as having "private consumption and investment as the two main driving forces".[32] Simultaneously, by the time television penetrated almost every household in Japan as shown in the Figure 1, the term "dual structure" had become obsolete.

Although the points raised opposite explain the change of circumstances or background of the productivity rise in the late 1960s, the factor that brought about the productivity rise is still remains to be investigated. The key to approaching the issue is investment.

29 OECD-HA, CPE/WP2(66)2, "Economic Growth, 1960-70, A Mid-Term Review of Progress towards the O.E.C.D. Growth Target (Note by the Secretariat)", Paris, 12th May 1966.
30 Charles Yuji Horioka, "Why is Japan's Household Saving Rate So High? A Literature Survey", in *Journal of the Japanese and International Economies,* vol.4, issue 1, p. 49-92, gives a through survey on the issue, including demographic and economic factors.
31 Hiroshi Yoshikawa, *Macroeconomics and the Japanese Economy,* Oxford, Oxford University Press, 1995.
32 OECD-HA, CPE/WP3(69)33, "Prospects for Current Balances (Note by the Secretariat)", Paris, 29th December 1969.

FIGURE 1 **PENETRATION OF DURABLE GOODS PER HOUSEHOLD, 1957-1977 (%)**

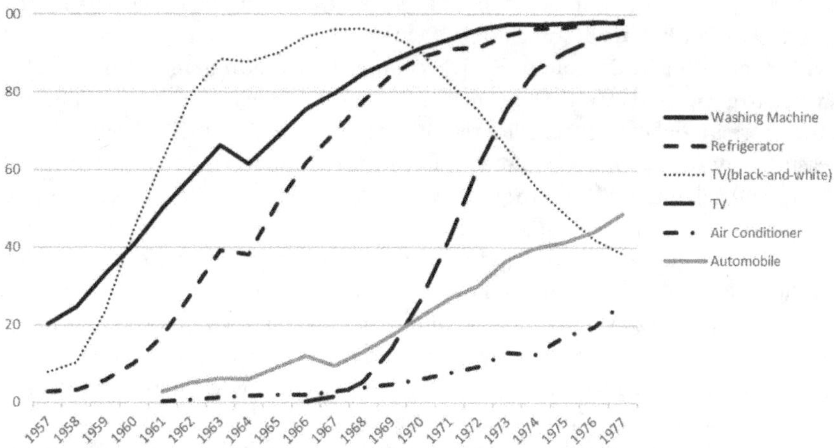

Source: Naikakufu [Cabinet Office], Shouhi Doukou Chousa [Consumer confidence Survey]
https://www.esri.cao.go.jp/jp/stat/shouhi/shouhi.html

3/ INVESTMENT AND INNOVATION: INSIDE THE "BLACK BOX"

Japanese investment had already seized a considerable share over the GNP during the 1950s and 1960s. Figure 2 below shows the rate of private and public investment over GNP of the period, reviewed by the WP2 in 1965, as follows: "The postwar growth of the Japanese economy was supported by a rapid increase of private investment in plant and equipment".[33]

FIGURE 2 **JAPAN, THE RATE OF PRIVATE/PUBLIC FIXED INVESTMENT TO GNP (1953-1968)(%)**

	Private investment on plant and equipment	Public invesment	Total
1953	11,3	9,1	22,2
1955	9,4	8,7	19,8
1958	15,9	8,9	27,1
1960	20,9	9,1	32,3
1963	18,5	11,2	33,0
1968 forecast	19,9	11,5	37,0

Source: OECD-HA, CPE/WP2(65)1/21, "A Mid-Term Review of Progress towards the O.E.C.D. Growth Target", *op.cit.*

33 OECD-HA, CPE/WP2(65)1/21, "A Mid-Term Review of Progress towards the O.E.C.D. Growth Target", *op. cit.* The report added a following reserve: "the fact of matter is that Japan still lags considerably behind most Western countries in the accumulation of social overhead capital".

Contemporary economists attempted to ascertain the return of growth over investment: while one study adopted by the WP2 suggested, according to the data for the period 1954 to 1962, that "some 50 per cent of the variation in rates of increase of GNP" of the major OECD countries, "is accounted for by the different shares of GNP devoted to grow fixed investment in machinery and equipment", "the part explicable in these terms is only 36 per cent" for the GNP per person employed.[34] Adopting these measurements to the Japanese case reveals curious outcomes: as for the structure of GDP calculated by the WP2 for the years 1950, 1960 and 1965 by 1964 prices, the rate of the items concerning manufacturing and services industries for Japan was almost the same as Canada, rather lower than most of the other major countries of the OECD. Another statistical study supports the view that the Japanese rate of growth of gross fixed investment was faster compared with that of GNP growth but was inferior to the countries grouped considerably faster, such as France, Germany, and the UK. Japan in the same statistics was put together with Canada, United States, Iceland, the Netherlands, and others.[35] The Japanese authorities, as cited above, were proud of the high rate of private investment, but the share in the GNP as well as its increase was not surprising. However, if one takes the annual rate of growth of output per employed person, Japan recorded the highest of its OECD peers, as shown in the Figure 3 below.

FIGURE 3 **JAPAN, THE RATE OF PRIVATE/PUBLIC FIXED INVESTMENT TO GNP (1953-1968)(%)**

	UK	US	Canada	France	Italy	Japan	Germany
1955-60 average	2,5	1,2	1,2	4,6	4,2	7,9	4,6
1960-61	2,3	1,8	1,0	4,4	n.a.	14,0	4,0
1961-62	0,3	4,5	3,7	6,9	n.a.	6,4	3,4
1962-63	4,6	2,5	2,3	3,5	n.a.	5,4	3,0
1963-64	4,0	2,8	2,8	4,7	n.a.	14,1	6,2
1964-65	2,2	3,0	2,5	3,3	4,4	2,0	4,0
1960-65 average	2,7	2,9	2,5	4,7	4,5	8,3	4,1

Source: OECD-HA, CPE/WP2(65)1/21, "A Mid-Term Review of Progress towards the O.E.C.D. Growth Target", *op.cit.*

What created this extraordinary productivity rise? As for the framework of productivity, a calculation by Nicholas Crafts underlined the importance of total factor productivity over the capital and labor inputs for the growth of advanced countries during 1950-73 in general and for Japan in particular.[36] Recent work by Kyoji Fukao supports this view, calculating that the contribution of the total factor productivity increase to total productivity as 43%.[37] So, which industry contributed to this productivity rise? Econometric analysis by Fukao coincides with the findings of business

34 OECD-HA, CPE/WP2(66)2, "Economic Growth, 1960-1970: A Mid-Term Review of Progress towards the OECD Growth Target", Paris, 12th May 1966; Yago, "Convergence and Divergence over the Growth Paradigm", *op. cit.*, p. 705-706.

35 OECD-HA, CPE/WP2(66)2, "Economic Growth, 1960-1970: A Mid-Term Review of Progress towards the OECD Growth Target", Paris, 12th May 1966.

36 Nicholas Crafts, "East Asian Growth Before and After the Crisis", *IMF Staff Papers*, vol. 46, no. 2, 1999.

37 Fukao, *Sekai Keizaishi karamita Nihon no Seichou to Teitai, [The Japanese Growth and Stagnation from the Global Economic History Perspective], op. cit.*, p. 182-183.

history studies: five industries (electrical appliances, vehicles, general machinery, precision machinery, and chemistry) demonstrated an annual rise of more than 10% of their total factor productivity from 1955 to 1970.[38] Those industries enjoyed special government support, including tax exemptions, limiting new entrants to the industries to avoid excess competition, as well as financial aid to introduce new technologies.[39] The World Bank aid also played an important role in introducing new technologies, along with the Japanese recipients who "translated" the aid donors' view.[40]

We could extend the list of factors which brought about successful productivity rise in Japan, from wise government intervention to ambitious investment in private firms, from favorable external conditions to a high-quality workforce. However, from the viewpoint of this chapter, dealing with the OECD view, the following reports of the WP3 at the beginning of the 1970s attract our attention.

In a report produced in 1970, the WP3 shared the notion that "The Japanese authorities have been faced with a less serious problem than those in other countries in maintaining tight monetary conditions at home without inducing capital inflows. Strict exchange controls have prevented a massive inflow of both non-monetary capital and banking funds".[41] The OECD often criticized the Japan's reluctance to open the door to freer capital movement, but the regulation secured the effective monetary policy run by the Bank of Japan, without interference by the capital inflows. Historical studies confirm this positive side of capital movement control: since foreign direct investment to Japan had been restricted during the 1960s, Western firms with higher technologies could only sell their knowledge through licensing. The Japanese government financially supported the introduction of these technologies.[42] Recent business history also emphasizes the role played by the Japanese general trading company (*sogo-shosha*) in introducing the license contracts.[43]

Another report presented in 1972 confirmed the above 1970 report from a longer perspective:

> "Until the late 1960s, the main factor motivating monetary policy – although domestic considerations were also important – was the need to protect the low level of reserves in response to overly fast domestic expansion or a weakening of demand in Japanese export markets. In this respect, monetary policy was remarkably successful".

The success was, according to the report, supported by the fact that "Japanese enterprises relied heavily on external finance, mainly bank credit. Alternative sources of

38 Fukao, *Ibid.*, p.186.

39 Haruto Takeda and Lim Chaisung, *Rekishi toshite no Kouseichou, Higashi Azia no Keiken [High-Speed Growth as a History, East Asian Experiences]*, Kyoto, University of Kyoto Press, 2019, p. 41-42.

40 Kazuhiko Yago, "Translated economic paradigms: World Bank lending and the Japanese growth in the 1950s and 1960s", in *Revue française d'histoire économique*, nos.9-10, 2018, p. 60-77.

41 OECD-HA, CPE/WP3(70)13, "Recent Monetary Developments (Note by the Secretariat)", Paris, 30th June 1970.

42 Takeda and Lim, *Rekishi toshite no Kouseichou, [High-Speed Growth as a History], op. cit.*, p. 41-43.

43 Tomoko Okawa, "Transformation of the Role of Shosha as Intermediaries in Japan's Fashion Industry", in *Entreprises et Histoire*, no.100, 2020, p. 39-55.

finance were scarcely available because Japan had no developed capital market, and had tight controls on foreign borrowing". The monetary authority could easily control the credit in the economy through banking, which they called a "direct transmission mechanism". The lack of a sufficient capital market and the lack of opportunity for capital introduction from overseas thus enabled the Bank of Japan to fight against inflation more easily than other OECD countries. The report also referred to investment and housing: "the share of investment in GNP was so high that depressing it temporarily by monetary restraint did not cause a painful dilemma", "Residential construction was financed largely out of accumulated savings, and monetary policy could be applied vigorously without any fear of disrupting this sector".[44]

The above reports from the OECD add a nuanced view on the conventional success story of the Japanese productivity: the total factor productivity rise, witnessed during the 1960s was enabled under strict control over foreign direct investment; The high rate of investment over the GNP was supported almost exclusively by bank credit, which allowed the smooth control of credit by the monetary authority. The fear of excess demand, which we referred to in the previous section, has been easily overcome through this "direct transmission mechanism".

Conclusion

Viewing the notion of productivity from the OECD archives led us to think about the issue slightly differently from the existing historiographies:

First of all, the notion of productivity was imperfect, as the OECD committee itself acknowledged. The framework of productivity, when they first settled the growth target in early 1960s, was limited to labor productivity. The residual factors have not been counted into national accounts. This starting point of a notion was coupled with the fear of unemployment. While pursuing increased productivity, the OECD WP2 had to pay attention to unemployment, with a certain contradiction between the two targets.

Secondly, the Japanese view has been constrained to a contemporary context. The huge rural population under low wage levels was regarded as a symbol of Japanese "backwardness", maintaining the dual structure. The Japanese authorities have been haunted by the fear of foreign reserves scarcity. This fear led to strict regulation of capital movement, credit control over the direct transmission mechanism, and cheap yen policy to protect the domestic market and secure the export market. The notion of investment and productivity, on the Japanese side, was also unclear by the mid-1960s.

Thirdly, however, the above understandings and misunderstandings occasionally enabled Japanese high growth. The "backwardness" of the rural population first supplied cheap labor, with strong propensity for saving, and finally turned into a vast market for household goods. They worked hard for emerging industries, saved a lot to support the financial system, and finally bought a lot to form a solid domestic

44 OECD-HA, CPE/WP3(72)12, "Secretariat Study of Monetary Policy in Japan (Introductory Note by the Secretariat)", Paris, 31st May 1972.

market. The role played by the government was essential in introducing foreign technologies, but one of the important backdrops was the capital movement regulation, which suggested the licensing and trade of intellectual properties, instead of direct investment. The direct transmission mechanism of banks, together with the high rate of household savings, enabled the Bank of Japan to fight against inflation more effectively than their OECD peers.

In a word, we could emphasize an "occasional" feature of Japanese growth: unlike the views appraising the "smart government" or "wise firms", this chapter sheds light on occasional factors, above all the demographic trend, which brought about the "black box" of productivity, i.e., virtuous circle of production, savings and consumption in Japan during the 1960s and the early 1970s.[45] Once this chain of logic is abandoned, a past virtuous circle may turn into a present vicious circle: a lower and elder population with lower productivity, consuming less, and reducing the past savings, while capital markets opened worldwide. The actual questions facing the Japanese economy thus present a mirror image of the growth and productivity during the high-growth era.

45 This view is partly shared with Juro Teranishi, *Rekishi tosihiteno Taishuu Shouhi Shakai [Mass Consumption Society as History]*, Tokyo, Keio University Press, 2017.

What is the local non-governmental management in economy?

a view on the commercial association during late Qing dynasty in China

Sun Rui
School of economics
Renmin University of China

1/ AN OVERVIEW ON THE CHINESE LOCAL COMMERCIAL ORDERS FROM 1500 TO 1911[1]

In the Ming and Qing dynasty, the government noticed that the commerce expanding was beneficial for the whole county. There was complex policy options. On one hand, the national government could intervene some industries actively, such as food grains and salt industries. because these mattered the whole people's welfare[2]. But the police effect was complicated. They got into these industries not for profits. And there was a large market in food and salt in private transactions. This means the center and local governments has responsibility on the keeping people's life in normal situation based on the Confucianism and the Chinese traditional culture—a source of govern legitimacy.

On the other hand, The was the official not much involved the commercial business. In ordinarily, the businessmen and local government has doing things together. Sometimes the local governments need them doing the marketing supervision or relieving the refugees. However we could not see the local official to intervene mar-

1 After middle of the Ming dynasty to the end of Qing dynasty.
2 The typical view come from R Bin Wong, *China transformed: Historical Change and the Limits of European Experience*, Ithaca (New York), Cornell University Press,1997.

keting regularly. There was a strong tension between the increasing transactional scale marketing and lack of enough official rulers. In eyes of local administration, the market belong to the "society things". which means government could not intervene actively. Influenced by the Confucian education, the local officials thought the government cannot make profit in market. They pay more attention on the whole social orders, education, local tax revenue or forbidding rebellion instead of commercial things. Business orders and rules, being as folk customs allowed, almost came from the commercial practice.

The national government considered that the marketing things should be treated as a civil matters not as a independent one like the modern value after 20 century. In traditional China, the supreme purpose was keep a regulated system in the whole society as the harmonious nature one. The top officers thought that they did not need and necessary influence too much on the private business. Business disputes and dissensions also be deal with the businessmen firstly, which almost depended on the business customs and commercial authority . The was a lot of organizations appeared.

The principal one was an organization called *Hui Guan* (会馆)[3]. It was born after the middle of Ming dynasty (about 1500), when the Great Geographical happened. With the overseas trade increasing, the business was boomed in China, as well as Southeast Asia. And the internal commerce was increasing, as well as the long-distance trade. Such as the Shanxi businessmen, one the most famous businessmen in Ming and Qing dynasty, doing the long-distance (over 1000km) trade with a large group together. These business way could also be regarded a social network, including traditional capital accumulation, finance and people turnover in business.

Hui Guan could be considered as a organization for persons from the same village, town or province living in a strange places far from their birthplace. It also as a society organization to keep balance between local public security and immigrant management, the economical function was just one of these functions. Then, *Hui Guan* developed two types: for businessmen and for the students preparing the Imperial examination (Keju,科举). There was a explanation that the commerce was not same with modern one. It include the handicraft industries. The handicraft was always in cities. They has a traditional business mode that the selling and making could not separate. The front opening a small shop in a street and you could found the producing and making was in the back of the shop. So the statistics in this paper was including the handicraft industries.

As the typical local commercial organization, *Hui Guan* was the basic factor for maintaining the local marketing orders[4]. It has emotional and feeling connections for businessmen living far from their hometown as well as respond positively to the government's asking for the social management. The centre and local government did not offer a framework in law on these organizations. There was a large space for *Hui Guan* to run by themselves. The environment and situations could lead to the

3 The base discussion about *Hui Guan* is Ho Ping-ti, *On the history of Chinese Hui Guan*, Taiwan student Bookstore, 1966.

4 The relationship between the business and the *Huiguan* research come from David Faure, *China and Capitalism: A History of Business Enterprise in Modern China*, Hong Kong University Press 2006. And Tang Li xing: *Businessmen and modern Chinese Society*, Zhejiang People's Publishing House, 1996.

mature and rational behaviors system made by *Hui Guan* on commercial, and the most industries could be accepted and kept rulers' willingness.

There is an example on the articles from Shanxi (山) and ShaanXi (陕西) (two province businessmen together as one group) *Hui Guan* in He Nan(河南) province, showing the guideline on department store commercial in 1785[5]:

[1] Selling goods should be weigh one by one, forbidding being as a tumble goods vaguely, if someone broken should be punished by 50 liang (两) (sliver unit, almost 1.875kg)

[2] Not being using hiring employers to work other stores, if someone broken should be punished by 50 liang

[3] Not attract business on the traffic road(fair competition), if someone broken should be punished by 50 liang

[4] Not allowed the price down when the commodity was already in store(not on the road) , if someone broken should be punished by 50 liang

[5] Not allowed disturb the customers, they should choices the store by themselves. if someone broken should be punished by 50 liang

[6] No alias or fake name to keeping customers, if someone broken should be punished by 50 liang

[7] Check out should be exactly on the small money unit, if someone broken should be punished by 50 liang

[8] Not allow get the customers in others stores, if someone broken should be punished by 50 liang

[9] Not keeping the store sign flag on the front of warehouse, just only the store name, if someone broken should be punished by 50 liang

[10] Each one of store should be prepare for play the drama every year at the fifteenth day of the first lunar month, if someone broken should be closed the store

[11] The new one should be get a banquet(50 liang).

There was 11 articles for the department store industry. Instead of entertainment or religion, most of the articles were the business things, involving trading rules fair compete and commercial honesty.ect. Compare with the guilds rulers in middle age in Europe, the articles were not monopoly on the whole industry, although not as free opening as modern marketing system.

2/ AN OVERVIEW ON THE GUILDS DURING THE 1787 TO 1909

The commercial associations in Hu Nan province was typical of the Chinese traditional society management. It also could tell us whether or not an autonomy orders exist before the modern times in China, which offered a basic rational behavior guideline on marketing affairs. The "autonomy" did not mean the government detached on the associations. The industries and national has a interaction in many ways as we discussed later. The "autonomy" could be understood that the major regulations and orders could be decided by the businessmen themselves---including making and modifying. As the authority to each one of the people and every inch land, the government could intervene all kinds of things happen in China. But in fact, they never

5 Zhang zheng ming, *The ShannXi Businessmen and the Culture*, Chicago (USA), World Book Publishing Press, 1998, p. 47.

did this. As far as the Ming and Qing dynasty, the government extend their power by indirect ways, such as rely on the gentry and big family to manage local society, which means the " centralized monarchy " was quiet diffidence compared with the Western countries in history. This is the point of understanding why the commercial associations running independently.

Hu Nan is an important province in the middle of China. It has 211,800 square kilometers and the population was about 19,000,000.Mao Ze Dong was born at this province, who is the founder of the People Republic of China. Hu Nan province was well place because its central location. This province situated at the transportation hub between North and south, being a distribution centre for all kinds of important goods and materials. The traffic was booming during the Qing dynasty as well as its commerce. Its provincial capital was Chang Sha (长沙) which has the biggest rice market around the country. And it also was closed the center of economy in China. But Hu Nan was not a political center and the political influence was not strong and sensitive as in Beijing or Shanghai. And there was not so much state-owned industries as Shanghai after 1860, the time of beginning in industrialize in China, especially in Military industry. The commercial associations in this place were a typical case study with a well development business market and the traditional market system still alive.

2.1/ A statistical analysis

The appendix in "The report of the Hu Nan Province on Business customs"[6] included the 269 commercial associations' regulations, 2636 clauses. The report classified 133 industries as Chinese traditional ways (such as Slaughter \ lodging\ umbrella\ Lettering.ect.) The report said these could be categorized 12 industries as modern industries, including the finance\ handicraft\Transportation\Service.ect. The time was from 1787 to 1909 because some of them had not the clear years. The regulations might be more early than 1787 the first year recording clearly.

TABLE 1 THE TIME OF COMMERCIAL ASSOCIATIONS 'REGULATIONS OF HU NAN PROVINCE

TIME	Qian Long 1736-1796	Jia Qing 1792-1820	Dao Guang 1821-1850	Xian Feng 1851—1861	Tong Zhi 1862—1874	Guang Xu 1875-1908	Xuan Tong 1909-1911
Number	2	2	11	3	9	121	32

Notes: There were 181 regulations having a clearly year written.

The 269 regulations(2636 clauses) could be classified as follow:

1/ The first type was the rules about the internal management. These rules were aimed at the public affairs among the members.

(1) The religion ceremonies. such as the activity and the items. For example: the publishing industry said "Need sacrifice to Emperor god of Wenchang (文昌帝) a

6 Peng Ze Yi, *The Data Collection about the Guilds of Commerce in China*, Ithaca (New York), Zhong Hua Book Company, 1995, p. 190-533.

FIGURE 1 **THE POSITION OF HU NAN PROVINCE IN CHINA(QING DYNASTY)**

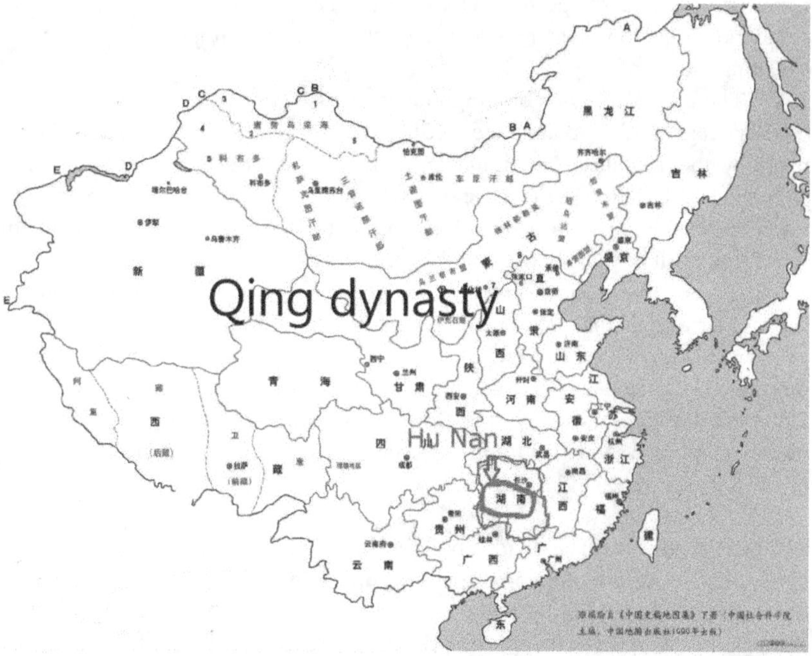

kind of god could manage the knowledge), each one of us should be join in with a well dress when the god's birthday"

(2) The arrangement on taking in the official Labour and tax Duty.

(3) Other expenses about the public things. For example: the sweet wine industry said "There are 60 members in our industry, each one of us should pay in 2000 qian (钱，close to sliver 74.6g) for public things, which is managed in turns"

(4) The guild internal structure and practice rules. such as the term of senior directors and the procedure to deal with dispute.ect. For example: same senior directors was for a three-year term and deputy directors for a one year. And they need collect dues, followed the rules about handover the power to next ones. The book stores industry said "The director should be by vote and this rule was passed by our assembly". Some clauses were concerned with the financial situation. If the new director found financial book was wrong, the current one should explain clearly and compensate for the unreasonable loss. And the duty of director was in a lot of clauses. They could be supervise the business in law and forbidden the unfair trade, or someone who broke the rules.

2/ The second one was the marketing rules.

(1) The standard measurement in local market. For example: the kinds of native products stores association regulated: "Balance of each store should be calibrated in every year on 16th March and get a mark into the balance. The standard is the same with the official one".

(2) The rules on how to deal with. such as money exchange and keeping business fairly. For example: the pawn on clothes said: "Not disturb the customers even they came into your door, let them choose freely and not do impolite behavior such as speaking too loud"

(3) The standard quality on the goods and craftworks. For example: the Pharmacy industry regulated: "No any fake medicine. If someone cheat customers and make profit by under quality, they should be closed and never get into our industry". The shoe shop said: "There are three levels on handing works. Not allowed making other lower level shoes with the right price and don't make fake shoes. If someone break the rule, he will be punished by a local opera for us".

(4) The standard prices on the goods and craftworks. The price of manual work was more rigorous than goods. The shop for selling the cake for religion said: "The prices of all kinds of cakes could be adjusted by the public discussion running by our director. The price tags were hanging in front of each door. We all follow the prices. Don't break the prices at any time. If someone selling with lower prices and making money in unfair way with a unqualified cakes, they will be punished by 4800 *qian* (close to sliver 180g)".

3/ The third one was the divide and inheritance on some marketing power. These kinds of rules were mainly on the practitioners and the industry admittance. The admittance included how to accept an apprentice and start a new business. And for the practitioners, the rules focus on the hiring\the forbidding of business\working time\some restrain on both of the employers and employees. Some of them regulated that one practitioner finished his apprenticeship and the master allowed his craft good with his moral character, the master could take a new one, which called "one finished one come in". Some industries also has a strict rulers that a new shop could not be opening without the fee to the industry for public things. For example the industry for banquet said: "The band just form the father to the son. It cannot taken to collateral relatives. If they want get into our industry, please taken money 7500 *qian* (钱, close to sliver 281.25g)". Some other regulations concerned about the unfair compete on the hire such as the recruiting from other shops with too higher salary.

4/ The fourth one was the rules showing a clearly notice on punishment and supervision, which were just a small part. In some sense, all the regulations had authority on punishment and supervision. These clauses always appeared the end of the regulations. This part just had a statistics meaning.

TABLE 2 **THE TABLE OF CLASSIFIED RULES**

Sorts of rules	Numbers	Proportion of all clauses	Proportion of each sort
The internal management	331	23%	100%
Religion ceremonies	42	2.92%	12.69%
Public management	158	10.98%	47.73%
Official duty	55	3.82%	16.62%

Sorts of rules	Numbers	Proportion of all clauses	Proportion of each sort
Fee and Fund	76	5.28%	22.96%
The marketing rules	494	34.33%	100%
Standard measurement	32	2.22%	6.46%
Standard currency	19	1.32%	3.85%
Keeping the measurement	13	0.90%	2.63%
Keeping dealings fairly	68	4.73%	13.77%
Standard quality	31	2.16%	6.28%
Prices on goods	50	3.47%	10.12%
Prices on labours	73	5.07%	14.78%
Others	208	14.46%	42.11%
Market power and inheritance	559	38.85%	100%
Admittance (hiring)	110	7.65%	19.68%
Admittance (practitioners)	125	8.67%	22.31%
Admittance (opening)	156	10.84%	27.91%
Restrict (working)	41	2.85%	7.33%
Restrict (hiring)	73	5.07%	13.06%
Restrict (running)	5	0.34%	0.89%
Restrict (employers\ employees)	37	2.57%	6.62%
Restrict (working times)	12	0.85%	2.20%
Punishment and supervision	55	3.82%	100%
Total	1439	100%	

Notes: The total number was 1439,not 2636.Because the table was a statistics on the one industry regulations could cover how many sorts of rules. For example: An association has 13 clauses in one regulation, but it just included 7 kinds of rules--- Religion ceremonies\ Official duty\ Standard currency\ Keeping dealings fairly\ Standard quality\ Punishment and supervision. So the number was 7,not 13---excepting the same sorts to exaggerated the data.

FIGURE 2 **THE SORTS OF RULERS**

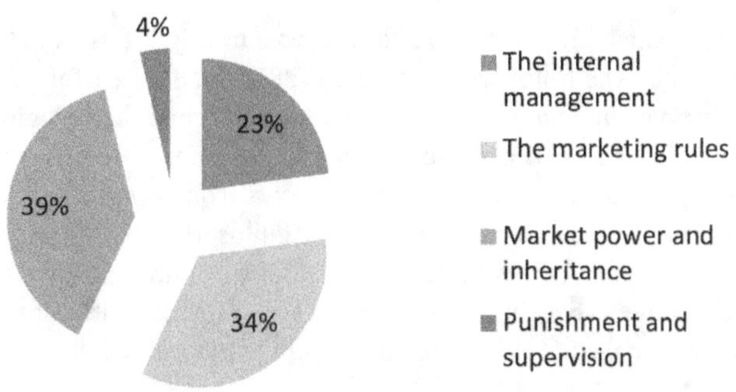

2.2/ An analysis on the inner structure and value of the guilds.

A/ The sense of identity and the rationality

The system of industry religion was important to enforced the loyal and dedicated spirit in the whole industry. At the same time, the religion festival was an opportunity to dealing with the public affairs. But the religion was not the core in the sense of identity, which was a small ratio--2.92% in all clauses.

FIGURE 3 **THE PROPORTION OF THE ALL CLAUSES IN THE INTERNAL MANAGEMENT**

The religion system in China was quiet different from western countries. The mainstream were Buddhism and Taoism, these were accredited from government. But there were thousands of local religions and industries ones. Some were came from famous person in history and became a legend. Such as the Shanxi group businessmen think the *Guan Yu* (关羽) who was a warrior dead in 220 AD and much loyal to his brother : the leader fight against the other warlords. The most important was his birthplace in Shanxi province. So the value from his behavior was a great example for worship. Some famous industries gods was also admitted by government. Other gods, such as in charge of the local things, safety sailing, marriage and healthy, were quiet different in different area. They owned their temples separately. Compared with Christianity, Chinese religion system seems more secular and not being a theology system. These characteristics means the religion should be understanding from the daily life, so as in commerce.

The religion did not mean the transcendence significances in one industry. The tendency could be testified by the follow research. At 1928, John Stewart Burgess (The guilds of Beking) observed in Beijing. He wrote "There was 9 guilds had religion ceremony among the 37 guilds. But all the nine guilds are stopped now", because the impaction was from industries declined and the new concepts from western world. And "The ceremony were not be treated seriously in some guilds". From the view of workers, they thought the religion "being a tradition, but not work now", "it means nothing"[7]. It might be challenged that the stereotypes on China history without the possible go further more rational and self management welling in local society.

7 John Stewart Burgess, *The Guilds of Peking(associate professor of Sociology*; Yenching University; China Member of staff of Princeton-in Peking), 1928, p. 151-155.

Actually, the sense of identity mainly came from the recognition on the relationship between the industry interest and the person's life supporting. In the 1928 researching, when asking the source of the guilds, the major answer was the "cooperative advantage on making a living". Furthermore, the association could keep a balance between the motivation for profit and the long-term interests. As the industry association, all the members could be follow the rules fairly, at the same time each of them should be taken the loss of profits in absolute marketing competition.

B/ The procedure principle and the rationality

The other source of the rationality was the procedure principle on public things. *The economy of China,* between 1907-1908 published in Japan by Tong-wen (东亚同文馆) in East Asia, has a chapter on Chinese guilds investigation. It said "Keeping a public discussion, which was one of the businesses customs in Qing dynasty, was a stable procedure ..... Almost kinds of regulations should be passed by public discussion".[8] It means the *Hui Guang* and commercial associations considered the rational rules should be passed through all of the members as the view of Japanese, which was the most important part of the business organizations in Ming and Qing dynasty. These were not only valuable but also some kinds of meaning on procedure principle, making sure a transparently fairly and impersonally running.

Except making the rules, these were some parts following the doctrine of publicity. The Chinese character "公"(*gong*) contented two different meaning on public activities: opening discussion and decision as well as the senior positions in turn among all the members.

The election should open and take turns in each members. There were sorts of requiring to the senior managers. The finance and items registers should hand over next ones clearly and openly. If something was wrong, the directors should make compensation. The religion items also has a serious accounting book, even about the lights and small tables. Others could not borrow them. The restricts to managers were mainly about the power exchanging and the prevention of corruption, as well as emphasizing the public affairs in a public way.

So the conclusion was certain that a principle hold and insisted by all member of the associations on dealing with the public affairs. The personal authority was not absolute. And the superior managers should be restriction and supervision.

On the other hand, Is the power structure could be called a certain of western democracy? The answer was no. In 1928 research, when asking the power of associations was coming from the" democracy requiring", the answer was blank. Burgess said "These guilds certainly thought that they were not a democracy group". The reason might be found from Chinese traditional practice.

Each of the individual doing the association's business. They views based on the private opinions. And all of the opinions exchanged, discussed and made public ones--- the industry viewpoint. It was not only a procedure but a process reaching a consensus. The general different from the western democracy was that the independent personal will would be neglected. The public standpoint will was quite different from each

8 Peng Ze Yi, *The Data Collection about the Guilds of Commerce in China*, Shanghai, Zhong Hua Book Company, 1995, p. 109.

person. The traditional Chinese to deal with the public things was a way of integration, not enforced the individual expression in local commerce.

C/ Punishment and rules implement

Punishment was not only a compensation but more enforced the recovery of the rules and feeling. Because the major ways were taken all members to watching traditional opera and banqueted. This means the misbehaviors hurting the industry feelings than the rules. These were a more harmonious solving than money punishment only----from Chinese etiquette culture. The offenders were not loss his prestige all and the value of industry could be followed. The spending on opera and banquette was higher than other punishments. The opera as being punished was one of the most serious ways followed the top one—ending of businesses.

The most important insure for the rules implement was the power of community exile. Each member never did businesses with the offenders. The indirect evidence was showing that the collective action was believable and available. In 1886, D. J. Macgowan's paper: *Chinese Gilds or Chambers of Commerce and Trades Unions,* said the guilds "boycotted did their best against every offender". "And the guilds has a great power during a boycotting action". H. B. Morse (1855-1934) graduated from Harvard University in 1847 and working in the Qing Customs. In 1909, his book: *The guilds of China,* based on his researching and observing in the cities of having the Customs, said that: "All of the guilds in China has the same way in protecting the members' interest and requires, which was a responsibility taken by every guild. The rules were not exist in name only. The regulations executed in practice. It was also the same point in all of them." Accordingly, it was certain believable that the rules could be considers seriously and taken in every local market.

D/ The government and the guilds

In Ming and Qing dynasty, the power structure has two different tendency. On one hand, the political power structure became more and more central. On the other hand, the society was growing up, having larger distance between the political and the people's life. Society had some kinds of organization or association, such as education, caring for baby and old man, financial assistance and businesses.

The Chinese associations could structure and maintain the industries' orders. And the whole system was taken by themselves instead of the official authority. How to understand the role of local government? H. B. Morse said: "In China, the government was just for taxing and maintaining social orders. As interfering into the business things, the government's motivations was on the ethical principles but not the economy and business things as well as not on the private interests of administrative officer. The guilds were developed independently under the watching from the government. They have their organizations, pursuing their purposes, making their rules and regulations, restricting themselves by their ways and methods". From the western observer, the government pay a very indirect role on the associations.

It was closed to the reality. The most direct things was the Labour and Tax duty between government and commercial industries. Therefore it was the heavy burden for one industry, especially in the Late Qing, as well as a hot focus on some disputations. Even after 1840,the traditional tax became much less on support the new expending such as reparation of war and the military industrialization[9]. The tax from the land tax and agriculture revenue were not enough. The commercial tax was increasing and being more important. The local high-ranking officials made the new commercial tax or Likin (厘金)being the key local tax as well as a part of their political capital.[10] So these duty and tax was also brought a "reasonable" excuse for these associations taking support from the government as a valuable chip.

The local officials confirmed the rules and regulations as a recording in the open or end of one chapter as an authority admitting way. We can see same sentences such as "following the government's orders to taken the duty of our industry, this rules has been agreed by local administers or officials". There were 54 chapters has the same kind of words among the 269 ones, about 20.07%. The agreement from government could be enforce the authority of associations.

On the other hand, the government was a final judgment in all kinds of commercial disputes. They did not intervene into disputations positively but they could choose some cases as a paradigm for solving the same ones, even between two different industries. In generally, the government had the same way to deal with the marketing and private business in early modern age. They never wanted to change the traditional possess and core structure of business groups. The most important was the government could enhance the authority of industries in keep orders fairly and recovering some kind of rules and customs that most of members admitted.

E/ The principle of marketing in modern China

FIGURE 4 **EACH PROPORTION OF THE MARKETING RULES**

9 The typical research is that Luo Zhi Tian, *The Expansion of State and the Shrinkage of Civil Society: A Continuing Tendency Emerging in the Qing Period*, Journal of Sichuan University (Social Science Edition), 2012 (5).

10 A study about the transform on political structure is Philip Kuhn, *Origins of the Modern Chinese State*, Stanford (California), Stanford University Press, 2003.

FIGURE 5 **EACH PROPORTION OF THE MARKET POWER AND INHERITANCE**

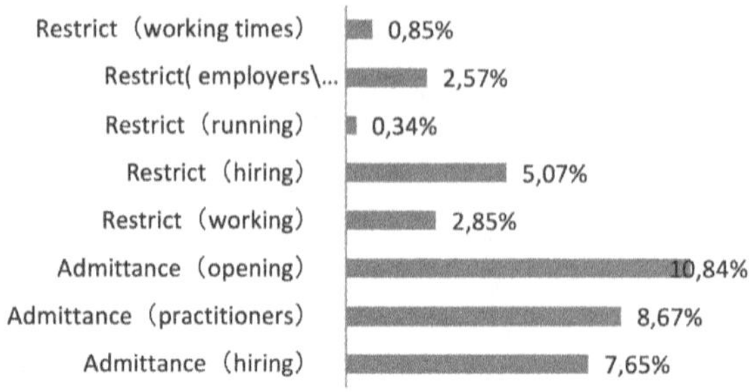

The figures 4 and 5 show a rational and piratical management making the market in order. Sometime the questions from the content in picture 5, which means the associations looks like same with the guild in the middle age in Europe. In this paper, the word "guild" was in the eyes of the western people. But the point different between the commercial associations and "guilds" was the monopoly power and the relationship with government. It was any official chapter or law to admit the association could own the franchise in one industry or local market. And there might be two or third associations in one industry with different hometown, such as the selling clothing store from west provinces and the same selling from other provinces. They cannot enforce someone should get into one association as the law to enter market. The marketing opportunity was fair and open to every single one of people. And they has no political rights from the local government ,although the local government need more support from them in Late Qing dynasty. In a word, the sp called "guilds" in China was just followed western historical paradigm in the 19-20 Century. If we research more careful and clear, we could found the "guild" was not the same things. So I used the word " association " replace the "guild" in this paper.

The rules concerned the question of price controlling. From modern economic theory, Price is a key factor for marketing system. Any of controlling behavior is wrong and unreasonable. Price also is the law to everyone get into the marketing system, which mean a free will to choice and a economic democratic. In this paper, some of the rules were about the price, which seems the commerce association system like conservative. It might be slow down the work stability. But from social perspective, controlling price means more fair and stable marketing. There was not a open and globe industrial manufactory system. And the produces were not the same standard as industry time. In Ming and Qing, even the marketing opening, the marketing system and the social foundation was the local and traditional. Price controlling means every member could alive and keeping a good quality in goods and services at a same time. The free competition was not on price but on other aspect, such as the service attitude and commercial honesty. One industry could not rely on the price controlling to keep the advantage. Marketing compete always working. In a word, although it was not same with modern market economy, the commerce association could be understanding a positive role in China at that time.

In picture 5, there was a lot of rulers on the market power and inheritance, it seems that there industries smell conservative and not any motivation to innovate and progress. The view was too much " modernism" and preconceived on the history process being only one forward as the right way. At any one of the pre-industrialization, the local market was not the same with the one in 20 Century. They had not multiple choices as the population growth. The first matter was keeping balance with the competed marketing and the surviving. These orders seem old and unacceptable on the perspective of modern marketing theory. But on the social-economy view, these could be understand. These also mean the tough circumstances in early modern China.

In picture 4, it seems a system of management on local market. Without any guideline or commercial laws from centre or local government, the market was healthy because of these associations[11]. Most of them concerned about the fair tractions and protecting the customers interesting, keeping a opening businesses orders. These all rules were came from the nongovernment ways and they did well in generally speaking. It might be possible that the marketing rules and orders might conform to the requirements of modern society at appropriate historical conditions. Unfortunately, these way of marketing and commercial self-management system became less influence after the Anti-Japanese war and the civil war between two Parties from 1945-1949.

3/ CONCLUSION

In the Ming and Qing dynasty, the basic business's orders came from the civil organizations. There was a system holding by the associations, which were including fair play principle and keep a stable trading circumstance as well as taking the official duty. The sense of identity was not any mysterious and transcendental things—such as religions, but rely on a clear consensus between the private interests and the long term developing benefit in one industry, as well as the public procedure dealing with group affairs. It was not only responded the great transformation in economical and social aspects, but could be a part of modern marketing system in China. The obvious different from the Ming and early Qing dynasty stage, the associations was less religions in the Late Qing dynasty (after 1840). Instead of religions, they became more reasonable in the sense of identity. The government play a indirect role on it. The businessmen could run and control their own organizations at that time of China. In some meanings, the marketing was management by themselves in a centralization of state power.

The power structure in economy things has two parts in Ming and Qing dynasty. One was the taxing system between the official and the people. The people has to undertake the tax demand even some labor duty. The country should be keeping the people living even in the war or nature disasters. On the other hand, the marketing system, which means could pursue profit directly, was always belong to the nongovernmental areas. The officials could not get involve into these things in the value of mainstream. It was a sham that a educational person get into a market straightly (In

11 A research about the traditional Chinese people's behavior is S. Sprinkle, *An introduction to the legal system in Qing Dynasty---a perspective on the sociological analysis (Chinese edition)*, Beijing, China University of Political Science and Law Press, 2000.

fact, they hold a business indirectly). As long as the businessmen could self regulation well and follow the local government's orders, the officials preferred to support them, not to speak the less numbers and scales of local official system lacking of the money to extending their functions. It also means there was a contradictory structure between large society and small government in the autocratic monarchy of China in Ming and Qing dynasty (about 1368-1911).It might be unique all over the word that the highly centralized authority was expanding of the substantial controlling power relying on the indirectly ways[12]. And the Hu Nan's associations could be a typical case to understand this. That was also a key point to understand the modern China, even the changing world in 20 Century.

Furthermore, there is a popular history concept come from modernity. Every county should become more free and independent. The explanation on history is not a process without any purpose but a transformation from traditional to modern. On this perspective to researching the non-Western counties history, the traditional based on their culture and institution was regarded kinds of impediments when they get into the modern world. There is only one direction from the old one to a new one. But from the Chinese commerce association research, the "old" is not a contradictious factor for social development. Historical process should be understand by their culture context even in the economical practice. The rationality is not a absolute evaluation criteria on explaining the social vicissitude. Multiple and critical perspectives might be the better choice.

12 A discussion about the political system thought in traditional China is Zhao Ding yang, *The Tianxia (the sky was covered beyond any national) system: an introduction on the philosophy of world system*, Beijing, Renmin University of China Press, 2011.

China's High-speed Rail:

From Technological Catching-Up to Innovation

Wang Qing
Institute of Finance & Banking
Chinese Academy of Social Sciences, Beijing

Wang Jue
Department of Economics
Renmin University of China, Beijing

1/ INTRODUCTION

High-speed rail (HSR) is now a symbol of China's technological progress and a significant source of national pride.[1] In less than a decade, China's HSR industry has experienced impressive growth both in running mileage and technological innovations. Analyzing the process from scratch of China's HSR network, we are shocked by the remarkable development speed: it only took China five or six years to enjoy half the world's total mileage, reaching 19,000 kilometers by 2015. (Figure 1). And according to the Medium and Long-Term Railway Network Plan of China (2016 version), an ambitious national strategy which was carried out by the central government to develop the railway infrastructure system, by 2020, the total mileage of China's over-250 kilometer-per-hour railway lines (high-speed rail lines) will reach 30,000 km and will link all provincial capital cities and cities with a population of more than 500,000 (Chen and Hayes, 2015).[2] In this ambitious plan, China's HSR network should consist of eight vertical rail lines linking north and south, and eight horizontal lines connecting east to west, meanwhile, adjacent large-sized and medium-sized cities should be connected by lines ranging from 1 to 4 hours.

1 Michelle Ker, "China's High-Speed Rail Diplomacy", *US-China Economic and Security Review Commission*, 2017, 8.

2 The so-called "Medium and Long-Term Railway Network Plan of China" was originally drafted by the MOR in 2004, and has been twice revived in 2008 and 2016 respectively under the supervision of the National Development and Reform Commission (NDRC).

FIGURE 1 **CHINA'S HSR OPERATING MILEAGE: 2008-2015**

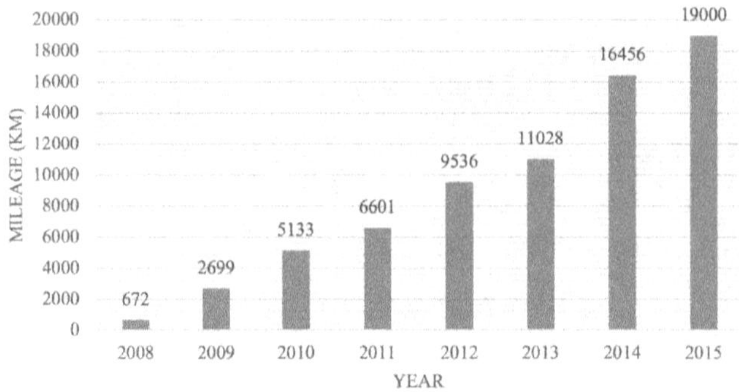

Data Source: China Statistical Yearbook (2015).

Undoubtedly, China has become a manufacturing giant of the HSR industry, however, there exists considerable evidence to suggest that its technological capacity is also soaring at the same time. According to Huang and Lü (2020), China has quickly absorbed the core technology of HSR that introduced from Japan, Germany, France, and other countries and cultivated the ability of independent innovation which leads to the successful invention and mass production of the EMU (CRH380A) with independent intellectual property rights.[3] In 2010, Davis Law Firm and the US Patent and Trademark Office evaluated the CRH380A EMU on more than 900 patents comprehensively and the results showed that there did not exist any property disputes, which provides possibility and legal protection for China South Locomotive and Rolling Stock Corp (CSR) to export the EMU to the United States.

Taking the railway patent applications as an example, China's railway technology began to take off in 2004 and in the same year, the Chinese government approved the Medium and Long-Term Railway Network Plan and started its large-scale technology import program, also known as the "Great Leap Forward" strategy which was proposed by the formal minster of MOR Liu Zhijun, also known as China's Shinji Sogō.

FIGURE 2 **NUMBER OF CHINA'S RAILWAY PATENT APPLICATIONS: 1996-2015**

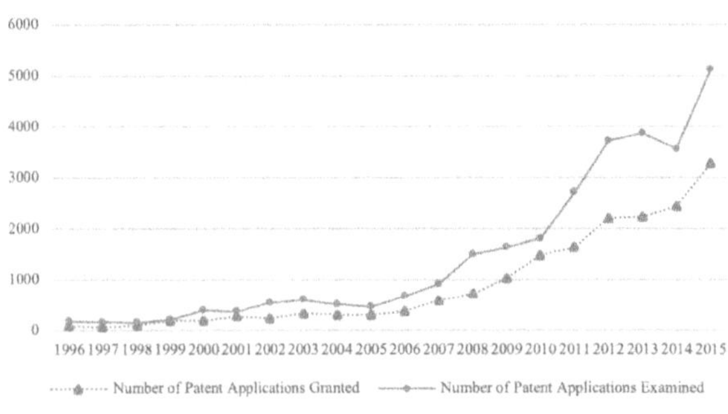

Data Source: State Statistical Bureau of China.

3 Huang Yanghua and Lü Tie, *Evolution of the Industrial Innovation System in the Deepening of System Reform: A Case Study of China's Catch-up in the World High-speed Rail Industry*, Beijing, Social Sciences in China, 2020 (5), p. 65-85.

The huge success of China's HSR industry, especially the technological success in catching up with and surpassing the OECD countries, has aroused continuous attention and discussion among scholars worldwide. In this paper, we adopt a historical perspective and examine the functional factors and organizations that have played an important role in the development process of China's HSR. Although there may be some disputes, we have to point out that the Chinese government, as the leading unit of technology introduction and innovation, is the most solid guarantee for its triumph. The HSR story shows that the night watchman metaphor may fail in a special situation and at a special time. And developing countries could seek their technological breakthroughs by formulating flexible industrial policies.

2/ A BRIEF HISTORY OF CHINA'S HSR

In the past decades, the railway has been in the absolute dominant position in China's transportation system and is the artery of the national economy. However, for quite a long time, China's railway network was underdeveloped due to the use of old technologies, and there was a huge discrepancy between transport capacity and actual demand which urged China to bolster railway capacity and increase railway supply continuously for maintaining economic growth and enhancing political legitimacy. In the case description, the technology progress of China's HSR industry has been divided into three periods, in each of which different strategies are implemented. We attempt to link these key strategies which greatly promote HSR technology development with the actions of the government, and study the role of the government in this process.

2.1/ Exploration period based on independent R&D: 1992-2003

In the 1980s, most of the major countries in the world had begun or even completed the upgrading of their railway systems. It runs into a common view that developing high-speed railway is the key to satisfying the growing demand for domestic passenger transport, nor is it surprising that China's policymakers share the same view. At that time, Changchun Passenger Car Works (CPCW), a state-owned railway locomotive manufacturer, introduced some overseas mature technology and crafts from the UK, Canada, and other countries. These techniques, however, were not commendably absorbed and digested due to the lack of supporting facilities and personnel, as well as financial support. As a result, policymakers of CCP decided to explore the HSR technology based on independent research and development.

In 1992, under the guidance of the Eighth Five-Year Plan of China, the former Ministry of Railway (MOR) launched the Ten Year Plan for the Development of Railway Science and Technology, which remarked that the government had put the construction of high-speed rail on its official agenda. At the same time, the feasibility demonstration of the Beijing-Shanghai high-speed railway project was in full swing under the auspice of the former MOR: "build" or "no build" and "wheel-rail" or "magnetic suspension" had become a social focus. After five years' demonstration and debate, the government finally decided to build a high-speed railway that operates at speeds over 200 km/h with wheel-track technology to connect the great metropolises of Beijing and Shanghai.

Relying on independent R&D and a small scale of technology import, China invented and manufactured several prototypes of EMU in this period, among which, the "China Star", led by Zhuzhou Electric Locomotive Works, had reached a record speed of 321.5 km/h on November 27th, 2002.[4] Although some parts, such as high-speed pantograph, vacuum breaker, deionized water pump, GTO device, high-speed bearing, and screw air compressor and other components still have to be imported from abroad, most of the design and components of the EMU have proprietary intellectual property rights.[5]

TABLE 1 **INDEPENDENT-DEVELOPED HIGH-SPEED PROTOTYPES**

	Blue Arrow	Pioneer	Mount Changbai	China Star
Trailing time	1999	2001	2003	2001
Maximum trail speed (km/h)	249	292	224	321.5
Maximum operational speed (km/h)	NA	250	235	270
Operational speed (km/h)	200	200	210	200
Quantity	8	1	1	2

Sources: Collected from the Internet

Unfortunately, the former Ministry of Railways abandoned the self-reliant technology R&D plan for various reasons.[6] One of the most important reasons is that the failure rate of China Star and other EMU projects remained high. A dramatic scene took place on November 28th, 2002, just the second day after the creation of "the first speed of China". Fu Zhixuan, the minster who was excited to learn the record-breaking news, wanted to get on the train himself and "experience the speed of China Star" with his deputies and other railway officials. According to the original arrangement, the test will start at 9 o'clock, but the test crew got up early to experiment ahead of schedule for the sake of security. Everything seemed to go smoothly, but the bogie fault diagnosis system installed on the EMU raised an alert just 17 seconds before the China Star returned to the experimental base and a cloud of smoke was seen from the bracket bearing for the axle shaft of the B power vehicle. After the analysis of data and the scene of the accident, the chief designer suggested that the following experiment must be stopped. The China Star met its Waterloo right under the noses of the senior leaders of MOR. Another reason is that the policymakers represented by Liu Zhijun believed that the current technology development of HSR is unable to bridge the technological gap and capture the core technology of EMUs that can be

4 Zhao Xiaogang, *Walking with Speed.* Beijing, China CITIC Press, 2014.

5 Leong Chan and Tugrul Daim, "Sectoral innovation system and technology policy development in china: case of the transportation sector". *Journal of Technology Management in China,* 2012, 7 (2), p. 117-135.

6 According to Zhao Xiaogang, many people had reservations about the decision of the MOR, especially the research and development staff represented by Zhuzhou Electric Locomotive Works.

operated at speeds over 300 km/h, as a result, they had lost patience with all these self-developed projects. [7]

This period has a very special meaning for the development of high-speed rail in China. Although "the products were sent to the museum", the staff and the talents who were involved in the independent researches had become the mainstay of the upcoming introduction of technology. As former chairman of the CSR Corporation Zhao Xiaogang said, "90% of the technical backbone of the construction of the Beijing-Shanghai high-speed railway had participated in the construction of Qin-Shen railway for supporting the R&D of China Star Project". This mature and high-level team had made a sustained contribution to the second phase of China's high-speed rail development.

2.2/ Large-scale technology introduction: 2004-2007

In 2004, the "Medium and Long Term Railway Network Plan" adopted by the State Council of China officially opened up the new chapter for the large-scale introduction of China's high-speed rail technology. The plan has put forward three basic principles, namely: introduction of advanced technology, joint design and production, and building the self-owned brand, carrying out an operation mode which is supporting domestic rolling stock manufacturing enterprises, introducing a small amount of original binding, assembling domestically and production domestically. The government had put the development of HSR to the height of the national strategy.

FIGURE 3 **ORGANIZATIONAL STRUCTURE OF EMUS RESEARCH IN CHINA**

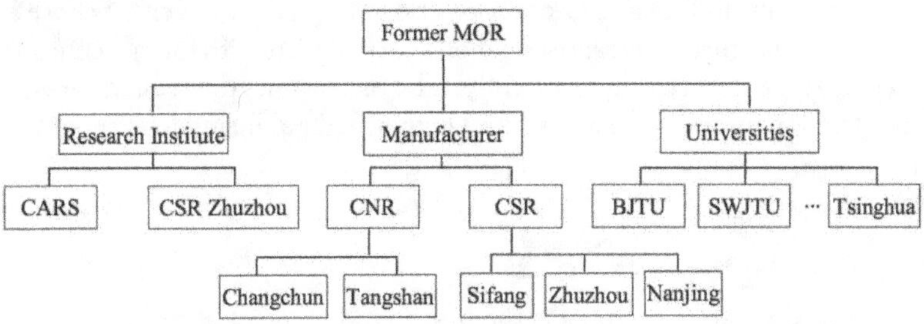

Note: On June 1st, 2015, the CNR and CSR were announced to be merged as a combined company named China Railway Rolling Stock Corp (CRRC), which had become the world's largest railway rolling stock manufacturer.

In this period, China has introduced complete procedures for high-speed train manufacturing on four main modes (CRH-1, CRH-2, CRH-3, and CRH-5) from four major companies (Alstom, Siemens, Bombardier, and Kawasaki). Well guided by "market for policy" or so-called "quid-pro-quo", the former MOR intentionally signed train

7 The new Minister, Liu, was a strong believer in railway development by utilizing foreign technologies. He repeatedly indicated that the process of Chinese Railway development could be accelerated by learning the advanced railway technologies of developed countries to achieve leapfrog development, as China was a latecomer to the HSR field. (Chen & Haynes, 2016)

procurement and technology transfer contracts with the targeted foreign firms at the same time for the benefit maximization. The tasks of developing indigenous technologies based on the acquired ones were then assigned to one of the subsidiaries of CSR or CNR. [8]

TABLE 2 **THE TECHNOLOGY TRANSFORMATION**

Mode	Contract Date	Operation Date	Chinese Enterprises	Foreign Enterprises	Order
CRH1	2004/2005/2007	2007.2	CSR Sifang	Bombardier (Canada)	80 EMU sets and no core technology transfers
CRH2	2004	2007.1	CSR Sifang	Kawasaki (Japan)	60 EMU sets and several core technology transfers
CRH3	2005	2008.4	CNR Tangshan	Siemens (Germany)	60 EMU sets and 9 core technology transfers
CRH5	2004	2007.4	CNR Changchun	Alstom (France)	60 EMU sets and 7 core technology transfers

Sources: Collected from the Internet

According to the official MOR reports as well as the interviews with engineers from the CSR and CNR, a standard technology transfer contract normally consists of four principles: (1) "Joint design" of train modes based on foreign prototypes that incorporate adaptation to the Chinese environment; (2) Access to blueprints; (3) Instructions on manufacturing procedures; (4) Necessary training of engineers.

The former MOR established a strict industrial policy and market access policy with high quality, making full advantage of the position of "strategic buyer". It chose only two vehicle manufacturing enterprises out of 35 to negotiate with foreign enterprises and organized the negotiating team uniformly; meanwhile, the "sellers" included Siemens, Alstom, Bombardier, and several high-speed rail manufacturers of Japan. The integration of domestic resources, the huge orders of 140 EMU units, and the attractiveness of the enormous market all guaranteed the implementation of these principles.

The most representative example is the first round of negotiation with Siemens, i.e. the "200 km/h EMUs Project", Siemens was kicked out of the door because of insisting the price of their technology transfer and returned home empty-handed. On the contrary, during the first tender, Alstom, Bombardier, and Kawasaki had all received a share of the orders. Learning from the lesson, the German giant agreed to sell its 300 km/h EMU prototype 250 million each and transfer its technology at 80 million euros during the second negotiation. In the end, it got an order of 60 EMU units and several technology transfers after a big concession to China's team and reached cooperation with CNR Tangshan in 2005.

8 There were 33 Chinese enterprises involving in the introduction of technology in 2004. Among them, 18 enterprises were subject to the CNR, and 15 were subject to the CSR, which were located in 25 cities including Beijing, Meishan, etc.

It's worth noting that, the MOR had implemented more active and promising government procurement to support independent innovation drawing the lessons of decentralized and competitive strategy before, which was considered as a major reason for the slow pace of R&D. In contrast, before the large-scale introduction of high-speed rail technology, China's domestic vehicle manufacturers did not enjoy the scale effect brought by "concentrating power to do big things." In 1998, the State Council of China began to implement institutional reforms to achieve "separation of government and enterprise" to improve administrative and economic efficiency. In this context, the State Council promulgated the "Regulations on the Ministry of Railways' Function Allocation, Internal Organizations and Staffing", which clearly stated The MOR is required to delegate the powers and responsibilities of production and operation accordingly to reduce and weaken the direct management of plans and projects. Railway bureaus, engineering bureaus, factories, etc., as corporate legal entities and market competition subjects, must operate independently, account for independently, and be responsible for their profits and losses. Although still restricted by the original MOR, in the tide of market reform, local railway bureaus had achieved the dominant position of market operation in name and had a lot of independent choice in actual operation. However, the delegation of the former MOR to local railway bureaus has had a profound but easily overlooked impact on the development of China's high-speed rail technology.

From 1998 to 2004, a number of vehicle manufacturing enterprises, including Zhuzhou Electric Locomotive Research Institute of the Ministry of Railways and Changchun Passenger Car Works, were engaged in the research and development of higher speed EMUs. During this period, China's high-speed railway technology research and development were more like a "championship" between enterprises, but the tournament is not only expensive to participate in but also very low in return.

TABLE 3 **THE HIGH-SPEED EMU CONTRACTS SIGNED BY CHINA'S MANUFACTURING ENTERPRISES AND RAILWAY BUREAUS BEFORE 2004**

EMU Mode	Railway Bureau	Enterprise	Quantity
Mount Changbai	Shenyang Bureau	CNR Changchun	2
Shark	Guangzhou Bureau	CSR Zhuzhou	1
Pioneer	Chengdu Bureau	CSR Nanjing	1
Tiansuo	Zhengzhou Bureau	CNR Datong	1
Blue Arrow	Guangzhou Bureau	CSR Zhuzhou	8

Sources: Collected from the Internet

As shown in Table 3, except for the 8 Blue Arrow EMUs ordered by the Guangzhou Railway Bureau to relieve the increasing passenger pressure on the Guangzhou-Shenzhen line, the orders placed by the other local railway bureaus were all less than 3. Such an order quantity cannot amortize the R&D cost of the enterprise and under the huge financial risks, the innovation incentives of vehicle manufacturers were seriously insufficient no surprisingly. Taking this failure as a lesson, while signing the "EMU that operates over 300 km/h project" with Siemens, the MOR ordered 60 EMU suits with CSR Sifang under great pressure, although CSR had not yet fully mastered the technology for producing 300 km/h EMUs. It is precisely this decision that actually embarked on China's HSR on a genuine road of independent innovation.

The large-scale technology introduction gave Chinese scientific and technical personnel a chance to come into contact with the advanced technology (although it was not the most advanced) of technologically sophisticated countries all over the world. [9] There was a great space for learning and absorbing for Chinese scientists and engineers from learning in the foreign factories to watching foreign engineers' demonstration, commissioning and guidance on-site after delivery of the EMUs. With great effort, China's scientific and technological personnel had made rapid progress in manufacturing technology, maintenance technology, management system, and operation experience, etc. Among the 160 units of the procured 200km/h foreign EMUs after the first tender in 2004, 9 units were produced and assembled by foreign partners. 151 units were produced and assembled domestically, all of which were completed at the end of 2007. The localization rate had reached 70%. The second procurement ordered 120 units of 300km/h EMUs in 2005, 60 of which were developed domestically by CSR Sifang based on the 200km/h EMU technology that was acquired through the first procurement. All train sets were completed in 2009 and the localization rate increased to 85%. The other 60 units were manufactured by the CNR Tangshan and were based on the acquired technology from Siemens. Only three units were imported whereas 57 units were manufactured domestically. The localization rate was increased from its initial level of 30% to the level of 70% at the end of 2009.

China had completed the digestion and absorption of HSR technology in just three or four years, gaining the ability of "manufacture according to design drawings", as critics said. There's no doubt that the most prominent problem at that stage is the lack of core technology, which manifested not only in the manufacture of specific components but also in the lack of key technologies, such as wheel-rail dynamics, aerodynamic, and the exploring experiences of higher speed EMUs. [10]

2.3/ Self-dependent innovation: 2008 to present

In order to meet the needs of China's railway development, the core technology innovation required by the HSR system prompted the Ministry of Science and Ministry of Railways to sign the "Independent Innovation of Chinese High-speed Train Cooperation Agreement Joint Action Plan" on February 26, 2008. Under the guidance of the agreement, the Natural Science Foundation of China had funded 55 kinds of research related to high-speed EMU, 33 of which were directly used to absorb and localize foreign technology. The Ministry of Science had invested nearly 10 billion

9 For example, the Japanese Union provided China with a "shrink edition" of the E2-100 which was operated at 275 km/h originally in northeast Japan, but 250 km/h in China.

10 Zhe Sun, "Technology innovation, and entrepreneurial state: the development of China's high-speed rail industry". *Technology Analysis & Strategic Management*, 2015 (6): 646-659.

in this science and technology plan, which was by far the largest investment program. The project had brought together a total of 25 universities, 11 research institutes, and national laboratories, and 51 engineering research centers.

TABLE 4 **PROJECT FOR HIGH-SPEED RAIL KEY TECHNOLOGY RESEARCH AND EQUIPMENT**

No.	Project	State funding (million)	Raise independently (million)	Total (million)	Unit
1	General technology and system integration technology	300	750	1050	CSR
2	Bogie technology of HSR	30	70	100	CNR
3	Aerodynamics of HSR	30	60	90	IM CAS
4	Bodywork technology of HSR	30	70	100	CNR
5	Traction drive and braking system of HSR	120	250	370	CRAS
6	The network control system of HSR	180	220	400	ISCAS
7	Reliability of key materials and components for HSR	50	120	170	CSR
8	Operation control system technology of HSR	160	330	490	BJU
9	Traction power supply technology of HSR	50	100	150	CREC
10	Operation plan of HSR	50	30	80	BJU
11	Total	1000	2000	3000	

Notes: IM CAS is short for Institute of Mechanics, Chinese Academy of Sciences; CRAS is short for China Academy of Railway Sciences; ISCAS is short for Institute of Software Chinese Academy of Sciences; BJU is short for Beijing Jiaotong University; CREC is short for China Railway Engineering Corporation.

Sources: Website of the Ministry of Science and Technology of China

The original railway development system was replaced by an innovative system that was much broader, more resourceful, and more in-depth with the involvement of the MOS. The R&D of high-speed rail had broken through the barriers between the departments and finally become a part of the state innovation system. On the one hand, more and more universities and research institutes, such as Tsinghua University, IMCAS, which had obvious advantages over the manufacturing enterprises on the conquest of cutting-edge technology, fundamental theory research, and simulation experiment, were involved in the technology innovation of HSR; on the other hand, the enthusiasm of scientific research institutes badly been better aroused by the support of large-scale research funds and their communication and technology transmission with enterprises was in much smoother progress. The original "championship contest" between the vehicle manufacturing enterprises has become a bridge game with the universities and research institutes during this period. Taking the "National Engineering Laboratory of HSR construction" as an example, the laboratory was based on four different units: China Railway Engineering Corporation, Central South University, Chinese Railway Science Research Institute, and the Third Railway Survey and Design Institute Group. The four units belonged to different management system comprising of university-industry-research collaboration, which represented the current HSR national innovation system of China to a certain extent.

At this stage, Beijing–Tianjin Intercity Railway, Wuhan-Guangzhou high-speed railway, and Beijing-Shanghai high-speed railway have been put into operation in 2008, 2009, and 2011 respectively. The opening of these lines was a powerful demonstration of China's ability to build, operate and maintaine the entire high-speed rail line, and this capability was maturing ceaselessly. In terms of high-speed EMU technology, the CRH380A that was designed and manufactured for high-speed operation at 380km/h was invented and produced massively by CSR in 2008. The reason why it was regarded as the decisive breakthrough of China's HSR was that the development of this EMU mode was completed by CSR independently, rather than by the union group made up of CSR and Kawasaki Heavy Industries, with independent intellectual property rights and able to withstands scrutiny. Besides, in order to adapt to different climates and regional geological features of China, the university-industry-research innovation system had carried out a number of critical re-innovations, based on the introduction of prototypes from Japan and Germany, etc. For example, the CRH380B developed by CNR served in the northeast region of China mostly and was nicknamed the "Alpine EMU" because it could be operated safely at minus 40 degrees Celsius.

The designing and manufacturing of more and more new modes of EMU, the impact on higher operating speed again and again, and most importantly, the birth of the HSR China Standard all revealed that China was not only a construction power but also a technology power of HSR. China has both interest and ability to participate in international competition with its former "teachers".

3/ CONCLUSION

Historically, it is not difficult to notice the important role of the government in the development of China's high-speed rail. Its role is so strong and complex that we can naturally associate and define it as an entrepreneur or something similar. It should be said that the development of China's HSR was directed by the State Council, led directly by former MOR, in close coordination with the National Development and Reform Commission, Ministry of Science and Technology, Ministry of Finance, and other departments and local governments of various levels, and achieved by the university-industry-research innovation system ultimately.

Especially in the process of technology introduction, as the leader, the former MOR exercised administrative and managerial functions representing the government and was also an active enterprise in the market in practice. Specifically, it was the strategy maker and executor; it was the rule-maker of all negotiation and contracts; it was manager of the technology introduction (with the acceptance mechanism); it was the funder of R&D; it was the creator of the market; at the same time, the guider of public opinions.[11] As for the construction of HSR, the MOR was responsible for

11 In 2011, China's HSR was suddenly under in the teeth of the storm because of a tragic accident near the city of Wenzhou, killing 40 passengers and injuring nearly 200 more and the investigation for corruption and abuse of power of Liu Zhijun.

raising money, investing and financing;[12] drafting plans and setting unified technical standards; bidding, construction, and acceptance of all the works; it was also responsible for the purchase and management of vehicles and other accessories. As for the operation, the MOR was responsible for the arrangement of operation plans, unified command and dispatch, and provision of transportation services.

Although, the development period of HSR had an intense color of the planned economy at the beginning: a series of flaws, like the loosing of credit constraints and over-lending, the mismatch and waste of resources, and the impatience with technological maturity did exist in the former MOR. However, when we enjoy the heritages of the mass construction of HSR lines, such as travel convenience, social mobility, and regional economic growth, the high efficiency and implementation capacity of the government should not be obliterated.

Before concluding, we must point out that the HSR industry is relatively special, and China is also a special country. Compared with other industries, HSR has three outstanding characteristics: large investment scale, high industry concentration, and wide social benefits, which lead to natural monopoly and strong positive externalities. And the rapid growth of HSR construction is closely related to China's huge economic scale and population size, as well as low infrastructure costs and land acquisition cost.[13] To be fair, there are not many countries in the world that can meet these conditions at the same time. Therefore, analyzing the history of China's HSR, we have to admit that it is very much like an old-fashioned story, that is, meeting the right person at the right time.

But it doesn't mean that the success of China's HSR is just a castle in the air without any theoretical and practical reference value. First of all, theoretically, the development of China's HSR technology has made a breakthrough in the boundary between the original national innovation system theory and the industrial innovation system theory and proposed a possibility of building a new analysis framework beyond these two theories. This success shows that the sectoral system of innovation theory initiated by Malerba and others has a bright future in explaining the economic miracle of emerging countries[14]; Secondly, from the practical point of view, the development of China's HSR technology also provides a successful example for how developing countries can do a good job in technology introduction and making full use of their second-mover advantages, that is, adhering to an open mind, using positive, prudent

12 According to the World Bank Report "High-Speed Railways in China: A Look at Construction Costs", the MOR "absorbed almost every financial risk of all the new-built high-speed railways".

13 It's no secret that China's land acquisition and resettlement costs are both relatively low. A survey on China's high -speed rail construction project funded by the World Bank in 2014 shows that these two costs only account for less than 8& of the total project cost. Correspondingly, the cost of on-site construction and right of way of the California high-speed rail is approximately 10 million dollars/km, accounting for 17.6% of the total cost. Part of the reason is that China's social and economic system has a strong ability to mobilize resources. The more important reason is that China has made full use of its low-cost advantages in the construction of viaducts. Although the relative cost of laying tracks on viaducts is slightly higher Roadbed, considering the economical substitution brought about by demolition, resettlement, and farmland protection, this strategy has been widely promoted, especially in the construction of high-speed railways with speeds exceeding 350km/h, which has reached 41%. Lower construction costs, especially land acquisition costs, have turned on the "green light" for China's large-scale high-speed rail construction.

14 Franco Malerba, "Sectoral systems of innovation and production", *Research policy*, 2002, 31(2), p. 247-264.

and pragmatic industrial and firmly taking the road of independent innovation. As a Chinese proverb goes, a man without foresight will have immediate worries. Although this voice may sound a little bit harsh in the context of today's globalization process, it must be pointed out that developing economies, especially large developing countries, must realize that the technological upgrading does not happen overnight. What they really need is a cool head and sustainable strategy.

The International Activities of the Chinese Construction Industry: The Case of "China Railway Group Limited"[1]

Zhou Xiaolan
South China Normal University

Introduction

After the declaration of the foundation of The People's Republic of China in 1949 by Mao Zedong, the construction industry suffered a serious "draw back" caused by the dreadful influence of the newly acquired state ideology on the economy.[2] After decades of under usage, the renewal of this long since stagnant industry only started with the arrival of a new leader: Deng Xiaoping, whose reforms were to propel China to a whole new economic rank.[3] The reforms of the public enterprises consisted of altering the planned economic system, giving more freedom to the construction companies, and research for more financial resources through the stock market.[4] However, in spite of numerous economic reforms the legacies of an outdated economic system have remained considerable.

1 Zhou Xiaolan, « The International Activities of the Chinese Construction Industry under the Context of China's Entry into WTO: The Case of China Railway Group Limited", communication to session S 10080 – *Multinational from Emerging and Developing Countries: Historical Roots*, 17th World Economic History conference, Kyoto, Japan, 3-7 August 2015. This communication has been updated in conclusion. See also : Zhou Xiaolan, « The Chinese Construction Industry in the Remaking since 1978 in the Context of the Important Reforms", *Revue française d'histoire économique*, n°1, 2014, p. 128-145.

2 Barry J. Naughton, *The Chinese Economy. Transition and Growth*, Cambridge (Mass.), MIT Press, 2007.

3 Wu Li, Sui Fumin and Zheng Lei, *China's Economy*, Beijing, Intercontinental Press, 2010; Wu Li and Wenli Rong, *Contemporary China's Economy*, Beijing, China Intercontinental Press, 2014.

4 Corinne Eyraud, *L'Entreprise d'État chinoise. De " l'institution sociale totale" vers l'entité économique ?*, Paris, L'Harmattan, 1999 ; Zuo Xuejin, Cheng Hansheng, *State-owned Enterprise Governance in China: An International Comparative Perspective*, Shanghai, Social Science Academic Press, 2005; Huang Yasheng, *Capitalism with Chinese Characteristics. Entrepreneurship and the State*, Cambridge (Mass.), Cambridge University Press, 2008.

Faced with China's entry into the World Trade Organization (hereafter WTO) since 2001, not only does the construction industry, still on its way to reform, has to compete against powerful rivals from all over the world, but also has to pass through national borders with the purpose of making profits on a larger scale of the international market.[5] In 2007 according to the statistics of the WTO, China was listed as the third biggest country in terms of output just after the USA and Japan;[6] also China and India, with expenses on construction growing annually by more than 8%,[7] both stand out as being the two biggest markets in the construction industry in the world.

The recently founded Asia Infrastructure Investment Bank (hereafter AIIB) which aims at exporting the exceeding capitals from China to support the construction of infrastructures, including railways, roads, bridges, ports and airports throughout Asia since November 2014, is largely depending on the construction industry. At the same time, China Railway Group Limited and China Railway Construction Corporation Limited the two biggest construction companies in China. These two companies are also the two biggest world-wide in term of capital. Alongside a third company, China State Construction, whose power is rapidly growing, is about to take the third place (become world number 1 in 2019).

In order to illustrate the rise of the Chinese construction industry on the global stage we will focus on two major companies: China Railway Group Limited and China Railway Construction Corporation Limited the two biggest construction companies in China. These two companies are also of the two biggest world-wide in term of capital. Alongside a third company, China State Construction, whose power is rapidly growing, is about to take the third place. In this paper, we will investigate the international activities of the Chinese construction industry, both in the economic battlefields where it dominates and the many defeats it suffered since the compulsory opening of the markets in China in 2001. This observation of its international activities will allow us to clearly visualize the strengths and the weaknesses of the industry and to forecast the tendency of its development.[8]

The argument will be divided in three parts: First of all, in 2000 on the occasion of the Third Session of the 11th National People's Congress, the Chinese government put forward the "go global" strategy in order to cope with the influx of foreign construction enterprises (equipped with more advanced technology and more efficient management system) expected to rise after its entry into the WTO. The interpretation of the policies was destined to draw the conclusion that the central government intended to facilitate the exportation of the domestic enterprises and encourage mergers and acquisitions with foreign enterprises. Secondly, we will look into the historical process of how one of the Chinese construction enterprises went global. The largest

5 Cheung Yin-Wong, Jakob de Haan, *The Evolving Role of China in the Global Economy*, Cambridge (Mass.), MIT Press, 2013.
6 The official site of the WTO: https://www.wto.org/english/tratop_e/serv_e/construction_e/construction_e.htm overviewed the 5th June, 2015.
7 https://www.wto.org/english/tratop_e/serv_e/construction_e/construction_e.htm overviewed the 5th June 2015.
8 Ilan Alon, John Child, Li Shaomin, John R. McIntyre, "Globalization of Chinese Firms: Theoretical Universalism or Particularism", *Management and Organization Review*, 7 (2), 2011, p. 191-200.

and most powerful construction group is going to be examined especially in two aspects: the countries or regions where it succeeded and where it failed (horizontal analysis), and the profit that it realized during its expansion in a larger scale market since 2001 (vertical analysis). Last but not least, we will present the successes of the giant corporation and the failures it suffered, as well as their origins.

1/ THE "GO GLOBAL" STRATEGY PROMOTED BY THE CENTRAL GOVERNMENT

The "go global" strategy was created to cope with the challenges that the country was facing after the conclusion of the contract between China and the WTO, even though the former put certain protective clauses into the treaty for the purpose of avoiding the destruction of the domestic industries.[9] Concerning the construction industry, the foreign enterprises who wanted to share a part of the Chinese market had to deal with many limitations set by the government, as they only could penetrate it by creating joint ventures. However, foreign-majority ownership was permitted. Within three years after China's access to the WTO, wholly foreign owned enterprises would no longer be permitted.

Wholly foreign-owned enterprises can only undertake the following four types of construction projects:

1. Construction projects entirely financed by foreign investment and/or grants.
2. Construction projects financed by loans of international financial institutions and awarded through international tendering according to the terms of loans.
3. Chinese-foreign jointly constructed projects with foreign investment equal to or more than 50 per cent; and Chinese-foreign jointly-constructed projects with foreign investment less than 50 per cent, implemented by Chinese construction enterprises alone.
4. Chinese construction projects with Chinese capitals which are difficultly implemented by Chinese construction enterprises alone can be jointly undertaken by Chinese and foreign construction enterprises with the approval of provincial government.[10]

This is considered in general as the "bring in" strategy, in contrast to the "go global" strategy which encouraged Chinese construction industry to exploit the foreign market. The official implementation of this strategy that began in 2000 was confirmed in the report of the chairman Jiang Zemin during the 16th Party Congress in November 2002:[11] "the 'go out' strategy is a great measure while the Reform and Opening policy (initiated by Deng Xiaoping in 1978) moved to a new phase. (We should) encourage and support both the state-owned and private enterprises to invest abroad, to export merchandise and service, consequently to form a number of transnational enterprises

9 Jean-Pierre Cabestan, *La Politique internationale de la Chine : Entre intégration et volonté de puissance*, Paris, Presses de Sciences Po, 2015.

10 http://itip.wto.org/services/(S(qklmwofmqxdo5ht2olchje4a))/DetailView.aspx/?id=China&isGats=1&sector_code=3.A, Overviewed the 9th June 2015.

11 The whole report can be read in the official site of the Party: http://news.xinhuanet.com/ziliao/2002- 11/17/content_693542.htm overviewed the 9th June 2015.

and famous brands. (We should) also take active part in regional economic exchanges and cooperation. "[12]

The "go global" strategy that has been carried out for more than 10 years accelerated the pace of Chinese overseas investments, from 2.7 billion dollars to 68.81 billion dollars (a thirtyfold increase over a relatively short period), while the number of enterprises investing abroad started to decrease after 2003.[13] The reason of this reduction was caused by the government urging enterprises of all types to merge and to turn themselves into competitive corporations ready to face the great competition of the international market. The foundation of the largest construction companies in China are the outcome of the mergers and acquisition of large scale implemented at the dawn of the 21th century.[14] As for the construction industry, in 2007, China State Construction, China Railway Group Limited and China Railway Construction Corporation Limited after the mergers and acquisition process led by the government went from 33.23 million dollars in 2006, to 1.072 billion dollars in 2010 with an average growth rate of 280%. Compared to the other sectors, the construction industry witnessed a spectacular rise.[15] This is why, in the next part, we would like to follow the historical trail of one of the biggest construction companies in China and to

TABLE 1 **THE PERFORMANCE OF THE "GO GLOBAL" AND "BRING IN" STRATEGIES FROM 1990-2010**

Year	Used Foreign Capitals (billion dollars)	Overseas Investment (billion dollars)	Overseas investment Reserve (billion dollars)	No. of new enterprises fit the "go global" strategy
1990	0.27	0.90		
1995	48.133	2.00		
2000	40.715	1.00		
2002	52.743	2.70	29.90	
2003	53.305	2.85	33.20	41081
2004	60.630	5.50	44.80	43664
2005	53.127	12.26	57.20	39679
2006	69.458	21.16	90.63	41485
2007	82.658	26.51	117.91	37888
2008	92.395	55.91	183.97	27514
2009	90.033	56.54	245.75	23435
2010	105.735	68.81	317.21	27406

Source: Yang Huan, Wu Dian and Wang Sansan, "The stages and tactics of China's 'go global' strategy", *International Business-Journal of University of International Business and Economics*, 2012, No.6, p. 78.

12 Nicolas Collett, Artie W. Ng, Jay Chatzel, K. F. Lau, Douglas Macbeth, "Dynamics of Chinese Emerging Multinationals in Cross-Border Mergers and Acquisitions", *Journal of Intellectual Capital*, 13 (3), 2012, p. 416-438.

13 "The direct overseas investment flow of different economic sectors from 2006 to 2010 (billion dollars)", in *China Statistical Yearbooks 2007-2011*.

14 Fan Jianting, *The Development of the Construction Industry and the Evolution of His Organization*, Shanghai, The Press of Shanghai University of Finance & Economics, 2008.

15 Yang Huan, Wu Dian and Sansan, "The stages and tactics of China's 'go global' strategy", *International Business-Journal of University of International Business and Economics*, 2012, No.6, p. 81.

particularly concentrate especially on its international activities since their founding in 2007. The most detailed information about their actions outside China can only be traced in the bulletins that they published for the stock market.

2/ INTERNATIONAL ACTIVITIES OF CHINA RAILWAY GROUP LIMITED

This company has lived through almost the entire contemporary economic history of China. Founded in March 1950, it had then a very official name: the General Bureau of Construction and Design, which was at that time a branch of the Railway Department. In 1958, the bureau was merged with other services and henceforth became the General Bureau of the Railway Infrastructures. Until 1989, the bureau remained under government's control, and its role was mainly to organize the many projects of constructions, which were always based on the state's need. Meanwhile, a nationwide reform spread throughout the country. Being indispensable for the economy, this bureau, regarded as responsible for the construction industry, launched its first steps with Deng Xiaoping's Open and Reform policy, and was then renamed as the General Company of the Railway Construction (the 1st July of 1989). Due to some difficulties in the implementation of the reform, during two years (1990-1991), the construction industry had to face with a severe economic stagnation which was spreading all over the country; but with the recovery of the national economy, the industry eventually rebounded. In May 2003, the Bureau became part of the National Resource Committee.

At the dawn of the 21st Century, with the success of Deng Xiaoping's Open and Reform policy and thanks to the government's support, this bureau was seated among the biggest national enterprises. In September 2007, the company was engaged in a movement of innovation, delete, "Company Laws" were put into application, was created and as we could see the birth of the China Railway Group Limited (hereafter CRGL). The company was organized in accordance with the principles of modern enterprises, but the company's investments were made in the majority of national capitals. The other giant national companies followed the same pattern as CRGL. At the very beginning, the government insisted on owning one hundred percent of the Group's shares which depended mainly or entirely on government's financial aids. With the purpose of developing business in the international scale and of having a closer connection with the domestic market, the Group, or the government, agreed to raise funds in the capital market. And in December of the same year, the Group was listed in Shanghai and Hong Kong's stock market. As the statistics show, at the end of June 2007, the group's activities were already covering 52 countries; the group had also installed 96 institutions abroad and gained 52 construction projects.

TABLE 2 **THE OVERSEAS PROJECTS REALIZED BY COVEC FROM 2003[16] TO 2011**

Year	In Africa	In Asia and Oceania
2003	Boundiali Highway, Côte d'Ivoire	Karkar Ring Road, Papua New Guinea
2004	Boundiali Highway, Côte d'Ivoire	Karkar Ring Road, Papua New Guinea
2005	1/Air Freight Center, Botswana 2/ Road of Koulikoro, Mali	
2006	1/House Renovation, South Sudan 2/Building of Congo (Kinshasa) Mining Co. Ltd.	
2007	1/Accra-Kumasi Highway, Ghana 2/Mahalapye District Hospital, Botswana	
2008	1/Irrigation and Water Conservancy Project, Mali 2/Headquarter Building of Department of Geological Survey, Botswana 3/House Renovation, South Sudan	
2009	1/Institute of Health Science, Botswana 2/Multi-functional Building, University of Botswana	
2010	Marrakech-Argana Tronçon Imintanout-Argana Section Highway, Equatorial Guinea	
2011	1/New Senior Secondary School, Botswana 2/Athi River-Namanga Highway, Kenya 3/Boulevard Sendwe-Triomphal, Democratic Republic of Congo 4/Boulevard du 30 Juin Kinshasa, Democratic Republic of Congo	

Source: The official site of COVEC: http://en.covec.com/about_us/&FrontComContent_list01-1330654682643ContId=10&comContentId=10.html overviewed the 15th June 2015.

It was the same year that we were given the possibility to dig into the detailed international activities of CRGL.[17] One of its branches: China Overseas Engineering Group Co., Ltd., (hereafter mentioned as COVEC), has been involved actively in the group's overseas expansion program with business spreading in Africa, Asia and Oceania. From 1991, one of the first overseas contractors in China, COVEC started its business based on the supporting programs in Africa initiated by Chinese government in the 1990s. Then Africa became the main destination of its investments and its construction works. The annual report of CRGL since 2007 shows a long-term cooperation between the group and the Democratic republic of Congo in the exploitation of mines of copper and cobalt, as well as the construction of highways with Congo National Mining Company and Congo Highway management Company. With the local capitals collected by Congo National Mining Company (28% of the total capital), China

16 In 2003, COVEC declared its affiliation to CRGL.
17 Zhang Kevin H., "Rise of Multinational Chinese Firms", *The Chinese Economy*, 42 (6), 2009, p. 81-96.

Railway Resources Group Co. Ltd (another branch of CRGL), holding 72% of the entire capital founded Lushia Mining Co Ltd in April 2006, which specialized in the production of cathode copper, cobaltous carbonate and sulphuric acid.[18]

In 2009, CRGL installed part of its capitals in Mali's textile industry through COVEC which created Mali Textile Co. Limited and gained some concessional terms from the government of the Republic of Mali: three years of exemption from paying 10% of value added tax (the government charged normally 18% for this tax) starting from the beginning of 2008.[19] In the same year, with the approval of the Ministry of Commerce, the COVEC invested in Madagascar Medical Service Company with 62% of the share (the local government holds 20%, a local company 16% and the independent physicians 2% of the share), aiming at medicine, veterinary medicine production as well as their sales. The medicine business extended to Cote d'Ivoire, marked by the creation of Sino-Cote d'Ivoirian Pharmaceutical Plant in 2009.[20] It was in 2010 that CRGL made progress in its primary business: the construction of railways, and design and consulting services. From 2003 to 2010, the Transtech Engineering Corporation, also affiliated to CRGL won the bid and signed a few contracts with the General Bureau of Railway of Morocco and the government of Angola.

The year 2004 marked a breakthrough in the exploitation of CRGL in South American markets: first in Venezuela and then in Ecuador and Columbia. In order to open the markets in the continent, China Tiesiju Civil Engineering Group Co. Ltd Venezuela Subsidiary Company was born with the slogan "grounded on Venezuela to explore markets in South America" on the 30th July 2008.[21] Meanwhile the company began its business there immediately: the contract for the construction of the railways in the mid-west of Venezuela was signed with the participation of the Instituto de Ferrocarriles del Estado.[22] However, this promising project was suspended in 2013 due to the death of Chávez (1954-2013) and the political turbulence that ensued.[23] The other two subsidiaries were registered in Ecuador and Columbia during the following years of 2008. In July 2010, the branch in Ecuador won the bid for the hydraulic engineering in Chone (a town in the province of Manabi) from Ecuador's water authority Secretaria Nacional del Aga (SENAGUA). With the geographical convenience, the company continued to explore the markets in Brazil, Mexico and Peru.

In Asia, according to the yearbook from 2007,[24] the group obtained the contracts for the bridge construction in Bangladesh, highway construction, drainage works in

18 See the official site of China Railway Resources Group Co. Ltd: http://www.crmrc.com.cn/News_View.asp?NewsID=249 overviewed the 14th June 2015.

19 Annual Report of CRGL, 2009, p. 139.

20 Annual Report of CRGL 2009, p. 145.

21 See the official site of China Tiesiju Civil Engineering Group Co. Ltd Venezuela Subsidiary Company : http://venezuela.crec4.com/list-876-1.html overviewed the 14th June 2015.

22 *Yearbook of China Tiesiju Civil Engineering Group Co. Ltd Venezuela Subsidiary Company 2009*, published on 15th February 2014 on the official site: http://venezuela.crec4.com/2014/dashiji_0215/150.html overviewed the 15th June 2015.

23 *Yearbook* of China Tiesiju Civil Engineering Group Co. Ltd Venezuela Subsidiary Company 2014, published on 15th February 2014 on the official site: http://venezuela.crec4.com/2014/dashiji_0215/155.html overviewed the 15th June 2015.

24 *Yearbook of CRGL*, Press of China Railway, 2008-2012.

Saudi Arabia, the construction of the building of China's embassy and the building for public employees in Nepal in 2007. The group participated in the programs for the renovation of the No.8 driveway in Cambodia, and the renovation of the Sabah railway in Malaysia in 2008. From 2009 the business in Asia surged in number, the construction of Bridge in the state of Johore in Malaysia, the construction of Hanoi railways and tramways and the Da Nang bridge in Vietnam, the construction of bridge in Pakistan in 2009. In 2010 and 2011, its business reached to Uzbekistan (electrified railways), Iran (metro), Tadzhikistan (driveway), Brunei (housing), Sri Lanka (driveway).

The performance of CRGL in Africa, South America and Asia in these recent years didn't satisfy the Chinese government. Their ambition has always been to conquer the markets in Europe and North America. The dream seemed to come true with the contract signed with the General Directorate for National Roads and Highways (GDDKIK) (during Jaroslaw Kaczynski's presidential term) for the construction of Warsaw-Berlin Motorway (known as A2 Program) on 28th September 2009. COVEC and China Railway Tunnel Group Co., Ltd allying themselves to Shanghai Construction Group and a local Polish design company, overcame the Polish government and the GDDKIK by the submitted price equivalent to less than half of the project's budget. However, this move which would have excited the parent group in China (CRGL) proved to be a blunder. The delay of the construction, the sky-rocketing price during the execution of the works and the scarce funding brought finally this project to a halt in 2011. The entry into European markets programmed by the giant CRGL for years failed. Legal actions followed the suspension of the project. In 2015, the two sides came to an agreement after 4 years of negotiation: COVEC had to pay an amount of about 33.67 million dollars to the GDDKIK. This marked a retreat for CRGL's expansion in Europe.

From the Annual Reports of CRGL 2007-2014, we can have a clear picture of the revenue realized in domestic, Hong Kong & Macao and abroad by different branches of CRGL. The profits made through its international activities, non-comparable to those earned at home (more than 91% of the total revenue), only represent a small part of the total income (from 2% to 5% of the total revenue). The overseas revenue was increasing at a stable speed and in 2010 it realized a remarkable growth, after which the profit stagnated until 2014. However, the group is still far away from being considered as a completely international enterprise. For the purpose of analyzing the future of this industry in regards of its international activities, of which CRGL gave us a vivid example, we would like to discuss the advantages and disadvantages of this industry that is in the way of widening its business outside China.

3/ THE ADVANTAGES AND DISADVANTAGES OF CRGL CONCERNING ITS INTERNATIONAL ACTIVITIES

From an historical perspective, between 1958 and 1978 CRGL depended purely on the domestic needs, more specifically on the country's needs under the strict regime of planned economy. Isolated from the market for more than twenty years, the group went with the flow of the Reform launched by Deng Xiaoping and realized gradually profits inside the giant country where the construction of infrastructure was urgently needed.

At the beginning of the 21th century, as a leading enterprise, CRGL with governmental supports behind has made some progress all over the world. Their branches have spread worldwide: in Africa, in Asia and in South America. The group's "going abroad" activities were stimulated by the government's "go global" strategy dealing with Chinese entry into the WTO. Its business didn't come from nowhere. All the construction projects were based on supporting projects since 1960s for the developing countries such as Botswana, South Sudan, Congo etc.,. With their social networks already long established, the Chinese construction enterprises could easily detect construction projects in countries which had long term diplomatic relation with the Chinese government, a situation rather favourable to the biggest enterprises eager to expand their influence abroad, with which can be regarded as their main advantage.

Then the state-owned groups after the process of mergers and acquisition became abundant in financial resources and qualifications in different domains, which could

TABLE 3 **THE NUMBER OF THE PROJECTS OF CRGL 2002-2011**

Years	Number of the projects (undertaken or accomplished)
2002	8
2003	16
2004	14
2005	12
2006	15
2007	18
2008	20
2009	12
2010	34
2011	43

Source: *Yearbook of CRGL*, Press of China Railway, 2003-2012.

give the branches charged of the international expansion the massive financial support from headquarters in China, for example, COVEC which violated the contract signed with GDDKIK and had to pay a fine of such a large an amount that it could have brought it to bankruptcy, was finally saved by its parent group CRGL in 2015 who unwillingly paid the fine of 33.67 million dollars. The same problems occurred among the other groups, such as China Railway Construction Corporation Limited which lost 67.7 million dollars in a tramway construction project in Saudi Arabia in 2010, whose damage was paid out by the parent department of the government, or by the national treasury.

Last but not least, the large-scale groups are competitive in developing countries like India, Vietnam, Malaysia, Madagascar and so on, countries without any local construction enterprises capable of accomplishing such large-scale projects with attractive coming price. This is the reason why Chinese construction enterprises are able to install their branches, enforce the networks and then win the biddings of local projects.

Meanwhile, the enterprises still have to face numerous difficulties due to the flaws that happened during the reform as well as their expansion in the world's markets. First of all, in order to create the gigantic groups and form the competitive units the Chinese government merged as many corporations of small or medium size as possible without revoking their independence, for instance, there are 57 branches within the CRGL group; in China Railway Construction Corporation Limited, 37 affiliated companies are counted; China State Construction, 63.[25] Normally these branches have their respective specialties; some are specialized in bridge, subway and highway constructions, others do well in dealing with almost all kinds of construction programs abroad.

That is to say, their activities are largely overlapping, which may cause numerous conflicts between the affiliated companies, especially after the publication of the "go global" policy in 2000 and also because of the fact that more and more companies realized that the domestic market became saturated. As a consequence, a number of companies that originally focused on the domestic market made their ways to overseas markets. When the dispatched engineer of COVEC Fu Tengxuan couldn't manage the accomplishment of the A2 program in Poland, it was the vice-manager of another affiliated company: China Railway Tunnel Group Co., Ltd. Sun Hang who took over the task. It seemed that the crew of Fu and that of Sun didn't get on well with each other. The conflict between the two companies was unapparent but admitted by the personnel who worked on the same project.

Secondly, Chinese construction enterprises were still under-equipped with new technology after the centralization of the enterprises of small and medium size. The competitiveness relies rather on the advantage of the intensive and cheap labour, than on that of the high technology. At last, Chinese construction enterprises with ambition of extending their business on a larger scale outside the country overlook the importance of abiding by the laws and customs in a rather legally well-framed country. This explains the reason why they had to experience a Waterloo-like failure in European countries like Poland.

Conclusion

Generally speaking, Chinese construction industry on one hand made remarkable progress in the overseas markets, mostly in developing countries. Their success is often marked by landmark buildings such as highways, hospitals and irrigation systems where the local governments are not capable of constructing these kinds of

25 Moustafa Benberrah, *L'assymétrie socio-politique d'une coopération économique. L'implantation dominatrice de la China State Construction Corporation (CSCEC) en Algérie*, doctoral thesis, superv. Josepha Laroche, Université Paris I Panthéon Sorbonne, École doctorale de science politique, 2020.

works. On the other hand, they still have difficulties in breaking through the markets in developed countries where the sanction of laws and contracts prevail over the governmental power. The case of "China Railway Group Limited" might be a perfect case for demonstrating the embarrassing situation of the construction industry in China nowadays. The eventual success of the industry in the international stage might rely on the deeper optimization on the structure of the state-owned groups, especially a better management of their branches, on the improvement of their Research and Development sector and on their consciousness of the legal systems in foreign countries if they still have intention to share the markets in Europe and North America. But what is the international situation of these Chinese companies today?

Since the end of the 2000s, Chinese companies have established themselves as world leaders in the construction and public works sector. In 2019, among the ten largest construction firms (or contractors), there were seven Chinese firms: China State Construction & Engineering Corp. (US$180 billion turnover, number 1 worldwide), China Railway Group Ltd (US$154.9 billion, number 2), China Railway Construction Corp. (US$123.4 billion, no. 3), China Communication Construction Group Ltd (US$89.5 billion, no. 4), Power Construction Corp. of China (US$57.0 billion, no. 5), China Metallurgical Group Corp. (43.6 billion, no. 8) and Shanghai Construction Group (40.2 billion).[26] Three Europeans were struggling to keep up with them: Vinci (France, 54.6 billion, no. 6 worldwide), Grupo ACS (Spain, 45.0 billion, no. 7) and Bouygues SA (France, 33.2 billion, no. 10), with Hochtief (Germany, 30.2 billion) ranking 11th in the world. For good measure, among the world's top 20 companies, there were still four Chinese companies: China Energy Engineering Corp. No. 12, Beijing Urban Construction Group Co. Ltd, No. 13, Shaanxi Construction Engineering Holding Group, No. 17 and China Chemical Engineering Holding Group Corp, No. 18. They faced two Japanese groups (Obayashi Corp., No. 15 and Kajima Corp., No. 19), one Austrian (Strabag SE, No. 14), one French (Eiffage, No. 16) and one Swedish (Skanska, No. 20).

The internationalisation of the Chinese champions is the fruit of a long-term strategy, rooted in the theory of the "Four Modernisations (industry, agriculture, defence, science and technology)", the policy of modernisation and openness promoted by Deng Xiaoping from 1979 onwards and continued by his successors, Jiang Zemin (going global), Hu Jintao, then Xi Jinping. Engineering and construction companies appear to be major beneficiaries of this strategy. Nevertheless, these large Chinese companies have not necessarily prevailed over their European, or even American, Japanese or South Korean competitors, given their levels of profitability and, above all, productivity. This is because these large Chinese companies remain largely focused on their domestic market. In fact, if we limit ourselves to international activities only, the 2019 world ranking appears to be very different.[27] The Europeans maintain their domination: 1 - Grupo ACS ($39.0 billion in international turnover), 2 - Hochtief ($29.3

26 "ENR TOP International Contractors", *ENR Rankings: Top 250 Global Contractors*, p. 5, enr.com/toplists/2020-Top-250-International-Contractors-Preview.
27 "ENR TOP International Contractors", *ENR Rankings: Top 250 Global Contractors, Ibidem*, p. 5.

billion), 3 - Vinci ($25.0 billion), 5 - Bouygues ($17.1 billion), 6 - Strabag (Austria, $15.7 billion), 9 - Skanska (Sweden, $12.9 billion), 10 - Technip FMC (United Kingdom, $12.8 billion). On the other hand, Chinese companies fell in the rankings: 4 - China Communication Construction Group (23.3 billion), 7 - Power Construction Corp. Of China (14.7 billion), 8- China State Construction & Engineering Corp. (14.1 billion). This clearly shows that the European leaders have not necessarily lost the game.[28]
The China Railway Construction Corporation (CRCC) is partially listed on the Shanghai and Hong Kong stock exchanges. However, it is based in Beijing. In 2017, it employed more than 261,000 people and achieved a profit margin of more than 2.7%. Present abroad, in sixty countries, it has notably built the first line of the Mecca metro and supplied the Montreal metro with double-decker cars. Most of its activity, however, concerns the immense Chinese railway network. It was listed on the stock markets in Shanghai and Hong Kong in 2007 and is controlled by the State. Its main competitor, the China Railway Group Ltd, is itself listed on the stock exchange in Shanghai and Hong Kong, but is controlled by the Chinese government through its main shareholder, China Railway Engineering (CREEC). CRG was recently created in 2007 and specialised in the construction of high-speed trains. In China, but also abroad (London-Birmingham, soon Manchester and Leeds). It still belongs to the CREEC group, founded in 1950 and based in Beijing. CREEC is also particularly active in Africa, notably in the Democratic Republic of Congo, and controls some thirty-one subsidiaries.

28 Dominique Barjot, "Why was the world construction industry dominated by European leaders?" The development of the largest European firms from the late 19th to the early 21st centuries", *Construction History International Journal of the Construction History Society*, vol.28, n° 3 (2013), p. 89-114.

The Korean Economic "Miracle" between the State and the Chaebols (1953-Today)

Dominique Barjot
Paris-Sorbonne University
& Renmin University of China

Park Rang-Ri
Paris-Sorbonne
University

Introduction

After the economic take-off of Japan, South Korea knew another "miracle".[1] She nevertheless suffered from a heavy inheritance: that of the "Hermit Kingdom" of the 19th century and of his technological, economic and social blockings, of the Japanese Occupation and of the Korean War.[2] Nevertheless, from 1960s, the country knew, from 1960s, a great economic development, based at the same time on the growth of exports and, with a certain delay, of the internal market of mass consumption. [3] We attribute it generally to the American aid, but also and especially to the excellent cooperation between the State and the big conglomerates appointed under the term of *chaebols* (from *chae*: wealth or property + *bol*: faction or clan). This is not false, but must be qualified. The various experiences of the steel industry, with Posco (and Hyundai Steel Corporation), shipbuilding and automobile industry (Hyundai in particular), clearly moves in this direction. On the contrary, the case of the electronics brings to put in perspective the importance of this connection, as show it the examples of LG

1 Dominique Barjot, « L'ascension économique de l'Asie : quels facteurs ? Quels modèles ? », *Entreprises et histoire*, vol. 90, no. 1, 2018, p. 6-24 ; « Le « miracle économique coréen (1953-2013). Réalités et limites », in *Outre-Terre. Revue européenne de géopolitique*, n° 39, avril-mai-juin 2014, p. 37-65.

2 The Korean Overseas Information Service, *Handbook of Korea*, Jung Moon Sa Printing Co., Seoul, 2003, 11e Edition; Li, O., *La Corée des origines à nos jours*, Léopard d'Or-Asean Kakhoe, Paris-Séoul, 1989.

3 Parc Jimmyn, *An eclectic approach to enhancing the competitive advantage of nations: analyzing the success factors of East Asian economies with a focus on the development of South Korea*, Dominique Barjot (Paris Sorbonne), co-supervisor, Moon Hwy-Chang (Seoul National University), co-supervisor, doctoral thesis in co-tutelle, Université Paris Sorbonne- Seoul National University, Seoul, 17 June 2014.

and, especially, Samsung. [4] Little as in Japan, two growth models thus coexisted, for the profit of the state economy. It is what wants to demonstrate the present paper. In this perspective, it is possible to handle successively two major aspects:

- Part 1 – The macroeconomic vision: the human resources at the heart of the "miracle";
- Part 2 – The microeconomic vision: the positive effects of the international specialization;

1/ THE MACROECONOMIC VISION: THE HUMAN CAPITAL AT THE HEART OF THE "MIRACLE"

From a macroeconomic point of view, the South-Korean major economic success largely resulted of a remarkable mobilizing of the human capital. [5]

1-1/ A major economic success

This major economic success was obtained in spite of a heavy inheritance. [6]

A/ A heavy inheritance

It resulted of three decisive historical experiences. [7] The first one corresponded to the marks left by the experiment of the "Hermit Kingdom" of the 19th century and of his technological, economic, social and cultural blockings. The second was the result of the Japanese Occupation. [8] This one had ambiguous modernization. [9] Finally, the considerable impact of the Korean War added to it: 150,000 deaths, 200,000 wounded persons and 3 millions of missing persons. [10]

B/ The Korean model; an industrialization based on exports

On the contrary, from 1961, South Korea opted for a new model of industrialization. It was not the case immediately. Indeed, between 1953 and 1960, South Korean rulers opted for an economic policy of substitution to imports.

4 Rang-Ri Park, *Samsung. L'œuvre d'un entrepreneur hors pair, Byung Chull Lee*, Paris, Economica, 2008; Dominique Barjot & Rang-Ri Park-Barjot, "Samsung: Lee Byung Chull, Créateur d'un modèle mondial, l'apport de la Business History", *Korea's Economic Development and the Role of Entrepreneurship, International Symposium to Commemorate the 100th Birthday of Lee Byung-Chull (Ho-Am), founder of Samsung Group*, Federation of Korean Industries, Korean Academic Society of Business Administration, Samsung Economic Research Institute, 2010, p. 171-219.

5 Alice H. Amsden, *Asia's Next Giant: South Korea and Late Industrialization*, New York, Oxford University Press, 1989; Lee Hyng-Koo, *The Korean Economy. Perspectives for the Twenty-First Century*, New York, State University of New York Press, 1996; Lee John W., *The Korean Economy and its Prospects, Lessons from a Developmental State*, East-West Research Institute, Washington DC, USA, 2003; Song Byung-Nak, *The Rise of the Korean Economy*, Hong Kong, Oxford University Press, 1997; Whang In-Joung, *Economic Transformation of Korea, 1945-95: Issues and Responses*, Seoul, The Sejong Institute, 1997.

6 Han Woo-Keun, *The History of Korea*, Seoul, The Eul-Yo Publishing Company, 22th edition, 1997.

7 Dominique Barjot & Rang-Ri Park-Barjot, « La société coréenne face à l'impérialisme japonais (1875-1945) : entre exploitation économique, modernisation forcée et assimilation », in Jean-François Klein, Claire Laux, *Les sociétés coloniales à l'âge des empires : Afrique, Antilles, Asie (années 1850-années 1950)*, Ellipses, 2012, chapter 7, p. 96-104.

8 Dominique Barjot (ed.), *Les sociétés, la guerre, la paix 1911-1946*, Sedes, coll. Regards sur l'histoire, Paris, 2003 ; George L. Hicks, *The comfort Women. Sex Slaves of the Japanese Imperial Forces*, Londres, Souvenir Press, 1995.

9 Alain Delissen, « Corée », in Harmut O. Rotermund (ed.), *L'Asie orientale et méridionale aux XIXe-XXe siècles. Chine, Corée, Japon, Asie du Sud-Est, Inde*, coll. Nouvelle Clio, Paris, PUF, 1999, p. 135-232.

10 Rang-Ri Park-Barjot, "Les conséquences économiques de la guerre : la Corée du Sud de 1950 à 1979, de l'économie assistée au Take-off", in Pierre Journoud (ed.), *La Guerre de Corée et ses enjeux stratégiques de 1950 à nos jours*, L'Harmattan, 2013, p. 303-318.

1°/ Indeed, the 1960s saw a strategic reorientation.[11] Until 1961, under the more and more authoritarian presidency of Syngman Rhee (1948-1960), this economic policy based itself on the substitution to imports, matched by a massive economic and technological aid of the United States.[12] It changed in a radical way with the coming to Power, in 1961, of the President Park Chung-Hee (1917-1979), a general trained in the Japanese military tradition. The new strategy settled a first to export with the purpose to reduce the outside trade deficit. It supposed to create and to develop the strategic industries, on the Japanese model and in front of North Korea, and then clearly more industrialized.

2°/ In the 1980s and 1990s, occurred a fast transformation, but it remained unfinished. During the Park Chung-Hee's period, South Korea knew a quickest development, comparable to that of Japan during the 1950s and 1960s. The military "coup d'état" of 1969 came along with a sensitive slowing down. But, firstly, this slowing down was also understand able by the impact of the second oil crisis and, secondly, the South Korean economic growth remained one of the strongest in Asia. From the middle of the 1980s, the national economy refounded the way of an extremely fast growth. During this period, South Korea asserted itself, as one the "Four Dragons", with Hong Kong, Singapore and Taiwan[13].

3°/ Although still very steady, the growth slowed a lot in the next year. This growth continued in fact with a very high rhythm, even after the coming to power of Kim Young-Sam (1927-2015), a civil President, in 1993. But this growth came along with economic imbalance more and more disturbing (inflation, excessive indebtedness of chaebols and all the banking system, corruption[14]). Thus, South Korea was seriously struck by the Asian crisis of 1997-1998 (-5% of growth during the year 1997). After this shock and in answer to requests of IMF, the growth model changed in a very deep way. Between 1998 and 2006, the annual average growth rate was 4.6% a year on average for the GNP and 4.3% of the GNP 2009, the South Korean growth remained steady, in spite of marked fluctuations. The period 1997-2012 was dominated by the liberation of the foreign exchanges and the international opening.

C/ Three key factors

Three key factors explain this economic success.

1°/ First factor. There exist powerful industrial and financial Korean groups.[15] They are organized most of the time in multi-diversified conglomerates (named *chaebols*). In 2010 the most important groups (see table 1) were:

11 Dominique Barjot & Rang-Ri Park-Barjot (ed.), « Aux origines du miracle coréen », *Conflits Actuels*, n° 22, 2008-2.

12 Park Tae-Gyun. « W. W. Rostow et son discours sur l'économie en Corée du Sud dans les années 1960 », *Histoire, économie & société*, vol. 25e année, no. 2, 2006, p. 281-289; *An Ally and Empire. Two Myths of South Korea-United States Relations, 1945-1980*, Seoul, The Academy of Korean Studies Press, 2012.

13 Ezra F. Vogel, *The four Little Dragons: The Spread of Industrialization in East Asia*, Cambridge: Harvard University Press, 1991; John Page, "The East Asian Miracle: Four Lessons for Development Policy", *The World Bank, National Bureau of Economic Research.*, Vol. 9, Cambridge (Mass.), MIT Press, 1994.

14 David Kang, *Crony Capitalism. Corruption and Development in South Korea and the Philippines*, Cambridge (Mass.), Cambridge University Press, 2002.

15 Myung-Hun Kang, *The Korean Business conglomerate. Chaebol then and now*, Berkeley, Institute of East Asian Studies, University of California, 1996; Moon Hwi Chang (ed.), *The Next Generation of Competition for Korean Firms*, Seoul, Seoul School of Integrated Sciences & Technologies, 2010.

1/ Samsung Group[16]
2/ LG Group
3/ Hyundai Kia Automobile Group
4/ SK Group
5/ GS Group

But, if we considered only companies and not group, the ranking became the following one:

1/ Samsung Electronics;[17]
2/LG;
3/SK Holding;
4/ Hyundai Motors;
5/LG Electronics;
6/ SK Energy;
7/GS Caltex;
8/ Hyundai Heavy Industries;
9/ Samsung Life;
10/SK Networks.

2°/ Second factor. The strategy of exports remains always profitable.[18] South Korea appears as a big exporter (seventh world rank in 2014). Her credit balance places her behind China, Germany, Japan and Netherlands and more or less at the level of Switzerland and of Sweden, other big exporting countries. This dynamism leans on a good competitiveness: the country was situated in the nineteenth world rank, behind Germany, the United States, the United Kingdom and Japan, but in the front of Canada, France, Australia, Spain, Italy, China and India.[19] On the industrial plan, South Korea always positions very well (electronics and NICT[20] or; shipbuilding; automobile industry, steel and iron industry).

3°/ Third factor. The government leads a voluntarist economic policy.[21] As Japan, South Korea obeys the model of development named "in flight of wild goose" :

1/ first step-textile industry;
2/ second step-steel and iron industry, shipbuilding and construction;
3/ third step-automobile and electronics.

16 Dominique Barjot & Rang-Ri Park, « Samsung. Le modèle de croissance entre exemplarité et originalité (1938-2007) », in Dominique Barjot (ed.), "Economic development, financing and business strategies (19th-21st century)". « Développement économique, financement et stratégies d'entreprises XIXe-XXIe siècle) », *Revue française d'histoire économique – The French Economic History Review*, n° 9-10 (n°1 et n° 2, janvier et septembre 2018), p. 78-111.

17 Rang-Ri Park-Barjot, "Samsung: an original case of knowledge transfer in economic organizations", in Dominique Barjot, Harm G. Schröter (eds), « La circulation de l'information et des connaissances », *Entreprises et Histoire*, n° 75, 2014, p. 91-101.

18 Rang-Ri Park-Barjot, « Mondialisation et avantage concurrentiel. La percée internationale de Samsung 1953-1986 », *Revue Économique*, vol. 58, n° 1, janvier 2007, p. 231-258.

19 Moon Hwi-Chang & Kim John Y., "Comparing the Competitiveness of Korea and Singapore after Ten Years of Asian Economic Crisis", *The Review of Business History*, 25 (1), 2010, p. 75-91; Moon Hwi Chang, M. Rugman Adam & Verbeke A., "A Generalized Double Diamond Approach to the Global Competitiveness of Korea and Singapore", *International Business Review* 7, 1998, p. 135-150.

20 New Information and Communication Technologies.

21 Jimmyn Parc & Rang-Ri Park-Barjot, « L'internationalisation comme facteur de développement économique : des dragons à l'envol de la Chine », in Dominique Barjot & Lu Yimin (eds), « Chine-Europe : perceptions croisées », *Géostratégiques*, n° 42, 2014, p. 81-108.

The Asian crisis of 1997 caused a decisive change to a more competitive internal market. The South Korean State was and today remains a strategist State). There show it:

1/ the agrarian movement Saemaul during the Park Chung-Hee's period;

2/ the "green growth" promoted by the former President Lee Myung-Bak during the second part of the 2000's;

3/ the development of technological universities, both by the state, as the Korea Advanced Institute of Science and Technology (KAIST)[22], and by the companies, for instance Posco, as the Pohang University of Science and Technology (Postech).

1-2/ The human capital: key factor of the South Korean model of development

South Korea today is a developed country. By her GDP (Gross Domestic Product) per capital in purchase power ratio, she is situated roughly at the level of Italy and Spain. A determining factor of this success lives in the mobilization of human capital (Schultze, Becker).[23] She is characterized by the highest performances of her school system (PISA surveys). His performances seem so high as regards R&D (fourth world innovator in 2013 behind USA, Japan and France).

A/ The human capital; the approaches

There are various manners to analyze the human capital.

1°/ The human capital takes place at the core of the global economic performance. South Korea is even in advance on Hong Kong, Singapore or Taiwan. The catching up, then advance were made in four stages (1945-1960, 1963-1978, 1979-1992, 1998-2012).

2°/ Was the Confucianism (is it still?) a brake or an accelerator of the progress? Indeed, there exist two opposite point of view between Max Weber (Confucianism constituted a factor of blocking) and Geert Hofstede (Confucianism played the role of a factor of progress).[24] It is advisable to distinguish between Confucianism and Neo-Confucianism renewed by the Christian influence, especially Protestant).[25]

3°/ Korea benefited and today benefits from an already cultural heritage. Korea possesses a very old scientific tradition (astronomy, printing system and system of education). From 1880s appeared the first modern schools.

22 "Korea Advanced Institute of Science and Technology, Computer graphics and visualization lab", http://www.cgv.kaist.ac.kr/medical_image, accessed 2 September 2016.

23 Rang-Ri Park & Jimmyn Parc, « Le capital humain : facteur clé du modèle coréen de développement », in *Outre-Terre*, n° 39, special issue « Corée du Nord, Corée du Sud : la guerre sans la guerre », 2014, p. 74-90.

24 Dominique Barjot, Rang-Ri Park-Barjot, « La Corée du Sud, un autre modèle Rhénan ? Samsung ou l'héritage de Lee Byung Chull », in Pierre Lamard et Nicolas Stoskopf (eds), *L'Entreprise rhénane. Mythe ou réalité ? Hommage à Michel Hau*, Paris, Picard, 2015, p. 95-109.

25 Dominique Barjot & Rang-Ri Park-Barjot, "Samsung, an original and competitive social model: The role of the founder, Lee Byung Chull", 14th EBHA conference Glasgow 2010, section 5F, *Alternative forms of business organization*, http://www.gla.ac.uk/departments/businesshistory/ebha2010/conferencepapers/; Rang-Ri Park-Barjot & Tae-Sik Rhee, « L'éthique confucéenne et l'esprit du capitalisme : l'exemple des cadres et dirigeants d'entreprises en Corée du Sud», in Flora Blanchon & Rang-Ri Park-Barjot (eds), *Le nouvel âge de Confucius*, PUPS, 2007, p. 211-233.

B/ Education and research: the specificities of the Korean model of development

As regards education and scientific research, there are marked specificities of the Korean model of development.

1°/ The school and university system seems successful, but at what price? The percentage of children in full time education is very developed, at the same because the effort of the state (table 4) and the highest spending level of families. But the system is discussing today (*Hagwons, Jeongsi*). The public school can assure to her alone the success of the children. Consequently, the parents entrust them to these *Hangwons* (institutes of training), most of the time deprived. The major objective lies in the university entrance (studies in four years) or in universitary colleges (two or three years) with professional purpose. The universitary entrance depends on the obtaining of *Jeongsi* (examination of the end of secondary education). The *Jeongsi* is constituted of two parts the notes obtained in *Sunning* (national wide competition) and the notes of three years of schooling at the high school, said *Naeshin*, establish both the determining elements of the admission of a candidate into university. The pupils stemming from secondary high schools can also enter on file (*Sussi*). Only a certificate of entrance to university establishes the proof that the candidate obtained the equivalent of a high school diploma. On the other hand, the South Korean university system appears very successful. All in all, South Korea counted, in 2012, 3.3 million students, more than in France, among which 2.3 in universities *stricto sensu*. South Korea counts a number of universities of world rank (KAIST, Postech, Yonsei, SNU, Sungkyunkwan, Koryo and so forth).

2°/ South Korea supplies a research and innovation massive effort.[26] South Korea is characterized by an intense effort of R&D (4.3% of GNP and the Sixth world rank in 2012). This effort is partially supported by the State (National Innovation System, National Science and Technology Council, Ministry of Education, Science and Technology, and so on.in rate, South Korea occupied the fourth rank of the OECD for the investments in R&D. (among which three quarters for companies). South Korea also develops an active policy of international cooperation. Indeed, always in 2013, the country took place in the fourth world rank for patents. More, South Korea knew the strongest progress regarding scientific publications.

2/ THE MICROECONOMIC VISION: THE POSITIVE EFFECTS OF THE INTERNATIONAL SPECIALIZATION

From a microeconomic point of view, South Korea benefited from positive effects of the international specialization. In this respect, shipbuilding is offering an excellent example of international conquest of the international leadership. Nothing would have been possible however without the emergence, in South Korea, of Posco, an

26 Romain Perroux et Pierre Thouverez, « La Corée du Sud, locomotive des technologies de santé », http://www.cvstene.fr, consulté le 24 mai 2020.

Asian leader of the steel industry. Nevertheless, it is in the electronics that is most situated Korean great success: the example of LG Electronics shows how a spectacular breakthrough was able take place in the electronics at the same time national and international.

2.1/ In the conquest of a world leadership: shipbuilding

In 2011, shipbuilding industry remained the four branch of export of South Korea (9.8% of the total of exports). It was more than in 1995 (5th post of exports and 4.3% of the total exports). [27] Shipbuilding arrived directly after semiconductors (1), automobile (2), and electronic displays (3). Shipbuilding played the role of a leading sector. They constituted a decisive key of the Korean economic by Rostow, Gerschenkron or Chandler. Well before the electronics, they took advantage of their closeness with the most powerful steel-making complex of the world (Posco at Pohang and Gwangyang, Hyundai Steel Group in Ulsan). From the early 2000s, the South Korean industry of the shipbuilding raised itself in the front row world in front of Japan, as the world leader. They competed with it seriously from the 1980s. Since 2009, they resist effectively in front of Chinese competition, thanks to a highly skilled workforce working a big number of hours (the longest annual duration of the work of all the OECD's countries) and an excellent strategic positioning of high-end products (terminals of liquefied gas, GNL, oil platforms, *etc.*). As a result, the Korean firms were able to benefit better than their Chinese or Japanese competitors, from the contraction of the global market: 48% of the order taking and 33% of the deliveries in 2011.This success was the fruit of a close cooperation between the State and the *Chaebols* begun in the 1960s.

A/ The ascent of an outsider: the Korean shipbuilding between 1945 and the eve of the 2000s

This increase in power came true in three periods.

1/The foundation of a shipbuilding industry in South Korea[28]

The foundation of a real industry of shipbuilding goes back to 1960s. After the attempts of the first one's reconstruction, from 1953 till 1960, the economic policy of Syngman Rhee was a failure. On the contrary, during the presidency of Park Chung-Hee, the State was the heart of an economical take-off.

2/ 1973-1979, planning and shipbuilding

Between 1960 and 1979, shipbuilding industry constituted a priority for the national planning. Such was the origin of the appearance of the Korean shipbuilding. It largely resulted of the government's commitment. However, the Korean shipbuilding industry was the result of an organized close co-operation between the State technocracy and the big business of *Chaebols*.

3/ 1980-1999, the times of imbalance

1980s and 1990 constituted a period of strong, but fragile and unstable growth. The State economic policy was more and more criticized, both inside the country

27 Dominique Barjot & Rang-Ri Park. « L'industrie des constructions navales : un secteur moteur stratégique pour le take-off économique de la Corée du Sud (1945-environs de 2000) », *Entreprises et histoire*, vol. 90, no. 1, 2018, p. 51-75.
28 Donatien Loret, « The Shipbuilding Industry in Korea, 1945-1990 », *Entreprises et histoire*, vol. 32, no. 1, 2003, p. 94-106.

(social tensions) and abroad (disputes with the European Union). At the same time, the shipbuilding depended more and more of foreign countries. But already the competitiveness of the Korean industry of shipbuilding allowed it to overcome the grave financial crisis of 1997-1998. Then the conquest of the world leadership began.

B/ The keys of the success:

The keys of the success held two major factors, as showed it the Hyundai's example.

1/ Constitution of a strong oligopoly of big firms.

The first one held the constitution of a powerful oligopoly of big firms. The biggest chaebols already occupied a dominating position. It was the case of Samsung (Samsung Heavy Industries) and Daewoo (Daewoo Shipbuilding & Marine Engineering or DSME). But important outsiders were also present on the market: Hanjin (since 1937), STX, and Hyundai Sambo Heavy Industries. The second liked the formation of very powerful clusters at the same time technical, organizational and financial. A small number of mega-shipyards were generating positive clusters effects (Michael Porter): so to Ulsan, Geoje, Busan, Gwangyang and Mokpo.

2/ The Hyundai's specific strategy.

The most spectacular fact lay however in the emergence of the Hyundai Group.[29] The major role fell to Chung Ju-Yung (1915-2001), his founder. At first repairer of cars, he entered the business in 1947. By that time, he founded a construction company intended for a beautiful future: Hyundai Construction. In 1967, he created the group Hyundai. It was the beginning of the diversification, continued until 1998. So was so born the most powerful of the Korean conglomerates (or *chaebols)*. It was present in car manufacturing, shipbuilding, precision engineering, petro-chemistry, consumer electronics, *etc.* In 1973, Hyundai entered the shipbuilding industry. It was at the beginning of a fast development, marked by a progressive diversification of the activities and the effective marketing strategies. On the site of Ulsan, Hyundai built the most powerful shipyard of the world, creating around this one there and of the most important automobile factory of Korea a model city. Today still Ulsan remains the world reference regarding shipyards. It was the result of a dynamics of productivity gains and an efficient management, but creating difficult industrial relations.

C/ The study ends in two major conclusions:

1/ Spectacular ascent up to the world leadership

First of all, the Korean shipbuilding industry made a success of a spectacular ascent up to the world leadership. This access to the world leadership came true, for the main part, between 1995 and 2003.It resulted of one convergence of favorable factors: fast growth of gross sales and employment, productivity gains exceeding the increase of the costs, increase in R&D expenditures, powerful developing clusters, competitive advantage of the three leading firms (Hyundai Heavy Industries, Samsung Heavy Industries, DSME) on the most expanding market segments. That is why the Korean shipyards were able resist in front of the competition until today (from 2003 to

29 Kwon Seung-Ho, O'Donnell Michael (eds.),*The Chaebol and Labour in Korea: The Development of Management Strategy in Hyundai*, London, Routledge, 2001.

2011). The role of the biggest groups seems decisive: Hyundai Heavy Industries, always leader, DSME, even Hanjin. The recent years however let guess a competitive advantage for Samsung, the company most regularly profitable.

2/ But a fragile leadership

These Korean companies are however threatened by two dangers. The first one is internal. It holds their high level of debts. STX appears in survival, thanks to the indestructible support of the Korean Bank of Development (KDB).[30] But the group had to disengage from its interests in Europe to restore a stable financial position. Besides DSME and same Hyundai Heavy Industries seem clearly more put into debt than Samsung Heavy Industries. The second danger was of external order. It lay in the conquest by China, but in tonnage only, of the world leadership in 2009 and 2010, then, again, in 2013. Much more, appear now new outsiders. Some benefited from a strong commitment of the State (Vietnam, India, Russia, and Brazil); others benefit from international investments (the Philippines, Romania, Malaysia); others finally take advantage of one dynamic private sector (Turkey, the sixth world producer). The South Korean firms set however a strong resistance against these threats. First of all, they become real multinationals. STX became established, from 2008, in Europe (STX Europe with subsidiaries in France, Finland and Norway) and in Canada, in Azerbaijan and, even, in China (Dalian) DSME did the same in Vietnam, in Romania, Oman and California (San Diego). As for Hyundai Group, it established Hyundai-Vinashin Shipyard Co. Ltd (70 % for Hyundai, 30 % for the public enterprise Vinashin). At the same time, Hyundai Mipo Dockyard entered into an alliance with Kvaerner Philadelphia Shipyards Inc. (USA). Finally, Hanjin started, in 2008 also, Philippines Hanjin Shipyards. Secondly, the Korean firms evolved towards activities at high rate of added value (containerships, methane carries, ferries and, more generally, ships for travelers).

2.2/ The emergence of an Asian leader of the steel industry: Posco (1968-2010)

South Korea remains even today the fifth world producer of steel (with 4.2 % of the world production in 2011). The steel industry thus establishes(constitutes) one of the engines of the economic development since the 1960s. This dynamism of the Korean steel industry rests(bases) mainly on POSCO, the third world producer in 2008, but fifth in 2010.[31]

A/ The take-off (1968-1981)

In the origins of Posco, there was undoubtedly a visit made by Park Chung-Hee in the United States. It resulted from it a joint-venture between the Korean government and Taegu Tech, then managed by Park Tae-Joon (1927-2011), with the support of the American company Koppers.

30 Moon, Woo-Sik. « Industrial bank in Korea: a legacy of German Banking or French Banking? », *Entreprises et histoire*, vol. 32, no. 1, 2003, p. 107-119.

31 Dominique Barjot & Rang-Ri Park-Barjot, « L'émergence d'un leader asiatique de la sidérurgie : Posco (1968-2010 », in Charles Barthel, Ivan Kharaba & Philippe Mioche (dir. /eds.), *Les mutations de la sidérurgie mondiale du XXe siècle à nos jours. The Transformation of the World Steel Industry from the 20th Century to the Present*, Bruxelles, P.I.E. Peter Lang, 2014, p. 299-319.

1°/ The creation (1965-1969)

The company was established the first of April 1968, under the company name Pohang Iron Steel and Co. But the real starting up was made only in 1972. The collaboration with Japan showed itself then decisive. It ensued in right line of the normalization of the relations with Japan which advocates Park Chung-Hee and which became a reality, in 1972, by an international agreement (credits of the Japan Export Import Bank, technical support of Japanese Steel).

2°/ The development (1970-1981)

From now on, the company knew a regular increase of its production capacities: the factory of Pohang could produce 1.03 million tons a year in 1973, but 9.1 in 1983. At that time, the Korean industries absorbed the major part of the products of Posco: the hot-rolled went to the automobile, the sheet steels in the naval or mechanical constructions and in the building and civil engineering works, the wires to the electricity and to the factories of processing. . If South Korea remained net importer of steel, she already showed competitiveness for certain products.

B/ A sustained economic growth (1981-1997)

During 1980s, Posco knew a very fast development.

1°/ Posco, the fifth world steel company

In 1985, began the construction of a second huge factory, that of Gwangyang. Next year, Posco created POSTECH (Pohang University of science and Technology). From this time, Posco put on the technology and the science. In terms of production capacity, the company passed from 11.8 million tons in 1987 to 20.8 million tons of capacity from 1992. Posco so became the fifth world steel company. She kept increasing her productivity, in a context marked by the decline of the steel industries American, then Japanese. In terms of productivity, Posco even stood out as the world leader. This evolution favored the development of Pohang, become an industrial complex making finished products from raw materials forwarded on the spot and intermediate products supplied by the steel industry

2°/ An increasing internationalization

At the same time, the firm knew an increasing internationalization: introduction in New York Stock Exchange (NYSE) and in 1994 in London Stock Exchange (LSE) one the year later. This internationalization came along with deep changes. In 1993, the founder, Park Tae-Joon, had to resign from his functions of chairman. A trial for mismanagement made a commitment against Park Tae-Joon, which turned out without fundament, but grew the former leader in a voluntary exile in Japan. Kim Dae-Jung's arrival to the Presidency of the Republic pulled the rehabilitation of Park Tae-Joon and, with him, the return of the former managers. Park Tae-Joon became Prime Minister of Korea. His successors at the head of Posco pursued its action in the sense of a strengthening of the decentralization and the diversification.

3°/ Park Tae-Joon (1927-2011), a great servant of the State

After studies to Waseda interrupted by the defeat of Japan, he made received a military training, to the Korea Military Academy, and university (Master's degree of Political science). Become a major general, he took part, in the side of Park Chung-Hee, in the coup d'état of May 16th, 1961. Almost immediately, of Park Chung-Hee named him responsible for the commercial and industrial division of the Council of Industrial Reconstruction. From 1963, Park Chung-Hee and Park Tae-Joon left the army. Most of the superior officers who had taken part in the coup d'état followed the first one in politics, but Park Tae-Joon preferred to turn to the affairs. After he straightened the Korean Tungsten company, in 1967, Park Chung-Hee called him to take the direction of Pohang Iron and Steel.

In 1980, Park Tae-Joon entered politics. He imposed upon it, becoming, in 1992, a president of the Liberal Democratic Party. For a long time, Park Tae-Joon had protected Posco of the hazards of the politics. But his disagreement with new president Kim Young-Sam and his government forced him, during October, 1992, to resign from its functions of executive president of Posco, as well as of those whom he occupied to the National Assembly. In 1997, reelected delegated and, again, president of the Liberal Democratic Party, he supported the election in Kim Dae-Jung's presidency. He became even, in 2000 but for a while rather in brief, a Prime Minister of South Korea at the request of Kim Dae-Jung. He ended his career as Honorary President of Posco. Considered by the Anglo-Saxons as "Korean Andrew Carnegie", it was one of the leading players of the Korean industrialization

B/ From the privatization to the multinationalization (1997-2007)

The history of Posco offered the example of a successful privatization, without real break with the past. She also constituted one of the keys allowing to understand the recovery of the Korean economy after the financial and economic crisis of 1997.

1°/ 1996-1998. From public to private company.

The idea of an opening of the capital to the public went back up in fact in 1988: it was simply a question then of opening the capital of the company to the financing deprived to limit the appeal to the bond debts. The decision to privatize Posco arose only in 1997. In the context of crisis striking the Korean economy, President Kim Young-Sam committed in a policy of privatization of joint stock companies to state capital. But, at the time of taking action, Kim Young-Sam's administration decided not to sell these shares controlled by the State. The election of Kim Dae-Jung relaunched the process. The decision was begun to privatize Posco. From 1998, the part of the government in the capital of Posco did not stop decreasing. From 2000, the privatization seemed complete.

The period lives an improvement of the coefficient of use of production capacities and a breakthrough in the export, even if the Korean internal market remained dominating. The development of sales and production came along with a deep progress of the profits. Three factors favored this evolution. The first one lives in a high level of investment. A second factor played in the same direction: the labour productivity gains. The last favorable factor held the importance of the effort of research and development, pressed the researchers of the research centers of Posco and, since 1997 at least, in a technical cooperation with Japanese Steel, main Japanese competitor.

2°/ After the crisis, a hesitating recovery (1998-2002)
During 1998s in 2002, the growth got out of breath. Sales knew then a quasi-stagnation. This situation is understandable by the rise of the competition.[32] From the years 1996-1998, Posco collided, on the world market, with the Japanese, American and Brazilian competition. She also shows itself on the internal market. Posco remained certainly in dominant position there, but the main competitor was Hyundai Group, avid to supply his own subsidiaries (automobiles, shipbuilding, construction).[33] This internal competition was encouraged by the support which brought, since 1996, the Korean government to the price of the steel. Posco did not stop giving ground on the internal market between 1998 and 2001.

In the face of the rise of the competition, Posco looked for the solution in a double diversification of its range of products and geographical (reorientation of sales for the benefit of China and emerging countries). Another way of facing the competition consisted in reaching agreements of cooperation with a lot of competitors or of major suppliers (Nippon Steel, Vale, BHP Billington, Mitsui Corporation). This strategy turned out paying, because the company protects its profitability. These good performances owed to the fact a lot that from 1998, the company made a commitment in an active policy of restructuring (and of external growth). This strategy of group came along with a diversification outside the sector.

3°/ A new phase of growth (2002-2007)
From 2002 till 2007, the company lives a clear relaunching of its production and its sales. The favorable evolution of the parity won / dollar still strengthened the trend. Nevertheless, the company kept facing an increasing competition. Such was the case on the internal market. In spite of an expanding domestic market, the company had to face increasing imports stemming from Japan, from China and from Russia, but also in the existence, in South Korea, of competitive competitors (Hyundai Steel in particular) Abroad, the major evolution concerned the scale of the unhooking in China arisen in 2005 and 2006. Posco surmounted partially the problem by agreements with the authorities of the country, where from the resumption of 2007. On the other hand, the company maintained well its positions in Japan and in North America and succeeded even in taking back foot on the European markets.

This activity of export based itself mainly on increasing sales of cold-rolled. The rise, within the exports, the electric steels and in silicone gave evidence of a will to boost the growth, by betting on the top of the range and the technological innovation to compensate for a decline of the competitiveness of basic products. Due to this reorientation, Posco became the most profitable steel company of the world. She owed it to the implementation of a strategy of export turned to China and India. Pushed by the too high level of salaries in South Korea, Posco was, in 2003, the first foreign firm to realize an integrated factory into China. Thanks to the set of its foreign (China,

32 Moon Hwi Chang (ed.), *The Next Generation of Competition for Korean Firms*, Seoul, Korea, Suny Stony Brook and Seoul School Of Integrated Sciences & Technologies, 2010.
33 Parc Jimmyn. « Does cartelization deteriorate or enhance industrial competitiveness? A case study of the Korean automotive industry », *Entreprises et histoire*, vol. 76, no. 3, 2014, p. 92-106.

India, Mexico, Vietnam) and Korean installations, Posco so stood out as the second world producer of sheet steels after Arcelor-Mittal.

C/ Conclusion: in search of the key factors of the growth

In its ascent, Posco benefited from specific assets, in particular from the development of service activities.

1°/ A lot of specific assets

The technological innovation constituted the first asset. Not only Posco supplies a vast range of diversified products, but the efforts of the company also concerned the trains of rolling mills, to increase the productivity and improve the quality of products. A second asset lies in the Asian and American setting-up of the group. The latter leans on six major sites. Two are Korean: Pohang (12.7 million tons of steel a year); Gwangyang, the most modern factory, endowed with an annual production capacity of 16.2 million tons. In Asia, are added to it: Zhangjiang in China, Phu My, in Vietnam; Paradip, in India, third bigger steel mill of the world. Outside Asia, Posco works on Altamira, in Mexico, and to Pitbara, in Australia, in search of a self-sufficiency in ore, according to a policy led also in Brazil.

2°/ A strong development of service activities

Benefiting from a world shareholding (45 % of foreign investors, 33 % of national), Posco stood out, with Samsung and Hyundai, as one of the world big companies of engineering, On the American model (Bechtel, Fluor), in 1994 was born Posco Engineering of Construction (Posec). This subsidiary knew, from 1995 till 2009, a rapid international breakthrough (Vietnam, China, Egypt, then Brazil, Iran, Taiwan, in Saudi Arabia, in Dubai and Cambodia). In April 2008, Posco acquired the rights of Daewoo Engineering, becoming one of the Korean leaders of the engineering.

Conclusion: a threatened, but boosted Korean model

Today, the Korean model seems ambivalent: threatened, it is so relaunched. Indeed, the international economic crisis of 2008-2011 pulled a crisis of Chaebols, as shows it the LG's example

1/ The international economic crisis of 2008-2011 pulled a crisis of Chaebols: The LG's example

This crisis of 2008-2011 was changing both general environment and the LG Electronics' growth. The consequence was a fall of the financial results: But with around 91,000 employee's in 2011, LGE remained the world's second largest television manufacture and the fifth largest mobile phone maker. In spite of the world economic crisis, LG Electronics aims to make the company one global top 3 in terms of shareholder return, profitability, growth, sales and market share. In this way, the LG Group adopted, in 2007, three specific values (1/ creating customer values through innovations and differential designs; 2/ maximizing shareholder values; 3/ building an organization worth benchmarking) and, consecutively, six strategies (1/ focusing on boosting ROIC[34] instead of simple growth; 2/ optimizing the portfolio; 3/ counter

34 Return on Invested Capital.

measuring the market bipolarization; 4/ technology innovation and design differentiation; 5/ strengthening brand investments; 6/ reinforcing global competencies): Indeed, the LG Group remains a strong economic actor. It controls very profitable subsidiaries. It is the case concerning LG Chem, LG display and, above all, LG Corp., the LG Group's holding.

2/ Today, the Korean model is weakened and threatened:
Today, the " Korean miracle " seems at the same time fragile and threatened. If we passed from the political risk to the ecological risk today, persist three major threats.

2.1/ Threaten number 1: North Korea. In the face of the military and geostrategic threat of the North Korea, South Korea keeps needing an outside help, at first American.

2.2/ Threaten number 2: the rise of the international competition. Certainly South Korea became the seventh commercial world power, with a double surplus of her trade balance as well as her balance of the invisibles. But she lost of her competitiveness, in particular in the face of China, Japan, Taiwan, India and Indonesia.

2.3/ Threaten number 3: a society under stress. Not only South Korea knows an inflation superior to the average of the OECD, but still and especially, it comes up against of grave societal problems. It is clear that the situation of the woman does not stop improving. On the other hand, the country knows an accelerated ageing, because of a low fertility, and the rate of suicide is one of the most higher of the developed world there.

3/ A relaunched economic model
South Korea benefits however from a good quality of life, comparable to that of Israel, Germany and the USA, but superior to that of Japan, from France or from the United Kingdom.[35]

3.1/ Priority to the new technologies. South Korea indeed gives an absolute priority to the new technologies.[36] She remains the number one in terms of using head by inhabitant for the uses of internet. It results from its peculiarities: the role played by the "netizens", but also institutions such as Naver[37] or Daum[38]. From 2008, the NICT represented 16 % of the GNP. Korea remains a country pioneer for the electronic government. At the same time, Samsung holds the place of number one of smartphones (24.2 % in 2015 against 30.4 in 2014). She is however more and more competed that by Apple (17.9 % against 15.3), by the Chinese (Lenovo, who acquired Motorola, 5.6 % against 5.9, Huawei, 5.4 % against 4.8) and the same LG Electronics (4.6 % against 4.0). Finally, the nuclear sector seems more and more competitive, with KEPCO[39],

35 *Korea. Economic Surveys. 2018 Overview*, Paris, OECD, 2018, http://www.oecd.org, consulté le 16 avril 2020.

36 Dominique Barjot, « La Corée du sud et la COVID-10 : un modèle de gestion sanitaire ? », *Outre-Terre*, vol. 57, no. 2, 2019, p. 143-168.

37 Naver was created in 1999. It is about the most powerful Korean search engine in South Korea, well before Google (in 2015, 75.9 % Naver, 15.4% Daum, 5.4% Google).

38 Daum is a Korean web portal, created in 1995 and fourth site in the country in terms of traffic.

39 Korea Electric Power Corporation, better known as KEPCO, is the largest electric utility in South Korea responsible for the generation, transmission and distribution of electricity and the development of electric power projects including those in nuclear power, wind power and coal. KEPCO is responsible for 93% of Korea's electricity generation The South Korean government (directly and indirectly) owns around 51.1% share of KEPCO.

the developer, Doosan Heavy Industries, the main supplier of boilers, and the South Korean participation to ITER[40].

3.2/ A voluntarist choice in favour of the "green growth".[41] It is necessary to underline here the personal role of president Lee Myung-Bak, at the origin of the Green New Deal and of the Plan of five years (2009-2013). This "green growth" comes along with economic realism: development of the industry of wind turbines (Doosan) and production of photovoltaic panels (Hyundai Heavy Industries). Finally, the objective was clearly expressed to catch up European Union as regards the reduction of greenhouse gases.

3.3/ Growing strength of the cultural model: the Korean Wave (or *Hallyu)*. There are a form of continuity between the Confucian tradition and the private sponsorship, especially that of companies (LG and, more still, Samsung). This cultural model concerns the artistic arts and the creation, but also the university and the sport. Especially, South Korea knew how to create a world craze for her cultural model. More shrink's global, but short-lived success and of his "Gangnam style" in 2012, asserts itself all over the world tea Korean Wave or *Hallyu*, where from the success of the famous K-pop, the jazz (Youn Sun Nah), dramas, cinema, the whole carried by very powerful studios such as SM Entertainment.

The result is appearing clear: today a fragile, but innovative and creative country. South Korea is a fragile economy, threatened in the long term by her demographic evolution (even if we observed recently a light increase). She is also an innovative country (the fourth world rank in the TOP Global 100 innovators ranking, behind the United States, Japan, France, but in front of Sweden, Switzerland, Belgium and Germany) and creative (*Hallyu*).

40 International Thermonuclear Experimental Reactor.

41 Romain Perroux, « La Corée du Sud, le pays du matin calme et des smart cities », *CVstene*, février 2016, https:/ /www.cvstene.fr, consulté le 8 avril 2016.

Việt Nam: The Rise of a New Industrialized Nation[1]

Dominique Barjot
Paris-Sorbonne University
& Renmin University of China

Introduction[1]

From the 1970s, Westerners have become aware of the rise of the "newly industrialized countries". These have emerged as an increasingly threatening economic competitors. Following the path opened by the Japan, the "four dragons" (South Korea, Hong Kong, Singapore, Taiwan) became in turn of the industrial powers[2]. Twenty years later, succeeded them the 'Asian Tigers' or 'new exporting countries"(Indonesia, Malaysia, Philippines, Thailand, Việt Nam)[3]. If some (Thailand, Philippines especially) have seen their growth broken by the economic crisis of 1997, confirming the reserves of Paul A. Krugman[4], others have bounced back with success (Malaysia, Indonesia and Việt Nam). They thus appeared to reproduce the Japanese way of development described in his time by Akamatsu Kaname "model in flight of the wild goose"[5]. It is therefore legitimate to ask the Việt Nam, in particular, if not by train, in turn, to engage in this same dynamic of growth.

1 Dominique Barjot and Jean-François Klein (eds.), *De l'Indochine coloniale au Việt Nam actuel*, Paris, Académie des Sciences d'Outre-Mer, Éditions Magellan, 2017. See especially: Dominique Barjot, « Introduction », p. 42-69.

2 Ezra F. Vogel, *The Four Little Dragons: The Spread of Industrialization in East Asia*, Cambridge, MA: Harvard University Press, 1991.

3 Kim Jong-Il, and Lawrence J. Lau, "The Sources of Economic Growth of the East Asian Newly Industrialized Countries", *Journal of the Japanese and International Economies*, Vol. 8, 1994, p. 235-71; World Bank, *The East Asian Miracle: Economic Growth and Public Policy*, Summary, New York, Oxford University Press, 1993.

4 Paul Krugman, "The Myth of Asia's Miracle", *Foreign Affairs*, Vol. 73, November-December, 1994, p. 62-78.

5 Kiyoshi Kojima, "The "flying geese" model of Asian economic development: origin, theoretical extensions, and regional policy implications", *Journal of Asian Economics*, 11, 2000, p. 375-401. See also: Akamatsu Kaname , "A theory of unbalanced growth in the world economy", *Weltwirtschaftliches Archiv*, 86, 196, p. 196-217; "Historical pattern of economic growth in developing countries", *The Developing Economies*, 1, 1962, p. 3-25.

Other models of European origin this time, could be questioned in the case of Việt Nam:

1/ the Rostow model, by the importance it places on the change of scale in investment (*take-off*) and effort to the ripple effect of the *leading sectors*[6];

2/ that of Kuznets, based on the reallocation of resources from low productivity sectors to high-productivity sectors[7];

3/ those of Perroux (role of development poles)[8] and Porter (effects of clusters)[9];

4/ evolutionist theory, insofar as the specific history of the Việt Nam must be taken into account in the analysis of its growth mode[10]. Even if points of convergence exist with the South Korea, or China, there are strong arguments in favour of phenomena of learning by doing and a specifically Vietnamese path dependency.

Việt Nam knew an eventful history, particularly in the 20th century, passing as the colonial State in that of a nation at war, then divided into two blocks, on the model of Germany and Korea, finally reuniting and committing, a little more than ten years later, in the way of a steady development[11]. According to partially the example of China, his very powerful neighbor, Việtnam joined the group of emerging countries today. Indeed, he is offering the example of the regular increase in power of a newly industrialized country[12]. Densely populated and marked by the imprint of the history, he established his national integration on a walking southward and the assimilation of the high lands[13]. In a country where the demographic transition is almost finished today, the population remains still young and feminized, particularly of the fact of the impact of the wars[14]. At the same time, the Vietnamese culture preserved a strong specificity, organized around the writing and around the language, profoundly marked by the Confucian influence, from where it resulted a narrow association of the knowledge and the language and the major role played still by the family[15]. Finally,

6 Walter W. Rostow, *The Stages of Economic Growth. A Non-Communist Manifesto*, Cambridge (Mass.), Cambridge University Press, 1960.

7 Simon Kuznets, *Modern Economic Growth: Rate, Structure and Spread*, New Haven and London, Yale University Press, 1966; *Towards a Theory of the Economic Growth with Refection on the Economic Growth of the Modern Nations*, New York, Yale University Press, 1966; *Economic Growth of Nations: Total Output and Production Structure*, Cambridge (Mass.), Harvard Univ. Press, 1971.

8 François Perroux, *A New Concept of Development* (presented by Basic Terek), London & New York, Routledge, 2015; Benjamin Higgins, Donald J. Savoie, *Regional Economic Essays in Honour of François Perroux*, London & New York, Routledge, 1986; François Perroux, *L'économie du XXe siècle*, Grenoble, PUG, 1961; *Indépendance de l'économie nationale et interdépendance des nations*, Paris, UGE, 1963.

9 Michael E. Porter, *The Competitive Advantage of Nations*, New York, Free Press, 1990.

10 Richard Nelson, Sydney G. Winter, *An Evolutionary Theory of Economic Change*, Cambridge (Mass.), Harvard University Press, 1982; Kenneth E. Arrow, "The Economic Implications of Learning by Doing", *Review of Economic Studies* 29 (June) 1962, p. 155-173.

11 Daniel Hémery, *Ho Chi Minh, de l'Indochine au Việtnam*, Paris, Gallimard, 1990; Philippe Delalande, *Vietnam, dragon en puissance*, L'Harmattan, 2007; Nguyễn Thế Anh, *Parcours d'un historien du Việt Nam. Recueil des articles écrits par Nguyễn Thế Anh* (presented by Philippe Papin), Paris, Les Indes savantes, 2008; Lê Thành Khôi, *Histoire du Việt Nam des origines à 1858*, Paris, Sudestasie, 1992.

12 Pierre Brocheux, *Une histoire économique du Việt Nam*, Paris, Les Indes savantes, 2009; Christian Taillard, « Le *Việt*-Nam, émergence d'un nouveau dragon », *Géographie universelle*, n° 12, Paris, Reclus-Belin, p. 183-213.

13 Philippe Papin, *Việt Nam. Parcours d'une nation*, Paris, Belin, 2003; Andrew Hardy, *Red Hills, Migrants and the State in the Highlands*, Honolulu, University of Hawaii Press, 2003.

14 Magali Barbieri, James Allman, Pham Bieh, Nguyen Minh Tang, « La situation démographique du *Việt* Nam », *Population*, 1995, n° 3, p. 621-651; Danièle Bélanger, *Rapport intergénérationnel et rapports hommes-femmes dans la transition démographique au Việt-Nam de 1930 à 1990*, thèse, Université de Montréal, 1997.

15 Nguyen Thê Anh, *Monarchie et fait colonial (1875-1925), le crépuscule d'un ordre traditionnel*, Paris, L'Harmattan, 1992; Andrew B. Woodside, *Việt* Nam and *Chinese model*, Cambridge (Mass.), Harvard University Press, 1988.

Việt Nam of today is confronted with a triple challenge: that of the relation between three powers that are the State, the Party and the Army, that of the evolution of the political frame and, of course, that of the transformation of the economic system [16].

1/ THE ECONOMIC SYSTEM: AN UNFINISHED TRANSFORMATION

In Việt Nam, the dead end of a system of centralized economy and the decisive influence of the Southern opened the way to a premature transition towards a free market economy characterized at the same time by the call for foreign aid, the rise of the informal activities and the progressive but unfinished privatization of the state sector [17]. Between 1954 and 1975, the Democratic Republic of Vietnam (in the North) made a commitment in the application of a socialist model: centralization of the processes of decision, socialization of the means of production, the collectivization of lands (5 000 cooperatives interesting 5 % of families with 1958, but 40 000 including 68 % of the population in 1960), adoption of the five year planning in 1960, under the double influence of the Soviet model of industrialization and of the Chinese agrarian communism [18]. In 1965, the private business supplied more than 11 % of the national income, limiting itself to the informal activities. Families hiding their asset holdings, the prices remained low (+ 2,5 % a year on average), and incomes too (rationing of the consumption of rice). If the executives of the *nomenklatura* could reach the international stores, the existence of the small and average state employees depended on their capacity to organize the distribution of the goods and that besides the population to...get in line.

1.1/ The shock of the reunification

Between 1965 and 1975, the country knew the war economy: agriculture destroyed by the system of cooperatives, draining of 20 % of the workforce for the benefit of the army, destruction of the industrial and transport infrastructures by the American bombings, with for result the excessive dispersal of the industrial sector and his reorientation towards the production of war material, from where the explosion of the imports (multiplied by 5 from 1964 till 1969) and the fall of the exports (divided by 2 in the same dates) [19]. With the entry in Brezhnev's power, the Soviet aid increased in power, whereas that of China was unimportant neither in quantity, nor in quality (clothes, sugar, medicine, meat) [20]. This contribution of the gifts, the loans and the subsidies of "brother countries" was immense: in 1975, they supplied about 50 % of

16 Pierre Brocheux, *Histoire du Việt Nam contemporain: La nation résiliente*, Paris, Fayard, 2011; Stéphane Courtois (dir.), *Việt Nam 1920-2012 : de l'insurrection à la dictature*, Paris, Vendémiaire, 2013; Christopher Goscha, Benoît de Tréglodé (dir.), *Naissance d'un État parti. Le Việt Nam depuis 1945*, Paris, Les Indes savantes, 2004.

17 Melanie Beresford et Dang Phong, *Economic transition in Việt* Nam, Paris, Gret-Karthala, 2002.

18 Vo Nhan Tri, « Croissance économique de la République démocratique du *Việt* Nam », *Tiers-Monde*, 1970, vol. 11, n° 42, p. 623-624.

19 Georges Boudarel, Van Ky Nguyen, *Hanoi, 1936-1996. Du drapeau rouge au billet vert*, Paris, Autrement, 1997; David Chanoff, Doan Van Toai, *Việt Nam. A Portrait of its People at War*, New York, Tauris Parke Paperbacks, 2009 (2nd edition).

20 Douglas C. Dacy, *Foreign Aid, War and Economic Development. South Việt Nam 1955-1975*, Cambridge (Mass.), Cambridge University Press, 1986.

the national income. But this financial support was not enough for needs. State corporations gave the priority to the quantity onto the quality (out-of-date wheat flakes, child's bikes for everybody), whereas developed the black market. Two fundamental elements of functioning of the economy settled at that time: the necessity of a foreign aid and an insertion of the black economy within the state apparatus.

The reunification of 1975 changed the situation. In the South, the inheritance was heavy: 10 million fugitives, 1 million widows and orphans, 1,5 million unemployed persons, 25 0000 drug addicts, of numerous mutilated, A third of lands sterilized by defoliants, 4 000 destroyed villages, a permanent threat of famine in spite of a partially successful agrarian reform under the previous regime. At the same time in the North, the discovery of the South shook the spirits: in a few months the goods come from Saigon flooded the market, evicting the Chinese and Russian products [21]. Because the Southern regions need ores, electricity and, especially, gasoline, was organized a vast traffic which revitalized the economy of the provinces of the North. This restart arose just when the Chinese aid stopped from April 1975 and just when that of the USSR decreased (50 % in 1980 compared with 1976). More Moscow required the refund of the debts, where from the sending, every year, of 2 000 Vietnamese workers in Soviet Union and in the satellite countries. The consequence was that the State lost its distributing function, had to give up the police control over products (radio sets, bikes, etc.) at the same time as exploded the black market.

It became necessary to soften the economic system [22]. In 1979, the Vietnamese troops eliminated regime of the Red Khmers. But the occupation of the Democratic Kampuchea (Cambodia) was expensive, isolated Việt Nam on the international scene, prevented the international assistance and cut it of the People's Republic of China which supported the of Angkar regime. It was translated by several border incidents which resulted in a brief opened conflict (in 17 February March 16, 1979[23]). So was understandable the choice made join Comecon in June, 1978[24]. Next August, the Central committee of the Party recommended the liberation of the trade and the integration of the private market within the planning. In October 1980, a decree authorized the provinces to constitute their own companies of import-export (IMEX) and to trade in a free way with the foreign countries. The exports exploded (+ 60 % in value from 1980 till 1985) for the benefit of ports, particularly that of Ho Chi Minh City. It resulted from it an acceleration of the imports (massive entry of the color television and the Japanese motorcycles). The integration in the South and the end of the Chinese and Russian assistances forced to soften the agrarian regime: A series of measures of liberalization led, in 1988, to the dismantling of cooperatives and to the distribution of the earth to families for five years, then in the land act of 1993 which

21 Nayan Chanda, *Brother Enemy: The War after the War*, New York, Macmillan, 1986.

22 Hy V. Luong (dir.), *Postwar Việt Nam. Dynamics of a Transforming Society*, Toronto, ISEAS-Roman & Littlefield Publ., 2003.

23 Laurent Cesari, *L'Indochine en guerres 1945-1993*, Paris, Belin, 1995.

24 Sophie Quinn-Judge (ed.), Odd Arne Westad, *The Third Indochina War: Conflict between China, Việtnam and Cambodia, 1972-1979*, New York, Routledge, 2006.

favored the mobility of the market of the earth. [25]. From 1988 moreover, the country became again exporter of rice, what it had been during all the colonial period. In a way, Việt Nam anticipated the Soviet perestroika, while taking place discreetly in a logic partially inspired by the policy led in nearby China at the instigation of Deng Xiaoping.

1.2/ Đổi mới: major consequences

In December 1986, after a complete renewal of governing bodies, the 6th Congress of the Party launched the strategy of *Đổi mới* ("change to make of the new"): It recognized the market economy, encouraged the individual initiative, rehabilitated the business, without abandoning the socialist frame [26]. It was a question at first of boosting the economy then plunged into the crisis: the inflation, amplified by the monetary reform of November 1985, reached 1 000 %, while 3 million farmers were threatened by the famine. It was impossible to an employee to live more than ten days with its wage. Moreover, the rationing was restored from January 1986. Drawing the conclusion that a step backward was suicidal, *Đổi mới* I also aimed at protecting the political control of a State impoverished, deprived of the outside aid (superior to 15 % of the budget in 1984) and excluded from formal or informal trade circuits engendered by the reunification. Wanted to reconcile the modernization of the economy and regaining control of this one by the state apparatus, the reforms committed within the framework of *Đổi mới* remained ambivalent.

On the other hand, his economic success was undeniable [27]. The Vietnamese economic reality associated, among other reforming elements, an extension of the coordination by the market and the development of the private property. The resurrection of the private sector, in a socialist frame, was so pushed very far by the Vietnamese as, ten years earlier, by the Chinese. Both, Việt Nam and China, knew an exceptional growth. On the contrary, the Eastern European countries and Russia sank into a profound economic crisis having suffered a shock therapy to try to go out of the socialist model. The gradual reforms undertaken from 1978 indeed allowed China as in Việt Nam to know growth rates close to 10 % in the decade 1990. This one lives the emergence of the famous "Babies Tigers" on Southeast Asia: Their growth was widely understandable by their links with the "Four Dragons" and their interconnection with the American and Japanese capital flows. The "economic miracle" of the center-world Asia-Pacific also played for the socialist countries of the zone.

In Việt Nam, quickly, the effects of the reform seemed significant [28]. From 1992, become member observer of the ASEAN - the big regional organization of the South-East Asia, Việtnam lived the growth of its GNP to overtake the 8 %, further to the reinstatement of the country in the circuits of the international trade, the construction

25 Brian J.T. Kerkvliet, *The Everyday Politics. How Việt Namese Peasants transformed National Policy*, Ithaca, Cornell University/SEAS, 2005.

26 Emmanuelle Paquet, *Réformes et transformation du système économique vietnamien, 1979-2002*, Paris, L'Harmattan, 2004.

27 Mazier Jacques, *L'économie vietnamienne en transition. Les facteurs de la réussite*, Paris, L'Harmattan, 1998.

28 Philippe Eglinger, *Genèse, situation actuelle et perspectives d'avenir des compagnies générales (Tổng công Ty) en République socialiste du Việtnam à travers les sources vietnamiennes*, thèse de Civilisation vietnamienne, tap., sous la dir. de Thi Kim Dung Pham, Inalco, 2005.

of infrastructures (roads and bridges), tourists' influx, the liberalization of the land market, to the boom of the building and the transport and, finally, the agricultural diversification. Certainly, social inequalities strengthened, but the State found its place as regulator of the foreign capital flows. Further to his reinstatement in the circuits of the Francophonie, then the levying of the American embargo in February 1994, Việt Nam benefited on a large scale from gifts, of loans at reduced rate and from foreign investments realized in joint-venture with state companies [29]. The country had so become one of the main beneficiaries of the development aid.

However, the most important was foreign-owned enterprises, which received ministerial licenses: in 2002, they accounted for about a quarter of the value of exports, 13% of GDP and 35% of industrial production[30]. Some of these investments - British particularly, from the Virgin Islands - certainly responded to short term financial strategies, but many also come from the Vietnamese diaspora and the income from the sending of labor in the countries of the former Soviet bloc. Result: in 1996, the state sector provided 40% of GDP against 32% in 1992. This development model nevertheless appeared fragile because of its dependence on the international situation and the explosion of private and informal sector, which is entirely outside the state. Yet it was, like China, which protects it from the stock market cataclysm sweeping East Asia and Southeast Asia in 1997.

The informal sector is defined both by the mobilization of capital escaping the tax and by a workforce doing the same with respect to regulation[31]. It is very important in developing countries, where it can occupy between one third and two thirds of employment (30% in Thailand, 45% in Indonesia, 50% in India). It covers mainly construction, services, retail and transport, and accounts for between 20% and 50% of national income (47% in India in 1992). In 1993, in Việt Nam, the state provided 39.2% of GDP, the foreigner 5.6% and the private sector, mostly informal, 55.2%. Multiform, this sector appears more developed in town than in the countryside, in the South than in the North. Between 1985 and 1996, it became the second largest employer sector, after the agricultural sector, but before the civil service. For the Vietnamese, the development of the informal sector has absorbed the majority of the 8.6 million workers who arrived on the labor market between 1996 and 2000. Not only it offered additional income, but also its high profitability (no taxes) drained popular savings. In addition, it provided work to demobilized soldiers returning from Cambodia, to rural cadres affected by the abandonment of cooperatives, to returnees from eastern countries, to workers who have been converted from large-scale socialist industry, to rural migrants and youths.

29 Philippe Eglinger, *Genèse, situation actuelle et perspectives d'avenir des compagnies générales (Tông công Ty) en République socialiste du Việtnam à travers les sources vietnamiennes, op. cit.*

30 *Ibidem.*

31 Philippe Papin, *Việt Nam. Parcours d'une nation, op. cit.*, p. 170-174.

The explosion of the private sector dominated the years 1992-2002: at this last date, it provided almost two thirds of the industrial production [32]. These were mainly small family businesses, but also, especially since the January 2000 law, more and more officially registered and taxable SMEs, characterized by a high growth rate. to the point of investing more per employee than the foreign sector. As of 1999, the private sector employed 61% of the 36 million assets, the consequence was a decline of the State. The revenues of the central budget decreased from 30% of GDP in 1990 to 20% in 1997 and the number of state enterprises from 12,000 to less than 5,000. Now, in 1997, foreign investments were collapsing. This is the starting point of an arm wrestling, from 1997 to 2000, between the Party and the government.

1.3/ A threatened economic model, but in process of renovation

In 1997-1998, Việt Nam went through a crisis: in 1998, growth fell to 3.5% per year. More seriously, the country appeared, with Cambodia and Laos, as an island of poverty in Asia, far behind Malaysia, Indonesia or China[33]. At the same time, the inter-regional inequalities are very strong: the GDP per capita of the South was double that of the North, while the mountains appear much poorer than the deltas and, especially, the cities. The informal sector and small private enterprise, if they have brought out a middle class, accentuated social differences. Disengagement of the state and subsequent privatizations had the effect of excluding the poorest from the health system, which remained of good quality. In fact, the gaps were widening between rich and poor: not only does growth benefit the rich much more, but it also increased the income gap between the city and the countryside. In 1999, poverty affected one-fifth of the Vietnamese population (less than 2,100 calories per day), but 45% of rural households, 53% of farmers in the highlands). In 2003, three quarters of minority populations were affected [34].

Certainly, in the countryside, the standard of living had increased since liberalization. Farmers owed it not to the increase in rice production, but to the diversification of crops (peanuts, corn, soybeans, tea, coffee, etc.). It followed a valuation of the high lands and those located along the busy axes. They were bought by the richest, thanks particularly to hidden savings. However, a significant part of the rural world faced serious difficulties with taxes, contributions and so-called «voluntary» contributions that strangle many peasant families. This was the origin of the uprisings of the provinces of Hà Tây, Thái Bình and Đồng Nai in 1997. Justified by local infrastructure works, these levies explained that, in most villages, farmers swung «between revolt, negotiation and resignation»[35]. In the city, the situations seemed more contrasted, because of a very strong social diversification, but also of the private appropriation of the residences of function granted to the civil servants. The social dividing line no longer separated public agents and ordinary citizens, but rich and poor. A middle

32 *Ibidem.*

33 Philippe Langlet, Quach Thanh Tâm, *Introduction à l'histoire de Việt Nam contemporain de la réunification au néocommunisme, 1975-2001,* Paris, les Indes savantes, 2001.

34 Carl Haub et Phuong Thi Thu Huong, « Population et développement au *Việt* Nam », *Population Reform Bureau,* 2015.

35 Philippe Papin, *Việt Nam. Parcours d'une nation, op. cit.,* p. 182.

class was emerging, however, driven sometimes by trade and employment in foreign companies, sometimes by scholarships and even petty corruption. Anxious to show its rank, it was she who buys motorcycles, automobiles, foreign fashion clothes, in a consumerist fever that affected all of Asia.

But the development continued. [36]. Without perhaps reaching the economic performances of some of its neighbors (China, India, Bangladesh), Việt Nam is fully integrated into Asian trade, particularly with Japan, South Korea, Singapore and Taiwan [37]. After joining ASEAN (Association of the South-East Asian Nation) in July 1995, the country joined in 1998 the Asia Pacific Economic Cooperation (APEC), which accounted for 58% of GDP and 47% of GDP at the time. world trade, before joining the World Trade Organization (WTO) in January 2007 [38]. Finally, all over Indochina Việt Nam participated with Cambodia, Laos, Myanmar (Burma), Thailand and the Chinese province of Yunnan in Great Mekong Sub-region program, to develop road connections, fluvial and electric. The Vietnamese industry was therefore facing competition, especially from China. This is the case of the textile industry, which is highly dependent on the North American market, but also very competitive on its own soil. This is also the case for televisions, fans, bicycles, furniture, mostly imported. This includes halting their smuggling.

Various indications suggest that between the preservation of an economic model out of breath and the risks of modernization, Việt Nam has chosen the second path [39]. Internationally, Việt Nam signed a border agreement with China in December 1999, without resolving the most crucial problems, namely those of the Paracel archipelago and that of Spratly, which opposes the Việt Nam not only to China, but also to Indonesia, Brunei and the Philippines [40]. They are largely occupied by China, which granted an oil concession in 1992, to an American company [41]. At the same time, Việt Nam is engaged in the in-depth reform of its business system: the new companies' ownership policy, implemented from February 1998, obtained significant results (600 public limited companies created in March 2003 compared to only 18 in February 1998); reform of the general companies, sectoral groupings of state enterprises, subject to a reinforced control, but also to imperatives of profitability; introduction of VAT since 1 January 1999; launching of a value-creating industry (construction of the Dung Quất refinery in Quảng Ngãi province, development of agricultural and food industries); setting up a modern infrastructure (role of hydroelectric plants, development of gas reserves, modernization of ports); insertion into global outsourcing networks (agreements with Samsung for the manufacture of mobile phones). As a result, the country has gradually built up credible development tools.

36 Tai Hue-Tam Ho, Mark Sidel (dir), *State, Society and the Market in Contemporary Việt Nam*, New York, Routlegde, 2012.

37 Brantly Womack, *China and Việt Nam. The Politics of Asymetry*, Cambridge University Press, 2006.

38 https://www.wto.org/french/thewto_f/acc_f/a1_ *Viet* Nam_f.htm, consulted on 28 December 2020.

39 Stéphane Dovert, Benoît de Tréglodé (dir.), *Việt Nam contemporain*, Paris, Les Indes savantes/IRASEC, 2009.

40 Pierre Journoud (dir.), « L'évolution du débat stratégique en Asie du Sud-Est depuis 1954 », *Études de l'IRSEM*, n° 14, 2012, p. 13-52. See also Sébastien Colin, *La Chine et ses frontières*, Paris, A. Colin, 2011.

41 Monique Chemillier-Gendreau (ed.), *Le Việt Nam et la mer*, Paris, Les Indes savantes, 2002.

2/ THE VIETNAMESE ECONOMY TODAY: PERFORMING, BUT STILL DEPENDENT ON RAW MATERIALS

Today, Vietnam's economy economically is booming [42].

2.1/ A successful economy

Populated country (89.7 million inhabitants in 2013), with a high average density (298 inhabitants / km2 at the same date), Việt Nam is experiencing a sustained demographic growth (+ 1% per year on average from the middle 2000s), but also, and above all, a high growth rate of gross domestic product (GDP) [43]. Between 2002 and 2010, it has been multiplied by three, the GDP per capita amounting to 1 298 USD, still in 2010. Since then, the growth rate has remained rapid:

TABLE 1 **EVOLUTION OF THE MAIN GROWTH INDICATORS OF VIETNAM BETWEEN 2010 AND 2013**

	2010	2011	2012	2013
GDP (average annual growth rate in %)	6,4	6,2	5,2	5,3
GDP per capita (USD)	1 298	1 532	1 753	1 896

Sources: IMF, World Economic Outlook Database.

In 2014, it is very likely that the USD 2,000 per inhabitant has been exceeded.

This strong economic growth is due particularly to the reforms launched in the framework of the Đổi mới and launched in 1986. This policy has made Việt Nam one of the Asian economies most open to international trade:

TABLE 2 **THE GROWTH OF VIETNAM'S FOREIGN TRADE 2009-2012**

	2009	2010	2011	2012
1) Average annual growth rates				
- Imports of goods and services	- 6,8	+ 8,2	+ 4,1	+ 9,1
- Exports of goods and services	- 5,1	+ 8,4	+ 10,8	+ 15,7
2) In % of GDP:				
- Imports of goods and services	73,3	80,2	83,5	76,5
- Exports of goods and services	63,0	72,0	79,4	80,0
3) Trade balance (excluding services in billions of USD)	- 7,6	- 5,1	- 0,5	+ 9,9

Sources: WTO, World Bank.

Her foreign trade represented about 136% of its GDP in 2009, 157 in 2012, twice the rate of China and four times that of India. Entering the WTO in 2007, the country has thus kept its commitment to liberalize its trade, signing Free Trade Agreements (FTAs) with the ASEAN nations and the United States, and concluding a commitment to cooperation with the European Union. This openness policy has resulted in a growing attraction for foreign investors. In fact, foreign direct investment (FDI) flows

42 Pierre Brocheux, *Une histoire économique du Việtnam, 1850-2007*, Paris, Les Indes savantes, 2009.
43 Pierre Brocheux, *Une histoire économique du Việt Nam, op. cit.*

increased from less than US $ 2 billion per year in the early 2000s to 10.5 in 2012. With a GDP growth rate of 5.5 2014, the outlook remains favorable.

Nevertheless, some sources of concern persist. There are persistent macroeconomic imbalances. The fiscal imbalance (around 7-8% in average during the early 2010s) is accompanied by persistent inflationary pressures and a significant level of government indebtedness:

TABLE 3 **FACTORS OF MACROECONOMIC IMBALANCES 2010-2014** (in%)

	2010	2011	2012	2013	2014
Inflation rate (% annual average)	9,2	18,7	9,1	8,8	7,4
State debt (in% of GDP)	51,7	47,9	51,3	50,4	50,5

Sources: IMF, World Economic Outlook Database.

Even the overall unemployment rate remains modest (4.5% on average per year from 2011 to 2014), it seems that underemployment, estimated at 30%, remains substantial.

The Vietnamese government has therefore imposed very strict imperatives: pursuit of the search for macroeconomic stability, reform of the banking system, restructuring of the private sector and modernization of the banking system. The significant drop in inflation since 2011 and the decline in the poverty rate (from 58% to 14% between 1999 and 2013) seem to indicate that the Vietnamese economy is moving in the right direction. In these circumstances, it is not surprising that Việt Nam is an attractive economy, or that, for example, South Korea has chosen to make it a major economic partner. The Vietnamese economy therefore seems to be engaged in a sustainable process of economic development, characteristic of intermediate countries with rapid and sustained industrialization. The American historian Joseph Buttinger has thus titled his book on Vietnam *The Smaller Dragon*[44], in comparison with the Chinese «big dragon». His point of view is widely shared by Western economists [45]. Although still very dependent on primary products, the country is indeed a rapidly growing and attractive economy for foreign investment, European and American, of course, but also Asian (Japan, Korea and India).

2.2/ An economy still highly dependent on raw materials

Agriculture still weighs heavily in the economy, even though it is declining. Dominated by crops and plantations (rice, coffee, cashew, corn, pepper, sweet potato, peanut, cotton, rubber, aquaculture), it is the sector that employs today, but in relative terms only, the largest number of workers.

A/ A highly exporting agriculture

Despite the existence of large urban agglomerations such as Ho Chi Minh City (7.1 millions inhabitants in 2012), Hanoi (6.5 millions) or Haiphong (1.9 million), the

44 Joseph Buttinger, *The Smaller Dragon. A Political History of Việt Nam*, New York, Praeger, 1975.
45 Michel Herlaud, *Le Vietnam en mutation*, Paris, La Documentation française, 1999.

country remains largely rural (32.3% of city dwellers at the same date)[46]. In these circumstances, it is not surprising that agriculture remains the most important sector in terms of employment:

TABLE 4 **DISTRIBUTION OF VIETNAMESE ECONOMIC ACTIVITY BY SECTOR IN 2005 AND 2014** (% of total)

	Agriculture	Industrie	Services
1) As% of total employment:			
- 2005	55,6	18,9	25,5
- 2014	47,4	21,1	38,4
2) As of GDP:			
- 2005	19,0	42,7	38,4
- 2014	18,4	38,3	43,3

Source: World Bank.

While it is no longer as dominant (- 8% of total employment in nine years), it still accounts for almost 20% of GDP, its weakest growth accompanied by significant gains in labor productivity.

More collectivized in the North than in the South, this agriculture benefits from the exceptional fertility of the two great deltas of the Mekong (38% of food production) and the Red River (18%). The most of arable lands (66%) remain used for rice. Improved irrigation has allowed the introduction of high-yielding seeds and the introduction of production, without intensive use of fertilizers and pesticides. In the North and Center, it is possible to obtain two harvests, usually in April and May, sometimes even a third (green manure or dry cultivation). While the Mekong Delta usually yields only one harvest per year, half of the Vietnamese rice fields yield two annual crops.

In addition to dry supplementary crops (maize, sweet potato, cassava, yam), which are favored by the abundance of water, rubber, tea, coffee and copra also provide abundant resources. Rubber plantations (for rubber production) are located north and west of the Mekong Delta. The coastal plains of central Viet Nam are engaged in fishing and growing rice, sugar cane and coconut. As for the highlands they produce tea and coffee (robusta). Moreover, the Vietnam coffee revolution is a model of development: today most of the freeze-dried coffee in the world comes from Việt Nam. A more diffuse addition is the cultivation of cashews and peanuts. If fish remains the main source of protein (especially through the factories of nước mắm), the breeding of pork and poultry gained importance. On the other hand, deforestation is becoming more and more of a problem: local practices (firewood and construction, shearing) are involved, as well as defoliation resulting from the war with the Americans. In fact, as in many countries in South-East Asia, forest cover has decreased considerably (16% of the territory in 2000, 23% in 1995, but 44% in 1943).

46 Philippe Papin et Laurent Passicousset, *Vivre avec les Vietnamiens*, L'Archipel, 2010.

Việt Nam also became again a big agricultural exporter. He takes place today in the second world rank of rice behind the Indian Union, but, since 2012, in front of the Thailand. He is also the second largest producer and exporter of coffee behind the Brazil. Production increased strongly in recent years to meet the demand of the East Asia. There are at least 500,000 coffee growers, especially in the Central Highlands, which has led to the installation of thousands of Vietnamese from the plains (Kinh) to the Central Highlands. It also exports cassava and seafood (live or prepared). But it also exports oil, benefiting from significant mineral and energy resources.

B/ Significant mineral and energy resources

Vietnam produces coal, including lignite and anthracite (Heng Gai and Cẩm Phả on Ha Long Bay), as well as iron ore. Iron and coal supply the steel complex of Thái Nguyên, the coal being exported to Japan. Việt Nam also produces bauxite, chromium, copper, tin, titanium, zinc, gold, apatite, phosphates and precious stones, most of which come from the North east of the country. Since 1986, the latter exploits submarine deposits of hydrocarbons, first with the participation of Russia (Vietsopetro), then by multiplying international cooperation. Since then, offshore surveys by other foreign companies have been disappointing, although there may be abundant natural gas resources. Four-fifths of current production is exported, gross, to Japan and Singapore. Indeed, the country has only one refinery in Ho Chi Minh City. Refined petroleum is then reimported, contributing to the trade deficit until 2011 and reducing the current account surplus (goods and services). This is all the more damaging as electricity production is still insufficient, especially in the South, despite significant hydropower potential. To try to overcome a North-South high-voltage line was made in 1994 but it is still the North that comes from the white coal while it could be produced on the spot as advocated by the many reports of the Commission of the Great Mekong.

C/ An industry still not very diversified

From 1987, the state industry, which had failed to gain ground in the South after reunification, has been replaced by a market economy that favors the production of consumer goods, especially for exports. This strategy has allowed rapid industrialization. As a result, in 2014, the industry provided nearly 40% of GDP and 20% of total employment, with a growth rate equal to that of the gross domestic product as a whole. Heavy industry and intermediate goods (iron and steel, fertilizer, paper, cement) still dominate in the North. Light and manufacturing industries, are developed mainly in the South, taking advantage of cheap labor. They supply mainly textiles, clothing and footwear, the main item of non-agricultural exports, but also, on a smaller scale, agro-food products and electronic components. In addition there is an electronic assembly activity. This is why foreign investors prefer the region of Ho Chi Minh City (45% of the total) to that of Hanoi (30%). The economic pre-eminence of the South is therefore tending to strengthen, along with the attractiveness of the country.

3/ THE VIETNAMESE ECONOMY TODAY: AN INCREASING ATTRACTIVENESS

The Vietnamese economy, through its rapid and sustained growth, can attract massive foreign investment.

3.1/ A rapidly growing economy

Since 1986, Việt Nam has experienced a sustained quick economic growth: per capita GDP, which was only 220 USD in 1994, has tripled from 2002 to 2010 and now stands at 2,064 in 2014 USD.

A/ Since the Đổi mới, a period of rapid growth

This growth is driven by the increasing dynamism of some leading sectors, such as textiles, footwear, electronics and seafood products. Although «newcomer» in the oil industry, Việt Nam is now the third largest producer in South-East Asia. But the country also remains very present in other basic industries (coal, electricity, cement, steel and shipbuilding). The country is also focusing more and more on high value-added industries such as automotive, electronics and computers (especially software).

The economy, however, appears increasingly driven by tourism and telecommunications. The service sector is dominated by the importance of its value added (38.4% of the total in 2005, but 42.2% in 2013 and even 43.3% in 2014). Even though the primary sector (agriculture, fishing and forestry) remains the most important in terms of jobs provided, from this point of view services significantly dominate the industry (31.5% of jobs in 2014 compared with 21.1% for industry): the gap has therefore increased since 2005 (respectively 25.5% and 18.9%). One of the fundamental reasons for this expansion of services is the resumption of tourism: in 2011, the country welcomed 6 million visitors, benefiting from the prestige of its sites classified on the World Heritage List of the world of Unesco. There are seven of them: all the monuments of the Hué Imperial Citadel, the Halong Bay, the Mỹ Sơn Shrine, the Ancient City of Hội An, the Phong Nha-Kẻ Bàng National Park, the central area of the imperial city of Thăng Long / Hà Nội and the citadel of the Ho dynasty (Thành nhà Hồ). A tourist manna that counts more and more in the contemporary Vietnamese economy.

B/ Reforms continued

To increase the attractiveness of the country, the Vietnamese government has launched and continues significant reforms [47]. One of these reforms is the partial privatization of state-owned enterprises, but because they affect key sectors of the economy, their implementation is gradual and remains limited. A tax reform has been initiated, aimed at offsetting the decline in customs revenue, which is the result of the country's entry into the WTO in 2007, and making the country more attractive to international investors. The results have been quite positive, as Việt Nam has not

47 Gilbert de Terssac, Truong An Quoc, Michel Catlla (dir.), *Việt-Nam en transitions*, Lyon, ENS Éditions, 2014.

suffered much from the economic crisis, although exports provide at least two-thirds of GDP (around 80% if services exports are included).

Indeed, to stem the effects of the global financial crisis, the government has put in place several recovery plans to encourage production and exports, boost consumption (remained strong in 2013) and investment, increase social security and reduce poverty, introduce effective monetary and fiscal policies. Recent reforms have also raised the standard of living of Vietnamese. The percentage of the population living on less than a dollar a day has decreased significantly. It is now lower than in China, India or the Philippines.

3.2/ An attractive economy for foreign investment

This rapid growth is driven by foreign trade, hence its attraction for foreign investors.

A/ Growth driven by foreign trade

Việt Nam benefits from the low relative cost of its workforce, particularly in the textile industry:

TABLE 5 **HOURLY LABOR COST IN THE INTERNATIONAL TEXTILE SECTOR IN 2011, IN USD**

1	France	31,3
2	Germany	28,3
3	Italy	21,9
4	Spain	18,7
5	United States	17,6
6	Portugal	10,2
7	Czech Republic	7,9
8	Turkey	4,5
9	Morocco	2,9
10	Tunisia	2,6
11	China	2,1
12	Bulgaria	2,0
13	India	1,1
14	Viêt Nam	0,6
15	Pakistan	0,6
16	Bangladesh	Less than 0,5

Source: Werner International.

It is thus able to export more and more: in 2010, 2011 and 2012, Vietnamese exports grew + 8.4, + 10.8 and +15.7, exceeding each time the pace of imports (see Table 2). The consequence was an increased rate of exports (80% in 2012 against 63% in 2009), but also, in 2013, the appearance of an excess balance of the balance of goods and services. The measures taken by the government from 2011 to reduce the current and current account deficits have thus proved effective.

The country's foreign trade, however, is unbalanced. Việt Nam is certainly in a trade surplus with Western countries, but it is experiencing a growing deficit with Asian neighbors. For exports, the situation is as follows:

TABLE 6 **MAIN CLIENT COUNTRIES OF VIETNAM IN 2009 AND 2012** (in% of total Vietnamese exports)

	2009		2012	
1	United States	20%	United States	17,2%
2	Japan	11,4%	Japan	11,1%
3	China	11,2%	China	9,5%
4	Swiss	4,4%	South Korea	4,9%
5	Australia	4,2%	Malaysia	3,9%

Source: WTO.

The relative share of the three largest partners, namely the United States, Japan and China, has decreased relatively, but more so for the first and third countries than for the second. The main beneficiaries seem to have been South Korea, which rose from 3.6 to 4.9 and Malaysia, while Singapore remained stable (3.6% in 2009 and 2012) while Switzerland's and Australia's respective shares declined slightly. and.

On imports, the main suppliers are all Asian countries in the region:

TABLE 7 **VIETNAM'S LEADING SUPPLIERS IN 2010 AND 2012 (% OF TOTAL)**

	2010		2012	
1	China	22%	China	25,5%
2	Singapore	10%	South Korea	13,7%
3	Japan	9,8%	Japan	10,2%
4	South Korea	9,6%	Singapore	5,9%
5	Thailand	6,4%	Thailand	5,1%

Source: WTO.

The United States was only in sixth place in 2010 (with a relatively low percentage of 3.9%). China's share seems to have been further strengthened (27% of imports in 2013) while South Korea has supplanted Japan, which maintains almost its positions, and Singapore in sharp decline, probably to the benefit of Taiwan, fourth Vietnam's supplier in 2013. Thailand, it regresses gradually. The gap seems to be narrowing between the two countries, even though in 2011, Thai foreign trade was ten times that of Vietnam, yet more populous.

As an exporter of simple and inexpensive primary or manufactured products, Viet Nam is very interested in African and Latin American countries. As an integral part of the Francophonie, it makes it one of the major axis of commercial expansion, without exclusivity and in diversification. France remains the first European partner and the second largest bilateral donor of Viet Nam in terms of official development assistance (ODA), behind Japan. With some 300 companies operating in the country in 2013 and bilateral trade rising (+ 13% in the first half of 2013, but with a strong imbalance in favor of Viet Nam), it focuses on ongoing negotiations to achieve a free trade agreement between the EU and Viet Nam. It is about strengthening its position as a privileged economic and trade partner of the country. But does France take all the means, in the face of the attraction enjoyed by Việt Nam from international investors?

B/ A positive change in foreign direct investment in Vietnam

After four successive years, from 2009 to 2013, of decreases in FDI commitments in Việt Nam, the latter posted in 2013 their best result since 2008 (+ 66.2% compared to 2012)[48]. These increased commitments are divided between 1,275 new projects (+ 81.7% new licenses compared to 2012) and the extension of projects in progress (+ 42.6%), for a respective amount of 14.3 billion USD and 7.3, or a total of 216. Three main factors contributed to this change: an ever more favorable domestic economic environment (with a 5.4% GDP growth rate in 2013); a spectacular increase in existing Japanese project extensions (+ 293% in 2013); massive new investments from South Korea[49]. FDI disbursements are high in 2013 at USD 11.5 billion (+ 9.9% in 2012).

These new projects are almost exclusively concentrated in the manufacturing industry. In 2013, this sector accounted for 77% of new FDI licenses launched (+ 83% in 2012, i.e. 47% of new projects). After a significant decline in 2012, FDI in utilities (electricity, gas and water) returned to levels of 2010 and 2011 (USD 2.1 billion, a seven-fold increase over 2012). It was now the second largest investment sector. Then comes residential and office real estate ($ 0.95 billion, or 4% of FDI commitments). In 2013, the latter recorded, following the difficulties encountered in the banking sector, which the real estate market is consubstantial.

In 2013, the top eight investors in Việt Nam were seven Asian countries and Russia: that year, they provided 90% of investment commitments against 75% in 2012. As in 2012, Japan remained the largest investor in Vietnam, with 5.7 billion USD, or 27% of FDI (+ 11.9% over 2012). In terms of new license allocation, however, it was outpaced by Singapore, the second largest investor ($ 4.4 billion, + 153.4%), South Korea ($ 4.3 billion, + 264, 5%) and China (USD 2.3 billion), which has increased its FDI by seven times compared to 2012. Fifth, Russia recorded the largest increase (only thirtieth in 2012). Then came more traditional Asian investors: Hong Kong (sixth, 0.7 billion USD), Taiwan (0.6) and Thailand (0.4). The European Union, meanwhile, has recorded only 0.85 billion USD (evening 4% of the total), divided between 100 projects. If we think in terms of stocks, the Asian countries represent 71% of the total (230,2 billion USD, that is + 7.7% on 2012). Japan retains first place (34.6 billion USD), ahead of Singapore (29.3), South Korea (29), Taiwan (27.9) and the British Virgin

48 « Évolution des investissements directs étrangers au Vietnam en 2013 », Ambassade de France au *Việt* Nam, *Note du Service économique, DG Trésor*, juin 2014.

49 Park Rang-Ri, « Les investissements sud-coréens au Vietnam : un exemple de l'attractivité des territoires francophones », dans David (François), « Les facteurs d'attractivité de la Francophonie », XVe Entretiens de la Francophonie, *Revue internationale des mondes francophones*, printemps-été 2015, p. 107-130.

Islands (first non-Asian with 15, USD 6 billion). The share of tax havens in the stock of FDI is decreasing (12.3% instead of 19% in 2012), but it remains relatively large. The EU, with 18 billion USD, provides only 8% of the total investment in Việt Nam.

Conclusion

Today, Việt Nam remains an emerging economy. With a GDP per capita (GDP per capita) of $ 2,305 in 2017 (but 6,925 at purchasing power parity or PPP), the country rest behind the other «Asian tigers» (respectively 3,895 and 12,433 for Indonesia, 6.265 and 17.750 for Thailand, 10.756 and 28.490 for Malaysia at the same date). Even the Philippines, whose population is roughly comparable, exceeds Việt Nam (£ 3,280 and $ 8,223, still in 2017) [50]. But of all these countries, apart from Indonesia, Việt Nam is without doubt the one with the highest growth potential. By 2017, Indonesia had risen to 36th in the world in terms of competitiveness and Việt Nam to 55th. In 2011, both of these nations ranked 44th and 75th, respectively.

Việt Nam benefits from an efficient labor market and strong innovation capacity in relation to its level of development [51]. If protectionism and bureaucracy slowed its expansion, the gradual opening of the borders wanted (or accepted) by the country's leaders could be the equivalent of what happened to nearby Guangdong in Southern China.[52]. There is no doubt that with the help of foreign capital, the country has achieved to a large extent its take-off and generated leading sectors (agricultural and food industries, textiles, chemicals, consumer electronics, but also oil , coal and tourism). Việt Nam has established itself as a preferred subcontractor for the Japanese and South Korean industries (40% of Samsung phones were manufactured there in 2014). According to Goldman Sachs, Việt Nam could become the 21st largest economy in 2025[53]. At that date, according to Price Waterhouse Coopers, the country would be the fastest growing emerging economy, with a potential for GNP growth of + 10% per annum [54].

At the same time, its rapid industrialization relies on large movements of capital, workers and skills from low to high productivity sectors. In the same way, the country benefits from the dynamism of the Saigon pole: very well placed in advanced technologies, it realized in 2014, 20,1% of the Vietnamese GNP, 27,9% of the industrial production and mobilized 34,9% of the national investments. But other centers of development: Da-Nang, Haiphong and, above all, Hanoi, also play a driving role: in 2013, the agglomeration of Hanoi benefited from 22% of the national investments, realized 12.6% of the GNP and supplied 7.5 Vietnamese exports. It is possible to conclude from the relevance of an analysis in terms of growth poles and clusters (Ho Chi Minh City, Hanoi or Da Nang are good examples), but also of path dependency.

50 By comparison, on the same date, the figures were $29,114 and $39,446 for South Korea, $38,577 and $42,314 for France and $38,231 and 42,860S for Japan.

51 Thomas Jandi, *Vietnam in the Global Economy*, New York, Lexington Books, 2013.

52 "Vietnam to be listed among top economics by 2050", HSBC, 14 janvier 2012.

53 Thomas Jandi, *Vietnam in the Global Economy, op. cit.*

54 "Vietnam may be fastest growing emerging economy", *Price Waterhouse Coopers,* 12 mars 2013.

While presenting in many respects the characteristics common to the Japanese model, Việt Nam is following its own path.

Expectations and Strategies of German Business in India

during Decolonisation & Import-Substitution-Industrialisation in the 1950s and 1960s

Julian Faust
University of Bochum

Introduction

During the Cold War that began in the late 1940s, India took the centre stage, both politically and economically. That the Cold War had a strong economic component is not new to our knowledge. Recently, this economic component has primarily been researched through the lens of development assistance and the fierce competition related to it. The battle of donor nations and thus the many government and non-government actors involved elicited an aid rush that was not confined to, but primarily focused on independent India. Much less is known about other actors in the economic realm, namely international private investors who (re-) established business links in a promising Indian market in the two decades that followed Indian Independence in 1947.[1]

The analysis looks at company examples from West-Germany to shift the focus from the superpowers who competed politically and economically in India. Before 1914, even though India was still quite firmly under British colonial rule, German business had successfully established business in India (Lubinski, Giacomin & Schnitzer 2018).

1 This chapter is based on a talk given at the conference held in Beijing in October 2017, jointly organized at Renmin University of China by professors Huang Chun, Wang Jue (Renmin University) and Dominique Barjot (Sorbonne Paris). A substantially enlarged paper dealing with German business investments and German development assistance in India from the 1940s to the 1970s is Julian Faust (2020): *Filling a colonial void? German business strategies and development assistance in India, 1947-1974*, DOI: 10.1080/00076791.2020.1802428.

After 1947, the large Indian market and an end of colonial rule proved attractive enough to quickly try to re-establish old links after the war. Relatively high export volumes in the early 1950s provided the basis for high expectations associated with the Indian market, e.g. in chemicals and pharmaceuticals. However, in the perception of German business, decolonisation, India's leaning towards socialist economic policies and state intervention made India a risky country – a view that was shared by the German government when Minister of Economics L. Erhard supported Germany's and its industry's 'Return to the World Market' (Erhard 1953).

Analysing German company examples, the analysis in this chapter tracks how business adapted their strategies for market (re-)entry when confronted with the economic and political challenges in an economy that, from 1951 onwards, operated within a system of five-year economic planning. The chapter investigates from a business history perspective of individual companies how German business (re-)built international business ties and tried to enter new or growing markets for their products. To confront western views of economic development and modernization with other frameworks development, e.g. on the Indian subcontinent, two cases of West German business and their strategies in India between the 1950s and 1960s are analysed. Linked to new strategies open to business from the 1950s onwards, this chapter deals with the relations business and official German development policy which evolved from the 1950s onwards through to the mid-1960s. Based on the hypothesis of a shared interest of German businesses and the German government in the early years of international development policy, this chapter analyses how the German origin of investing firms influenced the perception and treatment of their Indian joint-ventures. Here, imagined shared German and Indian backgrounds of second-mover industrialisation on the Indian side possibly helped to foster a positive image of German investments. Associations with National Socialism on the other side, may have prohibited an advantageous use of German company origin in Indian ventures after 1945, as companies had done in the interwar years with rising Indian Nationalism (cf. Lubinski 2015a; Frey 2003).

The paper elaborates on how German business built or re-established former networks to secure a positive climate in the wake of what became known as one of the most-regulated economies of the world by the mid-1960s with its so-called "Licence Raj" (Fitzgerald 2015, 382f.). India can serve as excellent case study of how foreign companies formally and informally dealt with non-tariff-barriers and restrictions for foreign investors in India which according to Roy adopted an "extreme" version of import-substitution-industrialisation (ISI)-strategies, which were generally used in other world regions, too (Roy 2017, p 72). At the same time, countries like India or Brazil were expected to become a "factor in the world economy" (BAL 059-402, 1953-1958, *Memorandum,* 3rd March 1955) within a period of roughly 20 to 30 years. High economic expectations within companies and economic observers were based on population growth and ambitious programs to foster industrial and overall economic growth. "Investing in India is foolish. Not investing in India is even more foolish", an observer summarised the economic expectations and challenges for foreign western companies dealing with India's planned economy and frequent crises in the year 1965. (F.A.Z. daily newspaper, 13th January 1965, p.21, *Partner-Betriebe in Indien)* Not investing early enough in order to jump regulative barriers to market entry and to not be excluded from a "future" market of the 1980s and 1990s was perceived to be a bigger threat than dealing with uncertainties of regulative policies and case-by-case decision on foreign investment projects.

How business has dealt with decolonization processes to secure business activities, property rights and legitimacy has recently been receiving more attention from business historical research (Decker 2008; Finsterhölzl 2015). That companies may face specific disadvantages in a foreign environment with other features such as a regime change during decolonization has been shown. By analysing such phenomena, research has shown the existence of "costs of doing business abroad" and a potential "liability of foreignness" (Zaheer 1995; Lubinski 2014; Johanson & Vahlne 2009; Stevens & Shenkar 2012). German companies in India before and during both world wars faced disadvantages due to their origin. During other phases, research points to the fact that the German origin proved to be an advantage that was used to expand business in India, while during World War II companies reverted to tactics of "cloaking" to disguise their business interests (Lubinski 2015a; Jones & Lubinski 2012; Kobrak & Wüstenhagen 2006). Risks in developing are perceived to be bigger than in nearby countries close to the home base of an internationally operating company (Casson & da Silva Lopes 2013). Apart from using ownership advantages, e.g. in technology or organization of production, companies built local and international networks to secure knowledge, legitimacy and reputation to avoid political and economic risks (cf. Bucheli & Kim 2015). Such strategies were used by MNE to cope with strong state regulation and bureaucratic delays in India (Jones 2013).

Research has pointed out that German business was eager to do business with the Soviet Union and adapted well and quick to an economic system fundamentally different from Western market economies by way of a well-tailored "political marketing" (Rudolph 2004). In other regions, too, German business was to gain from decolonisation as Germany was not in the first row of political Cold War confrontation and lacked a colonial past in some areas of the world (Kleinschmidt & Ziegler 2018). Little is known on German business in India after World War II, where the economic system shared features of Soviet style planning and state-led industrialisation. The focus of historical research in the realm of economic history has been on single, big projects financed by the German government implemented by German firm consortia in the steel sector (Unger 2008; Unger 2015). This contribution aims to shed more light on strategies and ways of German business interact with planned economies and how decolonisation influenced the positioning of large, foreign firms.

Historical evidence is gathered from company archives of German companies active in India from the 1950s onwards. The investigation primarily includes businesses from the chemical and automobile sectors, as these were of primary importance for the industrialization of the Indian economy which at the same time was increasingly regulated by government controls. The analysis of historical data from company archives of the chemical firm Bayer AG Leverkusen (BAL) and Robert Bosch GmbH (RB) from Stuttgart is combined with archival evidence from the Ministry for Economics (BMWi) in the Federal Archives of Germany in Koblenz (BAK).

1/ PLANNED INDUSTRIALIZATION, PRIVATE FOREIGN BUSINESS, AND INTERNATIONAL POLITICS IN INDIA AFTER 1947

Beginning in the late 1940s with India, more and more former colonies became independent and sought a new role in the global economic system. Indian political and economic leaders sought an economic policy of rapid modernization of the economy paired with the goal of a visible 'break' with old colonial economic patterns (Balakrishnan 2007; Chandra, Mukherjee & Mukherjee 2008, p. 442–474). The introduction of economic Five Year Plans starting from 1951 marked the start of an ambitious program for the industrialization of the Indian economy combined with import-substitution measurements requiring strict government controls as means to achieve plan targets, a balance of payments and the setup of stronger industrial capacities within the country (Chakravarty 1987). The 2nd Five Year Plan from of 1956 focused on the development of heavy and basic industries such as steel, chemicals, pharmaceutical products. The so-called Nehru-Mahalanobis strategy further postulated heavy investment outlays in infrastructure development to accompany investments in the mentioned industrial sectors (for a discussion of the so-called Nehru-Mahalanobis strategy, named after the first prime minister of India and Prasanta C. Mahalanobis, statistician and mind of the second Five Year Plan see Patnaik 2015).

From the 1950s onwards, decolonized economies received more interest by foreign trade and investors from Germany[2]. India offered new opportunities to foreign, non-British companies, as the formal colonial rule of the country and the economy had ended with independence in 1947. Although German businesses already had engaged in activities during India's colonial period, little is known about the extent and the ways of German business activity during the decades following the Second World War (see Lubinski 2014; Unger 2008). The realignment of German business interests along other regional lines has been observed as a common feature during the 1950s and early 1960s, as competition in traditional markets of German industry in industrial markets was stronger after the World War II (Schröter 2001; Schröter 1992). Apart from Asia, regions such as Latin America or the middle east provided a target for German business and investments (Nellißen 1997; Kleinschmidt & Ziegler 2018).

Roughly at the same time, India became important for the development and institutionalization of industrialized countries' development aid or assistance policy. India became specifically important as both perceived 'Blocks' in an intensifying

2 The term 'Germany' here in this paper refers to the Federal Republic of Germany.

'Cold War' tried to pull India on their sides, both ideologically and economically. The relatively new realm of development assistance and policy provided the West German governments with a new field where its foreign and economic policy could regain international strength, while leaving political confrontation to the large and powerful political leaders of the respective ideological sides (Unger 2010; McMahon 2012; Westad 2005). Furthermore, India and economic collaboration with the country became an important feature in the German Democratic Republic's (GDR) diplomatic goal of international recognition as well as for the Federal Republic's credibility of the so-called *Hallstein-doctrine* (Das Gupta 2014). During the period between 1950 and 1965, West German development aid was to a larger extent used to support German business activities and large industrialization projects with the aid of German firm consortia. In this realm, large-scale steelworks projects were to be showcases for western (or eastern) models of economic and political development. (Das Gupta 2004; Das Gupta 2012).

India provides a first example for the study of German companies' expectations in such developing and decolonized markets and the synchronization of such expectations with the reality on the ground when confronted with the economic, national and international political challenges.

2/ A CAUTIOUS ENTRY OF BIG GERMAN BUSINESS INTO THE MARKET IN THE WAKE OF AN ISI-ORIENTED ECONOMIC POLICY

Although Indian economic policy had envisioned a more rapid industrialization of the country together with a focus on domestic production and the propagated break with strong foreign economic influence from 1947 onwards, the Nehru-government was aware that a modernization of the Indian industry would only be possible through collaboration with foreign companies in a broad range of industrial sectors. As technical know-how and capital were scarce, India had to rely on foreign companies and foreign aid to realize its goals, thus opening up broader opportunities for foreign businesses to enter a market with tremendous growth potential and an expanding consumer base (see Haynes et al. 2010). Shortly after the war, internationally known German companies such as Bayer (chemicals) and Bosch (automobile ancillaries and parts) tried to re-establish international business links. German companies had had the experience of expropriation and losses due to war two times over a short period.

Although ideas and efforts were made by Bosch to take on business with India again from 1949 onwards, at first these efforts were on a smaller scale – financially and with regard to personnel. Many resources were bound in the reconstruction of the domestic production and the economy. Bosch had established closer business ties with India during the 1920s with the appointment of an Indian sole distributor for Bosch parts from Germany who also ran a Bosch service station, a customer service model which had been successful in Germany and in other parts of the world (RB 1 034

022, "Auslandsvertretung Indien / MICO"). Bosch, like Bayer, had contacted former German employees to gather first-hand information and evaluate the possibilities of a new market entry in India. With changed regulations, the only possibility after Indian independence was to enter into a licence agreement financial collaboration with Indian partners to set up foreign business. Hence, former and new distributors controlled by Indian business groups, together with former German and Indian personnel of Bayer and Bosch, were the logical contact points for re-entry into the market. They also provided first sources of economic information and, in the case of Indian partners, contact to actors in political decision-making, as is shown by a thorough market overview of India of Bosch (RB 1 034 023, "Auslandsvertretung in Indien / MICO). Personally, the departure for Bosch in India after 1947 and the formation of its joint-venture Motor Industries Company Ltd. was based on three individuals with different citizenships. With stronger expected regulation and "Indianisation" measures in mind, Bosch chose a local Indian industrial group with closer links to the freedom movement and the first Prime Minister of India J. Nehru. The general manager for MICO was a British citizen of German origin with close links to the German and British automobile industry and experience abroad. A leading engineer from Bosch in Germany provided the link between a newly established joint-venture and the headquarter in Germany to oversee Bosch's project in India. A former German employee of a distribution partner of Bosch in India assisted the sales development of the company strategically, as he was familiar with Bosch automobile products in India (RB 1 034 023).

The chemical firm Bayer also expected India to become a large potential market from the 1950s onwards. It had been a traditional market for Bayer exports of dyestuffs before the war. With the new political order, a rapidly growing population and ambitious targets of ISI the company expected a growing potential for its chemical and pharmaceutical business. According to a report of the board of directors, India was expected to become a "factor in the world economy" soon (BAL 059-402, Projekte Indien 1953-1958). While establishing government contacts through distribution partners' networks and visits of Bayer's director general Ulrich Haberland in 1954 to India, the firm actively promoted how its expertise and know-how could benefit the development of the envisioned fast modernization of the Indian industrial landscape, e.g. during a meeting with India's minister for industry Krishnamachari (*ibid.*). The use of old personal networks established during earlier business activities in Indian became useful. Bayer realized that success on the Indian market would take longer time and network building due to a highly regulated ISI-economy. Companies like Bayer and Bosch also realized that although there was a market for their products and core competencies these large companies had, that a one-to-one transfer of products developed in Germany for European markets would not be possible (BAL 302-235, Kurt Hansen – Indien 1956ff.).

Regarding staffing policies of German multinational companies in India, Bosch and Bayer in the 1950s and 1960s preferred to work with German engineers and commercial staff. Even with cultural clashes and complaints about qualification levels apparent in the company sources, the German headquarters were convinced that Indian calls for more Indian personnel in senior positions and trainings to transfer skills had to be satisfied on order not to cause harm to a foreign company's business in India's highly regulated environment (BAL 302-236; RB 1 034 023). Especially in the highly regulated and planned economy, capacity expansions and import licences were approved or rejected on a case-by-case basis. Thus, the integration of local senior staff and management was an important feature for success in government negotiations about production licences (NAI, Cabinet Secretariat, 8(2)-ECC/55; NAI, Commerce & Industry, 2-34/69-A.E.I.-II). Another approach made by the German chemical industry to form good political relationships with leading bureaucrats of Indian ministries to safeguard their investments was the engagement and political support of their home country's efforts concerning development assistance, as the next chapter will highlight.

3/ GERMAN BUSINESS PROJECTS AND STATE ASSISTANCE IN THE 1960S

Until the early 1950s, there hardly was any development assistance or development aid policy of the Federal Republic of Germany. Beginning in the 1950s, the FRG created a growing number of economic assistance programs to gain political influence and to secure business for German companies. Internationally, Germany was pressurized by its Western allies, foremost the United States of America, to step up assistance to developing countries like India during an intensifying 'Cold War', while the German economy had regained strength during the so-called 'Wirtschaftswunder' (McMahon 2012, 278ff.). By the end of the decade, the FRG had become one of the most important providers of international development aid funds (Lancaster 2007, pp 170–173). By 1965 the Federal Republic had become the second largest contributor of financial funds to the Aid India Consortium[3] for financing India's Five-Year Plans, overtaking the United Kingdom and providing more than Italy, France, Canada together (BAK B 102/122090).

Strategically, the Foreign Office and the Ministry for Economics tried to channel aid towards 'strategic' countries for German foreign policy and trade policy. India was placed at the forefront of 'strategic' countries (BAK B 136/2521). As an initiator of the non-alignment-movement, India became such an important factor in the foreign and foreign economic policy of Germany, as it was seen as the deciding country to upkeep and spread a western-style democracy and economic framework in Asia a. A cabinet bill of 1958 exemplifies this impression by stating that India was all the more important for German foreign policy and its Western allies "after the loss of China to the Soviet bloc" (BAK, B 102/91197).

3 The Aid India Consortium was led by the World Bank and the United States, who provided roughly 40% of the total funds of 4.5 billion US-$ between 1960 and 1965 for financing India's Five Year Plan. It was meant as an institution of multilateral aid to India of the Western countries.

Political interests were mentioned frequently here and in other sources from the German Federal Archives (BAK) as the reason to engage in a more substantial financial support for India in the 1950s. Such political motives translated into economic support for private German business. Especially larger German companies from the chemical industry had been amongst the first to gather information about the country and to establish new business contacts within India. In this way, they became important sources of knowledge when German development assistance policy from the mid-1950s onwards sought viable projects to be financed by state funds, because from the perspective of the German administration, the firms had more knowledge about economic needs and possible successes of projects. With bloc confrontation on the rise, failure of large economic projects funded by development aid were perceived to be major blows for a country's international political prestige and damaged the credibility of the respective economic and political ideology. By the end of 1958, India already was at the top of the list of recipients of German financial aid. The documents show that in 1958 future financial aid of the FRG was supposed to increase even more. The support of the government mostly came in the form of export credit guarantees for German companies and special support for large industrialization projects such as the Rourkela steel plant which was planned by a firm consortium, bringing together all major German companies of the steel sector under the leadership of Krupp (BAK B 136/2521; B 102/6403; B 102/122008; Unger 2010, pp 50-54). The support of German businesses and exports to foreign countries was in line with the minister for economics, Ludwig Erhard, who saw trade and private business initiative and investments in developing countries as the way of development assistance.

In other sectors, India was also keen on rapid industrial development and thus required assistance from outside. German companies from the chemical sector were approached by German and Indian officials to set up a large manufacturing complex for chemicals in the late 1950s (BAK B 102/122085, Vol. I-III). By that time, Bayer had re-established and strengthened business links with India again through a joint-venture called Bayer Agro Chem Ltd.[4] and had formed another joint-venture company to manufacture dyes together with its former partner Hoechst of the I.G. Farben. Within the directorate of Bayer in Germany, the support of a manufacturing complex for basic intermediate chemicals needed for the industrialization was perceived to be a good opportunity to demonstrate "good will" towards the Indian government and its ambitious industrialization program. The participation in such projects created "a good climate" for the firms' projects of Bayer Agro Chem Ltd. and Colour-Chem Ltd and it was urged to make full use of such a good climate in the course of developmental projects in the chemical sector in India (BAL 059-402, Projekte Indien 1960).

While creating a positive attitude within the higher administrative circles both in India and Germany, the company did not expect any direct monetary profits from such a developmental project. The company expected that a leading company of the size of Bayer was not able to deny its support for developmental projects that were

4 To become Bayer India Ltd. in 1963.

in line with the political strategies and goals of the federal government within the context of Cold War confrontation. Limited resources within the company for the development of foreign overseas markets made Bayer support development projects only in selected countries or regions that strategically provided a future market for Bayer products. India had been identified as one of such strategic markets with growth potential once industrialization would have picked up at an expected higher speed. (ibid.). Since Bayer had set up two joint-ventures with Indian partners after the mid-1950s where it held the majority in Bayer India Ltd., support and a good reputation within the regulating authorities was essential to expand in agrochemicals, rubber chemicals, dyes and pharmaceuticals. (BAL 318-33).

Increasing regulation within the Indian industry, especially towards foreign business after balance of payments crises and military conflicts with Pakistan and China led to internal conflicts about the decision of an early investment and the setup of a Bayer-led joint-venture in India. These political risks and conflicts severely dampened the company's future business outlook for the Indian market and its joint venture. In 1966, the CEO of Bayer Kurt Hansen stated that it would have been better not to have started business in India altogether against the background of increasing problems of the domestic Indian economy and a faster development of other markets in Europe (BAL 302-236. letter Hansen, 5th Sep 1966).

During such moments of crisis, German investors and their Indian joint ventures could regularly make use of German state assistance to finance imports needed for production and expansion. These funds were provided to India as development assistance loans and then partly and preferentially allocated to German businesses. Since the mid-1950s, German policy had been eager to attract more German private investment to the Indian subcontinent. Now, in a stagnating economy and tightening economic regulation from the mid.1960s onwards, the German administration could not deny support to private ventures. Here, not only pressure from private German business played a role. International politics and competition amongst western donor nations for influence and good development projects available to finance elicited state support. Western states were eager to support their own national industries, for example in chemicals (BAK B 102/122123, protocol of the interministerial steering committee, 3rd May 1966).

4/ THE PERCEPTION OF GERMAN COMPANIES AND THEIR ORIGIN IN INDIAN CONTEXTS OF DECOLONIZATION

Research has shown that during the first half of the 20th century the perception of German products and companies in India underwent significant changes during shorter time periods. Challenges arose through expropriation during the wars, while German companies could capture a good segment of the market during the interwar period. This was due to their ability to exploit the anti-colonialism struggle against the British and position themselves as a non-colonial alternative while British goods were boycotted. Here, the origin and the labelling of products as German could be beneficially used for business interests (Lubinski 2014; Lubinski 2015b). During the Second World War, the Nazi-regime and association with this regime posed threats to German companies' business abroad and many tried to conceal their identity abroad. In the early phase of re-establishing business links with India after 1945, evidence shows that companies were still very careful about their identity in Indian. For example, Bosch, when contacting former sole distributors in India again in July 1947, wanted to be seen as trustful businessmen only doing business and contribute to international cooperation, leaving aside political matters of the recent past (RB 1 034 023). Over the course of a few years after the war, such a more careful handling of the German identity was dropped. In 1953, Bosch was convinced that riskier investments in India would pay off in the long run, where Bosch according to company officials in Germany had "the best name". With this outlook, Bosch asked for support of German ministries to facilitate negotiations with Indian officials and to obtain German approval for a capital transfer to India to undertake first investments (RB 1 034 023).

On the political side the outlook of German companies was seen equally positive. The Foreign Office and the Chancellery pushed German companies to enter projects that were regarded as beneficial to the industrialization and hence the welfare and stability of India, both in political and economic terms. Apart from projects such as the Rourkela steel plant and a project for the manufacture of intermediate chemicals, the Foreign Office in 1960 urged Volkswagen to set up a plant to produce automobiles in India. It attached special political significance to a Volkswagen-project in India as the gain of trust in Germany associated with such a project could not be underestimated according to the state secretaries in the Foreign Office and Chancellery (BAK B 136/6578). Eventually, Volkswagen declined to undertake any project in India, as the market for small passenger cars was estimated to be too small with low levels of industrialization and related incomes (ibid.).

German foreign economic policy and diplomacy saw a specific advantage for German business in India because the country was not associated with colonialism in India, on the contrary, German companies enjoyed a good reputation due to the fact that the recovery of the German economy and industry had happened over a shorter period of time after the end of the war in 1945. Especially the large industry units were to be used by foreign policy and trade policy of the FRG as 'flagships' for Germany and its economy abroad in India. In relation to foreign companies from other origins, it seems that starting in the 1950s, German business actors could build on positive associations with their home country. A report from 1957 of the ministry of economics based on information from German diplomats in India stated that German firms had the political advantage of "being free of any colonial liability" which should be exploited both in a political and economical way (BAK B 102/91196). With this view, the government bodies had urged German companies to invest in projects in India from the mid-1950s onwards, primarily providing a guarantee for export and so-called 'commodity aid' to German companies in India to finance needed imports which had to be paid for in hard currency (BAK B 102/122123).

During the 1960s, German joint ventures in India employed a dual-sided strategy. With increasing regulation, especially of bigger and foreign firms, they highlighted their contribution to India's overall economic needs and industrial growth. At the same time, company boards in Germany and India realised that references to German origin, for example of automobile parts which were manufactured in India under a German license by a joint-venture of Indian and German partners helped sales and reputation. By the late 1960s, when expansion of production capacity was necessary to secure further growth and satisfy customer needs, Bosch and its Indian joint venture Motor Industries Company Ltd. (MICO) carefully used the mix of a German and Indian origin to negotiate expansion on the basis of Indian manufacturing and esteemed German quality in India, standards and worldwide German reputation for possible international sales of the affiliate company MICO. This was a crucial point, since Indian economic policy was eager to enhance exports from India in order to counter chronic balance of payments problems the economy faced due to costly imports of technology (Chandra, Mukherjee & Mukherjee 2008; Joshi & Little 1994).

Conclusion

For the analysed German companies India provided a promising target for trade activity and investment after the Second World War. Many big players of the German industry such as Bayer had established business links to India before the war. With a change in the political and economic system of India and an expected growing population, they expected India to become one of the most important and biggest markets in Asia in the future. The primary focus during the period of investigation was the domestic Indian market. Higher industrial and overall growth rates of the Indian economy were confirming such general expectations, that with ongoing industrialization and modernization, the Indian economy was to become a factor in the world economy.

While Five Year Plans and socialistic economic planning in general can be assumed to not have had much fit a market-oriented mindset of the West German company directorates, the analysed companies of the German large-scale industry did not retreat from the Indian market. Instead they developed strategies to cope with rising regulation of the market, barriers to entry such as production and import licenses, i.e. with the basic features of India's socialist economic model of planning. Alongside other foreign companies from West and East, companies like Bayer and Bosch were in competition to set up the first joint-venture production units within their specific business areas as the Indian government did only license the needed production capacity to one or very few firms. Thereafter the market was closed to other competitors, creating profit opportunities.

This infant-industry protection and India's need of foreign know-how and capital for industrializing the country without completely deterring its balance of payments provided the opportunity for foreign companies to step in. Bosch and Bayer could build former relationships in India and on the widely known quality of their products. A participation in industrial projects envisioned by the Indian and German governments and bureaucracy to develop the industrial capacity of the Indian economy helped to build networks within Indian administrative circles and provide showcases for the respective companies' capacities and their technological quality. Although they did not treat such activities as viable commercial projects, it allowed to demonstrate faith in Indian industrialization and its future success. In this way, they safeguarded what company boards regarded as their 'real', potentially profitable investments against stronger regulation, red tape and pressure to bring down stake holdings in their joint ventures to a minority.

This explains how investors, at the "heyday of the Cold War" in the late 1950s to mid-1960s (Engerman 2018), when the highest numbers of new Indo-German joint ventures were formed, secured their investment against broader political risks springing from geopolitical confrontation and economic ideologies they did not find on their home markets. Like when doing business in Eastern Europe and the Soviet Union, German businesses were able to cope with strongly regulated markets and operate in a socialist economic environment where actions of western private business could potentially have an explosive nature (Rudolph 2004). The analysis has shown that while firms were aware of the political Cold War that was also fought with economic weapons, they always sought to pursue their strategic business goals, even when engaging in activities that were not directly linked to their own business undertakings.

MNE like Unilever and its Indian affiliate Hindustan Lever managed to expand its Indian business and keep a majority shareholding due to a clear strategic decision and its positioning as a supplier of basic consumption goods which were not as 'political' as high-technology goods in important industries like chemicals, pharmaceuticals or computing technology (Jones 2013). This analysis has shown, for the case of Bayer and Bosch, that the companies managed to get a foothold on the market and successfully expand and even monopolise business in India because they were offering modern solutions in crucial sectors for the Indian economy – basic chemicals, agrochemicals, pharmaceuticals, diesel-engines and solutions for mobility and the transport of goods. With such offerings and investments in products that strategically provided an expanding market and the political support of German development assistance, e.g. Bosch's investment in its joint-venture MICO from 1959 until the 1980s provided a steady dividend of roughly 15% per annum to the German parent company, which was based on a near-monopoly in the area of fuel injection pumps (RB 1 017 455).

German participation in India's planned industrialization was actively encouraged until the end of the 1960s. Companies such as Bayer and Bosch positioned themselves as "German". In this regard, German firms provided a viable alternative to US-style capitalism, 'free enterprise' or British collaborators with a colonial past. The West German framework of the "social market economy" and its model of social welfare was less contested than images of liberal American capitalism within a "Socialistic Pattern of Society" that India's Prime Minister had put op on the political and social agenda.

With well-established joint ventures in the automobile and chemical sectors, the firms publicly highlighted their contribution to Indian development, called for continuous support from their home government during phases of strict economic regulation and macroeconomic crisis while attaining their first positive business results at that same time beginning in the late 1960s. Positive associations with the quality of German industrial goods served as an advantage over other competitors from other countries, despite the Nazi-regime which had only recently come to an end in 1945. The political imperative to cut ties with the former colonial power created not only created business opportunities. In a collaboration between private (big) German business, their Indian joint-ventures, foreign and economic policymakers were aiming to regain strength in the international political sphere and thus looked for speedy support of business investments in the 1960s. and political opportunities for companies as well as German foreign policy.

ARCHIVES / PRIMARY SOURCES:

Bayer Corporate Archives, Leverkusen (BAL)

Robert Bosch GmbH Archives, Stuttgart (RB)

German Federal Archives, Koblenz (BAK)

National Archives of India (NAI)

Frankfurter Allgemeine Zeitung (F.A.Z), national daily newspaper

REFERENCES

Balakrishnan, P 2007, 'The Recovery of India: Economic Growth in the Nehru Era', *Economic and Political Weekly*, vol. 42, 45-46, p. 52–66.

Bucheli, M & Kim, M 2015, 'Attacked from Both Sides. A Dynamic Model of Multinational Corporations' Strategies for Protection of Their Property Rights', *Global Strategy Journal*, vol. 5, no. 1, p. 1–26.

Casson, M & da Silva Lopes, T 2013, 'Foreign direct investment in high-risk environments: an historical perspective', *Business History*, vol. 55, no. 3, p. 375–404.

Chakravarty, S 1987, *Development planning. The Indian experience*, Clarendon, Oxford.

Chandra, B, Mukherjee, A & Mukherjee, M 2008, *India since independence*, Penguin Books, New Delhi.

Das Gupta, A 2004, *Handel, Hilfe, Hallstein-Doktrin. Die bundesdeutsche Südasienpolitik unter Adenauer und Erhard 1949 bis 1966*, Matthiesen, Husum.

Das Gupta, A 2012, 'Divided Nations: India and Germany' in *India in the world since 1947. National and transnational perspectives*, eds A Hilger & CR Unger, Peter Lang, Frankfurt am Main, p. 300–325.

Das Gupta, A 2014, 'The non-aligned and the German question' in *The non-aligned movement and the Cold War. Delhi-Bandung-Belgrade*, eds H Fischer-Tiné & N Boškovska Leimgruber, Routledge, London, New York, p. 143–160.

Decker, S 2008, 'Building Up Goodwill: British Business, Development and Economic Nationalism in Ghana and Nigeria, 1945-1977', *Enterprise & Society*, vol. 9, no. 4, p. 602–613.

Engerman, DC 2018, *The price of aid. The economic cold war in India*, Harvard University Press, Cambridge, Massachusetts.

Erhard, L 1953, *Deutschlands Rückkehr zum Weltmarkt*, Econ-Verl, Düsseldorf.

Finsterhölzl, R 2015, *Kommerzielle Werbung im kolonialen Afrika : die Werbebranche und der politische Wandel in Ghana 1930 - 1970*, Böhlau, Köln.

Fitzgerald, R 2015, *Rise of the Global Company. Multinationals and the Making of the Modern World*, Cambridge University Press, Cambridge.

Frey, M 2003, 'Control, Legitimacy, and the Securing of Interests. European Development Policy in South-East Asia from the Late Colonial Period to the Early 1960s', *Contemporary European History*, vol. 12, no. 4, p. 395–412.

Haynes, DE, McGowan, A, Roy, T & Yanagisawa, H (eds.) 2010, *Towards a history of consumption in South Asia*, Oxford University Press, New Delhi.

Johanson, J & Vahlne, J-E 2009, 'The Uppsala internationalization process model revisited. From liability of foreignness to liability of outsidership', *Journal of international business studies*, vol. 40, no. 9, p. 1411–1431.

Jones, G 2013, 'Learning to live with governments: Unilever in India and Turkey, 1950-1980' in *Entrepreneurship and multinationals. Global business and the making of the modern world*, ed G Jones, Cheltenham, p. 165–189.

Jones, G & Lubinski, C 2012, 'Managing political risk in global business. Beiersdorf 1914 - 1990', *Enterprise & Society*, vol. 13, no. 1, p. 85–119.

Joshi, V & Little, IMD 1994, *India - Macroeconomics and political economy, 1964-1991,* Washington, D.C.

Kleinschmidt, C & Ziegler, D (eds.) 2018, *Dekolonisierungsgewinner. Deutsche Außenpolitik und Außenwirtschaftsbeziehungen im Zeitalter des Kalten Krieges,* De Gruyter Oldenbourg, Berlin, Boston.

Kobrak, C & Wüstenhagen, J 2006, 'International investment and Nazi politics: The cloaking of German assets abroad, 1936–1945', *Business History*, vol. 48, no. 3, p. 399–427.

Lancaster, C 2007, *Foreign aid. Diplomacy, development, domestic politics,* Univ. of Chicago Press, Chicago, Ill.

Lubinski, C 2014, 'Liability of Foreignness in Historical Context: German Business in Preindependence India (1880-1940)', *Enterprise & Society*, vol. 15, no. 4, p. 722–758.

Lubinski, C 2015a, 'Global Trade and Indian Politics: The German Dye Business in India before 1947', *Business History Review*, vol. 89, no. 03, p. 503–530.

Lubinski, C 2015b, 'Local responsiveness in distant markets: Western gramophone companies in India before World War I', *Management & Organizational History*, vol. 10, no. 2, p. 170–188.

Lubinski, C, Giacomin, V & Schnitzer, K 2018, 'Internment as a business challenge. Political risk management and German multinationals in Colonial India (1914–1947)', *Business History*, vol. 11, no. 2, p. 1–26.

McMahon, RJ 2012, 'On the periphery of a global conflict: India and the cold war, 1947-1991' in *India in the world since 1947. National and transnational perspectives,* eds A Hilger & CR Unger, Peter Lang, Frankfurt am Main, p. 276–299.

Nellißen, FJ 1997, *Das Mannesmann-Engagement in Brasilien von 1892 bis 1995. Evolutionspfade internationaler Unternehmenstätigkeit aus wirtschaftshistorischer Sicht.* Zugl.: Diss., Beck, München.

Patnaik, P 2015, 'The Nehru–Mahalanobis Strategy', *Social Scientist*, vol. 43, 3/4, p. 3–10.

Roy, T 2017, 'The Origins of Import Substituting Industrialization in India', *Economic History of Developing Regions*, vol. 32, no. 1, p. 71–95.

Rudolph, K 2004, ‚Politisches Marketing im Kalten Krieg. Die westdeutschen Unternehmer in den Ost-West Beziehungen nach 1945' in *Marketing. historische Aspekte der Wettbewerbs- und Absatzpolitik,* eds C Kleinschmidt & F Triebel, Klartext-Verl, Essen, p. 207–220.

Schröter, HG 1992, ‚Außenwirtschaft im Boom: Direktinvestitionen bundesdeutscher Unternehmen im Ausland 1950-1975' in *Der Boom 1948 - 1973: gesellschaftliche und wirtschaftliche Folgen in der Bundesrepublik Deutschland und in Europa,* ed H Kaelble, Westdt. Verl, Opladen, p. 82–106.

Schröter, HG 2001, ‚Die Auslandsinvestitionen der deutschen chemischen Industrie 1930 bis 1965', *Zeitschrift für Unternehmensgeschichte*, vol. 46, no. 2, p. 182–197.

Stevens, CE & Shenkar, O 2012, 'The liability of home: institutional friction and firm disadvantage abroad' in *Institutional theory in international business and management,* eds. L Tihanyi, TM. Devinney & T Pedersen, Emerald, Bingley, p. 127–148.

Unger, CR 2008, ‚Rourkela, ein Stahlwerk im Dschungel. Industrialisierung, Modernisierung und Entwicklungshilfe im Kontext von Dekolonisation und Kaltem Krieg (1950 - 1970)', *Archiv für Sozialgeschichte*, vol. 48, p. 367–388.

Unger, CR 2010, 'Industrialization vs. Agrarian Reform: West German Modernization Policies in India in the 1950s and 1960s', *Journal of modern European history*, vol. 8, no. 1, p. 47–65.

Unger, CR 2015, *Entwicklungspfade in Indien. Eine internationale Geschichte 1947-1980,* Wallstein, Göttingen.

Westad, OA 2005, *The global Cold War. Third world interventions and the making of our times,* Cambridge University Press, Cambridge, New York.

Zaheer, S 1995, 'Overcoming the liability of foreignness', *Academy of Management Journal*, vol. 38, no. 2, p. 341–363.

PARTIE 3

Autres pays émergents

PART 3

Other emerging nations

Le développement économique péruvien durant les années 1950 et 1960 : distinguer deux modèles ?

Getsiva Cayo Durand de Geist[1]
Sorbonne université

Introduction

Depuis la crise de 1930, deux modèles de développement se sont confrontés en Amérique latine : le modèle primo-exportateur (guidé par le libéralisme) et l'industrialisation par substitution d'importations (ISI[2]). En prenant en compte les conditions internes et externes au développement, cette étude cherche à expliquer que les gouvernements péruviens n'ont pas été partisans d'un seul modèle de développement[3]. L'influence du modèle primo-exportateur a été interprétée comme un modèle orienté « vers l'extérieur », et celle du modèle ISI « vers l'intérieur ». Ce dernier modèle ne surgit pas en tant qu'idéologie, mais plutôt comme une nécessité[4].

Bien que la théorie de la dépendance dégagée par l'économiste argentin Raúl Prebisch ait été l'une des plus adoptées à l'époque, il ne s'agit pas d'une règle générale. L'Argentine, le Brésil, le Mexique, le Chili, la Colombie et l'Uruguay comportent des exemples classiques des pays latino-américains tournés « vers l'intérieur ». Cependant, le Pérou demeurait plutôt un partisan du modèle « vers l'extérieur[5] ». Il a fallu attendre les années 1960 pour témoigner de l'impact de la pensée de Prebisch[6].

1 Docteure en Histoire, chercheuse associée à l'UMR 8596 Centre Roland Mousnier de Sorbonne-Université, getsiva.cayo@posteo.de

2 Voir : Santos M. Ruesga et Julimar da Silva Bichara, *Modelos de desarrollo económico en América Latina: Desequilibrio externo y concentración de riqueza.* Madrid/Barcelona, M. Pons, Ediciones Jurídicas y Sociales S.A., 2005. Voir aussi : Osvaldo Sunkel, *El subdesarrollo latinoamericano y la teoría del desarrollo*, México, Siglo XXI Editores, Vigésima Edición, 1986, p. 73-78.

3 Chapitre II : El desarrollo económico y social en el Perú, Carlos Parodis Trece, *Perú, 1960-2000: políticas económicas y sociales en entornos cambiantes*, Lima, Universidad del Pacífico, 2000, p. 55-71.

4 Victor Bulmer-Thomas, *La historia económica de América Latina desde la independencia*, 2da Edición, México : FCE, 2010, p. 311-331.

5 Partie IV : El crecimiento orientado por las exportaciones laissez-faire : desilusión y reacción (1948-1977). Rosemary Thorp et Geoffrey Bertram, *Perú 1980-1977. Crecimiento y políticas en una economía abierta*, Lima, Universidad del Pacífico, 2013, p. 259-397.

6 Voir : Rigoberto García, F. Cordero et A. Izquierdo, *Economía y geografía del desarrollo en América Latina*, México, Fondo de Cultura Económica, 1987.

Quelle a été la politique économique préconisée au Pérou durant les années 1950 et 1960 ? Quels ont été les modèles de développement mis en œuvre et quels ont été leurs résultats? Pour dégager cette problématique, une approche de l'économie péruvienne sera effectuée en deux étapes. Tout d'abord, la politique économique péruvienne sera examinée sous le prisme de Rostow et ensuite sous celui de Prebisch[7]. Il s'agit de montrer les ambitions des modèles adoptés par les gouvernements en tenant compte de leurs limites et de leurs contradictions.

1/ UN PARTISAN DE ROSTOW ? LE PÉROU À LA RECHERCHE DU DÉCOLLAGE ÉCONOMIQUE

> « Il ne fait pas de doute que le Pérou bénéficie en Amérique du Sud d'une situation économique et financière à bien des égards privilégiée, qui a déjà des offres de crédits à des conditions surprenantes[8] ».

Les rapports d'études économiques rédigés par les diplomates français permettent de se faire une idée de l'image du Pérou à l'international au cours des années 1950 et 1960. Après la Seconde Guerre mondiale, les puissances économiques occidentales ont préconisé le libéralisme, dont le Pérou deviendra l'un des meilleurs partisans en Amérique latine. Le militaire Manuel Odría et son successeur Manuel Prado ont été convaincus que la meilleure voie de développement économique pour le Pérou était le libéralisme. Considéré comme un État « peu développé », mais libéral à la fois, le Pérou attirait l'attention des investisseurs étrangers tant du secteur public que privé. Il s'agissait d'un partenaire économique au marché ouvert et d'accès facile. Le taux de croissance du PIB du Pérou entre 1950 et 1960 s'est accru à un rythme de 5,5 % par an[9]. En conséquence, le Pérou était un pays attractif aux yeux des investisseurs étrangers et la concurrence ne fera que s'accroître.

Hernando de Soto affirme que, dès la Seconde Guerre mondiale, le Pérou a vécu les plus grandes transformations de son histoire depuis l'Indépendance. Ces transformations ont eu lieu au sein d'une politique économique imprécise et temporaire[10]. À la fin de 1945, le Pérou a confirmé son adhésion aux accords de Bretton Woods formalisant son entrée au sein du système multilatéral[11]. Même si, entre 1945 et 1948, le modèle primo-exportateur fut réformé par des politiques inspirées par le modèle ISI durant le gouvernement de José Luis Bustamante y Rivero, une crise économique, politique et sociale a changé la donne[12]. Le « pendule incertain » au sein de la vie politique de

7 Les ouvrages consultées les plus importantes de ces deux auteurs sont : W.W. Rostow, *Les étapes de la croissance économique*, Paris, Éditions du Seuil, 1960. Raúl Prebisch, *The economic development of Latin America and its principal problems*, New York, United Nations, Department of economic affairs, 1950.

8 « Pérou. Projets d'assurance-crédit », lettre n° 131, Ambassade de France en République argentine, B0061 432/1, Archives CAEF, Buenos Aires, 17 avril 1964, p. 2.

9 Capítulo I : Comportamiento de la economía peruana 1950-2015. *Panorama de la Economía Peruana 1950-2015*, Lima, INEI, 2016, p. 17-18.

10 Hernando de Soto, *L'autre sentier. La révolution informelle dans le tiers monde*, Paris, La Découverte, 1994, p. 11.

11 Teodoro Hampe Martínez, *El Banco Central de Reserva y la economía peruana (1922-1980)*, Lima, Banco Central de Reserva del Perú, Fondo Editorial,1995, p. 65-70.

12 « Note sommaire sur la situation financière du Pérou », Boîte 49, Finances du Pérou, Archives du Crédit Lyonnais, 1949, p. 1.

ce pays n'a pas uniquement continué à osciller au cours de la période étudiée, mais il s'est radicalisé[13].

Durant le gouvernement du dictateur Manuel Odría (1948-1956), la mission nord-américaine nommée « Mission Klein » (1949) a posé les bases d'une politique économique libérale progressive au Pérou en resserrant les relations avec les États-Unis. Dès lors, la suppression du contrôle des prix et du régime des changes a établi l'économie de marché[14]. La décision de mettre fin au contrôle des changes et du commerce patronnée en 1945 s'est consolidée en 1949 suite à la loi n° 11208, ce qui a donné lieu à une nouvelle politique de libéralisation économique[15]. Face aux déficits fiscaux, les dépenses publiques ont été réduites. L'investissement privé a été encouragé par la promulgation de nouvelles lois concernant les secteurs minier et pétrolier. Dès 1950, un changement perceptible s'est traduit par un excédent fiscal, une balance commerciale positive et la réduction de l'inflation.

Suite au coup d'État militaire de droite, le président Odría a montré que le Pérou préférait devenir un disciple du modèle libéral, voire de l' « américanisation[16] ». En suivant l'exemple des États-Unis et de pays européens d'occident, « les libéralismes » ont trouvé un écho incontestable[17]. Le Pérou est devenu le 35e membre du GATT en octobre 1951 lors du *Torquay Round* et a mis en place les réductions des tarifs douaniers exigées[18]. Les conditions pour les exportateurs de coton et de sucre sont devenues favorables. À Lima, une classe moyenne montante représentée par des ingénieurs, des techniciens et des administrateurs en a été la bénéficiaire. Les dépenses publiques ont entraîné un *boom* de la construction qui a fourni de la main-d'œuvre non qualifiée. Mais les conditions de vie des indigènes et des paysans n'ont pas fait partie de la politique de développement instaurée par M. Odría et la restauration de l'oligarchie péruvienne s'est installée[19].

En outre, les conditions internes des années cinquante ont été propices au développement du commerce extérieur. Un changement fondamental dans la politique commerciale et monétaire du pays en est la clef. Le Pérou a été l'un des pays latino-américains qui ont suivi les politiques les plus libérales en matière de commerce extérieur, d'où la dynamique de son commerce extérieur. Les exportations minières de grande envergure et l'élargissement de ses installations ont subi une augmentation substantielle d'investissements. La guerre de Corée (1950-1953) a favorisé les prix des produits agricoles et miniers et par rapport aux années 1940, les prix d'exportation ont doublé[20]. La « prospérité mondiale » de 1955 a eu un écho au Pérou. Les exportations

13 Le terme « pendule incertain » a été traduit de l'espagnol « péndulo incierto » employé par l'historien A. Flores Galindo. Voir : Alberto Flores Galindo, *La tradición autoritaria: violencia y democracia en el Perú*. Lima, APRODEH, 1999.

14 Voir: Capítulo VII : El informe presentado por la Misión Klein al Perú. Guillermo W. Coloma Elías, *El Perú a mediados del siglo XX*, Lima, Editor José Coloma Gygax/Instituto Latinoamericano de Cultura y Desarrollo, 2008.

15 Teodoro Hampe Martínez, *El Banco Central de Reserva y la economía peruana (1922-1980), op. cit.*, p. 77.

16 Voir : María Inés Barbero et Andrés Martín Regalsky. *Americanización: Estados Unidos y América Latina en el siglo XX: transferencias económicas, tecnológicas y culturales.* Universidad Nacional de Tres de Febrero, 2014.

17 À l'égard du libéralisme européen voir : Dominique Barjot, Olivier Dard, Fréderic Fogacci et Jérôme Grondeux, *Histoire de l'Europe libérale. Libéraux et libéralisme en Europe XVIIIe - XXIe siècle*, Paris, Nouveau Monde Éditions, 2016.

18 César Guzmán-Barrón, « Las nuevas reglas del GATT y la Organización Mundial de Comercio », *Agenda Internacional*, PUCP, n° 1, vol.1, 1998, p. 101-102.

19 Pour une étude plus approfondie sur les conditions sociales péruviennes, voir : François Bourricaud, *Pouvoir et société dans le Pérou contemporain*, Paris, Presses de Sciences Po (P.F.N.S.P.), 1967.

20 Winston Temple Seminario, *Guía Económica del Perú*, Lima, Instituto Peruano de Administración de Empresas (IPAE), 1968, p. 226.

se sont accrues de 10 % et les importations de 20 % par rapport à l'année précédente. L'acquisition de machines, d'équipements et de fournitures à la production sont devenues une priorité[21]. Néanmoins, les problèmes économiques accumulés par les dépenses publiques excessives et l'accroissement de l'endettement externe durant le gouvernement d'Odría n'ont pas tardé à se déclarer.

En 1956, Manuel Prado Ugarteche (1889-1967) a été élu démocratiquement à la présidence. La Banque centrale de réserve du Pérou (BCRP) a prôné la nécessité de mettre en place une politique d'ajustement monétaire, fiscale et de crédits. Mais les dépenses publiques n'ont pas été limitées. L'inflation a persisté, le déficit fiscal s'est accru et une situation d'instabilité s'est imposée. En 1958, la situation interne du pays était préoccupante et l'activité économique a subi une contraction. La production nationale a pâti d'une décroissance importante suite aux grèves qui ont causé la paralysie des industries. Seules les industries de la pêche, du café et l'industrie manufacturière n'ont pas été affectées[22]. Durant la présidence de M. Prado, les travaux publics ont continué à faire fondamentalement partie du programme de développement économique[23]. Le modèle de développement économique préconisé était orienté « vers l'extérieur ». Cependant, quelques mesures protectionnistes ont été envisagées. En juin 1958, le Comité d'intersession du GATT a examiné une demande faite par le gouvernement péruvien afin d'augmenter ses droits de douane pendant une période de trois ans, mais le GATT ne lui donna pas son accord[24].

En 1959, des modifications financières et monétaires ont été menées par l'un des principaux opposants du régime, devenu Premier Ministre : Pedro Beltrán. La loi de promotion industrielle n° 13270 a été promulguée[25]. Le déséquilibre de la balance des paiements a été corrigé et la hausse du coût de la vie contrôlée. Pour ce faire, des crédits de stabilisation ont été octroyés par le BCRP, le FMI, le Trésor américain et d'autres entités financières privées. En 1959, les exportations ont atteint une croissance annuelle de 7,8 % et en 1961 de 14,5 %. Le *boom* des produits de la pêche et la récupération des produits miniers ont été à la base de cette réussite. Il faut souligner que le Pérou était le premier exportateur mondial de farine de poisson. Les capitaux étrangers ont permis de récupérer les importations qui, en 1961, se sont accrues de 25 %, signe d'une activité économique majeure. Les biens de capitaux ont ainsi fait leur entrée sous forme d'investissement direct[26].

Le libéralisme édifié par ces deux présidents a connu ses limites. Les gouvernements conservateurs de Messieurs Odría et Prado se sont intéressés au développement économique, mais sans prendre en compte la dépendance croissante envers l'extérieur. L'investissement étranger était alors perçu comme la base de la modernisation du pays. Les entreprises privées ont été privilégiées. Cependant, les industries minière

21 Teodoro Hampe Martínez, *El Banco Central de Reserva y la economía peruana (1922-1980), op. cit.*, p. 88-91.

22 *Ibid.*, p. 93-96.

23 Annexe I : « Exposé du Général Romero Pardo », lettre n° 28, Série B-Amérique (1952-1963), Pérou (36), 13.9.1. Questions économiques (1952-1957), AMAE, Lima, 15 octobre 1957, p. 2-4.

24 « Du Comité d'intersession du GATT. Requête du Pérou », lettre N° 205, Direction des Finances Extérieures, Ministère des Finances, B-0061430/1, Archives CAEF, Paris, 9 juin 1958, p. 1.

25 En 1959, la loi sur la promotion industrielle favorisait l'importation de machines et autres biens de production dans le but de développer l'industrie de substitution, mais cette politique ne profitait qu'aux entreprises étrangères déjà en place. Cette loi arriva trente ans trop tard par rapport aux autres pays d'Amérique latine. Daniel Gilbert, *Le Pérou*, Paris, Karthala, 1997, p. 114.

26 Teodoro Hampe Martínez, *El Banco Central de Reserva y la economía peruana (1922-1980), op. cit.*, p. 97-100.

et pétrolière étaient contrôlées par des sociétés nord-américaines[27]. Si le début du démarrage économique péruvien aurait dû concerner « l'action d'un stimulus » sur des techniques nouvelles, la mise en marche des programmes de modernisation, la création de nouvelles industries, les termes de l'échange favorables et l'investissement direct extérieur, il est possible d'admettre que le Pérou était à la recherche de son décollage économique. Néanmoins, l'organisation économique de la société n'a évoluée que lentement. La croissance économique était stable, mais une transformation de l'économie n'a pas pu être accomplie avec des mesures strictement libérales.

2/ LA MONTÉE DES POLITIQUES DÉVELOPPEMENTISTES AU PÉROU : L'IMPACT DE LA PENSÉE DE PREBISCH

Le Pérou peut être considéré comme un pays en voie de développement qui s'est efforcé de faire décoller son économie en prenant comme fil conducteur la théorie de la modernisation, notamment entre 1948 et 1958. Cependant, Julio Cotler a constaté que l'accumulation des problèmes socio-économiques a éclaté lors de la seconde moitié des années cinquante. Le caractère contradictoire et anachronique de la société péruvienne s'est ainsi manifesté avec rudesse. Les changements structurels de l'organisation du travail, les vagues d'immigration de la population de la montagne (*sierra*) vers la côte, l'affluence de la population et le chômage à Lima, la négligence de l'éducation étatique de qualité, ont été quelques-uns des symptômes d'une société en mutation. La modernité et la croissance économique envisagées n'ont pas été menées sans une transformation sociale et politique[28].

Les conséquences de la modernisation des industries et des techniques péruviennes ont provoqué un impact dans la société péruvienne. Cette société en mutation n'a joui que partiellement des avantages du bonheur économique. La population indigène originaire de la montagne et de la forêt y était la moins favorisée. En revanche, l'oligarchie de la capitale et de certaines villes de la côte (Trujillo, Chimbote) a bénéficié d'un impact urbanistique et industriel exceptionnel. Ainsi, pendant que la population de la côte jouissait des avantages apportés par les capitaux étrangers, les habitants des villes de la *sierra* et de la *selva* ont préféré soit se rendre à Lima, soit s'isoler davantage[29].

Alors que le Pérou était reconnu pour le bon déroulement de ses activités économiques durant les décennies 1950 et 1960, les mécontentements sociaux ont persisté. La société péruvienne était composée de classes sociales très marquées[30]. Une société segmentée, fragmentée, confrontée et discriminée dans laquelle régnaient les grands écarts de revenus et l'hétérogénéité culturelle. La complexité de l'héritage culturel du Pérou a donné naissance à une société qualifiée par Arthur Lewis de « dualiste[31] ».

27 John Sheahan, *La economía peruana desde 1950: buscando una sociedad mejor*, Lima, Instituto de Estudios peruanos, vol. 19, 2001, p. 33.

28 Julio Cotler, *Clases, estado y nación en el Perú*, Lima, Instituto de estudios peruanos, vol. 17, 2005, p. 47.

29 François Bourricaud, *Pouvoir et société dans le Pérou contemporain*, Paris, Presses de Sciences Po (P.F.N.S.P.), 1967, p. 4.

30 « Pérou, Analyse du risque », Boîte 49, Archives du Crédit Lyonnais, janvier 1981, p. 4.

31 Arthur W. Lewis, « Economic development with unlimited supplies of labour ». *The Manchester School*, n° 2, vol. 22, 1954, p. 139-191.

Ce dualisme expliquait l'existence de deux secteurs contrastés au sein de la population péruvienne. Le secteur « moderne et dynamique » cohabitait avec un « secteur traditionnel dépourvu de ressources[32] ».

L'épuisement du modèle orienté « vers l'extérieur » s'est manifesté depuis les années 1958-1959, mais il a été plus net depuis le début de 1960. Jusqu'à cette date, le Pérou était un paradis pour les partisans du libre-échange en Amérique latine. Entre 1961 et 1962, la junte militaire dirigée par Pérez Godoy a mis en place un système de planification avec des conseillers locaux et régionaux dans les différents ministères. L'Institut National de la Planification (INP), le Conseil national pour le développement économique et le Conseil consultatif de planification ont été ainsi créés. La junte militaire a mis en place des réformes importantes : réduction des impôts sur les bénéfices, autorisation d'augmenter le taux d'amortissement annuel, garanties pour les entreprises étrangères (notamment intéressées par le développement des mines), etc.[33]. Même si les militaires avaient fait un coup d'État lors de la dernière année du gouvernement de Manuel Prado, le modèle « vers l'extérieur » y était toujours préconisé. Le système libéral adopté par les gouvernements péruviens entre 1948 et 1962 a enregistré une croissance économique assez stable, mais inégale.

La création d'un nouveau parti, Acción Popular, dirigé par Fernando Belaúnde Terry a fait de ce personnage un nouvel acteur politique. En effet, il a repris un programme nationaliste autrefois proposé par Haya de la Torre au sein de l'Alliance Populaire Révolutionnaire Américaine (A.P.R.A.[34]). Les politiques guidées par le modèle « vers l'extérieur » étaient de plus en plus combinées avec le modèle orienté « vers l'intérieur ». Durant le gouvernement de Belaúnde (1963-1968), le développement économique et social du Pérou s'est focalisé sur un programme ambitieux de travaux publics afin de réussir le décollage économique tant attendu. Ce président de centre-gauche a mis en œuvre plus de protection à l'industrie locale sans l'accord du GATT[35]. Un décret entré en vigueur en novembre 1963 a promulgué la loi n° 14729 créant de nouvelles taxes et de nouveaux droits d'importation (10 % CIF). Cette loi a été très critiquée et remise en question à l'international, mais aussi par certains organismes locaux au Pérou[36].

Le commerce extérieur, était pour le Pérou, l'un de facteurs les plus importants en vue du développement de son économie. Les échanges du Pérou avec l'extérieur se sont développés rapidement et régulièrement pendant la période 1950-1963. L'année 1963 a été considérée comme l'année « record » des chiffres d'affaires par rapport aux échanges commerciales. Ainsi, il a été constaté que durant la période 1950-1963,

32 « Pérou, Analyse du risque », Boîte 49, Archives du Crédit Lyonnais, janvier 1981, p. 4.

33 Ces bureaux étaient communs à ceux des systèmes de planification dans de nombreux autres pays d'Amérique latine. Ils ont été créés à la suite d'une pression des créditeurs tels que l'USAID et la BIRD au sein de l'Alliance pour le progrès. Il ne s'agissait pas d'une initiative de l'État péruvien, mais plutôt d'une obligation pour avoir reçu « l'aide au développement » puis des « projets de développement ». Victor Alba, *Peru*, Westview Press, Boulder, Colorado, 1977, p. 127. Voir aussi : Fitzgerald, E.V.K., *The State and Economic development. Peru since 1968*, Department of Applied Economics, London-New York-Melbourne, University of Cambridge, 1976, p. 78.

34 Julio Cotler, *Clases, estado y nación en el Perú*, *op. cit.*, p. 20-21.

35 « Nouvelles taxes sur les transactions et nouveaux droits d'importations », note n° 137, Ambassade de France au Pérou, B-0061430/1, Archives CAEF, Pérou, 13 décembre 1963, p. 1.

36 « Loi n° 14729 créant de nouvelles taxes et de nouveaux droit d'importation » Lettre N° 003, Ambassade de France au Pérou, B-0061430/1, Archives CAEF, Lima, 3 janvier 1964, p. 1-2.

les ventes du Pérou à l'étranger ont augmenté de 179,6% et ses achats de 198,7%[37]. De même, le Pérou était un grand récepteur de flux d'investissements variables et incertains, surtout après 1945. En 1924, les entreprises nord-américaines ont investi 124 millions de dollars au Pérou, mais en 1936 ce chiffre est tombé à 96 millions. Toutefois, ces investissements ont progressivement augmenté jusqu'à atteindre 295 millions de dollars en 1950 et 605 millions en 1967. À cette date, l'investissement des entreprises nord-américaines au Pérou représentait 5,2 % de tous les investissements américains à l'étranger. Des accords ont également été signés avec d'autres pays pour des investissements dans les entreprises péruviennes[38].

Les risques de l'investissement étranger ont fait l'objet d'un débat animé pendant près d'un demi-siècle au Pérou. D'une manière générale, ceux qui soutenaient l'investissement pensaient que les entreprises étrangères octroyaient de meilleurs salaires. Ces entreprises créaient des industries qui encourageaient le capital national et contribuaient généralement à la modernisation du pays. Les opposants assuraient que les entreprises privées entraînaient la discrimination des salaires et du traitement entre Péruviens et étrangers, en particulier dans le domaine des matières premières qui touchaient les intérêts d'autres pays et non pas ceux du Pérou, provoquant une politique nationale d'intervention. Malgré cette controverse, l'investissement américain a représenté 67,5 % du total de l'investissement étranger au Pérou entre 1950 et 1967[39]. À partir de 1960, la dynamique commerciale péruvienne s'est accélérée. La diversification des produits d'exportation a favorisé ce démarrage. L'expansion et la stabilité de l'économie péruvienne enregistrées entre 1960 et 1968 étaient fondées sur l'essor des exportations[40].

En effet, le modèle primo-exportateur et le modèle ISI n'ont pas été des stratégies économiques exclusives à suivre. Les gouvernements péruviens ont combiné et fusionné ces deux voies au fur et à mesure des conditions économiques, politiques et sociales présentées. Ainsi, Belaúnde a fondé les bases de la mise en œuvre de la réforme agraire. Les problèmes sociaux concernant la pauvreté et la classe moyenne marginale ont influencé son programme, qui donne la priorité aux affaires sociales internes. Les facteurs économiques ont cependant été négligés, car le financement de tels projets n'avait pas été prévu. La chute des prix internationaux, l'endettement extérieur accru, la crise de l'industrie de la pêche et la hausse des coûts de la vie ont remis en question le fonctionnement d'un modèle mixte[41]. Les promesses inachevées du président Belaúnde et le scandale d'un contrat de concession avec la société nord-américaine International Petroleum Company (IPC) ont consolidé un scénario propice à la naissance d'un autre coup d'État. Au début orienté « vers l'intérieur », il s'est finalement de plus en plus incliné « vers l'extérieur ». Certes, l'instabilité de la politique interne a joué en défaveur du développement économique péruvien.

37 « Le commerce extérieur péruvien », note n° 161, Ambassade de France au Pérou, B-0061430/1, Archives CAEF, Lima, mai, 1964, p. 1.

38 Victor Alba, *Peru*, Boulder, Colorado, Westview Press, 1977, p. 129.

39 Les partisans de la pensée « communiste » au Pérou se sont fortement opposés aux concessions des sociétés étrangères. Ils croyaient certainement que les entreprises américaines étaient les responsables du retard d'un pays. L'idée de « nationalisation » a été ainsi une lutte pour retrouver et redonner la première place au même pays qui s'est formé par des capitaux étrangers depuis l'époque coloniale. *Ibid.*, p. 127-130.

40 Winston Temple Seminario, *Guía Económica del Perú, op. cit.*, p. 225.

41 Teodoro Hampe Martínez, *El Banco Central de Reserva y la economía peruana (1922-1980), op. cit.*, p. 103-109.

De même, il faut prendre conscience de l'évolution d'une société très hiérarchisée et même raciste envers elle-même. La mauvaise distribution des revenus a créé un fossé de plus en plus profond entre les Péruviens. Les inégalités y étaient extrêmes. Les richesses naturelles ont donné naissance à une classe privilégiée qui a pris place à côté de la ploutocratie métisse déjà existante. Une classe moyenne essentiellement composée de métis s'est formée au fil des années, notamment après la Seconde Guerre mondiale. Le bien-être au Pérou était loin d'être homogène. En 1967, 46 % de la population faisait partie de la grande masse des indigènes considérée comme très pauvre, marginale et analphabète[42].

En octobre 1968 a eu lieu le coup d'État réformiste mené par un groupe d'officiers dirigés par le général Juan Velasco Alvarado. Le but était d'appliquer une doctrine de « progrès social et de développement intégral, nationaliste et réformiste ». Cette doctrine était influencée par les thèses de la CEPAL à propos de la dépendance et du sous-développement (modèle ISI). Quelques jours plus tard, J. Velasco nationalisait l'International Petroleum Company (IPC), filiale de la Standard Oil (New Jersey). Cette société nord-américaine exploitait le pétrole péruvien. Le projet suivant était la réforme agraire, qui engendra de nombreuses critiques. Cette réforme, assez mal menée, a mis fin aux latifundios et a exproprié les grands propriétaires étrangers[43].

La révolution péruvienne dirigée par le Général Velasco a voulu se montrer comme une « troisième voie : ni capitaliste, ni communiste[44] ». La première décision importante de la junte, qui vient de déposer le président Belaúnde, s'est focalisée sur la raffinerie de Talara et les gisements appartenant à l'IPC. La décision prise a été de nationaliser, sans indemnisation, les biens de cette compagnie nord-américaine. Puis le gouvernement a proclamé la date de l'occupation de Talara « Jour de la dignité nationale ». Cette expérience péruvienne a été autoproclamée comme un socialisme révolutionnaire[45]. Toutefois, les changements conduits par le dictateur Velasco Alvarado ont été très débattus[46].

Avant le coup d'État militaire de 1968, le gouvernement avait entamé des négociations à propos du refinancement de la dette extérieure. Devant l'impossibilité d'ignorer les obligations contractées par des crédits étrangers au cours d'une longue période, la junte militaire a ouvert des négociations avec les pays créanciers, en particulier les États-Unis, l'Allemagne de l'Ouest, la France et la Grande-Bretagne. À cette époque, le Pérou subissait un problème d'inflation, mais sa situation était moins grave que celle d'autres pays d'Amérique latine. Le coût de la vie avait augmenté, passant de l'indice 100 en 1958 à 190 en 1965, à 230 en 1970 et à 270 en 1975[47].

Cette réforme était considérée comme une opération de rationalisation économique pour permettre de fournir, entre autres, les capitaux nécessaires à l'industrialisation rapide du pays. L'ambiguïté du gouvernement révolutionnaire était questionnable. En

42 « Situation économique du Pérou. Relations commerciales franco-péruviennes », lettre n° 1054, Boîte 54915, CAEF, 6 juillet 1967, p. 5.

43 Alain Rouquié, *L'État militaire en Amérique latine*, Paris, Éditions du Seuil, 1982, p. 386.

44 Julio Cotler, *Clases, estado y nación en el Perú, op. cit.*, p. 24. Voir aussi : Jaroslav Vanek, « La Tercera Vía del Presidente Velasco », *Socialismo y Participación*, n° 5, 1978.

45 Alain Rouquié, *L'État militaire en Amérique latine, op. cit.*, p. 381.

46 Julio Cotler, *Clases, estado y nación en el Perú, op. cit.*, p. 25.

47 Victor Alba, *Peru, op. cit.*, p. 121.

effet, il proclamait la limite de la dépendance économique extérieure, mais en même temps il invitait les capitaux étrangers à exploiter les ressources naturelles du pays. Dès 1969, un calendrier d'exploitation rigoureux et un cahier des charges précis ont été imposés aux sociétés étrangères sous peine de perdre leurs droits. C'est ainsi que les grandes sociétés ont rendu leurs concessions inexploitées à l'État[48].

Entre 1968 et 1974, le gouvernement de la junte militaire avait consacré 40 % des recettes de l'État aux dépenses militaires. Le montant de la dette extérieure avait triplé[49]. Malgré l'accroissement de la dette, les réalisations du gouvernement révolutionnaire ont été considérables : réforme foncière radicale, réorganisation de l'industrie de la pêche, élimination du contrôle étranger sur les exportations, les finances et l'industrie lourde, renégociation des conditions de nouveaux investissements étrangers, création d'entreprises d'État dynamiques et début d'un ambitieux processus d'industrialisation comprennent quelques exemples positifs[50]. Néanmoins, la révolution péruvienne initiée en 1968 a plutôt échouée[51]. La politique économique menée par Velasco dirigée sur le modèle « vers l'intérieur » qui combinait politiques libérales n'a pas amélioré la structure économique du pays.

Le Pérou était un pays en développement hautement dépendant de l'extérieur, mais à la recherche de son articulation économique. Pour Efraín Gonzales, entre 1950 et 2007, l'histoire économique péruvienne avait un caractère « incomplet ». Depuis 1950, les réformes de la structure de production n'ont pas varié. L'exportation des matières premières était la base « inamovible » de l'économie péruvienne. Selon E. Gonzales, les transformations de la structure productive achevées par le gouvernement militaire de 1969 à 1980 sont à la base de la décennie perdue des années 1980[52]. L'analyse de la structure de l'économie a confirmé deux tendances opposées, mais aucune parmi elles ne se montra efficace. Face à la complexité de ses problèmes, l'économie péruvienne est toujours à la recherche de nouvelles propositions.

Conclusions

Les politiques mises en place par les gouvernements péruviens dirigés par le libéralisme et l'ISI ont été contrastées, mais pas totalement opposées. Depuis la fin des années cinquante, des politiques protectionnistes ont été mises en œuvre, révélant les limites de la tendance « vers l'extérieur ». Ces deux stratégies économiques ont réussi à cohabiter ensemble sans provoquer de rupture majeure.

Que ce soit sous le gouvernement des civils ou sous le gouvernement des militaires, de droite ou de gauche, ce pays n'a pas renoncé à son processus d'industrialisation. Cependant, aucun programme de développement n'a été mené à long terme. En tenant compte de la conjoncture locale et internationale, la mise en place des modèles orientés « vers l'extérieur », « vers l'intérieur » ou les « modèles mixtes » n'ont pas garanti la réussite.

48 Alain Rouquié, *L'État militaire en Amérique latine*, op. cit., p. 386-388 ; Voir aussi : Abraham Lowenthal, « Peru's ambiguous revolution », *Foreign Affairs* n° 4, vol. 52, 1974, p. 799-817.

49 Daniel Gilbert, *Le Pérou*, Paris, Karthala, 1997, p. 161.

50 Fitzgerald, E.V.K., *The State and Economic development. Peru since 1968, op. cit.*, p. 105.

51 Victor Alba, *Peru*, Boulder, Colorado, Westview Press, 1977, p. 239.

52 Efraín Gonzales de Olarte, *Una economía incompleta: Perú 1950-2007. Análisis Estructural*, Lima, Fondo Editorial PUCP/IEP, 2015.

Le décollage de l'économie péruvienne s'est vu retardé, voire bloqué par des problèmes de nature endogène et exogène. D'une part, l'instabilité politique, la corruption, l'économie dualiste, les conflits entre les classes sociales, une croissance démographique inégale, des contraintes géographiques et, d'autre part, la dépendance accrue du secteur commercial (termes de change) et financier (investissements, crédits) n'ont pas joué en faveur du *take-off.*

Références

1/ Bibliographiques

Alba, Victor, *Peru*, Colorado, Westview Press/Boulder, 1977.

Bourricaud, François, *Pouvoir et société dans le Pérou contemporain,* Paris, Presses de Sciences Po (P.F.N.S.P.), 1967.

BulmerThomas Victor, *La historia económica de América Latina desde la independencia,* 2da Edición, México, FCE, 2010.

Cotler, Julio, *Clases, estado y nación en el Perú*, Lima, Instituto de estudios peruanos, vol. 17, 2005

De Soto, Hernando, *L'autre sentier. La révolution informelle dans le tiers monde,* Paris, La Découverte, 1994.

Gilbert, Daniel, *Le Pérou*, Paris, Karthala, 1997.

Gonzales De Olarte, Efraín, *Una economía incompleta : Perú 19502007. Análisis Estructural,* Lima, Fondo Editorial PUCP/ IEP, 2015.

Guzmán Barrón, César, « Las nuevas reglas del GATT y la Organización Mundial de Comercio », *Agenda Internacional*, PUCP, n° 1, vol. 1, 1998.

Fitzgerald, E.V.K., *The State and Economic development. Peru since 1968*, Department of Applied Economics, London-New York-Melbourne, University of Cambridge, 1976.

Flores Galindo, Alberto, *La tradición autoritaria: violencia y democracia en el Perú*. Lima, APRODEH, 1999.

Hampe Martínez, Teodoro, *El Banco Central de Reserva y la economía peruana (1922-1980)*, Lima, Banco Central de Reserva del Perú, Fondo Editorial, 1995.

INEI, *Panorama de la Economía Peruana, 1950-2015*, Lima, INEI, 2016.

Parodi Trece, Carlos, *Peru, 1960-2000: políticas económicas y sociales en entornos cambiantes*, Lima, Universidad del Pacifico, 2000.

Rouquié, Alain, *L'État militaire en Amérique latine*, Paris, Éditions du Seuil, 1982.

Sheahan, John, *La economía peruana desde 1950: buscando una sociedad mejor*, Lima, Instituto de Estudios Peruanos, vol. 19, 2001.

Temple Seminario, Winston, *Guía Económica del Perú,* Lima, Instituto Peruano de Administración de Empresas (IPAE), 1968.

Thorp, Rosemary et Bertram, Geoffrey, *Perú 19801977. Crecimiento y políticas en una economía abierta,* Lima, Universidad del Pacifico, 2013.

2/ Archivistiques

Archives du Crédit Lyonnais : Boîte 49, années 1949 et 1981.

Archives Ministère des Affaires Étrangères (AMAE):
Série B-Amérique latine,
années 1952-1963.

Centre des Archives Économiques et Financières (CAEF) :
Boîte 0061 432/1, année 1964
et Boîte 0061430/1, années 1958 et 1963.

Networks of experts and political actors in the World Bank's early programs.

Loans in Colombia and their overall effects on aid to development (1940-1954)[1]

Elisa Grandi
Université de Paris - Laboratoire LIED
(UMR 8236)

Introduction

International financial organizations were peculiar actors in the post-1945 world context. They influenced financial relations among countries and elaborated economic models to be applied in the international order. They also played a fundamental role in defining "development" as a new field of intervention and international policies. The Export-Import Bank had financed development programs at the end of the 1930s. However, with the creation of the World Bank and the International Monetary Fund, financial aid became explicitly shaped and designed towards development plans, defining the international lending agencies mission. Among them, the World Bank not only pioneered these kinds of plans but contributed, with its expertise and practices, to the elaboration of models and policies specifically dedicated to tackling the backwardness of the so-called "Third World" countries.

This chapter aims to contribute to the literature on the World Bank history, by offering a novel insight into how the World Bank developed its lending policies. World Bank

1 I am grateful to my supervisors Zacarias Moutoukias, Maria Salvati and Stefano Magagnoli for their advice. Mario del Pero, Oliver Feiertag, Juan Flores Zendejas and Claire Lemercier, members of my PhD thesis committee, made fundamental remarks. Special thanks to Michele Alacevich, Pierre-Cyrille Hautcoeur and Angelo Riva for their invaluable support and suggestions.

historiography often explains the World Bank intervention in the so-called "developing" country as the result of the triumph of a model or a vision of development arising out of the different options generated within the Bank. (Mason and Asher 1973; Alacevich 2009). In particular, Michele Alacevich provided convincing findings on the multiple "voices" inside the Bank at its origins and how they gradually resulted in a standardized vision towards development.

Nonetheless, other elements proved to be equally important in orienting the Bank's early activities. Indeed, the local context in which it intervened, the different factions, interests and strategies carried by the actors oriented the Bank's loans and practices. World Bank's early missions in Colombia at the end of the Forties offer a perfect case study of local agency's relevance in orientating global development programs. The action of the Bank in the country was the result of negotiations between World Bank advisors and the Colombian politicians, experts, and businessmen. Bank's policies were not designed in Washington and applied further, neither were they uniquely the result of an intra-organization debate. Instead, given some peculiar historical circumstances, local actors played a significant role in deciding the programs to be financed and the ones to be abandoned. Bank's practices were indeed embedded in a network relying on both local and international advisors.

Local actors' interactions with international agencies did not start with the World Bank's missions. Previous loans and negotiations contributed to integrate local businessmen and politicians in the Inter-American system during the Forties and increase their international creditworthiness (Grandi 2017). By looking at the local actors' agency in which the Bank operated, this article contributes to the literature describing the interactions between Latin American and U.S. advisors in applying development programs (Olsson 2017; Offner 2019). Moreover, the relational approach applied in the study of the negotiations allows accounting for the microstructure and the organizational arrangements applied during the missions, which played a crucial role in defining the Bank's practices and crafting the role of the local economic and political leaders.

The chapter is structured as follows. The first section summarizes the literature on World Bank history and emphasizes the relevance of using microhistorical approaches in the study of global phenomena. The second section traces the World Bank's organizational framework and its early negotiations with Colombia. It argues that its practices in terms of loans' evaluation and implementation were defined through its early missions because of its fluid organizational asset. It describes Colombian actors' role in orienting the Bank towards the first General Survey mission in the country in 1949. The third section examines the World Bank's early missions in the country and its aftermaths through a relational approach. By visualizing the interactions between local and international advisors and their evolution through time, it accounts for the orientation of the Bank's early loans in the country.

1/ STATE OF THE ART AND THE CONTRIBUTION OF A MICRO-HISTORICAL APPROACH

Despite the relevance of international financial organizations both for the history of international financial aid and the recipient countries' economy, historical accounts of the World Bank activities are scarce. The vast economic literature tries to estimate the impact of its policies on national economies, but very few historical studies are devoted to the Bank's foundation, organization, and lending practices. In 1973, two former World Bank experts, Edward S. Mason and Robert E. Asher, wrote a fundamental contribution, collecting an impressive amount of documents and memories about its loans and policies (Mason and Asher 1973). This study combines the description of World Bank origins and an analysis of its functions, performance, and relations with other international institutions. More recently, the historiography became interested in the history of World Bank action toward underdeveloped areas. In particular, Michele Alacevich wrote the first account of its early policies, focusing on the central debates that took place inside the organization and defined its mission (Alacevich 2009), while other studies focused mainly on the loans the Bank disbursed in a specific area (Paganetto and Scandizzo 2010; Lepore 2013).

This chapter moves from these analyses but proposes different questions and applies a novel methodology. Indeed, it states that a comprehensive analysis of World Bank history needs to consider the role of local actors and the context in which it intervened. One of the most effective results of Alacevich' studies is the description of the multiple "voices" inside the World Bank, "below the official positions" (Alacevich 2009, 147). His analysis of the first General Survey Mission of the World Bank in Colombia shows how the international experts involved shaped their theories towards underdevelopment during the missions they worked in[2]. This is undoubtedly a key aspect to understand how the Bank evolved and gradually defined itself in its early years. But in this narrative, local actors appear to have a minor role in orienting the Bank's operations. Our study shows that the interaction between local and international actors plays a fundamental role in orienting the policies to be implemented and establishing a Bank's durable permanence in the country.

This study dialogues also with recent debates on Cold War history. It shares Odd Arne Westad's purpose to overcome traditional European boundaries in Cold War history (Westad 2007). This "geographical extension" of the Cold War studies is adopted here to underline the reciprocal influences among the regions and to describe how World Bank's policies and decisions resulted from local and international strategies. It is not a question of denying that the relations between international lending agencies and the countries concerned by their intervention were mostly asymmetrical. The aim is instead to focus on the local adaptation and reception of these broader hierarchies. For Latin American history, this perspective is particularly interesting because it

2 In particular his studies focused on Albert Hirschman and Lauchlin Currie, both working as international experts during the World Bank first loans in the country.

underlines the importance of linking Cold War historiography with debates on the evolution of the system of inter-American relations, as well as the contributions on the role and agency of local elites in dealing with the economic and political relations with the U.S[3].

Methodologically the way in which I stress the importance of dealing with local actors, follows Francesca Trivellato argument on "potential of a microhistorical approach for global history" (Trivellato 2009, 2). It is useful to recall the arguments advanced by Trivellato but also Giovanni Levi, about the relationship between microhistory and global history (Trivellato 2009; Levi 2019). They both underline that global history adopts a "macro-scale of analysis" (Trivellato 2009, 2), with broad generalizations that risk to simplify or hide the complexities, "distruptions [...] or incongruities that exist in the real world" (Levi 2019, 44). Some analyses of World Bank and U.S. programs in Latin America face the same problems when explaining the complexity of the interplay among the actors only in terms of a broader paradigm (such as the Cold War conflict or the US-Latin American relations). Far from denying the importance of the international context in which the World Bank operates, our view is that we can get essential elements to capture the frame of World Bank policies by looking at the interplay among the actors during the negotiations. Adopting a microhistorical approach in the study of the World Bank action in Colombia, therefore, does not mean looking at micro-phenomena, but focusing on the individuals, on their strategies, on the different options they had, and at how the resources and constraints they could mobilize oriented their rationality. World Bank's loans did not evolve in a deterministic and pre-designed way. They resulted from the interactions and strategies among the international experts and the local staff of each country concerned. To sum up, development programs are analyzed as a set of norms and practices, developed by the strategies of the actors involved, to be captured through the networks that connect them. The action of the Bank in the country is the result of negotiations between international experts recruited by the Bank and the Colombian politicians, experts, and businessmen. From the demand for Bank intervention in the country, in 1947, to the institutions established to implement his recommendations, in 1951, the Bank's advising resulted in a set of contacts and ties mobilized by the actors involved in the Mission, being them international experts or local staff.

Following this insight, the main challenge is to find a method able to get the strategies and practices put in place during World Bank missions and relate them to the missions' results. To this end, I apply the social networks analysis(SNA) to establish the individual and collective strategies in the negotiations. SNA allows to reconstruct the alliances and factions among Colombian political and economic elites and international experts. As described above, this method is adopted in dialogue with Italian microhistory (Levi 1985) and the so-called School of Manchester (Boissevain 1974). It also employs some sociological notions such as the one of "embeddedness" introduced

3 For a review of these contributions, see Friedman 2003 and Harmer 2011.

by Marc Granovetter (Granovetter 1985), and of "space of concrete action" proposed by Michel Crozier and Erhard Friedberg(Crozier and Friedberg 1977).

The use of SNA reveals how the nature of these ties affected the Bank's work. In more general terms, through the study of the microstructure of the Bank's missions, the strategies adopted by the actors demanding the loans, and the set of ties crystallized among the actors, I achieve a better understanding of the Bank's practices and programs. We have developed this method through networks' visualization and an analysis of the brokerage mechanisms on which the mission relied. To this end, the notion of "relational chain," introduced by Michel Grossetti, has been particularly useful (Grossetti, Barthe, and Chauvac 2011).

2/ DATA AND METHODOLOGY

This study tried to formalize the interactions among the actors involved and account for temporality to achieve a sort of "analytic narrative" (Bates et al. 1998), which uses networks to model the World Bank's practices and policies. Therefore, the historical account contextualizes the actors' behavior and illustrates the peculiar aspects of the World Bank organization and of the Colombian context, while the network analysis formalizes the actors' connections and interactions. Several types of primary sources have been exploited. The main source was the World Bank archives in Washington, well accounting for this organization's emerging nature and the importance of negotiations between international and local experts in implementing its strategies. Given the importance of local actors and local missions in our research, we also worked on local archives, through which we achieved a better understanding of the local dimension of World Bank loans and programs. The World Bank's missions have been retraced mainly through the letters exchanged among the international and local advisors. Some 1500 letters concerning the Bank's missions in Colombia were collected. More than 80% of them concern the period 1949-1959, and only 18% relate to the 1960s. Letters were the channels by which the Bank conceived its policy and set up its procedures in the interaction between the World Bank's management, in Washington, the World Bank staff hired for the missions, and the local politicians and businessmen that negotiated the loans with the Bank. Therefore, the correspondence is a particularly significant source, peculiar to this period and the Bank's on-going definition. In this context, local actors could intervene directly in the mission procedures and decision-making.

A relational database organizes the ties among the actors based on the documents examined. In particular, the exchanges among the advisors involved were analyzed as a set of relations between the sender and recipient and all the other actors mentioned in each exchange. A social network analysis of these negotiations shows that the demand for Bank intervention in the country and the institutions created to implement the report recommendations are embedded in a set of contacts and links mobilized by the actors involved in the Mission, both international and local. Having a broad set of letters available enlightens the peculiarity of this mission: the Bank's procedures were emerging and changing over time. Up to half of the 1950s, its organizational structure was still fluid. The numerous letters exchanged between Washington and Bogota during the mission reflects this creative process. In the 1960s, World Bank procedures were standardized: negotiations with local staff decreased and the material available to analyze those missions is limited to the reports compiled by the experts at different times in each mission.

While most of the letters were exchanged between the head of the mission, Lauchlin Currie, and the Bank's management in Washington, the existence of other recipients, such as the other members of the World Bank team or the Colombian experts and politicians involved is also essential. Moreover, the ties developed during the mission are not limited to individuals who exchanged letters. Of course, there was a wide range of oral exchanges that can be partially detected, considering the individuals mentioned by each sender during an exchange. Analyzing these ties, we can, therefore, illuminate each individual's role in the processes that led to the Bank's decisions.

TABLE 1 **SAMPLE OF THE SET OF RELATIONS ENLIGHTENED BY THE EXCHANGES**[4]

IDLetter	IDPerson1	IDPerson2	Date
210	122	4	28-apr-47
210	122	3	28-apr-47
58	2	127	15-may-47
161	162	164	19-may-47
160	163	164	02-jun-47
160	163	162	02-jun-47
209	86	4	25-feb-48
208	8	7	28-apr-48
207	7	8	30-apr-48
207	7	97	30-apr-48

3/ INTERNATIONAL FINANCIAL ORGANIZATIONS AFTER THE WWII: THE WORLD BANK STRUCTURE AND EARLY ACTIVITIES

Before focusing on the ties, though, it is essential to analyze the World Bank's organization. We will deal with two aspects: the relationship between the World Bank and other international organizations, and the organization of the World Bank concerning its governance, as well as its first interventions and the first loans approved (1945-1955).

4 Source: Sample extracted and elaborated from author's database.

After its creation through the Bretton Woods Agreements, the World Bank officially started its activities in 1947, disbursing a loan of 250 million USD to aid France's reconstruction. It was a significant loan, part of the U.S.- France negotiations for reconstruction aid that took place in 1946 (Wall 1987; Baubeau 2013). This inaugurated the first set of loans dedicated to reconstruction. After these first loans, the Bank started shifting its attention to development. Among the early missions towards the developing countries, the missions to Colombia played a fundamental role.

TABLE 2 **WORLD BANK EARLY LOANS (1947-1949)**[5]

Country	Approval Date	Project Cost (ml USD)	W.B. loan (ml USD)
France	09/05/1947	250	250
Netherlands	07/08/1947	195	195
Denmark	22/08/1947	40	40
Luxembourg	28/08/1947	12	12
Chile	25/03/1948	2,5	2,5
Chile	25/03/1948	13,5	13,5
Netherlands	01/07/1948	2	2
Netherlands	01/07/1948	2	2
Netherlands	01/07/1948	4	4
Mexico	06/01/1949	24,1	24,1
Mexico	06/01/1949	10	10
Brazil	27/01/1949	75	75
Belgium	08/02/1949	16	16

However, limiting the analysis to the international context, in terms of hierarchy between regions and the policy of containment in the Cold War context, would prevent to understand the action and the process of conception of problems and solutions related to finance development programs. The study of these organizations' microstructure (internal organization, staff, conventions, and) offers more insights to understand how its practices evolved. This type of approach to the study of international organizations is little applied on our subject. The article by Jeffrey Chwieroth, published in 2008, is, to our knowledge, the only study that develops an organizational analysis of the World Bank and its impact on the nature of loans (Chwieroth 2008). By working on the Bank's first loans, the author concludes that the practices related to loan disbursements are the products of intra-organizational dynamics. The author develops this thesis by highlighting a very important point for our analysis, namely the autonomy of the Bank's personnel management, which affects lending decisions and policies, intervention. Chwieroth notes, in particular, the transition between the first loans, aimed at the stabilization of the balance of payments (approved until the early 1950s), and the loans for the financing of specific projects

5 Source : Mason and Asher (1973, p. 812-826).

("project-oriented"). According to Chwieroth, this transition is explained by a shift in the Bank's departments' hierarchies.

Our study shares with Chwieroth the idea that Bank's organizational evolution and its practices and development policies are well-connected. However, we believe that the study of the hierarchy among the departments should be associated with a study of Bank's staff and hiring policies. In particular, the experts recruited to lead Bank's missions deserve more attention. The first mission to Colombia was announced on 10th January 1949, and it started at the end of June of the same year. Its significance has been nicely stated by Edward Mason and Robert Asher, according to which "in tracing the evolution of IBRD assistance to member countries in development programming, the historian quickly discovered that all roads lead not to Rome but to Bogota" (Mason and Asher 1973, 299). Indeed, World Bank's initial organization had an emergent and fluid character. The Bank started shaping its organization only in 1947 when John McCloy was appointed President of the Bank Robert Garner vice-President. Leonard Rist was head of the economic investigation office. Together they represented the core management of the Bank until the early 1950s. The rest of the staff was divided among the two offices that handled all bank's activities: the Loans Department and the Economic Research Department. McCloy, Garner and Rist recruited the members of Bank's missions directly based on personal and professional links. This means that at the beginning, the Bank did not have a stable staff and organization. Instead, when a mission was launched, the core management hired each member on ad hoc basis. In addition to the particular organization of the early years of the Bank's activity, this mission was the first "General Survey Mission" of the World Bank, i.e., a mission intending to report its overall economic conditions to launch a comprehensive development program.

In sum, World Bank early activities are characterized by a fluid organizational frame, through which the staff and heads of the missions were hired *ad hoc*; a gradual shift toward developing regions; and a practice leaving broad leeway to local actors in the negotiations in the countries involved. Nonetheless, these features alone would not explain this mission's importance in the Colombian economy and Bank's further interventions in Colombia and other countries. Therefore, it is crucial to analyze the Colombian economic context and its previous records with other international lending agencies to understand the impact of this mission both for the history of the Bank and the evolution of Colombian economic policies.

4/ THE INTERACTION AMONG LOCAL AND INTERNATIONAL EXPERTS DURING THE WORLD BANK MISSION: A SOCIAL NETWORK ANALYSIS OF THE NEGOTIATIONS

Before the World Bank mission, Colombian elites had already developed a well-established relationship with other international lending agencies. The expertise progressively developed in that way has been applied during the first contacts leading to the

Bank's intervention. Starting from the 1920s, a massive flux of foreign capital came to Colombia thanks to both private and international agencies. The details of this important turning point in Colombian economy goes beyond the purpose of this chapter[6], but it is important to recall that Colombian political and economic elites had already integrated a transnational network of businesses across the Inter-American space of action. These connections not only gave to national and local elites the resources to develop national and private enterprises, but promoted the rise of the economic groups leading the modernization programs, both at a local and national scale.

Indeed, the first negotiations with the World Bank in the Forties were inaugurated by the businessmen Alfonso Araujo and Jose Gutierrez Gomez, representing the Colombian Industrial National Association (ANDI), who required a first intervention in 1948 to finance agro-industrial projects. The ties they mobilized during the 1940s gave them the international creditworthiness to convince the leaders of the Bank of the opportunity to intervene in the country. At the same time, in 1948, Emilio Toro proposed to Vice-President Robert Garner to carry out the General Survey Mission. Therefore, on one side, a group of entrepreneurs directly activated the intervention of the experts from the World Bank, and on the other side, the negotiations led by Emilio Toro, within the World Bank. Therefore, the general survey mission resulted from the mobilization of different interests and actions, placed on multiple planes, from local to transnational.

Graph 1 shows indeed the 12 actors acting in the first negotiations and the organizations they belonged to. On the Colombian side, we have Emilio Toro; President Ospina; and Araujo, the ANDI's Representatives Gutierrez. On the World Bank side, we have Vice-President Robert Garner; President John McCloy Jacques Torfs, and William Iliff (and two other advisors). Nevertheless, reducing the negotiations on these two sides appears to be very reductive. Indeed, if we go deeper into the organizations and groups these actors belong to, we can observe a much more complex configuration. If we focus on Colombian actors, we find multiple political and social groups: Gutierrez and Araujo, coming from the industrial and conservative environment, consolidating and enlarging its influence, especially internationally. On the other side, Emilio Toro came from a completely different path: he can be considered the first "technician" who collaborated with the Bank. The mission offered him the opportunity to act as broker between the President of Colombia and the Bank. From its early negotiations, therefore, the General Survey mission appears as the result of the negotiations between local and international actors, pursuing different interests and logic. The social network analysis reveals the relational frame in which the mission took place and shows that the evolution of the Bank's policy cannot be analyzed only in terms of a confrontation of different ideas. To understand why a development model was established, we have to look at the interactions between individuals and their relative power in the negotiations.

6 A more detailed description of international credit in Colombia during the 1920s ans 1930 is provided by James Henderson (2001) and Elisa Grandi 2018.

Moreover, we can see from the actors' centrality that the hierarchy among the organizations involved is far from expected. We tend to consider the governments as the leading organizations managing the international financial credit, while we see here that the World Bank negotiated first with a socio-professional association, the Industrials' one. Similarly, the U.S. State Department does not recover a central role in these negotiations but is limited in receiving the information from the U.S. Executive Director, Emilio Collado. This is consistent with the World Bank studies showing that U.S. and World Bank interest were not superposed, even at the very beginning (Gwin 1997).

After these early negotiations, the World Bank General Survey mission began on 10th July 1949 with a team of 16 experts[22]. Only two of them belong to the Bank staff, while all the others were hired on purpose for that mission. In particular, the head of the mission was Lauchlin Currie, a new dealer economist previously employed as an advisor during the administration of Franklin Delano Roosevelt and a member of the Brain Trust of Harry Truman[23]. Thanks to the fluidity of the Bank's organizational structure, Currie could count on a large degree of autonomy in the decision-making process, for what concerns the team recruitment, the steps of the mission, and the pattern to follow in collecting data on the economic conditions of the country and preparing a set of recommendations to follow. The rest of the team referred mainly to him, and he was in charge of the communications with the Bank management in Washington.

FIGURE 1 **NETWORK AND ORGANIZATIONS CONFIGURATION BEFORE THE GENERAL SURVEY MISSION (1947-1949)**[7]

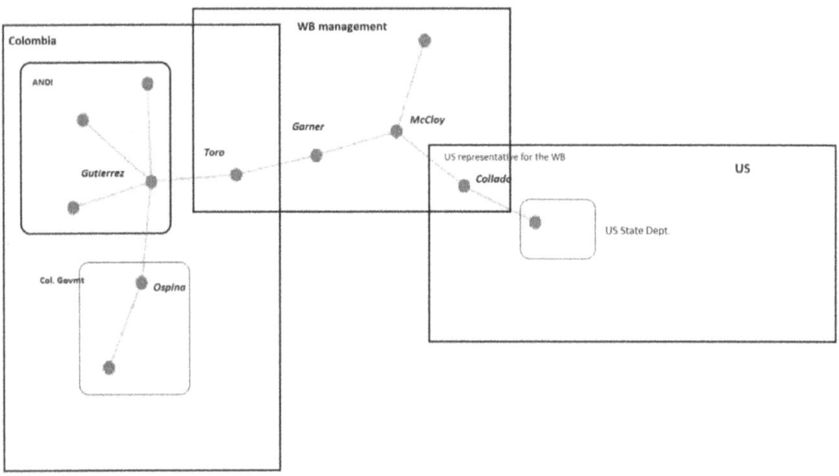

During the four months in Bogota, the mission collected data on all aspects of the Colombian economy. The report presented at the end of the mission, both to the

7 Source: Elaboration from author's database.

Bank management and the Colombian President in 1950, *The Basis of a Development Program for Colombia* (World Bank 1950), arose great interest and curiosity among the other international organizations. It marked a critical moment in the World Bank transition towards development policies. The report's general recommendations focused mainly on the increase of productivity, both for the agricultural and industrial sectors, on improving the transportation system and the development of a housing program. As a consequence, the first loans proposed and approved concerned the creation of hydroelectric plants (Loans 0038 and 0039, approved in 1951) and the construction of highways and railroads connecting the primary coffee production and industrial sites in order to facilitate these products' market (Loan 0043 and 0068, approved in 1952)[8].

FIGURE 2 **NETWORK CONFIGURATION DURING THE MISSION (1949-1951)**[9]

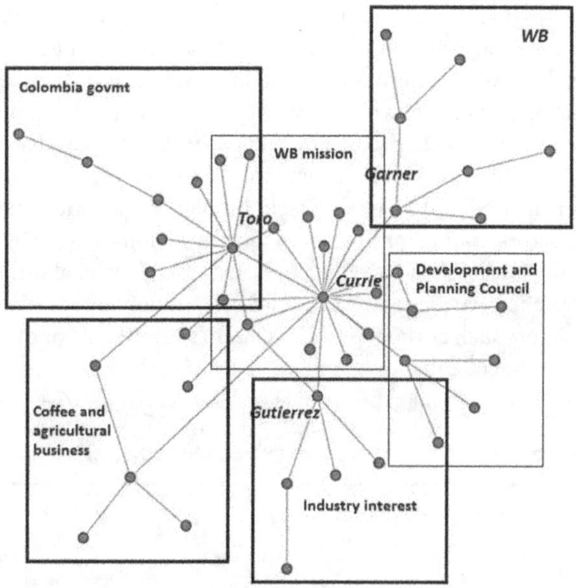

If we look now at the exchanges during the mission (Graph 2), Emilio Toro stands out as central in organizing the operations. He managed the staff's recruitment and in the decisions about the sectors (or regions) to study during the mission. He also ran the mission's operations with Currie. Therefore, the final report owes a lot to the intervention of local staff, instead of being the result of economic doctrines developed uniquely by international advisors. This is very significant for the understanding of the emergence of international economic advising and its reception. The historiography has already established that international development programs are re-adapted by the countries recipient (in contrast with the theory of "one size fits all"). However,

8 The complete list of loans disbursed by the World Bank, as well as the documentation regarding loan proposals and approval is disclosed and online on the World Bank website: http://www.worldbank.org/projects.
9 Source: Elaboration from author's database.

by looking at these ties, we understand that these policies resulted from the local staff's interaction. This is confirmed by the composition of the network of contacts crystallized during the mission. Graph 2 concerns the actors involved between 1949 and 195. It shows a network of 46 individuals, where almost half of the nodes are linked with a single node. We find Toro and other national political leaders and a strong presence of local politicians and entrepreneurs (mayors, head of local public enterprises, regional governors etc.), directly related to Currie. This implies that the mission has been a channel for the local elites to integrate a more comprehensive transnational network and access international credit.

If we turn now at the third period, reproduced in Graph 3, we noticed an even more complex articulation of actors and organizations. In this case, given the number of ties' density, it was impossible to overlap the organizations' structure and the network configuration. Therefore, we produced two parallel visualizations. Two aspects deserve to be detailed. On one side, the aftermaths of the World Bank's mission in terms of organisms created to manage the World Bank's loan and the fact that these same organisms were strongly connected with the World Bank. I am referring here to the Planning Council, created in 1952, in which we find two international advisors hired by the World Bank. Jacques Torfs, which participated also to the mission in 1949, and Albert Hirschman, hired in 1952 by the Bank. Moreover, we notice a progressive insertion of local actors, asking for loans on a local or regional basis. Given the same character of the mission, its chief Lauchlin Currie led several regional studies and surveys to get a comprehensive picture of the country's economic conditions. Through these dynamic, actors such as the representatives of Barranquilla or of the representatives of the Cauca Valley came to negotiate loans with the Bank without passing through the central Government support or supervision.

FIGURE 3 **NETWORK CONFIGURATION AFTER THE GENERAL SURVEY MISSION (1952-1954)**[10]

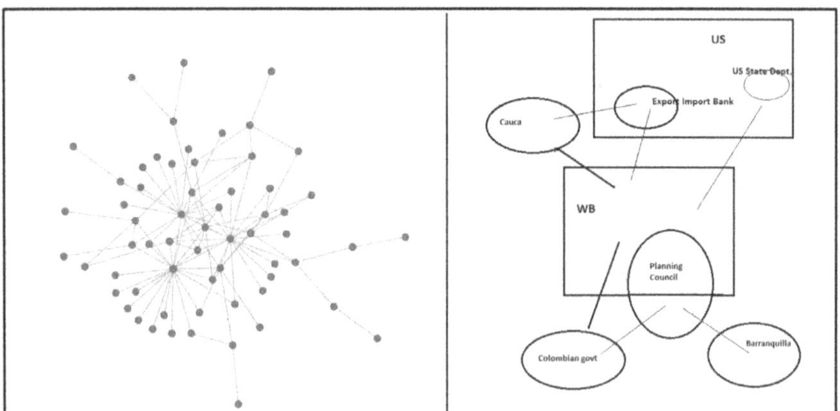

10 Source: Elaboration from author's database.

Conclusions

This paper aimed to reveal why the General Survey mission of the World Bank was seminal in orientating World Bank's loans in the country and how the relative position of each individual involved in negotiations influenced the mission's process, features, and aftermaths. The peculiarity of the early World Bank's intervention and the special relationship Colombian elites developed towards international lending agencies during the 1920s and 1930s allowed the local staff to have direct access to international credit, thanks to their direct intervention in mission's data collection, recommendations, and loans management and implementation. Moreover, the social and relational capital that some actors gained during the mission influenced the loan disbursement. Therefore, we the development programs' design and decision-making occur *during* and not *before* the organizational procedures. Personal ties play a fundamental role in the emergence and affirmation of these procedures.

Bibliography

Alacevich, Michele. 2009. *The Political Economy of the World Bank: The Early Years.* Washington, D.C.: Stanford University Press.

———. 2016. "Devising Routines for Project Appraisal at the World Bank, 1945-1975." In *The Emergence of Routines. Entrepreneurship, Organization, and Business History*. Oxford, Oxford University Press.

Bates, Robert H., Avner Greif, Margaret Levi, Jean-Laurent Rosenthal, and Barry R. Weingast. 1998. *Analytic Narratives*. Princeton, N.J, Princeton University Press.

Baubeau, Patrice. 2013. "La BIRD, la France et le dollar gap, 1946-1947." *Histoire@Politique* 19 (1), p. 66-82.

Boissevain, Jeremy. 1974. *Friends of Friends : Networks, Manipulators and Coalitions*. Oxford, Basil Blackwell.

Chwieroth, Jeffrey. 2008. "Organizational Change 'from within': Exploring the World Bank's Early Lending Practices." *Review of International Political Economy* 15 (4), p. 481-505.

Crozier, Michel, and Erhard Friedberg. 1977. *L'acteur et le système: les contraintes de l'action collective*. Paris, Éditions du Seuil.

Friedman, Max Paul. 2003. "Retiring the Puppets, Bringing Latin America Back In: Recent Scholarship on United States–Latin American Relations." *Diplomatic History* 27 (5), p. 621-36.

Grandi, Elisa. 2018. "Élites, modernización y redes de negocio transnacional en Colombia (1920-1935)." *Boletín americanista*, no. 76, p. 17-30.

Granovetter, Mark. 1985. "Economic Action and Social Structure: The Problem of Embeddedness" *American Journal of Sociology* (91), p. 481-510.

Grossetti, Michel, Jean-François Barthe, and Nathalie Chauvac. 2011. "Studying Relational Chains from Narrative Material." *Bulletin of Sociological Methodology/ Bulletin de Méthodologie Sociologique* 110 (1), p. 11-25.

Gwin, Catherine. 1997. "U.S. Relations With the World Bank, 1945-1992." In *World Bank's first half Century*, p. 195-274.

Harmer, Tanya. 2011. "Hal Brands, Latin America's Cold War." *H-Diplo Roundtable Review* 12 (17), p. 12-19.

Henderson, James D. 2001. *Modernization in Colombia: The Laureano Gomez Years, 1889-1965*. Gainesville, University Press of Florida.

Lepore, Amedeo. 2013. *La Cassa per il Mezzogiorno e la Banca Mondiale: un modello per lo sviluppo economico italiano*. Rubbettino.

Levi, Giovanni. 1985. *L'eredità immateriale: Carriera di un esorcista nel Piemonte del Seicento*. Torino, Einaudi.

———. 2019. "Frail Frontiers?" *Past & Present* 242 (Supplement_14), p. 37-49.

Mason, Edward Sagendorph, and Robert E. Asher. 1973. *The World Bank Since Bretton Woods: The Origins, Policies, Operations, and Impact of the International Bank for Reconstruction and*

Development and the Other Members of the World Bank Group. Washington, D.C.: Brookings Institution Press.

Offner, Amy C. 2019. *Sorting Out the Mixed Economy: The Rise and Fall of Welfare and Developmental States in the Americas*. Princeton, N.J., Princeton University Press.

Olsson, Tore C. 2017. *Agrarian Crossings: Reformers and the Remaking of the U.S. and Mexican Countryside*. Princeton, Princeton University Press.

Paganetto, Luigi, and Pasquale L. Scandizzo. 2010. *La Banca Mondiale e l'Italia: Dalla Ricostruzione Allo Sviluppo*. Bologna, Il Mulino.

Trivellato, Francesca. 2009. "Is There a Future for Italian Microhistory in the Age of Global History?" *California Italian Studies* 2 (1). http://escholarship.org/uc/item/0z94n9hq.

Wall, Irwin M. 1987. "Les Accords Blum-Byrnes. La Modernisation de La France et La Guerre Froide." *Vingtième Siècle. Revue d'histoire* 13 (1), p. 45-62.

Westad, Odd Arne. 2007. *La guerre froide globale : Le tiers-monde, les Etats-Unis et l'URSS*. Paris, Payot.

World Bank. 1950. "The Basis of A Development Program for Colombia. Report of a Mission Headed by Lauchlin Currie and Sponsored by the International Bank for Reconstruction and Development, in Collaboration with the Government of Colombia." Washington, World Bank.

CEMEX (1906-2008) Or the Rise of a Mexican Multinational

Dominique Barjot
Emeritus Professor of Modern Economic History
Sorbonne University

Introduction

Cemex was, in 2008, the fifth global cement production capacity and the fourth by the size of its turnover [1].

TABLE 1 **THE FIVE MOST IMPORTANT COMPANIES OF THE GLOBAL CEMENT INDUSTRY AT DECEMBER 21, 2008 (IN € BILLION)**

	Net Sales	EBITDA
Lafarge	19.0	3.5
Holcim	15.8	3.3
Cemex	14.5	1.7
Heidelberg Cement	14.2	2.4
Italcementi	5.8	1.1

Source: Annual reports of the concerned groups

But Cemex remained number one in Latin America, ahead of Holcim [2]and Lafarge[3]. Above all, the Group's was and, today, is the world leader for the ready-mix concrete

1 This study is based on a recount of the annual reports of the Group Cemex from 1999 to 2016. See particularly Cemex annual reports 1999-2016 and Cemex *Building the Future*, Sustainable Development reports 2004-2016.

2 Dominique Barjot, "Holcim: from the Family Business to the Global Leadership: an International Interfirm Comparison", in Dominique Barjot (ed.), "The Construction Industry in the xxth Century: an International Interfirm Comparison", *Revue française d'histoire économique – The French Economic History Review*, n° 1, septembre 2014, p. 56-85.

3 Dominique Barjot, « Lafarge : de l'entreprise internationale à la firme mondiale (1993-2007) », dans Dominique Barjot and Marie-Claude Esposito, *Mondialisation, modèles nationaux de développement et stratégies d'entreprises XIXe-XXIe siècles. Globalization, national patterns of development and strategies of firms (19th-21st centuries)*, Paris, SPM, 2016, p. 234-262; « Lafarge : l'ascension d'une multinationale à la française (1833-2005) », dans « Les mondialisations », *Relations internationales*, n° 124, hiver 2005, p. 51-67.

employment with 77 billion m3 per year instead of 48.5 to Holcim, 44.5 to Heidelberg Cement and 44 to Lafarge. Despite its global importance, Cemex remained still, in 2008, a Mexican group, whose headquarters stood at Mexico City, with a secondary office in New York, and all administrators remained Mexican. Cemex is an archetypal example of the rise of global firms from the third world, as Brazilian rivals Votorantim and Intercement or Chinese firms (CNBM, Anhui Conch, China Resources, Taiwan Cement)[4].

1/ A GRADUAL ASCENT

Cemex has first had a gradual rise, take advantage of the market-driven expansion[5].

1.1 / A market-driven expansion

The beginnings of Cemex was slow, because the start-up of the business had been slowed down, between 1906 and 1930, by the Mexican revolution.

A/ A startup slowed by the revolution (1906-1930)

Cemex was born in 1906. with the opening of the Hidalgo cement plant in the North of the Mexico: Cementos[6] Hidalgo produced then 33,000 tons per year. By 1909, the plant doubled its production capacity (i.e. 66,000 tons per year). In 1912, however, the Mexican revolution led to a stop in the production of cement. Indeed, the lack of available energy, of means of transport and workforce would cause the company to distribute the cement at profitable prices. In 1919, the company reduced partially its production to the factory of the Cement Hidalgo. It was only in 1921 when the factory returned to its full production. One year earlier, the Cementos Portland Monterrey Company had begun its operations with a 20,000 tons production capacity annual. Especially, she introduced in Mexico the first oven using the process of the wet way that was the most modern technology time. From then on, Cementos Portland Monterrey produced a mark, which satisfied the consumptions of the Northeast of Mexico. In 1930, this factory of Monterrey was equipped with a second oven: With a 40,000 tons production capacity a year, the company enabled to deal with the growing demand of the Northeast of Mexico. A new phase opened from now on, marked by a strategy associating organic and external growths.

B/ A strategy associating organic growth and external growth (1931 1975)

In 1931, Cementos Hidalgo and Cementos Portland Monterrey merged to form Cementos Mexicanos HIS (Cemex). This fusion gave birth to current Cemex, who, so restructured, crossed the big crisis of the 1930s. The restart of the request delayed

4 Dominique Barjot, "Introduction", in Dominique Barjot (ed.), "Globalization, national patterns of development and strategies of firms (19th-21st centuries) – Mondialisation, modèles nationaux de développement et stratégies d'entreprises (XIXe-XXIe siècles)", *Revue française d'histoire économique – The French Economic History Review*, n°1, mai 2015, p. 14-27.

5 Dominique Barjot, « Cemex (1906-2008). Le succès exemplaire d'une multinationale issue d'un pays émergent », in Cecena Blanca et Golib Felipe, *Cycle de conférences 2010*, Paris, Maison du Mexique. Cité internationale universitaire de Paris, 2010, p. 14-33.

6 Cemex *Milestones 1906-2006, The Company's 100th Anniversary. Cemex 100 years*, 2006.

however; in 1943, the Cemex de Monterrey factory increased its production capacity up to 250 tons a day (that is a little more than 78,000 tons a year). In the year 1948, the production capacity of Cemex carried in 124,000 tons, representing a fourfold increase compared with 1906. Year 1951 saw the start of the fourth oven to the factory of Monterrey (that was a 300 tons production capacity a day). Launched from now on in a process of steady growth, the Cemex company commemorated in 1956 the fiftieth birthday (anniversary) of the establishment of a cement industry the year Mexico. It was still only about organic growth. From 1959, thanks to the development of its factory of Monterrey, Cemex sold, in the year, 230,420 tons of grey cement and 14,692 tons of white cement (or aluminous cement). On one year later, the factory of Monterrey carried its production capacity in 500 tons a day (that is approximately 160,000 tons a year).

The year 1966 was a turning point, with the acquisition, in the Yucatán, of the factory of Cementos Maya to Mérida: It continued afterward to satisfy the demand of the South of Mexico under the brand Cemento Portland Maya. Next year, Cemex started the production of its new factory of cement of Torreon, to satisfy the increasing demand, which showed itself in the Northeast of Mexico. The company exploited the brands Cemento Portland Puzolona Monterrey and Cemento Portland Monterrey there. It was a success, because, from 1971, the factory of Torréon began the production of its second oven, with a 1250 tons production capacity a day (that is 390,000 tons a year). It was a successful equipment and allowing two phases of preheating. During the year, which followed, two ovens of the same model entered service, the one in Monterrey, the other one to Mérida. Thanks to these two phases of preheating, the company was equipped, in 1972, with 780,000 tons of additional production capacities. Pursuing its national setting-up, Cemex acquired, during year 1973, the factory of Cementos Portland del Bajio in Central Mexico. Especially, in the year 1974, the Cemex factory of Monterrey began the production of an eighth oven. It produced 1,300 tons a day (that is about 410,000 tons a year), thanks to his 4 phases of preheating and his electrostatic precipitator. Aspire to the national leadership became from now on of the order of the possible.

C/ Conquest of the national leadership (on 1976 1989)

From 1976, Cemex was side to the Mexico stock exchange and became the leader of the Mexican market, with the acquisition of Cements of Guadalajara. Two years passed. The factories of Monterrey and Mérida started respectively them ninth and second oven. The introduction of four phases of preheating reduced it the cost of the installations and allowed the collection of dusts thanks to the filters installed there. Thanks to the gains so realized of production capacity, ovens authorized an answer adequate to the expansion pursued by the demand of the regions of the South and of the North. In 1979, the Cemex's factories of Torréon and Ensenada started each the production of their third oven (with additional installed capacity of 1,300 tons a day and preheating in four phases).

The development of Cemex continued at a sustained pace. In the year 1981, with a production capacity installed by 2,200 tons a day, a new oven, more powerful, started its operations to the Cemex's factory Vallès (that is almost 690,000 tons a year). The year 1982 saw the starting up in Monterrey and Torréon respectively, their tenth and fourth ovens. Endowed with preheating processors in four phases, they represented an important technological advance for the company. By authorizing the decarbonation of about 90 % of the raw materials of factories and by reducing the size of ovens, they offered savings of cost price in the installations and the spare parts. Especially the capacity installed by every factory increased by 2,200 tons a day. From now on the program of exports doubled in volume. The next year, the factory of Guadalajara began, in its turn, the production of the fourth oven: Of a 2,200 tons production capacity a day, the new oven possessed at the same time a preheating in four stages and a precalcinator. The results were there: in 1989, for the first time, the annual sales of Cemex exceeded 6.7 million tons of cement and of clinker. Three factories dominated then the activity of the group, with each more than 1 million tons of sales annual of cement: Monterrey, Guadalajara and Torréon.

The year 1985 established a new decisive date. In a country where developed powerful conglomerates, Cemex decided then to diversify towards assets still not corresponding to its heart of business, but also to concentrate on the value chain of the cement. Pushed it his breakthrough to the export: 574,000 tons of cement and to clinker a year from 1985 also. It came along with the putting in production of its factory of Huichapan. Using the most advanced industrial technology, it distributed the cement to the builders of the central part of Mexico. With this new factory, endowed with a capacity installed by more than 1 million tons, the Cemex's capacity of production exceeded 10.7 million tons a year. During year 1986, thanks to common investments with North American cement companies, Cemex strengthened its program of export. In 1987, Cemex acquired a competitor, Cementos Anahuac, and sent the first team asked to work in the integration of the new subsidiary to operate the consolidation of the operation. At the same moment, Cemex began the deployment of a company exploiting a system of satellite communication, worth knowing Cemex Net. Especially 1989 let the repurchase of Cementos Toltecas, then the second more important Mexican producer. Cemex so entered the top 10 of the most important world cement makers.

1.2/ From the multinationalization to the world firm (1992-2006)

Cemex opted from then on for the multinationalization. The first stage lay in a breakthrough in the Iberian world and in the United States.

A/ Breakthrough in the Iberian World and in the United States

From 1992, with the acquisition of Valenciana and Sanson, two bigger Spanish companies of cement, Cemex started its international expansion on the international market, at the same moment of the signature of the North American Free Trade Agreement (NAFTA). Next year, Cemex established Neoris, formerly Cemtec, to serve as intern offer of services in technological information. In 1994, Cemex acquired

Vencemos, the biggest company cimentière of Venezuela. The group so began its operations in South America. Year 1994 also saw the repurchase of Cemento Bayano in Panama, through whom Cemex established in Central America. The year 1994 constituted well a turning point, because Cemex entered to the United States, thanks to the repurchase of an American cement works. In a simultaneous way, Cemex launched its strategy of alternative fuels and began to convert its factories to use some coke of oil there. The consequence was the establishment of an eco-efficiency program, from now on cornerstone of its strategy of sustainable development.

This modernization also concerned the sales management. In 1995, Cemex developed a digital system, Dynamic Synchronization of Operations, to manage in a more effective way and follow up to the end the orders of the customers. At the same moment, Cemex implanted its operations in the Caribbean world, thanks to the acquisition of Cementos Nacionales, producer of cement having the leadership on the market of the Dominican Republic. On one year later, Cemex took control of Samper and Cementeros Diamante in Colombia. These successive operations were worth to it reaching the third world rank of the producers of cement, but still far behind Holcim (ex Holderbank) and Lafarge. Within the NAFTA however, the leadership of Cemex became more and more a reality.

B/ Assertion as leader within the NAFTA (1997-2000)

During 1997, Cemex began operations in Asia, with the acquisition of 30% of the capital of Rizal Cement in the Philippines. At the same time, Cemex participated in the conference on climate change. The firm adhered to the Kyoto Protocol, which aimed to reduce emissions into the atmosphere of greenhouse gases. Continuing its strategy of multinationalization, the group took 25% of the capital of Indonesia's largest cement producer, Semen Gresik. Similarly, in 1999, Cemex bought APO Cement (99.9%) in the Philippines and increased its investments in Rizal Cement (with 40% of the capital now). 1999 marked a new milestone, with a first breakthrough in Africa, thanks to a majority stake in Assiut Cement Company, one of Egypt's largest producers. By acquiring Cementos del Pacifico (95%), the largest producer in Costa Rica, Cemex consolidated its presence in Central America and the Caribbean. Above all, the same year, Cemex entered to the New York Stock Exchange (NYSE) and founded Cemex Asia Holdings (CAH) to form partnerships and take stakes in cement business.

In 2000, Cemex launched its Cemex Way initiative to identify, incorporate and execute best practices across the organization. It encouraged the fact that Standard & Poor's raised Cemex's credit ratio to "recommended investments". Also, in 2000, Cemex formalized an exclusive long-term distribution agreement with Universe Cement of Taiwan and began construction of a new plant in Bangladesh, launched Cx Network, a new unit dedicated to creating innovative new business around the company's strengths. Above all, Cemex became the largest North American producer with the acquisition and integration of American Southdown Inc. During 2001, Cemex further strengthened its presence in Central America by launching operations in Nicaragua. Remained to assume the leadership.

C/ Taking on leadership (2000-2006)
That same year, 2001, Cemex strengthened its position in the Asian market, with the acquisition of Saburi Cement Company (99% of the share capital) in Thailand. The group set up its Construrama sales network, which at the end of the year grew to become the largest construction materials distribution chain in Mexico. Cemex also launched its online customer service, enabling them to place orders, purchases, place products and access services electronically. In 2002, Cemex strengthened its position in the Caribbean through the acquisition of the Puerto Rican Cement Company. The following year, the group successfully set up its global procurement system for all subsidiaries and holdings as well as its office for internationally consolidated negotiations.

The year 2005 was another decisive step towards the global firm. Indeed, the Cemex group doubled in size with the acquisition of Ready Mix Concrete (RMC), adding to its location twenty European markets. This resulted in greater global integration and increased geographic diversification in Europe, North America and Africa. One year later, in 2006, the company celebrated its 100th anniversary: at that time, firmly established in third place worldwide behind Lafarge and Holcim, the group employed more than 50,000 employees.

2/ IN SEARCH OF THE EXPLANATORY FACTORS OF MIRACLE

What were the explanatory factors for the "miracle" Cemex? This huge company founded in 1906 was a symbol of the success of capitalism in Monterrey and Mexico City. Originally, the family Zambrano was a trading house operating from the mid-nineteenth century. It had developed after the war with the United States, in 1846-1847, which had established the Rio Bravo line. This family established, between 1890 and 1910, with the families Garza, Ferrara, Madero, Meiz, Milmo and Sada, well studied by Mario Cerutti [7]. Analysis conducted here is based notably on research by Juan Ignacio Barragan (Urbis International Monterrey) and Mario Cerutti (Universidade Autonoma de Nueve Leon, Monterrey, Mexico) [8]. The central idea is that in 1982 there is a decisive economic crisis, which led to intense restructuring and internationalization.

2.1/ A breakthrough made in 1940 and 1982
During the period 1940-1982, Cemex experienced an early increase in its production capacity: in 1960, it reached 3.5 million tons against 1.5 in 1948. The company was

7 Cerutti Mario, *Proprietarios, Empresarios y Empresa en et Norte de Mexico,* Siglo Veintiuno Editores, Mexico, 2000 ; Marichal Carlos y Cerutti Mario, *Historia de las Grandes Empresas en Mexico, 1850-1930,* Mexico, Universidad Autonoma de Nuevo Léon & Fundo de Cultura Economica, 1997.

8 Barragán, Juan Ignacio and Mario Cerutti (2003). "Cemex: del mercado interno a la empresa global". Paper presented at the V Congresso Brasileiro de História Econômica e 6a Conferência Internacional de História de *Empresas*, Caxambu, Brazil, 7-10 September, mimeo. This case study traces the story of Cemex. See also: Barragán, Juan Ignacio and *Mario Cerutti* (2003). "Cemex: del mercado interno a la empresa global", in Marichal Carlos y Cerutti Mario (eds.), *Del Mercado Protegido al Mercado Global.* Monterrey 1925-2000, Mexico, Trillas, p. 55-80.

then facing stiff competition: Cementos Cruz Azul (Central and South Mexico), Cementes Guadalajara (West), Grupo Anahuac (Gulf of Mexico), Grupo Toltecas (Central) and San Luis Mining (Pacific). However, between 1970 and 1976, a first process of concentration took place around two groups: Cemex, by taking control of Cementos Guadalajara, and Cementos Toltecas, thanks to those of San Luis Mining and Cementos Atoyac.

A/ Change of scale, restructuring and vertical integration

The time first saw the change of scale of the company, passing from local to multiregional. It was part of an import substitution policy. Between 1948 and 1970, Cemex increased its Portland production capacity by 322%. In 1970, the firm supplied 15% of the national market, exercising a clear domination over the Northeast. Then followed a period of economic deceleration, which corresponded, in Mexico, to the presidency of Luis Echeverria Alvarez. Cemex was then a relatively small company: its tonnage production is no more than 3% of that of Blue Circle, 5% of Universal Atlas and 6% of Lone Star.

Such a situation pushed for reconstruction and vertical integration. Cemex adopted a more modern mode of governance. After a call to an American consultant Cresap, Mc Cormick & Paget, the firm adopted the staff and line, thus aligning itself with most of its major competitors worldwide. She was converting her production apparatus, engaging in a process of vertical integration. The purchase of Cementos Guadalajara allowed him to control 26% of the country's cement production capacity. In 1975, Cemex became the second largest producer after Cementos Toltecas (28.5%), a subsidiary of the British giant Blue Circle. The group was in a good position to take advantage of the new policy in favor of the cement industry.

B/ A new policy for investment and export

The arrival of President José Lopez Portillo (1976-1982) marked a political change. The rise in the domestic price was accompanied by Mexico's conversion into a major oil exporter, itself a result of OPEC policy. Then formed the Alianza para Produccion, an agreement between the federal government, the big industrialists and the central trade union CTM. The Programa de Fomento added to Industria Cementera. It was an ambitious project to triple the production capacity, from 1977 to 1984, involving a systematic transfer of foreign technology.

The crisis of 1982 changed the situation. During the crisis, Cemex inaugurated the country's most modern factory, Hidalgo in the Huichapan: with 10.7 million tons of annual production capacity, it delivered 32.5% of the national total. To finance itself, Cemex appealed to the great Mexicans (Mexicana Banca Serfin) and, above all, American (Bank of America, Chase Manhattan Bank, Citibank National Association, Crocker National Bank). The company could afford it because the debt represented only 16% of the assets. Despite the series of Mexican devaluations, Cemex did not have a serious financial problem. The group was looking for sound finances. It achieved this through a substantial drop in production costs: $ 42 per ton in 1987 instead of $ 55 in 1982.

2.2/ Successful entry on the international scene

Cemex thus had the means of a successful entry on the world stage. The context had changed since the 1970s. Before most of the major groups of the cement industry remained oriented towards their national markets, like Heidelberger Zement in Germany, CBR in Belgium, Ciments Français, and Italcementi or, in Japan, Onoda and Nihon. There were only four exceptions: Lafarge (Canada, Brazil, and Germany), Blue Circle, Holderbank and Lone Star[9]. Of these four groups, the most dynamic appeared Holderbank, unlike Lone Star who retired from Latin America in 1964. The turning point came in 1970: that year Lafarge acquired Canada Cement, dominating 70% of the Canadian market[10]. The French group opened the way for an offensive towards the American market and those of emerging countries. With the 1982 crisis, Cemex also had to look to foreign countries. The choice to export resulted from three main reasons:

1 / the Mexico City government abandoned, from 1985, the import substitution model in favor of an openness policy;

2 / European groups were showing increasing aggressiveness on the American continent. They bought plants in the United States, Canada and even South America. We were moving towards a small oligopoly of global firms;

3 / From then on, it became necessary to export looking for the competitive advantage. First, it was necessary to conquer absolute supremacy in Mexico.

A/ Conquest of absolute supremacy in Mexico

Cemex first consolidated its position in Mexico. In 1985, Cemex controlled 33% of the national production capacity (10.7 million tons produced per year). This strong position allowed for an active vertical integration strategy through which the group managed to control 23% of the national market for concrete. Cemex was already one of the world's leading companies and, in any case, was the leader in Latin America. Continuing its external growth, the group realized two major operations in quick succession. The first came in May 1987 with the acquisition of Cementos Anahuac (13% of the domestic market, thanks to its large factories in Barrientos, in the State of Mexico, and Tamuin, near San Luis Potosi). Especially Cementos Anahuac offered an excellent export platform, thanks to the first maritime terminal in Mexico (El Prieto, Veracruz) and another in Florida (West Palm Beach). In addition, the new acquisition had a small fleet through which it exported to the United States. Carried out through one of Cemex's subsidiaries, Cementos Maya, the operation enabled the group to produce 15.2 million tons, or 48% of the national total.

9 Dominique Barjot, "Lafarge : the keys of a successful internationalisation process (1946-1973)", in Hubert Bonin and *alii* (eds.), *Transnational Companies (19e-20e siècles)*, Bordeaux, Plage, 2002, p. 663-680 ; Léon Dubois, *Lafarge Coppée. 150 ans d'industrie*, Paris, Belfond, 1988.

10 Dominique Barjot, "The Americanization of the European Cement Industry: Lafarge in Comparative Perspective, from Fashion to a Structural Change", in William J. Haussman (ed.), *Business and Economic History On-Line*, Papers Presented at the BHC Annual Meeting, Vol. 7: The 209 Annual Meeting, 2009, ISSN 1941-7349.

Even more spectacular was the acquisition of Empresas Toltecas in Mexico City in 1989. With its 6.7 million tons of annual production capacity, this second acquisition was a transaction equivalent to Lafarge's absorption of Canada Cement. Empresas Toltecas dominated the Mexican cement industry for much of the 20th century. Cemex exceeded it in 1980, due to the difficulties of their largest shareholder, the Blue Circle group, victim of the fall of the British market and the technological obsolescence of its factories. As a result, from 1986 on, there was a profound restructuring, marked by a reorientation of its trade and the gradual disengagement of many of its activities in Australia and New Zealand, but also from Brazil and Mexico. In Mexico, the group had reduced its investments. During the 1982 crisis, its sales decreased by 50%. Between 1984 and 1988, it represented on average only between 8 and 13% of the total production capacity of Mexico, while Cemex spent, during the period, 21 to 30% of these same national capacities. The sale of Empresas Toltecas resulted mainly from the need to recapitalize Blue Circle. Cemex acquired a 49% stake in the capital against 31% in the Mexican group ICA.

The takeover of Empresas Toltecas meant a 44% increase in production capacity. It was one of the largest investments ever made by a national private group. Admittedly, it was an expensive acquisition ($ 95 per ton against 35 for Anahuac), because Toltecas was the largest concrete manufacturer in the country (with 70 plants supplying 2.8 million tons in 1989). However, Cemex now controlled 67% of the country's production capacity and opened the export route, with its facilities in California and Arizona and the Guyamas marine terminal, north of the island. State of Sonora. Cemex was positioned as the sixth largest producer in the world after, in order of importance, Holderbank, Lafarge, Blue Circle, Heidelberger Zement and Ciments Français, with, in 1989, a production capacity of 21.9 million tons per year and a production of 16.3, of which 4.2 export. Immediately, Cemex launched a new investment program. Between 1992 and 1994, it increased the group's production capacity by 8.8 million tons. In 1998, Cemex inaugurated the Tepeaca plant, then the most modern in the world, which produced four times more than the average of the group's factories. That same year, with a production capacity of 30.6 million tons, or 68% of the national total. Cemex thus offered a model then adopted in many countries, such as Italcementi in Italy (18.7 million tons of production capacity), Votorantim in Brazil (16.5 million tons) or Siam Cement in Thailand. (16.4 million tons). This model largely based on exports: as early as 1987-88, Cemex exported more than 27% of its production.

B/ A successful process of multinationalization (1997-2000)

Cemex then operated a breakthrough in the US market. It benefited from two favorable factors: the drop in Mexican domestic consumption, which was pushing for exports, and the expansion of demand in the United States, because of the favorable prices of Mexican cement. Mexico, before Canada, became the largest exporter of cement in the United States and sold 20% of its production there. To go in a sustainable way presupposed five conditions:

1 / establish a distribution network;

2 / impose an international image;

3 / strengthen the quality policy;
4 / ensure competitive prices;
5 / develop a sales infrastructure by sea.

To that end, Cemex relied on its presence in two US companies: South Western Sunbelt Cement, which had five terminals in California, Arizona and Texas, Texas Sunbelt Cement, which had five terminals in that state alone. The results of these takeovers gave immediate results: + 51% of exports in 1986. Further strengthened by the integration of TopTeco, Cemex exported, in 1987, 3.6 million tons, or 88% of Mexican exports and 22% of the group's total sales. The group settled in the United States, thanks to the integration of a series of companies in Texas, around Houston or California: in 1987, Gulf Coast Portland Cement Co and Houston Shell and Concrete, in 1988 - 89, Houston Concrete Products; in 1990, Pacific Coast Cement. At the same time, Cemex went from being a partner to being an owner. By 1990, the group had eighteen distribution terminals in Arizona, California, Florida, Kentucky, Minnesota, New Mexico and Texas.

Cemex also gained leadership in the Hispanic world. This was the case first in Spain, as early as 1992. The Spanish market offered two favorable factors: on the one hand, it was an emerging market with high growth potential; on the other hand, it was possible to acquire well-run and technologically competitive companies. An opportunity opened with the sale in 1992 of two groups: Compania Valenciana de Cementos Portland and Auxiliar de la Construction SA (SACSA). In total, Cemex acquired 28% of the Spanish production capacity and covers 70% of the country's territory from the outset. It was also the most important operation ever carried out in Spain by a Latin American company. At a cost of $ 160 per ton, Cemex became the world's largest exporter of white cement. From 1993 to 1995, it led to a major administrative restructuring (creation of exports, and in 1994 Cemex controlled 30% of the Spanish market and produced 10.8 million tons of it.

Cemex achieved another breakthrough in South America. In 1994, the Mexican firm bought the Corporation Venezulana de Cementos (Vencemos). Founded in the 1940s, this company gave birth to an authentic group. With 4.7 million tons of production capacity in 1995, it accounted for 46% of Venezuela. Cemex thus acquired a dominant position in the country, which was very useful for oil supplies and due to rapid population growth. Cemex realized 100% deliverability gains and now accounted for 71% of national exports. Similarly, again in 1994, Cemex took control of Cementos Bayano in Panama: the group immediately acquired 40% of the national market share, quickly increased to 55% after two years.

The process grew from 1996, with Cemex taking advantage of the Asian crisis. In 1995, the firm encountered serious difficulties in the Mexican market (-26% sales). It reacted by increasing its commitment to the global market. In 1996, Cemex bought Cementos Samper and Cementos Diamante in Colombia. Between 1992 and 1996, the group gained 3.5 million tons of additional capacity and 19,500 employees. However, the Asian crisis offered interesting opportunities: in 1997, a 30% stake in Rizal Cement (2.8 million tons) in the Philippines; in 1998, acquisition of 14% of the capital of PT Semen Gresik (Indonesia); the positions acquired in these two countries strengthened in 1999. The Cemex group was therefore gaining momentum worldwide, driven by the development of trading, the creation of a port terminal in Egypt (since 1998), the growth of its sales in China (1998), the acquisition in 1999 of Cementos Pacifico in Costa Rica (85% of the capital) and a significant stake in Cementos Bio in Chile (12%).

As a result, Cemex has become the world's third largest producer. In 1999, the group already had more than 60 million tons of production capacity, forty maritime terminals for trading and was establishing in sixty countries. The following year, Cemex strengthened by the acquisition of the giant US Southdown. With 77.2 million tons of production capacity, the firm ranked third in the world, with some 51 cement plants and 70 holdings, 464 concrete plants, 164 distribution centers and 55 marine terminals. Following the acquisition of Southdown, the pace of growth slowed down, but production capacity increased by 2.3 million tons in 2001, thanks to a merger in Thailand (Sarahari Cement) and stronger positions acquired in California. In total, under the leadership of Lorenzo Zambrano, production capacity increased by + 14% per year on average, from 10.5 million tons in 1985 to 79.5 million in 2001. One of the decisive factors the evolution was in the adoption in the United States, from 1989, of an anti-dumping policy against imports of Mexican cement. Abandoning the export strategy in a single country, Cemex therefore chose the path of international trading and global enterprise. To achieve this, the group had to build a solid base in emerging countries, dominate the most advanced technologies, set up an efficient organization and day the map of globalization.

C/ A global strategy: investment in technology and trading

Cemex realized, from the second half of the 1980s, an important technological investment. This included bridging the gap with Europe. In this perspective, in 1987, the group introduced the Cemexnet satellite communication system; 1993 saw the creation of Cemtec to provide technology services to all of the group's companies and in 1995, a digital system called Sincronizacion Dynamica from Operationes to satisfy customers. In 2000, Cemex established its Enabling Cx Networks process, bringing together former firms from Argentina, Brazil, Spain and Venezuela. The objectives of Cx Networks included the development of online portals for the construction industry (Construmix), the creation of a market for the supply of indirect goods and services (Latinnexes), the extension of Cemex consultancy in computer technology, logistics and internet, in order to increase the group's capacity as a trader.

In fact, Cemex became a global trader. In 1995, the group already accounted for more than 10% of global cement traffic. Starting in 1993, the group's leaders deliberately opted for a strategy to transform into an international trader: between 1992 and 1995, the quantities processed rose from 2.2 to 8.9 million tons. In 1995, Cemex's exports went to 54 countries on four continents: 40% to the United States, 19% to the Caribbean, 12% to Central and South America, 6% to Africa, 3% to Europe. As of 2001, emerged a trading model, specific to Cemex:

- sales of cement and pre-purchased concrete;
- focus on the world's most dynamic markets; maintaining a high rate of growth through pre-selected investments.

Three orientations explained this favorable position of the group:

1/ intensive development of information systems in procurement, marketing, management, logistics, customer service and staff capacity;

2 / the establishment of a permanent management training system, coordinated by the Instituto Technologico y Estadios Superiores de Monterrey (ISTEM), with the participation of professors from Stanford, Warton, Thunderbird and Carnegie Mellon;

3 / a graduated strategy. It was, at the international level, to establish itself as the world leader in trading (13.2 million tons in 2001). At the regional level, it was necessary to organize consumer information platforms and, at the local level, to establish distribution centers, always for the benefit of large consumers.

3/ CEMEX TODAY

Cemex was therefore able to define an ambitious strategy, but also to adapt to a more difficult situation while laying the foundations for an original strategy of sustainable development. She also affirmed the originality of her model.

3.1/ An ambitious strategy

Admitted to listing on the NYSE in September 1999, the Cemex share knew, until at least 2004, an exemplary course: on this last date, its price exceeded 90 index points the S & P 500 index. It was the result of a strategy based on four major axes:

1 / increase market share, particularly in Mexico and the United States;

2 / improve the system of knowledge flow;

3 / prepare new acquisitions for the leadership of tomorrow;

4 / define an efficient financial strategy.

A/ Towards global leadership in the concrete sector: the acquisition of RMC

The year 2004 saw the acquisition of the British group Ready Mix Concrete. This gave the opportunity to increase the scale of production, vertical integration and profitability of the group. The consequence was a clear rebalancing of sales by country (see Table 2):

TABLE 2 **DISTRIBUTION OF NET SALES BY COUNTRY IN 2004 (% OF TOTAL)**

	Before RMC acquisition	After acquisition
Mexico	36	18
U.S.A.	24	23
Spain	17	11

	Before RMC acquisition	After acquisition
Rest of Europe	08	22
South and Central America (including the Caribbean)	15	08
Others	0	06

Source: Cemex

This rebalancing reflected in the distribution of the workforce employed by country:

TABLE 3 **BREAKDOWN OF EMPLOYEES BY COUNTRY IN 2004 (% OF TOTAL)**

	Before RMC acquisition	After acquisition
North America	56	39
Europe	11	41
Africa and Middle East	03	03
Central and South America	19	10
Asia	07	04
Headquarters and other business	04	03

Source: Cemex

On the same date, Cemex set itself the goal of implementing an efficient financial strategy.

B/ In search of an efficient financial strategy

The first was to strengthen the financial structure. The improvement in the net debt / EBITDA ratio, which rose from 5% in 1994 to 2.2% in 2004, allowed for a rise in the dividend per share (US $ 0.31 in 1994, but 1.02 in 2003). The desire to become a growing global company had resulted in a doubling of the workforce: in 2004, with the absorption of RMC, the group had grown from 26,000 to nearly 50,000 employees. Nevertheless, to consolidate this model, it was necessary, in the minds of leaders, focus on the core business of the group (cement, ready-mix concrete, aggregates), provide more color to customers, increase profitability through integration, allocate capital more efficiently, improve the efficiency and productivity of the operation.

Until the absorption of RMC, Cemex remained primarily a cement producer (see Table 4).

TABLE 4 **DISTRIBUTION OF NET SALES BY PRODUCTS IN 2004 (% OF TOTAL)**

Cement	72
Ready mix concrete	19
Aggregates	04
Others	05

Source: Cemex

After the operation, the structure of the activity rebalanced strongly in favor of ready-mix concrete. This was the original framework for a sustainable development strategy.

C/ An original strategy for sustainable development

This strategy organized in four areas: employees and their families, communities close to business sites, business partners (suppliers, contractors, distributors, customers and investors), the global society. Regarding the staff, it was for Cemex, in 2008, to reduce direct employment and wasted time, offer courses and training online, provide twenty-one hours of training local per employee, to promote staff in 75% of cases. With respect to neighbors, three actions had priority: to reach 224,000 poorly housed families, thanks to a cheap housing program; locally recruit 28% of local staff in production sites; promote development by acting against natural disasters (Indonesia, Philippines).

With regard to business partners, three objectives were defining:

1/ to make 94% of the group's purchases made to the benefit of local suppliers;

2/ support the social and environmental performance of suppliers in 77% of the country in which Cemex operates;

3/ take part in a study from the University of Arizona to demonstrate the role of concrete pavements in reducing urban nuisances.

This led to support for sustainable construction as well as small and medium-sized local suppliers.

Finally, vis-à-vis the world, Cemex retained five objectives:

1/ to reduce by 15.8% the levels of carbon dioxide emissions;

2/ realize for 2015 the Cemex program for the use of alternative equipment;

3/ increase the share of alternative fuels from 7.6% in 2007 to 10.3% in 2009;

4/ cover all quarries in order to develop high biodiversity areas in collaboration with Birdlife International, an NGO advocating for sustainable development;

5/ to register two new biomass projects according to the United Nations own development mechanism.

Different achievements reflected these choices: the recovery of gases emitted (-40% at the Rugby plant in the United Kingdom), the development of wind turbines (Oaxaca in Mexico), a global partnership for Cemex sites, specific partnerships around biodiversity and sustainable transport (as in France). Nevertheless, the highly specialized nature of the group exposed it to the vagaries of the crisis that occurred in 2008.

3.2/ Faced with a more difficult situation, a strategic adaptation

In 2008, Cemex had further developed compared to 2004: present in more than fifty paces, the group employed about 57,000 employees worldwide. Thanks to the integration of RMC, this same group associated two main branches of activity (see Table 5).

TABLE 5 **DISTRIBUTION OF NET SALES BY PRODUCT IN 2008 (% OF TOTAL)**

	Net sales	EBITDA
Cement	40	67
Ready mix concrete	40	12
Aggregates	16	14
Others	04	07

Source: Cemex

The profitability of cement appeared much higher than that of ready-mixed concrete.

Geographically, between 2004 and 2008, the group's activity globalized, even though four countries accounted for 55% of sales and nearly 60% of profits:

TABLE 6 **DISTRIBUTION OF SALES BY GEOGRAPHIC AREA IN 2008 (% OF TOTAL)**

	Net Sales	EBITDA
Mexico	28.4	53.2
U.S.A.	28.4	9.5
United Kingdom	11.4	11.1
Rest of Europe	14.9	9.5
Rest of the World	16.9	16.7

Source : Cemex

Moreover, if Mexico remained the main source of profits, the group had achieved a spectacular breakthrough in Europe (36% of sales, 23% of profits).

Faced with an unfavorable economic situation and under the still strong leadership of Lorenzo H. Zembrano (born March 27, 1944 in Monterrey, died on May 12, 2014 in Madrid), Chairman of the Board of Directors and Chief Executive Officer, the group was committed to cost reduction measures (budget cuts, capacity reduction): diversification of its portfolio and divestment. Without renouncing the customer or product innovation, the group's strategy was to diversify these fuels (petroleum coke, fuel oil, natural gas) and reduce the investment program to promote deleveraging. This strategy organized around four actions: priority to the reduction of the debt; cost reduction (suspension of 27 furnaces, closure of 300 RMC plants and 50 aggregate sites); reduction of capital defenses; divestment of the business portfolio. This resulted in five objectives: meeting on the core business (cement, ready-mix concrete, aggregates); provide customers with value gains; increase profitability through integration; allocate capital efficiently; optimize the integration of acquisitions.

3.3/ Cemex: an original model

Cemex was therefore an original model, characterized by five elements. He was at the same time the world leader in white cement and trading, had the most advanced information and communication technology in the cement industry, was very creative in financial solutions, and the lowest cost of its sector. Cemex also appeared as the first global enterprise in Mexico. After having taken over the national market between 1982 and 1989, and achieved its international breakthrough, the group had established itself in culturally well-known areas: the United States, Spain and South America (1989-1994). He had broken into the trading market from 1992 to 2000, before joining the global firm (1997-2003). Its original trading system made it the direct competitor of Lafarge and Holderbank (then Holcim). Thus, it explained that Cemex had gone from the periphery to the center, demonstrating the incredible capacity of this entrepreneurial firm to adapt to the modes of organization of contemporary business.

The model, however, remained both dynamic and fragile. True, Cemex grew much faster than its major global competitors (Table 7).

TABLE 7 **AVERAGE ANNUAL GROWTH RATES OF CEMEX, HOLCIM AND LAFARGE (IN %)**

	Cemex 1990-2008	Holcim 1993-2008	Lafarge 1993-2008
Net Sales	+16.7	+ 7.3	+ 9.3
EBITDA	+12.9	+ 5.3	+ 10.7

Source : Cemex, Holcim, Lafarge.

On the contrary, of the Lafarge's case, it was clear that a gradual decline in margins for Cemex, also observable at Holcim, accompanied this faster growth. In fact, from 2004 onwards, this deterioration was obvious if one made a comparison with the competition (see Table 8). [11]

TABLE 8 **EVOLUTION OF THE OPERATING MARGINS OF THE MAIN WORLD CEMENT PRODUCERS (IN %)**

	2004	2008
CEMEX	31.1	20.0
Lafarge	20.8	18.6
Holcim	26.7	21.2
Heidelberg Cement	17.4	20.7
Italcementi	24.3	18.6

Source: Annual reports of each group.

Even though, in 2008, the group was only marginally outperformed by Holcim and Heidelberg Cement, in the long run the margin contraction had been very marked: in 1994, it was 34, 2% against only 20% in 2008. It was still an honorable figure showing a competitiveness despite everything preserved despite a heavy debt.

11 Dominique Barjot, « Lafarge (1993-2004). Comment on devient firme mondiale », dans Dominique Barjot, (dir.), « Où va l'histoire des entreprises ? », *Revue économique*, vol. 58, n°1, janvier 2007, p. 79-111.

Conclusion

In fact, in 2009-2010, the Cemex group experienced a very serious financial crisis. However, he managed to overmatch it by adapting its operations to the new market dynamics. Already listed on the stock exchanges of Mexico City, New York and London, the company was interested in new financial markets. In 2012, Cemex listed as South and Central American operations on the Columbian Stock Exchange, then, in 2016, its operations in the Philippines Stock Exchange.

1 / A family group with consolidated positions

In 2016, the group maintained its positions in its three dominant markets, but by reorienting its activity towards cement, the most profitable segment in the sector and by renouncing its diversification activities.

TABLE 9 **SALES DISTRIBUTION BY PRODUCTS IN 2016 (IN PERCENTAGE)**

Cement	45 %
Ready mix concrete	39 %
Aggregates	16 %

Source: Cemex

In addition, Cemex strengthened its positions in the United States, Latin America and the Caribbean, as well as in Asia, Oceania, the Middle East and Africa, to the detriment of Europe and, above all, Mexico.

TABLE 10 **SALES DISTRIBUTION BY REGIONS IN 2016 (IN PERCENTAGE)**

Mexico	22 %
U.S.A.	28 %
Europe	25 %
South, Central America and the Caribbean	13 %
Asia, Middle East and Africa	12 %

Source: Cemex

In this regard, the major operation was the 2007 acquisition of the Australian group Rinker, through which Cemex increased its breakthrough in the United States, the integration of this group ending in 2009, under financially difficult conditions. Nevertheless, the risk had paid off: in the 2010s, Cemex thus became the North American leader in the cement industry. In 2016, the group remained largely in the hands of the family. Led by a Mexican C.E.O., Fernando A. González, there were at least three representatives of the Zembrano family on its 15-member board of directors, including nine independent directors and all Mexicans.

2/ Faced with the threat of new competitors, a powerful and profitable group

Today, the group faces severe international competition from, among others, China and others:

TABLE 11 **GLOBAL CEMENT COMPANIES: 1-10 RANKED BY INSTALLED CAPACITIES AND NUMBER OF PLANTS IN 2016**[12]

Rank	Groups	Country	Capacity (million tons/ year)	Plants (number)
1	CNBM (Sinoma)	China	400.0	94?
2	Lafarge Holcim	Switzerland	386.5	180
3	Anhui Conch	China	285.0	32?
4	Heidelberg Cement Italcementi	Germany	205.7	139
5	Jidong Development	China	130.0	43
6	Sanshui (Sunnsy)	China	100.	?
7	Cemex	Mexico	94.0	55
8	China Resources	China	78.3	24
9	Taiwan Cement	Taiwan	69.0	23
10	Aditya Birth Group	India	68.9	14

Source: Annual reports of respective companies and their websites.

However, Cemex remains nevertheless the fourth world cement group:

TABLE 12 **THE SIX BIGGEST CEMENT GROUPS IN 2016**

Rank	Groups	Country	Net sales (billions of US $)	EBITDA (billions of US $)	Employees
1	CRH	Ireland	27.10	3.10	87,000
2	Lafarge Holcim	Switzerland	26.90	5.24	90,000
3	Heidelberg Italcementi	Germany	15.17	2.94	60,424
4	Cemex	Mexico	13.40	2.75	41,000
5	CNBM	China	11.88	1.68	106,989
6	Anhui Conch	China	08.10	2.49	44,859

Source: Annual reports 2016 of respective companies

12 Amy Saunders, "Top 75 global cement companies", Written by, *Global Cement Magazine*, 9 December 2013, p. 5-6.

Furthermore, Cemex took it on all its main European competitors in terms of profitability:

TABLE 13 **COMPARATIVE PERFORMANCE OF THE SIX LARGEST CEMENT GROUPS WORLDWIDE IN 2016.**

Groups	EBITDA/ Net Sales (in %)	Productivité annuelle du travail[13] Lafarge Holcim = 100
CRH	11.4 (6)	104.2 (1)
Lafarge Holcim	19.5 (3)	100.0 (3)
Heidelberg Italcementi	19.4 (4)	84.0 (4)
Cemex	20.5 (2)	103.9 (2)
CNBM	13.4 (5)	36.3 (6)
Anhui Conch	30.7 (1)	57.4 (5)

Source: Annual reports 2016 of respective companies

Today, in spite of its small size, Cemex remains largely competitive with its major European and Chinese competitors[14].

13 Net sales/ Number of employees.
14 Dominique Barjot, "Why was the world construction industry dominated by European leaders?" The development of the largest European firms from the late 19th to the early 21st centuries", *Construction History International Journal of the Construction History Society*, vol. 28, N° 3 (2013), p. 89-114.

Becoming a multinational mining company: the case of Vale (Brazil)

Hildete de Moraes Vodopives
Fellow Researcher Centre Roland Mousnier
Sorbonne University

Introduction

"Perhaps the biggest firm you have never heard of";[1] that is how *The Economist* defined the Brazilian mining company Vale. It was 2010 and Vale had recently became the second largest mining company in the world. With this achievement Vale also got into the Boston Consulting Group *Global Challengers* list: "a group of emerging challengers that are becoming important players in both developing and developed countries around the globe." Multinational companies from emerging countries such as Vale have drawn growing interest among historians and management scholars. In 2015, the section "Multinationals from emerging and developing countries, historical roots, organized by Judith Clifton and Pierre Lanthier[2], put forward the cases of Samsung, the Tata Group and Telmex.

Vale's business, mining, is a capital-intensive activity with political, environmental and social implications. It has become vital in modern societies, due to their intensive use in transportation, construction, manufacturing and communication. The industry encompasses a diverse group of businesses. Fossil fuels, namely oil and natural gas are reasonably uniform extraction wise. In contrast, metal ores vary in terms of chemical properties, method of extraction, or industrial use. Geography plays a vital

1 https://www.economist.com/business/2010/09/23/valuable-vale
2 17th World Economic History Congress in Kyoto, August 3-7, 2015.

role in both procurement and demand. Companies tend to explore mineral deposits that are closer to the consumer markets. The resources of industrialized European countries were the first to be explored in the 19th century[3]. The United States later surpassed Europe, becoming the leading producer of both iron and steel and forging a proto-type of the modern mass procurement system.

This article addresses the constitutive aspects of the company. They are: Brazil local constrains, political forces and the international alliances. It exams the strategic decisions that shaped the company over time. Three episodes are highlighted: 1. the technological definition phase and gain of scale involving transport. 2. the privatization of the company. 3. The strategic plan that defines the ambition of becoming a global player.

1/ CRAFTING A NATIONAL CHAMPION

From its foundation in 1942[4] to its privatization in 1997, Vale built muscles that made it a major iron ore producer and one of Brazil's leading companies. The steel industry would face radical changes in demand and technology.

1.1/ First challenges

Despite having abundant high quality iron ore deposits, from its early days Companhia Vale do Rio Doce faced challenges related to demand, technology and capital. The company was created at the confluence of Brazilian and foreign agendas. The Brazilian government was eager to launch an industrialization project. Brazil was a rural economy in need of technology, machinery and capital. Iron was not only an essential input for the industry it was also a promising economic activity capable of fostering economic development. The foreign drive was the war. The United States and Great Britain needed to outsource iron ore and Brazil rich high quality deposits was the ideal candidate. As shown in the next graph (figure 1), at that time Brazil was in the ascending mining countries.

When the war ended in 1945, both Great Britain and the United States relinquished their option to renew their contracts, leaving Vale without guaranteed markets. In the 20th century, steel demand skyrocket the widespread use of steel in urban construction, household appliances and railroads boosted demand. Vale needed to reach an adequate economy of scale, searching for foreign markets since Brazil remained a poor country with an insipient industry. However the lack of marketing structure and high maritime freight costs made it difficult for Vale to compete with companies that were closer to the consumer markets of Europe, United States and Asia. With

3 M. Ericsson, Trends in the Mining and Metals Industry. Mining's Contribution to Sustainable Development, ICMM, 2012.

4 Vale was established in 1942 by the nationalization and incorporation of two existing companies: Companhia Brasileira de Mineração e Siderurgia S. A. and Itabira de Mineração S. A.

the retraction of demand, financial limitations and infrastructure deficiencies the company was on to the brink of bankruptcy.

On top of its operational issues, Vale was loosing money with its sales organization that had initially been organized using a network of intermediaries. This system presented two problems. Not only Vale had no direct access to customers but also the company lost a big part of the margin. In Vale's main market, the United States, intermediaries bought from Vale for 8 dollars was resold for 14 to final customers[5].

FIGURE 1 **MINING ACTIVITY BY GEOGRAPHY IN THE WORLD 1850-2009**

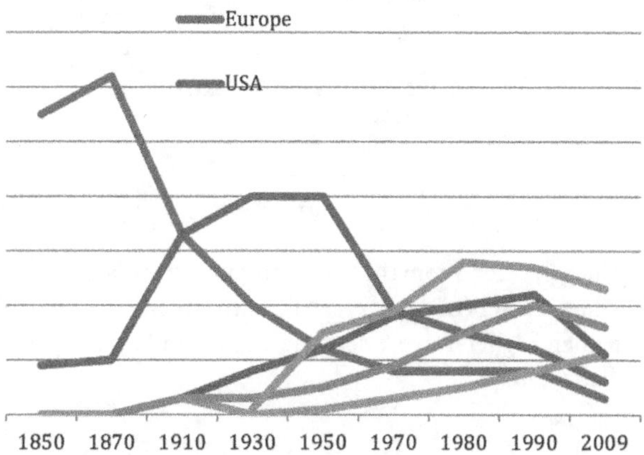

Source: Raw Materials Group, Stockholm, Sweden in M. Ericsson, ICMM. Trends in the Mining and Metals Industry. Mining's Contribution to Sustainable Development, 2012.

FIGURE 2 **VALE'S IRON ORE EXPORTS (TONS)**

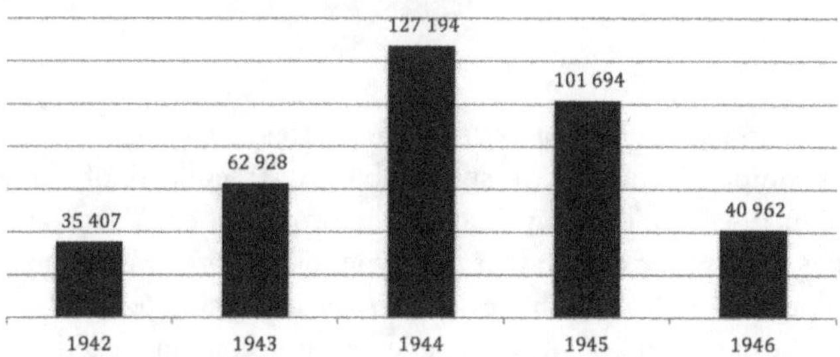

1.2/ Growing demand for steel and more competition

Along with the need to reconstruct after the war Japan became a major steel market. Steel consumption in Japan started to grow from 1956, reached an optimum level in 1970, peaked in 1973, declined in 1986, and stabilized from 1995[6]. The booming steel consumption stimulated the entry of new iron ore suppliers from Venezuela, Peru,

5 R. Penalva dos Santos, *op. cit.*, p. 163.

6 D. Gaspar, J. R. , L. Masiero, and A. Rachik, "Mining + Steel: How Will M&A Play Out? An analysis of internal consolidation in the steel and mining industries," A. T. Keaney, Chicago, 2010.

Liberia and India. The competition resulted in a reduction in mining prices. Brazilian iron ore had to compete with Australia, China, Soviet Union and India. With transport averaging around 30% of iron ore cost, Australia was better positioned to export to the rising Asian market. Brazil on the other hand was closer to the United States and Europe[7]. Vale's CEO at the time, Elieser Batista argued that Vale needed to face the problem of "economic distance". The challenge was to overcome the economic distance of a low cost commodity – iron ore – and deliver it to a distant market.

TABLE 1 **COMPARISON OF DISTANCES FROM JAPAN (OITA) TO BRAZIL AND TO AUSTRALIA**

Port	Nautical miles
Port Hedland, Australia	3.395
Ponta da Madeira, Brazil	12.030
Tubarão Brazil	11.105
Baia de Sepetiba, Brazil	10.591

Source : J.C.F Pinheiro, « *A Mineração brasileira de ferro e a reestruturação do setor siderúrgico*» [8]

Technology was the other game changer. From the 1960s onwards, the dissemination of new blast furnaces, called Linz - Dürer (LD) or oxygen furnaces, altered significantly the iron ore specifications; namely higher iron ore content, stricter and a more regular supply. Mining companies had to adapt.

2/ CHOICES LEADING TO THE LEADERSHIP IN IRON ORE

The way that Vale dealt with these challenges would craft the company's strengths in the following decades. They concerned sales, logistics, quality of the product and diversification.

2.1/ Competitive treats: superior iron ore and logistics

The first pillar of Vale's competitiveness was its sustainable investment in reinforcing the quality of its ores. In 1949, the company started the project of expansion and modernization of mines to meet the demand for new types of iron ores[9]. Vale chose the thermal process of pelletizing "to enrich the ore into iron and facilitate its subsequent treatment in blast furnaces. Free of impurities and high iron content, pelletizing offered a major opportunity to increase profitability. [10]

The second pillar of Vale strategy was to verticalize sales and logistics. Instead of intermediaries that were expensive, Vale established exclusive commercial represen-

7 M. L. Amarante de Andrade and M. da C. Da Silva Cunha, Luiz Mauricio; Martins Vieira, Jose Ricardo; Keller, "Mineral-metallurgical and steel sectors," BNDES , Rio de Janeiro, 1996.

8 *Ibid.*

9 O. R. De Medeiros, "The Economics of the World Iron and Steel Industry: 1950-1980," p. 1950-1980, 1999.

10 Vale, *Nossa Historia, op. cit.*, p. 115.

tatives. The company also constituted a subsidiary, Docenave, in charge of exports transportation[11]. Using large versatile vessels that transported iron ore and oil, Vale was able to cut transportation cost. The same ship that would take ore to Asia could come back to Brazil with oil from the Persian Gulf. Whereas between 1951 and 1954, the average price of ore from Vitória Port used to be $12.93 per ton (FOB), it fell to $7.99 for the period 1960-1972.

FIGURE 3 **DISTANCE FROM INDUSTRIALIZED MARKETS**

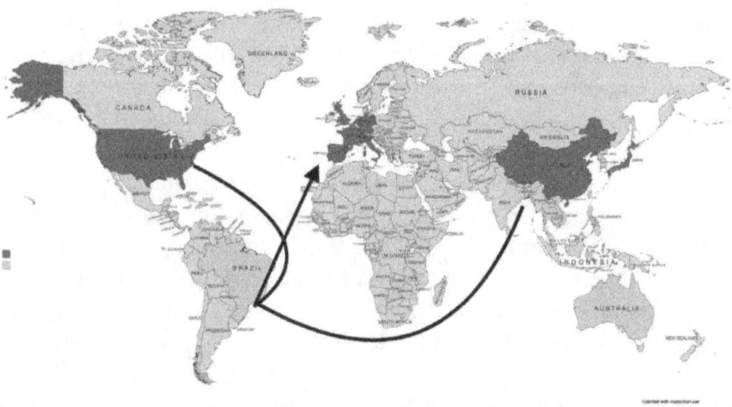

Vale succeeded in establishing long-term contracts (10 to 15 years) and expanded its clients from fourteen countries in 1960 to twenty-one in 1967.[12] That year, Vale was ranked among the six largest exporters in the world. The first long-term iron ore supply contracts were signed in 1961 with Italy and Argentina. But the most tangible achievement was the partnership established with Japan and Western Germany. The first long-term contract with Japan was signed in 1962. In 1967 the Germans consumed nearly 30% of Vale's exports, the Japanese 21%.[13]

FIGURE 4 **EVOLUTION OF LONG-TERM CONTRACTS, 1960-1976**

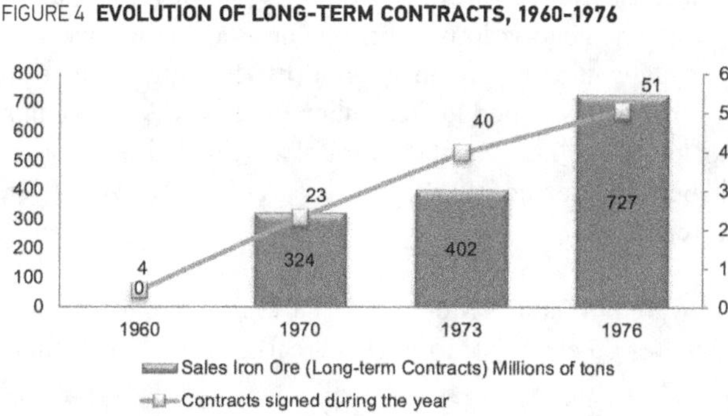

Source: Vale

11 Vale, "Our History", *op. cit.*, p. 103.

12 F. do Rego Fernandes (org.), "The largest miners in Brazil: per l entrepreneurial of the Brazilian mineral sector". São Paulo: EMEP, 1982, vol. 1, p. 30 (note) cité dans *Vale, Nossa Historia*, *op. cit.*, p. 104.

13 A. Dalla Costa, "La Vale in the New Context of the Internetization of Brazilian Companies," *Companies and History*, vol. I, no. 54, 2009, p. 20.

2.2/ Exploring the Amazon mineral wealth (with the government help)

The Amazon region became a new mining frontier when Bethlehem Steel-Icomi, found manganese deposit in the state of Amapá.[14] Further discoveries of rich deposits of bauxite and iron ore brought attention to the wild unexplored region in the North of Brazil[15]. The technical and economic viability of mining in this isolated region of northern Brazil was a huge challenge.

With the help of the Brazilian government, Vale not only set the Northern system with the implementation of Carajás but initiated an important new product: aluminum. Both enterprises illustrate the economic synergy involving the Brazilian government, the international companies and a local private sector. They were part of the plan to develop the Amazon region's infrastructure to explore its rich mineral reserves. It would also be necessary to adapt legislation and provide funding, encouraging the establishment of new enterprises, through partnership between foreign and national, state and private companies. Vale was interested in alumina and bauxite. Aluminum was seen as the metal of the future as the market anticipated a reduction in demand for steel and an increase in demand for these two materials in the world market. In 1973, this forecast was confirmed by the oil shock. Industries preferred using components manufactured with aluminum in order to reduce the use of oil and its derivatives.

In 1962, Alcan's subsidiary in Brazil, Aluminas, confirmed the existence of bauxite in the Trompetas river region (Pará). The initial project outlined a capacity of 1 million tons per year. This output would be entirely exported to Quebec. The goal was that eventually the Brazilian bauxite would completely replace the material imported from Guyana. However, Alcan had other priorities elsewhere. After the decision to shutdown the Trompetas project, the Brazilian government stepped in to mediate a solution. Aluminum fit into the Brazilian government's industrialization policy both in terms of nationalization of technology and substitution for imports. It was an opportunity to encompass a consortium to produce alumina with the participation of the Brazilian private sector. The negotiations to bring Vale as a partner began in May 1972. The feasibility study would be done in six months, defining production goals and timeline. An agreement was signed in December 1972, with Vale holding 41% of the shares and Alcan kept 19%. The rest of the capital was divided seven other partners[16]. The plant would be in a region near the navigable part of the Amazon River, which granted waterway integration.

Iron ore deposits were discovered in Carajás Mountains (Pará) by geologists from a subsidiary[17] of the United States Steel Corporation (US Steel) in 1967. Carajás had

14 Maria Cecilia Nunes Coelho and Maurilio de Abreu Monteiro, "Verticalização da produção e variedade de situações sociais no espaço funcional do alumínio nos baixos vales do Amazonas e Tocantins," *Rev. Territ.*, vol. VII, no. 11,12 e 13 set/out, p. 29-48, 2003.

15 H. de Moraes Vodopives, "Emerging multinationals, Alcan and Vale in Amazonia during the years 1960-1979", *French Economic History Review. Revue française d'histoire économique*, Paris, 2015 - II, p. 146-156.

16 Presently, MRN partners are: Vale 40%, BHP 14,8%, Alcan 12%, CBA 10%, Alcoa Brazil 8,58% Alcoa world alumina -5%, Abalco 4,62% - (Total Alcoa 18,2%) Norsk Hydro 5%. Alcan (19%).

17 Companhia Meridional de Mineração.

large quantities of high quality iron ore; 19.9 billion tons of iron ore with an average iron content of 66.1%. In 1970, a joint venture was formed with the intermediation of the Brazilian government forming the Amazônia Mineração S.A. (AMZA). The agreement gave Vale shareholder control of the company with 51% of the capital. The initial project was budgeted at US$ 930 million and aimed to reach capacities of 12 million tons annually from 1979 and 50 million tons annually in 1985. This production would be destined primarily for markets in the United States, Europe and Japan.

From 1975, the company took the lead in global iron ore exports, accounting for 16% of the seaborne market. By the late 1980s, Vale had consolidated the mining industry in Brazil and expanded its operations into two integrated systems of mines, railroads and port. The Southern System, based in the states of Minas Gerais and Espírito Santo had iron ore reserves of approximately 2.3 billion tons and the Northern System, Carajás, based in the states of Pará and Maranhão, had estimated iron ore reserves of approximately 1.2 billion tons[18]. Direct marketing, long-term contracts, the inauguration of the Tubarão Port, the creation of Docenave, and pelletization plants summarized Vale's strategic choices[19]. Vale also operated transportation (including rail and ports), steel and metallurgy plants as well as non-mining operations, such as wood pulp plants and paper. Portfolio diversification didn't work as well. Despite the company's efforts to explore other metals, in 1997 iron ore accounted for 89% of the Vale's output, with bauxite second with 8%. Manganese, gold and alumina do not exceed 1% each. All in all, the company's profile outside Brazil remains limited on the eve of its privatization in the 1990s.

FIGURE 5 **PORTFOLIO DIVERSIFICATION 1967-1997**

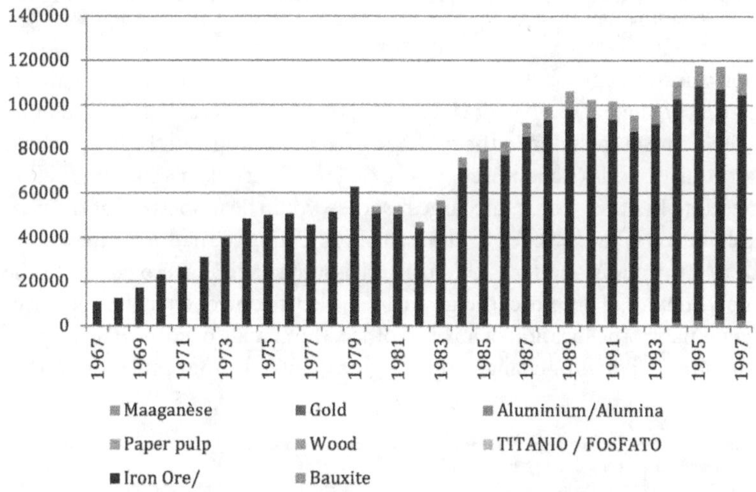

Source: Vale

18 www.vale.com
19 Companhia Vale do Rio Doce, Management Report 1967, p. 21. Cité dans *Vale, Nossa Historia, op. cit.*, p. 115.

3/ TRANSITIONING TO A PRIVATE MINDED GROUP

Vale's privatization officially began in 1995[20], when it was included in the national privatization program. In reality, the company initiated preparations in 1993 and ended in 2002.

3.1/ The privatization process

Three administrations were involved: the ones of presidents Itamar Franco, Fernando Henrique Cardoso and Luis Inacio Lula da Silva. The valuation of the company became a controversial topic. Vale was perceived at home as a national champion. The company's price tag should not only reflect that but also protect the national interest of a product considered strategic for the economic development of the country. Normally, the valuation methodology was the *discounted cash flow*. For mining companies it would take into account the profits projection of thirty years ahead[21]. However, Carajás was believed to have iron ore for 400 years. Such a long-term scenario was almost impossible to quantify. Furthermore, the global economy was slow and the price of iron ore, Vale's main product, was declining.

TABLE 1 **ORE PRICES 1991-1997**

USD/ ton	1991	1992	1993	1994	1995	1996	1997
Fine Iron Ore	19,3	18,7	16,6	15	16,2	16,3	16,7
Aluminium	1303	1254	1138	1479	1804	1507	1597
Pellets	33,8	31,9	28,9	28,6	30,7	32,7	33,3
Nickel	8179	7010	5291	6349	8223	7496	6907

Source: R. Reck Dias, "Capital structure - theory and evidence: the case of Companhia Vale do Rio Doce (1991-2000)," Federal University of Rio Grande do Sul, 2002.

The solution was to design a hybrid model addressing all these concerns. Regarding the price setting of mineral reserves, it was decided to separate potential and operating reserves. The first was included in the package of privatization and the latter would be object of equity bonds (debentures) [22] securing the rights of shareholders before the privatization. In other words, the large reserves would be monetized at the time of their exploitation in the future. The concern of protecting the national interest was addressed with the addition of a "golden share" issuing special prerogatives to the Brazilian government. Therefore, the government kept control over the change of the company's name, the location of its head office, the change of corporate purpose regarding mining activities or changes in the rights granted by the regulations on the

20 The decree that included the company in the PND was signed by President Fernando Henrique Cardoso on June 1, 1995, after the subject had been thoroughly discussed in the National Congress.

21 Eduardo Almeida Gazzola, interview, Projeto Vale Memoria, Museu da Pessoa, 12/06/2000, Rio de Janeiro.

22 A debenture is a financial instrument that has the same characteristics as a bond, however the debenture does not offer any collateral. A total of 388,559,056 debentures were issued at a par value of R$ 0.01 (one cent), whose value will be restated in accordance with the variation in the General Market Price Index ("IGP-M"), as set forth in the Issue Deed As at December 31, 2012 the total amount of these debentures was US$1,653 (US$ 1,336 in December 31, 2011). Source: Vale , "Consolidated Financial Statements for the year ended December 31, 2012," Hong Kong, 2013.

preferred shares issued by Vale. In addition, it protected against the risk of liquidation of the company, including any disposal or partial liquidation of the iron ore and integrated mining logistics systems businesses[23].

The privatization was carried out in three parts: the auction, the sale to the employees[24] and finally the sale to the public[25]. The process took place between 1997 and 2002. The first round was the most important one. It regarded the auction of 41.73% of the outstanding common stock (ON)[26], equivalent to the controlling stake of the company. The second round regarded Vale's employees. They used their severance funds and social security contributions to purchase 4.45% of the common shares and 6.3% of the preferred shares. The third stage regarded the remaining common shares (25%-30%), to the public. It was part of Cardoso's objective of promoting the democratization of the stock market. The auction date was set for April 29, 1997, but due to the 127 actions and injunctions filed in court[27], it was not held until May 6. The Brazilian government set a minimum price for the controlling block of the company of R$10.4 billion. It was based on the average price of the company's shares (R$26.67[28]) on the stock exchange immediately prior to the pricing date[29].

There were two contenders for Vale. The favorite, Consortium Valecom[30], was led by Antonio Erminio de Moraes, head of the Brazilian industrial group Votorantim[31], and involved the participation of Anglo American (mines), Centrus (pension fund of the Central Bank of Brazil), Sistel (pension fund of Telebras), and a Nippon-Brazilian consortium formed by Caemi-Mitsui and twelve companies. The outsider, Consortium Brasil[32], was formed at the last minute under the leadership of Benjamin Steinbruch, CEO of steel company Companhia Siderurgica Nacional (CSN).

The bidding ended in five minutes. Consortium Brasil won, offering $3.338 million ($32 per share)[33]. It was a 20% premium. Antonio Erminio de Moraes, leader of the

23 Prospecto Definitivo de Debentures da Vale . Accessible on .vale.com.br the 21/02/2011

24 On May 20, 1997, the Treasury sold 5.1%, (4.5% of ordinary actions and 6.5% of privileged actions of catégorie A) of the company's shares for R$ 179 million to Investvale, the employees' investment club, using the severance fund, social contributions and with an additional loan from BNDESPAR Investvale also had the option of exchanging these shares for those held by the controlling group. Source : Companhia Vale do Rio Doce. 2002. "Prospectus for Public Trading of 6th Issue Participative Debentures of CVRD". Rio de Janeiro. p. 372.

25 There are two interpretations in the literature on the privatization of Vale . Often, the authors consider the auction and the sale to employees as belonging to the first phase.

26 Website da Vale . 10/03/11.

27 C. M. Borges Costa Pinto, " The process of privatization and destabilization of the Brazilian State". http://.egov.ufsc.br/portal/sites/default/files/anexos/30159-30685-1-PB.pdf

28 This was equivalent to a price 10% lower than the price of Vale's common shares traded on April 29, 1997.

29 Ediméia Maria Ribeiro de Mello " The structural conditions of the steel industry in Minas Gerais: Natural Resources, State and Educated Elite. «These de doctorat. Sour l'orientation de Ralfo Edmundo da Silva Matos. Universidade Federal de Minas Gerais. 2010. Available on the internet:http://.bibliotecadigital.ufmg.br/dspace/bitstream/1843/MPBB8BZMCT/1/tese_final_02.12.01.pdf , p. 196.

30 *Folha Online,* " Understand the case of the privatization of Vale do Rio Doce ", 07/05/2002, Accessible le 12/12/2015 http://www1.folha.uol.com.br/folha/brasil/ult96u32222.shtml

31 Antonio Erminio de Moraes, President of the Votorantim Group .

32 Consorsio Brasil is constituted by a subsidiary of Companhia Siderúrgica Nacional (CSN); Brazilian pension funds: Banco do Brasil (PREVI), Petrobrás (Petros), CESP (Fundação CESP) and Caixa Econômica Federal (Funcef); and the banks: Bradesco , Opportunity and Nations Bank.

33 The company's value was R$12.431 billion. E. M. R. de Mello and S. Mendes de Paula, "Iron mining and enclave. Case study of Companhia Vale do Rio Doce.", p. 613-636.

Valecom Consortium, said later that he was initially prepared to bid up to 31.30 per share. He was ready to cover CSN's bid, but his Japanese partner stopped him[34]. Consortium Brasil became Valepar SA, a holding company formed to act solely as Vale's majority shareholder.

FIGURE 6 **VALEPAR'S SHAREHOLDERS**

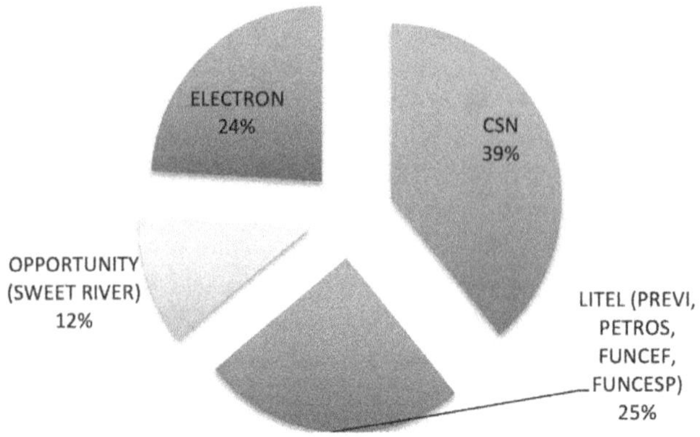

The sale to the public of the remaining common shares completed the privatization of Vale on March 20, 2002. The Treasury and BNDES sold 20.3% of Vale's capital[35] to thousands of people who used part of their Government Severance Indemnity Fund (FGTS) resources.

3.2/ Accommodation phase

Free from the State supervision, the company faced political and economic instability. A succession of crises in Asia, the technology bubble and finally the 2001 terrorist attacks dramatically increased the Brazil risk [36]. At the same time, the election of a left-wing president Luiz Inacio Lula da Silva Workers' Party (PT) takes the index to its highest level, reaching 2,446 points in September 2002, more than double the average for the years 1994-2001. The U.S. dollar reached the record level of R$ 4.00/ US dollar[37] and weighs on Brazilian company's cost of capital with negative impacts on Vale's competitiveness.

Internally, the conflict among Valepar's shareholders punctuated the period 1997-2000. Without a long-term strategic consensus, the board directive focus on cost reduction and to continue projects already underway in logistics, copper and aluminum. The contention among partners was settled by CSN's withdraw from the group. A transition is set in motion under the direction of Jorio Dauster Magalhães e Silva

34 *O Globo Newspaper*, "Vale is sold with 20% premium and will have national capital control" 7/05/1997.

35 INFORM-SE. No. 45 - July 2002. BNDES . Available on the Internet 10/03/11. (33% of the common stock, according to Vale's 2002 Administration Report).

36 The EMBI + Risco-Brasil (JP Morgan - JPM366_EMBI366) corresponds to the average premium paid by Brazilian bonds on equivalent U.S. Treasury term securities. Source: http://hcinvestimentos.com/2011/03/28/risco-pais/

37 The currency reached R$ 2.06 at the end of February 1999, reaching a valuation of 70% against the real. The quotation on 12/31/1999 was R$ 1.79. Ipeadata.

(2000-2001). Vale accomplished the consolidation of its leadership in Brazil. After acquiring Brazilian mining companies Samitri, Samarco Socoimex, and Caemi[38]. Gross revenues from iron ore increased by 24.0% in 2003[39].

TABLE 2 **ACQUISITIONS IN BRAZIL 2001-2003 ($ MILLIONS)**

Company	Product	Year	Value paid1
Caemi	Iron Ore and Kaolin	December 2001 and March 2003	705
Salobo	Copper	2002	51
Alunorte	Alumina	2002	42
MVC	Bauxite	2002	2

Source : Economatica database

At that time mining, with the exception of aluminum, was a local, low-value business. But the game would soon change with China's ascent stimulates demand for commodities. With iron ore prices recovering after a 30-year low[40] mining companies become eager for acquisitions. M&A activity went from 5% of American GDP in the 1970s to rose to 25% in 1999[41].

FIGURE 7 **IRON ORE DEMAND, 1990-2009**

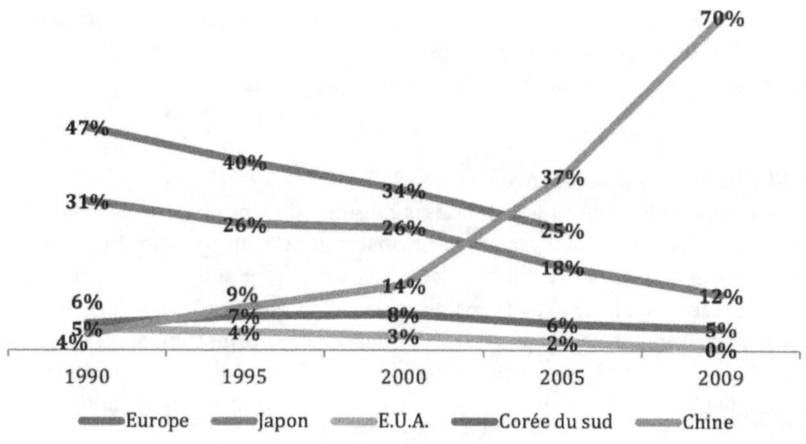

Source : IISI Steel Statistical Yarmouk.

At Valepar grew the influence of the bank Bradesco who appoints the successor of Dauster, Roger Agnelli. The bank had influence on the board through two investment holdings: Electron and Babié/Bradespar. At the same time, a diagnosis was commis-

38 Companhia Vale do Rio Doce, "CVRD: Corporate Governance and Strategic Guidelines, Press Release (October 25, 2001)." Rio de Janeiro, p. 1-5, 2001.

39 Vale, Report 20F, 2004, *op. cit.*, p. 82.

40 A.T. Kearney Inc, "Mining + Steel: How Will M&A Play Out," Chicago, 2010.

41 E. Amiel Pfiffer, *Adequação estratégica dos processos de fusões e aquisições no setor de minério de ferro: estudo de caso da Companhia Vale do Rio Doce,* thèse, PUC-RIO, 2004, http://www2.dbd.puc-rio.br/pergamum/biblioteca/php/mostrateses.php?open=1&arqtese=0212262_04_ P.2

sioned from McKinsey consulting firm in 2000 to evaluate Vale's strategy and governance perception[42]. The objective was to maximize value for its shareholders over the long term. Of the seven largest mining companies, Vale was the only one at the time that did not have an *investment grade*[43]. The risk was reflected in two factors: concentration on one product and a single geographic footprint. The lack of strategy and poor communicating were seen as problems[44].

3.3/ Setting the course for 2002-2010

The extensive scrutiny resulted in the elaboration of a strategic plan. The goal was to increase the company's value from $10 billion to $25 billion and make Vale figure among the world's three largest mining companies in 2010[45]. The diagnosis highlighted that mining was no longer a local business and Vale had to compete in a global environment. Three aspects stood out: a corporate governance model with well-defined roles, the need to guarantee quality deposits, located in countries other than Brazil, portfolio diversification and lowering the cost of capital. Reducing the cost of capital implied minimizing factors impacting income generation. Portfolio diversification was set to minimize risk dependence on a single product. Divesting in non-core businesses such as pulp and paper initially financed opportunistic acquisitions. Expansion priorities were copper and nickel, next came thermal and coking coal, cobalt, platinum group metals, and fertilizers. In 2003, acquisitions were made in Chile and Peru. Between 2004 and 2006, international expansion accelerated in other neighboring Latin American countries, Africa, and Asia[46]. Gradually, the idea of buying a major North American miner was taking shape.

3.4/ The acquisition of Inco in Canada

The acquisition of Inco for $18.68 billions is considered as the point of order of Vale's internationalization. Canada was a traditional mining country, with high quality assets and qualified workforce. It has also a mature market and a gateway to North America. Established in 1916 as a subsidiary of an American company, Inco was one of Canada's champions. Inco had a solid international footprint[47] and was the largest nickel producer in the world, accounting for about 25% of the global production. The company had a growth pipeline of nickel, cobalt, copper and precious metals projects[48].

42 G. Stoliar, "Strategy and Governance: The CVRD Case". *National Congress of Management Update*, Joinville, SC, p. 0-41, 2005.

43 Investmentgrade corresponds to a low level of risk. They correspond to ratings from rating agencies ranging from AAA to BBB- according to the Standard & Poor's scale. Also called High Grade, these are the ratings established by the rating agencies for borrowers that are between AAA and BBB-. Source: www.verminen.net

44 *Ibid.*

45 Gabriel Stoliar , director of Vale interview, Rio de Janeiro, 15/01/2009.

46 R. de Rezende Penalva Santos, "Impacts of privatization on the organization's healthy longevity: the case of CVRD/Vale . UFRJ, Rio de Janeiro, 2011, p. 133.

47 Inco had operations in the United Kingdom, Indonesia and New Caledonia as well as refineries in Japan, South Korea and Taiwan, commercializing through a marketing network in over 40 countries.

48 H. de Moraes Vodopives, "The globalization wave rolls over Canada with Vale's acquisition of Inco", *French Economic History Review. Revue française d'Histoire Economique*, 2015, p. 80-91.

FIGURE 4 **VALE ACQUISITIONS 2003-2006**

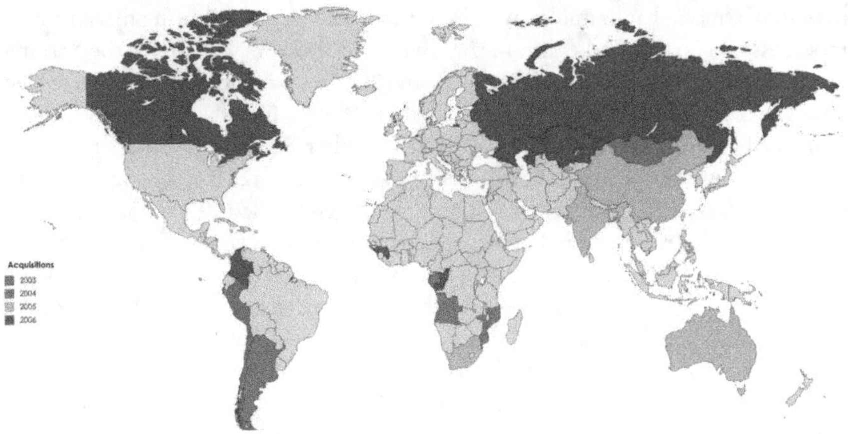

Note: 2003: Chile, Peru. 2004: Mozambique, Angola, Gabon, Argentina, Mongolia. 2005: Australia, China, India, South Africa. 2006: Kazakhstan, Colombia, Canada, Russia, Congo, Guinea. Source: Vale , Administration Reports.

It was however, a bold move. Vale would take on a high debt ratio. The company was relying on its solid cash flow could to get by in a stress scenario. The valuation considered Inco's assets and the synergies expected after the merger. Four banks worked in the transaction: ABN Ambro, Credit Suisse, UBS, and Santander. Nevertheless, the financial community had doubts. Although analysts acknowledged the benefits of diversification, they feared that the company was taking risks by shifting its focus away from its core business, iron ore, which had the advantage ofbeing marketed with long-term contracts[49]. In the long run, results confirmed the company's assumptions and even exceeded the market capitalization goals.

Conclusion

Vale's becoming a multinational mining company is the crowning of a long cycle. The large-scale nature of the mining industry had a determinant role in pushing Vale toward internationalization. Instigated by the need to secure the supply of mineral resources, the mining industry became a global business. The growing international capital flows relates to the standardization of accounting rules opening doors to international acquisitions and capital flows. Vale also had a significant stakeholder: the Brazilian State. The Brazilian government in important played a decisive role in important episodes: the company's foundation, the Carajás and Aluminum projects. But Vale had to deal with political interests and bureaucracy limiting its autonomy[50]. The strategic positioning implemented after the company's privatization constitutes the leap towards internationalization. Vale achieved (for a while) its goal of figuring among the world's three largest diversified mining companies, alongside BHP Billiton and Rio Tinto.

49 B. Simon and T. Benson, "Brazil Mining Giant Said to Seek Noranda Stake," *New York Times*, New York, p. 1-2, 2004.

50 R. de Rezende Penalva Santos, "Impacts of privatization on the organization's healthy longevity: the case of CVRD/Vale". UFRJ, Rio de Janeiro, 2011, p. 199.

The mining consolidation was put on hold with the 2008 financial crisis, but its effects persisted. On one hand, miners were rewarded with larger operating margins with repercussions on the market capitalization of consolidators. Except for the Xstrata-Falconbridge (2006), and Rio Tinto-Alcan (2007), consolidated groups excelled after the mergers. Vale for example, gained 110% after Inco's acquisition while the industry benchmark index lost 14%[51]. On the other hand, steelmakers remained small local ventures. In 2011, the iron ore market had the five largest companies with 90% of market share. The five largest steelmakers controlled 19% of their segment. This imbalance translated in low negotiation power of steelmakers with suppliers and consumers[52]. However, the making of this *global challenger* was full of ups and downs. Doing business abroad proved to be a challenging experience. When dealing with Canadian states, government agencies, employees or unions, Brazilians under-estimated cultural differences and tried to impose their point of views. Recurrent conflicts resulted in Vale loosing precious work force and ultimately jeopardizing expected synergies at Inco.

51 Bank of America Merrill Lynch, *Big Global Miners*, 31 August 2010.
52 M. P. de Mello Lopes, "A industria do aço no Brasil e no Mundo." *Instituto do Aço*, 2011.

L'Égypte : réalité et limites d'une voie nationale de développement

(XIXe- XXe siècles)

Caroline Piquet
Sorbonne Université

Au début du XIXe siècle, l'Égypte présente un modèle d'affirmation nationale original au sein de l'Empire ottoman. S'inscrivant dans le mouvement de réformes engagé par les sultans ottomans, le gouverneur Muhammad Ali, conscient de la supériorité militaire et technique des pays européens, cherche à développer l'économie égyptienne en favorisant les investissements étrangers. L'Égypte devient ainsi une destination privilégiée des capitaux européens. Toutefois, à l'image d'autres pays du Moyen-Orient, ces capitaux jouent un rôle ambigu : ils contribuent à moderniser les infrastructures en développant dans le même temps des logiques de domination politique. En effet, leur essor s'accompagne d'une lutte d'influence des puissances européennes, débutée en 1798 par l'expédition de Napoléon Bonaparte et dont le processus s'achève avec l'occupation militaire du pays par la Grande-Bretagne en 1882. Au XIXe siècle, la pénétration des capitaux européens se fait donc au prix d'une tutelle étrangère sur le pays. Jacques Berque parlait alors de l'Égypte comme d'un modèle d'impérialisme[1].

L'ombre du passé colonial continue à peser sur le pays tout au long du XXe siècle, d'autant plus qu'un fort parallèle se dessine avec les marges de manœuvre de l'Égypte du siècle précédent : une dette publique énorme, une économie dépendante des capitaux étrangers et des aides non dénuées d'intérêt dans un pays qui occupe une position géopolitique centrale au Moyen-Orient[2]. La dépendance aux économies et aux capitaux européens est fortement remis en cause par l'affirmation du mouvement

1 Jacques Berque, *Égypte. Impérialisme et révolution*, Paris, Gallimard, 1967.

2 De l'ordre de 2 milliards par an à la fin du XXe siècle, une aide internationale considérée par ailleurs comme vitale pour l'économie égyptienne. http://www.diplomatie.gouv.fr. M. Selmani, « Les relations égypto-américaines entre logique globale et vision étatique de l'Égypte », *Le Débat Stratégique*, n°42, Janvier 1999. http://www.ehess.fr/cirpes/ds/ds42/Égypte.html

nationaliste durant l'entre-deux-guerres, puis par la révolution nassérienne en 1952 et par les régimes militaires qui lui succèdent sous la présidence d'Anouar el-Sadate et d'Hosni Moubarak. Cependant, l'Égypte est en butte à de sérieux problèmes de déficit de financements et de compétences. Le pays cherche une voie développement propre, partagé entre une logique de réforme nationale sous la coupe d'une politique dirigiste et une ouverture aux investissements extérieurs, indispensable mais suscitant de fortes craintes.

1/ DE L'AFFIRMATION D'UN MODÈLE NATIONAL SOUS MUHAMMAD ALI À LA TUTELLE COLONIALE

Face aux convoitises étrangères qui s'expriment avec l'expédition de Napoléon Bonaparte, Muhammad Ali (1769-1849), nommé gouverneur de l'Égypte en 1805 par le pouvoir ottoman, cherche à défendre un modèle de souveraineté qui passe par la réforme de l'armée, de l'administration et de l'économie.

1.1/ Ouverture du marché égyptien aux capitaux européens

Muhammad Ali s'inscrit dans la même démarche que les réformateurs ottomans, pour lesquels il s'agit de combattre l'Occident par l'emprunt de ses méthodes et de ses techniques. Il s'entoure ainsi des compétences d'ingénieurs et de savants étrangers pour favoriser la pénétration de pratiques et de connaissances étrangères[3]. Dans le domaine économique, il veut assurer à la production égyptienne une résistance aux produits européens. Il soutient la création de manufactures et d'industries textiles, contribuant à l'essor du secteur cotonnier. Il appuie également le développement des industries alimentaires avec les sucreries et les ateliers de décorticage du riz. L'agriculture demeure toutefois le secteur le plus important : les réformes cherchent à développer les cultures nouvelles et accroitre les rendements. De grands travaux hydrauliques sont lancés sur le Nil ; le barrage sur le Nil dans le delta est confié à Eugène Mougel, ingénieur en chef des ponts et chaussées français passé au service de l'administration égyptienne. L'effort se porte également sur la construction d'un réseau de canaux destinés à l'irrigation. Le creusement du canal Mahmoudieh qui débute en 1818 est confié à l'architecte français Pascal Coste : reliant Alexandrie au reste du pays, il provoque l'extension des terres agricoles et la croissance des implantations rurales. Alexandrie, de simple bourgade, se hisse au rang de grands ports du bassin Méditerranée et attire de nombreux marchands européens[4].

Par ailleurs, le pays s'ouvre aux capitaux étrangers avec la multiplication des traités de libre-échange : les premiers accords de commerce anglo-turcs sont signés entre le Royaume-Uni et l'Empire ottoman en 1838. Ces traités abolissent tous les monopoles économiques et ouvrent ainsi la porte à l'influence commerciale britannique dans l'Empire ottoman. Dans les années 1840, les traités de libre-échange sont étendus à

3 Ghislaine Alleaume, *L'École Polytechnique du Caire et ses élèves. La formation d'une élite technique dans l'Égypte du XIXe siècle*, thèse de doctorat d'État, Lyon II, 3 t., 1993.
4 Robert Ilbert, *Alexandrie, 1830-1860. Histoire d'une communauté citadine*, Le Caire, IFAO, 1996.

la France, à l'Autriche et à l'Italie. Entre 1884 et 1909, viennent s'y greffer les accords bilatéraux passés entre les puissances européennes et l'Égypte ; ils imposent au marché égyptien une ouverture totale aux produits étrangers, en particulier à ceux en provenance de l'empire britannique.

Dans le même temps, les successeurs de Muhammad Ali poursuivent son action réformatrice : son fils Muhammad Saïd autorise le chantier du canal de Suez qui commence en 1859. Dix ans plus tard a lieu la cérémonie d'ouverture du canal, présidée par le khédive Ismaïl (1830-1895), petit-fils de Muhammad Ali. Cet événement inaugure la période qualifiée de « l'Égypte des Khédives[5] » qui se caractérise par une forte pénétration des capitaux étrangers. Les ressortissants des puissances européennes bénéficient alors de privilèges fiscaux et de protection juridique avec le système des capitulations. Ce système, d'abord obtenu par les consuls puis étendu au XIXe siècle aux ressortissants des puissances étrangères, facilite l'installation des entreprises européennes : l'absence d'impôts directs, une législation sans règlementation rigide entre employeurs et employés et un coût de la vie peu élevé sont autant de facteurs favorables à leur développement. Nombre de sociétés concessionnaires étrangères britanniques français et belges investissent alors dans les concessions de tramway et de chemin de fer, les services publics d'eau et d'électricité[6]. Le pays devient ainsi une colonie de capitaux où les étrangers s'illustrent dans le crédit hypothécaire, la commercialisation du coton et les sociétés concessionnaires[7].

De plus, le règne d'Ismaïl (1863-1879) se caractérise par une entrée en masse de capitaux dirigés vers les emprunts d'États contractés auprès de créanciers anglais, français ou belges pour l'essentiel, avec des taux d'emprunts allant de 12 à 20 %[8], si bien que la dette explose : estimée à 4 millions de livres au début du règne, elle se monte à 91 millions de livres en 1875. Cette dépendance financière a un coût politique. L'État fait banqueroute en 1875 et tombe sous tutelle européenne avec la mise en place d'une Commission internationale de la dette. Cet organisme chargé de contrôler les recettes du pays et leur affectation au remboursement des emprunts ouvre la voie à la domination européenne du pays. La Commission internationale des finances devient en 1878 une commission composée de deux fonctionnaires, un Français et un Anglais délégués pour assurer la gestion de budget de la Dette. En 1882, l'occupation militaire des Britanniques achève le processus de domination du pays, malgré de fortes oppositions nationalistes[9]. La domination britannique se traduit par la protection des capitaux étrangers et des sociétés concessionnaires, ainsi que par la priorité donnée à la culture et au commerce du coton, contribuant à maintenir le pays dans un faible développement industriel.

5 Titre donné en 1867 par le sultan ottoman au vice-roi d'Égypte Ismaïl, puis conservé par ses successeurs jusqu'en 1914.

6 Ghislaine Alleaume, « La production d'une économie nationale : remarques sur l'histoire des sociétés anonymes par actions en Égypte de 1856 à 1956 », *Les Annales Islamologiques*, t. XXXI, 1997, p. 1-16.

7 Samir Saul, *La France et l'Égypte de 1882 à 1914. Intérêts économiques et implications politiques*, Paris, Comité pour l'histoire économique et financière de la France, 1997.

8 David Landes, *Banquiers et pachas, Finances internationales et impérialisme économique en Égypte*, Paris, Albin Michel, 1993, p. 65.

9 La révolte d'Urabi Pacha en 1882est dirigée contre le khédive et les étrangers dénoncés comme trop puissants dans l'appareil d'État et l'économie. Elle est considérée en Égypte comme la première révolte nationaliste.

1.2/ La dénonciation d'une économie sous dépendance étrangère

Au sortir de la Première Guerre mondiale, les élites égyptiennes affirment leur volonté de démanteler le système colonial instauré au XIXe siècle pour construire une économie indépendante, préalable à l'indépendance politique. La déclaration de la souveraineté du pays en 1922 ne met pas fin à l'occupation britannique et les mécanismes de contrôle de l'économie par les Européens se poursuivent. Mais l'Égypte connaît un mouvement d'industrialisation qui se traduit par l'affirmation d'une bourgeoisie nationale. Alors que l'administration coloniale anglaise contrôle l'appareil d'État, les acteurs privés se penchent sur la réforme industrielle et sociale du pays à travers des associations comme la Société khédivale d'économie politique, de statistique et de législation et la Fédération des industries d'Égypte. Les élites européennes et égyptiennes y partagent un projet commun : sortir le pays de son arriération économique et le faire entrer dans la marche des pays développés.

Néanmoins, leurs intérêts sont divergents : pour l'élite étrangère, il s'agit avant tout de conserver ses positions, alors que la bourgeoisie égyptienne entend conquérir le marché national[10]. En outre, la performance et la prospérité des firmes étrangères reposent sur des privilèges conférés par le système des capitulations. Pour la bourgeoisie égyptienne, ces privilèges créent une situation discriminatoire inacceptable. Le fonctionnement des sociétés étrangères fait également l'objet de vives contestations : leur capital est constitué par un actionnariat majoritairement européen et elles ne permettent, le plus souvent, que de drainer des capitaux provenant de l'extérieur ; le patronat étranger s'appuie en outre sur l'administration britannique pour garantir ses intérêts financiers ; enfin, trop peu d'Égyptiens parviennent à siéger dans les conseils d'administration de ces entreprises.

Les grandes sociétés concessionnaires concentrent les critiques du fait de la faiblesse des investissements réalisés dans le pays. La presse les présente comme les plaies de la nation et les accuse d'être un contrepoids dangereux à l'autorité du gouvernement. Parmi elles, se distinguent la Compagnie des eaux d'Alexandrie et du Caire, la Compagnie des tramways d'Alexandrie, la Cairo Electric Company, la Compagnie de gaz et d'électricité Lebon ou encore la Compagnie du canal de Suez. Cette dernière représente la plus importante société concessionnaire du pays du fait de ses bénéfices et du territoire concédé : depuis sa création en 1858, elle est devenue un symbole de l'exploitation étrangère et de l'impérialisme économique dans le pays[11].

10 Caroline Piquet, « Patronat colonial, entrepreneurs étrangers et élites égyptiennes dans la réforme et l'industrialisation de l'Égypte libérale », dans Hubert Bonin, Catherine Hodeir et Jean-François Klein (dir.), *L'Esprit économique impérial (1830-1970). Groupes de pression & réseaux du patronat colonial en France & dans l'empire*, Paris, Publications Société française d'histoire d'Outre-mer, 2008, p. 633-646.

11 En 1854, le diplomate Ferdinand de Lesseps avait obtenu du vice-roi égyptien Muhmmad Saïd (1854-1863) une concession pour creuser et exploiter le canal de Suez. L'Égypte finance environ la moitié du coût du creusement du canal mais perd progressivement ses droits d'actionnaire sur ce dernier. En 1875, au bord de la banqueroute, elle vend ses actions (44 %) à l'État britannique ; les 56 % restants dont détenus par des actionnaires européens, en grande majorité français. En 1882, les Britanniques occupent le pays et se déclarent *de facto* les gardiens de la sécurité du canal. Enfin, le coup de grâce à la souveraineté égyptienne concernant le canal est porté en 1888 lorsque la convention de Constantinople lui accorde un statut de voie maritime internationale. Caroline Piquet, *La Compagnie du canal de Suez. Une concession française en Égypte (1888-1956)*, Paris, PUPS, 2008.

1.3/ L'offensive de la bourgeoisie égyptienne durant l'entre-deux-guerres

Malgré la crise économique mondiale, les années trente inaugurent une période nouvelle pour l'industrie égyptienne. En 1930, le dernier des accords commerciaux passés entre les puissances et l'Égypte prend fin ; le pays retrouve ainsi sa liberté tarifaire. Cela renforce la position de la bourgeoisie égyptienne, d'autant plus que les capitaux se détournent d'un secteur agricole en crise pour alimenter le secteur industriel. En outre, la crise des années trente fait crûment apparaître la question sociale avec la baisse des niveaux de vie et l'apparition du chômage. Dès lors, le cheminement vers une économie nationale repose sur deux postulats : l'Égypte doit développer son industrialisation en favorisant les investisseurs et les employés égyptiens en se débarrassant des privilèges accordés aux étrangers.

Ces deux points trouvent en l'homme politique Ismaïl Sidqi un défenseur pragmatique et résolu. Celui-ci prend les rênes de l'industrialisation du pays en présidant en 1916 la Commission gouvernementale sur le commerce et l'industrie ; son rapport en 1917 met l'accent sur la nécessité de l'industrialisation en proposant notamment la création d'une banque de développement industriel. Ce rôle est tenu par la première banque égyptienne, la banque *Misr*, dont le fondateur Talaat Harb crée en 1923 un compte destiné aux filiales commerciales et industrielles. Ismaïl Sidqi préside également à partir de 1922 la Fédération des industries d'Égypte, avant de prendre la tête de deux ministères successifs de juin 1930 à septembre 1933 sous le sigle des Indépendants[12]. Ces efforts se traduisent par des avancées notables : dès 1928, une commission est chargée par le gouvernement d'étudier une législation prenant en compte la situation économique du pays et les premières mesures sociales concernant le travail des enfants et des femmes sont votées en 1932 et 1933.

Par ailleurs, se développe dans la presse nationaliste un discours dénonçant les rapacités du capital étranger. En 1930-1931, se crée l'association L'Égyptien pour l'Égyptien qui anime une campagne de boycott des produits britanniques sur le modèle de Gandhi en Inde ; l'appel au boycott est associé à la promotion de la production égyptienne. L'intellectuel d'origine copte Salama Musa en prend la direction ; son action rencontre beaucoup d'échos parmi la jeunesse éduquée et sensibilise au thème de la mobilisation économique[13]. L'action de l'association est en outre soutenue par la Banque Misr et son fondateur, Talaat Harb. D'autres groupuscules comme Jeune Égypte défendent un nationalisme farouche et appellent à un « djihad économique ». Les attaques sont dirigées vers les étrangers : les Britanniques qui demeurent toujours très présents dans la gestion de l'État, mais aussi les Européens et les Syro-Libanais installés en Égypte depuis le XIXe siècle. Le patronat étranger devient la cible de la presse nationaliste, présenté comme un élément parasite ; il est accusé de maintenir

12 Hélène Cottenet-Djoufelkit, « L'industrialisation de l'Égypte au XXe siècle » dans *L'Égypte dans le siècle 1901-2000*, Égypte / monde arabe n°4-5, 2 /2000-1/2001, p. 135-171.

13 Didier Monciaud, « *L'Égyptien pour l'Égyptien* (1930-1931), campagne nationaliste économique et controverses sur l'identité » dans *Débats intellectuels au Moyen-Orient dans l'entre-deux-guerres*, Revue des mondes musulmans et de la Méditerranée, Edisud, n° 95-96-97-98, 2002, p. 355-380.

l'Égypte dans la dépendance économique en limitant ses investissements dans le pays et en freinant le recrutement des nationaux. À ces invectives, le patronat étranger ne réagit que peu, se sentant protégé par la tutelle britannique. Le traité anglo-égyptien de 1936 change la donne.

2/ LUTTES D'INDÉPENDANCE ET RÉVOLUTION : À LA RECHERCHE D'UN MODÈLE NATIONAL DE DÉVELOPPEMENT

2.1/ Affirmation de l'État dans la sphère économique : le tournant des années 1930

Le traité anglo-égyptien de 1936, avec la reprise en main des affaires intérieures par les Égyptiens, redonne à ces derniers la possibilité d'intervenir dans le domaine économique. Quelques mois plus tard, en mars 1937, la conférence de Montreux entérine la fin du régime des capitulations. Cette abrogation n'a rien d'inattendu puisque ce régime avait déjà été supprimé après la Première Guerre mondiale dans les anciennes provinces arabes de l'Empire ottoman ; l'Égypte fait ainsi figure de retardataire. Mais le patronat étranger se sent lâché par les Britanniques qui jusque-là avaient assuré la protection d'un statut leur accordant immunités et privilèges.

Ce climat est favorable à l'expansion du contrôle égyptien dans la sphère économique. Ce phénomène se traduit par l'organisation d'une législation fiscale, d'un système d'imposition sur les entreprises ainsi que par la création d'une banque centrale égyptienne. L'État affiche désormais une orientation nettement plus interventionniste que dans la décennie précédente et le rapport de force entre les Égyptiens et les Européens s'inverse. La négociation avec la plus grande entreprise étrangère du pays en est un signe fort : au printemps 1936, pour la première fois depuis l'époque de l'obtention de la concession (1855), le gouvernement négocie la question de la participation de l'Égypte aux revenus et à la gestion du canal de Suez ; le gouvernement obtient de l'entreprise le reversement d'une redevance annuelle de 200 000 livres égyptiennes et deux Égyptiens sont autorisés à siéger dans son conseil d'administration.

D'autre part, la question de l'égyptianisation des entreprises devient le thème dominant de l'action de l'État vis-à-vis des entreprises étrangères, à un moment où la crise économique mondiale met en exergue la question du sous-emploi et le peu de possibilités réservées à la jeunesse égyptienne. Les entreprises étrangères emploient en priorité des ressortissants de leurs pays, ou bien des Grecs, Italiens et autres Européens réputés plus qualifiés. Dès 1934, une commission supérieure est créée au sein du ministère des Travaux publics pour examiner les plaintes reçues sur les questions de discrimination et d'égyptianisation. Après le traité anglo-égyptien de 1936, la pression se renforce sur les entreprises étrangères. Le gouvernement emporte une victoire symbolique cette même année en soumettant la plus puissante d'entre elles, la Compagnie du canal de Suez, à un accord l'obligeant à recruter 25 % de nationaux au sein de ses employés. Le gouvernement vise une égyptianisation qualitative avec l'emploi et la formation de catégories de cadres, ceux-là même qui pourront assurer la transition vers une réappropriation de l'économie nationale en brisant le cercle vicieux de la dépendance technique.

La Seconde Guerre mondiale marque une pause de l'action de l'État dans le domaine économique en raison de la reprise en main du pays par les Britanniques. Dès 1945, l'offensive repart dans un climat alourdi par la décolonisation. Les négociations avec la puissance impériale demeurent dans l'impasse jusqu'en 1954, ce qui engendre au sein de l'opinion égyptienne un rejet plus violent de tout ce qui est occidental. Les gouvernements qui se succèdent après la guerre poursuivent l'action engagée contre le fonctionnement des entreprises étrangères, avec notamment le vote de la loi n° 138 sur les sociétés anonymes en 1947. Ce vote produit un véritable choc parmi les milieux d'affaires étrangers ; il représente une nouvelle étape vers un nationalisme économique et une appropriation de l'appareil productif. La loi stipule que 40 % des membres du conseil d'administration doivent être égyptiens ; de plus, 75 % des postes d'employés et 90 % des postes d'ouvriers doivent être réservés aux Égyptiens. Enfin, il est prévu que 51 % des actions soient détenus par des nationaux[14]. Les milieux d'affaires étrangers crient à la discrimination et à l'entrave à la liberté de commerce.

Les conséquences de l'égyptianisation des entreprises étrangères se font sentir au sein des personnels, au moment où le pays en est butte aux mouvements sociaux menés par les étudiants, ouvriers, Frères musulmans et communistes ; l'agitation sociale se traduit par une vague de grèves de l'automne 1947 au printemps 1948 qui touche les usines de Shubra al-Khayma, Mehalla el-Kubra ou encore les filatures d'Alexandrie[15]. Dans la région du canal de Suez où dominent trois grands employeurs étrangers – les camps militaires britanniques, la Shell et la Compagnie du canal de Suez –, la lutte sociale se double d'une lutte politique dénonçant l'exploitation coloniale du pays. En octobre 1951, lors de la dénonciation du traité de 1936 par le gouvernement égyptien, la région devient le terrain d'une guérilla opposant les militants nationalistes aux soldats britanniques. Le 26 janvier 1952, après un incident intervenu à Ismaïlia, un immense incendie ravage Le Caire ; la colère est dirigée contre les symboles de la domination coloniale ; les enseignes étrangères tombent en cendre. Le gouvernement est incapable de rétablir une situation de stabilité ; dans la nuit du 22 au 23 juillet, un groupe d'officiers de l'armée prend le pouvoir.

2.2/ Le régime nassérien : le dilemme entre l'action révolutionnaire et l'accumulation du capital

La prise de pouvoir des Officiers libres annonce la fin de la monarchie parlementaire et constitue une rupture politique majeure. En revanche, du point de vue économique, les Officiers libres poursuivent le processus de démontage de l'héritage colonial amorcé depuis les années trente. Lors de son arrivée au pouvoir, le comité révolutionnaire des jeunes officiers avec à sa tête le colonel Nasser, est placé face à un dilemme : se

14 Ghislaine Alleaume, « La production d'une économie nationale : remarques sur l'histoire des sociétés anonymes par actions en Égypte de 1856 à 1956 », art. cit., p. 14-16.

15 Joel Beinin, "Islam Marxism and the Shubra al-Khayma textile workers: Muslim brothers and Communists in the Egyptian Trade union movement" in *Islam, Politics and social Movement*, E. Burke et I.M. Lapidus (dir.), London, I.B Tauris, 1988, p. 207-226.

réapproprier les structures de l'économie nationale et mener une réforme profonde du système tout en poursuivant l'accumulation du capital nécessaire au développement du secteur industriel[16]. Or, les investissements étrangers sont tout à fait essentiels à ce processus. Nasser espère par ailleurs un soutien important des États-Unis dans ce domaine. C'est ainsi que les premiers gestes du régime vont dans le sens de l'ordre : les Officiers libres s'illustrent dans les premières semaines de pouvoir par un geste de répression contre les ouvriers des usines de textile en grève à Kafr el-Dawwar, près d'Alexandrie.

Dans le même temps, les mécanismes de contrôle sur les entreprises étrangères se durcissent. Les Officiers libres poursuivent la politique d'égyptianisation des sociétés anonymes dans le sens défini par la loi n° 138 de 1947. Pour le régime, dépendance économique et dépendance politique vont de pair, toutes deux étroitement liées à la dépendance technique. Le cas de la nationalisation du pétrole en Iran en 1951 est à ce titre représentatif : faute de techniciens locaux, les Iraniens ont dû remplacer les techniciens anglais par des techniciens américains. Le gouvernement égyptien ne veut pas se retrouver face à un pareil scénario. C'est ainsi que la loi n° 26 en 1954 renforce la législation sur l'égyptianisation du personnel ; elle exige en outre des sociétés anonymes qu'au moins 40 % des membres du conseil d'administration soient égyptiens. Ces mesures sont un moyen de se débarrasser des hommes de l'ancien régime et de placer au sein des conseils des grandes entreprises les protégés des Officiers libres. Au cours de l'année 1955, la pression se renforce puisque deux arrêtés prévoient la publication du bilan des sociétés et le résumé des activités de leur conseil d'administration. En mars 1955, les entreprises se voient obligées de tenir à la disposition de l'inspecteur du Département du travail des registres du personnel respectant des barèmes précis.

L'objectif du gouvernement consiste à faire participer les revenus des entreprises étrangères à l'économie nationale. Il fait en particulier pression sur la plus puissante entreprise étrangère : la Compagnie du canal de Suez ; il souhaite évoluer vers le modèle de partage à égalité des revenus appliqué par les compagnies pétrolières depuis le début des années cinquante. Au même moment, Nasser nourrit l'espoir d'un financement de son projet du haut-barrage d'Assouan par la Banque mondiale. Cependant, le 20 juillet, celle-ci, sous pression des Etats-Unis, lui refuse cette aide ; quelques jours plus tard, le 26 juillet, Nasser annonce la nationalisation de la Compagnie du canal de Suez ; il compte récupérer les revenus générés par l'exploitation de la voie maritime pour les affecter au projet du barrage et, plus largement, les mettre au service du développement économique du pays.

La nationalisation de la Compagnie du canal de Suez et la crise militaire qui s'en suit à l'automne 1956 inaugurent une nouvelle époque en Égypte. Les biens britanniques et français sont placés sous séquestre, ce qui permet au gouvernement de mettre la main

16 John Waterbury, *The Egypt of Nasser and Sadat: the Political Economy of the two Regimes*, Princeton, Princeton University Press, 1983.

sur les activités où les étrangers s'illustraient : les banques, les compagnies d'assurances et les sociétés commerciales. D'autre part, la communauté juive subit les conséquences de l'agression d'Israël en octobre 1956 au côté de la France et de la Grande-Bretagne ; une hostilité croissante se développe à l'égard de ses ressortissants qui fuient le pays en masse. La victoire du canal, en faisant sauter le verrou des intérêts étrangers, constitue un pas de plus vers un dirigisme planifié. Entre 1956 et le début des années 1960, des milliers d'affaires commerciales sont abandonnées par les étrangers quittant le pays. La nationalisation des biens belges après la crise du Congo en 1960, le rapprochement avec Moscou et le programme de socialisme arabe entrepris par le régime nassérien à partir de 1962 finissent par décourager les derniers entrepreneurs européens. Ces derniers cèdent alors la place aux techniciens russes qui vont s'illustrer en particulier dans la construction du haut-barrage d'Assouan.

2.3/ Les années Sadate et Moubarak : une libéralisation de l'économie sous condition

La période nassérienne apparaît comme une tentative désespérée pour sortir du sous-développement ; elle se traduit par la nationalisation des grandes sociétés industrielles étrangères et d'un contrôle de l'État accru sur ces dernières. Cependant, le tournant socialiste du régime en 1962 et l'étatisation de l'appareil productif provoquent des effets ravageurs sur les performances de l'économie nationale[17]. De plus, celle-ci présente un aspect rentier, basé sur les revenus du pétrole, ceux du canal de Suez, les transferts des travailleurs émigrés et les aides extérieures[18]. Un changement de politique, l'*Infitah* (ouverture économique), est décidé au cours des années 1970 par Anouar el-Sadate pour rapatrier les capitaux privés égyptiens et attirer les investisseurs étrangers. En 1974, dans un document qualifié de « Charte d'octobre », Anouar el-Sadate annonce officiellement le retour à une économie de marché ; le capital étranger est invité à revenir dans le pays, politique soutenue par les institutions financières internationales ; le relâchement du contrôle étatique sur les échanges commerciaux avec l'étranger redonne sa liberté au secteur privé[19].

En 1982, Hosni Moubarak succède à Anouar-el Sadate à la tête de l'État et poursuit sa politique d'ouverture économique. Il présente un nouveau plan de libéralisation et de restructuration d'ensemble du système où il affiche sa volonté de faire évoluer l'économie rentière dirigiste vers une économie de production internationalisée[20]. Au début des années 1990, apparaissent aussi des associations militant pour la libéralisation du système ; c'est le cas de l'association el-Nida el-Gadid, soutenant le libéralisme tant dans le domaine de l'économie que de la politique[21]. Or, le passage à une économie de

17 Hélène Cottenet-Djoufelkit, « L'industrialisation de l'Égypte au XXe siècle. Des volontés politiques aux réalisations économiques », art. cit., 2001, p. 150-152.

18 Bruno Cabrillac, « Les spécificités de l'économie égyptienne », *Égypte/ Monde arabe*, 12/13, 4e trimestre 1992/ 1er trimestre 1993, p. 11-19.

19 Maurice Martin, « L'Égypte après Sadate », *Notes et articles sur l'Égypte, Études*, août-septembre 1982, p. 155-170. CEDEJ-Égypte/Soudan, 2018 ; http://www.openedition.org/6540

20 Louis Blin, « introduction » à *Une économie en transition, Égypte/ Monde arabe*, 12/13, 4e trimestre 1992/ 1er trimestre 1993, p. 7-9.

21 Ben Nefissa Sarah, « L'association el-Nida' el-Gadid, un nouvel acteur sur la scène politique égyptienne », *Égypte/ Monde arabe* n°20, 4ème trimestre 1994, p 155-166 ; Imco Brouwer, « Les élites économiques et les groupes de pression égyptiens », *Égypte/*

production repose sur la part des investissements étrangers, qui présentent en outre l'avantage d'offrir une forme de financement extérieur ne générant pas d'endettement. Leur déploiement dans le pays reste toutefois laborieux car pèse sur eux le soupçon de dépendance économique du pays, en souvenir des logiques coloniales du siècle précédent. À la fin du XXe siècle, le poids de l'État dans l'économie demeure important ; le régime favorise plutôt l'émergence d'un secteur intermédiaire, « le secteur public des affaires », qu'un véritable secteur privé. Cela explique à la fin du XXe siècle une action contradictoire de l'État : « une libéralisation sans libéralisme[22] », où pèse toujours les craintes d'une mainmise étrangère sur la souveraineté nationale.

Conclusion

Durant les deux derniers siècles, les capitaux étrangers investis en Égypte ont joué un rôle ambivalent : ils ont favorisé l'intégration du pays dans l'économie mondiale, mais, associé au pratiques coloniales des puissances européennes, ils ont aussi provoqué une réaction de repli et d'isolement de l'économie nationale sur elle-même. Le processus d'intégration de l'Égypte à l'économie mondiale amorcé au XIXe siècle s'est ralenti durant la période de la décolonisation et du nassérisme. Il a été ensuite nettement réenclenché dans le dernier quart du XXe siècle par les présidents Anouar el-Sadate et Hosni Moubarak. Après la parenthèse des Frères musulmans de juin 2011 à juin 2013, il est à nouveau poursuivi par le président Sissi depuis son accès au pouvoir en 2014. Ce dernier encourage les capitaux étrangers à investir massivement dans le pays avec la création de partenariats ou de zones franches[23]. Mais ce processus se réalise plus péniblement qu'à la période coloniale, en raison de la forte instabilité politique et économique de la région. L'économie reste entravée par les traumas du XIXe siècle qui contribuent à maintenir les logiques d'un système dirigiste où l'État demeure perçu comme un rempart à une mondialisation économique menaçante pour la souveraineté nationale.

Monde arabe, n° 21, 1er trimestre 1995.

22 Louis Blin, *L'économie égyptienne, Libéralisation et insertion dans le marché mondial*, Paris, L'Harmattan, 1993, p. 9.

23 Citons par exemple la zone économique du canal de Suez, zone franche de 460 km² créée en 2015 où la Chine a conclu un contrat d'exploitation sur 7,3 km², quand l'Arabie saoudite ou la Russie ont investi dans des concessions de respectivement 5 km² et 2 km². www.suezcanal.gov.eg

Oil and development in Algeria

Marta Musso
Research Fellow at King's College London and at the Archives Portal Europe Foundation

Introduction

At a first glance, compared to many other post-colonial countries, Algeria reached a good level of development. It is an upper-middle-income country and the third most important economy in the MENA region, above its North-African neighbours.[1] According to the World Bank, it is also one of the few countries to have achieved a 20% poverty reduction in the past two decades.[2] The country ranks 82 in Human Development Index, with constant improvements over the last 25 years in life expectancy, schooling, and GNI per capita (see Figure 1).[3]

FIGURE 1

	1990	1995	2000	2005	2010	2015	2018
Life expectancy at birth	66.7	68.1	70.2	72.2	73.8	75	76.7
Expected years of schooling	9.6	9.8	10.9	12.3	14	14.4	14.7
GNI per capita (PPP $)	9,895	8,825	9,776	11,799	12,875	13,533	13,639
HDI value	0.577	0.6	0.644	0.686	0.724	0.745	0.759

In 2017 its GDP was $612.5 billion, 55th in world ranking; with a 3.3% annual growth between 2015 and 2016, the country had a larger GDP growth than the EU average, and levels of unemployment down to 11.2% (from almost 30% in 2000), lower than

1 The World Bank, "The World Bank in Algeria. Overview." Text/HTML, World Bank, April 21, 2018, http://www.worldbank.org/en/country/algeria/overview.

2 *Id.*

3 United Nations Development Programme, "Human Development for Everyone. Briefing Note for Countries on the 2016 Human Development Report. Algeria.," 2016, http://hdr.undp.org/sites/all/themes/hdr_theme/country-notes/DZA.pdf.

a highly industrialised country like Italy.[4] Though official data are scarce, its Gini coefficient in 2011 was 27.6, significantly lower than the 40.20 registered in 1988, and closer to that of Sweden (26.9) than France's (33.3).[5]

These positive results, however, must be compared to the fragility of the country *vis-à-vis* an economy in which deep inequalities persist. The quantitative optimism of the Gini index must be put into the context of a heavily centralised and subsidized economy, in which personal and political freedoms are severely curtailed. The good performances of Algeria change dramatically if the benchmark for poverty is pushed to \$2.75/day rather than \$1.25, raising the percentage of people living below the poverty line to 23%.[6] Within the high employment datum, vulnerable employment (underpaid or unpaid own-account workers), still counted for more than a third in 2009.[7] Furthermore, youth unemployment currently reaches 28.3%, adding pressure to a political climate that remains uncertain.[8] The wounds of the civil war between the government and Islamist groups are still open, and the geopolitical crisis of the MENA region contributes to generate instability in the country.[9]

Furthermore, the overall economy and State budget are still largely dependent on the volatile revenues of the hydrocarbon sector. In 2016, oil and gas accounted for 96% of the exports – a surprising datum if compared to the 35% of non oil and gas GDP at the end of the 1980s (the decade of low crude prices), and even more surprising if compared to the aggressive industrialisation plan launched by the Algerian authorities in the aftermath of independence, which aimed to fill the gap between Algeria and its European neighbour within a decade. A gap that is not only far from being filled, but has strongly widened since the departure of Algeria from the European Economic Area in 1962 (see Figure 02).[10]

4 The World Bank, "GDP (Current US\$) | Data," accessed April 27, 2018, https://data.worldbank.org/indicator/NY.GDP.MKTP.CD?locations=DZ&year_high_desc=true.

5 Knoema.com, "Algeria GINI Index, 1960-2017," *Knoema*, accessed April 27, 2018, https://knoema.com/atlas/Algeria/topics/Poverty/Income-Inequality/GINI-index.2018, https://knoema.com/atlas/Algeria/topics/Poverty/Income-Inequality/GINI-index.","plainCitation":"Knoema.com, "Algeria GINI Index, 1960-2017," Knoema, accessed April 27, 2018, https://knoema.com/atlas/Algeria/topics/Poverty/Income-Inequality/GINI-index.","noteIndex":5},"citationItems":[{"id":2354,"uris":["http://zotero.org/users/1634819/items/CG9S6JC3"],"uri":["http://zotero.org/users/1634819/items/CG9S6JC3"],"itemData":{"id":2354,"-type":"webpage","title":"Algeria GINI index, 1960-2017","container-title":"Knoema","abstract":"In 2011, GINI index for Algeria was 27.6 index. GINI index of Algeria fell gradually from 40.2 index in 1988 to 27.6 index in 2011. Gini index measures the extent to which the distribution of income or consumption expenditure among individuals or households within an economy deviates from a perfectly equal distribution. A Lorenz curve plots the cumulative percentages of total income received against the cumulative number of recipients, starting with the poorest individual or household. The Gini index measures the area between the Lorenz curve and a hypothetical line of absolute equality, expressed as a percentage of the maximum area under the line. Thus a Gini index of 0 represents perfect equality, while an index of 100 implies perfect inequality.","URL":"https://knoema.com/atlas/Algeria/topics/Poverty/Income-Inequality/GINI-index","language":"en-US","author":[{"family":"Knoema.com","given":""}],"accessed":{"date-parts":[["2018",4,27]]}}}],"schema":"https://github.com/citation-style-language/schema/raw/master/csl-citation.json"}

6 See: African Development Bank, "The Search for Inclusive Growth in North Africa: A Comparative Approach," 2013, https://www.afdb.org/fileadmin/uploads/afdb/Documents/Publications/Economic_Brief_-_The_Search_for_Inclusive_Growth_in_North_Africa-_A_Comparative_Approach.pdf. and O El-Kikhia, M., "Algeria: The Challenge of Poor Choices," *Al Jazeera*, April 17, 2014, https://www.aljazeera.com/indepth/opinion/2014/04/algeria-challenge-poor-choices-201441661717332782.html.

7 African Development Bank, "The Search for Inclusive Growth in North Africa: A Comparative Approach."

8 Ibarra, G.L., "Putting One More Piece in the Global Poverty Puzzle: The Case of Algeria," Text, *Voices and Views: Middle East and North Africa*, (May 31, 2017), http://blogs.worldbank.org/arabvoices/global-poverty-puzzle-case-algeria.

9 Guerid, D., *L'exception algérienne : La modernisation à l'épreuve de la société*, Casbah Editions, Algiers, Algiers-Casbah, 2010.

10 The World Bank, "GDP (Current US\$) | Data." accessed April 27, 2018, https://data.worldbank.org/indicator/NY.GDP.MKTP.CD?locations=DZ&year_high_desc=true.

FIGURE 2

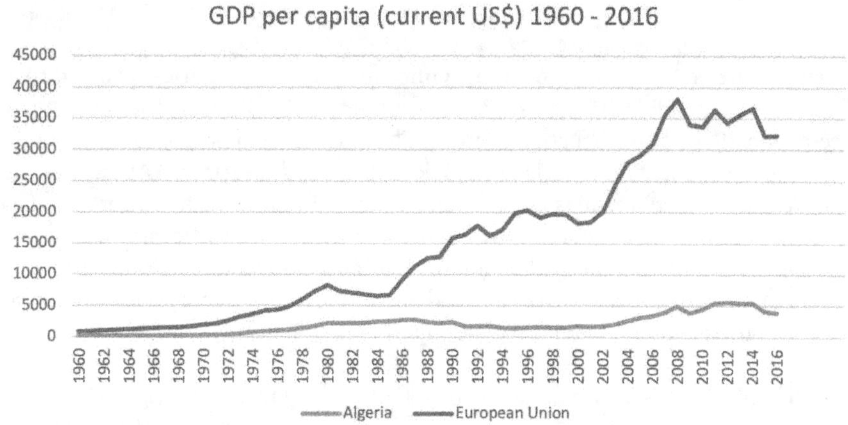

Despite efforts over time, to these days sixty percent of the government's budget still depends on hydrocarbons revenues, and the positive results obtained in the last years could not survive a prolonged period of low oil prices.[11] In 2017 alone, the State had to cut spending and subsidies by 14%, increasing the prices of fuel, electricity, and food, and inflation reaching 7.6% in February 2017. At the same times, taxes were raised and the public sector, still the larger employer in Algeria, was frozen.[12] While it is still too early to quantify the impact of the Covid-19 pandemic, the oil prices crash will most likely have a strong negative impact on the country's economy.

Only in recent years the private sector has started to expand. Since independence, agriculture has been the neglected sector of Algeria's economy, suffering from underinvestment, poor organization, and scarce access to water supplies, which have been preferentially used for the heavy industry. A substantial area of fertile land has gone out of production because of the civil strife in the country since the early 1990s. The fishing industry, which has high potential, is underdeveloped because of the lack of refrigeration and canning facilities. While the government has taken steps to invest in this sector, investments are made uncertain by the volatile prices.[13]

Other sectors operating in the country are leather and footwear, textiles, food processing and pharmaceuticals. However, this private sector is largely informal, characterised by partial or complete tax evasion, and unprotected workforce. Interpersonal relations strongly prevail over contractual rules: in 2011, a survey of 7500 SMEs found that 42% of the workforce was off the books, and 30% of the companies' revenues were not declared.[14] According to the UGCAA (Union Générale des Commerçants &

11 The World Bank, "The World Bank in Algeria. Overview."

12 "Stability or Stagnation in Algeria?," *The Economist*, April 20, 2017, https://www.economist.com/news/middle-east-and-africa/21721155-algerians-see-little-reason-vote-coming-general-election-stability-or.

13 Central Intelligence Agency, "The World Factbook — Algeria," 2018, https://www.cia.gov/library/publications/the-world-factbook/geos/ag.html.

14 Mebtoul, A., "Bilan Des Politiques Économiques de 1963 a 2010," in *Le Développement Économique de l'Algérie*, by Taïeb Hafsi, Algiers, Casbah Editions, 2011, p. 47-74.

Artisans Algériens), in 2009 two thirds of local consumption came from the informal economy, with a loss of 200 billion DA (2.6 billion dollars).

Furthermore, a 2010 survey from the Office for National Statistics reported that 80.1% of workers did not enjoy any type of social security: 79.8% in the agricultural sector and 79.7% of construction workers. The informal economy accounts for 25% of employment and 20% of the DGP outside of the oil and gas sector. [15] At the present, the Algerian society remains divided between an elite of specialised workforce in administration and the heavy industry sector, particularly the hydrocarbon industry, and a second stratum of informal economy in precarious working conditions. The shift from an informal economy to a structured one will be fundamental for the economic differentiation and development of the country.

The reasons for this dual structure can be found in the history of Algeria as an independent country, which is intertwined with its oil and gas industry. Hydrocarbon resources have affected the development model of the country, and still cover an important role in the economic and political life of Algeria. For this reason, the country may appear as a manual case of the so-called "oil curse", the poor economic and social performances of countries rich in oil and gas reserves. Oil is sometimes generically indicated in the press as a reason for the Algerian failure to industrialise and to achieve a more differentiated and stronger economy, as well as a freer and more inclusive society. A closer analysis, however, reveals that the country does not fit any oil-curse model, and it has been used mostly to debunk the literature on the subject.[16]

As a matter of fact, at independence Algeria was considered a country full of potential precisely *because* of its oil and gas resources. In general, up until the countershocks of the 1980s, oil was considered an important opportunity of global development, and the best tool at disposal for newly independent countries to solve the problem of capital formation.[17] Oil was also an opportunity to promote industrialisation, thanks to the abundance of a cheap energy source, making potential enterprises competitive against Western companies. Finally, oil was considered a diplomatic tool in the negotiations with Europe, a leverage in negotiations with industrialised countries. All in all, the history of post-independence Algeria suggests that while oil has surely had a significant impact in the history of the country, the reasons for Algeria's poor performances are not attributable to its hydrocarbon industry.

15 *Ibid.*

16 See Chekouri, S.M., Chibi, A., and Benbouziane, M., "Algeria and the Natural Resource Curse: Oil Abundance and Economic Growth," *Middle East Development Journal*, 2017, doi:10.1080/17938120.2017.1366772.; Henry, C.M., "Algeria's Agonies: Oil Rent Effects in a Bunker State," *Www.La.Utexas.Edu*, accessed April 27, 2018, http://www.la.utexas.edu/users/chenry/pmena/mats03/HenryAlgeria2.htm.; Fardmanesh, M., "Dutch Disease Economics and the Oil Syndrome: An Empirical Study," *World Development* 19, no. 6, 1991, p. 711-717.

17 In 1957 alone for example, a period of relatively low commodity prices, oil companies paid to Middle East countries about $2,200 million in royalties: more than the entire sum invested by the United States and Europe in all underdeveloped areas up to that date. See "Fresh Attack on Under-Development"," *Petroleum Press Service*, May 1961, London Edition. In Musso, M., "Inequality and History," *Inequality and History*, 2016, http://inequalityandhistory.blogspot.com/search?q=Marta+Musso.4,27]]}}}],"schema":"https://github.com/citation-style-language/schema/raw/master/csl-citation.json"}

1/ THE ALGERIAN ECONOMY IN THE EVE OF INDEPENDENCE

Plans for the economic development of the area date back to the beginning of the 20th Century, interrupted by the two world wars and the 1929 global financial meltdown. In 1940, 80% of the Algerian population was poor or very poor. [18] In the aftermath of World War II, the French authorities launched a series of development plans, particularly for the Sahara, to counteract the mounting opposition to colonialism in the region; however, none of the projects activated virtuous economic cycles. In 1953, the GDP of the country was 24 times smaller than the metropole's.[19] When three years later French companies discovered large amounts of oil and gas reserves, however, both France and the Algerian independence fighters welcomed them as the answers to the problems of underdevelopment of the area. In 1958, together with oil production, France launched the last development plan in Algeria before independence, the Constantine Plan. The plan envisaged the redistribution of 250,000 hectares of land to Muslim farmers, the recruitment of more Muslims in the civil service, so that they would represent at least 10% of the public administration, and investments in schooling and housing. The bulk of the plan, however, was the fast industrialisation of the country through the establishments of large industrial poles, with metallurgic and chemical factories fuelled by Saharan oil and gas.[20] Furthermore, gas was supposed to promote more diffused local development, providing a cheap energy source to remote areas in the countryside, thus encouraging light industries and local manufacturing.

The first concrete actions under the plan de Constantine were the expansion of the electricity network, the construction of two production plants in Hassi R'Mel and Tlemcen, and a gas pipeline to connect Hassi R'Mel to Algiers and Oran.[21] At the end of 1959, 157 companies had established themselves in Algeria or extended operations there, with a £25 million-investment that created 11,000 new jobs. International observers welcomed the Constantine plan: the *New York Times* wrote that the development of the oil industry in Algeria could be an important vehicle for peace;[22] the *Petroleum Press Service* agreed that after decades of failed development plans, the Saharan discoveries could finally "radically alter the economic background [of Algeria]."[23] The French oil industry, however, did not share the enthusiasm of its government. In a series of reports, the Compagnie Française de Pétrole (CFP) considered that basing the development of Algeria on hydrocarbons and heavy industry was as a fundamental mistake, because the large investments required did not promote jobs creation, and the short-terms improvements for the Muslim population would be insignificant.[24]

18 Samir Saul, *Intérêts économiques français et décolonisation de l'Afrique Du Nord (1945-1962)*, Genève, Droz, 2016.

19 *Ibid.*

20 Lefeuvre, D., *Chère Algérie : La France et Sa Colonie, 1930-1962* (Flammarion, 2005). and Lefeuvre, D., "Les Réactions Patronales Au Plan de Constantine," *Revue Historique*, 1986, p. 167-189.

21 Cotta, A., "Les Perspectives décennales du développement économique de l'Algérie et Le Plan de Constantine," *Revue Économique* 10, no. 6 (November 1959): 913, doi:10.2307/3498606.

22 ADF. Press Releases. *L'information*, summary of the New York Times, 25 November 1959.

23 "Algerian Opportunity", *Petroleum Press Service*, Dec. 1959, London Edition.

24 TOTAL Archives. Archive de Vincent Labouret. Note without date or signature, probably from 1959.

CFP proved to be right. Many of the jobs created rotated around the oil industry, with skilled workers imported from France and very little impact on the local areas; furthermore, the oil industry was the only one to attract international capital. Land redistribution, on the other side, made very little progress, for fear of alienating the *grands colons*.[25] Despite the aim of decentralisation and promotion of Small and Medium Enterprises (SMEs), the Constantine plan was eventually shaped around the oil industry and large industrial conglomerates. As government analysts explained, decentralisation was not profitable, and it was postponed to a second stage of the plan that never saw the light.[26] In June 1961, the employment data were disappointing, and the government had to admit that the Constantine plan was a half-failure (Figure 03).[27]

FIGURE 03

Employment in Algeria in 1959[28]	
Agriculture	1700000
Industry	214000
Construction	130000
Services	360000
Administration	123000

Jobs created by the Constantine Plan, June 1961[29]	
Food processing	1766
Construction material	2788
Minerals e metal working	972
Engineering and electrical	11.765
Chemical industry	1998
textile	2341
other	2191
TOTAL	23.821

Yet the independence fighters shared France's enthusiasm for the hydrocarbon industry, hailed as the only opportunity for Algeria to reach economic independence after the political one. Between 1956 and 1962 *El Moudjahid*, the newspaper of the Front de Libération Nationale (FLN), dedicated many articles to the importance of the FLN to gain control over the Saharan reserves. The recent literature on the Algerian war shows that "oil diplomacy" played an important role in the independence war;[30] since the Saharan discoveries, the FLN built relations with oil companies in the United States, Italy, Germany, and Russia, promising concessions in a future independent Algeria in exchange for data on the Saharan oil industry, the training in oil management of the Algerian personnel, and petrol for the Armée de Libération

25 Davis, M.H., "Restaging Mise En Valeur: 'Postwar Imperialism' and The Plan de Constantine," *Review of Middle East Studies* 44, no. 2 (2010), p. 176-186.

26 Cotta, "Les Perspectives décennales du développement économique de l'Algérie et Le Plan de Constantine."

27 ADF. Secrétariat d'Etat aux Affaires Algériennes. Affaires Politiques. *Note*, December 1960.

28 Saul S., *Intérêts Économiques Français et Décolonisation de l'Afrique Du Nord (1945-1962)*, Genève-Paris, Droz, 2016.

29 NARA. General Records of the Departments of State, Central Decimal Files, 1960-63 Economic, Economic Affairs French Africa. Labor Rep*ort*, 1 June 1961.

30 See: Cantoni, R., *Oil Exploration, Diplomacy, and Security in the Early Cold War*, London, Routledge, 2017; Beasley, B., "White-Collar Wildcatters and Wildcat Strikes: Oil Experts, Global Contracts, and the Transformation of Labor in Postwar Houston," in *Working for Oil. Comparative Social Histories of Labour in the Global OIl Industry*, by Touraj Atabaki, Elisabetta Bini, and Kaveh Ehsani, London, Palgrave, 2018, p. 257-84.; Malti, H., *Histoire secrète du pétrole algérien*, Paris, La Découverte, 2012; Kouzmine, Y., 1981-, *Le Sahara Algérien: Intégration nationale et développement régional*, Paris, Harmattan, 2012; Horne, A., *A Savage War of Peace: Algeria 1954-1962*, Pan Macmillan, 2012; Musso, M., "'Oil Will Set Us Free': The Hydrocarbon Industry and the Algerian Decolonization Process," in *Britain, France and the Decolonization of Africa*, UCL Press (Taylor & Francis Ltd), 2017, doi:10.14324/111.9781911307730.

Nationale (ALN). Through a series of informal networks, secret negotiations, and bursaries, students selected by the UGEMA (the Algerian students' association) and the UGTA (the Algerian trade union) trained in energy and oil management during and immediately after the war, creating a class of experts ready to fill key positions in the newly established Algerian government.

During the negotiations for the peace agreements, the problem of sovereignty and management of the oil resources was one of the most heated points of debate. France tried to retain the Saharan areas as an independent area, a *mer riverain* in which other countries, particularly Tunisia and Morocco, would be able to claim the benefits of the development of oil resources thanks to French businesses. This strategy succeeded in breaking the solidarity front within Maghreb, and was one of the reasons for the troubled relations between Algeria and its neighbours in the aftermath of independence. In fact, the FLN negotiators at Evian did not agree to any concessions that would not grant to the Algerian State full sovereignty over the Sahara according to the borders indicated by the FLN; in the end, France had to back down, in exchange of a series of guarantees over French companies' investments in the Sahara.

2/ 1962-1972 – THE BIRTH OF A STATE

After a century of institutions developed to serve the metropole and the minority of European citizens, and after seven years of war, in 1962 Algeria was in dire conditions. The only non-French institutions in place were the provisional government, the Conseil Nationale de la Révolution Algérienne (CNRA), similar to the Parliament; the UGTA, and the UGEMA. In the intentions of the 1956 Tripoli programme, which laid out the guidelines for future independence, the People's Democratic Republic of Algeria would become a democratic State based on the socialisation of the means of production, and the integration of the *pieds noirs* within the Muslim population. On an economic and social level, the priorities were the redistribution of land and the construction of cooperatives, through an industrialisation plan based on the needs of the agricultural sector.[31] After the war, however, divisions behind unity against the common goal exploded to the point of civil war; the one-party system, which had not been envisaged in Tripoli, eventually prevailed.[32]

The national economy displayed all the characteristics of a colonial economy: agriculture was divided in a modern sector for export (particularly wine and citrus) and a traditional sector based on self-sufficiency.[33] More than 40% of the population still lived in total misery, and only 10% of the children went to school. The majority of the population, especially from the countryside, did not speak French.[34] In June

31 Stora, B., *Histoire de la Guerre d'Algérie (1954-1962)*, vol. 115, Collection Repères, Paris, La Découverte, 1993.
32 *Id.*
33 Addi, L., "Algeria's New Oil Strategy," in *H. Clement-Moore and Gillipsie. Oil in the New World Order*, Florida, Florida University Press, 1995, p. 89-102.
34 Stora, B., *Histoire de l'Algérie depuis l'indépendance*, vol. 140, Repères, Paris, La Découverte, 1995.

1962 alone, five hundred thousand *pieds noirs* fled the country, abandoning the land and hundreds of small businesses. Amongst Muslim Algerians, at least two million unemployed and underemployed men fled the countryside, quickly expanding the slums in the cities' peripheries. French colons owned about one third of the cultivable land; after their sudden departure, farmhands started to work the land collectively, encouraged by the UGTA and by Ahmed Ben Bella's government, to avoid the concrete risk of famine.[35]

In the immediate aftermath of the independence, three principles guided the political economy of Algeria: the nationalisation of the economy; the establishment of a strong centralised State; and an industrialisation à *marche forcée* based on State-controlled heavy industry. Control over the oil and gas revenues was seen as a fundamental prerequisite for the State to raise the capitals needed for its industrial plans. While the Evian accords openly forbade nationalisations in the Sahara, the government concentrated on gaining as much control as possible over the industry. Within 18 months from the end of the war, the first Algerian company was established, Sonatrach (Société Nationale pour le Transport des Hydrocarbures), controlled by those FLN militants that had studied abroad during the war. Initially, Sonatrach was established for the construction of a new pipeline, thanks to loans granted by English banks; however, the company became the centre of Algeria's first industrial strategy, based on acquiring gradual control over its oil reserves - between 1963 and 1967, a series of successive nationalisations of the mining and other private sectors precluded to the nationalisation of the oil industry, and by 1967 Sonatrach counted more than 5000 employees.[36] At the same time, between 1960 and 1963, the country's GDP contracted by 35%,[37] while the French financial help to Algeria was being reduced: one billion new francs in 1963, 690 in 1964, 490 in 1965.[38] Ben Bella could not really control the country, and protests against his government were mounting. Finally, in June 1965, colonel Houari Boumédiène, who was now serving as Minister of Defence, staged a coup against Ben Bella and took power directly.

The new government implemented a further authoritarian turn in Algerian politics, and a more aggressive foreign politics. In 1967, right after the nationalisation of the Anglo-Saxon oil companies, Boumédiène launched the first quadrennial plan, based on four steps: the full *mise-en-valeur* of the hydrocarbon resources; the development of the heavy industry; the development of light industry; investments in education and professional training for the population. The plan was inspired by the work of French economist Gérard Destanne de Bernis, and his theory of the *industrie industrialisante*, industrialising industry. In the literature on Algeria, De Bernis' theories are often reduced to the idea that the State should only invest in State-directed heavy industry and large infrastructures, which would then organically bring about general economic development.

35 Santacroce, P., "La Riforma Agraria in Algeria," *Monthly Review. Edizione Italiana* 6, no. 7-8, 1973, p. 35-40.

36 Rebah, A., *Sonatrach: Une Entreprise pas comme les autres*, Algiers, Casbah editions, 2006.

37 Ruedy, J., *Modern Algeria: The Origins and Development of a Nation*, Indianapolis, Indiana University Press, 1992.

38 Centre des archives économiques et financières (CAEF). *Trésor-Action régionale-Outre-mer. Algérie*, 1965.

However, for de Bernis, the *industrie industrialisante* was such if it met two criteria: the final product had to be consumed locally; and it had to be a product "porteurs de progrès", carrier of progress, a stimulation for the other sectors and for the promotion of local technical development, which added general value to a territory. Particularly in reference to Algeria, de Bernis used the expression "non-industrialising industry" in relation to the type of industry set up by France before independence: industrial areas that did not create a diffused development system, and therefore did not add real value to the territory – precisely those developed through the oil industry and the Constantine plan. Furthermore, de Bernis advised that a programme for industrial expansion was not divisible from that of social reforms.[39] The Algerian authorities were aware that oil was not an industrialising industry in itself, and that its direct impact on the territory was limited; however, it was the only source at disposal to raise the capitals needed for other projects.[40]

In 1969, Algeria joined OPEC, pushing an aggressive agenda to impose higher crude prices. Despite the country being a small producer compared to giants like Saudi Arabia, it became the hawk of the organisation, pushing for nationalisations and radical changes in the international oil industry. Finally, in 1972, thanks to a joined action within OPEC, Boumédiène was able to break from the Evian accords and to gain direct State control over the Saharan oil and gas sources.[41] In reality, Sonatrach only acquired 51% control over the oil industry, with similar terms to those that most European countries required in the local mining industry. The Algerian nationalisation was therefore not the extreme socialist move portrayed at the time, but a simple acquisition of control over a strategic industry. However, Algeria started a domino effect amongst oil producers, which rushed to nationalise their assets. Following this process of nationalisation, the golden decade of OPEC started.

3/ 1972-1982: THE GILDED YEARS

The three quadrennial plans of 1967, 1970, and 1974 were ambitious industrial plans based on large-scale complexes that largely exceeded internal demand, and focussed on export. The 1973 oil boom and the easy credit allowed by petrodollar recycling made enormous investments possible; throughout the 1970s, the Algerian economy seemed to boom beyond the most optimistic expectations. Between 1967 and 1978, the government invested a total of 300 billion DA, and created 1.1 million jobs.[42] Sonatrach became a powerful international player, both in the upstream and downstream sector, and the first African company. Other sectors also took off, from chemical and petrochemical, particularly fertilisers, to smelting, industrial vehicles

39 See Bernis, G.D. de, "L'industrialisation en Algérie," in *Problèmes de l'Algérie indépendante*, by F. Perroux ed (Paris: Institut d'étude du développement économique et social, 1963). and G.D. de Bernis, "Les Industries Industrialisantes et Les Options Algériennes," *Tiers-Monde* 12, no. 47 , 1971, http://www.persee.fr/docAsPDF/tiers_0040-7356_1971_num_12_47_1802.pdf.
40 Fosset, R., "Pétrole et Gaz Naturel Au Sahara," *Annales de Géographie* 71, no. 385, May 1, 1962, p. 279-308, http://www.jstor.org/stable/23445027 and Nordine Aït-Laoussine, Interview with Nordine Aït-Laoussine, by author, 2016.
41 Rebah, *Sonatrach*.
42 Addi, "Algeria's New Oil Strategy."

and agricultural machinery, hydraulic and the electronic industry. The light industry also expanded, particularly food processing, textiles, wood, glass, and ceramics. Annaba became the capital of steel production, Arzew of petrochemicals, Sidi Bel Abbes of electronics.

Between 1976 and 1982, employment rose in the latter from 4750 units to 14210, in Setif from 3560 to almost 28000, and in Biskra from 630 to 11250. In 1954, the Algerian Muslims enrolled in university were 500; in 1970 they were 12500.[43] Between 1970 and 1978, the country's GDP grew from 40 billion to 86.8 billion DA, more than doubling, and the urbanisation went from 31% in 1966 to 50% in 1987.[44] Population also doubled, from 11.5 million in 1962 to 23 million in 1985. French sociologist Robert Linhart, who visited Algeria in 1964 and again ten years later, wrote that in 1974 "the physical transformation of the landscape was striking, as it was the appearance of a new generation of young managers passionately engaged with technology and research."[45]

The world looked at Algeria with optimism, and the country was hailed as a successful example of non-aligned Socialist State. The country gained importance in the international scene, too. After being one of the leading forces behind OPEC's defiance of the commodity markets in 1973, it became one of the strongest promoters of the New International Economic Order (NIEO), a set of proposals to create a permanent table between industrialised and developing countries, promoting the restructuring of the world's economy in favour of underdeveloped countries. During the 1973 crisis, interestingly, the debate within OPEC was split between doves, such as Saudi Arabia and Kuwait, that with sparse population did not face heavy financial requirements for industrialisation, and did not want to weaken the economies of consumer countries with prolonged high prices; and hawks, such as Algeria, Iran, and Iraq, which desired the highest possible prices to support their programmes of industrial development.[46]

While the country reclaimed a new world economy, however, within its borders neither colonel Boumédiène nor his successors altered the pre-independence structure of the country. On the contrary, the rapid but uneven pace of industrialisation exacerbated the divisions between the elites linked to the industrial projects, and the millions of farmers left behind, for which independence did not improve their living conditions. The agricultural sector, at the centre of the pre-independence plans of the Tripoli congress, did not enjoy the revolution it was promised, neither a serious reform. At independence, as already mentioned, French colons owned about one third of the arable land; these were seized by farmers working in the fields, which established a self-managed sector under the control of the UGTA; effectively, State-controlled (and subsidised) large agricultural enterprises. However, for lack of investments and expansion by the early 1970s the self-managed sector was exploited at full capacity, creating

43 Guerid, *L'exception algérienne*, *op. cit.*, p. 107.
44 Addi, "Algeria's New Oil Strategy."
45 Le "Transfert de technologie" et ses contradictions: quelques aspects de l'industrialisation algérienne, *Revue française d'administration publique*, n. 4, oct-dec 1977, p. 835-836, quoted in Guerid, *L'exception algérienne*.
46 Basosi, D., *Finanza e Petrolio. Gli Stati Uniti, l'oro Nero e l'economia Politica Internazionale*, Venezia, La Toletta, 2012.

a privileged farmer position, with minimum wage, healthcare, and family assistance; against a myriad of farmhands and of mini-owners (10 hectares or less per family), the *fellaheen*, which kept living below the poverty line. Furthermore, another third of the land was owned, since before independence, by a 0.3% of large Muslim owners, which occupied alone as much land as the small owners, and were able to maintain their privileges.[47] In 1971, Boumédiène launched the "agrarian revolution", based on the modernisation of the agricultural sector and land redistribution to the farmers. This was, however, organised with a top-down approach, by the government representatives in the local municipalities, which promoted patronage and often remained dead letter. The large owners, often part of the pre-independence Algerian urban elite that constituted the backbone of the FLN, were able to block large-scale redistribution, which only amounted to 2.5 hectares per family, below subsistence level and well below the possibility of using intensive industrial techniques to exploit the land.[48]

The failure to modernise the agricultural sector was a major setback for industrialisation, too. The growth rate in the countryside remained zero or negative, blocking the expansion of a domestic consumption market. Already in 1970, the production of fertilisers (one of the most common usage of gas resources) largely exceeded consumption, causing stockpiling problems. The *fellaheen* did not have the capital to buy fertilisers, and lived mostly outside of the monetary system, without being able to afford the 10 DA (one day of salary for a farmer of the self-managed sector) required to install an electricity meter. More than 5 million *fellaheen* kept living of self-consumption and migrant remittances – almost every family had one relative abroad, particularly in France.[49] Throughout the 1970s, Algeria produced tractors for which it was not able to find a market, and farmers that were too poor to afford the shovels - which were in return imported, because the artisanal sector also lagged behind.
The failure of modernising the agricultural sector caused deep social consequences. While during the revolution the *fellaheen* remained allied with the urban elites that guided the independence process, this alliance broke soon after independence. Similar divisions emerged in the urban landscape, where landless *fellaheen* poured in an attempt to join the industrial sector. A *fellah* without land lived on a salary between 150 and 300 DA per year; a small owner on 900 DA; a farmer from the self-managed sector (about 1.4 milion people) on 2800-3300 DA; a construction or factory worker had an annual salary of about 4800-9000, up to 11000 if specialised. A practitioner such as a doctor would enjoy a starting salary of at least 72000 DA.[50] Throughout the 1970s, the salaries of the urban bureaucracy grew three times more compared to the urban working class.[51] In the analysis of sociologist Lahouari Addi, without incentives and no other possibility to express their discontent, workers boycotted productivity.[52] Despite the improvements in schooling and professional training, there was a lack of

47 Santacroce, "La Riforma Agraria in Algeria."
48 *Id.*
49 *Id.*
50 *Id.*
51 Benbitour, A., "Un regard historique sur le rééchelonnement de la dette extérieure", in *Le Développement économique de l'Algérie*, by Taïeb Hafsi, Algiers, Casbah editions, 2011, p. 75-117.
52 Addi, "Algeria's New Oil Strategy.", art. cit.

specialised personnel. The lack of economic freedom and controlled prices also did not incentivise the creation of small businesses; the small and medium urban middle class put their savings in maintaining some family members at university, possibly abroad.[53]

The economic boom, then, relied solely on the hydrocarbon and heavy industry – however, the latter mostly failed to reach independence from the subsidies allowed by the former. Despite the million jobs created, this was a small result compared to the capitals invested and the demographic pressure, with large sums wasted in enormous complexes that were too big for the economy of the country or its export markets. Projects were set up without general planning, with strong unbalances between investments, markets, and returns. Furthermore, the State subsidy system created a culture of unaccountability for banks and industry executives, with no separation between political and industrial power.[54] Finally, and perhaps most importantly, apart from its oil and gas resources Algeria failed to find an export market for its products.

While European countries were establishing the common market, Algeria failed to create commercial agreements with its neighbours, while worsening relations with its biggest importers, France and the US, in the aftermath of the nationalisations. The opportunity of creating a common Maghreb economic area, often advocated by the Algerian fighters in the pre-independence years, and in which Algeria could have played a predominant role, failed to realise. At the same time, the country refused the "open door policy" adopted by many Arab countries towards the international private sector, closing the door to Western investments and pursuing a confrontational policy on international trade agreements through the NIEO agenda. Throughout the 1970s, in the West, Algeria was considered a rogue State. This strategy was revised already in the second half of the 1970s, when the need for market outlets brought the country to rekindle relations with both the United States and the Soviet Union; for example, the intervention of the USSR saved the wine industry from collapse, after France stopped buying.[55]

While exports did not take off, Algeria remained dependent on imports of all sort of goods, particularly food. The country needed to import about half of its food supplies, which were heavily subsidised by the State to remain at an affordable price. The cost of food subsidies grew from 731 million dinars in 1967, to close to 9 billion in 1984.[56] As a result of these imbalances, and in spite of the oil windfalls, public debt grew from 1 billion US dollars in 1970, to 17 billion in 1980, more than 17 times in 10 years. When oil prices stopped being favourable, all the contradictions and weaknesses of the Algerian development system were laid bare.

53 Benbitour, "Un regard historique sur le rééchelonnement de la dette extérieure"; Santacroce, "La Riforma Agraria in Algeria."

54 Addi, "Algeria's New Oil Strategy.", art. cit.

55 Harrigan, J., Wang, C., and El-Said, H., "The Economic and Political Determinants of IMF and World Bank Lending in the Middle East and North Africa", *World Development* 34, no. 2, 2006, p. 247-70.

56 Addi, "Algeria's New Oil Strategy.", art. cit.

Already before the 1986 oil crash, the Algerian debt was the object of a series of measures. In 1980, in order to keep borrowing and to alleviate the burden of an inefficient industrial sector, the country embarked in a partial liberalisation programme. However, Algeria did not encounter the favour of the IMF. While Morocco and Tunisia had more than a third of their annual external debt on concessional terms, Algeria had only access to market-based loans, which caused further ballooning in foreign debt.[57] At the same time, after the death of colonel Boumédiène in 1978 there was a lack of strong political governance. The situation exploded in 1986, when the oil counter shock provoked a fall in GDP that did not recover for the next 25 years (Figure 04).[58]

FIGURE 04

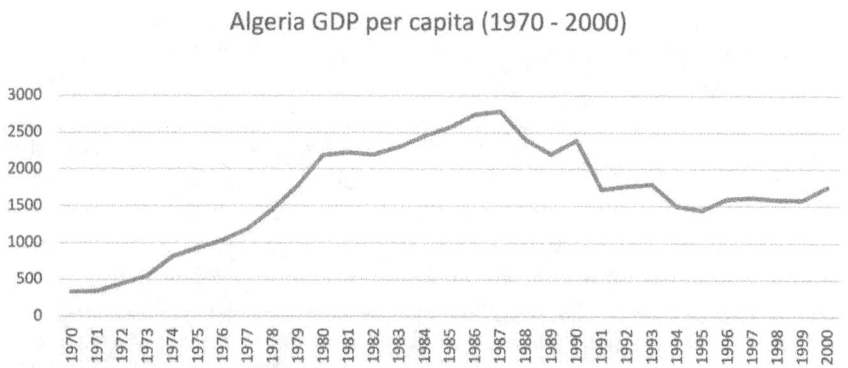

When the shock hit, overall unemployment went up to 22%; youth unemployment reached 75%.[59] Inflation escalated, with more and more Algerians not being able to afford essential goods. Opposition to the regime mounted, until the October 1988 riots caused more than 500 deaths.[60]

The economic and political crisis prompted a shift in both domestic and international policy. President Chadli Bendjedid opened to a multi-party system, and a new Constitution passed in 1989. In order to attract foreign investments, a new law partially liberalised the oil industry. Other reforms, following the indications of the IMF, regarded new fiscal laws and the liberalisation of commerce and enterprises, without abolishing the Socialist agenda but turning "the private sector [a] complement of the State sector."[61] In 1989 Algeria also joined the newly-established Arab Maghreb Union (UMA), a trade agreement aiming to foster future political unity in Maghreb and closer commercial links with the European Community. In May, the World Bank

57 Harrigan, Wang, and El-Said, "The Economic and Political Determinants of IMF and World Bank Lending in the Middle East and North Africa.", art. cit.
58 The World Bank, "GDP (Current US$) | Data."
59 Chekouri, Chibi, and Benbouziane, "Algeria and the Natural Resource Curse: Oil Abundance and Economic Growth.", art. cit.
60 United Nations High Commissioner for Refugees (UNHCR), "Refworld | Algeria: Riots of October 1988," *Refworld*, April 27, 2018, http://www.refworld.org/docid/3ae6aba95c.html.
61 Mebtoul, "Bilan des politiques économiques de 1963 a 2010.", art. cit.

granted to Algeria a $ 300 million structural adjustment loan. In the course of the next ten years, the country received four stabilisation loans, the largest ever bank program loan to any country in the MENA region.

However, the agreement with the creditor came to a cost; the dinar was devaluated by 75%, and some of the liberalisation had strong social ramification, such as the removal of state subsidies on foodstuffs, increased unemployment, and reduced income for the working class.[62] In the void left by the State, Islamist forces started to flourish, helping the informal economy and providing welfare to the mass of young unemployed people in the peripheries of urban areas. In the 1992 elections, the Islamic Salvation Front won; in return, the army stepped in and deposed the government. The Front was banned and its members arrested; while the army cracked down on the Islamist group, guerrilla emerged in a civil war that only ended at the beginning of the 2000s. While the army placed firmer control over the country, a series of Sonatrach executives became head of governments, such as Sid Ahmed Ghozali, Belaid Abdessalam, and Redha Malek.

Throughout the 1990s, in a situation of civil war and without the capability of either investing nor passing structural reforms, the main changes in the economic system were therefore partial liberalisations to welcome foreign investments – however, the most interesting and lucrative sector to the foreign eye was always the oil industry. At the same time, the government continued to invest in the development of oil and gas resources as the main source of capital to tackle its budgetary problems. The series of confused and weak political reforms did not allow to establish clear institutional frameworks in which businesses could operate. The adjustment plans from the IMF and World Bank were carried out to the detriment of the middle class, with further rises in inequality and the expansion of the informal economy.[63] Only at the end of the 1990s, thanks to the recovery of hydrocarbon prices, the overall economic situation improved. From the beginning of the 2000s, significantly higher levels of oil prices allowed for a new wave of public investment programmes. After two lost decades, in 2000 the government has started a National Plan for agricultural development, and in 2005 a free exchange agreement was signed with Europe.[64] In 2014, the Algerian economy expanded by 4% and unemployment fell to 15% - the 2016 price drop has again brought about a contraction, but not as strong as that of the 1980s.[65] However, it is still too early to determine whether the Algerian economy will be able to thrive in a future decarbonised economy.

62 Harrigan, Wang, and El-Said, "The Economic and Political Determinants of IMF and World Bank Lending in the Middle East and North Africa.", art. cit.

63 Addi, "Algeria's New Oil Strategy.", art. cit.

64 Ministère de l'Agriculture et de l'Alimentation, "Les Politiques Agricoles à travers le Monde. Algérie," July 18, 2016, http://agriculture.gouv.fr/algerie.

65 World Bank, "Algeria's Economic Outlook - April 2018," Text/HTML, *World Bank*, accessed April 26, 2018, http://www.worldbank.org/en/country/algeria/publication/economic-outlook-april-2018.

Conclusions

This short panoramic on the economic history of Algeria shows that while the presence of important quantities of hydrocarbons has significantly influenced the economy of the country, its social and economic underperformance can hardly be attributed to the oil industry. While Sonatrach clearly holds strong connections with the government and the military elites of the country, these influences are definitely not an Algerian exception – one recent example is the appointment of former Exxon CEO Rex Tillerson as Secretary of State in the US, from 2016 to 1018. The reasons for the weakness of the country outlined in this paper are largely independent from the oil industry: the lack of reforms in the agricultural sector; the inability to create a differentiated economic system; the failure to establish a self-sufficient industry; the isolation of the country from international markets.

There are no indications that a counter history of Algeria, in which oil and gas reserves were never found, would have brought about a better economic system. On the contrary, the bibliography utilised in this paper suggests that Algeria could have remained an agricultural society based on exports from large properties; and that the oil and gas sector did allow to raise national capitals that would have otherwise been never at disposal. Finally, while the optimism about the future of Algeria in the 1960s and early 1970s was followed by deep disappointment for the collapse suffered in the 1980s and 1990s, compared to the immediate post-colonial period the country shows to have overall improved its course; and future planning in the light of the common global objective to decarbonise the economy may unleash Algeria's potential.

Bibliography

Addi, L. "Algeria's New Oil Strategy." In *H. Clement-Moore and Gillipsie. Oil in the New World Order*, Florida, University Press Florida, 1995, p. 89-102.

African Development Bank. "The Search for Inclusive Growth in North Africa: A Comparative Approach," 2013. https://www.afdb.org/fileadmin/uploads/afdb/Documents/Publications/Economic_Brief_-_The_Search_for_Inclusive_Growth_in_North_Africa-_A_Comparative_Approach.pdf.

Aït-Laoussine, N. Interview with Nordine Aït-Laoussine. In person, 2016.

Basosi, D. *Finanza e Petrolio. Gli Stati Uniti, l'oro Nero e l'economia Politica Internazionale*. Venezia: La Toletta, 2012.

Beasley, B. "White-Collar Wildcatters and Wildcat Strikes: Oil Experts, Global Contracts, and the Transformation of Labor in Postwar Houston." In *Working for Oil. Comparative Social Histories of Labour in the Global OIl Industry*, by Touraj Atabaki, Elisabetta Bini, and Kaveh Ehsani, London, Palgrave, 2018, p. 257-84.

Benbitour, A. "Un regard historique sur le rééchelonnement de la dette extérieure." In *Le Développement Économique de l'Algérie*, by Taïeb Hafsi, Algiers, Casbah editions, 2011, p. 75-117.

Bernis, G.D. de. "L'industrialisation en Algérie." In *Problèmes de l'Algérie Indépendante*, by F. Perroux ed. Paris: Institut d'étude du développement économique et social, 1963.

Cantoni, R. *Oil Exploration, Diplomacy, and Security in the Early Cold War.* London: Routledge, 2017.

Central Intelligence Agency. "The World Factbook — Algeria," 2018. https://www.cia.gov/library/publications/the-world-factbook/geos/ag.html.

Chekouri, S.M., Chibi, A., and Benbouziane, M. "Algeria and the Natural Resource Curse: Oil Abundance and Economic Growth." *Middle East Development Journal*, 2017. doi:10.1080/17938120.2017.1366772.

Cotta, A. "Les Perspectives décennales du développement économique de l'Algérie et le Plan de Constantine." *Revue économique* 10, no. 6 (November 1959), p. 913. doi:10.2307/3498606.

Davis, M.H. "Restaging Mise En Valeur: 'Postwar Imperialism' and The Plan de Constantine." *Review of Middle East Studies* 44, no. 2 (2010), p.176-86.

Fardmanesh, M. "Dutch Disease Economics and the Oil Syndrome: An Empirical Study." *World Development* 19, no. 6 (1991), p. 711-17.

Fosset, R. "Pétrole et gaz naturel au Sahara." *Annales de Géographie* 71, no. 385 (May 1, 1962), p. 279-308. http://www.jstor.org/stable/23445027.

"Fresh Attack on Under-Development"." *Petroleum Press Service*, May 1961, London edition.

Guerid, D. *L'exception algérienne : La modernisation à l'épreuve de la société*. Casbah Editions. Algiers, Casbah, 2010.

Harrigan, J., Wang, C., and El-Said, H. "The Economic and Political Determinants of IMF and World Bank Lending in the Middle East and North Africa." *World Development* 34, no. 2 (2006), p. 247–70.

Henry, C.M. "Algeria's Agonies: Oil Rent Effects in a Bunker State." *Www.La.Utexas.Edu*. Accessed April 27, 2018. http://www.la.utexas.edu/users/chenry/pmena/mats03/HenryAlgeria2.htm.

Horne, A. *A Savage War of Peace: Algeria 1954-1962*. Pan Macmillan, 2012.

Ibarra, G.L. "Putting One More Piece in the Global Poverty Puzzle: The Case of Algeria." Text. *Voices and Views: Middle East and North Africa*, May 31, 2017. http://blogs.worldbank.org/arabvoices/global-poverty-puzzle-case-algeria.

Knoema.com. "Algeria GINI Index, 1960-2017." *Knoema*. Accessed April 27, 2018. https://knoema.com/atlas/Algeria/topics/Poverty/Income-Inequality/GINI-index.

Kouzmine, Y., 1981-. *Le Sahara Algérien: Intégration Nationale et Développement Régional*. Paris: Harmattan, 2012.

Lefeuvre, D. *Chère Algérie : La France et Sa Colonie, 1930-1962*. Flammarion, 2005.

———. "Les Réactions patronales au Plan de Constantine." *Revue Historique*, 1986, p. 167–89.

Malti, H. *Histoire secrète du pétrole algérien*. Paris: La Découverte, 2012.

Mebtoul, A. "Bilan Des Politiques Économiques de 1963 a 2010." In *Le Développement Économique de l'Algérie*, by Taïeb Hafsi, Casbah Editions. Algiers, 2011, p. 47-74.

Ministère de l'agricolture et de l'alimentation. "Les Politiques Agricoles à travers le Monde. Algérie," July 18, 2016. http://agriculture.gouv.fr/algerie.

Musso, M. "Inequality and History." *Inequality and History*, 2016. http://inequalityandhistory.blogspot.com/search?q=Marta+Musso.

???. "'Oil Will Set Us Free': The Hydrocarbon Industry and the Algerian Decolonization Process." In *Britain, France and the Decolonization of Africa*. UCL Press (Taylor & Francis Ltd), 2017. doi:10.14324/111.9781911307730.

O El-Kikhia, M. "Algeria: The Challenge of Poor Choices." *Al Jazeera*, April 17, 2014. https://www.aljazeera.com/indepth/opinion/2014/04/algeria-challenge-poor-choices-201441661717332782.html.

Rebah, A. *Sonatrach: Une Entreprise Pas Comme Les Autres*. Alger: Casbah editions, 2006.

Ruedy, J. *Modern Algeria: The Origins and Development of a Nation*. Indianapolis, Indiana University Press, 1992.

Santacroce, P. "La Riforma Agraria in Algeria." *Monthly Review. Edizione Italiana* 6, no. 7–8 (1973), p. 35-40.

Saul, S. *Intérêts économiques français et décolonisation de l'Afrique Du Nord (1945-1962)*. Genève: Librairie Droz, 2016. https://www.droz.org/france/fr/6333-9782600018999.html.

"Stability or Stagnation in Algeria?" *The Economist*, April 20, 2017. https://www.economist.com/news/middle-east-and-africa/21721155-algerians-see-little-reason-vote-coming-general-election-stability-or.

Stora, B. *Histoire de la Guerre d'Algérie (1954-1962)*. Vol. 115. Collection Repères ; Paris, La Découverte, 1993.

Stora, B. *Histoire de l'Algérie depuis l'indépendance*. Vol. 140. Repères ; Paris, La Découverte, 1995.

The World Bank. "GDP (Current US$) | Data." Accessed April 27, 2018. https://data.worldbank.org/indicator/NY.GDP.MKTP.CD?locations=DZ&year_high_desc=true.

???. "The World Bank in Algeria. Overview." Text/HTML. *World Bank*, April 21, 2018. http://www.worldbank.org/en/country/algeria/overview.

United Nations Development Programme. "Human Development for Everyone. Briefing Note for Countries on the 2016 Human Development Report. Algeria.," 2016. http://hdr.undp.org/sites/all/themes/hdr_theme/country-notes/DZA.pdf.

United Nations High Commissioner for Refugees (UNHCR). "Refworld | Algeria: Riots of October 1988." *Refworld*, April 27, 2018. http://www.refworld.org/docid/3ae6aba95c.html.

World Bank. "Algeria's Economic Outlook - April 2018." Text/HTML. *World Bank*. Accessed April 26, 2018. http://www.worldbank.org/en/country/algeria/publication/economic-outlook-april-2018.

The North-South Negotiations in the Sixties: The Case of Tunisia with the EEC[1]

Mohamed SASSI
University of Tunis

Introduction

After Tunisia's independence in 1956, relations between Tunisia and the European Union certainly developed, but not without fluctuations and difficulties. The first «exploratory conversations» started quite late in the year 1963. It was not until 1976 that Tunisia and the European Commission experienced their first more or less rewarding contractual relations[2], whereas the Treaty of Rome had been signed twenty years earlier (in 1957). However, Tunisia seemed to have worked tirelessly, since its independence, to strengthen its relations with all European countries[3]. Several problematic questions can be asked as to the reasons for the difficulty in establishing stable and lasting economic links with the European Community.

Can we draw a parallel between Tunisia's colonial past and the difficult beginnings of relations with Europe?[4] Did this difficulty arise from a purely economic logic, based on competition and promoting efficiency, linked to a neoclassical conception of regional relations? Or would it be the victim of an exacerbated subjectivity or of the conception of a unilateral rationality which consists in putting aside the economic and social conditions which form the necessary condition for establishing effective

1 This paper is an extension of the following article : Mohamed Sassi, « Les relations de la Tunisie avec la CEE : les débuts difficiles (1957-1976) », in Mohamed Sassi (dir.), *Espace Méditerranéen : diversité et évolution*, Tunis-Paris, ATHE/SPM, 2020, p. 235-262.

2 This is the cooperation agreement signed on April 25, 1976 and entered into force on November 1, 1978.

3 In 1995, Tunisia was the first Mediterranean country to sign an Association Agreement with the EU. Then in 2008, Tunisia becomes the first country to join the free trade area ...

4 ... Although it is difficult to determine with exactitude the impact of colonial period on the future of relations between the two shores.

partnership links? We will try to answer these various questions in order to better illustrate the circumstances of the relations between Tunisia and the EEC from 1957 to 1970, putting in perspective North-South relations in the Mediterranean context.

Tunisia's independence (in 1956) has already preceded the signing of the Treaty of Rome in 1957[5]. When signing this Treaty, the French Government, seeking to avoid referring the colonial question to the National Assembly, provided for a specific framework for relations with its former protectorates having already resumed their autonomy[6] - the adhesion of those two countries to Europe being, in any case excluded, because the new community was only open to the countries of the continent. However, inter-community customs unification had been accompanied by specific measures with regard to Tunisia and Morocco. That resulted in special provisions aimed at maintaining a preferential trade regime within the framework of the «Declaration of intent for the association with the EEC of the independent countries of the franc zone»[7] and the "Protocol relating to goods originating in and coming from certain countries and benefiting from special arrangements for importation into one of the Member States"[8]. It was in this particular context that the first negotiations between Tunisia and the Europe of the Six take place[9].

1/ TUNISIA FACING THE NEW EMERGENCIES OF THE EUROPE OF THE SIX

The formation of a new geopolitics within Europe itself could not be done without having consequences for third countries. In a context of diverging intra-European interests, Tunisia found itself confronted with real difficulties as to its positioning on the new regional geopolitical chessboard. Those difficulties were as much linked to endogenous reasons, related to Tunisia's difficult economic situation during the first years of independence, as to exogenous reasons, due to the complexity and entanglement of international pressures on Europe. In consequence, reviewing the geopolitical circumstances of Europe itself is necessary to extend the analysis to possible collaboration options for Tunisia.

1.1/ Geopolitical pressure on the Europe of the Six

The EEC, in gestation, underwent during its first years of multiple influences. We know that under the Treaty of Rome, Tunisia was able to join the Common Market, France

5 As a reminder, this treaty constitutes the birth certificate of the EEC (European Economic Community) and the EAEC (European Atomic Energy Community), after the establishment of the ECSC (European Coal and steel) on the occasion of the Treaty of Paris (1951).

6 The 1958 Treaty of Rome includes a specific protocol for Tunisia and Morocco, then independent for a year. Algeria, still French territory, was included in the fourth part of the Treaty of Rome on association with overseas territories.

7 Archives of the Ministère des Affaires étrangères de France (MAE), Papiers Wormser, Dossier 31, Conférence intergouvernementale pour le Marché commun et l'Euratom-Acte final.

8 Treaty establishing the EEC - Protocol relating to goods originating in and coming from certain countries (Rome, 25 March 1957), Available on the web: https://www.cvce.eu/content/publication/1999/1/1/48618174-c68f-4cfb-9211-e0bdcd6fdf68/publishable_fr.pdf, website consulted on October 20, 2019.

9 The Europe of Six of 1957 brings together France, Germany, Italy, the Netherlands, Belgium and Luxembourg.

wishing to provide the Maghreb countries with the possibility of benefiting from the perspective of preserving its predominant influence over their economies. Likewise, the African countries dependent on France, Belgium and Italy were associated from the outset. However, having regained their independence, those two groups would continue to be treated as partners, from January 1963 and for a period of five years, negotiating a new global association agreement on a case-by-case basis.

On the other hand, the United Kingdom and Greece had been particularly active in preserving their consecutive interests. The first was able to get the Six to offer the same association to the African Commonwealth countries. Greece, whose economy had been and remained one of the least developed in Europe, literally forced the hand of its allies, putting forward the scarecrow of communism to which it could move in if it was not taken care of by the Six. Thus, the Association Agreement with Greece was designed with a view to subsequent full integration into the Common Market. Steps were planned to achieve that goal. That treatment prompted Turkey, a "European country", to request the same treatment. The United States, for its part, was asking to enter into negotiations with the EEC, when their exports had been largely favorable to the European Community since its formation[10].

The EEC, therefore, found itself animated by a reflex of self-defense in the face of the demands which were seized by all the countries of Western Europe, and even by the most Western of the communist countries: Yugoslavia. That also explains the reluctance towards neutral countries (Sweden, Switzerland and Austria) and the very clear opposition to the demands of Spain and Portugal, about which reservations of an essentially political nature were added. Another eastern country, Israel, also happened to be asking to be associated, which was clearly refused. However, given the support it had with the governments of most of the Six, it could not be completely rejected. The Community then imagined negotiating a trade agreement with that country. Tunisian economic diplomacy, for its part, faced with the obligation to opt for an adequate partnership formula, could it have found in the option of a «trade agreement» a possible alternative?

1.2/ Preeminence of trade agreements: a choice or an obligation?

According to the Tunisian ruling elite, economic cooperation with member countries of the Common Market had been fruitful. It included assistance likely to equip and industrialize the country. It opened up new perspectives for Tunisian productions, which needed a larger market than that of France. However, Tunisian officials feared that it could inevitably lead to blind competition that would have affected domestic production, given the deterioration in terms of trade. At the end of 1962, Tunisian diplomacy seemed genuinely aware that the alternative of forging trade agreements was attractive. It was enough to deal with the Community, instead of dealing with each of the six member countries. However, the latter were also part of the GATT (General Agreement on Tariff and Trade), which obliged them to extend, to all signatory members, the advantages they grant in their bilateral agreements (unless is not

10 In 1958, the United States exported goods worth 2.8 billion dollars to the Community (importing 1.7 billion dollars). In 1971, US exports increased to $ 9 billion (compared to imports of $ 7.7 billion). Cf. Karl Kaiser, *L'Europe et les États-Unis*, Robert Laffont, 1973, p. 48.

a customs union). At that time, the United States was preparing to negotiate «tariff agreements» and wanted to establish an Atlantic partnership with the Community, as soon as the British negotiations were completed.

However, America, the initiating country of the GATT and a fervent supporter of the promotion of the freedom of international trade, would be the element which would influence the Community and the GATT, with a view to a new balance of trade in what we call the free world. The Mediterranean agricultural policy of the EEC was directly called into question with the appeal filed by the United States before the GATT against the system of preferences enjoyed on entry into the EEC, citrus exports from associated Mediterranean countries[11]. It was in the face of this situation, which called for rapid changes that were difficult to predict, that Tunisia, then living internally under the impetus of a collectivist economic power, had to find a way to actively impose itself.

Thus, in the circumstances and the concerns that Europe was experiencing at the beginning of the 1960s, and given the apparently socialist orientation of Algeria after independence in 1962 and the setbacks in relations with the Nasserian Egypt, the situation was becoming more complex for Tunisia. Its room for maneuver was also limited at the international level: the European side considered that it did not really interest the United States, unlike Morocco which benefits from its geostrategic position between the Mediterranean and the Atlantic and of its condition of land passage between Europe and Africa. Moreover, in a global geopolitics dominated by East/West dynamics, it was not supposed to be of more interest to the USSR, unlike Algeria. This was to say if, for the Europeans and their policy of progressive integration, Tunisia seemed to be the poor relation of the Maghreb ... – it is also to say in passing, how short the political vision may be[12].

Added to that, we can mention the few difficulties in diplomatic relations with France. In reality, the situation is paradoxical: it is such that the negotiating power of Tunisian diplomats seems weakened. Exploratory conversations are starting, in fact, at a time when the country's economic start-up largely depends on France. Due to the historical link between the two countries, having led to stable trade flows, European integration should have a negative and definite influence on Tunisian politics and economy. On the political level, the economic union of the Six tended towards a political union, and, in any case, towards a complete liberalization of trade. Tunisia risked finding itself, therefore, in a situation of weakness and facing a *fait accompli*. Accordingly, the interest of such a step, in the eyes of Tunisian diplomacy, was to gain favorable status from the start.

On the economic level, again in the eyes of Tunisian diplomats, the effects of the common market on the Tunisian economy couln't be known *a priori*. Several scenarios were to be seen, some of which were foreseeable (the complete abolition of customs duties, the gradual merger into a single European economy, and therefore with common economic and social policies which were completely combined, etc.) and others were to be foreseen (monetary union, even political, etc.). Member States

11 Laurence Tubiana, « Menace sur la politique agricole méditerranéenne », *Le Monde Diplomatique*, Août 1986.

12 To note the recent Turkish offensive in the Mediterranean, Tunisia's place turns out to be decisive in today's geopolitics.

would be less and less able to enter into bilateral agreements with third countries, those agreements having to be concluded with the whole Community. Thus, it was recommended by the diplomatic services to the Ministry of Planning to foresee the influence of economic relations with Europe.

It is for those reasons that Tunisia would request, on October 8, 1963, the opening of «exploratory talks» with the Community. The purpose of these was «to explore the possibilities and conditions offered by the conclusion of a trade agreement with the EEC ... and to envisage the establishment of organic links with the common market, such as association or the customs union"[13]. As for the other Maghreb countries, and in the absence of sufficient coordination between them, requests would be expressed respectively by Morocco and Algeria on December 14 and 18 of the same year. Added to that delay was the difficult start of negotiations.

2/ DIFFICULTIES OF THE FIRST NEGOTIATIONS AND DISAPPOINTING RESULTS (1963-1969)

As negotiations with the EEC took place, conditions were not very favorable for Tunisia. Relations between France and Tunisia between 1956 and 1965 were certainly marked by a mutual desire to pursue a policy of cooperation, but the Bizerte crisis in 1961 caused a breakdown in relations for a year. And the resumption of diplomatic relations would not be without incidents.

2.1/ The instability of relations with France explains the delays in the negotiations

Since the abrogation of the customs union on September 5, 1959, relations between Tunisia and France had been governed by a trade and tariff agreement which applies the reciprocal most-favored-nation clause throughout the customs territory. The basic principle remains that of the free movement of goods, but with the possibility of derogation, especially for Tunisia. Thus, for three quarters of Tunisian products imported into France, customs exemption was total. On the other hand, two thirds of imports into Tunisia of French products benefited from customs duties lower than the ordinary customs tariff. From 1961[14], the convention would undergo numerous revisions.

13 Confidential letter from the Tunisian Ambassador in Brussels to the Secretary of State for Foreign Affairs, December 15, 1962. Archives Nationales de Tunisie de Tunisie (A.N.T.), Versement du MAE N°33/2012.

14 The strategic importance of the Mediterranean naval base of Bizerte encouraged France to keep it, even after the independence of Tunisia, in 1956. In the spring of 1961, France refused to leave the naval base of Bizerte, at the request of the Tunisian President Habib Bourguiba. This caused a crisis between the two countries. A blockade by the Tunisians led to a military intervention by France which would be followed by a cease-fire on July 23. Bizerte would finally be evacuated by France in October 1963. See Sébastien Abis, « L'affaire de Bizerte, une crise géopolitique méconnue », in *Confluences Méditerranée*, 2008/4 (n°67), p. 129-146. See also, Samya El Machat, « La crise de Bizerte 1960-1962 », in *Revue française d'histoire d'outre-mer*, 2000, p. 299-326.

The context of the Tunisian economic transition being difficult, because of the internal complications[15] and following the incidents with France[16], President Habib Bourguiba was forced to delay the re-entry into negotiations of Tunisia with the EEC in order to settle certain first-rate disputes[17]. Reciprocal claims between Tunisia and France had still not been settled. On July 20, 1962, the French and Tunisian governments decided to renew diplomatic relations at the ambassadorial level[18]. Then, on January 8, 1963, a protocol, established on a lump sum basis, provides for general compensation and payment of charges by Tunisia over a period of fifteen years.

Thus, on March 2, 1963, an agreement was signed allowing concerted decolonization (initiated under May 18, 1957 and the protocol of October 13, 1960), preserving the interests of French agricultural owners in Tunisia and allowing the acquisition of 127,000 hectares of lands. Those territories, located in regions where the maintenance of French farms created certain problems, were sold to the Tunisian State. From April 9, 1963, the French ambassador launched new negotiations with Tunisia with a view to obtaining interests other than agricultural ones. Subsequently, on August 9, 1963, the two countries signed a protocol in Paris relating to economic and financial cooperation, with a loan of 90 million francs and aid of 35 million, all for the realization of industrial projects. Some new advantages, on occasion, were offered to Tunisia:

- The labor agreement concerning Tunisian workers in France and vocational training for Tunisian adults.
- The suspension of visas between the two countries for stays of less than three months from January 29, 1964.
- The renewal of the protocol of cultural and technical cooperation of April 15, 1959, from October 1, 1964.

The event coming after was the withdrawal of the French government, of its own accord, of the last military elements on October 15, 1963, thus normalizing Franco-Tunisian relations. It is a date that almost coincides with Tunisia's request to open negotiations with the EEC for a partnership agreement. Then, on February 25, 1964, wishing to put an end to the ongoing disputes, France granted some advantages to Tunisia within the framework of new agreements: aid of 100 million francs, of which 55 million was reserved for industrial projects. That was when the unilateral decision of the Tunisian government (May 12, 1964) to nationalize lands belonging to foreigners came in[19], and on which the French reaction was unequivocal[20].

Indeed, since that date, trade has been subject to the common law regime applied to third countries. Tunisian sales to France are down to 40% of what they were before. In

15 Mohamed Sassi, « La question économique de la Tunisie indépendante : les contraintes d'une transition difficile », *Colloque international : 1956 en Tunisie et dans le monde arabe*, organised by the Institut Supérieur de l'Histoire de la Tunisie contemporaine et le Laboratoire DIRASET, le 24-25-26 novembre 2016.

16 In particular the mutual complaints of Tunisia and France to the UN Security Council. See: Abdelaziz Chneguir, *La politique extérieure de la Tunisie 1956-1987*, Paris, L'Harmattan, 2004, p. 42.

17 The autonomy of the Tunisian dinar (1958), Tunisia's support for Algeria during the war with France, the presence of French troops on Tunisian territory, the occupation of agricultural land by settlers, etc.

18 Abdelaziz Chneguir, *La politique extérieure de la Tunisie 1956-1987, op. cit.* p. 89.

19 It should be emphasized here that the internal pan-Arab and union pressure was such that President Bourguiba could not do better on the issue of nationalizations. See Mohamed Sassi, «The economic question of independent Tunisia: the constraints of a difficult transition», *op. cit.* Article in publication. To view it, please contact the author by email: msassi@live.com

20 Cancellation of untied aid of 45 million francs, cancellation of the unallocated portion of tied aid, ie 15 million francs. Abdelaziz Chneguir, *La politique extérieure de la Tunisie 1956-1987, op. cit.* p. 91.

return, French sales in Tunisia suffered only a slight reduction. That was explained by the continuation of industrial projects in progress and, therefore, by the maintenance of purchases in France at a high level. But that would not work without compromising the observed imbalance over time. The problem was that Tunisia should experience an almost complete shutdown of cultural and technical cooperation programs, including:

- the recall of 61 agricultural experts and contingent soldiers assigned to agricultural education colleges;
- suspension of the expanded technical cooperation program;
- non-replacement of teachers at the end of the contract;
- stopping the recruitment of experts for technical cooperation missions.

To all this must be added the postponement of conventions related to social security, legal aid, consular aid, tax, etc.

2.2/ Tunisia in the ideological crossroads of Europe: the distance from France

During Tunisia's first talks with EEC countries, the Tunisian position remained mixed. Some countries like the Netherlands, not having economic interests in North Africa (and in Algeria in particular), found themselves in contradiction with the French vision of Europe. Those countries find themselves in perfect alignment with British and American interests and were pulling towards Great Britain's membership of the Community. That was a subject on which France had vetoed. It also happened that the attitude of Tunisian diplomacy was very suspicious of French foreign policy following the incidents of 1961 and out of fear of any form of neo-colonialism. The breakdown of the England-Common Market negotiations denoted an autarchic vision (as to his conception of Europe), if not «neocolonialist», of Charles de Gaulle[21]. This attitude, expressed in terms of the desire for French hegemony within the Europe of the Six, was rejected by the Five, thus causing real differences of vision. The EEC, in the view of some of its members, should offer similar possibilities and should not practice a discriminatory policy against the ex-colonies. Tunisian officials have apparently remained neutral, but do not hide their preference for a Europe that was more open to itself, to the world and to the developing countries.

The permanent representative of the Netherlands to the EEC (Mr. Dirk Spierenburg) expressed his country's position to the Tunisian ambassador during an interview the day after the hundredth Council of Ministers of the Common Market (April 1 and 2, 1963). According to him, «the Netherlands can only conceive of the Community as an institution open to the world and as an instrument of peace and progress», adding that the French Government should kept its commitments regarding the raising of difficulties in the face of negotiations between the Common Market and the USA on the basis of the Trade Expansion Act, as well as on the acceptance of the principle of resuming contact with the United Kingdom[22]. Moreover, Tunisia,

21 « Lettre confidentielle de l'Ambassadeur de Tunisie à Bruxelles au Secrétaire d'État aux Affaires étrangères, du 2 Février 1963 ». Archives Nationales de Tunisie, Versement du ministère des affaires étrangères, 33/2012.

22 Rapport confidentiel de l'Ambassadeur de Tunisie à Bruxelles du 6 avril 1963, « Entretien avec le représentant permanent des Pays-Bas auprès du Marché Commun », Archives Nationales de Tunisie, Versement du ministère des Affaires étrangères, 33/2012.

wanting to count on its good historical relations with the United States[23], opted for the idea that the economic world would be better with the rapprochement between the United States and the EEC.

The formation of a large economic unit, with great facilities for economic exchanges, would be more favorable for a country the size of Tunisia. Be that as it may, the difficult relations with France did not encourage an acceleration of the negotiations for a «Tunisian statute» in its relationship with Europe and even less help to prepare the conditions favorable to a good negotiation.

2.3/ Rather asymmetric and difficult negotiations

The first wave of debates went through three stages of negotiation. The first of these was the initiation of debates between Tunisia and the EEC, which required Tunisian diplomatic efforts for the opening of «exploratory conversations»; the second was summed up in a first period of negotiations between 1963 and 1965, without any successful results; the third, finally, were the negotiations of 1967, which resulted in an agreement in 1969.

A/ The Tunisian initiative and the difficult beginnings

The first discussions between Tunisia and the European Commission took place in 1959, but those conversations did not follow. It was only in the fall of 1963 that Tunisia requested the opening of exploratory conversations with the Common Market, in the letter of intent of October 8, 1963, addressed to the European Commission. Tunisian diplomatic action then turned to the exploration of relations with the EEC in order to study the form that economic relations between Tunisia and the European Community could take in the future. The Commission was quick to agree, stressing the favorable position of each member country, despite some reluctance[24].

The representatives of Belgium and Luxembourg both assured Tunisia of their support. That of Italy, although showing certain coldness in considering the Tunisian request, agreed that the case of Tunisia did not raise major problems. Indeed, the quantity of exported Tunisian citrus fruits, the quality of which intended them for a clientele other than that targeted by the Italians, remained relatively modest. Olive oil was not an insurmountable problem either, as Italy was one of the main buyers. Likewise, the grain issue could be resolved through a general negotiation or a global agreement[25]. The Permanent Representative of Germany also expressed his country's good attitude towards Tunisia and said that the case of Tunisia did not seem to him to encounter any great difficulties. On the other hand, the position of Mr. Spierenburg, Permanent Representative of the Netherlands, remained hesitant, in view of the concern already expressed by Belgium and Luxembourg regarding the «slide of

23 Relations between Tunisia and the United States had remained intense since Tunisia's independence in 1956. President Eisenhower said in 1957 that the policy embodied by Habib Bourguiba was the best chance for the free world. President Bourguiba, finding himself backed by the US, was considered «the most independent and enthusiastic friend in the Arab world ...». Cited in Abdelaziz Chneguir, *La politique extérieure de la Tunisie 1956-1987, op. cit.*, p. 38.

24 « Rapport de l'Ambassade de Tunisie à Bruxelles du 26 octobre 1963 », Archives Nationales de Tunisie, Versement 33/2012, Boîte 1.

25 « Lettre confidentielle du 9 novembre 1963 de l'Ambassadeur de Tunisie à Bruxelles au Secrétaire d'État aux Affaires étrangères (à Tunis) », Archives Nationales de Tunisie, Versement du ministère des Affaires étrangères, 33/2012.

Algeria towards communism»[26]. The Netherlands could not then declare itself before examining the outcome of the conversations with the Commission.

It was in that climate of relative mistrust that the first exploratory conversations began between the Commission and the three Maghreb countries. They would take place between 1963 and 1965. But the talks did not proceed according to the hoped-for pace. As the EEC was in a launch phase, the European partners favored a rather wait-and-see position towards all the Maghreb countries. Some members of the EEC, including France, considered any negotiations with third countries as still premature. As a result, the first step towards opening the talks was thwarted by a procedural reaction: it would involve bringing Tunisian diplomacy into play in territory that was not its own.

Indeed, the intention of Tunisian diplomacy was to address both the Council and the Commission. This was because at Commission level alone the discussions would have been of a technical nature which should be avoided, with decisions ultimately resting with the Member States. However, the Tunisian request did not seem to have been taken in the first degree of interest and would have to go through the «Commission» and not by the «Council». So the first session of the exploratory conversations, which took place on December 13, 1963, ended in failure, if not «humiliation,» if one considers the Embassy's report[27]. Although subsequent meetings were going to be better, the first discussion sounded like a ridiculous 'job interview', as Tunisia, emerging from a long colonial period, did not yet benefit from a level of experts sufficiently high and, above all, at that scale of economic and diplomatic relations.

A few days later, a summary of the minutes[28] was communicated by the Commission delegation[29] to the Tunisian Ambassador[30], giving more volume and content to the «asymmetric» meeting. Axel Herbst, President of the European Delegation, underlined, among other things, the importance of supporting Tunisia so that it could develop, sell its products and cover its trade deficit with Europe. But the report ruled out any form of partnership. He therefore proposed «to find a very broad formula which would bring together the association, without being the association, and which would be in accordance with GATT rules»[31]. Without going further into the details, the first meeting was synonymous with a double failure: in its form, given that it was devoid of any political will on the part of the European side, and in substance, insofar as it did not did not meet Tunisian political aspirations and did not provide concrete answers.

26 *Ibid.*

27 « Compte-rendu de la première séance des conversations exploratoires avec la CEE », Rapport confidentiel de l'Ambassadeur de Tunisie à Bruxelles du 18 décembre 1963, Archives Nationales Tunisiennes, Versement du ministère des Affaires étrangères, 33/2012.

28 « Compte-rendu des conversations préliminaires tenues le 13 décembre 1963 entre la Délégation tunisienne et la Délégation de la Commission de la CEE », fait à Bruxelles le 17 décembre 1963, Archives Nationales de Tunisie, Versement 33/2012.

29 The European delegation was composed of MM. Herbst (Chairman), Director General of External Relations (German), Divers Martino, Director of Trade Agreements (Italian), Mr. Roussel, Head of Division of Associations and Special Agreements (French), Westhof, Head of Agriculture Division (Dutch, Maltzham, Chief Customs Officer (German), Tavitian, Chief Financial Officer (French).

30 The Tunisian delegation was made up of MM. El Goulli, Ambassador of Tunisia in Brussels; Ghezel and Fayache, Secretary and Ambassador Attaché respectively.

31 « Compte-rendu des conversations préliminaires tenues le 13 décembre 1963 entre la Délégation tunisienne et la Délégation de la Commission de la CEE », *op. cit.*

Afterwards, the echoes and the general impression suggested that Tunisia should not face objections in principle to the idea of establishing a Free Trade Area (FTA). It remained a possible convergence option and would remain a basis for future discussions. Another working hypothesis was that proposed during the exploratory conversations of January 22, 1964[32]. That would involve expanding the regime defined between Tunisia and France in 1959.

The years 1964 and 1965 were not economically easy years for Tunisia. The deterioration of its relations with France in 1964 caused difficulties in the flow of its products and in its external finances. The devaluation of the dinar carried out by the Tunisian government, however, enabled it in 1965 to maintain the volume of its sales, at the cost of reduced revenues. It should be noted the almost total halt in the export of wine. Admittedly, the resumption in 1966 of preferential relations with France, although targeting a smaller number of products than that of the 1959 Convention, will contribute to the absorption of the difficulties experienced in 1965. But Tunisian diplomatic action in 1965, as far as Europe is regarded, did not go away and was more oriented towards urgency. Obviously, President Bourguiba spared no effort to support Tunisian diplomatic efforts in Brussels. He confirmed that in his rather appeasing speeches for the West and with his intermediate positioning as a man of peace in the Middle East[33].

Tunisia's vision of economic relations with Europe could clearly be summed up in Bourguiba's speech in an interview with the ORTF :

> "... Because our economy is closely linked to one of the largest countries in the Common Market, that is to say France, and we wish to extend our trade to the other five countries in the Common Market to promote our development. We believe that the assistance that the developed countries and particularly France could bring us, could not be limited to credits, funds, technicians, but go beyond this framework to include trade... If we were given the possibility of selling our products at a suitable price, to buy the equipment we need to industrialize ourselves, to develop our agriculture at equally suitable prices, which would also be a way of promoting our development ..."[34]

Thus, the Tunisian request would ultimately relate to the development of a preferential customs regime, particularly in the agricultural sector, financial assistance to facilitate industrial investments, and technical support for manpower training. However, Tunisian economic diplomacy would again face other obstacles or barriers than the relationship of tension and instability with France. In particular, it was a

32 « Conversations exploratoires entre la Tunisie et la CEE, Deuxième session du 22 janvier 1964 », Archives Nationales de Tunisie, Versement du ministère des Affaires étrangères, 33/2012.

33 Bouguiba's speech in Jericho (Ariha) in March 1965 condemned the "all or nothing" solution and advocated a solution for the first time in stages. His speech was presented by the Egyptian media (among others) as the most abject betrayal of the Palestinian cause. See B. Etienne et N. Sraieb, « Bourguiba et Israël », *Annuaire de l'Afrique du Nord (AAN)*, 1965, p. 151-162.

34 Feuille documentaire N°67/1965 du 12 avril 1965, « La Tunisie et la CEE : Extraits d'une interview de son Excellence Habib Bourguiba, Président de la République tunisienne, à l'O.R.T.F., Archives Nationales de Tunisie, Versement du ministère des Affaires étrangères, 33/2012. It should be noted in this regard that, according to the point of view of the Tunisians and their president, the aid sought is hardly assimilated to any form of begging, but rather to a form of compensation, because of the spoliations which were the lot and the feeling of colonial times.

question of securing the hard-to-obtain unanimity among the Six. The negotiations would be oriented in such a way that no comprehensive agreement would be possible.

B/ Tunisia faced with the long «intergovernmentalization»[35] process within the EEC

The second half of the 1960s were, for the Six, years of «internal crises» which impacted economic activity during this period. Charles de Gaulle's refusal to strengthen the powers of the Commission and the European Parliament led to the empty chair crisis in 1965 and tensions would continue over the following years[36]. There was also the refusal of certain countries to allow the advantages to accumulate for France, monopolized until then thanks to unclear relations with its former colonies. Those facts had had a negative impact on the volume of trade between the countries of the EEC. In 1967, therefore, European economic activity slowed down significantly compared to that of the previous year. The average GDP of the EEC grew only by 2.5% in real terms, against more than 4% in 1966.

It was in this precise context that Tunisia would also experience great difficulties in adopting a mandate allowing it to re-enter negotiations with the EEC. In effect, given the «accumulated urgencies» for member States, the EEC Council of Ministers would only grant a partial mandate to the Commission. Questions of technical and financial assistance to Tunisia would then be excluded from the negotiations, and those relating to products subject to negotiation would remain restricted. That can be explained, in part, by the divergent positions of Italy and France. In fact, as early as 1964, Italy presented a memorandum to the Council which defined the guiding principles of the foreign policy to be followed by the Community, in particular with regard to the Mediterranean countries. Positioning itself on the side of Tunisian interests, Italy wanted to put an end to the different statuses of the Maghreb countries vis-à-vis France and the other countries of the Community. It so happened that at that date, France's position illustrated a certain lack of interest in Tunisia, probably linked to the tensions of decolonization and the crisis in Bizerte. Thus, the negotiation session of July 1965 did not lead to any agreement, two products fundamental to the economy of Tunisia, olive oil and citrus fruits, being excluded from the list of products subject to the negotiation.

Commission delegates admitted to representatives of Tunisian diplomacy in Brussels that «the discussions were not easy» and that the EEC «still has the difficult task of finding solutions capable of reconciling the sometimes divergent interests of the economies of (our) member countries". Since then, and until December 1966, negotiations remained in abeyance, due to differences within Europe over the Tunisian (and Moroccan) question[37].

On 23 November 1966, finally, the Commission of the EEC adopted an opinion recommending the resumption of negotiations with Tunisia. Some points concer-

35 This neologism clearly reflects the procrastination between the European partners as to the definition of relations between the EEC and Tunisia.

36 Paolo Caraffini, "De Gaulle, the "Empty Chair Crisis" and the European Movement", *Perspectives on Federalism*, Vol. 7, issue 2, 2015, p. 163-189.

37 « Lettre confidentielle du 5 février 1967 » of the Tunisian Ambassador in Brussels to the Ministry of Foreign Affairs, Archives Nationales de Tunisie, Versement 33/2012.

ning agriculture, however, are not settled, such as the question of «oranges». But the attitude of the EEC States was starting to soften and the majority was fully in favor of a rapid resumption of negotiations. The Benelux and Germany unanimously and unreservedly support the Tunisian candidacy. France assured that its support goes without saying, but demanded the regrouping of the three Maghreb countries in a single mandate, while underlining the specific character of each one.

As for Italy, its attitude remained characterized by good dispositions in terms of principles (due to its good relations with Tunisia) and reluctance as to concrete solutions. Italy no longer formulates total reservations on a particular product, but seek to limit the preferential margins to be granted to the Maghreb countries in general. In fact, the Italian government strongly opposed any dissociation between the Tunisian and Algerian issues, for two main reasons:

- France's maintenance of total exemption for Algerian olive oil in defiance and violation of the sampling system established at the borders of the Six for this product. That clearly showed a concern on the part of France to preserve bilateral relations (treatment on a case-by-case basis) with its former colonies.
- The huge tariff and quota preferences granted by Germany to Algerian wines.

That was the reason why Italy continued to speak, in a constant manner, of sometimes «global», sometimes «regional» or «Mediterranean» problems, so as to highlight the weight of the competition to which its products would be submitted, in case of association of the Maghreb countries, Spain and Israel, after that of Greece and Turkey. Other reasons for that delay can be explained by the differing positions of the member States regarding the granting of trade advantages to third countries without any real stake, with regard in particular to Belgium and Germany. We should also highlight the new differences, which appeared in 1968 in the face of French intransigence over the British candidacy for the EEC, which would be at the origin of a state of tension which reigned within the Community.

Thus, during the work of the experts, the Netherlands were particularly reluctant to reach an agreement with Tunisia for reasons of technical nature: the Dutch tended to want to link the resumption of the Tunisia-EEC negotiations with the EEC-Great Britain ones. The Italian position, on the other hand, suggested that the development of that agreement be seen from a broader perspective, that is, by placing it in the Mediterranean area. In short, the repeated delays in the progress of the negotiations can be explained by the existence of a certain form of general indifference on the part of the EEC states. The process of political decision-making at European Community level did not promote a consistent position-taking[38].

Adding all of those factors together fostered a climate that was not conducive to fair and equal negotiation, given the limited scope of products covered by the agreement in question. Indeed, the agreement, supposed to be comprehensive, was in fact limited to the commercial aspect alone. At that level, Tunisia, given its economic dependence until then, did not enjoy much leeway in terms of negotiation and persuasion. The pressures on Europe were such that the idea of Tunisia's important

38 Mohamed Sassi, « Les relations de la Tunisie avec la CEE : les débuts difficiles (1957-1976) », in *op. cit.*

geostrategic position, at the heart of the Mediterranean and at the gates of Europe, was still not unanimous.

On the other hand, the efforts to «inter-governmental» decisions, to fill the lack of coordination and the divergences of interest, after the passage through the CAP, were only beginning, because some questions remained unanswered. Indeed, intergovernmental debates often took place with a background specific to the economic interests of each member country. Thus, on the specific problem of olive oil, the subject of diverging views among experts and permanent representatives of the Six, France's position in October 1967 with regard to Tunisia was then of a financial nature, while that of Germany was more of a commercial one.

Indeed, for France, it was a question of paying Tunisia a rebate equivalent to the shortfall. Not having been supported by the other countries, France was trying by all means to pass this measure through a political decision (by the Council of Ministers). The German representative, for his part, proposed a compromise solution and preferred instead to defend a solution of conventional prices. Belgium, in a perspective of a realistic solution, supported the German solution, while the Italian delegation thought that France was making difficulties with the sole aim of delaying the adaptation of a negotiating mandate.

On the other hand, in the eyes of Italy and the Netherlands, Algeria was a problem. For them, the Maghreb formed a unit. During the negotiations, therefore, there was a confusion between the advantages offered to Algeria and the particular situation of Tunisia or Morocco. In other words, the confusion between the interests drawn by Algeria, thanks to its particular relations with France, had a negative impact on the interests of other Maghreb countries, insofar as the European countries wished to deal uniformly with the entire Region.

C/ The problem of the integration of Algeria and its consequences for Tunisia

The legal starting point of relations between Algeria and the EEC was the former statute of the French Department of the first and the provisions of the Treaty of Rome or its annexes. Algeria continued to benefit from almost all the member States of the same advantages that they granted between them. That situation was increasingly difficult to justify in law. In the economic and social fields, Algeria was experiencing widespread difficulties (problems of economic organization, very high unemployment, shortage of executives at all levels, etc.). On the other hand, it had, thanks to oil and gas, potential and substantial resources which facilitated the formation of capital and provide it with appreciable means of external payment.

Of the three Maghreb countries, it was Algeria that depended most on its relations with France, for understandable reasons. Since the mid-1960s, it had been trying to diversify its business relationships. Thus, wine and citrus represented respectively more than half and one sixth of Algeria's exports to the EEC. Tunisia, on the other hand, has a significant economic and social infrastructure, both material and human. That country was less affected by unemployment than the other two Maghreb countries, pursuing an accelerated development program. It was, of course, a collectivist program of socialist inspiration whose limits would appear very quickly, but it had the merit of opening a significant number of industrial sites to the point that Tunisia reached the thresholds defined for an economic take-off.

As for Morocco, it continued, as much as Tunisia, to benefit from the trade advantages concluded with France, but the structure of its economy revealed, just as much as that of Algeria, problems of unemployment and shortage of executives. However, the EEC failed to regulate and harmonize its relations with the Maghreb countries and to put an end to certain anomalies in order to achieve the Common Market. Each Community country applied a different regime to imports from the Maghreb. Moreover, these regimes were not even uniform, depending on whether it is Algeria, Morocco or Tunisia. Those differences made it impossible to abolish border controls between the Six.

In fact, Algerian goods returning to France, benefiting from a special regime, caused traffic distortions when they freely enter the markets of other member States. Thus, despite its positive attitude towards Tunisia, Italy had had to maintain its position regarding the association of the cases of Tunisia and Algeria, in order to be able to request more substantial compensation on the basis of the "balance of charges" between the Six. That was a policy which bore fruit in the last months of 1966, since the latest regulations adopted by the EEC provided Italy with sufficient advantages and shielded Italian producers from competition. In the process, the Algerian affair took a different turn, in January 1967, when Algeria refused to enter into negotiations with the EEC[39]. On January 27, Jean-Marc Boegner, representative of France to the EEC, declared that, Algeria not being ready to take part in the new negotiations, it would be advisable to speak with those who are ready to do so![40]

This is how the Tunisia-EEC negotiations in 1967 turned out to be relatively better: a second term introduced olive oil and citrus fruits into the negotiations, but excluded other products such as wine. In the meantime, cooperation with France has started to resume a reasonable pace since 1966. However, the question of technical and financial assistance will not be discussed, France having ended all financial assistance to Tunisia since the nationalizations of 1964[41]. This explains why the cooperation policy between the two countries remained relatively improvised until 1968.

The negotiations were finally resuming, but without any real stakes for the EEC, because of political reasons (political stability in the western Mediterranean, development aid, respect for the declarations of intent annexed to the Treaty of Rome). They took place from November 14 to 16, 1967, but it was not until March 1969 that the association agreements were signed. That delay was due, in particular, to the establishment of the process of a common agricultural policy (CAP) placing reservations on certain products, including wine. That explains, of course, one of the underlying reasons for the mixed progress of Tunisia's negotiations with the EEC. As a result, the 1969 agreements would have a life of only five years, but provided for the opening of new negotiations on a broader basis.

39 Algeria, finding itself in a position of strength by its offer, and thanks to the support from France, "was all the less eager to negotiate an agreement at the beginning of its independence, because it had benefited from an advantageous status quo, until 1968". Houda Ben Hammouda, « Le rôle de la France envers le Maghreb au sein de la Communauté européenne (1963-1969) », in *Matériaux pour l'histoire de notre temps*, 2010/3 (n°99), p. 90-97.

40 « Lettre confidentielle du 5 février 1967 » , *op. cit.*

41 Houda Ben Hammouda, « Le rôle de la France envers le Maghreb au sein de la Communauté européenne (1963-1969) », *op. cit.*

3/ THE 1969 AGREEMENT AND ITS EFFECTS

Those bilateral agreements aimed, as a whole, to develop trade relations between the contracting parties on the basis of the principles of equality and reciprocity of benefits. As such, the main provisions of those agreements recommended the need to facilitate and develop trade in goods between the parties concerned, while taking into account the provisions and requirements of the General Agreement on Tariffs and Trade, known under the name of GATT. Those agreements essentially enshrine the principle of reciprocity and most favored nation (MFN)[42] treatment with regard to customs duties and customs formalities. Joint commissions, made up of representatives of the two contracting parties, were formed to ensure the proper functioning of the said agreements.

Tunisia's trade balance vis-à-vis the EEC had steadily deteriorated since the entry into force of the 1969 agreement. In 1970, the coverage rate even fell to 44.7% for as regards Tunisia, while it was 52.4% in 1961, a year of catastrophic drought[43]. The Tunisia-EEC trade balance deficit more than doubled between 1968 and 1971, going from 31.6 million Tunisian dinars (MTD) to 66.6 MTD[44]. Indeed, Tunisian imports from the EEC increased by 18.6% in 1970 and 14.5% in 1971, ie at rates higher than the growth rates of total Tunisian imports. There were two explanations for the reasons for that deterioration in trade:

- The limited scope of products covered by the 1969 agreement, in particular that of agricultural products. Products such as «wine and derivatives, cereals and derivatives and essentials of fruits and vegetables» were outside the 1969 Association Agreement and were subject to various and high protectionist measures by the EEC. The case of wine is the most significant. From 670,000 hl in 1969-1970, wine explorations plummeted to 37,000 hl in 1971-1972, due in particular to the ban on wine blend imposed on Tunisian wine.
- The prohibitive nature of obstacles of all kinds: "Tunisian products, whether or not they are covered by the 1969 agreement, exported to the markets of the Six, not only encounter customs and trade obstacles arising from the regulations Community but also the problem linked to their low competitiveness, such that their access to the EEC markets is considerably limited"[45], said the tunisian delegation to Brussels in october 1972.

To this are added two crucial problems: first, the weakness of the "Tunisian offer" as regards the negotiation of the partnership contract and, secondly, the obvious delay in the definition of support policies, from both sides, as regards the progressive economic integration of a country emerging from a long colonial period. The deterioration in trading conditions was set to become more pronounced with the enlargement of the Community.

42 Most-favored-nation clause (in public international law): clause in a treaty by which each signatory State undertakes to grant to the other any advantage that it would grant to a third State. See : François Perroux, *L'Univers économique et social*, t. IX de l'Encyclopédie française, Paris, Larousse, 1960, p. 3812.

43 Moncef Guen, *La Tunisie indépendante face à son économie*, PUF, Paris, 1961, p. 137.

44 *Mémorandum de la délégation tunisienne auprès de la CEE en date du 26 octobre 1972 au sujet de l'établissement des relations futures entre la Tunisie et la CEE*, October 1972, p. 9, Archives Historiques de l'Union Européenne, 205-I/72-F

45 *Ibid.*, p. 11.

Conclusions

The first exploratory discussions were marked by the lack of interest on the part of the members of the EEC – the European issues went far beyond the framework of relations with third countries and the former colonies - but also by the lack of preparation and experience on the part of Tunisian diplomats. Rather, we expected a political negotiation and we find ourselves facing the economic experts of the European Commission. To this was usually added the «surprise effect» during each negotiation. The lack of timely information was costly to diplomats, especially in a turbulent economic environment such as it was in the 1960s.

The international coordination mechanisms in the Euro-Mediterranean case, and more particularly in the case of Tunisia, had been confronted with major obstacles: those were the positioning in relation to American interests in the region, on the one hand, and the divergence of interest vis-à-vis third countries, on the other hand. The relative failure of the American project in terms of economic openness had not favored Tunisian economic interests – Let us recall that Tunisia is an agricultural country - especially with the intervention of the CAP. On the other hand, the conflicts with France, and particularly agricultural decolonization, did not allow fair and lasting negotiations with all of the Six. Although Tunisia enjoyed the clear support of most of the Six when launching the European project, the tension with France was causing enormous losses in terms of synergies.

As a result, following the deficiency noted in the 1969 agreement, the European Commission invited further debates within the EEC with a view to redressing the situation and providing a framework favorable to North-South trade. On the Tunisian side, the deterioration of Tunisia-EEC trade, the modesty of investment flows and the non-existence of large-scale partnerships, once again relaunch diplomatic efforts opting for a new framework of equitable cooperation and for a global approach that would only end in 1976 with a more or less promising new agreement.

Afrique de l'Ouest : deux modèles de développement comparés, le Sénégal de Léopold Sédar Senghor et la Côte d'Ivoire de Houphouët-Boigny

Joseph-Pierre E. Diouf
Sorbonne Université, UMR 8596 Centre Roland Mousnier

Introduction

Le Sénégal et la Côte-d'Ivoire étaient les deux colonies privilégiées de l'ancienne puissance coloniale française en Afrique de l'Ouest. Après la Seconde Guerre mondiale, dans le processus de décolonisation, leurs leaders de ces territoires que sont respectivement Léopold Sédar Senghor et Félix Houphouët-Boigny condamnent la politique coloniale. Ils contribuent à la création du Rassemblement Démocratique Africain (RDA) en 1946 à Bamako. Le RDA est le parti des colonies françaises d'Afrique qui devaient fournir 29 députés africains représentant l'Afrique Occidentale Française (AOF). Tandis que Senghor crée le Bloc Démocratique Sénégalais (BDS), Houphouët-Boigny crée le Parti Démocrate de Côte-D'ivoire (PDCI), qui sont des antennes locales du RDA. Grâce à ces formations politiques et leur militantisme, les deux leaders ont successivement occupé des postes de député puis ministre, dans le cadre de l'Union française et la Communauté. Ces expériences leur ont, par ailleurs, conféré permis d'être en première ligne des négociations ayant conduit à l'indépendance et d'avoir une certaine légitimité politique. De même, Léopold Sédar et Félix Houphouët-Boigny ne souhaitent pas l'indépendance immédiate et sont de fervents partisans du maintien du lien avec l'ancienne puissance coloniale. En outre, ils pèsent de tout leur poids pour avaliser et signer les accords de coopération ayant précédé l'accession de leur pays à la souveraineté. Ainsi, le premier devient Président de la République du Sénégal tandis que le second est élevé à la présidence de la Côte-d'Ivoire.

Toutefois, les deux hommes ont des visions différentes du développement de leur pays et ont hérité de la colonisation des structures économiques également différentes. Par conséquent, les deux pays ont eu des trajectoires de développement différentes et opposées dans la forme et le fond. Léopold Sédar Senghor défend et théorise un modèle de développement fondé sur le socialisme africain[1]. Celui-ci qui se veut original prône une rupture totale avec l'héritage colonial et rejette le socialisme marxiste-léniniste ainsi que le modèle capitaliste occidental dans un contexte de guerre froide. De surcroît, Senghor conçoit et met en œuvre une théorie de développement endogène. Quant à Félix Houphouët-Boigny, il fait le choix du libéralisme hérité de la politique de « mise en valeur » coloniale et inscrit la Côte-d'Ivoire dans le camp occidental. Par ailleurs, les cultures commerciales restent les piliers du développement. En effet, tandis que les cultures arbustives, en particulier le cacao et le café, constituent la principale richesse de la Côte-d'Ivoire, le Sénégal fonde son développement sur la monoculture arachidière. Cependant, si ces cultures ont fait la richesse de ces deux pays comme en atteste le « miracle ivoirien », elles les ont néanmoins conduits à la faillite à la fin des années soixante-dix. Comment expliquer cette trajectoire de développement ? En quoi ces deux expériences socialistes du développement sont-elles révélatrices de l'inadaptation des structures économiques et des difficultés de ces deux pays à s'insérer dans l'économie mondiale tout en amorçant une véritable dynamique de développement ? C'est à ces questions que cette étude comparée tente de répondre.

1/ LE POINT DE DÉPART : UNE RECHERCHE SUR LES RELATIONS ÉCONOMIQUES ET FINANCIÈRES ENTRE LA FRANCE ET LE SÉNÉGAL DE 1960 A 1974

On le sait, les débats contemporains le confirment il est d'affronter avec objectivité la difficile question des relations économiques et financières entre la France et ses anciennes colonies ou ses anciens protectorats[2]. Celles entre le Sénégal et la France n'échappent pas à la règle. À travers ce dernier exemple, il est possible en effet d'aborder la question, plus large, des rapports entre l'ancienne métropole et l'Afrique sub-saharienne d'expression française. Il a été décidé ici de centrer l'étude sur la présidence de Léopold Sédar Senghor, en s'appuyant sur un thèse de doctorat récemment soutenue avec succès[3]. Mais, restreignant le projet initial, il a été préféré se limiter aux années 1960 à 1974, avec un terme correspondant au décès de Georges Pompidou et à la crise de l'énergie.

1 Jacques Droz (dir.), *Histoire générale du socialisme, tome 4 : de 1945 à nos jours*, Paris, Presses universitaires de France, 1978, p. 321-328.

2 Benjamin Stora, *Les Questions mémorielles portant sur la colonisation et la guerre d'Algérie*, Rapport au Président de la République, Paris, janvier 2021, 160 p. https://www.viepublique.fr/sites/default/files/rapport/pdf/278186.pdf

3 Joseph-Pierre E. Diouf, *Les relations économiques et financières entre la France et le Sénégal de 1960 à 1974)*
804 p., 1 vol. Thèse de doctorat d'histoire sous la direction de Dominique Barjot en cotutelle avec le professeur Boubacar Barry (Université Cheikh Anta Diop de Dakar) soutenue à l'Université Paris-Sorbonne, le lundi 12 décembre 2015.

1.1/ La démarche

Joseph Diouf, l'auteur, centre son approche sur une révision de l'historiographie. Il part d'un constat simple : au moment de l'indépendance, le Sénégal apparaît comme le pays le plus développé d'AOF, avec la capitale et le port les plus modernes, un tissu industriel non négligeable, des élites bien formées et une tradition démocratique. En même temps, il est le premier bénéficiaire de l'Aide Publique au Développement (APD). En 1974 au contraire, le pays se trouve affronté à un déclin sans précédent, à une hausse de la pauvreté, au vieillissement des infrastructures, aux difficultés de l'activité productive et à une dette colossale, au contraire de la Côte d'Ivoire. Le choix de 1960 s'est donc imposé comme date de départ, avec l'indépendance et l'arrivée au pouvoir de Léopold S. Senghor. Quant à 1974, cette date marque l'arrivée à la Présidence de la République de Valéry Giscard d'Estaing, la révision des accords de coopération et une priorité donnée aux pays jugés les plus intéressants.

Le Sénégal se situe au cœur d'un vaste débat historiographique, marqué par la naissance de « l'École historique de Dakar », à la fois scientifique et militante, que la thèse a pris en compte, mais dans une perspective révisionniste, associant les approches macro- et microéconomiques. Elle apporte ainsi des informations sur l'action des entreprises françaises au Sénégal, mais aussi sur le secteur public créé dans ce pays. La thèse s'appuie sur des sources archivistiques abondantes. Ont été dépouillées les archives publiques françaises (CAC, CAEF de Savigny-le-Temple, fonds le plus riche, CAOM d'Aix-en-Provence, CAMT de Roubaix) et sénégalaises (Agence Nationale de la Statistique et de la démographie du Sénégal ou ANDS et Centre d'Études de Politique pour le Développement ou CPOD). Les archives privées aussi se sont avérées riches d'informations. J. Diouf a largement parcouru celles des banques. La Banque de France (notamment sur le Sénégal et la coopération) recèle des fonds très importants concernant les relations financières extérieures des États de l'Union Économique et Monétaire Ouest-Afrique (UEMOA), le Crédit du Sénégal, les infrastructures, les mines et l'agriculture. D'autres archives bancaires se sont révélées d'un très utile recours : Banque Centrale des États de l'Afrique de l'Ouest (BCEAO), Crédit Agricole et Crédit Lyonnais, Société Générale (notamment la filiale sénégalaise SGBS, la Banque Commerciale Africaine ou BCA) ou la Banque Nationale de Développement du Sénégal ou BNDS). D'autres fonds d'entreprises ont également été consultés : sociétés de commerce (Maurel et Prom, CFAO), firmes de travaux public (Colas, Fougerolle), et, bien sûr, EDF (pour la Société Nationale d'Électricité du Sénégal). La consultation de très nombreuses sources imprimées a nourri aussi un grand nombre de développements originaux.

1.2/ Une démarche en trois temps

La démarche s'articule autour de trois thèmes. En premier lieu, les mobiles des relations économiques et financières entre les deux pays ont connu une réadaptation permanente entre le XVIIIe siècle et les années 1960. Il s'est produit une uniformisation de l'espace par le contrôle politique du territoire. Mais, en raison du pacte colonial et de l'incapacité de l'État colonial à arbitrer, il en a résulté des évolutions défavorables : marginalisation des activités commerciales des autochtones, difficulté à accroître les revenus tirés de l'arachide, priorité à la politique fiscale, absence de politique sociale. En second lieu, après la Seconde Guerre mondiale s'est produit une remise en cause, d'où d'importants investissements, mais pour l'essentiel destinés à promouvoir la production et les échanges avec la métropole. Les plans de modernisation, dont le Sénégal a beaucoup bénéficié, ont conduit à des formules d'association, telles que proposées par De Gaulle et Michel Debré, et à la création d'organisme mis en place après les indépendances (FAC, CCCE, puis CCFOM). Mais ces politiques, si elles ont ouvert la voie aux entreprises, ont aussi favorisé l'endettement du pays. En troisième et dernier lieu, il n'est pas déraisonnable d'affirmer que les accords de coopération ont prolongé la politique de développement colonial des années 1946-1953.

La seconde partie traite de « l'impact des relations économiques et financières dans l'organisation et le fonctionnement des structures politiques et du système productif du Sénégal ». L'argumentation se développe en trois chapitres : le cadre stratégique de la construction nationale du Sénégal, associant planification et réformes institutionnelles (chapitre 4) ; une économie agricole inadaptée, budgétivore et vecteur de dépendance, d'où la généralisation de la pauvreté (chapitre 5), diversification et redéploiement (chapitre 6). Joseph Diouf en conclut qu'il y a eu juxtaposition d'une part du modèle de développement libéral prôné par la France et fondé sur la coopération et, de l'autre, de celui, socialiste, défendu par les élites sénégalaises. Cette contradiction a constitué l'un des principaux obstacles à l'instauration d'un véritable régime démocratique, à la diversification de la production agricole et au redressement de l'industrie au service du développement. L'adoption d'un modèle socialiste a cependant constitué la première faiblesse du programme de construction nationale. Fondé sur le parti unique, mais dirigé par deux personnalités aux divergences nombreuse, il a donné la priorité à l'idéologie sur la recherche d'un consensus autour de priorités communes : M. Dia revendique une décolonisation économique et la rupture avec la France, au contraire de L.S. Senghor, tenant d'une décolonisation culturelle et au maintien d'une étroite coopération avec la France.

L'échec d'une action administrative rationalisée et de la planification a profité à la France et aux intérêts privés. En effet, le nationalisme économique de M. Dia voulait rompre avec l'économie coloniale afin de promouvoir le bien-être de la population, mais il est entré en conflit avec les intérêts des notables et chefs coloniaux locaux, mais aussi des opérateurs économiques métropolitains tout en s'opposant de façon radicale aux intérêts stratégiques de la France en Afrique. Dès lors, il n'y a pas d'autre issue que l'éviction, en 1963, de M. Dia avec la complicité de L.S. Senghor. Celle-ci marque l'abandon du modèle de développement participatif et la restauration du modèle dirigiste, technocratique et productiviste mis en place par la France après 1945. Le renforcement du poids de l'arachide, des pouvoirs des industriels de l'huilerie, du contrôle des coopératives et des populations par les autorités religieuses et les notables s'est accompagné d'une affirmation de la présence des anciens administrateurs et technocrates de la période coloniale. Parce que l'action de L.S. Senghor s'est trouvé ainsi limitée et que les secteurs en difficultés ont été occupés par l'État, les accords de coopération ont pu constituer un obstacle au développement d'institutions démocratiques et à l'essor et à la diversification du secteur productif.

Quant à la troisième partie, elle analyse « un développement du Sénégal sacrifié sur l'autel de la stabilité politique de la dissymétrie des relations commerciales à la spirale de l'endettement ». La juxtaposition des deux voies précitées a abouti à la création de deux secteurs productifs non articulés d'une part une agriculture investie par l'État et les acteurs locaux, de l'autre des secteurs dynamiques, dont la pêche, dominés par la prépondérance du capital étranger. L'État s'est avéré ainsi incapable à réformer les secteurs agricole et industriel pour les mettre au service de la construction nationale. C'est pourquoi les activités commerciales, le système bancaire et l'aide au développement n'ont pas pu empêcher le déclin économique d'un pays engagé dans la spirale de l'endettement. Cette partie comporte aussi trois chapitres : dissymétrie et marginalisation des relations commerciales (chapitre 7) ; polarisation du système bancaire et privatisation des relatives financières : la prépondérance des banques françaises et la spirale de l'endettement du pays (chapitre 8) ; une construction national du Sénégal au bilan mitigé (chapitre 9).

Le résultat est une quasi-faillite de l'État. En effet, la structure dualiste des systèmes bancaires n'a pas permis de drainer toutes les ressources vers la construction nationale. L'indépendance des banques françaises n'a pas permis non plus de mobiliser toutes les ressources pour financer l'économie : elles ont donné priorité au financement des activités les plus rentables, elles-mêmes dominées par les entreprises françaises, d'où une marginalisation des acteurs sénégalais des secteurs les plus dynamiques (commerce de gros). Le gouvernement sénégalais s'est donc avéré incapable de mettre les ressources de ces banques au service de l'économie locale, compte tenu des règles de fonctionnement de la zone franc jusqu'en 1973 (faiblesse des contraintes relatives au rapatriement des devises et libre circulation des capitaux entre les deux pays).

S'est donc créé un système économique dualiste. Il découle des accords de coopération, du statut particulier des opérateurs économiques français, de la présence des administrateurs coloniaux au sein des administrations publiques et de la proximité de ceux-ci avec les hommes d'affaires français. Il en a résulté d'abord une faiblesse de l'État face au lobby colonial français, aux grands marabouts et aux notables locaux, amis aussi l'échec de la stratégie de Mamadou Dia[4] et l'incapacité de l'État à créer une synergie entre les différents secteurs de l'économie. L'inadaptation du système éducatif n'a fait qu'aggraver la situation. La domination des sciences humaines et sociales a attiré les nouveaux diplômés vers une fonction publique et des entreprises parapubliques aux effectifs pléthoriques. En augmentant sans cesse le budget de fonctionnement alors que l'aide au développement se réduisait, la politique de « sénégalisation » de la fonction publique a ouvert la voie à la spirale de l'endettement et à l'échec de la politique de développement.

4 Philippe Bernard, « Mamadou Dia », *Le Monde*, 29 janvier 2009.

1.3/ Trois conclusions majeures

De la thèse ressortent trois enseignements :

1/ entre le Sénégal et la France, les relations économiques et financières ont été ambigües et contradictoires. Entre L.S. Senghor et De Gaulle, l'équivoque a porté notamment sur la signification du mot indépendance. Pour le second, la primauté est allée à l'affirmation de la « grandeur de la France », d'où une volonté développementaliste visant à concilier les intérêts métropolitains avec uns des nouveaux États indépendants. Mais le pacte colonial et les pratiques des maisons françaises de commerce ont constitué un obstacle de taille à une politique d'investissements sociaux. La politique de coopération a été donc ambivalente. Tandis que les accords de coopération proclamaient l'égalité juridique entre deux pays indépendants, le modèle libéral fondé sur le libre-échange et les effets de spécialisation se révélait inopérant.

2/ des explications plausibles permettent d'éclairer cette ambigüité. En premier lieu, le rôle de l'État a été d'abord conçu comme celui d'un facilitateur d'affaires. Dans ces conditions, l'État a opté pour la conquête, la stabilisation du territoire, la mise en place d'une administration coloniale et d'un système bancaire et l'adoption d'une vision mercantiliste, visant à faire rentrer le maximum d'impôts possibles. En second lieu, avec l'affirmation de libre-échange et de la mondialisation, s'est ouverte l'ère des États « entrepreneurs, banquiers et commerçants ». La crise des années 1930 a poussé l'État à l'intervention économique, puis la Seconde Guerre ouvre la voie à l'essor de la diplomatie multilatérale (ONU, FMI, BIRD, OCDE) et à l'affirmation des multinationales, surtout dans les années 1960.

Ainsi s'expliquent les dilemmes du Sénégal dans le contexte de la Guerre froide. Ce dernier a influencé de façon négative les relations économiques et financières entre les deux pays. De fait, le Sénégal demeurait un partenaire essentiel de la France, d'où l'incompréhension française vis-à-vis de la politique de M. Dia et son éviction avec le feu vert de L.S. Senghor. Ce dernier était partagé entre socialisme africain et panafricain d'une part, attachement à la France de l'autre. C'est pourquoi, en fin de compte, L.S. Senghor rallia finalement la France, d'où la division des élites sénégalaises entre M. Dia et L.S. Senghor, et le retour à un système néocolonial.

3/ L'État sénégalais s'est avéré incapable d'impulser une dynamique de développement. Elle résultait de trois causes : la monoculture de l'arachide, l'inefficacité de l'intervention de l'État et la défaillance du secteur privé. En effet, l'abandon du développement participatif et l'impossible sortie de l'arachide ont conduit à une impasse dans la construction nationale[5]. M. Dia, Premier Ministre. Ce dernier veut sortir de l'arachide, grâce à un système coopératif, mais se heurte aux intérêts des industriels de l'arachide. Le Sénégal s'engouffra donc dans l'impasse arachidière, d'où le retour à une économie agricole de type colonial et la dérive technocratique de l'État. Il s'ensuit une série d'erreurs : le système coopératif n'admet pas d'augmentation conséquente de la production, d'où son absorption par l'ONCAD dès 1966 ; politique et économie se confondent, d'où un clientélisme généralisé, le détournement des structures coo-

5 Joseph-Pierre E. Diouf, « Développement économique du Sénégal et cycle de l'arachide (1960-1970) », dans Dominique Barjot, Phan Thi Hoai Trang (dir.), *Économie et Développement durable : Héritages historiques et défis actuels au sein du monde francophone*, Paris, Publications de la Société Française d'Histoire d'Outre-Mer (SFHOM), 2016, p. 250-265.

pératives par les notables locaux, les marabouts et les politiciens locaux, d'où l'échec du crédit rural ; l'aggravation du sort des paysans, d'où la « grève de l'arachide » et le retour aux cultures vivrières d'autosubsistance ; la perte de marge de manœuvre de l'État se traduisit notamment par l'amplification de l'exode rural et, par suite, la dégradation des conditions de vie urbaines.

À cela s'est ajoutée l'hypertrophie d'un secteur parapublic budgétivore et à la rentabilité faible. En effet, l'État opte pour le développement d'entreprises industrielles parapubliques. De nombreuses entreprises mixtes se sont créées où l'État restait l'actionnaire principal, à l'instar de la BNDS, principal organe du financement de l'économie. Elles restèrent inefficaces, du fait notamment de l'incapacité du secteur privé à promouvoir une dynamique économique. En résultèrent la montée des protestations, d'où les troubles sociaux de mai 1968 et de mars 1969 ainsi que le problème des revendications étudiantes. Par ailleurs, la politique de relance par l'industrialisation a échoué. Le IIIe Plan (1969-1973) a péché par son optimisme excessif. Même si la demande restait entretenue par un niveau de salaire élevé, le secteur moderne manqua cruellement de salaires levés. À une politique basée sur l'endettement s'ajouta l'absence d'insertion des diplômés sur le marché du travail et des populations issues de l'exode rural[6].

Ces stratégies ont révélé de nombreuses limites. Le cadre idéologique de la construction nationale induisait le choix de l'arachide comme modèle de développement, conduisit l'économie dans une véritable impasse, échoua à faire naître des opérateurs économiques locaux et à relancer l'industrie. La faiblesse de l'État et son incapacité à promouvoir une véritable politique de développement sont le reflet et la conséquence de la cohabitation entre trois types de pouvoirs : d'abord l'État, dont les fondements sont investis par le second pouvoir, chefs religieux (marabouts) et chefs traditionnels[7] et, troisième pouvoir, le grand patronat (grands industriels coloniaux, grandes maisons de commerce, banques privées). Cette situation a engendré le développement de l'économie informelle[8].

Le développement de l'économie informelle n'était pas une nouveauté. Elle s'est diffusée à partir de l'éviction des marchands locaux par les maisons de commerce durant l'époque coloniale. Avec l'indépendance, les secteurs du commerce de gros et de demi-gros demeurèrent aux mains des acteurs coloniaux[9]. Cette économie informelle tenait à deux phénomènes. D'abord, elle constituait la destination naturelle de ruraux venant en ville chercher un emploi. Ensuite, la législation sociale gonfla le secteur : la complexité des procédures d'embauche et de licenciement poussait les entrepreneurs à préférer le recrutement des travailleurs temporaires au lieu de

6 Louis Verrière, *La population du Sénégal (Aspects quantitatifs)*, Dakar, Université de Dakar, 1965 (thèse doctorat Sciences économiques)

7 Sheldon Gellar, *Senegal: an African nation between Islam and the West*, Westview Press, Oxford, Boulder (Colorado), 1995 (1re éd. 1982).

8 Ndongo Samba Sylla, *Le secteur informel au Sénégal : sa structure, ses caractéristiques, sa contribution à l'emploi et aux revenus des ménages*, Mémoire DEA en Économie du développement, Université Paris 1, 2003.

9 Catherine Boone, *Merchant Capital and the Roots of State Power in Senegal, 1930-1985*, Montréal, McGill, 1995.

salariés permanents. Par suite, une partie importante de la population connut une précarité croissante. En définitive, la thèse de Joseph Diouf aborde des problèmes fondamentaux : celui de la mise en place de la « Françafrique », celui des enjeux du développement et celui du socialisme africain.

2/ DEUX MODÈLES DE DÉVELOPPEMENT BIEN TYPÉS: LE SÉNÉGAL DE LÉOPOLD SÉDAR SENGHOR ET CÔTE D'IVOIRE DE FÉLIX HOUPHOUËT-BOIGNY, DE 1960 À 1980.

À ce double égard, les modèles du Sénégal et de la Côte d'Ivoire apparaissent radicalement opposés, de par leurs spécificités respectives.

2.1/ Deux expériences aux spécificités bien marquées

Le Sénégal est évidemment marqué par la personnalité très forte de son premier Président, Léopold Sédar Senghor (1906-2001)[10].

A/ Au Sénégal, Léopold Sédar Senghor

Léopold Sédar Senghor, né le 9 octobre 1906 à Joal, au Sénégal, et mort le 20 décembre 2001 à Verson (Calvados), en France, est un poète, écrivain, homme d'État français, puis sénégalais et premier président de la République du Sénégal. Il fut aussi le premier Africain à siéger à l'Académie française. Il fait figure de symbole de la coopération entre la France et ses anciennes colonies pour ses partisans, mais aussi du néocolonialisme français en Afrique pour ses détracteurs. C'est aussi l'un des plus grands poètes de la littérature francophone. Sa poésie se fonde sur le chant de la parole incantatoire. Chez ce catholique, elle se construit autour de l'espoir de créer une Civilisation de l'Universel, fédérant les traditions par-delà leurs différences. Par ailleurs, L. S. Senghor approfondit le concept de négritude, notion introduite par Aimé Césaire qui la définit ainsi : « La négritude est la simple reconnaissance du fait d'être noir, et l'acceptation de ce fait, de notre destin de Noir, de notre histoire et de notre culture[1]. »

Quant au Sénégal lui-même, il convient de rappeler que c'est en 1850 que débute véritablement la colonisation française. Ancien comptoir de commerce stratégique dans la traite atlantique de la première mondialisation, le Sénégal est l'une des grandes réussites du régime impérial (Joseph Diouf[11]). Depuis sa rétrocession à la France par le Royaume-Uni, en 1815, celle-ci a décidé d'en faire une colonie d'exploitation agricole. Le Français y expérimentent avec succès la culture de l'arachide qui devient très vite un produit stratégique pour l'industrie métropolitaine, d'où l'avènement de relations commerciales florissantes entre les deux territoires.

Le projet de transformation du comptoir du Sénégal en colonie d'exploitation agricole est un succès, résultat lui-même d'une convergence d'intérêts entre de la politique

10 Christian Roche, *Léopold Sédar Senghor : le président humaniste*, Toulouse, Privat, mars 2006.

11 Joseph Diouf, « Le Sénégal des années 1860 », chapitre 17 dans Dominique Barjot et Éric Anceau (dir.), *L'Empire libéral. Essai d'histoire globale* , Paris, Éditions SPM, 2021, p. 265-295.

expansionniste de l'Empire libéral, la volonté des Maisons de commerce de créer un marché de libre-échange nécessaire au développement de leurs activités commerciale et des ambitions individuelles de conquête des responsables militaires. Cela permet de relancer l'économie locale par la culture de rente de l'arachide et l'essor des relations commerciales avec la métropole, la modernisation économique, le développement d'infrastructures, la naissance d'un système administratif moderne et l'essor de l'urbanisme. En outre, cette politique coloniale libérale fait du Sénégal une expérience formative de la colonisation française en Afrique subsaharienne.

En revanche, ce modèle fondé sur la production et l'exportation de l'arachide crée une économie extravertie fortement dépendante du cette monoculture de rente et du marché métropolitain. En fait, la colonie du Sénégal des années 1860 souffre d'un manque crucial de mesures sociales et assimilationnistes. C'est en partie la conséquence de la forte influence des maisons de commerce sur la politique coloniale de la métropole visant à l'orienter uniquement vers la création de conditions favorables à l'essor des activités commerciales et à la préservation de leur monopole sur l'import-export de marchandises. En fin de compte, le Sénégal des années 1860 est le symbole même des ambiguïtés de l'Empire libéral, en matière économique. Le contexte est à la fois celui de l'abolition de la traite négrière et d'une crise économique qui conduit les colonisateurs à faire du Sénégal une colonie d'exploitation spécialisée dans l'arachide.

La Seconde Guerre mondiale contribue à une prise de conscience qui ouvre la voie à une autonomie progressive des colonies, puis aux indépendances [12]. L'Empire colonial français cède d'abord la place à l'Union française en 1946 qui confère au Sénégal un statut de territoire d'outre-mer. Ces avancées sont pourtant jugées insuffisantes et la montée de l'anticolonialisme dans de nombreux pays aboutit au vote de la loi-cadre du 23 février 1956 qui permet au gouvernement de modifier le statut de ces territoires. Comme d'autres, le Sénégal conquiert une autonomie accrue, ainsi que le suffrage universel pour les hommes et les femmes. En 1958, après son retour dans l'arène politique à la suite du putsch d'Alger, le général de Gaulle propose un projet de constitution soumis à un référendum dans tous les États africains. Lors du référendum constitutionnel du 28 septembre 1958, 97,2 % des Sénégalais optent pour le statut d'État membre dans le cadre de la Communauté et le pays se dote d'une constitution proche du modèle français.

Soucieux de préserver l'unité régionale, la République soudanaise (actuel Mali) et le Sénégal fusionnent en avril 1959 pour former la Fédération du Mali , qui devient complètement indépendante le 20 juin 1960 et dont la capitale est Dakar[13]. Cette indépendance est la conséquence des transferts de pouvoirs convenus dans l'accord signé en France le 4 avril 1960. Un déséquilibre économique et des rivalités personnelles provoquent le démembrement de la fédération le 20 août 1960. Le Sénégal et le Mali déclarent leur indépendance et entrent séparément à l'ONU le 28 septembre

12 « Sur la voie de l'indépendance » in Gerti Hesseling, *Histoire politique du Sénégal : institutions, droit et société*, Paris, Karthala, 2000, p. 151-187.
13 Gerti Hesseling, *Histoire politique du Sénégal : institutions, droit et société*, *op. cit.*, p. 173-175

1960. Le Sénégal adopte un régime parlementaire[14]. Mamadou Dia est le Président du Conseil[15]. Léopold Sédar Senghor, alors poète de renommée mondiale, est lui président de la République. L'un et avaient fondés ensemble, en 1958, l'Union progressiste sénégalaise (UPS)[16]. La voie politique choisie est celle d'une coopération avec la France, mais, en même temps de l'adoption d'un modèle de développement socialiste sans pour autant renoncer à la monoculture arachidière.

Le Président du Conseil, Mamadou Dia, inscrit son action dans une vision de l'État héritée de quatrième République, à savoir un système parlementaire bicéphale : la politique économique et intérieure pour lui, la politique extérieure pour Senghor. Mais ses relations avec le Président de la République se dégradent peu à peu. En effet, Dia souhaite une rupture plus nette avec la France. Il oriente le pays vers une sortie planifiée de l'économie arachidière. Cette volonté heurte les intérêts français. Elle inquiète aussi les puissants marabouts présents sur le marché de l'arachide et qui ont tiré profit de l'expansion importante de la culture de l'arachide dans les années 1940 et 1950[17]. Dans son discours sur « les politiques de développement et les diverses voies africaines du socialisme », prononcé le 8 décembre 1962 à Dakar, le Président du Conseil Mamadou Dia opte pour le « rejet révolutionnaire des anciennes structures » et une « mutation totale qui substitue à la société coloniale et à l'économie de traite une société libre et une économie de développement ». Cette déclaration heurte de front la vision de Senghor, qui pousse les députés qui lui sont favorables de déposer une motion de censure contre le gouvernement [18].

Mamadou Dia jugeant cette motion irrecevable. Il tente alors d'empêcher son examen par l'Assemblée nationale au profit du Conseil national du parti. Il fait évacuer la chambre le 17 décembre et en fait empêcher l'accès par la gendarmerie. En dépit ce qui a été qualifié de « tentative de coup d'État » et de l'arrestation de quatre députés, la motion est votée dans l'après-midi au domicile du président de l'Assemblée nationale, Lamine Guèye (1891-1968)[19]. Mamadou Dia est arrêté le lendemain par un détachement de paras-commandos, avec quatre autres ministres. Ils sont traduits devant la Haute Cour de justice du Sénégal du 9 au 13 mai 1963. Même si le procureur général ne requiert aucune peine, ils sont condamnés à 20 ans d'emprisonnement au centre spécial de détention de Kédougou (Sénégal oriental).

Le procureur général de l'époque, Ousmane Camara, revient sur le déroulement du procès dans une autobiographie publiée en 2010 : « Je sais que cette haute cour de justice, par essence et par sa composition (on y retrouve des députés ayant voté la motion de censure), a déjà prononcé sa sentence, avant même l'ouverture du procès

14 Sur les dirigeants politiques sénégalais, voir notamment Babacar Ndiaye et Waly Ndiaye, *Présidents et ministres de la République du Sénégal*, Dakar, 2006 (2e édition).

15 Abdoulatif Coulibaly, *Le Sénégal à l'épreuve de la démocratie*, Paris, L'Harmattan, 1999.

16 Jacques Mariel Nzouankeu, *Les partis politiques sénégalais*, Dakar, Clairafrique, 1984 ; François Zuccarelli, *Un parti politique africain, l'Union progressiste sénégalaise*, Paris, Librairie générale de droit et de jurisprudence, 1970.

17 Jean Copans, *Les Marabouts de l'arachide*, Paris, L'Harmattan, 1980.

18 Roland Colin, *Sénégal notre pirogue, au soleil de la liberté*, Paris, Présence Africaine, 2007.

19 Nicole Bernard-Duquenet, « Lamine Guèye : De l'ancienne Afrique au Sénégal nouveau », dans Charles-André Julien *et alii*, *Les Africains*, Paris, Jeune Afrique, 1977, III, p. 143-169.

(...) La participation de magistrats que sont le Président, le juge d'instruction et le procureur général ne sert qu'à couvrir du manteau de la légalité une exécution sommaire déjà programmée » [20]. Lors de leur incarcération, des personnalités comme Jean-Paul Sartre, le pape Jean XXIII ou encore François Mitterrand demandent leur libération. Mais Senghor reste sourd jusqu'en mars 1974, année à laquelle il les gracie et les libère. Ils sont amnistiés en avril 1976, un mois avant le rétablissement du multipartisme au Sénégal. Parmi leurs avocats durant cette période, on compte Abdoulaye Wade[21] et Robert Badinter. Aujourd'hui encore cet épisode de l'histoire du Sénégal demeure un sujet délicat dans un pays qui passait alors pour un modèle de démocratie.

Le 7 mars 1963 une nouvelle constitution est adoptée par référendum, instaurant un régime présidentiel qui attribue tous les pouvoirs au chef de l'État et fait de l'UPS le parti dominant, voire unique[22]. Le Sénégal s'engage dès lors dans la voie de l'économie mixte et d'une diplomatie active, notamment en négociant avec l'Afrique du Sud. Organisé à Dakar en 1966 à l'initiative du président Senghor, le premier Festival mondial des arts nègres affirme pour la première fois la négritude de façon solennelle et festive. De plus, le 14 juin 1966, l'UPS – le parti du pouvoir – fusionne avec le Parti du rassemblement africain (PRA), alors seul parti d'opposition légal. Une nouvelle révision de la constitution est effectuée le 20 juin 1967. Senghor est réélu le 25 février 1968, personne ne s'étant présenté contre lui. De même, pour les élections législatives, une seule liste se présente, celle de l'UPS. Néanmoins, la situation économique est mauvaise et des troubles sociaux éclatent, notamment à l'Université. Ils sont sans rapport avec les événements de mai 68 en France [23]. Un mot d'ordre de grève générale est même lancé, mais le gouvernement parvient à enrayer le mouvement. Les étudiants se remettent en grève en avril-juin 1969[24]. L'état d'urgence est alors proclamé le 11 juin. Face à la nécessité de démocratiser le pays, une nouvelle révision constitutionnelle, celle du 26 février 1970, instaure un régime présidentiel modéré. Elle crée un poste de Premier ministre, confié à Abdou Diouf (1935-)[25].

La sécheresse de 1972 provoque de nouveaux troubles sociaux. De plus, l'agitation augmente fortement dans les milieux scolaire et universitaire [26]. Cependant, Senghor remporte à nouveau l'élection présidentielle du 8 janvier 1973 (97 % des suffrages exprimés). Abdou Diouf reste Premier ministre. En juillet 1974, la fondation du Parti démocratique sénégalais (PDS) est autorisé. Il est dirigé par Abdoulaye Wade (1926-)[27]. De plus, plusieurs prisonniers politiques, dont Majhemout Diop (1922-2007)[28], sont libérés. La révision constitutionnelle de 1976 n'autorise que trois partis politiques, nécessairement rattachés à l'une des trois idéologies suivantes : démocratie libérale,

20 Ousmane Camara, *Mémoires d'un juge africain. Itinéraire d'un homme libre*, Paris, Karthala, 2010, p. 122.

21 Souleymane Jules Diop, *Wade : L'avocat et le diable*, Paris, L'Harmattan, 2007.

22 Gerti Hesseling, *Histoire politique du Sénégal : institutions, droit et société, op. cit.*, p. 256.

23 Abdoulaye Bathily et Francis Kpatindé, « Mai 68 a contraint Senghor à accepter le pluralisme politique », *Le Monde*, 8 mai 2018.

24 Gerti Hesseling, *Histoire politique du Sénégal : institutions, droit et société, op. cit.*, p. 262.

25 Mody Niang, *Abdou Diouf. 40 ans au cœur de l'État socialiste au Sénégal*, Paris, L'Harmattan, 2009.

26 Gerti Hesseling, *Histoire politique du Sénégal : institutions, droit et société, op. cit.*, p. 270.

27 Abdou Latif Coulibaly, *Wade, un opposant au pouvoir : l'alternance piégée ?*, Dakar, Éditions sentinelles, 2003.

28 Thierno Diop, *Léopold Sédar Senghor, Majhemout Diop et le marxisme*, Paris, L'Harmattan, 2010.

démocratie socialiste, communisme ou marxisme-léninisme, et désigne le Premier ministre comme successeur du Président en cas de défection de celui-ci[29]. Les autres partis existants luttent pour obtenir leur reconnaissance officielle. Le 26 février 1978 Senghor est réélu pour la cinquième fois avec 82,5 % des voix. Son parti, l'UPS qui, après son adhésion à l'Internationale socialiste, est devenu le Parti socialiste (PS), l'emporte avec un score comparable devant le Parti démocratique sénégalais (PDS) de Abdoulaye Wade. Le troisième parti, le Parti africain de l'indépendance (PAI), conduit par Majhemout Diop, n'obtient aucun siège à l'Assemblée nationale. Abdou Diouf demeure premier ministre. La Constitution est modifiée une sixième fois le 28 décembre 1978 [30]. Aux côtés du français, langue officielle, six langues nationales sont désormais reconnues : lediola, le malinké, le poular, le sérère, le soninké et le wolof. Un quatrième parti politique est autorisé. le Mouvement républicain sénégalais (MRS) de Boubacar Guèye, qui s'identifie alors au courant conservateur.

En décembre 1980, Senghor démissionne. Conformément à la Constitution, il désigne comme son successeur Abdou Diouf, qu'il a préparé à cette fonction depuis longtemps. Ce retrait volontaire en cours de mandat présidentiel revêt un caractère exceptionnel tant en Afrique que dans le monde. Habib Thiam[31] est nommé Premier ministre. Mais cet héritage n'est pas de tout repos. Suite à un incident dans une école de Ziguinchor, en Casamance, la situation dégénère. L'agitation gagne dès lors les milieux de l'enseignement dans tout le pays. De plus, la situation économique est particulièrement critique, de par le cumul de phénomènes naturels, d'une conjoncture internationale défavorable, mais aussi des erreurs de gestion imputables au gouvernement. Abdou Diouf prend ses fonctions le 1er janvier 1981[32]. Il promet le pluralisme politique et la consolidation de l'ouverture démocratique. Dès avril, il met fin à la limitation du nombre des partis politiques. Remaniant le Code électoral, il met en place un scrutin mixte est adopté pour les législatives et augmente le nombre de députés de 100 à 120. Il réduit aussi les interventions du gouvernement dans l'économie et élargit les engagements diplomatiques du Sénégal, en particulier vis à vis des autres pays en développement.

B/ En Côte d'Ivoire, Félix Houphouët-Boigny

Pour la Côte d'Ivoire, 1893 constitue une date-clé. En effet, le pays devient officiellement une colonie française le 10 mars 1893. Le capitaine Binger, parti de Dakar pour rallier Kong[33], devient le premier gouverneur. La capitale se situe à Grand-Bassam : dès 1842 a été signé le traité de protectorat de Grand-Bassam. Binger négocie des traités frontaliers avec le Royaume-Uni (pour le Liberia), puis engage une campagne

29 Gerti Hesseling, *Histoire politique du Sénégal : institutions, droit et société, op. cit.*, p. 274.

30 Gerti Hesseling, *Ibidem*, p. 282.

31 Mamoudou Ibra Kane et Mamadou Ndiaye, *Habib Thiam, l'homme d'État*, Paris, L'Harmattan, 2010.

32 Mamadou Diouf, *Le Sénégal sous Abdou Diouf*, Karthala, 1990.

33 Kong est une ville du nord-est de la Côte d'Ivoire, située à proximité du Parc national de la Comoé. C'est une ancienne ville marchande qui fut détruite par Samory Touré en 1897, puis reconstruite. Georges Niamkey Kodjo (éd.), *Côte d'Ivoire : 1894-1895 : la ville de Kong et Samori, d'après le journal inédit du Français Georges Bailly*, L'Harmattan, Paris, 1991 ; Louis Tauxier, *Les États de Kong (Côte d'Ivoire)*, Ed. Karthala, 2003.

qui dura jusqu'en 1898 contre Samory Touré (1830-1900)[34], un chef guerrier malinké originaire de la Guinée actuelle. De 1904 à 1958, le pays est inclus dans la Fédération de l'ouest africain français appelée Afrique-Occidentale française (AOF). C'est une colonie et un territoire d'outre-mer pendant la Troisième République. Il s'agit du territoire le plus intéressant de l'Afrique occidentale française, car associant un sous-sol riche et une végétation luxuriante. Très vite, le territoire trouve sa spécialisation dans le café et le cacao. Jusqu'au lendemain de la Seconde Guerre mondiale, « l'association » faisait des habitants des colonies des sujets français sans droit de représentation. La capitale du territoire est Bingerville jusqu'en 1933, puis Abidjan.

Pendant la Seconde Guerre mondiale, l'AOF reste sous le contrôle du Régime de Vichy jusqu'à la fin 1942 , puis se rallie ensuite à l'exécutif d'Alger, et passe, un an plus tard, sous l'autorité du Comité français de Libération nationale. Dans la droite lige de la conférence de Brazzaville en 1944 et de la première assemblée constituante de 1946, la citoyenneté française est accordée, la même année, aux sujets africains. Le droit de s'organiser politiquement leur est reconnu. Surtout le travail forcé est aboliepar la loi du 11 avril 1946, proposée par Félix Houphouët-Boigny (1905-1993)[35]. La répression contre son parti, le Parti démocratique de Côte d'Ivoire (PDCI)[36], s'accentue à la fin des années 1940. Des militants sont régulièrement arrêtés et battus par des policiers, avec parfois des actes de tortures ; d'autres sont renvoyés de leurs emplois. L'un des principaux dirigeants du parti, le sénateur Biaka Boda, est retrouvé pendu et déchiqueté dans la foret, alors qu'il était recherché par la police. Les tensions culminent au début de l'année 1950, quand, à la suite d'un incident, la quasi-totalité de la direction du PDCI est arrêtée. Des rassemblements de protestation sont organisés ; alors que la police tire à blanc pour disperser la foule, des colons le font à balles réelles, tuant treize manifestants. Au lieu de rechercher les auteurs du massacre, les autorités, craignant des émeutes, font arrêter des milliers de militants indépendantistes . En 1956, la loi-cadre de réforme de l'outremer décida du transfert de pouvoirs de Paris vers des autorités locales, sans pour autant freiner le mouvement vers l'indépendance.

En décembre 1958, la Côte d'Ivoire devient une république autonome suite au référendum créant la Communauté française entre la France et ses anciennes colonies. Elle est alors dirigée par un premier ministre, Auguste Denise, auquel succède Félix Houphouët-Boigny en avril 1959. Grâce à cette autonomie la Côte d'Ivoire ne doit plus partager ses richesses avec les autres territoires pauvres du Sahel. Le budget de l'administration ivoirienne augmente ainsi de 152%. Le 7 août 1960 l'indépendance devient effective. Le pays reste cependant très lié à la France dans le cadre de la politique de Coopération : sa monnaie est dirigée par la Banque de France, par le biais de l'union

34 Julie d'Andurain, *La capture de Samory, 1898 : l'achèvement de la conquête de l'Afrique de l'Ouest*, Soteca, Saint-Cloud, 2012 ; Ibrahima Khalil Fofana, *L'almami Samori Touré, empereur : récit historique*, Paris, Dakar, Présence africaine, 1998.

35 Frédéric Grah Mel, *Félix Houphouët-Boigny : biographie*, Paris Abidjan Abidjan Paris, Maisonneuve et Larose Servedit CERAP, Karthala, 2003.

36 Le Parti démocratique de Côte d'Ivoire (PDCI-RDA) est un parti politique ivoirien fondé en 1946. Il succéde au Syndicat agricole africain fondé dès 1944 par F. H.-Boigny et se fixe pour objectif affiché « l'émancipation du peuple noir » Il est membre du Rassemblement démocratique africain dès sa création. Voir notamment Pierre Kipré, *Histoire de la Côte d'Ivoire*, Abidjan, Éditions AMI/Bordas 1992, tome 2.

monétaire d'Afrique occidentale (franc CFA), tandis que de nombreux investissements français rendent l'économie ivoirienne d'autant plus dépendante de la France.

Médecin et « Premier Paysan-Planteur », le président-fondateur est donc Félix Houphouët-Boigny. Il le reste à vie, grâce à son parti unique, le Parti démocratique de la Côte d'Ivoire (PDCI). En tant que l'un des fondateurs du Rassemblement démocratique africain (RDA), parti politique d'avant l'indépendance pour toute l'Afrique occidentale française (exceptée la Mauritanie), il commence sa carrière en 1944 en fondant le Syndicat agricole africain, qui fut le noyau du PDCI. Après la Seconde Guerre mondiale, il est a été élu de peu à la première assemblée constituante. Il représente ensuite la Côte d'Ivoire à l'Assemblée nationale de 1946 à 1959. Il s'y consacre pour l'essentiel aux organisations politiques interterritoriales au sein de l'AOF, et à l'amélioration des conditions de travail. Il est même ministre de la République trois ans durant. Élu président en 1960, il est ensuite constamment réélu de cinq ans en cinq ans à partir de 1965, son parti unique, le PDCI-RDA, occupant tous les sièges de l'Assemblée nationale. Il est très actif en politique étrangère. Dès mai 1959, il crée le Conseil de l'entente avec le Niger, la Haute-Volta (Burkina Faso), le Togo, et le Dahomey (Bénin), organisation de développement économique. Il affirme que la seule voie pour la solidarité africaine est le développement économique progressif et la coopération politique, reconnaissant ainsi le principe de non-intervention dans les affaires internes des États africains. Le 21 avril 1961, il signe un accord d'assistance militaire avec la France. Cet accord est également signé par le Dahomey et le Mali.

Ayant aboli la polygamie en 1964, Félix Houphouët-Boigny fait le choix, payant dans l'immédiat, d'un modèle de développement libéral. En effet, les années 1970 à 1985 bénéficient d'une bonne situation économique. Néanmoins, sa dégradation, au cours des années 1980, provoqua une agitation étudiante, la révolte de barons du régime et la naissance d'une opposition clandestine. Les manifestations étudiantes du 9 février 1982 révèlent en le Professeur Laurent Gbagbo (1945)[37] un leader d'opinion (l'interdiction d'une de ses conférences est la cause immédiate du mouvement)[38]. Ce dernier fonde le Front populaire ivoirien (FPI), et s'exile en France. Le 21 mars 1983, Yamoussoukro devient la capitale politique et administrative de Côte d'Ivoire. À la fin de sa vie, Félix Houphouët-Boigny prépare la voie à une démocratisation en 1990 par quelques réformes importantes : autorisation des partis politiques le 5 mai (il s'en crée 14) ; pour la première fois, présentation de deux candidats à l'élection présidentielle (Laurent Gbagbo obtient 18 % des voix face au président sortant) ; élections pluralistes, où les étrangers, notamment burkinabés, peuvent voter, ont lieu (le PDCI-RDA remporte 175 sièges, contre 8 au FPI). En dépit de ces avancées, Laurent Gbagbo est arrêté après les manifestations étudiantes de février 1992 et emprisonné pendant quelques mois, ainsi que son épouse, Simone Ehivet Gbagbo[39].

37 Laurent Gbagbo, *La Côte d'Ivoire : économie et société à la veille de l'indépendance (1940-1960)*, Paris, L'Harmattan, 1982 (livre de poche 2006).

38 Raymond Borremans, *Le grand dictionnaire encyclopédique de la Côte d'Ivoire*, Tome 3 : E-F-G-H, Abidjan, NEA, 1987, p. 109.

39 Viviane Gnakalé, *Laurent Gbagbo : pour l'avenir de la Côte d'Ivoire*, Paris, L'Harmattan, 2006 ; Guillaume Soro, *Pourquoi je suis devenu un rebelle : La Côte d'Ivoire au bord du gouffre*, Paris, Hachette, 2005.

Félix Houphouët-Boigny meurt le 7 décembre 1993. D'une comparaison des expériences des deux pays sous la houlette des deux leaders, il ressort une problématique simple : en quoi la trajectoire de développement des deux pays est-elle révélatrice des limites leur expérience du socialisme et du libéralisme?

2.2/ Cadre idéologique et institutionnel de la construction nationale dans les deux pays

Il convient, dans ce but, d'analyser le cadre idéologique et institutionnel de la construction nationale dans les deux pays. Ils représentent chacun une vision différente du développement.

A/ Deux visions différentes du développement : le socialisme sénégalais

De leur côté, Léopold S. Senghor et Mamadou Dia apparaissent comme des théoriciens du socialisme africain. Ils partagent en effet une vision anticoloniale et panafricaine du développement. Il s'agit, pour eux, d'enclencher un processus de croissance de l'économie, mais accompagné d'une transformation positive des structures sociales, culturelles, institutionnelles ainsi que d'une amélioration du bien-être. Dans cette perspective, le projet adopté est celui d'un système coopératif visant à un « développement inclusif à la base » et basé sur l'animation rurale. Il s'ensuit, au Sénégal, trois orientations majeures :

1. l'adoption de plans quinquennaux de développement, avec un accent sur la culture de l'arachide ;
2. la création de l'Office National de Commercialisation de l'Arachide (OCA) ;
3. la fondation de la Banque Nationale de Développement du Sénégal (BNDS).

Léopold S. Senghor et Mamadou Dia, en tant que théoriciens du socialisme africain adoptent une vision anticoloniale et panafricaine du développement. Ils rejoignent largement la vision de Samir Amin (1931-2018).

Né au Caire d'une mère française et d'un père égyptien, tous deux médecins, S. Amin a passé son enfance et son adolescence à Port-Saïd. Il y suit les cours d'une école française et y obtient son baccaalauréat (de type français) en 1947. De 1947 à 1957, il étudie à Paris et y passe avec succès un second baccalauréat option « mathématiques élémentaire » au lycée Henri IV à Paris. Ayant obtenu un diplôme de sciences politiques à Sciences Po Paris en 1952, puis deux autres en statistique (1956) et en économie (1957), il devient professeur agrégé en sciences économiques. Par la suite, il enseigne plusieurs années à l'université Cheikh-Anta-Diop de Dakar[40]. Il assure également des responsabilités dans différentes institutions, par exemple Secrétaire exécutif du Conseil pour le développement de la recherche en sciences sociales en Afrique (CODESRIA) entre 1973-1975, directeur de l'Institut africain de développement et de planification (IDEP), ou encore président du Forum du Tiers-Monde.

À son arrivée à Paris, Samir Amin a rejoint le Parti communiste (PCF), mais il se distancie plus tard du communisme soviétique et est tenté, un certain temps, par

40 Samir Amin, *Le monde des affaires sénégalais*, Paris, Éditions de Minuit, 1969.

le maoïsme. Sa théorie majeure est celle du développement inégal différenciant les centres du capitalisme, où l'appareil de production s'est développé et où le prolétariat peut accéder au statut de classe moyenne consommatrice, et leurs leurs périphéries, où sont produites ou extraites les matières premières transformées et valorisées dans les centres et où le prolétariat ne peut accéder à l'autonomie matérielle[41]. Théoricien de l'antimondialisme, puis de l'altermondialisme, il préconise un « développementisme marxiste » comme prolongement au tiers-mondisme de ses années maoïstes. Moins connu est le fait que sa grille de lecture économiste en fait un historien des « formes précapitalistes » des pays colonisés, notamment africains[42], mais aussi à propos du cas chinois.

B/ Deux visions différentes du développement : le libéralisme ivoirien

Félix Houphouët-Boigny, quant à lui, a fait le choix assumé du libéralisme, adhérant ainsi à la vision du développement, telle que développée par Walt W. Rostow. Dans *The Stages of Economic Growth*, Walt W. Rostow propose une vision alternative[43]. Il montre que toutes les économies développées passent par cinq étapes successives : la société traditionnelle, l'accumulation des conditions préalables, le *take-off*, la marche à la maturité, l'ère de la consommation de masse. La société traditionnelle correspond une structure déterminée par des fonctions de production limitées, elles-mêmes fondées sur la science et la technologie prénewtonienne. Productivité agricole et productivité industrielle butent sur des limites infranchissables. La plupart des ressources servent à acheter des produits agricoles. En conséquence de quoi les propriétaires fonciers dominent la hiérarchie sociale. Il ne s'agit pas toutefois d'une société immobile, car elle autorise des augmentations de production.

L'accumulation des conditions préalables précède le *take-off*. Elle implique trois conditions :
1. une augmentation de la productivité agricole. Celle-ci permet de nourrir une population croissante, en particulier urbaine et d'accroître le revenu des agriculteur, donc les débouchés de l'industrie. Le surplus agricole met ainsi à la disposition de l'industrie les capitaux nécessaires aux investissement (directement, mais aussi par le biais de la fiscalité et de l'exportation)
2. la mise en place d'une infrastructure de transports, souvent par intervention de l'État
3. l'apparition d'une nouvelle élite, en particulier de chefs d'entreprises.

Le *take-off* (ou décollage) peut être déclenché par des stimuli technologique (Grande-Bretagne), politiques ou économiques. Il ouvre la voie à la croissance auto-entrete-

41 Samir Amin, *Le développement inégal, essai sur les formations sociales du capitalisme périphérique*, Paris, Éditions de Minuit, 1973.

42 Samir Amin, *L'Afrique de l'Ouest bloquée. L'économie politique de la colonisation. 1880-1970*, Paris, Éditions de Minuit, 1971. Voir aussi : Samir Amin, *Trois expériences africaines de développement : le Mali, la Guinée, et le Ghana*, Paris, P.U.F., 1965 ; *Le développement du capitalisme en Côte*-d'Ivoire, Paris, Les Éditions de Minuit, 1967 ; Samir Amin, Catherine Coquery-Vidrovitch, *Histoire économique du Congo 1880-1968*, 1970 ; *L'Afrique de l'Ouest bloquée. L'économie politique de la colonisation. 1880-1970*, Éditions de Minuit, 1971.

43 Walt W. Rostow, *The Stages of Economic Growth: A Non-Communist Manifesto*, Cambridge, Cambridge University Press, 1960.

nue. Il présente trois caractéristique : un changement d'ordre de grandeur du taux national d'investissement net, résultat de facteurs d'origine variable (l'accumulation par le commerce extérieurs dans le cas de la Grande-Bretagne) ; le développement de *leading sectors* (activités motrices), comme l'industrie cotonnière (Grande-Bretagne) ou, surtout, le chemin de fer ; l'existence ou les mise en place d'un appareil politique, social et institutionnel exploitant les tendances à l'expansion.

L'apport de Rostow est double. En premier lieu, il propose une chronologie du *take-off* (1783-1802 pour la Grande-Bretagne, pays le plus précoce), qui a fait l'objet de nombreuses discussions. En second lieu, il a défini deux notions essentielles : le *take-off* et le *leading sector*. Le premier offre une alternative à la notion de révolution industrielle : alors que celle-ci consiste en une transformation progressive de l'organisation de la production et du monde du travail, le *take-off* implique une accélération forte du taux de croissance du produit national brut ainsi que du taux d'investissement. Il peut donc y avoir révolution industrielle sans *take-off*, mais pas l'inverse. La notion de *leading sector* découle du fait que l'effet multiplicateur de l'investissement n'est pas le même suivant le secteur où s'applique cet investissement. Pour Rostow, le développement des sociétés et populations sous-développées peut être obtenu pourvu qu'on y appliquent les politiques qui ont permis aux pays développés d'atteindre ce stade actuel du développement. C'est pourquoi Félix Houphouët-Boigny opte pour un choix assumé du libéralisme. À l'inverse, Léopold S. Senghor préfère une construction nationale fondée sur le Socialisme sénégalais, déclinaison locale du Socialisme africain.

C/ Une communauté de choix politiques : deux « démocraties » dirigées par un parti dominant

Les deux pays ont un commun d'être des « démocraties » formelles, dirigées chacune par un parti dominant. Au Sénégal, le pouvoir est contrôlé par l'Union Progressiste Sénégalaise (UPS) de Léopold S. Senghor (*vide supra*)[44]. En Côte-d'Ivoire, il existe un pouvoir monopolisé par le Parti Démocrate de Côte-d'Ivoire (PDCI) de Félix Houphouët-Boigny[45]. Il s'ensuit une caractéristique commune : une répression et des emprisonnements arbitraires comme mode de gouvernement des deux leaders et, ceci, au nom de la stabilité politique, économique et sociale[46].

2.3/ Deux économies extraverties dépendantes de cultures commerciales vulnérables

La similitude ne concerne pas que les modèles politiques. Il existe en effet des effets de dépendance communs, tant vis à vis des monocultures agricoles que des exportations.

44 François Zuccarelli, *Un parti politique africain : l'Union Progressiste sénégalaise*, Paris, Librairie de droit et jurisprudence, 1970.

45 Marcel Amondji, *Côte d'Ivoire. Le P.D.C.I. et la vie politique de 1945 à 1985*, Paris, L'Harmattan, 1986.

46 Doudou Sidibé, *Démocracie et alternance politique au Sénégal*, Paris, L'Harmattan, 2006.

A/ Une dépendance majeure vis à vis des monocultures agricoles
Cette dépendance est évidente à l'égard des monocultures agricoles[47]. Le poids de l'arachide est ainsi considérable dans l'économie sénégalaise. Sous Léopold Sédar Senghor, l'agriculture occupe environ 85% de la population active[48]. Le Sénégal se caractérise par une agriculture de type familial aux pratiques culturales primaires et rudimentaires. Cette agriculture reste dominée par la production de l'arachide. En Côte-d'Ivoire, on peut dire la même chose des cultures arbustives, en l'occurrence le café et le cacao[49]. L'économie de plantation ivoirienne repose sur deux leviers de: les plantations industrielles et les plantations dites villageoises. Le gouvernement met en œuvre une politique incitative pour l'expansion de l'arboriculture de café et de cacao. Elle confère un rôle crucial au Syndicat Agricole Africain (SAA), se traduit par le développement des palmeraies à huile et de l'hévéa et la création de la Caisse de stabilisation des prix à l'exportation (ou Caistab).

B/ Des exportations dominées par les cultures commerciales dans les deux pays
Le résultat en est simple : dans les deux pays, les exportations restent dominées par les cultures commerciales. Au Sénégal, le poids de l'arachide induit des conséquences très lourdes. Cette même culture de l'arachide représente 80 à 90 % des exportations en 1960, et plus de 75% jusqu'en 1967. En revanche, à partir de 1970, cette part chute à 48%. La chute est imputable à la fin des tarifs préférentiels survenue en 1967. Il s'ensuit l'apparition et l'aggravation du malaise paysan. Ce dernier se fonde sur la baisse progressive du pouvoir d'achat des paysans, soit 75 % de la population en 1970[50]. En effet, le prix moyen du kilogramme d'arachide payé au producteur connaît une forte baisse : 22 F CFA en 1967, 17,60 F CFA en 1968, 17,95 en 1969. De même le revenu brut engendré par la vente de l'arachide chute : 18,7 milliards de francs CFA, en 1965-1966, à 15,5 milliards, en 1966-1967, puis 13 milliards en 1967-1968 et 10,1 milliards en 1968-1969. De ce fait, les paysans se trouvent dans l'incapacité de recouvrer les crédits contractés auprès de la Banque Nationale de Développement en vue de l'achat de matériels agricoles. La crise de 1968 doit se comprendre dans ce contexte. Le malaise est général est : le recul de l'arachide s'accompagne du début d'un exode rural massif en direction de la capitale, Dakar[51].

En Côte d'Ivoire, un phénomène similaire s'observe à propos du poids du café et du cacao et ses conséquences. De 1960-1978, il est possible de parler du « miracle ivoirien ». Durant ces années les exportations augmentent en moyenne de 7% par an. En 1974, l'excédent commercial est considérable, avec un taux de couverture élevé des importations par les exportations, à savoir 25,9 %.

47 Boubacar Ba, *Agriculture et sécurité alimentaire au Sénégal*, Paris, L'Harmattan, 2008.
48 Mamadou Keita, *Évolution de la population et de la production agricole du Sénégal (1920-1968)*, Dakar, Université de Dakar, Faculté de Droit, 1970 (Diplôme d'Études Supérieures).
49 Dian Boni, *L'économie de plantation en Côte-d'Ivoire forestière*, Abidjan, Nouvelles éditions africaines, 1985.
50 Pierre Biarnès, *La fin des cacahuètes*, Paris, L'Harmattan, 2005.
51 Cheikh Guèye, *Analyse spatiale des migrations internes au Sénégal 1960-1980*, Louvain, Université de Louvain, 1986, 100 + 12 p. (Thèse de Démographie).

TABLEAU 1 **LA BALANCE DES ÉCHANGES EXTÉRIEURS DE LA CÔTE D'IVOIRE EN 1974**

Recettes d'exportation 1974	Coûts des importations 1974	Excédent commercial 1974
292 milliards f. CFA	232 milliards f. CFA	60 milliards f. CFA

Cette même année 1974, le PIB par habitants de la Côte d'Ivoire s'élève à 120.000 francs CFA.

Ce dynamisme se poursuit dans les années 1970[52]. Le taux de croissance est alors d'environ 4% par an de 1970 à 1979. L'euphorie est en particulièrement forte dans les années 1975-1977, notamment en raison de la hausse des prix du cacao. Durant ces années, le taux de croissance du PIB global atteint même 10 % par an. Le taux de croissance de la demande publique et privée est même plus élevé encore 20 % par an. Avec un PIB par habitant de 2237 dollars en 1977, la Côte-d'Ivoire est élevée au rang de Pays à Revenu Intermédiaire dès l'année suivante, en 1978. En revanche, à partir de 1980, se produit l'avènement du « cauchemar ivoirien » . Il résulte de la conjonction de deux facteurs clés : la désépargne et la hausse progressive des dépenses publiques. La première découle d'une brutale augmentation de 10 % de la consommation des biens importés, d'où résulte une hausse du déficit extérieur. En parallèle se produit une hausse progressive des dépenses publiques : elles atteignent en moyenne 42% du PIB dans les années 1970 au lieu de 30 % dans les années soixante. En conséquence, la dette publique quadruple dans les années soixante-dix, passant de 18,5 % du PIB en 1970 à environ 45 % au début des années quatre-vingt. Tout cela conduit à un échec de la politique de développement libérale[53].

Conclusion

La spirale de l'endettement est la conséquence du caractère extravertie des deux économie et donc l'échec de la politique de développement dans les deux pays. D'une part, le Sénégal et la Côte-d'Ivoire ont, depuis les Indépendances, vécu au-dessus de leurs moyens. D'autre part les dirigeants des deux pays ont péché par excès d'optimisme, en particulier Félix Houphouët-Boigny, obnubilé par la « manne cacaoyère ». En outre, la forte croissance démographique que connaissent les deux pays dans la période a sapé les effets de la croissance tout en augmentant la dépense publique.

Aujourd'hui encore, la croissance du Sénégal demeure fragile[54]. La croissance moyenne a été relativement forte entre 1995 et 2005 et accompagnée d'une forte baisse de l'incidence de la pauvreté. En revanche, et en raison notamment d'une série de chocs exogènes, cette croissance a diminué pour tomber à une moyenne de 3,3 % en 2006-11. En conséquence, le revenu par habitant n'a augmenté que modestement. Par suite, l'incidence de la pauvreté a à peine diminué au cours de cette période et reste élevé. En outre, de grandes disparités existent entre les zones rurales, où l'incidence

52 Paul Koffi Koffi, *Le défi du développement en Côte d'Ivoire*, Paris, L'Harmattan, 2008.
53 Christian Grootaert, *Réformes économiques et analyse de la pauvreté : l'expérience de la Côte d'Ivoire*, Paris, L'Harmattan, 1996.
54 Salifou Issoufou, Andrew Jewell, Alexei Kireyev, and Gaston Mpatswe, Senegal, *Achieving High and Inclusive Growth While Preserving Fiscal Sustainability*, International Monetary Fund, Publication Services, 2013.

de la pauvreté est plus élevée que la moyenne, et les zones urbaines. Dans le même temps, les déficits budgétaires ont augmenté, ce qui a réduit la marge de manœuvre budgétaire et la dette ont augmenté, ce qui soulève des préoccupations quant à la viabilité de cette même dette. Le déficit budgétaire, qui était inférieur à 4 % du PIB en 2007, s'est approché de 7 % du PIB en 2011. Les déficits plus élevés ont été justifiés dans une large mesure par la réponse aux chocs successifs. Entre-temps, le ratio de la dette publique au PIB s'est élevée en continu. En raison de ces évolutions, la marge de manœuvre budgétaire a diminué, et cela limite la capacité des autorités à mener des politiques anticycliques. De tels niveaux de déficit budgétaire sont incompatibles avec une durabilité à long terme. Le principal défi à moyen terme pour le Sénégal est donc d'atteindre un niveau élevé de croissance, mais une croissance inclusive tout en préservant la viabilité budgétaire. Il y a un relativement large consensus sur le fait que la croissance au Sénégal n'est pas entravée par un seul, mais plutôt par une série de problèmes, notamment les lacunes en matière d'infrastructures, l'accès à la terre et au financement, la protection des droits de propriété ; l'inefficacité des politiques économiques de l'État.

La situation apparaît bien meilleure pour la Côte d'Ivoire[55]. Avec un taux de croissance moyen estimé à 9,2 % sur la période 2012-2016, l'économie ivoirienne est l'une des plus dynamiques du monde. Le plan national de développement (PND) prévoit une croissance moyenne de 8,7 % entre 2016 et 2020. La croissance prévue sera robuste, inclusive, durable et résistante. La croissance reste vigoureuse, avec un taux de croissance de 8,5 % prévu pour 2017. Le FMI et les agences de notation soutiennent les autorités et prévoient une croissance solide en 2017. La croissance de 2016 a atteint 8,8 %, tirée par les secteurs secondaire et tertiaire. Malgré des chocs exogènes en 2016, dont une baisse de 35 % du prix du cacao, le secteur primaire continue de bénéficier d'un mix agricole diversifié. Une croissance résistante est soutenue par l'investissement (privé et public) et la consommation. La consommation privée a représenté 65 % de la demande interne, soutenue par une démographie favorable.

55 Republic of Côte d'Ivoire, *Accelerating 2030 Agenda*, April 2018, https://www.un.org/development/desa/dspd/wp-content/uploads/sites/22/2018/05/8-1.pdf

Index Nominum

Abstracts - Résumés

Introduction
Dominique Barjot

Abstract

"To what extent are European development-theories on industrialization valid from a World point of view?"

To what extent can the traditional theories be meaningfully applied to non-European countries? Traditional theories on the World's development, especially industrialization, have a Western Europe-biased design. Consequently, it is valuable to mobilize the recent achievements in business history and of microeconomic research on companies, the state and consumers. The purpose is evaluating the role of business, both large and small, in the growth dynamic of both industrialized and emerging nations, by exploring their performance, strategies and types of organization, together with the social, cultural and environmental implications of their behaviour as actors. The issue of the emergence of globalization bears upon many fundamental questions: the growth of mass consumption and Americanization; public policy, both cyclical and structural; firms' investment policies and, more broadly, operational and strategic decisions, taking into account transaction costs; the interaction of social networks and/or techniques, spatial dynamics (industrial districts, local productive systems and clusters); path dependency.

From the actual collective work come three main conclusions:

1/ It has been possible to make a useful comparative review and a no less useful inventory of the research carried out on the subject.

2 / In general, theoretical models of Western origin, whether macro- or microeconomic, are useful and even indispensable, because they are the basis of possible typologies, but also likely to provide explanatory models. Such were the case of the Rostow, Kuznets and Gerschenkron's analyzes in the macroeconomic field, or, in terms of technology, the Schumpeterian or Neo-Schumpeterian approaches. As far as regional economic development is concerned, Michael Porter's cluster vision offers the advantage of providing the better explanatory elements.

3 / Under a number of conditions, Western theoretical models can be applied in a relevant way to the interpretation of the development of today's emerging countries.

Keywords: Globalization, internationalization, multinationalization, industrialized countries, emerging countries, global players, path dependency, performances, strategies, structures, state intervention

JEL Classification: B0, D22, F5, F6, N1, N6, N8

Résumé

« Dans quelle mesure les théories du développement européen sur l'industrialisation sont-elles valables d'un point de vue mondial ? »

Dans quelle mesure les théories traditionnelles peuvent-elles être appliquées de manière significative aux pays non européens ? Les théories traditionnelles de l'industrialisation mondiale témoignent d'un tropisme ouest-européen. Il est donc intéressant de mobiliser les réalisations récentes de l'histoire des entreprises et de la recherche microéconomique sur les entreprises, l'État et les consommateurs. L'objectif est d'évaluer le rôle des entreprises, grandes et petites, dans la dynamique de croissance des pays industrialisés et des pays émergents, en examinant leurs performances, leurs stratégies et leurs types d'organisation, ainsi que les implications sociales, culturelles et environnementales de leur comportement en tant qu'acteurs. La question de l'émergence de la mondialisation soulève de nombreuses questions fondamentales: croissance de la consommation de masse et l'américanisation; politiques publiques, tant cycliques que structurelles ; politiques d'investissement des entreprises et, plus largement, décisions opérationnelles et stratégiques, en tenant compte des coûts de transaction; l'interaction des réseaux et / ou des techniques sociales, les dynamiques spatiales (districts industriels, systèmes de production locaux et clusters); dépendance de sentier.

Du travail collectif proprement dit, trois conclusions principales se dégagent :

1 / Il a été possible de faire un bilan comparatif utile et un inventaire non moins utile des recherches menées sur le sujet.

2 / En général, les modèles théoriques d'origine occidentale, qu'ils soient macro ou microéconomiques, sont utiles et même indispensables, car ils constituent la base de typologies possibles, mais sont également susceptibles de fournir des modèles explicatifs. C'est le cas des analyses de Rostow, Kuznets et Gerschenkron dans le domaine macroéconomique, ou, en termes de technologie, des approches schumpétérienne ou néo-schumpétérienne. En ce qui concerne le développement économique régional, la vision du groupe de Michael Porter offre l'avantage de fournir les meilleurs éléments explicatifs.

3 / Dans un certain nombre de conditions, les modèles théoriques occidentaux peuvent être appliqués de manière pertinente à l'interprétation du développement des pays émergents d'aujourd'hui.

Mots clés : globalisation, internationalisation, multinationalisation, nations industrialisées, pays émergents, acteurs globaux, dépendance de sentier, performances, stratégies, structures, intervention de l'État

Chapter 1 - **L'Économie européenne au prisme du projet politique des États-Unis. Du Plan Marshall au Grand dessein de Kennedy**

François David

Abstract

The European Economy through the lens of the US political project. From the Marshall Plan to Kennedy's Grand Project

We illustrate here the thesis of the primacy of politics on the economy, through the American policy towards Europe, after 1945. In the reorganization of the world demanded by the United States since Woodrow Wilson, the economy is a means; politics, an absolute goal. In the founding years 1945-1963, the major economic and commercial projects conceived by the United States for the benefit of Western Europe have a strategic aim: to create an interdependent international society, with the rejection of stubborn sovereignty, so as to dissolve the aggressiveness of the Westphalian Nation-State. The Marshall Plan, the ECSC and then the Common Market successively pursue this goal. About the method, the United States has been able to adapt, passing from a kind of blackmail (dollar diplomacy), to a finer diplomacy summed up as follows: neither isolationism nor open intrusiveness. In any case, the United States of Europe remains the ultimate objective.

Keywords: Multilateralism, Woodrow Wilson, Marshall Plan, Economic Community of Coal and Steel (ECCS), Common Market,

JEL Classification: N11, N12, N14, N42, N44

Résumé

Nous illustrons ici la thèse du primat du politique sur l'économie, à travers la stratégie américaine en direction de l'Europe, après 1945. Dans la réorganisation du monde voulue par les États-Unis depuis Wilson, l'économie est un moyen ; la politique, une fin. Dans les années fondatrices 1945-1963, les grands projets économiques et commerciaux pensés par les États-Unis au profit de l'Europe occidentale revêtent une visée stratégique : créer une société internationale interdépendante, avec des abandons de souveraineté, de façon à dissoudre l'agressivité belligène de l'État-nation westphalien. Le plan Marshall, la CECA puis le Marché commun poursuivent successivement ce but. Sur la méthode, les États-Unis ont su s'adapter, passant d'une forme de chantage à coups de dollars, à une diplomatie plus fine se résumant au slogan : ni isolationnisme, ni ingérence ouverte. Dans tous les cas, les États-Unis d'Europe demeurent le but ultime.

Mots-clés : multilatéralisme, Woodrow Wilson, Plan Marshall, Communauté Économique du Charbon et de l'Acier (CECA), Marché commun

Chapter 2 - **Modern Corporate Growth after the Modern Economic Growth: A Comparative Study of General Electric and Westinghouse Electric, 1946-2000**

Kenichi Miyata

Abstract

This chapter explores the process of corporate change for growth and path dependence during the second half of the twentieth century, using GE and WH as case study subjects. Although the two firms had similar structures after the war, they both incrementally changed their respective business structures during the period under study. The distinct corporate changes that evolved were the result of a divergence in top management behaviors arising from their respective perceptions of environment, conceptions of prospects and actions taken to pursue unrelated diversification. The findings seek to raise the understanding of emerging another form of growth and the influence of path dependence, in order to flag the limits to change for business organizations during the period.

Keywords: modern industrial enterprise, corporate transformation, diversification, corporate strategy, path dependence,

JEL Classification: N82

Résumé

La croissance moderne des entreprises après la croissance économique moderne : Une étude comparative de General Electric et Westinghouse Electric, 1946-2000

Ce chapitre explore le processus de changement des entreprises en faveur de la croissance et de la dépendance à l'égard de la trajectoire au cours de la seconde moitié du XXe siècle, en utilisant GE et WH comme sujets d'étude de cas. Bien que les deux entreprises aient eu des structures similaires après la guerre, elles ont toutes deux progressivement changé leurs structures commerciales respectives au cours de la période étudiée. Les changements distincts des entreprises qui ont évolué sont le résultat d'une divergence dans les comportements des cadres supérieurs découlant de leurs perceptions respectives de l'environnement, de leurs conceptions des perspectives et des mesures prises pour poursuivre une diversification sans rapport. Les résultats cherchent à mieux comprendre l'émergence d'une autre forme de croissance et l'influence de la dépendance à la trajectoire, afin de mettre en évidence les limites du changement pour les organisations commerciales au cours de la période.

Mots-clés : entreprise industrielle moderne, transformation de l'entreprise, diversification, stratégie d'entreprise, dépendance à l'égard des chemins de fer,

Chapter 3 - **The Canadian experience in business: the case of the St. Maurice Valley from 1890 to 1975**

Pierre Lanthier

Abstract

Canada owes a substantial part of its industrialization to foreign investors, British and American especially, mainly interested in the exploitation of natural resources. The staple theory, formulated by two Canadian historians, describes this reality. However, the analysis of a Quebec region, the Mauricie, gives a more nuanced portrait: if the presence of foreign investors is crucial, it is humanly and financially tied with the Canadian business world; moreover, far from only exporting raw material, the Mauricie companies underwent its initial transformation. After 1945, they carried out their vertical integration up to finished product, but with limited results that did not favour the Mauricie area. This regional case dissociates itself from the theses of Smith and those of Gerschenkron. It matches better, although not completely, 's approach. At any rate, it provides a complement to the staple theory.

Keywords: Canada, natural resources, industrialization, regional history, foreign investment

JEL Classification: N1

Résumé

L'expérience canadienne des affaires industrielles : le cas de la vallée du Saint-Maurice de 1890 à 1975

Le Canada doit son industrialisation en bonne partie aux investisseurs étrangers, notamment britanniques et américains, principalement intéressés par l'exploitation des ressources naturelles. La théorie du *staple*, conçue par deux historiens canadiens, rend compte de ce phénomène. L'analyse d'une région du Québec, la Mauricie, donne toutefois un portrait plus nuancé : si la présence étrangère est notable, elle est accompagnée humainement et financièrement par le monde des affaires canadien ; par ailleurs, loin de n'exporter que de la matière première, les entreprises mauriciennes ont procédé à leur première transformation. Après 1945, ces dernières ont poursuivi leur intégration verticale jusqu'au produit fini, mais avec des résultats limités et peu favorables à la Mauricie. L'exemple mauricien se démarque des thèses de Smith et de celles de Gerschenkron. Il correspond davantage, mais incomplètement, à l'approche de Chandler. Il apporte en tout cas un complément à la théorie du *staple*.

Mots-clés : Canada, ressources naturelles, industrialisation, histoire régionale, investissements étrangers

Chapter 4 - **Germany's economic development 1950-1990: its significance for development economics**

Harm Schröter

Abstract

Instead of simply re-telling the story of German economic development once more, this contribution looks for its underlying factors. These factors have been mentioned by previous authors, but never systematically collected and categorized. In our analysis we apply the theories of Douglas North emphasising continuous, incremental change and Joseph Schumpeter's focus on discontinuous ruptures; in other words, we juxtapose factors of predominantly path-dependency with factors of predominantly creative destruction. In a few cases neither category fits, so we created a third composite category. Which factor category was responsible for German economic development? Clearly, all three played a role. But the proposition that especially discontinuous factors promoted the country's exceptional growth in these years has much attraction.

Keywords: Germany, economic development, theoretical explanation, 1950-1990

JEL Classification: N14, N34. N44, O14, O40

Résumé

Le développement économique de l'Allemagne 1950-1990 : son importance pour l'économie du développement

Au lieu de simplement raconter une fois de plus l'histoire du développement économique allemand, cette contribution cherche ses facteurs sous-jacents. Ces facteurs ont été mentionnés par les auteurs précédents, mais n'ont jamais été systématiquement collectés et catégorisés. Dans notre analyse, nous appliquons les théories de Douglas North, qui mettent l'accent sur le changement continu et progressif, et celles de Joseph Schumpeter, qui mettent l'accent sur les ruptures discontinues ; en d'autres termes, nous juxtaposons les facteurs de dépendance prédominante des voies d'accès avec les facteurs de destruction créative prédominante. Dans quelques cas, aucune des deux catégories ne correspond, nous avons donc créé une troisième catégorie composite. Quelle catégorie de facteurs a été responsable du développement économique allemand ? Il est clair que les trois ont joué un rôle. Mais la proposition selon laquelle des facteurs particulièrement discontinus ont favorisé la croissance exceptionnelle du pays au cours de ces années est très intéressante.

Mots-clés : Allemagne, développement économique, explication théorique, 1950-1990

Chapter 5 - **A "French Miracle"? The Economic Growth of France 1949-1969**

Dominique Barjot

Abstract

After the WW2, production increased greatly in France : from 1949 to 1969, the GDP growth rate was + 5.1% per year on average. In this way, the use of a Cobb-Douglas function leads to interesting results. According to Jean-Jacques Carré, Paul Dubois and Edmond Malinvaud, the growth in production was due to a number of factors It resulted first of all from the increased labor efficiency. Labor resources have increased slightly: + 0.2% per year. The total population has gone from Malthusianism to the renewal of the birth rate. If the activity rate has decreased compared to 1918, the level of employment remained very high since 1949, in spite of a very limited deterioration since 1965 and the duration of work strongly grew between 1946 and 1969. At the same time, the quality of the labor force has improved because of the higher level of education. Consequently, labor productivity accelerated slowly before the war, strongly thereafter. It also resulted from the increase in the stock of productive capital due to a considerable investment effort. Indeed, the growth of productive capital was indisputable. Nevertheless, after 1945, labor and capital growths only explained a limited part of the growth of GDP. Since 1945, the growth was mainly due to a residue. It was explained by economies of scale, better management methods and the development of technical progress and measured by total factor productivity gains. The level of this one was low in 1949 but was characterized by a rapid growth from 1949 to 1966. In conclusion, the French growth resulted from a series of favorable factors: catching up the birth rate, shock of 1939-45, institutional reforms parallel to the efforts of instruction of the French population, reconversion of the industry, release of the demand, environment favorable. Some factors were decisive: firstly, the French gave some priority to work; secondly during the 1960s, France benefited from a modernized productive apparatus and a dynamic, coherent and efficient economic policy was conducted then.

Keywords: French GDP growth 1949-1969, Cobb-Douglas function, productive capital, investment effort, total factor productivity gains, technical progress, catching up

JEL Classification: N14, N24, N34, N44, O47

Résumé

Un « miracle économique français ? La croissance économique de la France 1949-1969

Après la seconde guerre mondiale, la production augmente fortement en France : de 1949 à 1969, le taux de croissance du PIB est de + 5,1% par an en moyenne. Ainsi, l'utilisation d'une fonction Cobb-Douglas conduit à des résultats intéressants. Selon Jean-Jacques Carré, Paul Dubois et Edmond Malinvaud, la croissance de la production est due à un certain nombre de facteurs. Elle résulte tout d'abord de l'augmentation de l'efficacité du travail. Les ressources en main-d'œuvre ont légèrement augmenté : + 0,2 % par an. La population totale est passée du malthusianisme au renouvellement de la natalité. Si le taux d'activité a diminué par rapport à 1918, le niveau de l'emploi est resté très élevé depuis 1949, malgré une détérioration très limitée depuis 1965 et la durée du travail a fortement augmenté entre 1946 et 1969. Dans le même temps, la qualité de la main-d'œuvre s'est améliorée grâce à un niveau d'éducation plus élevé. Par conséquent, la productivité du travail s'est lentement accélérée avant la guerre, beaucoup plus après. Elle résulte également de l'augmentation du stock de capital productif due à un effort d'investissement considérable. En effet, la croissance du capital productif était incontestable. Néanmoins, après 1945, les croissances du travail et du capital n'ont expliqué qu'une partie limitée de la croissance du PIB. Depuis 1945, la croissance est principalement due à un résidu. Il s'explique par les économies d'échelle, l'amélioration des méthodes de gestion et le développement du progrès technique et se mesure par les gains de productivité totale des facteurs. Le niveau de celle-ci était faible en 1949, mais a été caractérisé par une croissance rapide de 1949 à 1966. En conclusion, la croissance française résulte d'une série de facteurs favorables : rattrapage de la natalité, choc de 1939-45, réformes institutionnelles parallèles aux efforts d'instruction de la population française, reconversion de l'industrie, libération de la demande, environnement favorable. Certains facteurs ont été décisifs : d'une part, les Français ont donné une certaine priorité au travail ; d'autre part, au cours des années 1960, la France a bénéficié d'un appareil productif modernisé et d'une politique économique dynamique, cohérente et efficace.

Mots-clés : croissance du PIB français1949-1969, fonction de Cobb-Douglas, capital productif, effort d'investissement, gains de productivité globale des facteurs, progrès technique, rattrapage

Chapter 6 - **The cement market during the 20th century**: **between cartels and regulation**

Cécile Coursiéras-Jaff

Abstract

The aim of this paper is to understand the evolution of the cement market especially in Europe and France during the twentieth century and to show how the cartels played a major role toward this market building. This evolution finds an explanation in the particular structure of the cement market but also because of economic and political reasons. The cement industry is a heavy industry with a low value product. Therefore, one of the key issues consists in limiting storage and transportation costs to preserve a competitive end product cost on the market. This paper will analyze how each producer manages to combine investment in productivity, capacity and spatial location to remain competitive.

Keywords : Cement, cartels, oligopoly, firms, regulation
JEL Classification: N60, N64, 014, P17, P52, R38

Résumé

L'objectif de cet article est de comprendre l'évolution du marché du ciment notamment en Europe et en France au cours du vingtième siècle et de montrer comment les cartels ont joué un rôle majeur dans son élaboration. La structure particulière du marché du ciment tout autant que des facteurs politiques et économiques contribuent à façonner ce marché. L'industrie du ciment est une industrie lourde aboutissant à la commercialisation d'un produit de faible valeur. L'un des enjeux clés consiste donc pour les producteurs à limiter les coûts de stockage et de transport pour préserver un coût de produit final compétitif sur le marché. Cet article analyse comment chaque producteur parvient à combiner coûts de productivité, capacité de tonnage et localisation spatiale pour rester compétitif.

Mots-clés : ciment, cartels, oligopoles, entreprises, régulation

Chapter 7 - **L'Union Européenne. L'évolution économique des pays d'Europe occidentale et la spécificité française depuis les années 1960**
Michel Hau

Abstract

The European Union. The economic evolution of Western European countries and the French specificity since the 1960s

Treaty of Rome brought together six countries, but only two economic models. On one side, the interventionist and protectionist system of France. On the other, the of the liberal and free-trade oriented system of its five European partners. The French model was characterized by a social security system which was mainly financed by enterprises et deprived them of resources for investments. On the contrary, the five partner countries came after 1945 in reaction against state interventionism and chose an economic model based on autonomy of enterprises. The fathers of Europe, even on the French side, were proponents of a market economy. Few resources were allocated for common policies. The supranational authorities acted above all to remove distortions of competition. Since 1974, the French model entered into a crisis caused by deindustrialisation, monetary weakness and public deficit. France requested for more monetary cooperation and, after the creation of the euro, for more financial cooperation. The European partners were in situation of imposing a convergence towards their model.

Keywords: Protectionism, planning, globalization, free trade, common market
JEL Classification: E, F, H, N et P.

Résumé

Le traité de Rome a réuni six pays, mais seulement deux modèles économiques. D'un côté, celui, dirigiste et protectionniste, de la France, de l'autre, celui, libéral et libre-échangiste, des cinq autres pays partenaires. Le modèle français était caractérisé par un financement de la sécurité sociale qui pesait principalement sur les entreprises et les privait de ressources pour les investissements. À l'inverse, les cinq partenaires de la France réagirent après 1945 contre le dirigisme et optèrent pour un modèle économique centré sur l'entreprise. Les pères de l'Europe, même du côté français, étaient partisans de l'économie de marché. Peu de ressources furent consacrées aux politiques communes. Les autorités supranationales agirent prioritairement pour éliminer les distorsions de concurrence. À partir de 1974, le modèle français entra

dans une crise causée par la désindustrialisation, l'affaiblissement monétaire et le déficit des comptes publics. La France demanda alors une coopération monétaire accrue puis, après la création de l'euro, une coopération financière plus poussée. Les partenaires européens de la France furent alors en mesure de lui imposer une convergence vers leur modèle
Mots clés : protectionnisme, planification, mondialisation, libre-échange, marché commun.

Chapter 8 - **The double diamond and the state-backed path of industrialization in small, open economies: Two Hungarian companies on the world market 1867-1989**
Mária Hidvégi

Abstract
The goal of this chapter is to identify some factors that may be useful to apply the theory of state-backed path of industrialization to small, open and late industrializing countries in the analysis of entrepreneurial contribution to national economies' performance on the long run. The case study displays experiences of the two national champions of the Hungarian electro-technical industry useful to this end using insights from the generalized double diamond model.
Keywords: Electro-technical industry, Hungary, transnational networks, structural change, socialism, competitiveness
JEL Classification: L16, L22, N84, O12, O38

Résumé
Le double diamant et la voie de l'industrialisation soutenue par l'État en petites économies ouvertes : deux entreprises hongroises sur le marché mondial 1867-1989
L'objectif de ce chapitre est d'identifier certains facteurs qui peuvent être utiles pour appliquer la théorie de la voie d'industrialisation soutenue par l'État aux petits pays à industrialisation ouverte et tardive dans l'analyse de la contribution des entreprises aux performances des économies nationales sur le long terme. L'étude de cas présente les expériences des deux champions nationaux de l'industrie électrotechnique hongroise, utiles à cette fin, en utilisant les connaissances du modèle généralisé du double diamant.
Mots-clés : industrie électrotechnique, Hongrie, réseaux transnationaux, changement structurel, socialisme, compétitivité

Chapter 9 - **Russia in the 19th century, Russia today: the permanence of technology transfer**

Boris Vinogradov

Abstract

This article analyses the influence of the occidental technologies on the Russian industry. Focusing attention on the automobile, oil and aluminum industries we examine the reasons, motifs and describe the process of Western technology transfer. In this paper, we examine the results of the Western technology transfer on the efficiency and productivity of the Russian economy. The Soviet industry machine tool industry had insufficient capacity to produce special machines and automatic lines for mass production. The Europeans manufacturers have largely contributed to the development of the Russian industry. The success of today's Russian industry is largely due to the transfer of Western and especially French technologies.

Key words : Russian industry, automobile, technology transfer, France, french enterprises

JEL Classification: O33, N13, N14, N74, N84

Résumé

Russie du XIXe **siècle, Russie d'aujourd'hui : la permanence du transfert de technologie**

Cet article analyse l'influence des technologies occidentales sur l'industrie russe. En concentrant l'attention sur les industries de l'automobile, du pétrole et de l'aluminium, nous examinons les raisons, les motifs et décrivons le processus de transfert de technologies occidentales. Dans cet article, nous examinons les résultats du transfert de technologie occidental sur l'efficacité et la productivité de l'économie russe. L'industrie soviétique des machines-outils avait une capacité insuffisante pour produire des machines spéciales et des lignes automatiques pour la production de masse. Les fabricants européens ont largement contribué au développement de l'industrie russe. Le succès de l'industrie russe actuelle est en grande partie dû au transfert de technologies occidentales et surtout françaises.

Mots clés : industrie russe, automobile, transfert de technologies, France, entreprises françaises

Chapter 10 - **The "black box" of Japanese growth (1945-1973): The origins of productivity**

Kazuhiko Yago

Abstract

This chapter aims to present an alternative view on Japanese growth, referring to contemporary debates in the OECD in order to review how contemporaries understood productivity, with updated historiography. Viewing the notion of productivity from the OECD archives, the followings have been discovered: The notion of productivity was imperfect, and the Japanese view has been constrained to a contemporary

context, in particular the foreign reserves. However, the above understandings and misunderstandings occasionally enabled Japanese high growth. The "backwardness" of the rural population first supplied cheap labor, with strong propensity for saving, and finally turned into a vast market for household goods. The role played by the government was essential in introducing foreign technologies, but one of the important backdrops was the capital movement regulation, which suggested the licensing and trade of intellectual properties, instead of direct investment.
Key Words: Productivity, growth, OECD, Japan, investment, capital movement
JEL classification: B22, N15, N35, O40, O43

Résumé

La «boîte noire» de la croissance japonaise (1945-1973) : les origines de la productivité

Ce chapitre vise à présenter un point de vue alternatif sur la croissance japonaise, en se référant aux débats contemporains au sein de l'OCDE afin de revoir la façon dont les contemporains ont compris la productivité, avec une historiographie actualisée. En examinant la notion de productivité à partir des archives de l'OCDE, les éléments suivants ont été découverts : la notion de productivité était imparfaite, et le point de vue japonais a été limité à un contexte contemporain, en particulier les réserves de change. Toutefois, les interprétations et les malentendus susmentionnés ont parfois permis au Japon de connaître une forte croissance. Le « retard » de la population rurale a d'abord fourni une main-d'œuvre bon marché, avec une forte propension à l'épargne, et s'est finalement transformé en un vaste marché pour les biens ménagers. Le rôle joué par le gouvernement a été essentiel dans l'introduction des technologies étrangères, mais l'une des arrière-plans importantes a été la réglementation des mouvements de capitaux, qui a suggéré l'octroi de licences et le commerce de la propriété intellectuelle, au lieu de l'investissement direct.
Mots clés : productivité, croissance, OCDE, Japon, investissement, mouvement de capitaux

Chapter 11 - **What is the local nongovernmental management in economy? a view on the commercial association during late Qing dynasty in China**

Sun Rui

Abstract

This paper focus on the local commercial management in Hu Nan(湖南) Province during 1787 to 1909 of China. The research is the 269 regulations, including 2636 clauses,133 industries as Chinese traditional ways. There was a commercial autonomy in these regulations. And the core industry interests was noticed and kept in each one of them, which was the most important things instead of religions. Procedural justice could be insist on election and interior finance management. There also had rules about supervising the top directors. They must be responsible for their association. The associations has great marketing authority that made the transaction regulations as well as the punishments. And the local government's influence was important but not the essential. This research could be another perspective to understand the Chinese social structure in history.

Key words: Local business management; commercial associations; commercial autonomy; Social structure

JEL Classification: N85, N45, O17, P23

Résumé

Cet article se concentre sur la gestion commerciale locale dans la province de Hu Nan(湖南) entre 1787 et 1909 en Chine. La recherche porte sur 269 règlements, y compris leurs 2636 clauses, et 133 industries classées selon les conventions traditionnelles chinoises. Il y avait une autonomie commerciale dans ces règlements. Et les intérêts fondamentaux de l'industrie ont été codifiés et conservés dans chacun d'entre eux, ce qui était la chose la plus importante quelques soient les religions. La justice procédurale pouvait insister sur l'élection et la gestion des finances intérieures. Il y avait également des règles portant sur la supervision des directeurs principaux. Ils doivent être responsables de leur association. Les associations disposent d'une grande autorité en matière de marketing qui établit les règles de transaction ainsi que les sanctions. L'influence du gouvernement local est importante mais pas essentielle. Cette recherche pourrait être une autre perspective pour comprendre la structure sociale chinoise à travers l'histoire.

Chapter 12 - **China's High-speed Rail: From Technological Catching-Up to Innovation**

Wang Jue & Wang Qing

Abstract

This paper reviews the development history of China's high-speed rail, which can be divided into three periods: the exploration period based on independent R&D, the massive technology introduction period and the self-dependent innovation period. Through the description of the history and achievements of this special industry, this paper reveals the role that the Chinese government had played during the introduction of technology and the formulation of the strategy of innovation.

Keywords: High-speed rail, technology introduction, innovation, Ministry of Railway (MOR)

JEL Classification: D22, N45, N65, N75

Résumé

Le train à grande vitesse chinois : du rattrapage technologique à l'innovation

Ce texte passe en revue l'histoire du développement du train à grande vitesse en Chine, qui peut être divisée en trois périodes : la période d'exploration basée sur la R&D indépendante, la période d'introduction massive des technologies et la période d'innovation autonome. Grâce à la description de l'histoire et des réalisations de cette industrie particulière, ce papier révèle le rôle que le gouvernement chinois a joué

pendant la phase d'introduction de la technologie et la formulation de la stratégie d'innovation.
Mots-clés : train à grande vitesse, introduction de la technologie, innovation, Ministère des Chemins de fer (MOR)

Chapter 13 - **The International Activities of the Chinese Construction Industry. The Case of "China Railway Group Limited"**
Zhou Xiaolan

Abstract
With China's entry into the World Trade Organization since 2001, not only does the construction industry, still in the process of reform, have to compete against powerful foreign rivals, but it also has to go beyond national borders in order to make larger scale profits in the international market. The recently created Asia Infrastructure Investment Bank, which aims to export surplus capital from China to support the construction of infrastructure, including railways, roads, bridges, ports and airports throughout Asia from November 2014, is heavily dependent on the construction industry. At the same time, China Railway Group Limited and China Railway Construction Corporation Limited are the two largest construction companies in China. These two companies are also the world's two largest companies in terms of capital. Alongside a third company, China State Construction, whose power is growing, is taking third place. Overall, the Chinese construction industry has made remarkable progress in foreign markets, mainly in developing countries. However, it is having difficulty penetrating developed country markets, as the case of China Railway Group Limited shows.
Keywords: WTO, Asia Infrastructure Investment Bank, Chinese construction enterprises, China Railway Group Limited, China Railway Construction Corporation Limited, China State Construction
JEL Classification: F14, L24, L74, L92, N65, N85

Résumé
Les activités internationales de la construction chinoise. Le cas de la « China Railway Group Limited »
Face à l'entrée de la Chine dans l'Organisation mondiale du commerce depuis 2001, non seulement l'industrie de la construction, encore en cours de réforme, doit se battre contre de puissants rivaux étrangers, mais elle doit aussi sortir des frontières nationales dans le but de réaliser des profits à plus grande échelle sur le marché international. L'Asia Infrastructure Investment Bank, récemment créée, qui vise à exporter de Chine les capitaux excédentaires pour soutenir la construction d'infrastructures, notamment de chemins de fer, de routes, de ponts, de ports et d'aéroports dans toute l'Asie depuis novembre 2014, dépend largement de l'industrie de la construction. Dans le même temps, China Railway Group Limited et China Railway Construction Corporation Limited sont les deux plus grandes entreprises de construction en Chine. Ces deux entreprises sont également les deux plus grandes entreprises mondiales en

termes de capital. À leurs côtés une troisième entreprise, China State Construction, dont la puissance est en pleine croissance, a pris la troisième place. D'une manière générale, l'industrie chinoise de la construction a fait des progrès remarquables sur les marchés étrangers, principalement dans les pays en développement. Mais elle a des difficultés à percer les marchés des pays développés, comme le montre le cas de la China Railway Group Limited.

Mots-clés : OMC, Asia Infrastructure Investment Bank, entreprises de construction chinoises, China Railway Group Limited, China Railway Construction Corporation Limited, China State Construction

Chapter 14 - **The Korean Economic "Miracle" between the State and the Chaebols (1953-Today)**

Dominique Barjot & Rang-Ri Park

Abstract

Together with Taiwan, South Korea is therefore one of the best illustrations of Rostow's theories. After Japan's economic takeoff, South Korea experienced another "Miracle". From the 1960s onwards, the country benefited from rapid economic development, based on the growth of exports and, with some delay, the domestic market for mass consumption. From the point of view of the dominant historiography, the most important factors of success were American aid and cooperation between the state and the large conglomerates (or *chaebols*). This is not untrue, but must be qualified. The different experiences of the steel industry, shipbuilding and the automobile industry clearly point in this direction; on the contrary, the case of electronics leads us to relativize the importance of this link, as shown by the examples of LG and Samsung: two growth models have coexisted. The economic success of South Korea is largely due to a remarkable mobilization of human capital. The school and university system seems to have succeeded. Above all, South Korea has a massive research and development effort. At the microeconomic level, South Korea has benefited from the positive effects of international specialization, as shown by the example of shipbuilding or that of Posco, the fifth largest steel company in the world. At the same time, South Korea has made a successful breakthrough in the field of electronics, thanks to LG and Samsung. Today South Korea still benefits from strong assets: a good quality of life, an absolute priority given to new technologies, a voluntarist choice in favor of "green growth" and the growing strength of the Korean cultural model.

Keywords: Korean Economic Miracle, Rostow, *chaebols*, shipbuilding, Posco, Samsung, LG, human capital, green growth

JEL Classification: B25, D22, H52, L22, N15, N35, N45, N65, N85

Résumé

Le « miracle » économique coréen entre l'État et les Chaebols (1953-aujourd'hui)

Avec Taiwan, la Corée du Sud est donc l'une des meilleures illustrations des théories de Rostow. Après le décollage économique du Japon, la Corée du Sud a connu un autre « Miracle ». À partir des années 1960, le pays a bénéficié d'un développement économique rapide, basé sur la croissance des exportations, et, avec un certain retard, du marché intérieur de consommation de masse. Du point de vue de l'historiographie dominante, les facteurs de succès les plus importants ont été l'aide américaine et la coopération entre l'État et les grands conglomérats (ou *chaebols*). Cela n'est pas faux mais doit être nuancé. Les différentes expériences de la sidérurgie, de la construction navale et de l'industrie automobile vont clairement dans ce sens ; au contraire, le cas de l'électronique amène à relativiser l'importance de ce lien, comme le montrent les exemples de LG et de Samsung : deux modèles de croissance ont coexisté. La réussite économique de la Corée du Sud est en grande partie due à une remarquable mobilisation du capital humain. Le système scolaire et universitaire semble avoir réussi. Surtout, la Corée du Sud fournit un effort massif de recherche et de développement. Sur le plan micro-économique, la Corée du Sud a bénéficié des effets positifs de la spécialisation internationale, comme le montre l'exemple de la construction navale ou celui de Posco, la cinquième entreprise sidérurgique du monde. Dans le même temps, la Corée du Sud a réalisé une percée réussie dans le domaine de l'électronique, grâce à LG et Samsung. Aujourd'hui la Corée du Sud bénéficie toujours d'atouts forts : une bonne qualité de vie, une priorité absolue donnée aux nouvelles technologies, un choix volontariste en faveur de la «croissance verte» et la force croissante du modèle culturel coréen.

Mots-clés : Miracle économique coréen, Rostow, *chaebols*, constructions navales, Posco, Samsung, LG, capital humain, croissance verte

Chapter 15 - **Việt Nam: The Rise of a New Industrialized Nation**
Dominique Barjot

Abstract

Vietnam belongs to the group of "Asian Tigers", but like China, Indonesia or Malaysia, it has overcome the 1997-98 financial crisis quite well. The regularity of its growth raises questions about the relevant interpretative model(s). Densely populated and marked by history, Vietnam has established its national integration on a southward march and highland assimilation. Despite an unfinished demographic transition, the population has remained young and feminized. At the same time, Vietnamese culture, marked by the Confucian influence, developed around the original language and writing. In Vietnam, the end of a centralized economic system and the decisive influence of the South paved the way for a premature transition to a free market characterized by the call for foreign aid, the rise of informal activities and the gradual but incomplete privatization of the state sector. The consequence has been a profound change. In December 1980, the *Dôi moi* strategy was adopted, which recognized the market economy, encouraged individual initiative, rehabilitated the company without abandoning the socialist framework. The success is undeniable. Despite the financial crisis of 1997-98, Vietnam became fully integrated into Asian trade. From 1986 onwards, Vietnam experienced a high GDP growth rate. As a result, it has become one of the most open Asian economies to international trade. Among the "Asian Tigers", with the exception of Indonesia, Vietnam is the one with the highest

growth potential, as it has an efficient labor market, a strong capacity for innovation, a progressive economic opening, and a position as a privileged subcontractor for Japanese and South Korean industries.
Keywords: Asian Tigers, *Dôi moi*, socialist market economy, privatisations, informal economy, international subcontracting
JEL Classification: B24, F15, F54, L32, N15, N45, N55, N65

Résumé

Việt Nam : L'émergence d'une nouvelle nation industrialisée

Le Vietnam fait partie du groupe des « Tigres asiatiques », mais comme la Chine, l'Indonésie ou la Malaisie, il a assez bien surmonté la crise financière de 1997-98. La régularité de sa croissance soulève des questions sur le ou les modèles d'interprétation pertinents. Densément peuplé et marqué par l'histoire, le Vietnam a établi son intégration nationale sur une marche vers le Sud et une assimilation des hautes terres. Malgré une transition démographique inachevée, la population est restée jeune et féminisée. En même temps, la culture vietnamienne, marquée par l'influence confucéenne, s'est développée autour de la langue et de l'écriture originales. Au Vietnam, la fin d'un système d'économie centralisée et l'influence décisive du Sud ont ouvert la voie à une transition prématurée vers un marché libre caractérisé à la fois par l'appel à l'aide étrangère, la montée des activités informelles et la privatisation progressive, mais inachevée du secteur d'État. La conséquence a été un changement profond. En décembre 1980, est adoptée la stratégie du *Dôi moi*, qui reconnaît l'économie de marché, encourage l'initiative individuelle, réhabilite l'entreprise sans abandonner le cadre socialiste. Le succès est indéniable. Malgré la crise financière de 1997-98, le Vietnam s'est pleinement intégré dans le commerce asiatique. À partir de 1986, le Vietnam a connu un taux de croissance élevé du PIB. En conséquence, il est devenu l'une des économies asiatiques les plus ouvertes aux échanges internationaux. Parmi les « Tigres asiatiques », à l'exception de l'Indonésie, le Vietnam est celui qui a le plus fort potentiel de croissance, car il dispose d'un marché du travail efficace, d'une forte capacité d'innovation, d'une ouverture économique progressive, d'une position de sous-traitant privilégié pour les industries japonaises et sud-coréennes.
Mots-clés : Tigres asiatiques, *Dôi moi*, économie socialiste de marché, privatisations, économie informelle, sous-traitance internationale

Chapter 16 - **Expectations and Strategies of German Business in India during Decolonization & Import-Substitution-Industrialization in the 1950s and 1960s**

Julian Faust

Abstract

The internationalisation of European firms outside of the continent after 1945 took place within the broad context of Cold War and decolonisation. This chapter analyses German MNE in postcolonial India. It deals with the ways and strategies of private business to re-enter a market that was defined by a socialist model of economic

planning. India became a metaphor for a future market. This led to early investments to build networks despite an economic framework in India which did not fit well with western economic ideologies. Business networks, state support and a careful positioning of joint ventures as German helped to secure market shares. This analysis supports the findings that German business was flexible enough to adapt to differing economic systems and ideologies.
Keywords: Multinational enterprise, development assistance, decolonisation, business history, India

JEL Classification: N8, N84, N86, O25

Résumé

Attentes et stratégies des entreprises allemandes en Inde pendant la décolonisation et la subdivision des importations dans l'industrialisation des années 1950 et 1960

L'internationalisation des entreprises européennes hors du continent après 1945 s'est déroulée dans le contexte général de la guerre froide et de la décolonisation. Ce chapitre analyse les entreprises multinationales allemandes dans l'Inde postcoloniale. Il traite des moyens et des stratégies des entreprises privées pour réintégrer un marché qui était défini par un modèle socialiste de planification économique. L'Inde est devenue une métaphore d'un futur marché. Cela a conduit à des investissements précoces pour construire des réseaux malgré un cadre économique en Inde qui ne correspondait pas bien aux idéologies économiques occidentales. Les réseaux d'entreprises, le soutien de l'État et un positionnement prudent des entreprises communes en tant qu'allemandes ont contribué à garantir les parts de marché. Cette analyse confirme les conclusions selon lesquelles les entreprises allemandes étaient suffisamment flexibles pour s'adapter à des systèmes économiques et des idéologies différents.
Mots-clés : entreprise multinationale, aide au développement, décolonisation, histoire des affaires, Inde

Chapter 17 - **Le développement économique péruvien durant les années 1950 et 1960 : distinguer deux modèles ?**

Getsiva Cayo Durand de Geist

Abstract

Peruvian economic development during the 1950s and 1960s: distinguishing two models?

This article contemplates the economic models favoured by the governments of Peru throughout the 1950s and 1960s. While the majority of Latin American countries adopted protectionist policies after World War II, Peru initially decided to become a firm disciple of economic liberalism. The Peruvian governments strived to initiate the *take-off* of the Peruvian economy by following the concepts of W.W. Rostow. Nevertheless, the impact of R. Prebisch's protectionist thought was constantly increasing and the implementation of respective measures expanded since the early 1960s. Is it possible to distinguish only between those two antagonistic models? In reality, the successive Peruvian governments applied a particular mix of economic policies. In this context, it was possible to envisage a Peruvian "third way" to accomplish the economic *take-off*. The analysis of the conditions, and results of Peru's contradictory quest for economic development, therefore, requires a more nuanced perspective.

Keywords: Latin American models for economic development, economic policy of Peru, 1950s-1960s.

JEL Classification: H11, N16

Résumé

Cet article s'interroge sur les modèles économiques préconisés par les gouvernements péruviens au cours des années 1950 et 1960. Tandis que la plupart des pays d'Amérique latine adoptaient des politiques protectionnistes après la Seconde Guerre mondiale, le Pérou préférait devenir un partisan ferme du libéralisme. Au sein du système multilatéral, les gouvernements cherchaient le *take-off* de l'économie péruvienne en suivant les concepts de W.W. Rostow. Néanmoins, la pensée de R. Prebisch s'installa progressivement. La montée des politiques protectionnistes a été mise en œuvre dès le début des années soixante. Ce pays était à la recherche de son modèle de développement économique, mais peut-on distinguer deux modèles de développement économique uniquement ? Les gouvernements successifs péruviens ont adopté aussi des modèles mixtes. Une « troisième voie » à la péruvienne a vu le jour en vue de réussir le démarrage économique. Il s'agit de mettre en discussion les conditions, les contradictions et les résultats de cette recherche.

Mots clés : modèles de développement économique Pérou-Amérique latine / politique économique Pérou / 1950-1960.

Chapter 18 - **Networks of experts and political actors in the World Bank's early programs. Loans in Colombia and their overall effects on aid to development (1940- 1954)**

Elisa Grandi

Abstract

This chapter studies the World Bank's early loans in Colombia from its early missions and until 1954. After describing the World Bank's organizational structure, it focuses on Colombian missions to uncover its advisors' networks and how they affected the loans' orientation. To analyze these interactions, I built a relational database collecting some 1500 letters exchanged among the actors involved, in which more than 900 actors appear. The network analysis on these actors, combined with a study of the World Bank missions' microstructure, conveys new insights on World Bank policies. Specifically, it enlightens some local actors' role in the decision-making process concerning the loans' approval and orientation and shows the impact of the World Bank's early missions on Colombian economic institutions.

Keywords: World Bank, Columbia, experts and missions

JEL classification: N00, N26, N86, O20

Résumé

Réseaux d'experts et d'acteurs politiques dans les premiers programmes de la Banque mondiale. Les prêts en Colombie et leurs effets globaux sur l'aide au développement (1940- 1954)

Ce chapitre étudie les premiers prêts de la Banque mondiale en Colombie depuis ses premières missions jusqu'en 1954. Après avoir décrit la structure organisationnelle de la Banque mondiale, il se concentre sur les missions colombiennes pour découvrir les réseaux de ses conseillers et la manière dont ils ont affecté l'orientation des prêts. Pour analyser ces interactions, j'ai construit une base de données relationnelle rassemblant quelque 1500 lettres échangées les plus de 900 acteurs impliqués. L'analyse des réseaux de ces acteurs, combinée à une étude de la microstructure des missions de la Banque mondiale, éclaire le rôle de certains acteurs locaux dans le processus décisionnel concernant l'approbation et l'orientation des prêts et montre l'impact des premières missions de la Banque mondiale sur les institutions économiques colombiennes.

Mots clés : Banque mondiale, Colombie, missions d'experts

Chapter 19 - **Cemex (1906-2008) or the Rise of a Mexican Multinational**

Dominique Barjot

Abstract

Cemex was the fifth largest cement production capacity in the world in 2008 and the fourth largest company in the world in terms of turnover. Above all, the group is now the world leader in ready-mixed concrete. Cemex is an archetypal example of the rise of emerging global companies. This company, founded in 1906, is a symbol of the success of capitalism in Monterrey and Mexico City. It was originally owned by the Zambrano family, a trading house operating since the mid-19th century. In 1982, a decisive economic crisis led to intense restructuring and internationalization. Cemex thus became an original model. It appears to be the world leader in white cement and trading, has the most advanced information and communication technologies in the cement industry, is very creative in financial solutions, and benefits from the lowest costs in its sector. Cemex has also established itself as Mexico's first true multinational. In 2009-2010, the Cemex group experienced a very serious financial crisis, which it overcame by adapting to the new market dynamics. In 2020, the group remains largely in the hands of the Zembrano family. Today, despite its smaller size, Cemex remains highly competitive compared to its main European and Chinese competitors.

Keywords: cement industry, ready-mixed concrete, Zembrano family, Monterrey, multinational firm

JEL Classification: D22, F61, L13, L62, L74, N66, N86

Résumé

Cemex (1906-2008) ou la naissance d'une multinationale mexicaine

Cemex était la cinquième capacité de production de ciment au monde en 2008 et la quatrième entreprise mondiale en termes de chiffre d'affaires. Surtout le groupe est aujourd'hui le leader mondial du béton prêt à l'emploi. Cemex constitue un exemple archétypal de la montée en puissance des entreprises mondiales émergentes. Cette entreprise fondée en 1906 constitue un symbole du succès du capitalisme à Monterrey et à Mexico. À l'origine, se trouve la famille Zambrano, une maison de commerce opérant depuis le milieu du XIXe siècle. En 1982, une crise économique décisive a conduit à une restructuration et une internationalisation intenses. Cemex est devenu ainsi un modèle original. Il apparaît à la fois comme le leader mondial du ciment blanc et du négoce, dispose des technologies de l'information et de la communication les plus avancées dans l'industrie du ciment, est très créatif en matière de solutions financières, et bénéficie des coûts les plus bas de son secteur. Cemex s'est également imposée comme la première véritable multinationale du Mexique. En 2009-2010, le groupe Cemex a connu une très grave crise financière, qu'il a surmontée en s'adaptant à la nouvelle dynamique du marché. En 2020, le groupe reste largement entre les mains de la famille Zembrano. Aujourd'hui, en dépit de sa plus petite taille, Cemex demeure largement compétitif par rapport à ses principaux concurrents européens et chinois.

Mots-clés : industrie cimentière, béton prêt à l'emploi, Famille Zembrano, Monterrey, firme multinationale

Chapter 20 - **Becoming a multinational mining company: the case of Vale (Brazil)**

Hildete de Moraes Vodopives

Abstract

The internationalization of companies from developing countries is a novel feature of contemporary globalization. Inverting the trend of capital flows, they represent what the Boston Consulting Group calls the *Global Challengers*: "a group of emerging challengers that are becoming important players in both developing and developed countries around the globe." Among them is the Brazilian company Vale. Taking into account the specificities of the mining industry, this paper exams the factors influencing the company's road towards internationalization. As a state controlled company, Vale had the support of the government, interested in developing the Brazilian economy. However, since its foundation in 1942, Vale experienced a number of challenges: a small local market, deficient infrastructure and lack of Brazilian capital. The company had no alternative but to focus in the international market. When the company was privatized in 1997, Vale was by far the mining leader in Brazil, but the company's international presence remained modest. After defining a long-term strategy, the company announced a strategic plan where the main goal was to transform Vale into a global player.

Keywords: Emerging countries, Brazil, mining, strategy, globalization
JEL Classification: D22, G34, L25, L26, L61, L72, N66, N86

Résumé

Devenir une société minière multinationale : le cas de Vale (Brésil)

L'internationalisation des entreprises des pays en développement est une caractéristique nouvelle de la mondialisation contemporaine. Inversant la tendance des flux de capitaux, elles représentent ce que le Boston Consulting Group appelle les «Global Challengers» : «un groupe de challengers émergents qui deviennent des acteurs importants à la fois dans les pays en développement et dans les pays développés à travers le monde». Parmi eux, on trouve la société brésilienne Vale. En tenant compte des spécificités de l'industrie minière, cet article examine les facteurs qui influencent le cheminement de l'entreprise vers l'internationalisation. En tant qu'entreprise contrôlée par l'État, Vale bénéficiait du soutien du gouvernement, intéressé par le développement de l'économie brésilienne. Cependant, depuis sa fondation en 1942, Vale a dû faire face à un certain nombre de défis : un marché local restreint, des infrastructures déficientes et un manque de capitaux brésiliens. L'entreprise n'avait d'autre choix que de se concentrer sur le marché international. Lorsque l'entreprise a été privatisée en 1997, Vale était de loin le leader de l'industrie minière au Brésil, mais la présence internationale de l'entreprise est restée modeste. Après avoir défini une stratégie à long terme, l'entreprise a annoncé un plan stratégique dont le principal objectif était de transformer Vale en un acteur mondial.

Mots clés : pays émergents, Brésil, exploitation minière, stratégie, mondialisation

Chapter 21 - **L'Égypte : réalité et limites d'une voie nationale de développement**

Caroline Piquet

Abstract

Egypt: Reality and limits of a national path of development

Under the leadership of Muhammad Ali, Egypt experienced significant economic development in the 19th century, supported by European capital. The latter contribute to the economic opening of the country and to its modernization in terms of equipment, but associated with political domination, they also generate violent tensions. The link between economic openness and colonial domination that developed at the end of the 19th century had strong implications for 20th century economic models. Successive regimes are faced with the difficulty of finding a path of economic development that can both rely on the necessary external financing while being at the service of national reform.

Keywords: Muhammed Ali, European capital, Canal Company, Great Britain, France, Colonel Nasser, Anwar-el Sadat, Hosni Mubarak

JEL Classification: N45

Résumé

Sous l'impulsion de Muhammad Ali, l'Égypte connait au XIXe siècle un développement économique important, soutenu par les capitaux européens. Ces derniers contribuent à l'ouverture économique du pays et à sa modernisation en termes

d'équipements, mais associés à une tutelle politique, ils génèrent aussi de violentes tensions. L'association entre ouverture économique et domination coloniale qui se noue à la fin du XIXe siècle a de fortes implications sur les modèles économiques du XXe siècle. Les régimes qui se succèdent sont confrontés à la difficulté de trouver une voie de développement économique qui puisse à la fois s'appuyer sur les nécessaires financements extérieurs tout en étant au service de la réforme nationale.
Mots clés : Muhammed Ali, European capital, Compagnie du canal de Suez, Grande-Bretagne, France, colonel Nasser, Anouar-el Sadate, Hosni Moubarak

Chapter 22 - **Oil and development in Algeria (1956-2000)**
Marta Musso

Abstract

This paper analyses the economic history of Algeria as an independent country, and the relations between the economic policies adopted by the governments in the first 50 years of its independence and the oil and gas industry. The Algerian hydrocarbon industry is intertwined with the independence process; while oil and gas have always played an important role in the economic and political history of the country, it is important to adopt a multi-faceted approach rather than the mechanistic outlook offered by the "oil curse" theories. The history of Algeria offers the opportunity to analyze the case of an oil-producer country in the wider international, social, and political context in which a newly-independent country operated.
Keywords: development, Algeria, industrialization, post-colonial economies, oil curse

JEL Classification: 013

Résumé

Pétrole et développement en Algérie (1956-2000)

Ce papier analyses l'histoire économique de l'Algérie en tant que pays indépendante, et les relations entre la politique économique adopté par le gouvernement dans les premiers 50 ans d'indépendance et l'industrie du gaz et du pétrole. L'industrie des hydrocarbures en Algérie est profondément liée au procès d'indépendance, et le gaz e le pétrole ont toujours joué un rôle importante dans l'histoire économique et politique du pays. Pour cette raison, il est important d'adopter une approche multi-facettes plutôt que les perspectives mécanistes offertes par les théories sur la « malédiction du pétrole ». L'histoire de l'Algérie offre la possibilité de conduire une analyse sur un pays producteur dans le complexe contexte internationale, sociale, et politique dans lequel un pays de nouvelle indépendance opérait.
Mots-clés : développement, Algérie, industrialisation, économies postcoloniales, malédiction du pétrole

Chapter 23 - **The North-South Negotiations in the Sixties: The Case Of Tunisia With The EEC**

Mohamed Sassi

Abstract

The awareness of Tunisia's re-entry into negotiations with the European Economic Community (EEC) was only made, at the level of Tunisian diplomacy, following the relative recovery in relations with France, independence of Algeria and especially the establishment of a new agricultural regime at the level of the EEC, the common agricultural policy (CAP) in 1962. Tunisia being mainly an agricultural country, the CAP posed a real problem for the Tunisian economy. In addition, the multilateral challenges for the Europe of the Six since 1957 were not without risk for the future of traditional trade flows, and particularly of agricultural exports from Tunisia to France and Europe. Exploratory conversations for a new status for Tunisia with the (EEC) only began a few years after independence in 1956. The long process of discussions and negotiations led to a first agreement only in 1969, the results of which were largely negative for Tunisia. That opens up a second stage of negotiation, within the framework of the Global Mediterranean Policy designed by the European Commission in 1972 for the benefit of the EEC. Those were circumstances which would condition the future of relations between Tunisia and Europe.

Keywords: North / South, negotiation, bilateral, multilateral, international relations, economic history, EEC, EEC-Tunisia, Tunisia, Tunisia-Maghreb

JEL Classification: E65, H12, F02, F31, N47, N80, N87, O01, O11, O19, O52, O55, O57, P33, P45

Résumé

Les négociations Nord-Sud dans les années 60 : Le cas de la Tunisie avec la CEE

La prise de conscience de la rentrée en négociation de la Tunisie avec la Communauté Économique Européenne (CEE) ne s'est faite, au niveau de la diplomatie tunisienne, qu'à la suite du redressement relatif des rapports avec la France, l'indépendance de l'Algérie et surtout l'instauration d'un nouveau régime agricole au niveau de la CEE, la politique agricole commune (PAC) en 1962. La Tunisie étant principalement un pays agricole, la PAC pose un véritable problème pour l'économie tunisienne. De plus, les enjeux multilatéraux pour l'Europe des Six depuis 1957, ne sont pas sans risque pour l'avenir des flux traditionnels des échanges et particulièrement des exportations agricole de la Tunisie vers la France et l'Europe. Les conversations exploratoires pour un nouveau statut de la Tunisie avec la (CEE) n'ont commencé que quelques années après l'indépendance de 1956. La longue marche de discussions et de négociations n'aboutira à un premier accord qu'en 1969 dont les résultats sont largement négatifs pour la Tunisie. S'ouvre ainsi une deuxième étape de négociation, dans le cadre de la politique méditerranéenne globale conçue par la Commission européenne en 1972 au bénéfice de la CEE. Il s'agit de circonstances qui conditionneront l'avenir des rapports entre la Tunisie et l'Europe.

Mots clés : Nord/Sud, négociation, bilatérale, multilatérale, relations internationales, histoire économique, CEE, CEE-Tunisie, Tunisie, Tunisie-Maghreb.

Chapter 24 - **Afrique de l'Ouest : deux modèles de développement comparés, le Sénégal de Léopold Sédar Senghor et la Côte d'Ivoire de Houphouët - Boigny**
Joseph-Pierre E. Diouf

Abstract

West Africa: two models of development in comparison, the Senegal of Léopold Sédar Senghor and the Ivory Coast from Houphouët - Boigny

Senegal and Côte d'Ivoire were the two privileged colonies of the former French colonial power in West Africa. After the Second World War, which was in the process of decolonization, their leaders in these territories, Léopold Sédar Senghor and Félix Houphouët-Boigny, condemned colonial policies. While Senghor created the Senegalese Democratic Bloc (BDS), Houphouët-Boigny founded the Democratic Party of Côte d'Ivoire (PDCI). Through these political parties and their activism, the two leaders were at the forefront of the negotiations that led to independence. Strong supporters of maintaining the link with the former colonial power, they did not want immediate independence. Thus, the former became president of the Republic of Senegal while the latter was elevated to the presidency of Côte d'Ivoire. However, the two men had different visions of the development of their countries and had also inherited different economic structures from the colonization. As a result, the two countries had different development trajectories. Léopold Sédar Senghor defends and theorizes a development model based on African socialism. He advocates a total break with the colonial legacy, but both reject Marxist-Leninist socialism and the Western capitalist model in the context of the Cold War. Furthermore, Senghor conceives and implements a theory of endogenous development. At the same time Félix Houphouët-Boigny, he chose the liberalism inherited from the colonial development policy and placed Côte d'Ivoire in the Western camp. Nevertheless, cash crops (cocoa and coffee in Côte d'Ivoire, groundnuts in Senegal) remain the pillars of development. However, if these crops have made the wealth of these two countries as witnessed by the "Ivorian miracle", it nevertheless led to bankruptcy at the end of the 1970s.

Keywords: Senegal, Ivory Coast, Léopold Sédar Senghor, Félix Houphouët-Boigny, African Socialism, "Ivorian Miracle".

JEL Classification: B24, N17, N37, N47, N57

Résumé

Le Sénégal et la Côte d'Ivoire étaient les deux colonies privilégiées de l'ancienne puissance coloniale française en Afrique de l'Ouest. Après la Seconde Guerre mondiale, en voie de décolonisation, leurs dirigeants dans ces territoires, à savoir Léopold Seder Senghor et Félix Houphouët-Boigny, ont condamné les politiques coloniales. Tandis que Senghor crée le Bloc Démocratique Sénégalais (BDS), Houphouët-Boigny fonde le Parti Démocrate de Côte-d'Ivoire (PDCI). Grâce à ces partis politiques et à leur militantisme, les deux dirigeants ont été à l'avant-garde des négociations qui ont conduit à l'indépendance. Fervents partisans du maintien du lien avec l'ancienne puissance coloniale, ils n'ont pas voulu d'une indépendance immédiate. Ainsi, le premier est devenu président de la République du Sénégal tandis que le second a été élevé à la présidence de la Côte d'Ivoire. Cependant, les deux hommes avaient des visions différentes du développement de leur pays et avaient également hérité, de la colonisation, de structures économiques différentes. En conséquence, les deux pays ont eu des trajectoires de développement différentes. Léopold Seder Senghor défend et théorise un modèle de développement basé sur le socialisme africain. Il prône une rupture totale avec l'héritage colonial, mais tous deux rejettent le socialisme marxiste-léniniste et le modèle capitaliste occidental dans un contexte de guerre froide. En outre, Senghor conçoit et met en œuvre une théorie du développement endogène. Quant à Félix Houphouët-Boigny, il choisit le libéralisme hérité de la politique coloniale de développement et a inscrit la Côte d'Ivoire dans le camp occidental. Néanmoins, les cultures de rente (le cacao et le café au Côte d'Ivoire, l'arachide au Sénégal) restent les piliers du développement. Cependant, si ces cultures ont fait la richesse de ces deux pays comme en témoigne le «miracle ivoirien», celui-ci a néanmoins conduit à la faillite à la fin des années 1970.

Mots-clés : Sénégal, Côte d'Ivoire, Léopold Sédar Senghor, Félix Houphouët-Boigny, Socialisme africain, « Miracle ivorien »

Table of authors

Dominique Barjot is Professor Emeritus of Contemporary Economic History at the Sorbonne University of Letters and a member of the French Academy of Overseas Sciences. Former Deputy Director of the SHS at the CNRS (1994-1997) and French representative on the Standing Committee of the European Science Foundation (1994-1998), he was also Scientific Director of Human Sciences and Humanities at the Ministry of Higher Education and Research (2003-2007) and Director of the Doctoral School of Modern and Contemporary History (ED 188) at the University of Paris-Sorbonne (Paris-IV) (2002-2010). President, since 2017, of the French Committee of Historical Sciences, former president of the French Association of Economic Historians (1998-2001), he is the author of numerous books and journal articles, among which, in 2019 and 2020 : (dir.), with Anna Bellavitis, Olivier Feiertag and Bertrand Haan, *Regards croisés sur l'historiographie française aujourd'hui*, Paris, Éditions SPM, 2020, 302 p.; (ed), "Theory and Empirical Performance. Economic Paradigm and Performance in the Long Run (18th to 21st century)", *Revue française d'histoire économique - The French Economic History Review*, n° 11-12 (n°1-, 2019), 354 p.

Née à Cuzco (Pérou) en 1986, **Getsiva Cayo Durand de Geist** est issue d'une famille d'entrepreneurs et d'enseignants résidant depuis des siècles dans la capitale des Incas. Après avoir effectué ses études à l'université San Antonio Abad, elle décide de se spécialiser en histoire récente. Son premier mémoire s'est penché sur la problématique des mouvements religieux non catholiques à Cuzco entre 1980 et 2008. Son intérêt pour l'histoire des relations internationales la conduira à s'installer en France. Elle est diplômée d'un master (2010) à l'université Paris-Sorbonne dans la spécialité « Enjeux, conflits et systèmes internationaux à l'époque moderne et contemporaine ». À la suite de la réalisation de son mémoire, dirigé par M. Dominique Barjot, elle a constaté l'importance de l'histoire économique au sein des relations Nord-Sud. Mme Cayo, désirant élargir ses travaux de master, est actuellement étudiante en dernière année de doctorat. Sa thèse intitulée *Les relations économiques, financières et commerciales entre le Pérou et la France (1945-1975)* est constituée de dix chapitres issus d'années de recherche auprès d'archives en France, au Pérou, en Italie et en Belgique.

Chercheuse associée au Centre Roland Mounier de Sorbonne Université, chargée d'enseignement à l'ICP et professeure d'Histoire dans l'enseignement secondaire, **Cécile Coursiéras-Jaff** est docteure en histoire économique de l'Université Paris Sorbonne (Paris IV), elle a soutenu une thèse sur l'histoire de l'entreprise cimentière Poliet et Chausson. Ses travaux portent sur l'histoire des entreprises et l'histoire industrielle, plus particulièrement celle de l'aluminium et du ciment. Elle a rédigé plusieurs articles notamment sur les rapports entre les entreprises et les banques et sur les cartels du ciment à l'échelle européenne et mondiale.

Agrégé d'histoire, ancien élève de l'École normale supérieure (Ulm), ancien pensionnaire de la Fondation Thiers (Institut de France - CNRS), **François David** est maître de conférences, habilité à diriger des recherches, à l'Université Jean Moulin, Lyon 3. Il y dirige le laboratoire E.A. 4586 «*Francophonie, mondialisation et relations internationales*». Il travaille, entre autres, sur les relations transatlantiques (*John Foster Dulles, secrétaire d'État,* Cold Warrior *et père de l'Europe*, PUPS, 2010), les questions diplomatiques et militaires, ainsi que sur le renseignement américain (*L'aigle et le vautour – La naissance de la CIA 1945-1961,* Nouveau monde Éditions, 2016). Son prochain ouvrage, *Le XXIe siècle sera-t-il wilsonien ?* (PUPS) traitera du devenir du multilatéralisme et de la démocratie libérale dans le système international de l'après-Guerre froide. Un autre versant de ses recherches porte sur les influences culturelles et les rapports de puissances dans les aires francophones, en contexte multilatéral. Il est directeur-adjoint de l'*Institut international pour la Francophonie*, chargé de la recherche.

Joseph-Pierre Diouf est professeur d'histoire-géographie en classes de BTS commerce. Chercheur associé à l'UMR 8596 Centre Roland Mousnier, il est docteur de Sorbonne Université, avec une thèse en cotutelle (Sorbonne Université - Cheikh Anta Diop de Dakar) sur les relations économiques et financières de la France et du Sénégal à l'époque de la présidence de Léopold Sédar Senghor.

Julian Faust holds a B.A. in *Philosophy & Economics* from the University of Bayreuth and M.A. in *Economic & Social History* from the University of Göttingen (Germany). He pursued his doctoral dissertation at the University of Marburg (Germany) on the re-internationalisation of German companies in India after the Second World War until the end of the 1980s during a phase of decolonisation. This work evolved within a research project funded by the German Research Foundation on German companies in India at Institute for Economic and Social History, University of Marburg (2017-2020).

Elisa Grandi is Associate Professor (Maitre de Conferences) at the University of Paris and PIERI Institute since 2020. She holds a PhD Thesis from the University of Paris Diderot and University of Bologna and she is specialized in economic and business history; international financial organizations; social network analysis and digital humanities. Her research covers two main fields: 1) the history of international financial organizations and their loans in Latin America and Europe and 2) the financialization of the French firms in the Twentieth century. She analyzes firms' organization, networks and governance, as well as the international programs and institutions financing them.

Born in 1943 at Reims (France), **Michel Hau** has studied History at the Sorbonne from 1960 to 1965 and then at the University Paris 10-Nanterre (Ph D in 1973). Recruited as assistant at Strasbourg University in 1970, he achieved in 1985, under the direction of Prof. Maurice Levy-Leboyer, at University Paris 10-Nanterre, a thesis on the industrialization of Alsace from 1803 to 1939.He became professor of economic and social history at Strasbourg University in 1987. Michel Hau has published articles and books about regional long-term growth in France, history of entreprises in the Rhenish regions, German economy and deindustrialization in Europe from 1974 to the present day.

Mária Hidvégi is a historian of Tungsram Group. She wrote her PhD thesis about Tungsram and Ganz & Co. at Leipzig University. In her thesis (Anschluss an den Weltmarkt – Ungarns elektrotechnische Leitunternehmen 1867-1949, Vandenhoeck & Ruprecht, Göttingen, 2016) and in various presentations and articles (e.g. "Crises and Responses: Government Policies and the Machine-Building Cartels in Hungary, 1919-1949", in *Enterprise and Society* Vol. 20, No. 1, March 2019, 89-131.) she has dealt with various topics concerning the role of international and national cartels for small countries using the example of these companies, electrification in East-Central Europe, and the role of statistical knowledge production in the development of economic thought in Hungary before 1848.

Pierre Lanthier est professeur retraité au département des Sciences humaines de l'Université du Québec à Trois-Rivières et membre du Centre interuniversitaire d'études québécoises depuis sa création. Il a obtenu son doctorat en 1988 de l'Université de Paris-X (Nanterre). Il a publié en histoire des entreprises (en particulier celles liées à l'électricité et à l'aluminium en France et au Québec) et en histoire municipale et régionale (notamment les villes et villages dans les régions de la Mauricie et de Lanaudière). Depuis quelques années, il s'est intéressé à l'économie de l'Inde contemporaine, et plus spécifiquement à la production d'énergie dans ce pays.

Kenichi Miyata is a Senior Assistant Professor of Business History at the School of Business Administration, Meiji University, Tokyo, Japan. He received his Ph.D. in 2016 from the Graduate School of Business Administration, Meiji University. His main research interests includes corporate diversification and manager's beliefs. He is currently working on projects on the global business history of heavy electrical equipment firms in twentieth century, evolution of content industries in the twentieth century in Japan, history of media industries in the United States. He has published several scholarly articles dealing with business enterprises of electrical equipment and PC industries in the United States.

Hildete de Moraes Vodopives, is a fellow researcher of the Centre Roland Mousnier, at Sorbonne University. She holds a PhD in economic history (Sorbonne) an MBA in capital markets (PUC) and a certificate in administration and management (Harvard). Her PhD dissertation focused on the internationalization of the Brazilian mining company Vale. Research topics include: emerging multinationals, natural resources regulation, cost of capital optimization, and long-term strategy planning. She participated in numerous scientific publications addressing: global competitiveness, market entry strategies, emerging markets, foreign direct investments, mega events intangible impacts (COPPE / UFRJ - Paris XI), sustainability and urban challenges. She participated in the organization of sessions on competitiveness in Brazil (Brazilianists association Congress, 2019), development of large industrial food groups (Rural History Congress, 2019), regulation and competition in Brazil, (Pre-conference for the World Economic Congress, 2017). Hildete has a background in asset management and works with companies and government investment agencies in Latin America and Europe. She is partner of Investor Asset Management, served in the board of the Brazilian Analysts Association (APIMEC). She is member of the Ivy League Speakers.

Marta Musso is a historian working on energy history and digital humanities. She specialises in energy policies and State/company relations, as well as methodologies for research in a digital environment. As a research fellow of the Royal Institute of Technology (KTH), she is currently studying the development of the European oil industry in the background of the evolution of international markets after decolonisation. She is also the editor of the Resources section of the Journal of Energy History / Revue d'Histoire de l'Énergie (JEH/RHE), and Research Manager for Archives Portal Europe, as well as visiting fellow at the Grantham Research Institute (London School of Economics)

Rang-Ri Park-Barjot est docteur en Histoire de l'Université Paris-Sorbonne (aujourd'hui Sorbonne Université). Chercheure associée à l'UMR 8596 Centre Roland Mousnier, elle a publié deux livres : *La Société de Construction des Batignolles : des origines à la première guerre mondiale (1846-1914),* Presses de l'Université de Paris-Sorbonne, 2005, 542 p. ; *Samsung. L'œuvre d'un entrepreneur hors pair, Byung Chull Lee*, Paris, Economica, 2008, 266 p. Elle en a codirigé deux autres : (avec Dominique Barjot), « Aux origines du miracle coréen », *Conflits Actuels*, n° 22, 2008-2 ; (avec Flora Blanchon), *Le nouvel âge de Confucius*, PUPS, 2007, 367 p.. Elle est l'auteur de nombreux articles, parmi lequels, comme seule auteure : « Samsung : an original case of knownledge transfer in economic organizations », in Barjot (Dominique), Schröter (Harm G.), eds, “La circulation de l'information et des connaissances”, *Entreprises et Histoire*, n° 75, 2014, p. 91-101 ; “Les conséquences économiques de la guerre : la Corée du Sud de 1950 à 1979, de l'économie assistée au Take-off”, in Pierre Journoud (dir.), *La Guerre de Corée et ses enjeux stratégiques de 1950 à nos jours*, L'Harmattan, 2013, p. 303-318 ; « Mondialisation et avantage concurrentiel. La percée internationale de Samsung (1953-1986) », *Revue Économique*, vol. 58, n° 1, janvier 2007, p. 231-258 ; avec Dominique Barjot : « L'industrie des constructions navales : un secteur stratégique pour le take-off économique de la Corée du Sud (1945-

environs de 2000 », *Entreprises et Histoire*, n° 90, avril 2018, p. 51-75 ; « La Corée du Sud, un autre modèle Rhénan ? Samsung ou l'héritage de Lee Byung Chull », dans Lamard (Pierre) et Stoskopf (Nicolas) (dir.), *L'Entreprise rhénane. Mythe ou réalité ? Hommage à Michel Hau*, Paris, Picard, 2015, p. 95-109. « L'émergence d'un leader asiatique de la sidérurgie : POSCO (1968-2010) », in Charles Barthel, Ivan Kharaba, Philippe Mioche (dir.), *Les mutations de la sidérurgie mondiale du XXe siècle à nos jours*, PIE Peter Lang, 2014, p. 299-319.

Agrégée et docteur en histoire, **Caroline Piquet** est maîtresse de conférences en histoire contemporaine à Sorbonne-Université. Spécialiste de l'histoire économique et sociale de la Méditerranée et du Moyen-Orient et membre du centre Roland Mousnier (UMR 8596), elle est l'auteur de nombreux ouvrages et articles dont *Histoire du canal de Suez*, Perrin, Paris, 2009 (nouvelle édition complétée en 2018) et *Les pays du Golfe, de la perle à l'économie de la connaissance. Les nouvelles terres du libéralisme*, Paris, Armand Colin, 2013.

Mohamed Sassi est enseignant-chercheur en histoire économique contemporaine à l'Université de Tunis et directeur du Département des Sciences humaines et l'Institut Préparatoire aux Études Littéraire et des Sciences Humaines de Tunis (IPELSHT). Il est l'auteur d'une thèse de doctorat en Histoire économique à Paris-Sorbonne sur l'histoire pétrolière française et d'un post-doctorat à Paris IV en collaboration avec l'université de Genève. Auteur de l'ouvrage : *La politique pétrolière de la France de 1861 à 1974*, Paris, Éditions SPM, 2018, 641 p. Il a publié plusieurs articles liés à l'histoire des relations économiques en Méditerranée, l'histoire bancaire en Tunisie (Histoire de la banque publique, la STB) et l'histoire énergétique et pétrolière en France et en Tunisie. Il mène actuellement des recherches sur l'Histoire des relations économiques et diplomatiques entre le Maghreb et l'Union européenne.

Dr. Harm G. Schröter has worked as a professor in Departments of Economics, History, and in Business Schools at Universities in Germany, USA, Norway, especially at the University of Bergen. His published on European economic and business history (cartelization, cultural conditions of economic development, FDI, co-operatives, labour movement, Americanization, and business groups). He served as President of European Business History Association and organized the First World Congress on Business History in 2016.

Sun Rui is now lecturer of School of Economics, Renmin University of China. She got PhD from the Chinese Academy of Social Sciences. And the dissertation is "Market order and Industries Organization: a study of Tianjin local private bank industry association in modern times". Her post-PhD research is the traditional private banks and the relationship between the modern banks. Her recent research interests include the traditional economic institutions, the Chinese economic transformation and the comparative study on 19-20 century between China and Western countries. And the new book is "Organization, market and state: Modern Tianjin local private bank Association with the construction of economic rules and orders".

Boris Vinogradov, doctorate in History. Works on themes related to economic history, history of relations between Russia, France and European countries. Postdoctoral researcher at the University of Nantes (UMR 6025 CENS). Scientific secretary of the international research group EURUS, Centre Roland Mousnier (UMR 8596). Author of the following contributions : "French banks in the USSR 1950-1990 and their participation in the East-West industrial projects", in. David Feest, *Geld Prestige, Verantwortung*, Kiel, Édition Solivagus, 2020, p. 181-195 ; « Transferts de technologie entre l'URSS et la France, 1954-1991 », in. Dominique Barjot, *Transmission et circulation des savoir scientifiques et techniques*, Paris, Édition de CTHS, p. 327-338.

Wang Jue is now Professor of School of Economics, Renmin University of China and head of its Department of Economic History. She's also the Vice-President of the Society of Foreign Economic History in China. As a specialist in economic history, she has written 3 and translated 5 books, two of which have become recommended textbooks for Chinese universities. Her recent research interests include development economics and political economics of technology transfer, and the achievements can be seen in her new book *Technology and Status of State Power: The World Economy from 1200 to 1945, Social Sciences Academic Press(China), 2019*.

Wang Qing is now PHD candidate of School of Economics, Renmin University of China. He is the recipient of the China Development Research Scholarship in 2018 awarded by the China Development Research Foundation. He has published several papers on technology transfer and cross-border e-commerce industry in mainstream Chinese journals including Economist(China), Economic Review Journal and Science and Technology Management Research, etc.

Kazuhiko Yago, Professor at Waseda University, Faculty of Commerce, defended his doctoral dissertation "L'épargne populaire comme fonds de placement public : Caisse des Dépôts et Consignations" at Université Paris X in 1996. Pursuing historical studies on international financial organizations such as the BIS and the IMF, his recent researches focus on the role played by the World Bank on growth and development of the capitalist world around the 1960s and the 70s. Recent publications include : *History of the IMF: Organization, Policy, and Market* (with Yoshio Asai and Masanao Itoh), Springer, 2015 ; *Asian Imperial Banking History* (with Hubert Bonin and Nuno Valério), Pickering and Chatto, 2014 ; *The Financial History of the Bank for International Settlements,* Routledge, 2012 ;"La Banque du Japon dans le système monétaire international (1945-1985)", in Olivier Feiertag et Michel Margairaz, dirs., *Les banques centrales à l'échelle du monde,* Presses de la Fondation nationale des sciences politiques, 2012.

Xiaolan Zhou is a professor at the School of History and Culture of the South China Normal University. She holds a PHD in history (Sun Yat-sen University and Paris-Sorbonne University), a MA in history (University of Lyon 3). She is specialized in the 19th century history of France and contemporary history of the Chinese industry.

Table of abbreviations

AIIB (Asia Infrastructure Investment Bank)
ALN (Armée de Libération Nationale)
APD (Aide Publique au Développement)

BDS (Bloc Démocratique Sénégalais)
BRICs (Brasil, Russia, India, China, South Africa)

CAP (Common Agricultural Policy)
CEE (Communauté Économique Européenne)
CEO (Chief Executive Officer)
CGT (Confédération Générale du Travail)
CGTU (Confédération Générale du Travail Unitaire)
CICE (Crédit d'Impôt Compétitivité Emploi)
CNR (Compagnie Nationale du Rhône)
CNR (Conseil National de la Résistance)
CoCom (Coordinating Committee for Multilateral Export Controls)
COMECOM (or CAEM : Conseil d'Assistance Économique Mutuelle)
CSG (Contribution Sociale Généralisée)

DA (Dinar Algérien)
DM (Deutche Mark)

ECSC (European and Steel Community)
EDC (European Defense Community)
EDCC (External Development Cooperation and Development)
EEC (European Economic Community)
ERP (European Recovery Reconstruction)

FCSFCCF (Fédération des Chambres Syndicales des Fabricants de Chaux et Ciments de France)
FDI (Foreign Direct Investment)
FF (French Franc)
FLN (Front de Libération Nationale)

GAFAM (Google, Amazon, Facebook, Apple, Microsoft)
GATT (General Agreement on Tariffs and Trade)
GDP (Gross Domestic Product)
GDR (German Democratic Republic)
GNP (Gross National Product)

HSR (High-Speed Railway)
HSR (High-Speed Rail)

IBRD (International Bank for Reconstruction and Development)
IMEX (Vietnamese Companies of Import-Export)
IMF (International Monetary Fund)
ISI (Import-Substitution-Industrialization)

LME (London Metall Exchange)

MIST (Mexico, Indonesia, South Korea, Turkey)
MNF (Multinational Firm)
MNFs (Multinational Firms)
MOR (Ministry of Railways)

NAFTA (North American Free Trade Agreement)
NATO (North Atlantic Trade Organization)
NIEO (New International Economic Order)
NYSE (New York Stock Exchange)

OECD (Organization for Economic Cooperation Council)
ONCAD (Office National de Coopération et d'Assistance au Développement)
OPEC (Organization of the Petroleum Exporting Countries)

PDCI (Parti Démocratique de Côte d'Ivoire)

R & D (Research and Development)
RDA (Rassemblement Démocratique Africain)

SNA (Social Networks Analysis)
SOEs (State-Owned Enterprises)

UEMOA (Union Économique et Monétaire Ouest-Afrique)
USD (United States Dollar)
USSR (Union of Soviet Sovereign Republics)

WTO (World Trade Organization)

Table of contents

OTHER EMERGING NATIONS / AUTRES PAYS ÉMERGENTS

www.ingramcontent.com/pod-product-compliance
Lightning Source LLC
LaVergne TN
LVHW050051061026
849532LV00001BA/67
9782379990137